Economic Growth and Sustainable Development

Economic growth, reflected in increases in national output per capita, makes possible an improved material standard of living. Sustainable development, popularly and concisely defined as "meeting the needs of the present generations without compromising the ability of future generations to meet their needs," directly addresses the utilization of natural resources, the state of the environment, and intergenerational equity.

Fundamental questions addressed in this textbook include:

- What causes economic growth?
- Why do some countries grow faster than others?
- What accounts for the extraordinary growth in the world's population over the past two centuries?
- What are the current trends in population and will these trends continue?
- Are there limits to economic growth and population growth due to resource constraints and environmental thresholds?
- Is sustainable development compatible with economic growth?
- Can sustainable development be attained without addressing the extreme poverty that afflicts over a billion of the world's population?

This interdisciplinary textbook uses a blend of formal models, empirical evidence, history and statistics to provide a coherent and comprehensive treatment of economic growth and sustainable development.

Peter N. Hess is Gail M. and Ernest G. Doe Professor of Economics at Davidson College, North Carolina, USA. He is the co-author of undergraduate texts on economic principles and economic development and the author of an undergraduate text on mathematical economics. In addition to this, he has published journal articles on the fertility transition, military spending in developing economies, and sustainable development. He also serves as president of Nepal Orphans Home, an international nonprofit with operations in Nepal.

ROUTLEDGE TEXTBOOKS IN ENVIRONMENTAL AND AGRICULTURAL ECONOMICS

Economic Growth and Sustainable Development

Peter N. Hess

Routledge
Taylor & Francis Group

LONDON AND NEW YORK

First published 2013
by Routledge
2 Park Square, Milton Park, Abingdon, Oxon OX14 4RN

Simultaneously published in the USA and Canada
by Routledge
711 Third Avenue, New York, NY 10017

Routledge is an imprint of the Taylor & Francis Group, an informa business

© 2013 Peter N. Hess

British Library Cataloguing in Publication Data
A catalogue record for this book is available from the British Library

Library of Congress Cataloging in Publication Data
Hess, Peter N.
  Economic growth and sustainable development/by Peter N. Hess.
    p. cm.
  Includes bibliographical references and index.
  1. Economic development. 2. Sustainable development. I. Title.
  HD75.H4583 2013
  338.9–dc23   2012030672

ISBN: 978-0-415-67948-0 (hbk)
ISBN: 978-0-415-67949-7 (pbk)
ISBN: 978-0-203-07051-2 (ebk)

Typeset in Perpetua
by Sunrise Setting Ltd, Paignton, UK

Printed and bound by CPI Group (UK) Ltd, Croydon, CR0 4YY

Dedication

To my wife, Boo, our grandchildren,

my brother, Michael, and the children of Nepal Orphans Home

I dedicate this book.

Peter Hess

Contents

List of illustrations

FIGURES

TABLES

BOXES

Preface

As we entered the twenty-first century, over one fourth of the human race lived in extreme poverty. Many lived under oppression. Across the continents, there were signs of environmental deterioration. And, the world seemed increasingly smaller. More than ever before, we were aware of the welfare of those living in other nations. Yet, overall, the human condition was improving.

The last two centuries have witnessed more profound change for the human race than the previous hundred centuries combined. Population growth, economic growth, and climate change have all been unprecedented. Consider that the human population did not reach 1 billion in size until the beginning of the nineteenth century. Since then, rapid population growth has pushed the earth's population beyond 7 billion. And, the population is projected to increase by another 2 billion over the next few decades. More than 90 percent of this growth is expected to occur in the less developed countries.

Poverty has also defined the vast span of human existence. Minimal economic growth accompanied the minimal population growth until fairly recently. For the developed nations of Western Europe, the United States, Canada, Australia, Japan, and New Zealand, economic growth over the past two centuries has delivered a high material standard of living. Within the last quarter century, however, the most rapid economic growth has occurred in the less developed countries, especially China and India, the two most populous nations of the world.

Moreover, there are increasing concerns with the environment and sustaining development, so that the ability of future generations to meet their needs is not compromised. The United Nations Development Program in its *Human Development Report 2007/2008* warned:

> Climate change is the defining human development issue of our generation. . . . One of the hardest lessons taught by climate change is that the economic model which drives growth, and the profligate consumption in rich nations that goes with it, is ecologically unsustainable.

Global warming, rising sea levels, increasing droughts, greater volatility and severity of storms all portend possible ecological tipping points, threatening future livelihoods.

Perhaps no subject deserves our attention more than sustainable global development, encompassing the universal fulfillment of basic human needs and the effective stewardship of common resources and the environment. This is our focus. Some of the fundamental questions we address include:

■ What causes economic growth?

- What accounts for the extraordinary growth in the world's population over the past two centuries from 1 billion to 7 billion?
- What are the current trends in population and will they continue?
- Are there limits to economic growth and population growth due to natural resource constraints and environmental thresholds?
- How do we measure sustainable development?
- Is sustainable development compatible with economic growth?
- Is sustainable development possible when extreme poverty afflicts much of the human race?
- Why should we be concerned with the welfare of future generations?

THE OBJECTIVE

In the social sciences, the ultimate objective of theory should be enlightened policy. Therefore, we begin with theories of economic growth, population change, and sustainable development. Various types of models are used to convey the theory—from the fairly simple, largely descriptive models of the earlier classical economists, to more complex simulation models, macroeconomic models, and formal growth models. Throughout the text, we try to show not only how each theory added to our understanding, but also how the limitations of the models contributed to the development of new theories and ultimately more informed policies.

Theories should be confronted with the evidence. Combined with the presentation of the theories is a history of the human experience. We refer to significant events of the past two hundred years, particularly in the post-World War II era, when economic development was first recognized as a distinct discipline in economics. We will see that while economic growth and demographic change have accelerated in the last two centuries, concerns about sustainability have persisted.

Throughout the text, statistics on economic growth, population, and sustainable development are presented for countries grouped according to the World Bank's per capita income classification (low-income, middle-income, and high-income economies) and for regions of the less developed countries (sub-Saharan Africa, Middle East and North Africa, Europe and Central Asia, South Asia, East Asia and the Pacific, and Latin America and the Caribbean). The diversity of experience across income classes and regions will be evident.

To illustrate how theories are tested, the fundamentals of regression analysis are presented. From the theories, and based on the evidence, policy implications are derived. In particular, what policies will promote economic growth? What would be required for sustainable development? These issues are unsettled and even controversial. In many of the chapters, boxes are included to elaborate on key concepts or to illustrate the theory with brief case studies of countries. For example, in Chapter 10, the economic success and demographic tragedy of Botswana, a small sub-Saharan African nation, is profiled.

In short, the organizing principle of specifying the theory, reviewing the evidence, and discussing the policy implications promotes a natural progression within—and consistency across—the chapters of the text. In addition, the integration of relevant history further enhances the progression of material and is important for drawing lessons from experience. The goal is to impart not only a better understanding of the phenomena of economic growth and sustainable development, but also recognition of the challenges ahead and the opportunities for progress.

CHAPTER OUTLINE

We begin in Part I with an introduction to economic growth and population growth. In Chapter 1 the unprecedented economic growth over the past two centuries is reviewed. The primary sources of economic growth are set forth and the relationship between economic growth and poverty alleviation is discussed. Evidence on the differential rates of economic growth and poverty across nations illustrate the theory. Policies to promote economic growth are outlined. The extraordinary economic growth of China and India is highlighted in a case study on growth accounting.

In Chapter 2 the measurement and sources of population growth are examined. A brief overview of the history of world population growth is provided, incorporating demographic transition theory and the different experiences of the developed and contemporary developing nations. The relationship between population growth and economic growth is summarized. We introduce the concept of carrying capacity and explain why the world population is expected to stop growing in the next half century.

In Part II theories of growth are examined from an evolutionary perspective. In Chapter 3 insights of the great classical economists of the late eighteenth and early nineteenth century are discussed, including: Adam Smith's international specialization with a simple model illustrating the gains from trade; Thomas Malthus's law of population and his famous prediction that population growth would outpace the food supply; and David Ricardo's diminishing returns to labor and theory of rent, which elaborated on the classical concern with land constraints. In the long run, the classical economists envisioned a stationary state with zero economic growth, zero population growth, and subsistence level incomes.

Roughly a century later, economists were again focused on economic stagnation, as described in Chapter 4. In contrast to the classical fear of unchecked population growth, however, macroeconomists in the 1930s worried about insufficient population growth in the developed economies. John Maynard Keyes, the great British economist, revolutionized macroeconomics with his theory of aggregate demand and supply and his advocacy for expansionary policy in a depressed economy. The importance of investment and physical capital formation for economic growth is emphasized. We contrast the general economic growth under the pre-World War I gold standard with the economic turbulence and lack of international cooperation following the war, particularly during the Great Depression.

In Chapter 5 we pick up the narrative with the international institutions established after World War II to foster a new world order: the International Monetary Fund, World Bank, and General Agreement on Tariffs and Trade. The emergence of the Cold War in the 1950s, the growth of the less developed nations of Asia, Africa, the Middle East, and Latin America, and the stagflation in the 1970s occasioned by sharply higher oil prices are reviewed in this chapter. Expanding on the classical concern with land constraints on food production is the limits to growth simulation model that suggested the ecological footprint of the global economy has already exceeded the carrying capacity of planet Earth. Herman Daly's theory and institutions for steady-state economics are also presented. The debt problems of the developing economies in the 1980s and the uneven economic progress in the closing decade of the twentieth century are discussed. In particular, the difficult transitions of the former socialist economies during the 1990s and the East Asian currency crisis in 1998 are highlighted.

Part III of the text deals with macroeconomic models. In Chapter 6 an overview of business cycles is given and an aggregate demand–aggregate supply model is set forth to explain short-run macroeconomic fluctuations—in particular, the absence of deflation during recessions. While the focus is on the United States, especially with an account of the Great Recession of 2008–09, the history of the European Union and the economic turmoil in the euro zone in the aftermath of this recession are also provided. Lessons from the severe recession conclude the chapter.

Chapter 7 turns to longer-run economic trends. A simple neoclassical growth model is presented and then extended to include technological progress, natural resources, and qualitative change in the primary factors of production. Policies for promoting economic growth, including increasing saving, controlling inflation, reaping the demographic dividend, and encouraging technological progress, are reviewed. Convergence theory, which implies that the gaps between the high- and low-income nations are decreasing, is confronted with the evidence. Reasons for economic divergence drawing on endogenous growth theory are considered. The topic of income distribution follows naturally from economic growth and convergence theory. A case study of the growing income inequality in the United States is presented.

Chapter 8 is devoted to testing economic theory. The basics of regression analysis are provided, and then empirical analysis of the determinants of economic growth, derived from macroeconomic theory, both the short-run aggregate demand–aggregate supply model in Chapter 6 and the enhanced Solow growth model in Chapter 7, are tested for a cross-section of low- and middle-income economies. The policy implications from the regression analysis follow, drawing on the World Bank's market-friendly strategy of development introduced in the 1990s and comprehensive development framework promoted in the 2000s.

The two chapters on demography in Part IV provide a good transition to the study of sustainable development. In Chapter 9 population dynamics and the key components of population change, mortality and fertility, are examined. Different measures of mortality are given and the construct of life tables for modeling mortality and projecting populations is explained. Then, different measures of fertility are presented. Specific examples for individual nations as well as more aggregate statistics are used to illustrate. The importance of the age and sex structure of populations is conveyed through population pyramids and the related phenomenon of population momentum. Finally the mechanics of population projection are outlined.

Chapter 10 deals with population transitions. The epidemiological transition describes the changing pattern of mortality that accompanies economic development and the aging of populations. The potential consequences for morbidity and mortality from climate change are noted. The fertility transition captures the decline in birth rates with economic development. A model based on utility maximization is derived to explain the demand for children and fertility rates. Post-World War II trends in fertility are reviewed, including the baby boom in the high-income nations, which was followed by a return to low fertility. The consequences of low fertility for economic growth and the challenges of aging populations are discussed. Possible lessons from Europe, where fertility rates have been well below replacement level for some time, and from China, where the authoritarian government imposed a stringent birth control policy, are explored. The chapter concludes with the determinants of migration, the third source of population change. International migration, already a major important force in many national economies, is likely to become even more consequential, if no less controversial.

The five chapters on sustainable development constitute Part V of the text. Chapter 11 provides an introduction to the various definitions, indicators and underlying philosophy of sustainable development. A basic ecological identity and the Millennium Development Goals are used to illustrate the importance of achieving sustainable development. Three indicators of sustainable development are examined: the World Bank's adjusted net saving rate, which is a more comprehensive measure of capital formation; the United Nations Development Program's Human Development Index; and a new Index of Youth Investment. Also addressed is the practice of child labor, prevalent in some poor societies, which not only represents disinvestment in youth but also serves to perpetuate poverty. A case study of indentured child labor in Nepal is given to illustrate. A key to sustainable development is managing physical, human, natural, and social assets. The degree of substitutability across assets significantly affects this management.

Natural resources and climate change are the main topics in Chapter 12. The evidence for natural resource scarcities, both nonrenewable and renewable, is reviewed. The natural resource intensive sectors of mining and forestry are profiled. The use of natural resources for economic growth and the ironies of the Dutch disease, a development distortion brought on by a boom in natural resource exports, and the natural resource curse, a failure of leadership in nations especially well endowed with fossil fuels or minerals, are all addressed. Current energy use, including the reliance on fossil fuels and the consequent challenges with climate change, are examined.

Chapter 13 deals with the global food supply. Globally, the Malthusian specter has not come to pass. There is more than enough food produced in the world to provide adequate diets for all populations. Thanks largely to advances in agricultural technology with the green revolution of the 1960s and the more recent gene revolution, food supplies have greatly increased. And, the declines in population growth with the demographic transition and birth control have moderated the demands for food. Nevertheless, hundreds of millions in poor countries suffer from malnutrition. At the same time, obesity is a growing problem in rich countries—and even in some developing nations. Moreover, there are renewed concerns with resource depletion, likely to be exacerbated by global warming. Policies to promote sustainable agricultural development are suggested. An overview of fishing, an industry increasingly under environmental stress, and of the rising phenomenon of aquaculture, a blue revolution, closes this chapter.

Chapter 14 examines the economic role of the government. The basic market mechanism embodied in perfect competition, while yielding allocative and productive efficiencies—in contrast to monopoly and imperfect competition—does not often prevail. Moreover, there are market failures that warrant government intervention, including public goods and merit goods and the regulation of business for the common good. The externalities or spillover effects on social welfare are a major market failure. In particular, the negative externalities that often accompany the use of natural resources in the production and consumption of goods and services are examined. Policy options for managing natural resources to achieve sustainable development, including carbon taxes and marketable pollution permits, are set out. The existence of poverty, even in the richest nations, is seen by many as another market failure. The role of the government in stabilizing the economy and promoting growth and development is discussed, especially in light of the recent difficulties in the major capitalist economies and the rapid growth in some of the more heavily managed economies, such as China. The chapter concludes with an overview of international cooperation in managing the global commons, including the oceans, atmosphere, and biodiversity.

The concluding Chapter 15 directly addresses the challenges in attaining sustainable development. Two guidelines, the precautionary principle and Rawls's veil of ignorance, should inform the policies for sustainable development. Success will require international cooperation, in alleviating poverty, in supporting measures both to mitigate and adapt to climate change, and to continue the research and development into environmentally sustainable technologies. Hardest of all—but arguably the most important—for achieving sustainable development in the world will be a fundamental evolution in human behavior, reflected in a shift from materialism to conservation, respect for the natural environment, and greater concern for the welfare of the less fortunate. To this end, evidence on the relationship between income and happiness is discussed, and a model for utility maximization is offered that embodies the shift in human priorities.

Throughout the text we strive for balanced presentation, blending theory, evidence and policy. We draw on many fields, including microeconomics and macroeconomics, economic development, international economics, econometrics, economic history, as well as demography. Controversies as well as consensus are noted. In the end, achieving sustainable development will require informed judgments and sound policies, guided by science, enlightened by lessons from the past, and carried forth with good will—not an easy task, but absolutely essential for our future.

NOTE TO INSTRUCTORS

There is a lot of material here, perhaps too much for one semester. Instructors have considerable flexibility, however, in the choice of chapters to cover in order to best fit the interests of their classes. Indeed, this text could be used in a number of courses: from undergraduate classes in economic development and environmental studies to master's level programs in public policy and international development. Mindful of the different backgrounds of students, care has been taken throughout the text to review the underlying fundamentals, whether perfect competition for analysis of markets, descriptive statistics for regression analysis, or matrix multiplication for population projection.

Nevertheless, if time constraints are binding and there is less interest in economic history and classical thought, Chapters 3 and 4 might be skipped. Or Chapter 6 and the aggregate demand–aggregate supply analysis might be passed over if short-run macroeconomic fluctuations are deemed relatively less important. The empirical analysis with a review of econometrics in Chapter 8 and the formal demography, including population projection, in Chapter 9 may be omitted if the treatments are deemed too technical. In short, the core chapters that are most essential for understanding economic growth and sustainable development are Chapters 1–2, 5, 7, and 10–15.

Acknowledgments

Usually the motivation for writing a text is the belief (and hope) that you can improve on the current offerings in the field. I first offered the course, Economic Growth and Sustainable Development, in the spring semester of 2004. Combining these two major topics, usually treated separately, in one course seemed both intuitive and challenging. Not finding a text suitable for this course, I decided to write one, drawing on the class lectures, discussions, and my research over the years. I have learned a lot in writing this book and I now better appreciate how vast, complex and important the topics of economic growth and sustainable development are.

Any project like this is only made possible with the contributions of many others—both directly and indirectly. I would like to begin with my students. In trying to fashion the best course possible in economic growth and sustainable development, I have been inspired by my students, who are talented, diligent, and ambitious and who, I think, will go on to be game-changers. I have been fortunate to teach at Davidson College for my entire career, since the fall of 1980, always in the company of outstanding colleagues. With respect to this book, I am grateful to all the good people at Routledge, beginning with Rob Langham, Senior Publisher, who from the beginning has been both encouraging and insightful. I have enjoyed working with Natalie Tomlinson, Editorial Assistant, and Lisa Salonen, Senior Production Editor.

Finally, I hope that the students who use this text will work toward the goal of sustainable development for all.

Peter Hess
Professor of Economics
Davidson College
Davidson, North Carolina

Part I
Introduction

Chapter 1

Introduction to economic growth

المدى الواسع هم أدنى

The vast span of human existence has been defined by poverty, with minimal economic growth and minimal population growth.[1] **Economic growth**, a rise in per capita incomes, allows for an improved material standard of living, tending to reduce absolute poverty. Throughout history, most people have been able to earn only enough income to meet their most basic needs for shelter, food, water and clothing. Good health and the opportunity for education have been lacking for many more.

As noted by the World Bank (2001b: 45), "Until the mid-18th century, improvements in living standards worldwide were barely perceptible. . . .As late as 1820 per capita incomes were quite similar around the world—and very low." Average incomes at the turn of the nineteenth century might have ranged from $700 in China and South Asia to between $1,400 and $2,100 in the richest countries of Europe. Three-quarters of the world's population likely lived on less than $500 a year.[2]

Two centuries of economic growth later, per capita real income for the world averaged nearly $10,000 in 2010. But there were great differences across nations. In the high-income nations average per capita income in 2010 was $33,600. In contrast, in the low-income nations, average per capita income was $1,200 (World Bank 2012: Table 1.1). And roughly 1.3 billion of the world's population were living in extreme poverty—on $1.25 a day or less (World Bank 2012: Table 2.8).[3]

We begin with a brief history of modern economic growth. The measurement of economic growth and the relationship between economic growth and poverty are illustrated. The sources

---

[1] According to one economic historian (Clark, 2007: 1), "the average person in the world in 1800 was no better off than the average person of 100,000 BC." Clark attributes the lack of any sustained economic growth to the Malthusian trap, to be discussed later in Chapter 3. Basically, any increases in income and living standards would be offset by population growth, plunging the societies back into subsistence. It should be noted, however, that there are no reliable economic records of early human experience, especially extending back a thousand centuries. Clark's *A Farewell to Alms: A Brief Economic History of the World* is widely read, but a number of his interpretations are controversial. In particular, Allen (2008: 955) concludes: "Economic growth before the Industrial Revolution was not rapid, but it did generate a higher standard of living for most people than that enjoyed by ancient foragers and early farmers." Allen provides a fairly comprehensive critique of Clark's work.

[2] These incomes, converted to 2005 internationally comparable dollars, are derived from estimates reported in the World Bank (2001b: 45). The initial figures, expressed in 1990 constant internationally comparable or purchasing power-adjusted dollars, were $500 in China and South Asia and $1,000–$1,500 in the richest countries of Europe. These were converted to constant (2005) dollars by multiplying by 1.38, which is the ratio of the 2005 to the 1990 implicit price deflators for US gross domestic product, and then rounded to the nearest hundred dollars. The following incomes for 2010 are also converted to 2005 internationally comparable dollars, by dividing the nominal incomes reported in World Bank (2012, Table 1.1) by 1.11, which is the ratio of the 2010 to the 2005 implicit price deflator for US gross domestic product, and then rounded to the nearest hundred dollars. We should emphasize that averages understate the range of incomes across and within the countries. In each nation there would be the relatively high-income nobility and large landowners coexisting with the mass of peasants and agrarian households.

[3] The international poverty line for extreme poverty is set at $1.25 a day (in 2005 purchasing power parity-adjusted dollars). In 2008, the latest year available for regional estimates, 74 percent of the extremely poor lived in South Asia and sub-Saharan Africa.

of economic growth are then identified using an aggregate production function. The differential progress of the nations of the world in generating economic growth and reducing poverty will be examined.

BRIEF HISTORY OF ECONOMIC GROWTH

Maddison (2005: 5, 8) estimates that over the past millennium, world population rose 23-fold and per capita income rose 14-fold—in contrast to the first thousand years AD when world population grew by only a sixth and per capita income was stagnant. The economic growth, however, had been uneven. Real per capita income in Western Europe, the United States, Canada, Australia, New Zealand and Japan increased, on average, nearly threefold between 1000 and 1820, the beginning of the "capitalist epoch." In these areas, economic growth then accelerated, with incomes increasing nearly 20-fold from 1820 to 2001. For the rest of the world, economic growth was comparatively modest, with average per capita incomes rising by a third between 1000 and 1820 and then "only" sixfold from 1820 to 2001.

While there are a number of underlying factors, the extraordinary economic growth over the past two centuries has largely been attributed to technological progress—with advances in science and engineering yielding inventions and innovations. This is not to imply that technological progress was absent in the centuries before the industrial era. For example, Maddison (2005: 5, 16) cites major developments in shipbuilding and navigation that contributed significantly to the economic growth in Western Europe between 1000 and 1820. And the invention of the printing press in the fifteenth century helped spread ideas. Clark (2007: 251) lists other innovations in Europe during this medieval period, including: the windmill (c.1200), mechanical clock (c.1285), arabic numerals (c. 1450), the potato (1532), knitting frame (1589), telescope (1608), and microscope (1665). In general, though, there was little investment in physical or human capital that would raise labor productivity.

The genesis of the modern era of economic growth was the Industrial Revolution, initially centered in England in the late eighteenth century.[4] Indeed, Sachs (2005: 33) calls the invention of the steam engine the "decisive turning point of modern history." Primarily fueled by coal, the steam engine facilitated mass production under the factory system, particularly in textiles and steel. In turn, steel was used in the production of machinery. The steam ship reduced transportation costs and promoted international trade. Fossil fuels also were used in the production of chemical fertilizers, contributing to the gains in agricultural output.

Sachs (2005: 42) notes a second wave of technological breakthroughs in the middle of the nineteenth century in transportation (with the expansion of railroads) and communications (with the telegraph), linking markets across countries and promoting economies of scale in production. The opening of the Suez Canal (1869) and the Panama Canal (1914) reduced transport costs.[5] A third wave of technological progress came at the end of the nineteenth century with the widespread use of electricity and the internal combustion engine. The application of nitrogen-based fertilizers further boosted agricultural productivity in the early twentieth century.

---

[4] Sachs (2005: 32–35) explains why the Industrial Revolution began in England. The main reasons were the relatively free British society with the protection of personal property rights, the encouragement of science, favorable geography with a sovereign island and a climate conducive to agriculture, rich coal deposits essential to the production of energy, and extensive rivers for transportation. England's location between North America and continental Europe was also advantageous.

[5] Kenwood and Lougheed (1992: Chapter 4) provide a good overview of the movement of nations, especially Great Britain, toward free trade during the nineteenth century.

Economic growth in the industrial nations was interrupted by World War I (1914–18). The war was followed by uncertain economic recoveries, the Great Depression and economic stagnation in the 1930s, and then World War II (1939–45). Important institutions, however, were established in the mid-1940s: the International Monetary Fund, International Bank for Reconstruction and Development (World Bank), and the General Agreement on Tariffs and Trade, with the intent of promoting economic growth and fostering international cooperation. Soon thereafter, a Cold War between the United States and the Soviet Union emerged, lasting through the 1980s.

Still, the decades following World War II saw significant economic growth in both the industrial nations and the developing economies of Latin America, Asia, Africa, and the Middle East. International trade grew faster than national outputs.[6]

Maddison (2005: 9) labels the period from 1950 to 1973 a "golden age of unparalleled prosperity. . . with world per capita GDP rising at annual rate near 3 percent." In the developing nations, however, explosive population growth accompanied the economic growth, and soon became a global concern.

The 1970s brought rising natural resource prices—in particular, sharply higher fuel prices sparked by the Organization of Petroleum Exporting Countries oil embargo. The industrial economies experienced stagflation, a combination of recession and inflation. Indeed, all oil-importing nations suffered significant setbacks. As will be discussed later, the industrial nations resumed economic growth fairly quickly. The oil-importing developing nations, seeking to continue their economic growth, took on substantial external debt, a burden that resulted in a lost decade of development for many of these nations in the 1980s.

With the dissolution of the Soviet Union and end of the Cold War, the difficult transitions of former socialist states and command economies of Russia and Eastern Europe toward democracy and market-oriented systems characterized the 1990s. This last decade of the twentieth century also witnessed steady economic growth for the United States, fueled in part by the information technology revolution, and somewhat slower growth, but increased integration, of the European economies.

Soon into the first decade of the twenty-first century, the industrial economies slowed down. The shock of the terrorist attacks on September 11, 2001 turned the attention of the United States to homeland security. The US launched incursions into Afghanistan and Iraq. And toward the end of the decade, the US economy fell into a deep recession, prompted by a financial crisis that originated in the overextended housing market. Other high-income economies with similar excessive spending and financial recklessness also suffered sharp downturns. Unemployment rates soared and government budget deficits mushroomed. The sovereign debt problems of some of the weaker economies in the European Union, particularly Greece, not only threatened the nations of the euro zone, but cast a pall over the entire international financial system, significantly hindering the recoveries of the industrial economies. The developing economies too experienced slowdowns in their growth, in large part due to the reduced international trade. Progress in reducing extreme poverty was hampered.

Subsequent chapters will elaborate further on key historical developments in the global economy. And, in Chapter 2, a brief history of the world population growth will be given. We now turn to the measurement and sources of economic growth.

---

[6]The World Bank (2009: 13) shows the share of international trade in global GDP increasing from 6 percent in 1900 to 12 percent in 1950 and 26 percent in 2000. In part, the increase in the number of sovereign nations reflects the emergence of new nations with their independence from former colonies in the post-World War II decades and later the dissolution of the Soviet Union. The number of international borders doubled from 104 in 1900 to 200 in 1950 and then tripled again to 600 by 2000.

MEASURING ECONOMIC GROWTH

Real national output measures the market value (adjusted for inflation) of all final goods and services produced in an economy over a year. Producing a dollar's worth of output generates an equivalent dollar's worth of income, so we can use real national output and real national income interchangeably.[7] Economic growth occurs with increases in real national output and real national income per capita. If we let Y be real national output (real national income) and P be population, then $y = Y/P$ is per capita real national output (per capita real national income).

In order for economic growth to occur, real national output has to increase faster than population. That is, differentiating per capita real national output, and then dividing through by per capita output, we obtain the economic growth rate, dy/y.[8]

$$dy = \frac{dY \cdot P - Y \cdot dP}{P^2}$$
$$= \frac{dY}{P} - \frac{Y}{P}\frac{dP}{P}$$
$$\frac{dy}{y} = \frac{dY}{Y} - \frac{dP}{P}$$

If real output increases faster than population, i.e., $dY/Y > dP/P$, then we have positive economic growth with a rise in per capita income, $dy/y > 0$. It is possible to have negative economic growth, or economic decline, even with positive output growth, if the growth rate of population exceeds the growth rate of output, i.e., if $dP/P > dY/Y > 0$, then $dy/y < 0$. For example, from 2000 to 2009, the average annual growth rates in real national output and population for Haiti were 0.7 percent and 1.7 percent, respectively, yielding approximately an average annual decline in per capita income of 1.0 percent (World Bank 2011a: Table 4.1; 2011b: Table 1). This decline occurred even before the devastating earthquake that hit Haiti in early 2010, setting the nation back years, if not decades.

ECONOMIC GROWTH AND POVERTY

There are numerous measures of income poverty, including the **headcount index** (the absolute number of poor in a country or region), the **incidence of poverty** (the percentage of a population that is poor), and the **poverty gap** (the mean shortfall as a percentage of income from the poverty line). The headcount index illustrates the absolute magnitude of poverty, while the incidence of poverty accounts for the relative prevalence of poverty in a population. The poverty

---

[7] Strictly speaking, **gross domestic product** (GDP) and **gross national income** (GNI) are distinct, but similar, measures of aggregate output. The underlying basic idea is that producing a dollar's worth of output generates a dollar's worth of income. GDP measures the total market value of the final goods and services produced in an economy over a year, i.e., within the borders of a nation. GNI measures the income earned by residents of a nation in producing final goods and services over a year. The difference between GDP and GNI is net factor income payments (e.g., wages, interest, profits) to the rest of the world. GDP includes the output (and income) produced by foreign capital and labor in the nation. GNI includes the income (and output) produced abroad by the nation's capital and labor. For most countries, GDP and GNI are quite similar. For some countries, though, GDP could significantly exceed GNI if, for example, there was considerable foreign labor working and foreign capital invested in the national economy. For other nations, GNI could significantly exceed GDP when a substantial amount of their labor was working abroad or if there had been significant foreign investment of capital in other nations.

[8] Actually this derivation holds only for infinitesimal changes in income and population. Nevertheless, the rate of economic growth, the percentage change in per capita national income (dy/y), is approximately equal to the difference between the growth rates in real national income (dY/Y) and population (dP/P).

gap measures the depth of poverty, i.e., how poor, on average, are the poor in a population. Box 1.1 provides a simple illustration for these different measures of poverty.

BOX 1.1: MEASURES OF POVERTY

To illustrate the three measures of poverty with a simple example, consider two countries, A and B, each with a population of 4 (million), poverty lines of $1 a day and given per capita daily incomes of:

	Population A	Population B
Poorest million	$0.80	$0.50
Second million	$0.90	$0.60
Third million	$4.00	$3.00
Richest million	$8.00	$9.60

The average per capita incomes in the two countries are the same: $y_A = \$3.425 = y_B$.

The poverty headcount, given the poverty line of $1 per day, is 2 (million) in each nation, here the bottom two quartiles of the populations. The incidence of poverty is 50 percent in both nations. Despite the same per capita incomes, poverty headcount, and incidence of poverty, the poverty gaps are different. The depth of poverty, indicated by the poverty gap, in country B, at 22.5 percent, is three times that for country A, at 7.5 percent. The poverty gap calculations, based on mean shortfalls in income from the poverty line, are:

$$\text{Country A} = 0.25 \cdot [0.20 + 0.10 + 0 + 0]/1.00 = 0.075 = 7.5\%$$

$$\text{Country B} = 0.25 \cdot [0.50 + 0.40 + 0 + 0]/1.00 = 0.225 = 22.5\%$$

To illustrate for Ecuador in 2010, we use $1.25 per day (in PPP dollars), the international measure for extreme poverty, as the poverty line. Ecuador had a poverty gap in 2010 of 2.1 percent, meaning the average shortfall of income was $0.026 (2.1 percent of $1.25 = $0.026). In 2010, 4.6 percent (or 0.67 million) of Ecuador's population of 14.5 million fell below this poverty line. It would take then approximately $377,000 per day to lift the 0.67 million up to the poverty line (i.e., $0.026 times 14.5 million population), or daily transfers of $0.56 per extremely poor person (see World Bank 2012: Table 2.8).

Note that if the poverty line is set at $2 per day (PPP dollars), then the incidence of poverty in Ecuador in 2010 rises to 10.6 percent (1.54 million), and the poverty gap is 4.1 percent, meaning an average shortfall of income of $0.082. To lift the 1.54 million out of poverty then would take approximately $1,189,000 per day in the aggregate or transfers of nearly $0.77 per poor person.

The first Millennium Development Goal, adopted by 189 nations in the Millennium Declaration of the United Nations in September 2000, called for cutting in half the percentage of people living in extreme poverty, then defined as less than $1.08 in 1993 **purchasing power parity-adjusted** (PPP) dollars, between 1990 and 2015. A new extreme poverty line has since been set at $1.25 a day in 2005 PPP dollars. This represents the mean of the poverty lines found in the poorest 15 countries ranked by per capita consumption. PPP incomes are used to estimate global poverty since they take into account the local prices of goods and services not traded internationally (see World Bank 2012: 73.)

Purchasing power parity-adjusted incomes

Incomes converted to dollars using market exchange rates tend to understate the real incomes in poor countries where the cost of living is lower. Exchange rates reflect the demands and supplies of national currencies, in turn, derived from the demands and supplies of internationally traded goods, services, and assets.[9] In less developed economies, nontraded goods and services, i.e., not entering into international trade but consumed only domestically, may be relatively inexpensive. In these labor-abundant nations, wages are low and the costs of production are less. Further, with lower incomes, the demands for goods and services may be lower, which also reduces market prices. In short, a US dollar will purchase more goods and services in less developed countries than implied by the exchange rates used to convert incomes from the local currencies into dollars. Therefore, internationally comparable or PPP dollars should be used when presenting incomes across countries with different costs of living. (See Box 1.2 for an illustration of the calculation of PPP income.)

BOX 1.2: EXAMPLE OF CONVERSION TO INTERNATIONALLY COMPARABLE (PPP) NATIONAL INCOMES

If India's GDP is 40,000 billion rupees and the current exchange rate is 50 rupees = $1.00, then India's GDP is 40,000 billion rupees/(50 rupees/$1) = $800 billion. But if, say, a haircut (not internationally traded) in India cost 50 rupees (or $1 at the current exchange rate), while a similar haircut in the US costs $10, and, in general, prices of nontraded goods and services are one tenth as expensive in India compared to the US, i.e., 50 rupees in India purchases the same quantity of goods and services as $10 would in the US, which implies a PPP exchange rate of 5 rupees = $1.00, then there needs to be an adjustment upwards in the value of India's national output and national income to take into account the lower cost of living in India (or the real purchasing power of the rupee).[a]

Not all of a country's national output would enter into international trade, however, so the differences in the cost of living and the calculation of the purchasing power adjusted national income should reflect the openness of the economy. If, say, 80 percent of India's GDP does not enter into world trade, then the actual purchasing power adjusted exchange rate can be calculated as:

$$0.8 \cdot (5 \text{ rupees}/\$1) + 0.2 \cdot (50 \text{ rupees}/\$1) = 4 \text{ rupees}/\$1 + 10 \text{ rupees}/\$1$$

$$= 14 \text{ rupees}/\$1$$

---

[9]Some nations set official exchange rates which may not reflect market equilibrium exchange values of their currencies. When the World Bank converts national incomes expressed in national currencies into current US dollars a three-year average of real exchange rates is used to smooth the effects of transitory fluctuations in exchange rates. When official exchange rates are deemed to be unreliable or unrepresentative of the effective exchange rate during the period, the World Bank uses alternative estimates of the real exchange rate between the national currencies and the US dollar.

So, to calculate India's national output and national income in internationally comparable dollars, we use this PPP-adjusted exchange rate. Thus, India's GDP (in PPP dollars) is

$$40,000 \text{ billion rupees}/(14 \text{ rupees}/\$1) = \$2,857 \text{ billion}$$

[a] For internationally traded goods and services there is one common world price (before any import tariffs or trade barriers and transportation costs). For example, one bushel of wheat costing 100 rupees in India would trade for \$2 at the current exchange rate; otherwise arbitrage would be profitable. Arbitrage refers to (simultaneously) purchasing a good or asset in one market and selling it in a second market (for a higher price and profit). For example, if a bushel of wheat only costs 75 rupees in India, then at the exchange rate of 50 rupees = \$1.00, arbitrageurs could buy Indian wheat for \$1.50 and sell it in the world market for \$2.00, a profit of \$0.50 per bushel. Consequently the purchases of wheat in India would bid up the Indian price to the world price. Moreover, if India could produce wheat for 75 rupees a bushel, less than the world price of 100 rupees or \$2, then India would be an exporter of wheat and in increasing the production of wheat for export, move up the domestic supply curve of wheat, which raises the Indian supply price of wheat to the world price of 100 rupees.

Diversity in the incidence of poverty

The World Bank (2001b) provides evidence that the incomes of the poor also tend to increase with economic growth (see especially Chapter 3 of that report). Rates of economic growth, however, vary across and within countries over time. Moreover, the extent to which economic growth reduces poverty depends in part on the distributions of income within the countries and the institutions in place and economic policies implemented. As noted by the World Bank (2006: 9):

On average, for countries with low levels of income inequality, a 1 percentage point growth in mean incomes leads to about a 4 percentage point reduction in the incidence of \$1 per day poverty. That power falls close to zero in countries with high income inequality.

See Table 1.1, for example, where extreme poverty is defined as living on less than \$1.25 a day. This income threshold is adjusted for inflation and differences in the costs of living across countries. Globally, the incidence of extreme poverty in the developing nations, i.e., the low- and middle-income nations of Asia, Africa, the Middle East, Latin America, and Eastern Europe, has been reduced between 1990 and 2008 from 43.1 percent to 22.4 percent of the populations, or from 1.9 billion to less than 1.3 billion people. This mostly reflects China's extraordinary success. Overall, outside China, the absolute number of extremely poor in developing nations decreased between 1990 and 2008 by 110 million.

China, with an average economic growth rate of over 9 percent between 1990 and 2008, was able to reduce the incidence of extreme poverty from 60 percent (683 million) in 1990 to 13 percent (173 million) of its population in 2008. South Asia, dominated by India, has also reduced the incidence of poverty with its economic growth, although this region still had over 44 percent of the extremely poor in the world in 2008. The doubling of the incidence of poverty in Europe and Central Asia over the 1990s reflected the difficulties the former socialist states experienced in transforming their economies to more market-oriented systems. On average, output growth, not

Table 1.1 *Statistics on world poverty*

	GNI per capita in 2008		Ave. annual growth rates in per capita GDP		Extreme poverty incidence, % of population (millions)		
	$	PPP$	1990–99	2000–08	1990	1999	2008
East Asia & Pacific	$2,644	$5,421	6.2%	8.3%	56.2% (926)	35.6% (656)	14.3% (284)
China	$2,940	$6,010	9.6%	9.8%	60.2% (683)	35.6% (446)	13.1% (173)
Europe & Cen. Asia	$7,350	$11,953	−2.5%	6.1%	1.9% (9)	3.8% (18)	0.5% (2)
Lat. America & Car.	$6,768	$10,312	1.7%	2.7%	12.2% (53)	11.9% (60)	6.5% (37)
M. East & N. Africa	$3,237	$7,343	0.8%	2.9%	5.8% (13)	5.0% (14)	2.7% (9)
South Asia	$963	$2,695	3.7%	5.7%	53.8% (617)	45.1% (619)	36.0% (571)
India	$1,040	$2,930	4.2%	6.5%	51.3% (448)	45.6% (473)	37.4% (445)
Sub-Saharan Africa	$1,077	$1,949	−0.4%	2.7%	56.5% (290)	57.9% (376)	47.5% (386)
All low- & middle-income countries	$2,780	$5,303	1.9%	5.1%	43.1% (1,909)	34.1% (1,743)	22.4% (1,289)

Notes: Gross national income (GNI) is the total market value of the final goods and services produced by residents of a nation. GNI per capita is gross national income divided by the total population. Extreme poverty is measured by persons living on less than $1.25 a day in 2005 PPP dollars.

Sources: World Bank (2001a, Table 4.1; 2001b: Table 3; 2010a: Tables 1.1 and 4.1; 2010b: Table 2.8; 2012: Table 2.8). See also http://iresearch.worldbank.org/povcalnet for country and regional estimates of poverty.

just economic growth, was negative in these nations over the last decade of the twentieth century. Sub-Saharan Africa had not seen much economic growth over the last quarter of the twentieth century. In the first decade of the twenty-first century, however, sub-Saharan Africa did generate some economic growth, with its aggregate output rising faster than its population, and did reduce the incidence of extreme poverty, but not the numbers. Still in 2008, nearly half of sub-Saharan Africa's population lived on less than $1.25 a day. The global recession of 2009 likely slowed the progress in poverty alleviation in many developing nations.[10]

In general, then, economic growth makes possible a reduction in the incidence of poverty. Conversely, with economic recessions, poverty rates tend to rise. The type of development strategy followed by a nation can affect the degree of poverty reduction realized from economic growth.

---

[10] In 2009 world GDP fell by 1.9 percent, with declines of 2.6 percent and 3.3 percent in the real outputs of the upper middle- and high-income economies, respectively. Regionally, aggregate real outputs declined 5.8 percent in Europe and Central Asia and 1.9 percent in Latin America and the Caribbean (World Bank 2012: Table 1.1). In addition, increases in food prices over the last few years have especially hurt the poor in developing countries. Nevertheless, the World Bank (2012: 2) refers to preliminary estimates for 2010 that indicate continual progress such that the Millennium Development Goal of halving the global incidence of extreme poverty is likely to be reached five years before the 2015 target date.

For example, to the extent that a nation has invested in human capital and institutions to promote socioeconomic mobility, the degree of absolute poverty might be less, the income distribution would be more equal and the economic growth that occurs would more likely be equitable. The East Asian success stories, such as South Korea and Taiwan, reflect this growth-with-equity approach to development. The recent explosive economic growth in China, however, has been accompanied by growing inequalities; although, as noted, the rise in per capita incomes has also significantly reduced extreme poverty in the nation. So, too, the former socialist and relatively egalitarian economies of Eastern Europe have experienced increasing inequalities during their transformation to more market-oriented systems; and in the initial decade of transformation in the 1990s, the incidence of poverty increased with the negative economic growth.

On the other hand, to the extent that wealth is concentrated, often the case with countries well endowed with mineral resources, the extent of poverty may be relatively high, institutions may not be as developed or progressive, and the economic growth that occurs would be less likely to improve the conditions of the majority of the population. The oil-rich nations in the Middle East might be examples, as average incomes there are fairly high, but the distributions of incomes are relatively unequal. Latin American nations have also been characterized by unequal distributions of income and significant poverty for the levels of per capita incomes. In fact, income inequality may hinder economic growth:

> Unequal societies are more prone to difficulties in collective action, possibly reflected in dysfunctional institutions, political instability, a propensity for populist redistributive policies, or greater volatility in policies—all of which can lower growth. And to the extent that inequality in income or assets coexists with imperfect credit markets, poor people may be unable to invest in their human and physical capital, with adverse consequences for long-run growth. (World Bank 2001b: 56)

Returning to Table 1.1, we note the relatively low economic growth rates for Latin America and the Caribbean over the past two decades, and the significantly higher poverty incidence, particularly in contrast to the Europe and Central Asia, a region with similar average per capita incomes.

Income distribution

As stated, economic growth will more likely alleviate poverty when the distribution of income is more even. To illustrate this stylized fact of economic growth, refer to Table 1.2, where the incidence of extreme poverty (the percentage of the population living on less than $1.25) and the poverty gap (the average percentage shortfall in income below the poverty line) is given for selected Latin American nations.

To begin, observe the difference between per capita incomes in dollars and PPP dollars, which accounts for differences in the cost of living across countries. For example, in 2010 we see that Panama had significantly higher per capita national income than Peru, both in US dollars and PPP dollars. The incidence of poverty and the poverty gaps in Peru, however, are lower than those in Panama, reflecting, in part, Peru's somewhat less unequal income distribution.

For another example, in 2010 Colombia and the Dominican Republic had similar per capita incomes, but Colombia had a much higher incidence of extreme poverty and poverty gap. Colombia's highly unequal distribution of income is reflected in the shares of income (e.g., 60.2 percent

Table 1.2 *Poverty incidence and poverty gap: selected countries in Latin America and the Caribbean, 2010*

Country	GNI per capita		% of population below	Poverty gap at	Population share of income		
	$	PPP$	$1.25 a day	$1.25 a day	Bottom 20%	Top 20%	Gini Index
Colombia	$5,510	$9,060	8.2%	3.8%	3.0%	60.2%	55.9
Dominican Rep.	$5,030	$9,030	2.2%	0.5%	4.7%	52.8%	47.2
Ecuador	$3,850	$7,880	4.6%	2.1%	4.3%	53.8%	49.3
Panama	$6,970	$12,770	6.6%	2.1%	3.3%	56.4%	51.9
Paraguay	$2,720	$5,080	7.2%	3.0%	3.3%	56.4%	52.4
Peru	$4,700	$8,930	4.9%	1.3%	3.9%	52.6%	48.1

Notes: Gross national income (GNI) is the total market value of the final goods and services produced by residents of a nation. GNI per capita is GNI divided by the mid-year population. Data are in current US dollars converted using the World Bank *Atlas* method where GNIs in national currencies are converted into dollar values using a three-year average of real exchange rates to smooth the effects of transitory fluctuations in exchange rates.

Gross national income in PPP dollars is GNI converted to international dollars. An international dollar has the same purchasing power over GNI as a US dollar in the United States. PPP rates provide a standard measure allowing comparisons of real levels of income and expenditures between countries.

The incidence of extreme poverty is measured by the percentage of the population living on less than $1.25 a day in 2005 PPP dollars.

The *poverty gap* is the mean shortfall from the poverty line (counting the nonpoor as having a zero shortfall), expressed as a percentage of the poverty line. This measure reflects the depth of poverty as well as its incidence. Inequality in the distribution of income is reflected in the percentage shares of personal income received by quintiles of the population.

The Gini Index is a measure of the inequality of the income distribution, ranging from 0 (perfect equality) to 100 (perfect inequality).

From: World Bank (2012: Tables 1.1, 2.8, and 2.9).

of the income received by the top 20 percent of the population) and more comprehensively in the high Gini Index of 55.9 (see World Bank 2012: Table 2.9). The **Gini Index**, a comprehensive measure of income inequality, can range from 0 (perfect equality, where everyone in the population has the same income) to 100 (perfect inequality, where one individual receives all the income).[11]

As remarked, Latin America is characterized by relatively unequal income distributions. And, for a given per capita income, the incidence of poverty and poverty gap will be affected by the distribution of incomes and the types of economic policies, e.g., social welfare expenditures. In particular, Mexico and Brazil, with their conditional cash transfers programs, have effectively used income redistribution to promote human capital formation, a key not only to poverty alleviation but also to economic growth.

As we will discuss later, there are other consequences for economic growth besides increases in the average standard of living and the reduction of absolute poverty. We now turn to the determinants of output growth.

---

[11] In contrast, the Gini indices in the egalitarian northern European nations of Sweden and Norway in 2000 (the latest year available) were respectively 25.0 percent and 25.8 percent. As will be discussed in Chapter 7, the United States, on the other hand, has a relatively unequal distribution of income. In 2000, the Gini Index for the US was 40.8. We should add a note of caution that data on income distribution are based on surveys of households and may be subject to considerable error, with differences in the accuracy of measurement across nations and over time.

PRIMARY SOURCES OF OUTPUT GROWTH

As noted, the economic growth rate is given by the difference between the growth rate in real national output (dY/Y) and the growth rate in population (dP/P). We begin with the sources of output growth. In Chapter 2 we will discuss the sources of population growth.

Using a nation as the unit of analysis, we begin with an aggregate production function, which can be generally written as

$$Y = A \cdot F(\underline{K}, \underline{L}, \underline{R})$$

where Y is real national output, A is an index of technology, $\underline{K} = q_K \cdot K$ is effective physical capital (with q_K an index of the quality of physical capital and K the physical capital stock), $\underline{L} = q_L \cdot L$ is effective labor (with q_L an index of the quality of labor and L the quantity of labor), and $\underline{R} = q_R \cdot R$ is effective natural resources (with q_R an index of the quality of natural resources and R the quantity of natural resources available). That is, real national output, the production of final goods and services in an economy, depends on the state of technology and the supplies of the **effective factors of production**.[12] Each primary factor of production (physical capital, labor, and natural resources) is multiplied by an index of the quality or inherent productivity of that physical factor.

Technological progress reflects advances in science and engineering that enhance the production of goods and services. An increase in the index A allows for greater output for a given set of effective factors of production. Invention of new goods and innovation of production processes improve the productive capacity of a nation. Moreover, gains in knowledge can be shared and built upon to generate further advances in technology. As represented here, the index A reflects **neutral technical change**, i.e., total factor productivity is enhanced by an increase in the index A, but relative factor productivities are unaffected. As we will see, technological progress also promotes economic growth through improvements in the quality of physical capital and increased efficiencies in using natural resources.[13]

The **physical capital** stock (K) consists of the human-made aids to production, or the buildings, machinery, and equipment used to produce goods and services. If gross fixed domestic investment (total expenditures on new capital goods) exceeds depreciation (the loss in the capital stock due to wear and tear and technological obsolescence), then net fixed investment is positive and the value of the nation's physical capital stock rises, augmenting the productive capacity of the economy.

Much of new technology is embodied in the new capital goods, e.g., improved fuel efficiencies in trucks, more energy-efficient machines, and faster and more powerful computers. The index of the quality of capital, q_K, captures this source of growth. For example, if the initial value of q_K is 1.0 (the reference period), and the quality of capital increased by 0.5 percent, on average, with the replacement of depreciated machinery and equipment with improved versions, then q_K would increase to 1.005. Even if the level of the physical capital stock were unchanged, the effective capital stock would be scaled up by 0.5 percent. An example might be personal computers. Replacing a three-year-old personal computer with a new version that embodies the latest technology (e.g., increased speed, more memory, improved word-processing, and enhanced spreadsheet applications) would leave the physical capital stock unchanged, but would increase the effective physical

---

[12] We could also use the world economy as the unit of analysis, and consider a global production function for gross world output.

[13] Note that, if we regard $Y = A \cdot F(\underline{K}, \underline{L}, \underline{R})$ as a global production function, then an increase in A, the global index of technology, may reflect not just technological progress which tends to originate in the developed countries, but also the spread of technology to less developed countries which raises total factor productivity there.

13

capital stock. Moreover, these advances in technology have been so significant that the new and improved personal computers may well cost less. Overall, the growth rate in effective physical capital is equal to the sum of the growth rates in the quality of capital and the quantity of capital: $d\underline{K}/\underline{K} = dq_K/q_K + dK/K$.

Effective labor represents the input of human resources. The physical labor force, L, reflects the population of working age and the labor force participation rates. The index of the quality of labor, q_L, captures the inherent productivity of a unit of physical labor. With human capital formation and investments in education, health, and nutrition, the quality of labor increases. A more experienced labor force may also be more productive. The growth rate in effective labor is equal to the sum of the growth rates in the quality and quantity of labor: $d\underline{L}/\underline{L} = dq_L/q_L + dL/L$.

The third primary factor of production is effective natural resources or "gifts of nature." We should distinguish renewable from nonrenewable natural resources. **Renewable natural resources** (e.g., farmland, forests, aquifers, and fishing stocks), if not drawn on beyond their regenerative capacities, can be used in production continuously, so $dR/R = 0$. Overuse or misuse of renewable natural resources, however, can result in a decrease in their availability, as with soil erosion, deforestation, and depletion of fishing stocks. In contrast, **nonrenewable natural resources**, also known as exhaustible resources, such as fossil fuels and minerals, have finite stocks. While all the deposits might not be known at present or, with the current technologies, accessible for use in production, the use of nonrenewable resources will nevertheless draw down the total stocks in the world, so $dR/R < 0$. A nation might increase its use of nonrenewable natural resources, at the expense of other nations, and in the short run any nation can overuse its renewable natural resources; however, in the aggregate for the world and in the long run, the contribution of natural resources to output growth will be declining.

Improvements in the quality of natural resources, a rise in q_R, however, would increase the effective supply. For example, investment in land with the use of fertilizers and irrigation can increase soil fertility. On the other hand, misuse of natural resources and pollution can reduce their average productivity (e.g., waterlogging and salinization of soils or emission of pollutants into the atmosphere or waste into the ocean). As De Souza et al. (2003: 22) note for forests:

> The loss of forests in recent decades had been partially offset by new plantations. But the substitution of planted forests for natural forests is a net loss for Earth's biodiversity. Replanted forests often consist of few tree species, making forests more vulnerable to disease, drought, and other natural stresses. And less-diverse tree plantations cannot support as many species of other plants and animals.

For nonrenewable resources, given the profitability of using the richest deposits first, the average quality may decline as the resources are extracted. For example, the quality of coal varies with the age of the deposits. The older is the coal, the higher the carbon content and the more valuable for use in energy. Generally, anthracite is the oldest coal, followed by bituminous and lignite. In sum, if stocks of nonrenewable natural resources are declining, then to maintain effective natural resources, $d\underline{R}/\underline{R} = 0$, the index of the quality of natural resources would have to be rising, $dq_R/q_R > 0$.

Before deriving the growth equation, we should note the invaluable and virtually irreplaceable services provided by the natural environment. The air we breathe, the water we drink, and the soil we use for growing our food are all essential for sustaining life. In addition, the natural environment absorbs the wastes generated by human activity.

OUTPUT GROWTH ACCOUNTING

Moving from a static aggregate production function to the growth rate in real national output requires a bit of math. Beginning with the aggregate production function, $Y = A \cdot F(\underline{K}, \underline{L}, \underline{R})$ and totally differentiating gives:

$$dY = dA \cdot F(\underline{K}, \underline{L}, \underline{R}) + A \cdot [(\partial F/\partial \underline{K}) \cdot d\underline{K} + (\partial F/\partial \underline{L}) \cdot d\underline{L} + (\partial F/\partial \underline{R}) \cdot d\underline{R}]$$

Dividing through by $Y = A \cdot F(\underline{K}, \underline{L}, \underline{R})$ and simplifying, we get

$$dY/Y = dA/A + \sigma_{\underline{K}} \cdot (d\underline{K}/\underline{K}) + \sigma_{\underline{L}} \cdot (d\underline{L}/\underline{L}) + \sigma_{\underline{R}} \cdot (d\underline{R}/\underline{R})$$

That is, the growth rate in real national output, dY/Y, is equal to the sum of the growth rate in the index of technical change, dA/A, and the products of the growth rates of effective capital, labor, and natural resources with their respective partial output elasticities: $\sigma_{\underline{K}}$, $\sigma_{\underline{L}}$, and $\sigma_{\underline{R}}$.

The growth rates of the effective factors of production are, in turn, equal to the sums of the growth rates in the indices of the quality or inherent productivity of the factors and the physical quantities of the factors:

$$d\underline{K}/\underline{K} = dq_{\underline{K}}/q_{\underline{K}} + dK/K = \text{growth rate in effective physical capital}$$

$$d\underline{L}/\underline{L} = dq_{\underline{L}}/q_{\underline{L}} + dL/L = \text{growth rate in effective labor}$$

$$d\underline{R}/\underline{R} = dq_{\underline{R}}/q_{\underline{R}} + dR/R = \text{growth rate in effective natural resources}$$

The partial output elasticities, the σs, are equal to the partial derivatives of the growth rates of output to the growth rates of the effective factors. In discrete terms, the partial output elasticity for effective capital indicates the percentage change in real output resulting from a one percentage point change in effective capital, *ceteris paribus*, i.e., holding constant technology and the other effective factors of production:

$$\frac{\delta(dY/Y)}{\delta(d\underline{K}/\underline{K})} = \sigma_{\underline{K}} = \text{partial output elasticity with respect to effective capital}$$

$$\frac{\delta(dY/Y)}{\delta(d\underline{L}/\underline{L})} = \sigma_{\underline{L}} = \text{partial output elasticity with respect to effective labor}$$

$$\frac{\delta(dY/Y)}{\delta(d\underline{R}/\underline{R})} = \sigma_{\underline{R}} = \text{partial output elasticity with respect to effective natural resources}$$

To illustrate with a specific example, consider a Cobb–Douglas production function: $Y = A \cdot \underline{K}^{\alpha} \underline{L}^{\beta} \underline{R}^{\gamma}$ $(0 < \alpha, \beta, \gamma < 1)$. To identify the sources of output growth we can totally differentiate this production function:

$$dY = dA \cdot \underline{K}^{\alpha} \underline{L}^{\beta} \underline{R}^{\gamma} + A \cdot [\alpha \underline{K}^{\alpha-1} \underline{L}^{\beta} \underline{R}^{\gamma} d\underline{K} + \beta \underline{K}^{\alpha} \underline{L}^{\beta-1} \underline{R}^{\gamma} d\underline{L} + \gamma \underline{K}^{\alpha} \underline{L}^{\beta} \underline{R}^{\gamma-1} d\underline{R}]$$

To find the growth rate, divide both sides by $Y = A \cdot \underline{K}^{\alpha} \underline{L}^{\beta} \underline{R}^{\gamma}$ to give

$$dY/Y = dA/A + \alpha \cdot (d\underline{K}/\underline{K}) + \beta \cdot (d\underline{L}/\underline{L}) + \gamma \cdot (d\underline{R}/\underline{R})$$

where α, β, and γ are the partial output elasticities with respect to effective capital, effective labor, and effective natural resources, respectively. Note that each of these partial output elasticities, indicated by the exponents of the effective factors of production, is assumed to be positive and less than 1. For example, if the growth rate in effective labor were to increase by 1 percent, then holding constant technology and the other effective factors of production, the growth rate in output would increase by β percent, where $0 < \beta < 1$.

In sum, the production of real national output can increase with advances in technology, improvements in the quality, and increases in the quantity of the primary factors of production. We have identified physical capital, human capital (adding to the inherent productivity of labor), and natural capital (i.e., natural resources) as important factors of production. We should note a fourth type of capital, **social capital**, which refers to interpersonal trust, shared values, and social networks that give cohesion to society and foster cooperation, identification with the nation, and promotion of the common good. Social capital is undermined by discrimination, ethnic rivalries, corruption, and crime. The erosion of social capital can result in political instability and, in the extreme, civil war. In contrast, social capital formation, while less tangible than physical capital formation, can contribute to economic growth and may be essential for sustainable development.

Other influences on output growth include returns to scale, economies of scale, international integration, and aggregate demand. Each will be discussed, in turn, below.

Returns to scale

Returns to scale refer to the change in output resulting from an across-the-board change in the factors of production for a given technology. If an increase (decrease) in the factors of n percent results in a greater than n percent increase (decrease) in output, then **increasing returns to scale** are indicated. If output increases (decreases) by less than n percent when the factors of production increase (decrease) by n percent, then **decreasing returns to scale** characterize the production function. Finally, if an n percent increase (decrease) in the factors of production results in an n percent increase (decrease) in output, then **constant returns to scale** apply.

We can illustrate with the Cobb–Douglas aggregate production function,

$$Y = A \cdot \underline{K}^\alpha \underline{L}^\beta \underline{R}^\gamma,$$

where $(0 < \alpha, \beta, \gamma < 1)$. The sum of the exponents, α, β, and γ, indicating the partial output elasticities with respect to effective capital, effective labor, and effective natural resources, determines the returns to scale. If $\alpha + \beta + \gamma > 1$, then increasing returns to scale apply, if $\alpha + \beta + \gamma < 1$, then decreasing returns to scale apply, and if $\alpha + \beta + \gamma = 1$, then constant returns to scale apply.

For example, let $\alpha = 0.3$, $\beta = 0.6$, and $\gamma = 0.2$. The aggregate production function is $Y = A\underline{K}^{0.3}\underline{L}^{0.6}\underline{R}^{0.2}$. Now, if we increase the effective factors of production by 50 percent, i.e., multiply each of the effective factors of production by 1.5, then

$$A(1.5\underline{K})^{0.3}(1.5\underline{L})^{0.6}(1.5\underline{R})^{0.2} = A(1.5)^{0.3+0.6+0.2}\underline{K}^{0.3}\underline{L}^{0.6}\underline{R}^{0.2} = (1.5)^{1.1}A\underline{K}^{0.3}\underline{L}^{0.6}\underline{R}^{0.2} = 1.56 \cdot Y$$

That is, increasing the effective factors of production across the board by 50 percent increases output by 56 percent, due to increasing returns to scale.[14]

---

[14] A simple example from packaging might be a cube with 2-foot-long sides. The area of each side of the cube is 4 square feet, giving a total surface area of 24 square feet of material (say, cardboard). The volume of this cube, which gives the capacity to store material, is 8 cubic feet. Now, increasing the length of the sides by 50 percent to 3 feet would increase the surface area of each side by 125 percent, from 4 to 9 square feet. The total surface area of the cube increases also by 125 percent, from 24 square feet to 54 square feet. The volume of the cube, however, increases by 237.5 percent, from 8 to 27 cubic feet. In sum, increasing the surface area of this cube (inputs into the production function) by 125 percent, increases the volume (output of the cube or storage capacity) by 237.5 percent, illustrating increasing returns to scale.

Economies of scale

Returns to scale, however, may be of limited relevance since as firms increase production the factor proportions might change. More relevant might be the **economies of scale** reflected in the decreasing long-run average cost of production as the rate of production increases. The long-run average cost curve for a firm is generally believed to be U-shaped. As a firm expands its output in the long run, where all factors of production are variable, the average cost of production might fall—at least up to a point. The lower unit cost of production reflects the **division of labor**, the principle behind the assembly line, and the substitution of capital for labor (e.g., with automation). As the rate of production increases for a firm, it becomes more efficient to break down the production of the good into different stages, with specialized labor and capital responsible for different parts of the production process.

For example, on the automobile assembly line, rather than having a small group of workers producing a car from start to finish, the workers are organized with specific tasks, installing windshields, fitting bumpers, etc. Thus the product moves along the assembly line with workers in place at different stations, becoming very efficient in their particular tasks and requiring one set of specialized tools to do their jobs and not having to change tools to do additional tasks. Moreover, as the volume of production increases, automation or the replacement of labor with high-speed, expensive machinery and equipment becomes cost-effective. For both reasons, the unit cost of production may decline as the volume of production rises.

Whether this division of labor is good for the human soul is another question. E.F. Schumacher, in his classic work, *Small Is Beautiful: Economics as if People Mattered* (1973: 38), described the mass production of the assembly line as "soul-destroying, meaningless, mechanical, monotonous, moronic work. . .an insult to human nature which must necessarily and inevitably produce either escapism or aggression, and. . .no amount of 'bread and circuses' can compensate for the damage done." We will discuss Schumacher's approach to development later.

There can be **diseconomies of scale**, where further increases in the rate of production lead to increases in the average cost of production, i.e., the long-run average cost curve slopes upwards (the right-hand side of the U-shaped curve). This can occur if larger firms encounter difficulties in management, communication, and supervision of workers. Moreover, as Schumacher would argue, the morale and productivity of workers might decline as the volume of production rises above a certain level due to the self-perception of each worker as an insignificant "cog" in the production process. Labor shirking might rise with the size of the company.

Nevertheless, larger countries, with greater populations and aggregate incomes, may have an advantage over smaller countries, where the domestic demands for goods and services may be too small for firms to capture all the economies of scale. With economic growth and development, cities emerge as centers of industry, commerce, and government. Favorable for output growth are the agglomeration effects with urbanization, including the concentration of firms, producing both final goods and services as well as supplying intermediate goods, and the large pools of labor (see World Bank 2009, especially Chapter 4). Complementary industries provide essential services in transportation, communications, and finance. Larger markets promote such specialization in production and occupations. That is, when serving sufficiently large markets, firms can specialize in the production of goods and services (e.g., construction firms that specialize in building schools, or hospitals, or water treatment plants), and the variety of goods and services produced increases (e.g., models of automobiles and electrical appliances).

Closely associated will be the **specialization of labor**, justified again by the greater markets served. For example, in rural areas of the US you may find the few doctors practicing family medicine. In urban areas, with hospitals and many doctors, you will find more specialization (e.g., orthopedic surgeons and oncologists). The specialization of firms and labor will increase productivity as such specialization increases expertise and motivates continual improvement. So, too, larger and wealthier economies with graduate universities can generate more scientists and engineers and afford more research and development. It is not surprising that most of the advances in technology come from the larger and richer nations.

While "bigger may be better" for the growth in aggregate output for the reasons noted above (i.e., economies of scale, specialization, and research and development), when we consider natural resource constraints (e.g., the drawing down of nonrenewable resources or the ability of environments to absorb the wastes from the output produced), there may be limits to the growth. As we will discuss in the following chapters, there is considerable controversy over this issue.

International trade and investment

Both theory and evidence support international trade and investment as promoters of growth through a more efficient allocation of resources. Nations producing based on comparative advantages (lower opportunity costs) and engaging in international trade will increase the aggregate output of the world and allow these nations to consume beyond their production possibilities boundaries. (In Chapter 3 we will illustrate the gains from trade with a simple model.) Indeed, small nations can escape the constraints on production imposed by their limited domestic demands by engaging in international trade and producing for export. The East Asian economies are noted for their export expansion strategies of economic growth. In contrast, the South Asian and Latin American economies, as well as the former socialist economies of Eastern Europe and the Soviet Union, with more inward-looking policies and less international integration, were not as successful in engaging economic growth.

Increased integration into the international economy is one of the four major components of the World Bank's Market Friendly Strategy of development (see World Bank 1991), which will be discussed in Chapter 8.[15] All economies are becoming more integrated into the international economy, particularly since the dissolution of the Soviet Union in the late 1980s and the conversion of command and socialist economies to more market-oriented economies. International factor mobility, with freer flows of capital seeking better returns without regard to national borders and increased immigration of labor, complements the efficiencies realized through increased trade in goods and services.

Aggregate demand

So far we have focused on the production of national output. The primary sources of output growth from the aggregate supply side (i.e., technological progress and increases in the quantities and qualities of the primary factors of production) were identified. We discussed the importance of economies of scale, increased specialization, and the efficiencies gained through international trade.

---

[15] The other three components are competitive domestic markets, stable macroeconomies, and human capital formation.

Aggregate demand, Y^D, the total quantity of real national output demanded by consumers, businesses, the government, and the rest of the world, is also important. The major components of aggregate demand are: C, personal consumption expenditures; I, gross private domestic investment; G, government purchases of goods and services; and net exports, or X, exports of goods and services, less M, imports of goods and services. That is, $Y^D = C + I + G + X - M$.

Equilibrium real national output is jointly determined by aggregate demand and aggregate supply. Aggregate demand, however, need not equal aggregate supply at full employment or where all the labor and capital are fully utilized.

Moreover, the composition of aggregate demand is important. Nations with a higher rate of gross capital formation or gross domestic investment (GDI $= I + G_I$, where G_I is government capital expenditures) have higher potential growth. For example, China and India have experienced among the highest output growth rates in the world over the past quarter century. The remarkable economic growth of China and India reflects, among other factors, the high rates of gross capital formation. For China, annual growth rates in GDI averaged 10.8 percent and 13.3 percent for 1990–2000 and 2000–10, respectively. For India, the average annual growth rates in GDI were 6.9 percent and 12.9 percent. Both significantly exceeded the period averages for all low- and middle-income economies of 2.6 percent and 9.6 percent (World Bank 2012: Table 4.9). Greater gross domestic investment not only adds to current aggregate demand but also increases aggregate supply with the physical capital formation enhancing the productive capacity of the economy. For an accounting of the growth of China and India see Box 1.3.

BOX 1.3: GROWTH ACCOUNTING: CHINA AND INDIA

China and India, with 1.34 and 1.22 billion people respectively, together account for 44 percent of the population of the low- and middle-income economies and 37 percent of the world's population. Over the last two decades, China has experienced one of the highest economic growth rates in the world. India has also enjoyed significant economic growth. For 1990–2000 the average annual growth rate in per capita gross domestic product was 9.5 percent and 4.1 percent for China and India, respectively. Over the period 2000–10, even with the global recession of 2009, China and India's average annual economic growth rates actually increased to 10.5 percent and 6.8 percent. The corresponding economic growth rates for all low- and middle-income economies were 2.3 percent (1990–2000) and 5.3 percent (2000–10). The extraordinary growth of the Chinese and Indian economies has already had, and will continue to have, profound effects on the world's resources.

Bosworth and Collins (2008) use a simple aggregate production function with constant returns to scale, $Y = A \cdot K^{\alpha} \cdot (LH)^{1-\alpha}$, to account for the growth in real national output (Y). The scalar A represents an index of neutral technical change or total factor productivity, K is physical capital (here also including land), L is labor, and H is a proxy for labor force skills, indicated by the average years of schooling for the labor force. The partial output of elasticity, α, is assumed to be 0.4, and a constant annual return of 7 percent is assumed for

19

each additional year of schooling. Differentiating this production function, the growth rate in labor productivity can be derived as the sum of the growth rate in total factor productivity and a weighted average of the growth rates in the physical capital–labor ratio (indicating physical capital deepening) and the labor skills (indicating human capital deepening):

$$\frac{d(Y/L)}{Y/L} = \frac{dA}{A} + \alpha\frac{d(K/L)}{K/L} + (1-\alpha)\frac{dH}{H}$$

For the period 1978–2004, when China's annual output growth per worker averaged an exceptional 7.3 percent and India's an impressive 3.3 percent, Bosworth and Collins calculate the contributions from these factors. For China, the contribution of increases in physical capital deepening, education, and total factor productivity were approximately 3.2, 0.3, and 3.6 percent respectively. For India's average annual output growth per worker, the respective contributions were 1.3, 0.4, and 1.6 percent.

To compare the experiences of these two giants over the last two decades, refer to Table 1.1B. The average for all low- and middle-income economies is also given. With the accelerated declines in its fertility rate to below replacement level (an average of less than two children per woman) in the last three decades, China has reaped a demographic dividend, illustrated by the rising share of its population in prime labor force years (roughly ages 15–64). India's birth rate declines have been much slower and, at the end of the first decade of the new century, on average a woman in India still would bear nearly three children.

Both economies have high savings rates. The share of gross capital formation (gross domestic investment) in GDP has risen in China from 36 percent in 1990 to a remarkable 48 percent in 2010. India too has successfully increased the share of its national output for physical capital formation from 24 percent in 1990 to 35 percent in 2010.

Table B1.1 *Selected statistics on economic growth: China and India*

	China	India	Low- and middle-income economies
Ave. annual growth rate in GDP			
1990–2000	10.6%	5.9%	3.9%
2000–2010	10.8%	8.0%	6.4%
Ave. annual growth rate in population			
1990–2000	1.1%	1.8%	1.6%
2000–2010	0.3%	1.2%	1.1%
Share of population aged 15–64			
1990	67%	59%	60%

Table B1.1 *continued*

	China	India	Low- and middle-income economies
2000	68%	62%	63%
2010	72%	64%	65%
Share of gross capital formation in GDP			
1990	36%	24%	26%
2000	35%	24%	24%
2010	48%	35%	29%
Share of agriculture/ industry in GDP			
1990	27%/42%	31%/28%	18%/37%
2000	15%/46%	23%/26%	12%/35%
2010	10%/47%	19%/26%	10%/35%
Share of exports/imports of goods and services in GDP			
1990	19%/16%	7%/9%	20%/20%
2000	23%/21%	13%/14%	27%/25%
2010	30%/26%	22%/25%	28%/28%
Life expectancy at birth			
1990	69 years	58 years	63 years
2000	70 years	63 years	64 years
2010	73 years	65 years	68 years

Notes: Agriculture also includes forestry and fishing. Industry covers mining, manufacturing, construction, electricity, water, and gas. The residual share of gross domestic product, not attributed to agriculture or industry, is services.

Sources: World Bank (1992: Table 26; 2002a: Tables 2.1, 2.20; 2002b: Table 1; 2007: Tables 4.2, 4.8; 2012: Tables 2.1, 2.23, 4.1, 4.2, 4.8).

Both nations realized higher productivity in agriculture with the Green Revolution that began in the 1960s. One of the hallmarks of economic development is a shift in labor out of agricultural employment to the higher-productivity employment in industry and modern services. China has been more successful than India, reducing the share of GDP coming from agriculture from 27 percent in 1990 to 10 percent in 2010 versus a decline in India from 31 percent to 19 percent. China has a much higher share of GDP coming from industry: 47 percent in 2010. The share of industry in GDP for India has been fairly stable over the last two decades, and in 2010 stood at 26 percent.

China has also more successfully engaged in international trade, as evidenced by higher shares of exports in national output than India (although not in comparison to low- and middle-income economies in general). Moreover, China tends to run balance of trade surpluses (4 percent of GDP in 2010), while India remains a net importer of goods and services (balance of trade deficit of 3 percent in 2010).

Finally, as a measure of investment in human capital, China's life expectancy at birth of 73 years in 2010 is significantly higher than India's of 65 years, which is below the average of 68 years for all low- and middle-income countries.

There are other differences between these two nations that affect their economic growth. Fundamentally, China is a communist country with still extensive state control over the economy. India, a democracy, with less ability for government to direct its economy, still suffers from inefficiencies from its state bureaucracy, despite considerable economic liberalization over the past two decades.

Xu (2011) offers an explanation for the "China puzzle," or China's prolonged superior economic growth despite a seemingly weak legislative system (with restricted political participation) and judicial institutions (with arbitrary rule of law and private property rights), as well as prevalent corruption. He characterizes China as a "regionally decentralized authoritarian regime," a combination of political centralization and regional economic decentralization. The Communist Party appoints the regional and state government officials, who in turn have autonomy to pursue policies that promote economic growth. While the central government still controls and directs investment toward key sectors of the economy, such as banking, energy, transportation and communications, regional authorities have considerable sway. As Xu (2011: 1099) explains:

> When the reform era started in the late 1970s [after the death of Mao Zedong], regional governments were encouraged to find ways to develop faster than other regions. Policies on special economic zones and other economic development zones were implemented, enabling subnational governments' competition for investments. Regions competed for economic growth and for attracting FDI [foreign direct investment]... Government statistics and mass media regularly publish rankings of regional performance, which become an important part of evaluations for determining the promotions of subnational government officials.

Such regional competition allowed for best practices to spread, furthering economic growth. Agrarian reform brought greater incentives for individual farmers and township-village enterprises were developed to supply growing markets. This has combined with the Communist Party's guidance of the macroeconomy—including priority investment in key infrastructure, increased integration with the international economy, and authoritarian population policy–to generate impressive economic growth, and China has progressed from a low-income economy at the end of the twentieth century to an upper-middle income economy today. And, as we noted earlier, the unprecedented economic growth has dramatically reduced poverty. As we will discuss later, China still faces important challenges, including environmental deterioration (an adverse consequence of rapid economic growth), a soon-to-be rising elderly burden of dependency (an inevitable consequence of the accelerated fertility transition), not to mention issues of human rights.

Kotwal et al. (2011: 1152) open their study of India as follows: "By the end of the 1970s, India had acquired a reputation as one of the most protected and heavily regulated economies of the world." Unlike China, India has been a democracy since its independence in 1947. State control over commerce and inward-looking import substitution policies, however, discouraged the development of private enterprise and the efficient allocation of resources. Consequently, until the adoption of more liberal and open economic policies, particularly in the early 1990s, India had experienced little economic growth. While the Green Revolution in agriculture has helped to feed the large population, India remains largely rural and agrarian. Growth poles in the major cities, however, have emerged with services, not manufacturing, as leading sectors of growth. In particular, with international integration, its English-speaking population (a significant number of whom are well educated) and location (in a time zone half-way around the world from the United States), India has taken advantage of the growing outsourcing of business services. Whether it has been the development of software or the staffing of call centers, India has generated considerable export revenues in the telecommunications sector. Yet, after two decades of strong growth, India remains a poor country, with over a third of its population living in extreme poverty. Kotwal et al. (2011: 1196) conclude:

> there are two Indias: one of educated managers and engineers who have been able to take advantage of the opportunities made available through globalization and the other—a huge mass of undereducated people who a making a living in low productivity jobs in the informal sector—the largest of which is still "agriculture."

From their growth accounting study, Bosworth and Collins (2008: 64–65) conclude:

> Overall...the supply-side prospects for continued rapid growth in China and India, in terms of labor, physical capital, and reallocation across sectors are very good. Ultimately, India will need to redress its inadequate infrastructure and to broaden its trade beyond the current emphasis on services. Only an expansion of goods production and trade can provide employment opportunities for its current pool of underemployed and undereducated workers. China has performed well in the international dimension, but now needs to focus on development of internal markets, reducing inefficiencies in its financial sector, and achieving a more balanced trade position. However, none of these concerns can diminish the amazing accomplishments of both countries and the progress they have made in lifting two and a half billion people from abject poverty.

In short, an increase in real national output can reflect an increase in aggregate demand, as well as in aggregate supply. Usually, both aggregate demand and aggregate supply increase over time; however, sometimes nations experience negative output growth, or a decline in real national output, which can be caused by a decrease in aggregate demand or aggregate supply. (In Chapter 6 a simple model of aggregate demand and aggregate supply is used to illustrate fluctuations in real national output.)

LABOR PRODUCTIVITIES AND PER CAPITA INCOMES

We can disaggregate per capita income into the average product of labor and the share of the population that is economically active:

$$y = Y/P = (Y/L) \cdot (L/P)$$

where L is labor force. Economic growth can occur with an improvement in labor productivity (a rise in Y/L, or output per unit of labor) or with a greater share of the population in the labor force (L/P). Increases in the average product of labor could reflect capital deepening (increases in the physical, human, or natural capital per unit of labor) or increases in technology. Increases in the share of the population in the labor force tend to occur with the fertility transition, a **demographic dividend** associated with the sustained declines in birth rates that accompany economic development.

For evidence, see Table 1.3, where we have arranged countries according to the World Bank's per capita income classification. In addition, the three largest nations in the world—China (now an upper middle-income economy), India (a lower middle-income economy), and the United States (a high-income economy)—are distinguished. The aggregate statistics are weighted by population shares and these three countries dominate their respective income groups. In fact, the two demographic billionaires, China and India, account for over a third of the world's population. If we add the United States, these three nations account for more than two out of every five persons on the planet.

We can see the highly unequal distribution of income across the world. One sixth of the world's population living in the high-income economies (including the United States, Western Europe, and Japan) accounted for 70 percent of the world's income in 2010. At the other end, one-ninth of the world's population living in the low-income nations (most of sub-Saharan Africa and South Asia) generated less than 1 percent of the world's income. Correspondingly, the average per capita income in the high-income nations is over 70 times that of the low-income nations. Averages understate the actual ranges in income between the richest and poorest nations, so the gaps between the richest and poorest nations are even greater.

As noted, per capita incomes converted to dollars using market exchange rates tend to understate the real incomes in poor countries where the cost of living is lower. We can see that, expressed in PPP dollars, the per capita incomes for the low- and middle-income countries increase significantly, often doubling or even tripling. Accordingly, the gaps in average per capita incomes between the high- and low-income economies, while still large, are reduced from a ratio of over 70 : 1 to a ratio closer to 30 : 1 (in PPP dollars).

The gaps in per capita incomes largely reflect gaps in labor productivities, as comparisons of gross national income (GNI) per laborer reveal. Labor is more productive, on average, in the high-income economies due to the higher capital to labor ratios, the greater human capital per laborer, superior technologies, and more efficient economic systems. Also contributing to the higher per capita incomes are higher labor force to population ratios in the high-income economies compared to the low-income economies. China's labor force share in total population in 2010 is nearly 60 percent. The sharp declines in fertility in China over the past three decades have yielded a demographic dividend that significantly contributed to China's extraordinary economic growth.

Two considerations should be noted in presenting these statistics. First, a relatively greater share of national output in less developed countries is not measured, due to the greater prevalence of subsistence agriculture and the informal economies. Thus, the per capita output and income figures for low- and middle-income economies are somewhat understated. Secondly, not all of the labor force in any country will be employed, so the ratios of the average productivities of employed labor will be understated by the ratios of GNIs to labor forces. Nevertheless, the orders of magnitude between the high-income and low-income economies are significant.

Table 1.3 *Selected statistics on economic growth, by income*

2010	World	Low	Lower Middle	India	Upper Middle	China	High	US
	Economies by income classification							
Gross national income, trillion $ (% of world)	62.53	0.42 (0.7%)	4.08 (6.5%)	1.55 (2.5%)	14.43 (23.1%)	5.72 (9.1%)	43.68 (69.9%)	14.65 (23.4%)
Population, millions (% of world)	6,895	796 (11.5%)	2,519 (36.5%)	1,225 (17.8%)	2,452 (35.6%)	1,338 (19.4%)	1,127 (16.3%)	309 (4.5%)
Labor force, millions (% of world)	3,223	364 (11.3%)	994 (30.8%)	473 (14.7%)	1,314 (40.8%)	800 (24.8%)	551 (17.1%)	158 (4.9%)
GNI per capita ($)	$9,069	$528	$1,619	$1,270	$5,884	$4,270	$38,745	$47,340
GNI per laborer ($)	$19,401	$1,154	$4,105	$3,277	$10,982	$7,150	$79,274	$92,722
Labor force/Population	0.467	0.457	0.395	0.386	0.536	0.598	0.489	0.511
GNI per capita (PPP$)	$11,066	$1,307	$3,632	$3,400	$9,970	$7,640	$37,317	$47,340
Ave. ann. growth rates: GDP (2000–10)	2.7%	5.5%	6.3%	8.0%	6.5%	10.8%	1.8%	1.8%
Population (2000–10)	1.2%	2.1%	1.6%	1.5%	0.7%	0.6%	0.7%	0.9%
Energy use per capita, kg of oil equiv. (2009)	1,788	365	665	560	1,848	1,698	4,856	7,051
Carbon dioxide emissions per capita metric tons (2008)	4.8	0.3	1.5	1.5	5.3	5.3	11.9	18.0
Female life expectancy at birth, years (2010)	72	60	67	67	75	75	83	81
% of population undernourished (2006–08)	13%	29%	17%	19%	9%	10%	<5%	<5%

Notes: These statistics are based on weighted averages for the countries in the designated income categories.

Low-income economies ($n = 35$) have per capita gross national incomes (GNIs) in 2010 of $1,005 or less) and include mostly sub-Saharan African and South Asian nations.

Lower middle-income economies ($n = 57$) have per capita GNIs in 2010 between $1,006 and $3,975) and include mainly the less developed Latin American, North African, Middle Eastern, Eastern European and South Asian nations, and former Soviet republics. India is a lower middle-income economy.

Upper middle-income economies ($n = 54$) have per capita GNIs in 2010 between $3,976 and $12,275 and include mainly the more developed Latin American, East Asian, Middle Eastern, and East European nations and the Russian Federation. China is an upper middle-income economy.

High-income economies ($n = 70$) have per capita GNIs in 2010 of $12,276 or more. In addition to the United States, Canada, Japan, Australia, New Zealand, Greece, and the nations of Western Europe, included among the high-income nations are: Bahrain, Cyprus, Czech Republic, Estonia, Hungary, Israel, Kuwait, Oman, Poland, Puerto Rico, Qatar, Saudi Arabia, Singapore, Slovak Republic, Slovenia, South Korea, Trinidad and Tobago, and United Arab Emirates.

GNI or gross national product (GNP) is the total market value of the final goods and services produced by residents of a nation. Data are in current US dollars converted using the World Bank *Atlas* method where GNIs in national currencies are converted into dollar values using a three-year average of real exchange rates. GNI per capita is gross national income divided by the total population. GNI per laborer is gross national income divided by the labor force.

Gross domestic product (GDP) is the total market value of the final goods and services produced within the borders of a nation. GDP = GNI + net payments of factor income to foreigners.

Purchasing power parity-adjusted dollars (PPP$) are expressed in internationally comparable dollars, adjusted for differences in price levels, where an international dollar has the same purchasing power over output as a US dollar has in the United States.

Table 1.3 *continued*

Notes Continued

Energy use refers to the use of primary energy before transformation to other end-use fuels, which is equal to indigenous production plus imports and stock changes, minus exports and fuels supplied to ships and aircraft engaged in international transport. Primary energy includes petroleum (crude oil, natural gas liquids, and oil from nonconventional sources), natural gas, solid fuels (coal, lignite, and other derived fuels), and combustible renewables and waste (solid biomass and animal products, gas and liquid from biomass, and industrial and municipal waste) and primary electricity, all converted into oil equivalents. Biomass is any plant matter used directly as fuel or converted into fuel, heat, or electricity. Here energy use is expressed in per capita kilograms of oil equivalent.

Carbon dioxide emissions are emissions from the burning of fossil fuels (coal, oil, petroleum, and natural gas products) and the manufacture of cement, and include carbon dioxide produced during consumption of solid, liquid, and gas fuels and gas flaring.

Female life expectancy at birth is the number of years a newborn infant girl would live if prevailing patterns of mortality at the time of her birth were to stay the same throughout her life.

Prevalence of undernourishment is the percentage of the population whose dietary energy consumption is continuously below a minimum requirement for maintaining a healthy life and carrying out light physical activity with an acceptable minimum weight for height.

Source: World Bank (2012: Tables 1.1, 1.5, 2.1, 2.2, 2.20, 3.7, 3.9, 4.1.).

Convergence

As we know, the economic growth rates can be approximated by the difference between the average annual growth rates in GDP or GNI and population. If a low-income nation is growing faster than a second, higher-income nation, then the relative gap in per capita income will decrease.[16] An important question is whether per capita incomes are converging between countries. From the table we can see that over the period from 2000 to 2010, the average annual growth rate in per capita income for the world was 1.5 percent (i.e., $dy/y = dY/Y - dP/P \approx 0.027 - 0.012$). For the low-income, lower middle- income, and upper middle-income, economies the economic growth rates were 3.4 percent, 4.7 percent (pulled up by India's rapid growth), and 5.8 percent (augmented by China's extraordinary growth), respectively, compared to 1.1 percent for the high-income economies—suggesting convergence in general. In Chapter 7 we will discuss theories of convergence in detail.

Turning to Table 1.4, where we present selected statistics on economic growth by geographical region, with the high-income economies also present for comparison, the diversity across regions of the developing world is again apparent. Sub-Saharan Africa and South Asia are the poorest regions, together with over one third of the world's population, but generating only 5 percent of the global income in 2010. Nevertheless, the average growth rate in per capita income for South Asia, including India, in the period 2000–10 of 5.8 percent was exceeded only by East Asia and the Pacific, including China, (8.6 percent) and exceeded Europe and Central Asia (5.2 percent). The high economic growth rates in East Asia and the Pacific are, in part, due to the demographic dividend of a rising share of the population in the labor force. South Asia has yet to reap this dividend fully, while the European and Central Asian economies, with the prolonged low fertility, have nearly expended this favorable age structure effect. The global recession in 2009, however, reduced economic growth rates around the world. In Chapter 6 we will discuss the Great Recession which originated in the United States.

---

[16] We hasten to add that a reduction in the relative gap need not mean a reduction in the absolute gap. To illustrate, consider the following. The per capita incomes of country A and country B are $y_A = \$1,000$ and $y_B = \$20,000$ and the annual economic growth rates are $r_A = 0.04$ (4 percent) and $r_B = 0.01$. Since country A is growing faster, the relative gap (y_B/y_A) is reduced next year from 20 to 1 ($\$20,000/\$1,000$) to 19.4 ($\$20,200/\$1,040$); however, in this case, the absolute gap ($y_A - y_B$) increases from $\$19,000 to \$19,160$.

Table 1.4 *Selected statistics on economic growth, by region*

2010	ECONOMIES BY REGION						
	Sub-Saharan Africa	Middle East & N. Africa	Europe & Central Asia	South Asia	East Asia & Pacific	Latin America & Caribbean	High Income Economies
Gross national income,	1.00	1.28	2.95	1.92	7.25	4.51	43.68
trillion $ (% of world)	(1.6%)	(2.0%)	(4.7%)	(3.1%)	(11.6%)	(7.2%)	(69.9%)
Population, millions	853	331	405	1,633	1,962	583	1,127
(% of world)	(12.4%)	(4.8%)	(5.9%)	(23.7%)	(28.5%)	(8.5%)	(16.3%)
Labor force, millions	340	105	192	639	1,118	278	551
(% of world)	(10.5%)	(3.3%)	(6.0%)	(19.8%)	(34.7%)	(8.6%)	(17.1%)
GNI per capita ($)	$1,176	$3,874	$7,272	$1,176	$3,696	$7,733	$38,745
GNI per laborer ($)	$2,941	$12,190	$15,365	$3,005	$6,485	$16,223	$79,274
Labor force/Population	0.399	0.317	0.474	0.391	0.570	0.477	0.489
GNI per capita (PPP$)	$2,148	$8,068	$13,396	$3,124	$6,657	$10,926	$37,317
Ave. Ann. Growth Rates:							
GDP (2000–10)	5.0%	4.7%	5.4%	7.4%	9.4%	3.8%	1.8%
Population (2000–10)	2.5%	1.8%	0.2%	1.6%	0.8%	1.2%	0.7%
Energy use per capita, kg of oil equiv. (2009)	689	1,399	2,831	514	1,436	1,245	4,856
Carbon dioxide emissions per capita metric tons (2008)	0.8	3.8	7.8	1.2	4.3	2.8	11.9
Female life expectancy at birth, years (2010)	55	74	75	67	74	77	83
% of population undernourished (2006–08)	22%	7%	6%	20%	11%	9%	<5%

Notes: Sub-Saharan Africa comprises all the African countries south of the Sahara.

Middle East and North Africa comprises the low- and middle-income economies of Algeria, Djibouti, Egypt, Iran, Iraq, Jordan, Lebanon, Libya, Morocco, Syria, Tunisia, West Bank and Gaza, and Republic of Yemen.

Europe and Central Asia comprises the middle-income economies of Albania, Armenia, Azerbaijan, Belarus, Bosnia and Herzegovina, Bulgaria, Georgia, Kazakhstan, Kosovo, Kyrgyz Republic, Latvia, Lithuania, Macedonia FYR, Moldova, Montenegro, Romania, Russian Federation, Serbia, Tajikistan, Turkmenistan, Turkey, Ukraine, and Uzbekistan.

South Asia comprises Afghanistan, Bangladesh, Bhutan, India, Maldives, Nepal, Pakistan, and Sri Lanka.

East Asia and the Pacific comprise all of the low- and middle-income economies of East and Southeast Asia and the Pacific.

Latin America and the Caribbean comprises all American and Caribbean economies south of the United States.

Even sub-Saharan Africa, a region with stagnant per capita incomes over the last three decades of the twentieth century, generated a higher economic growth rate (2.5 percent) than the high-income economies in the first decade of the twenty-first century. Kenwood and Lougheed (1992: 134) provide an interesting historical perspective for sub-Saharan Africa's generally lagging performance, attributing the relative backwardness of many of its nations to late integration into the world economy:

Although there was a rapid expansion of African exports in the late nineteenth century, the extent of the continent's integration into the world economy was seriously limited by transport difficulties. In a continent with few navigable rivers, where the ravages of the tsetse fly restricted the use of animal power, and where, as a result, porterage was the chief means of transport, the transition from an economic system based on slave labor to one based on wage labor tended to have a paralyzing effect on transport and through it on internal trade. Apart from gold and ivory, there were few commodities that could bear the high cost of porterage from the interior.....This transport deficiency blunted the impact of world demand on the African economy and accounts for the persistence of a substantial African subsistence economy which, through its low productivity and lack of monetization, slowed down the overall economic growth of the continent.

Doubling times

An intuitive way to comprehend growth rates is to use doubling times. That is, if the given annual growth rates were maintained, how long would it take for the per capita incomes to double? A useful approximation is the 'rule of 69.3.' Dividing the growth rate in percentage points into 69.3 gives the approximate doubling time.[17] For example, returning to Table 1.3, if China were to continue with an economic growth rate of 10.2 percent (the average annual rate for 2000–10), its per capita income would double approximately every 7 years ($69.3/10.2 = 6.8 \approx 7$). For the high-income economies, maintaining an economic growth of 1.1 percent would double per capita incomes every 63 years ($69.3/1.1 = 63$). In 2010 the per capita national incomes in the high-income economies ($38,745) were over nine times greater than China's ($4,270). Extrapolating the respective average annual economic growth rates for 2000–10, it would take China around 24 years to catch up to the average per capita income of the high-income economies—around 2034, when real per capita incomes in China and the high-income economies would average approximately $50,600. We hasten to add that this extrapolation is not a prediction. Economic growth rates vary over time. It is arguable, however, whether China and other developing countries will be able to attain an average income and consumption that the high-income nations even now enjoy. As Chapter 5 discusses, there may be limits to growth due to natural resource constraints and environmental thresholds.

From Tables 1.3 and 1.4, we can see the direct relationship between per capita incomes and energy use per capita and carbon dioxide emissions per capita. We see that higher incomes are associated with lower incidence of undernourishment and higher life expectancies. Public policies on health, education, the environment and economic opportunity, as well as economic growth, are important for human welfare. In particular, we observe the far greater gaps in per capita incomes than in life expectancies. For example, in 2010, India's per capita income (in PPP dollars) was only 7 percent of that of the United States; yet India's female life expectancy at birth of 67 years

---

[17]The 'rule of 69.3' reflects exponential growth. Let y_T and y_0 be the per capita incomes in a nation at time T (in the future) and time 0 (initially) and assuming per capita income is growing continuously at an annual rate of r percent. Then $y_T = y_0 \cdot e^{rT}$, where e is the base of the natural exponential function,

$$e = \lim_{m \to \infty} [1 + (1/m)]^m \approx 2.71828$$

The intuition behind the irrational number, e, is that $1, compounded continuously over 1 year at an annual rate of 100 percent, would equal e dollars, or approximately $2.72, at the end of the year. To find the doubling time for per capita income growing continuously at the annual rate of r percent, we write $y_T/y_0 = 2 = e^{rT}$. Taking the natural logarithm (ln), we find $\ln 2 = 0.693 = rT$. Solving for $T = 0.693/r$, where the growth rate, r, is expressed in decimal, gives the doubling time.

For example, if per capita income is growing at an annual rate of 2 percent ($r = 0.02$), then the doubling time in years would be $0.693/0.02 = 34.65$. Using the 'rule of 69.3,' we express the annual growth rate in percentage points.

was 83 percent of the 81 years in the US, which was actually lower than the average for the high-income economies.

The demands on resources will depend not only on economic growth (in particular, rising standards of living) but also on population growth. Before turning to the determinants of population growth and trends in the world population, we should discuss negative output growth.

NEGATIVE OUTPUT GROWTH

We noted earlier that negative economic growth could result even with positive output growth if the population growth exceeded the output growth. While even the high- income or developed economies experience periodic recessions, prolonged declines in real national output are unusual.[18] Prolonged declines in output growth in low- and middle-income economies, however, have been observed more often. Of the 150 nations with populations of 1 million or more, 23 (all low- and middle-income economies) experienced negative output growth over the decade of the 1990s. In the first decade of the twenty-first century, however, only one nation (Zimbabwe, with -6.0 percent) experienced negative average annual growth rates in real national output.[19] Before reviewing this evidence, we will identify the possible explanations for negative output growth.

Accounting for negative economic growth

Return to the earlier example of an aggregate production function, given by $Y = A \cdot \underline{K}^{\alpha} \underline{L}^{\beta} \underline{R}^{\gamma}$, where the growth rate in real national output can be written as $dY/Y = dA/A + \alpha \cdot (d\underline{K}/\underline{K}) + \beta \cdot (d\underline{L}/\underline{L}) + \gamma \cdot (d\underline{R}/\underline{R})$. Negative output growth, $dY/Y < 0$, could result from inefficiencies in production or general declines in total factor productivity (reflected here in $dA/A < 0$), decreases in supplies of the effective factors of production, or declines in aggregate demand (as in a recession or depression).

Technological regress and misuses of technology are not likely over an extended period of time. What may happen, though, are institutional breakdowns (e.g., with political instability or shocks to the economic system). For example, there may be a lack of incentive to produce for the market due to overregulation of business or oppressive taxes. High inflation can encourage rent-seeking (attempts to profit from anticipated or real price discrepancies) rather than productive activities. High inflation also blurs relative price signals in the market, resulting in less efficient allocations of resources. With hyperinflation, triple-digit or higher annual inflation rates, the national currency ceases to function not only as a store of value but also as a medium of exchange. Economic exchanges may increasingly take place through bartering, an inefficient means for conducting transactions.

Political instability, crime, corruption, and ineffective institutions (judicial, legislative, administrative) for allocating resources, honoring contracts, and protecting private property can undermine an economy. Although not an explicit factor of production, social capital will be eroded with corruption, ethnic conflict, and discrimination. Such internal dissension can not only divide a nation state, but also cripple an economy—as, in the extreme, a civil war can do.

---

[18] During the Great Depression, US real national output fell by over a quarter in 1929–33.

[19] Including the 56 nations with populations under 1 million, there are over 200 nation states. Some countries, perhaps with negative output growth during the 1990s, are not reported due to lack of data. The same holds for the 2000–10 period. For example, data on growth rates for real GDP for both periods are missing for North Korea, Somalia, and Myanmar.

Significant structural change with economic transformation (e.g., conversion from command economies and socialist systems to more market-oriented, capitalist economies and democracies) can cause negative output growth during the transitions. A shortage of key inputs (raw materials and intermediate goods) may occur due to wars, embargoes, or lack of foreign exchange.

Declines in total factor productivity might be accompanied by declines in the supplies of the effective factors of production, contributing to the negative output growth. For example, the physical capital stock would decline, $dK/K < 0$, with negative net fixed investment, i.e., insufficient gross fixed investment due to the lack of savings for investment or depressed business confidence reducing the incentive to invest, or with accelerated depreciation of the capital stock. Destruction of physical capital stock may occur with war or natural disasters. A decline in the index of the quality of capital, $dq_K/q_K < 0$, might occur with the replacement of depreciated capital with lower-quality capital.

A decrease in effective labor $d\underline{L}/\underline{L} < 0$, might happen with a decline in labor force, $dL/L < 0$, due to heavy net outmigration or earlier low fertility or unusual mortality (e.g., AIDS or war) or with a decline in the average quality of labor, $dq_L/q_L < 0$ (e.g., less experienced workers replacing more experienced workers).

A decline in effective natural resources, $d\underline{R}/\underline{R} < 0$, would take place with depletion of nonrenewable resources and overuse of renewable resources, $dR/R < 0$. Natural disasters (e.g., forest fires, tsunamis, earthquakes) or war can also reduce the supplies of effective natural resources. A decline in the quality or inherent productivity of the natural resources, $dq_R/q_R < 0$, could take place with pollution and poor conservation, (e.g., acid rain destroying forests, pollution of water from industrial discharges overgrazing of pastures, or water logging or erosion of farmland).

Finally, negative output growth could reflect a decline in aggregate demand, as in a recession. Whether one or a combination of the above factors would be sufficient to reduce output for a prolonged period, of course, depends on the severity of the shocks to the economy and on the policies undertaken to address the economic declines.

Recent evidence of negative economic growth

Turning to Table 1.5 and the 23 nations that experienced negative output growth over the decade of the 1990s, 18 of these nations are former socialist economies of Eastern Europe or republics of the former Soviet Union that underwent massive structural change during the decade. In addition to the difficulties in overhauling their command economies, a number of these nations experienced negative labor force growth, primarily due to chronically low fertility rates. Twelve of these 18 economies experienced declines in spending on gross capital formation, likely resulting in decreases in effective physical capital stocks. Four of the other the 23 nations with negative output growth are from sub-Saharan Africa, and in each case these countries were beset by civil war and political instability. Cuba, the other nation with declining output over the last decade of the twentieth century, also experienced difficulties with its controlled economy and the withdrawal of support from the former Soviet Union.

When we look at inflation, we see that the negative output growth during this period was accompanied by high inflation—and almost always hyperinflation. Average annual inflation rates in this last decade of the twentieth century for these 18 transition economies ranged from 48 percent (Latvia) to 408 percent (Turkmenistan). For the four sub-Saharan African countries with negative output growth, inflation was lower, except for the Democratic Republic of the Congo (for all purposes a failed state), but still in the double digits. A fall in real national output with inflation is consistent with a fall in aggregate supply.

We notice that all 23 nations rebounded in the next decade, with positive output growth—all above the world average for 2000–10. The annual growth rates for gross capital formation (gross domestic investment) for these nations dramatically reversed from an average of −3.9 percent (1990–2000) to 9.0 percent (2000–10). Critical for restoring growth was reducing inflation. The average annual inflation rate for these economies fell from 196 percent to 12 percent. Nevertheless, while these economies resumed output growth, real per capita incomes may not have recovered to their 1990 levels.

Table 1.5 *Negative output growth: recent experience*

	Average Annual Percentage Growth Rates							
	Real GDP		Population		Gross Capital Formation		Inflation	
Country	1990–2000	2000–10	1990–2000	2000–10	1990–2000	2000–10	1990–2000	2000–10
Armenia	−1.9%	9.2%	0.8%	0.1%	−1.9%	16.3%	212.5%	4.6%
Azerbaijan	−6.3%	17.1%	1.2%	1.2%	41.7%	13.9%	203.0%	9.8%
Belarus	−1.6%	8.0%	−0.2%	−0.5%	−7.5%	18.1%	355.1%	21.5%
Bulgaria	−1.1%	4.8%	−0.7%	−0.8%	−5.3%	11.2%	102.1%	5.9%
Burundi	−2.9%	3.2%	2.2%	2.7%	−0.5%	. . .	13.4%	10.7%
Congo DR	−4.9%	5.3%	3.2%	2.8%	2.6%	. . .	964.9%	26.7%
Cuba	−0.7%	6.7%	0.6%	0.1%	0.7%	8.8%	6.4%	3.3%
Georgia	−7.1%	6.9%	0.0%	0.1%	. . .	. . .	356.7%	6.9%
Kazakhstan	−4.1%	8.3%	−0.9%	0.9%	−19.0%	15.2%	204.7%	15.1%
Kyrgyz Rep.	−4.1%	4.4%	1.2%	1.1%	−4.5%	9.1%	110.6%	8.6%
Latvia	−1.5%	4.8%	−1.0%	−0.6%	−3.7%	3.7%	48.0%	8.1%
Lithuania	−2.5%	5.3%	−0.1%	−0.6%	11.1%	5.6%	75.0%	3.9%
Macedonia	−0.8%	3.3%	0.7%	0.3%	3.6%	4.8%	79.3%	3.7%
Moldova	−9.6%	5.2%	−0.2%	−0.2%	−15.5%	7.5%	119.6%	10.8%
Romania	−0.6%	5.0%	−0.3%	−0.5%	−5.1%	10.6%	98.0%	14.7%
Russian Fed.	−4.7%	5.4%	−0.2%	−0.3%	−19.1%	7.6%	161.5%	15.1%
Rwanda	−0.2%	7.6%	2.0%	2.7%	0.4%	. . .	14.3%	10.4%
Serbia	−4.2%	4.1%	. . .	−0.3%	. . .	18.1%	. . .	15.3%
Sierra Leone	−5.0%	8.8%	2.3%	3.5%	−5.6%	. . .	31.9%	9.6%
Tajikistan	−10.4%	8.6%	1.8%	1.1%	−17.6%	5.8%	235.0%	19.7%
Turkmenistan	−4.9%	13.6%	2.8%	1.1%	. . .	5.7%	408.2%	12.6%
Ukraine	−9.3%	4.8%	−0.5%	−0.7%	−18.5%	1.6%	271.0%	16.6%
Uzbekistan	−0.2%	7.1%	1.8%	1.4%	−2.5%	4.7%	245.8%	24.0%
Average	**−3.9%**	**6.8%**	**0.8%**	**0.7%**	**−3.9%**	**9.0%**	**196.2%**	**11.9%**
World	**2.9%**	**2.7%**	**1.4%**	**1.2%**	**3.3%**	**2.8%**	. . .	. . .

Notes: Low-income economies (2010 GNI per capita of $1,005 or less): Burundi, Congo Democratic Republic, Kyrgyz Republic, Rwanda, Sierra Leone, and Tajikistan.
Lower middle-income economies (2010 GNI per capita from $1,006 to $3,975): Armenia, Georgia, Moldova, Turkmenistan, Ukraine, and Uzbekistan.
Upper middle-income economies (2010 GNI per capita from $3,976 to $12,275): Azerbaijan, Belarus, Bulgaria, Cuba, Kazakhstan, Latvia, Lithuania, Macedonia, Romania, Russian Federation, and Serbia.
Gross capital formation (gross domestic investment) includes outlays on additions to fixed assets of the economy and net changes in inventories. Fixed assets include land improvements; plant, machinery and equipment purchases; and construction (roads, railways, schools, buildings, etc.).
Inflation rates refer to the average annual percentage changes in the implicit price deflators for GDP.
Sources: World Bank (2002b: Table 1; 2012: Tables 2.1, 4.1, 4.9, and 4.16).

CONCLUSION

This first chapter has introduced the concept, measurement, and consequences of economic growth. The importance of economic growth for reducing extreme poverty was highlighted. In addition, the determinants of national output growth were discussed. Statistics on economic growth for the nations of the world grouped by per capita incomes and geographical regions were presented not only to illustrate the concepts, but also to portray the diversity in experience. In later chapters we will discuss theories of economic growth and macroeconomic models. And in Chapter 8 we will present an empirical analysis of the determinants of economic growth in developing nations. In Chapter 2 we turn to the determinants and trends in population growth.

KEY TERMS

constant returns to scale

demographic dividend

division of labor

economies of scale

Gini Index

gross national income

incidence of poverty

neutral technical change

physical capital

purchasing power parity adjustment

social capital

decreasing returns to scale

diseconomies of scale

economic growth

effective factor of production

gross domestic product

headcount index

increasing returns to scale

nonrenewable natural resources

poverty gap

renewable natural resources

specialization of labor

QUESTIONS

1. Does negative economic growth necessarily mean real national output has declined? Explain. For example, in Venezuela, the growth rates in real gross domestic product for 2009 and 2010 were −3.3 percent and −2.3 percent, respectively. Specifically, what factors could account for Venezuela's decreases in real national output?

2. Suppose that for a country, Atlantica, gross national income (GNI) equals $100 million; labor income earned by residents of Atlantica working abroad equals $1.5 million; labor income earned by foreigners (nonresidents) working in Atlantica equals $0.6 million; interest and dividends paid by Atlantica to foreign investors equals $0.8 million; and interest and dividends received by residents of Atlantica from foreign investments equal $0.1 million. Calculate Atlantica's gross domestic product. Show your work.

3. Suppose that for a country, Pacifica, GNI per capita is 8,000 pesos and that the foreign exchange rate between the peso and the US dollar is 10 pesos to $1.00. What would be the per capita GNI for Pacifica expressed in US dollars?

    If prices in Pacifica for goods and services not entering into international trade are exactly 40 percent of the prices for similar commodities in the United States, i.e., any item costing $1 in the US costs 4 pesos in Pacifica, estimate the per capita GNI for Pacifica in international or purchasing power parity-adjusted dollars. Assume that 60 percent of Pacifica's national output is not internationally traded.

4. Suppose that the per capita incomes for 2010 for Bangladesh and Belgium of $700 and $45,840, and assume that the average growth rates in real national outputs and population for 2000–10 are maintained into the future:

	Average growth rate (2000–10)	
	Real GDP	Population
Bangladesh	5.9%	1.4%
Belgium	1.6%	0.6%

In what year would the per capita income in Bangladesh equal the per capita income in Belgium? What would be the level of the per capita incomes at that point?

5. Suppose that there are two nations, A and B, each with 5,000 population, with the following distributions of income (in PPP dollars per capita per day):

	Population A	Population B
Poorest thousand	$0.50	$0.60
Second thousand	$1.30	$0.80
Middle thousand	$2.00	$1.50
Fourth thousand	$4.00	$2.50
Richest thousand	$8.00	$6.00

Assume an international poverty line of $1.00 a day.

(a) Determine the average daily per capita incomes in each nation.

(b) Determine the poverty headcount and incidence of poverty in each nation.

(c) Determine the poverty gaps in each nation.

REFERENCES

Allen, Robert. 2008. "A Review of Gregory Clark's *A Farewell to Alms: A Brief Economic History of the World*," *Journal of Economic Literature*, 46(4): 946–973.

Bosworth, Barry and Susan Collins. 2008. "Accounting for Growth: Comparing China and India," *Journal of Economic Perspectives*, 22(1): 45–66.

Clark, Gregory. 2007. *A Farewell to Alms: A Brief Economic History of the World.* Princeton, NJ: Princeton University Press.

De Souza, Roger-Mark, John Williams, and Frederick Meyerson. 2003. "Critical Links: Population, Health, and the Environment," *Population Bulletin*, 58(3).

Kenwood, A.G. and A.L. Lougheed. 1992. *The Growth of the International Economy: 1820–1990,* 3rd edition. New York: Routledge.

Kotwal, Ashok, Bharat Ramaswami, and Wilma Wadhwa. 2011. "Economic Liberalization and Indian Economic Growth: What's the Evidence?" *Journal of Economic Literature,* 49(4): 1152–1199.

Maddison, Angus. 2005. *Growth and Interaction in the World Economy: The Roots of Modernity.* Washington, DC: AEI Press.

Sachs, Jeffrey. 2005. *The End of Poverty: Economic Possibilities for Our Time.* New York: Penguin.

Schumacher, E.F. 1973. *Small is Beautiful: Economics as if People Mattered.* New York: Harper & Row.

World Bank. 1991. *World Development Report 1991: The Challenge of Development.* New York: Oxford University Press.

World Bank. 1992. *World Development Report 1992: Development and the Environment.* Washington, DC: World Bank.

World Bank. 2001a. *World Development Indicators 2001.* Washington, DC: World Bank.

World Bank. 2001b. *World Development Report 2000/2001: Attacking Poverty.* New York: Oxford University Press.

World Bank. 2002a. *World Development Indicators 2002.* Washington, DC: World Bank.

World Bank. 2002b. *World Development Report 2002: Building Institutions for Markets.* Oxford: Oxford University Press.

World Bank. 2006. *World Development Report 2006: Equity and Development.* Washington, DC: World Bank.

World Bank. 2007. *World Development Indicators 2007.* Washington, DC: World Bank.

World Bank. 2009. *World Development Report 2009: Reshaping Economic Geography.* Washington, DC: World Bank.

World Bank. 2010a. *World Development Indicators 2010.* Washington, DC: World Bank.

World Bank. 2010b. *World Development Report 2010: Development and Climate change.* Washington, DC: World Bank.

World Bank. 2011a. *World Development Indicators 2011.* Washington, DC: World Bank.

World Bank. 2011b. *World Development Report 2011: Conflict, Security, and Development.* Washington, DC: World Bank.

World Bank. 2012. *World Development Indicators 2012.* Washington, DC: World Bank.

Xu, Chenggang. 2011. "The Fundamental Institutions of China's Reforms and Development," *Journal of Economic Literature,* 49(4): 1076–1151.

Chapter 2

Introduction to population growth

Approximately one out of every 15 people ever born on this planet is now living.[1] In 2012 an estimated 134 million babies were born and 56 million deaths occurred, adding 78 million (or one fourth the current population of the United States) to the world population. Every day the world population increased by approximately 214,000.[2] For the vast majority of human experience, however, population growth has been minimal. And, while the world has experienced unprecedented population increase over the past two centuries, rising from 1 billion at the beginning of the nineteenth century to 6 billion at the turn of the twenty-first century and to over 7 billion by 2012, this growth is unlikely to continue for much longer. The world population is expected to stabilize at less than 10 billion before the end of this century.

Demographers predict a leveling off of the world population not just because continued population increase on a finite planet is unsustainable. In fact, history shows a demographic transition where, with economic growth and development, populations move from a traditional state of slow population growth, with high birth rates, on average, only minimally above death rates, to a modern equilibrium of zero population growth with low birth and death rates. In Chapter 1 we identified the sources of output growth; now we turn to the sources of population growth.

COMPONENTS OF POPULATION CHANGE

For any initial population for a given area, such as a nation or region of the world, additions to that population will occur through births and immigration (or in-migration). Deductions from the population will occur with deaths and emigration (out-migration).[3] That is, let P_T be the population of an area at time T, the end of a period of duration t (where t equals 1 year); P_{T-1} is the population of the area at time $T - 1$, the beginning of the period. Let $\bar{P}_T$ be the mid-point

---

[1] This is based on a rough estimate by Carl Haub, "How Many People Have Ever Lived on Earth?" http://www.prb.org/Articles/2002/HowManyPeopleHaveEverLivedonEarth.aspx. Actually Haub goes back to 50,000 BC (roughly when modern *Homo sapiens* appeared) and begins with a human population of 2. With assumptions about birth rates over the millennia, Haub estimates there have been approximately 107.6 billion births up to 2011, which, divided into the mid-2011 world population of 6.99 billion, yields 6.5 percent of the population ever born currently living in 2011.

[2] These estimates are from the US Census Bureau: see http://www.census.gov/population/international/data/idb/worldvitalevents.php.

[3] Population size is a **stock** variable, measured at a point in time. Births, deaths, and net migration, however, are **flow** variables defined over periods of time, such as a day or a year. That is, in measuring flows we need to define the period of time to provide context for the magnitudes. For example, a wage of $100 would be high for an hourly rate, modest for a daily wage, and low for a weekly salary in a high-income economy. Changes in stocks reflect flows over the period. If you have $1,000 in a savings account at the beginning of the year (stock) earning 4 percent annual interest, then after 1 year the new level of savings in the account is $1,040 (stock), with the difference being the $40 interest earned over the year (flow).

population of the area, given by $\bar{P}_T = 0.5(P_{T-1} + P_T)$. Let B_t and D_t be respectively the number of births to and deaths in the population during the period of duration t. Let NM_t be the net in-migration to the area during the period of duration t. Net in-migration equals the difference between the migration to the area (in-migration or immigration) and the migration from the area (out-migration or emigration). Assuming constant flows of births, deaths, immigration, and emigration over the period, the mid-point population equals the average of the beginning-of-period and end-of-period populations. The convention in demography is to express population change relative to the population at the mid-point of the period in question (usually a year) and to express the change per thousand mid-point population.

The population at time T, the end of the period of duration t, equals the initial population plus the births less the deaths plus the net migration to this population over the period:

$$P_T = P_{T-1} + B_t - D_t + NM_t$$

Subtracting the initial population from both sides of the equation and dividing through by the mid-point population gives the population growth rate, r_t:

$$r_t = \frac{P_T - P_{T-1}}{\bar{P}_T} = \frac{B_t}{\bar{P}_T} - \frac{D_t}{\bar{P}_T} + \frac{NM_t}{\bar{P}_T}$$

$$r_t = CBR_t - CDR_t + NMR_t = CRNI_t + NMR_t$$

The population growth rate (r) is the sum of the crude rate of natural increase (CRNI) and the net in-migration rate (NMR). The **crude rate of natural increase**, in turn, is equal to the difference between the **crude birth rate** (CBR), measured as births per thousand mid-point population, and the **crude death rate** (CDR), measured as deaths per thousand mid-point population. The **net in-migration rate** is the difference between the immigration and emigration rates.

For example, assume: $P_{T-1} = 50,000$, $B_t = 1,200$, $D_t = 450$, and $NM_t = -120$.
Then:

$$P_T = 50,000 + 1,200 - 450 + (-120) = 50,630$$
$$\bar{P}_T = 0.5(50,000 + 50,630) = 50,315$$
$$r_t = \frac{50,630 - 50,000}{50,315} = \frac{1,200}{50,315} - \frac{450}{50,315} + \frac{-120}{50,315} = \frac{630}{50,315} = 0.0125$$
$$0.0125 = 0.0238 - 0.0089 + (-0.0024) = 0.0149 + (-0.0024)$$

or $CBR_t = 23.8$ (per 1,000) and $CDR_t = 8.9$ (per 1,000), yielding $CRNI_t = 14.9$ (per 1,000) and with $NMR_t = -2.4$ (per 1,000), and the population growth rate is $r_t = 1.25$ percent.

Since the world is a closed population, the crude rate of natural increase equals the world population growth rate. Some nations may be virtually closed to immigration and emigration, for example, North Korea.

MEASURING POPULATION GROWTH RATES

There are three basic assumptions that can be made when measuring population growth rates. The implications for annual population change and the growth rate will differ.

Linear growth

The linear assumption will yield a constant absolute annual increase in population and a decreasing annual growth rate. To illustrate, let P_T be the population at time T and P_0 the initial population (at time 0). Let a be the annual change in population size and T be the number of years (or periods). If we assume linear growth, $P_T = P_0 + a \cdot T$, then the annual absolute change in the population is constant and equal to a.

For example, let $P_0 = 50,000$, $a = 630$, and $T = 5$. The population is adding 630 people each year. The populations for the first five years are $P_1 = 50,630$, $P_2 = 51,260$, $P_3 = 51,890$, $P_4 = 52,520$, and $P_5 = 53,150$. With a constant annual increase of population equal to 630, the annual population growth rate is continually declining: from 1.25 percent in the first year ($r_1 = 630/50,315 = 0.0125$) to 1.19 percent in the fifth year ($r_5 = 630/52,835 = 0.0119$).

Geometric growth

With geometric growth under simple annual compounding, the annual growth rate is constant, but the absolute increase in the annual population rises. Assuming exponential growth with a base of $(1 + r)$, where r is the annual population growth rate, gives $P_T = P_0(1 + r)^T$.

We illustrate using the same initial and final population sizes. As before, let $P_0 = 50,000$, $P_T = 53,150$, and $T = 5$. Solving for the annual growth rate in population, r_t, we find $P_T = 53,150 = 50,000(1+r)^5 = P_0(1+r)^T$. Dividing the equation by the initial population size gives: $53,150/50,000 = 1.063 = (1 + r)^5$. Taking the fifth root of both sides of the equation, we can solve for the average annual population growth rate: $r = (1.063)^{1/5} - 1 = 0.012294 \approx 0.0123$. The following table illustrates this population progression:

Annual population size	Population change: $P_T - P_{T-1}$
$P_1 = 50,615 = 50,000(1 + r)^1$	+615
$P_2 = 51,237 = 50,000(1 + r)^2$	+622
$P_3 = 51,867 = 50,000(1 + r)^3$	+630
$P_4 = 52,505 = 50,000(1 + r)^4$	+638
$P_5 = 53,150 = 50,000(1 + r)^5$	+645

Geometric growth with continuous compounding

The geometric growth under simple compounding, however, is not very realistic since births, deaths, and migration occur throughout the period, not just at the very end of the period. Thus, when measuring population growth, continuous compounding is the most appropriate assumption.

The geometric assumption with continuous compounding yields $P_T = P_0 e^{r'T}$, where $e \approx 2.71828$ is the base of the natural exponential function (see Chapter 1, note 17). Here the average annual growth rate is r'. If we assume the same initial population of $P_0 = 50,000$ and final population of $P_5 = 53,150$, then to find the average annual growth rate under continuous compounding we solve for r' as follows: $53,150 = 50,000e^{5r'}$ or $1.063 = e^{5r'}$. Taking the natural logarithm of both sides and solving for r' gives $r' = \frac{1}{5} \ln 1.063 = 0.012219 \approx 0.0122$. The same population increases illustrated in the table above under simple annual compounding are realized with continuous compounding, but the annual growth rate is lower. That is, assuming continuous growth takes a lower annual rate of population growth (here $r' = 0.0122 = 1.22$ percent) to reach a given population size than with simple annual compounding ($r = 0.0123 = 1.23$ percent).[4] Or, in other words, for the same annual rate of population growth, continuous compounding, the more realistic assumption, would increase an initial population faster than simple annual compounding.

BRIEF OVERVIEW OF WORLD POPULATION GROWTH

Estimates of the world's population are largely speculative, especially before the nineteenth century. Even today, there has never been a census of the world's population. One fact is clear, however: over the vast span of modern human existence, from at least 35,000 years ago, since *Cro Magnon* man, up until the last two centuries, the growth of the world's population has been minimal.[5] Early humans essentially foraged for their sustenance. Weeks (2008: 39) cites research that life expectancies of primitive hunter-gatherer populations might have averaged around 20 years, with only half of the children born surviving through their first 5 years of life. For such populations to be maintained would require women, on average, to bear seven children.

Around 8000 BC, the time of the first agricultural revolution with the discovery of agriculture and the cultivation of crops, much of humankind changed from hunting and gathering food to producing food. The estimated size of the human population then was roughly 5 million.[6] With the growing of crops and raising of livestock, both death and birth rates likely increased. Death rates rose with the greater vulnerability of the more sedentary populations to local conditions (e.g., severe weather and crop failures). And the greater densities of agricultural populations—as opposed to nomadic populations—may have increased the transmission of diseases and contamination of food and water supplies. Birth rates increased, not only to maintain populations subject to higher mortality rates, but also with the greater food supplies from harvested crops, on average, diets improved and fecundity increased. Moreover, with the more stationary lifestyle, children were easier to rear and more valuable for helping in farming. Hunting and gathering populations had to be continually on the move, so very young children would have to be carried, naturally limiting family sizes. With the shift to growing crops and raising livestock, mothers might have weaned their infants earlier, in turn reducing the natural contraception provided by breastfeeding. In general, then, birth rates increased more than death rates, raising the population growth rate. Nevertheless, average annual growth rates were still only marginally above zero, as periods of population increase alternated with periods of depopulation. In some areas, populations grew in size and in other areas populations vanished.

By AD 1, the world population had grown to perhaps 300 million. Over the first five centuries of the new millennium, however, the size of the world population might have even declined. As noted by Weeks (2008: 34), population declines in the third through the fifth centuries reflected increases in mortality, with plagues, and the collapse of the Roman Empire in the Mediterranean and the Han Empire in China. By the end of the first modern millennium, the size of world population might have been only 10 million greater than a thousand years earlier (see Table 2.1). In fact, for the first thousand years AD, the implied average annual population growth rate was

---

[4] Setting $1 + r = e^{r'}$, we can write $r = e^{r'} - 1$. Here $r = 0.012294 = e^{0.012219} - 1$.

[5] *Cro Magnon* man, standing about $5\frac{1}{2}$ feet tall and anatomically nearly identical to modern man, began to appear some 35,000 years ago in Europe. See http://www.historyworld.net/wrldhis/PlainTextHistories.asp?history=ab12.

[6] Haub, "How Many People Have Ever Lived on Earth?"

Table 2.1 *World population estimates and projections*

Year	World population (millions)	Average annual increase (millions)	Average annual growth rate (%)	Doubling time (years)
1 AD	300	0.01	0.03%	2100
1000	310	0.38	0.10%	720
1500	500	1.60	0.22%	309
1800	980	6.70	0.52%	133
1900	1,650	18.14	0.88%	79
1950	2,557	63.23	1.85%	37
1980	4,453	82.05	1.57%	44
2000	6,095	77.40	1.20%	58
2010	6,869	72.70	0.96%	72
2030	8,323(proj.)	55.90	0.63%	110
2050	9,441(proj.)			

Sources for the population estimates and projections: up to 1900, United Nations Secretariat (1999); for 1950–2050, US Census Bureau, "World Population," http://www.census.gov/population/international/data/worldpop/table_population.php (both accessed June 8, 2012).

To calculate the average annual growth rate, continuous population growth is assumed, $P_T = P_0 e^{rT}$, so $r = (1/T)\ln(P_T/P_0)$. For example, from 1800 to 1900, the average annual rate of population growth is $r_t = (1/100)\ln(1650/980) = 0.0052 = 0.52\%$.

The average annual increase is calculated as $(P_T - P_0)/T$. For example, from 1800 to 1900 the average annual increase is $(1650 - 980)/100 = 6.70$.

only 0.03 percent (i.e., $r = 0.0003$), yielding an average annual increase in numbers of 10,000. To put this growth in perspective, during 2012, the world population size increased by 10,000 people every 68 minutes.

Although the average annual population growth rates rose, the doubling times remained high, at several centuries. Not until the beginning of the nineteenth century did the world's population reach 1 billion. The second billion was attained in a little over a century, around 1930. The growth rate of the world's population is estimated to have peaked in the 1960s at around 2 percent per year, implying a doubling time of 35 years. Again, we should be mindful that these are averages for the world: some countries were growing much faster, while other nations were experiencing slower population growth.

The Western European experience

In Western Europe during the Middle Ages (c.500–1500 AD), conditions were generally improving. Both birth and death rates likely declined, although death rates remained volatile with outbreaks of disease, war, and occasional famines. For example, the bubonic plague, a highly contagious, usually fatal epidemic transmitted by fleas from infected rats, swept through Europe during the fourteenth century. The Black Death, as it was known, arrived in 1347, with the first wave leveling the European population by over a third.[7] Periodically, the plague would return and mortality rates would again soar.

---

[7]See Clark (2007: 99–101) for a discussion of the bubonic plague. Clark notes that the frequency and virulence of plagues diminished in Europe after the late seventeenth century, but remained endemic in Asia.

The emergence of a custom of late marriage and significant celibacy in Western Europe after the Middle Ages helped suppress fertility and reduced crude birth rates from the 45–50 range to the 35–40 range. The system of primogeniture (the right of the first child, especially the eldest son, to inherit the parent's estate) tended to postpone marriage for that son until he acquired the land. This, in turn, would delay the marriages for his younger brothers, who might then have been forced off the family land to migrate into towns for work. As Ronald Lee (2003: 169) notes:

> In western Europe in the centuries before 1800, marriage required the resources to establish and maintain a separate household, so age at first marriage for women was late, averaging around 25 years, and a substantial share of women never married. . . Although fertility was high within marriage, the total fertility rate. . .was moderate overall at four to five births per woman. . . Mortality was also moderately high, with life expectancy at birth between 25 and 35 years. . . .Population growth rates were generally low, averaging 0.3 percent/year before 1700 in western Europe. . . .In Canada and the United States, marriage was much earlier because land was abundant, and population at first grew rapidly, but then decelerated in the nineteenth century.

In the early eighteenth century a second agricultural revolution began in England and spread to the European continent and colonies. Changes in farming techniques with new crops, improved strains of plants and seeds, advances in animal husbandry, investment in irrigation systems and changes in land tenure through enclosures all increased food supplies.[8] With improvements in transportation (canals, railways, and shipping), better storage facilities, and the commercialization of crops, localized food shortages due to crop disease or poor weather could be alleviated. And with the Industrial Revolution emerging in the latter part of the century, manifested in a series of inventions and innovations, including steam engines and iron production, and the development of the factory system with the mechanization of textile production, the demand for labor increased. Real wages rose. The general increase in per capita incomes and improved nutrition yielded healthier populations, with increased work capacities. A related factor which likely reduced death rates may have been genetic, in the form of the decreasing virulence of diseases. With hardier populations surviving past epidemics, immunities built up.[9]

Interestingly, medical advances and improvements in the environment and sanitary conditions, while eventually contributing to declining mortality, probably had little to do with the initial declines. In the mid-eighteenth century medical knowledge and practices were still primitive.

---

[8] According to John Cannon's *Dictionary of British History*, there were three phases to this second agricultural revolution. In the first half of the eighteenth century, new crops, especially root crops like turnips and rutabagas, were introduced and could be grown between grain crops, which increased the productivity of land. Additional livestock could be fed and the manure used for fertilizer. During the second phase, roughly from 1750 to 1830, land was enclosed, farm size grew, and agricultural productivity increased with some regional specialization. During the third phase, extending several decades after 1830, farmers began purchasing inputs such as fertilizers and feed for their animals. With the introduction of improved methods of drainage, further gains in agricultural productivity were realized. See http://www.encyclopedia.com.

[9] With improvements in agriculture, food supplies may have become more reliable, nevertheless average nutrition levels remained low. The economic historian, Robert Fogel (1994: 371), noted in his 1993 Nobel Prize in Economics lecture that:

> for many European nations before the middle of the nineteenth century, the national production of food was at such low levels that the poorer classes were bound to have been malnourished under any conceivable circumstance, and that the high disease rates of the period were not merely a cause of malnutrition but undoubtedly, to a considerable degree, a consequence of exceedingly poor diets.

McKeown et al. (1972: 350) maintain that "Virtually nothing was known about...the natural history of disease before the late 19th century. Effective measures were few and their use was largely misunderstood. Surgery was limited without anesthesia and dangerous without knowledge of antisepsis." It was not until the mid-1860s that the English surgeon Lister pioneered the use of antiseptics in surgery. While the smallpox vaccine discovered by Jenner in 1798 did help reduce mortality in the nineteenth century, vaccines to prevent cholera and typhoid were not developed until the 1890s. Penicillin, discovered in the 1930s, was not widely available until after Word War II.

The urbanization which accompanied the industrialization of economies, as labor was released from growing food to working in factories, may have initially worsened sanitary conditions. During the first half of the eighteenth century, excrement was dumped on the streets, as sewer systems were underdeveloped. Water closets (invented toward the end of the century) emptied either into large vaults under houses or directly into sewers that flowed into rivers which were used for water supplies. Disease spread easily in congested populations.

Nevertheless, the trend in death rates was decidedly down with gains in nutrition and the average standard of living.[10] Then, with a lag of several decades, birth rates began to decline. Initially fertility may have risen in the face of the sustained declines in mortality with improved health and nutrition increasing fecundity. The lag in the birth rate declines reflected the underlying customs and traditions which were slower to change. As summarized by Lee (2003: 170, 173),

> The beginning of the world's demographic transition occurred in northwest Europe, where mortality began a secular decline around 1800... Between 1890 and 1920, marital fertility began to decline in most European provinces, with a median decline of about 40 percent from 1870 to 1930.

We should note, however, that this generalized description of the demographic transition, centered on Western Europe, does not adequately portray the diversity of human experience, even in Western Europe.[11] In particular, the fertility transition took place under a variety of socioeconomic conditions. It was France, not England where the Industrial Revolution began, that saw the first declines in fertility near the beginning of the nineteenth century, several decades at least before the general declines in fertility in England and the rest of Western Europe. And the declines in French birth rates took place before much industrialization. Moreover, fertility fell under a variety of infant mortality conditions. For example, in Germany marital fertility tended to decline earlier in areas of higher infant mortality. Infant mortality, in fact, may have been an accommodation to high and unwanted fertility, with infanticide from abusive child care, including the "laying over" and suffocating of infants in the parental bed.

Although the traditional methods of birth control might have been recognized (e.g., abstinence, rhythm, and withdrawal), the majority of populations likely did not exert any deliberate control over their fertility until the latter part of the eighteenth century. Nevertheless, once begun by

---

[10] Guinnane (2011: 599) offers a useful assessment of the improving mortality conditions:

Most European countries also experienced a significant mortality decline in the nineteenth century. Historians and others still debate the causes of the historical mortality decline, but most scholars stress some combination of better food supplies, improvements in public health systems (such as clean water supplies and food-safety measures), and modest results from medical interventions (such as vaccines against small pox).

[11] See Knodel and van de Walle (1982) and Coale (1973). Guinnane (2011) also provides a good survey of the historical fertility transition, profiling England, France, Germany, Italy, and the United States.

the more educated and upper middle classes, the innovative behavior of fertility limitation spread. Guinnane (2011: 595) in his study of the fertility transition observes that the positive relationship between fertility and income in England and Wales broke down after the early nineteenth century. And, by the latter half of the nineteenth century, birth rates were generally declining across Europe. It was arguably more a cultural phenomenon, though, with the diffusion of the idea and practice of birth control across populations sharing common languages and normative beliefs that promoted lower fertility.

Stabilization of the world population

While it took around 130 years for the world's population to double from 1 to 2 billion, it took less than half a century to double again to 4 billion, attained around 1975. In the next quarter century, the world population added another 2 billion, to reach 6 billion at the turn of the twenty-first century. As pointed out in Chapter 1, two countries, China and India, are now themselves demographic billionaires.

At some point, likely in the next few decades, the world population will cease to grow, returning on average to the near zero population growth that has characterized the vast span of human experience. Exactly when this limit will be reached, and whether the world population may then decline in size, is open to speculation. We will discuss the possible scenarios later. Here with a simple extrapolation we can show that population growth cannot continue indefinitely on a finite planet.

Begin with the world population in 2011, estimated to be 7 billion in number. Dividing by the total land area of the nations of the earth, approximately 130 million square kilometers (50 million square miles), yields an average population density of 54 persons per square kilometer, which is roughly half again the population density of 35 persons for the United States in 2011.[12] If we project this population forward at an annual rate of growth of 1.2 percent, the average annual rate of population growth for the world for 2000–10, corresponding to global crude birth and death rates of 20 and 8, respectively, then in 200 years the world population will have increased to 77 billion, yielding a population density of 590 per square kilometer (nearly 20 percent greater than the 2011 population density of the Netherlands). In another 58 years (in 2269) under an annual population growth rate of 1.2 percent, the world population would have doubled to 154 billion, with a density of approximately 1,180 persons per square kilometer (65 percent greater than the population density of the West Bank and Gaza in 2011 and over 90 percent of Bangladesh's, by far the most densely populated nation on earth with 1,285 persons per square kilometer in 2011).

Of course, this projection is not a likely scenario. But consider that not all of the world's land area (e.g., some mountainous regions and deserts) is habitable, and that some land is needed to grow food. And, while 258 years may seem like a long time, compared to the 35,000 years modern humans have inhabited the earth, two and a half centuries is equivalent to about 10 minutes in a day. It should be clear that any significant rate of population growth is unsustainable on this planet.

From Table 2.1, we can see the world population growth rate is projected to continue to decline. Moreover, in the twenty-first century annual net additions to the world population are declining.

---

[12]The population density figures are based on land area, not surface area. Surface area refers to "a country's total area, including areas under inland bodies of water and some coastal waterways." See World Bank (2011: Table 1) for this definition and statistics on population density for 2009, which were extrapolated forward to 2011 for this illustration. Surface area differs from land area, which excludes bodies of water. This total for land area refers to the aggregate for the nations of the world and does not include Antarctica, which would add approximately 5.5 million square miles to the total.

Logistic curve

This phenomenon of initially increasing then diminishing growth can be captured by a **logistic curve**, a well-known growth curve in demography. As Shryock and Siegel (1975: 382) explain:

> Some species of animals and some bacterial cultures have been observed to grow rapidly at first when placed in a limited environment with ideal conditions of food supply and space for their initially few numbers, and then to grow more slowly as the population approaches a point where there is pressure on available resources. There may be an upper limit to the numbers that can be maintained, whereupon the population ceases to grow.

A simplified, general equation for a logistic function is given by

$$P(T) = \frac{K}{1 + e^{a-bT}}$$

where K is the maximum value that the dependent variable P approaches, i.e., the upper asymptote, e is the base of the natural logarithm, P is a dependent variable and T an independent variable, and a and b are parameters ($a, b > 0$).

For example, assume $P(T) = 50/[1 + e^{2-T}]$, where T refers to 60-year intervals and P is the size of the world population (billions); see Table 2.2 for the projection of this population forward. The population at time 0, say the year 2000, is 6 billion, or 12 percent of the upper limit of 50 billion, a limit which likely far exceeds the carrying capacity of the world.

Carrying capacity refers to the maximum number of people that can be supported in an area given the available resources, technology and resource utilization rate. In this example, although the population growth rate is declining the population rises by an increasing amount until the year 2120 (when $T = 2$, the inflection point of this logistic curve). At this point the world population would be 25 billion, or 50 percent of the maximum possible in this illustration (i.e., the upper limit of $K = 50$). Beyond this point the population increases per period diminish; still by the year 2300, the population reaches 95 percent of this upper limit. As with the earlier population projection, this is not intended as a realistic scenario. Rather, the example illustrates that even with modest and declining population growth over the next two centuries the world would rapidly approach any imaginable carrying capacity.

Indeed, a graph of the world population size does follow a logistic curve (see Figure 2.1). To explain this population growth, we turn to the demographic transition.

DEMOGRAPHIC TRANSITION THEORY

The theory of the **demographic transition** draws on human experience to explain the transition between the two equilibrium states of population growth. Figure 2.2 gives a stylized representation of the three stages of the demographic transition.[13]

In the **traditional stage** (also known as the Malthusian stage) that has characterized most of human history, birth rates are high and fairly stable, while death rates are high and more variable.

---

[13] Some scholars identify four stages of the demographic transition, dividing the second stage of rapid population growth into two phases: the first dominated by the declining mortality rates and the second with declining fertility rates converging to the lower mortality rates. Haub and Gribble (2011) illustrate the four phases with contemporary case studies of countries: phase 1 (Uganda, with high birth rates and fluctuating death rates); phase 2 (Guatemala, with declining death and birth rates); phase 3 (India, with birth rates approaching replacement level); and phase 4 (Germany, with very low birth rates and death rates).

Table 2.2 Logistic growth of a population: $P(T) = 50/[1 + e^{2-T}]$

Year	T	$P(T)$	$\Delta P(T)$	% of limit	Average annual growth rate
1940	−1	2.4		5%	
			3.6		1.46%
2000	0	6.0		12%	
			7.5		1.35%
2060	1	13.5		27%	
			11.5		1.03%
2120	2	25.0		50%	
			11.5		0.63%
2180	3	36.5		73%	
			7.5		0.31%
2240	4	44.0		88%	
			3.6		0.13%
2300	5	47.6		95%	

Population growth, on average, is minimal. Periods of population increase alternate with periods of depopulation. Exogenous shocks such as severe shifts in weather, famine, outbreaks of disease and violence account for the volatility in mortality. Fertility, although somewhat affected by economic and environmental conditions, is more set by custom and tradition and has to remain high to offset the high death rates. Moreover, in traditional agrarian societies, large families are advantageous. Extra hands to work the fields and do chores are always welcome. With no social security system, parents depend on their children for old age support. In this traditional stage, populations are young: life expectancy is short and there is a relatively high percentage of the population under age 15.

The second stage is the **transitional stage** of population disequilibrium. Declines in death rates precede declines in birth rates, opening up historically high rates of population growth. Fertility rates remain high for some time, and might even rise with improvements in health. Eventually, though, birth rates fall. The historical delays in fertility rates declining reflect recognition and response lags. First, it takes time for parents to comprehend that improved survival rates for children make it no longer necessary to have so many births to achieve a desired family size. Urbanization makes larger families more expensive since the costs of food and shelter are higher in cities. Moreover, child labor laws and compulsory education reduce the opportunities for children to work. Rising standards of living change attitudes. Merit and achievement become more important than birth right and privilege for socioeconomic mobility. Consumer aspirations are stimulated with discretionary income and new products. Fertility falls first for the educated and upper-middle classes. Then the middle classes see the possibilities for socioeconomic mobility

World population size	Approximate date
1 billion	1804
2 billion	1927
3 billion	1960
4 billion	1974
5 billion	1987
6 billion	1999
7 billion	2011
8 billion (projected)	2025
9 billion (projected)	2041

Population (in billions)

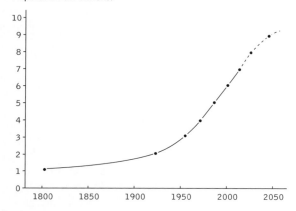

Figure 2.1 *World population by the billion*

Estimates of the size of the world population are from: "The World at Six Billion," Population Division, Department of Economic and Social Affairs, United Nations Secretariat (p. 8). [See http://www.un.org/esa/population/publications/sixbillion.] Population projections for reaching 7, 8, and 9 billion are from US Census Bureau, "Total Midyear Population for the World: 1950–2050." [See http://www.census.gov/ipc/www.idb/worldpop.php, accessed 11/08/2011].

with education and smaller families. Eventually, falling birth rates catch up with the lower death rates and the modern demographic equilibrium is reached. In Chapter 10, a behavioral model of the fertility transition will be presented.

In the third stage, the **modern stage**, birth rates, while low and somewhat responsive to economic cycles, again offset death rates. Population growth is minimal, average life expectancy is high, and populations are older. The crude death rate may even rise slightly as populations age. This is not to say that modern societies have not experienced spikes in mortality in the twentieth century, for example, with the influenza pandemic in 1918 and the two world wars; rather that improved standards of living and health care otherwise extended life expectancies. Nevertheless, as will be discussed in Chapter 10, affluence may also bring obesity and reduced physical fitness, undermining the gains in health.

Contemporary developing nations

There are important differences between the historical demographic transition experiences of Western Europe and the contemporary developing nations of Asia, Africa, the Middle East, and Latin America. For the latter regions of the world, the population growth rates during the

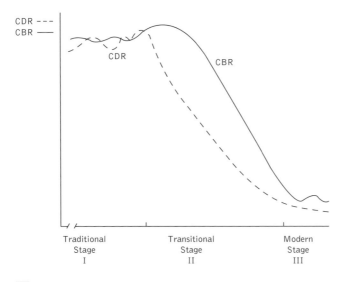

Figure 2.2 *The demographic transition*

There are three stages to the demographic transition. In the traditional stage, high birth rates offset, on average, high and variable death rates, yielding minimal population growth. In the transitional stage, death rates decline before birth rates, resulting in significant population growth. In the modern stage, birth rates are low, somewhat variable, and largely offset low death rates, again yielding minimal population growth.

transition from the traditional stage of high birth and death rates to the modern stage of low birth and death rates have been much greater (for a concise overview, see Teitelbaum 1975).

First, the source and pace of the initial sustained declines in mortality differed. Unlike the earlier experiences of Western Europe, the source of mortality decline was not indigenous economic development with a general improvement in the standard of living during the eighteenth and nineteenth centuries. Rather the discovery and application of new methods of disease control and treatment significantly reduced death rates in the developing world in the twentieth century. Imported medical technologies financed and administered through international agencies, Western governments, and private foundations initiated a revolution in public health that was possible without much indigenous economic development in the poor recipient nations. Examples include the eradication of disease-carrying insects through the spraying of insecticides, vaccinations for smallpox, diphtheria, polio, and tetanus, and new drugs such as penicillin and antibiotics.

The declines in death rates that began in the developing world in the first decades of the twentieth century accelerated after World War II. A dramatic illustration is Ceylon (now Sri Lanka), where the crude death rate fell by 34 percent in just one year (1946–47), and then continued to decline thereafter. The main reason was malaria eradication from the spraying of DDT against mosquitoes (Davis 1956: 307). In Latin America, the life expectancy at birth at the beginning of the twentieth century was comparable to what it had been in Europe during the Middle Ages. But when death rates began to decline, it took only a half-century for mortality in Latin America to fall to a point that had taken some five centuries in Europe (Weeks 2008: 153).

Second, the levels of fertility were much higher in the contemporary developing nations of Asia, Africa, Latin America, and the Middle East when their sustained declines in mortality commenced.[14] In these developing regions early and nearly universal marriages were the tradition. Thus the periods of childbearing were longer. While crude birth rates in Europe in the eighteenth and nineteenth centuries might have been 30–35 births per thousand population, in the developing nations in the twentieth century, crude birth rates were perhaps half as much again, 45–50 births per thousand.

The combination of the sharper declines in mortality through imported medical technologies and initially higher fertility led to population "explosions" in Africa, Latin America, Asia, and the Middle East. Where the population growth rates might not have reached 1.5 percent during the earlier demographic transitions, the population growth rates in the developing nations in the twentieth century often rose above 3 percent, with attendant doubling times of 20–30 years.

Moreover, while international migration had been largely free up to World War I, increasingly restrictions on migration were imposed after the war. And ever since, the legal movement of population has been regulated. Therefore, not only did the contemporary developing nations in the twentieth century have significantly higher crude rates of natural increase, but also the outlet of emigration was limited. The high rates of population growth experienced during their demographic transitions have created high youth burdens of dependency, hampering the generation of savings and productive investments in human and physical capital important for economic growth.

Nevertheless, there are factors that contribute to the contemporary developing nations completing their fertility transitions much faster. Foremost might be the international demonstration effect. That is, with increased exposure to the West, populations in low- and middle-income nations are more aware of the smaller family norm and greater consumption possibilities. With more education, female socioeconomic mobility is enhanced and marriage and childbearing are delayed. Consequently the demand for children decreases and the practice of contraception increases. Secondly, with modern contraceptive techniques (e.g., the birth control pill, intrauterine devices, injections, and sterilization), the ability to limit fertility is enhanced.

Sweden and Mexico illustrate the historical and contemporary demographic transitions (see Gelbard et al. 1999: 5–8). Sustained declines in mortality began in Sweden in the early 1800s, with crude death rates falling from between 25 and 30 to below 15 by the early 1900s. The crude birth rate in Sweden, between 30 and 35 in the early 1800s, did not decline until two or three generations later. In contrast, for Mexico, the crude death rate was higher, between 30 and 35 at the outset of the 1900s, and soared to over 40 from the violence of the Mexican Revolution (in the 1910 decade), before declining sharply to under 15 by 1950. The Mexican crude birth rate at the onset of the sustained mortality declines was between 40 and 45. But, when fertility began to fall a half-century later, the decline was much faster, and in one generation the crude birth rate was halved. Consequently, during Mexico's demographic transition, the rate of population growth has been significantly greater than was Sweden's a century earlier.

For another example, the fertility transition experiences of the United States and Bangladesh can be contrasted. The fertility rate in the US declined from seven children to three, on average, between 1800 and 1920. For Bangladesh, the fall in fertility from seven to three children took only 40 years, between 1960 and 2000 (see Kent and Haub 2005: 6–7). And, the fertility rate continued to decline to 2.2 by 2010. The dramatic decline in fertility in Bangladesh, a low-income economy with a gross national income per capita of $1,810 in 2010 (in PPP dollars), less than

---

[14]Recall the custom of later marriages and the relatively high incidences of celibacy in Europe, largely due to the practice of primogeniture and the delay of marriage until adequate means to support a family had been attained. In the United States, however, with abundant land to be settled, birth rates were much higher than in Europe. As Guinnane (2011: 599) notes, in the early nineteenth century in the US the average fertility rate was around seven children.

the average for sub-Saharan African nations ($2,148), is attributed, in large part, to effective family planning. By the early 2000s, over half of the married women in Bangladesh were using contraception.[15]

Progress in the demographic transition

The unprecedented population growth during the demographic transitions of the developing economies is dramatically reflected in the accelerated increases in the world population since 1950.

Figure 2.3 illustrates the differential progress the developing regions of the world through their demographic transitions. While birth rates have fallen in all regions, sub-Saharan Africa has made the least progress. The crude birth rate of 37 in 2010 in sub-Saharan Africa was still quite high, and the crude rate of natural increase has declined only modestly, from 29 to 24 between 1980 and 2010. The crude birth rates for East Asia and the Pacific and the former socialist economies of Europe and Central Asia are near those for the high-income economies. Note that the crude death rates in the Middle East and North Africa, Latin America and Caribbean, and East Asia and the Pacific are all lower than in the high-income economies. As we will discuss in Chapter 9, crude death rates and crude birth rates are sensitive to age distributions in the populations. There are more comparable measures of mortality and fertility across populations.

From Table 2.3 we can see, in general, that crude birth rates decline with economic growth. While crude death rates also decline with economic growth and, as discussed, precede the decreases in fertility, there is little difference in the crude death rates across income groups, despite significant differences in life expectancies. The low crude death rates in the developing regions largely reflect young populations.

The low-income economies are fairly early in the transition stage, with crude birth rates well above crude death rates. The high-income economies have essentially completed their demographic transitions, indeed most have reduced fertility to below replacement level and any positive crude rates of natural increase reflect some remaining population momentum from their post-World War II baby booms. Some developing countries—in particular, China and most of the transition economies of Eastern Europe and the former Soviet republics—are also well below replacement level fertility.

In sum, population growth rates are declining across the board, consistent with the demographic transition. Differential progress in the demographic transitions, however, means that the shares of the world population accounted for by low-income economies, especially sub-Saharan Africa, will rise, while the share of the high-income economies will fall. For example, between 2010 and 2020, the share of sub-Saharan Africa in the world population is projected to increase from 12.4 percent to 14.2 percent, while the share of the high-income economies is projected to decline from 16.3 percent to 15.4 percent. Regionally, East Asia and the Pacific's share is expected to decline from 28.5 percent in 2010 to 27.1 percent in 2020, reflecting the low fertility in these countries.

Some nations even have negative crude rates of natural increase, which, in the absence of net in-migration, would result in depopulation. As we did with negative output growth, we can identify

---

[15]These statistics are from World Bank (2012: Tables 1.1 and 2.19). The **total fertility rate** measures the average number of live births a woman would have if she lived through the childbearing years and adhered to the prevailing probabilities of giving birth at each age. In Chapter 9 we will discuss the total fertility rate and other measures of fertility in greater detail. The **contraceptive prevalence rate** measures the percentage of women aged 15–49, married or in union, who are practicing, or whose sexual partners are practicing, any form of contraception. For Bangladesh for 2005-2010 it was 53 percent; for sub-Saharan Africa it was 22 percent, and the 2010 total fertility rate averaged 4.9.

recent experiences with negative population growth (see Table 2.4). Fifteen nations with populations of at least 1 million had greater crude death rates than birth rates in 2010. Twelve of the 15 are transition economies, all with crude birth rates between 9 and 12, yet with a range of per capita incomes. For example, Bosnia and Herzegovina with a per capita income (in PPP dollars) in 2010 of $8,910 had the same vital rates as the high-income economies of Japan ($34,610) and Italy ($31,810). The nation with the lowest crude birth rate in the world in 2010 is Germany, with a per capita income of $38,100 in 2010. In all 15 nations, except Italy, negative population growth is projected for the 2010–20 period.

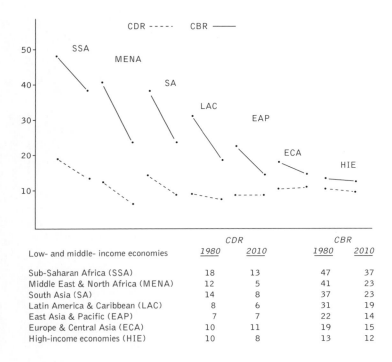

Low- and middle- income economies	CDR		CBR	
	1980	*2010*	*1980*	*2010*
Sub-Saharan Africa (SSA)	18	13	47	37
Middle East & North Africa (MENA)	12	5	41	23
South Asia (SA)	14	8	37	23
Latin America & Caribbean (LAC)	8	6	31	19
East Asia & Pacific (EAP)	7	7	22	14
Europe & Central Asia (ECA)	10	11	19	15
High-income economies (HIE)	10	8	13	12

Figure 2.3 *Progress in the demographic transition*

The developing regions of the world are at different stages in the demographic transition. Sub-Saharan Africa has made the least progress. Europe and Central Asia have nearly completed the transition.

Data From: World Bank, World Development Indicators 2000, 2012, Tables 2.1 and 2.2

The [demographic] transition began around 1800 with declining mortality in Europe. It has now spread to all parts of the world and is projected to be completed by 2100...Since 1800, global population size has already increased by a factor of six and by 2100 will have risen by a factor of ten. There will then be 50 times as many elderly, but only five times as many children; thus the ratio of elders to children will have risen by a factor of ten.

Ronald Lee, "The Demographic Transition: Three Centuries of Fundamental Change,"

Journal of Economic Perspectives (Fall 2003), p. 167.

Table 2.3 Selected statistics on population growth

Country	Population (millions) 2010	CBR 2010	CDR 2010	Population growth rate (annual average) 2000–10	2010–20	Population (millions) 2020
WORLD ($11,066)	6,895	20	8	1.2%	1.0%	7,635
Low-income economies ($1,307)	796 (11.5%)	33	11	2.1%	2.1%	979 (12.8%)
Lower middle-income economies ($3,632)	2,519 (36.5%)	24	8	1.6%	1.4%	2,902 (38.0%)
India ($3,400)	1,225 (16.8%)	22	8	1.5%	1.2%	1,385 (18.1%)
Upper middle-income economies ($9,970)	2,452 (35.6%)	14	7	0.7%	0.5%	2,576 (33.7%)
China ($7,640)	1,338 (19.7%)	12	7	0.8%	0.6%	1,382 (19.0%)
High-income economies ($37,317)	1,127 (16.3%)	12	8	0.7%	0.4%	1,178 (15.4%)
United States ($47,310)	309 (4.5%)	14	8	0.9%	0.8%	335 (4.4%)
LOW & MIDDLE-INCOME ECONOMIES						
Sub-Saharan Africa ($2,148)	853 (12.4%)	37	13	2.5%	2.4%	1,084 (14.2%)
Mid. East & N. Africa ($8,068)	331 (4.8%)	23	5	1.8%	1.6%	387 (5.1%)
Europe & Cen. Asia ($13,396)	405 (6.0%)	15	11	0.2%	0.2%	414 (5.4%)
South Asia ($3,124)	1,633 (23.7%)	23	8	1.6%	1.3%	1,861 (24.4%)
East Asia & Pacific ($6,657)	1,962 (28.5%)	14	7	0.8%	0.5%	2,069 (27.1%)
Lat. Amer. & Carib. ($10,926)	583 (8.5%)	19	6	1.2%	1.0%	642 (8.4%)

Notes: Population estimates are usually based on national censuses, but the frequency and quality vary by country. Estimates for the years before and after the census are interpolations or extrapolations based on demographic models. Per capita gross national incomes for 2010 in PPP dollars are listed in next to the country classification or region. The population growth rates for 2010–20 and the populations for 2020 are projections.
Crude birth rate (CBR) is the number of live births during the year per thousand mid-year population.
Crude death rate (CDR) is the number of deaths during the year per thousand mid-year population.

Source: World Bank (2012: Tables 1.1 and 2.1).

Table 2.4 *Negative crude rates of natural increase in 2010*

	Population (millions) 2010	CBR 2010	CDR 2010	Population growth rate (annual average) 2000–10	2010–20	Population (millions) 2020
Belarus ($13,590)	9.5	11	15	−0.5	−0.4	9.2
Bosnia & Herz. ($8,910)	3.8	9	10	0.2	−0.4	3.6
Bulgaria ($13,440)	7.5	10	15	−0.8	−0.7	7.0
Croatia ($18,890)	4.4	10	12	0.0	−0.3	4.3
Germany ($38,100)	81.8	8	11	−0.1	−0.2	79.8
Hungary ($19,550)	10.0	9	13	−0.2	−0.2	9.8
Italy ($31,810)	60.5	9	10	0.6	0.1	60.8
Japan ($34,610)	127.5	9	10	0.0	−0.3	123.6
Latvia ($16,380)	2.2	9	13	−0.6	−0.4	2.1
Lithuania ($18,060)	3.3	11	13	−0.6	−0.5	3.1
Moldova ($3,360)	3.6	12	13	−0.2	−0.6	3.3
Romania ($14,290)	21.4	10	12	−0.5	−0.3	20.9
Russian Fed. ($19,240)	141.8	13	14	−0.3	−0.2	139.3
Serbia ($11,090)	7.3	9	14	−0.3	−0.2	7.2
Ukraine ($6,620)	45.9	11	15	−0.7	−0.6	43.3

Notes: Per capita gross national incomes (PPP dollars) in 2010 are listed in parentheses next to each country. International migration is the only other factor besides birth rates and death rates that directly determines a country's population growth. Annual data on net migration rates, however, were not reported. About 195 million people (approximately 3 percent of the world's population) live outside their home country (World Bank 2012: 45).

The population for 2020 is projected using the cohort component method using assumed fertility, mortality, and net migration rates.

Source: World Bank (2012: Tables 1.1 and 2.1)

LOW POPULATION GROWTH

Recall that population growth rates are the sum of the crude rates of natural increase and net migration rates. Negative crude rates of natural increase can be offset by net in-migration so that population growth is positive. There are a number of concerns with depopulation, however, as we will discuss in Chapter 10 in greater detail.

Briefly, the demographic dividend of an increased share of the population in the labor force that accompanies the fertility transition will be depleted. In turn, with an increased elderly share of the population, the share of the population in the labor force will decline. Lower fertility will eventually result in declines in the growth of the labor force, unless offset by higher labor force participation rates, and even declining output growth, if not economic stagnation. Prolonged low fertility, *ceteris paribus*, results in an older population and increased elderly dependencies, involving provision for the social security and health care needs of the retired population. This can also reduce the ability to generate savings for investment, further restricting economic growth. As will be examined in Chapter 4, macroeconomists were concerned in the 1930s with insufficient population growth.

There are additional concerns with an older population (i.e., an increased share of the population aged 65 or older) being more conservative and less innovative, which can stifle technological progress. Countries facing natural depopulation, however, can compensate with immigration, which can offset the natural declines in the labor forces and rising old-age dependency burdens, with inflows of younger workers and families. There has been resistance in many countries, however, to increased immigration, reflecting the perception that immigrants are different (the vast majority of immigrants to the developed countries are from the developing nations) and might undermine the national identity and culture.

In sum there are two equilibrium states in the demographic transition. The traditional low-level equilibrium with high, relatively stable, birth rates and high variable death rates yields, on average, minimal crude rates of natural increase. This equilibrium state has characterized most of the human experience, with populations subsisting well below the low natural carrying capacities. The modern equilibrium characterizes the developed economies of the twentieth century, with low, somewhat cyclical, birth rates and low and more stable death rates, again yielding minimal crude rates of natural increase, on average, but with much larger populations living with greater carrying capacities. Prolonged low fertility rates, well below replacement levels, in the nations of Europe, Canada, Japan, Australia, and New Zealand, however, may portend a fourth disequilibrium stage in the demographic transition: one defined by declining populations, before eventually reaching a fifth stage of a long-run equilibrium of zero population growth.

As stated, we will explore these issues in more depth later. We conclude this introduction to population growth with a discussion of the impact of population change on economic growth.

POPULATION CHANGE AND ECONOMIC GROWTH

Recall that economic growth, the growth rate of real per capita output, can be measured as the difference between the growth rates of real national output (dY/Y) and population (dP/P), i.e., $dy/y = dY/Y - dP/P$. *Ceteris paribus*, a one percentage point increase in the population growth rate would decrease the economic growth rate by one percentage point. Not all population growth, however, will have the same implications for economic growth, since accompanying the population growth may be changes in output growth.

For example, if the growth in population is due to an increased crude birth rate, then there may be no significant impact on output growth for roughly two decades when the labor force growth rate then might increase. In this case, the decrease in the economic growth rate would be comparable to the increase in the population growth rate. On the other hand, if the population growth reflects increased immigration of labor, especially skilled labor, into the economy, then output growth will increase and may even exceed the population growth, yielding greater economic growth. Or if the increase in population growth reflects a decrease in the crude death rate, which also results in a healthier and more productive population, then the gains in the supply of effective labor would increase output growth and may lead to economic growth.

Conversely, declines in the growth rate of population may have differential consequences for economic growth depending on the sources of the decreased population growth (e.g., falling birth rates, greater emigration, or increased death rates).

CONCLUSION

We have discussed the measurement and sources of economic growth, output growth, and population growth in these two introductory chapters. We have also reviewed global trends in economic and population growth. We will return to the components of population growth in Chapters 9 and 10, examining the measures and determinants of mortality, fertility, and migration in greater detail. We turn now to theories of economic growth, beginning in Chapter 3 with the classical economists, writing two centuries ago when some nations of the world first experienced significant economic growth and population increase. As we will see, the classical economists expected neither to continue in the long run.

KEY TERMS

carrying capacity	contraceptive prevalence rate
crude birth rate	crude death rate
crude rate of natural increase	demographic transition
flow	logistic curve
net in-migration rate	modern stage of demographic transition
stock	total fertility rate
traditional stage of demographic transition	transitional stage of demographic transition

QUESTIONS

1. In mid-2010 the world population was estimated to be 6.89 billion, with the population of sub-Saharan Africa estimated to be 0.85 billion. Assuming that the world population grows at the annual rate of 12 per thousand, while the population of sub-Saharan Africa grows at an annual rate of 25 per thousand (the annual average population growth rates for the 2000–10 period), when would the population of sub-Saharan Africa constitute 50 percent of the world total? At that time (the nearest year), what would be the size of the world population? Discuss whether you think this is likely to happen.

2. Discuss why in the demographic transition model it is intuitive that mortality rates would decline before fertility rates. Even so, in France during the early nineteenth century, it appears that mortality and fertility rates declined concurrently. Discuss possible explanations.

3. If the logistic curve mirrors the historical trend in population growth, what would happen if there were a fourth stage to the demographic transition, where crude birth rates fell below crude death rates? Do you think this is likely? Discuss.

    If there were a fourth stage in the demographic transition with negative crude rates of natural increase, would there then have to be a fifth stage? Discuss.

4. If the contemporary developing nations had not experienced the significant declines in mortality largely due to imported medical technologies and disease control in the middle of the twentieth century, what might have been the consequences for the world population at the beginning of the twenty-first century?

5. Do you think in the long run a zero rate of population growth for the world is inevitable? Explain why or why not. If so, would or should all the nations of the world have a zero crude rate of natural increase?

REFERENCES

Clark, Gregory. 2007. *A Farewell to Alms: A Brief Economic History of the World*. Princeton, NJ: Princeton University Press.

Coale, Ansley. 1973. "The Demographic Transition," in *International Population Conference, Liège*, Vol. 1. Liège: International Union for the Scientific Study of Population: 53–72.

Davis, Kingsley. 1956. "The Amazing Decline of Mortality in Underdeveloped Areas," *American Economic Review*, 46(2): 305–318.

Fogel, Robert. 1994. "Economic Growth, Population Theory, and Physiology: The Bearing of Long-Term Processes on the Making of Economic Policy," *American Economic Review*, 84(3): 369–395.

Gelbard, Alene, Carl Haub, and Mary Kent. 1999. "World Population Beyond Six Billion," *Population Bulletin*, 54(10).

Guinnane, Timothy. 2011. "The Historical Fertility Transition: A Guide for Economists," *Journal of Economic Literature*, 49(3): 589–614.

Haub, Carl, and James Gribble. 2011. "The World at 7 Billion," *Population Bulletin*, 66(2).

Kent, Mary and Carl Haub. 2005. "Global Demographic Divide," *Population Bulletin*, 60(4).

Knodel, John and Etienne van de Walle. 1982. "European Transition," in John Ross (ed.), *International Encyclopedia of Population*, Vol. 1. New York: Free Press: 268–275.

Lee, Ronald. 2003. "The Demographic Transition," *Journal of Economic Perspectives*, 17(4): 167–190.

McKeown, Thomas, R.G. Brown, and R.G. Record. 1972. "An Interpretation of the Modern Rise of Population in Europe," *Population Studies*, 26(3): 345–382.

Shryock, Henry and Jacob Siegel. 1975. *The Methods and Materials of Demography*, Vol. 2. Washington, DC: US Bureau of the Census, Department of Commerce.

Teitelbaum, Michael. 1975. "Relevance of Demographic Transition Theory for Developing Countries," *Science*, 188: 420–425.

United Nations Secretariat. 1999. *The World at Six Billion*. New York: Population Division, Department of Economic and Social Affairs, United Nations. http://www.un.org/esa/population/publications/sixbillion/sixbillion.htm.

Weeks, John. 2008. *Population: An Introduction to Concepts and Issues*, 10th edition. Belmont, CA: Thomson Wadsworth.

World Bank. 2000. *World Development Indicators 2000*. Washington, DC: World Bank.

World Bank. 2002. *World Development Indicators 2002*. Washington, DC: World Bank.

World Bank. 2011. *World Development Report 2011: Conflict, Security, and Development*. Washington, DC: World Bank.

World Bank. 2012. *World Development Indicators 2012*. Washington, DC: World Bank.

Part II
Theories of growth

Chapter 3

Classical theories of economic growth

Can the world continue to produce enough goods and services to accommodate an increasing population with rising aspirations for consumption? Will advances in technologies and human ingenuity allow for population growth and economic growth to continue? Or are there limits to the growth in people and output, due to either resource constraints or environmental thresholds?

Economists have been concerned with economic growth for some time. The major classical economists of the eighteenth and nineteenth centuries believed that the long run would be characterized by a stationary state, with, on average, subsistence-level income and zero economic and population growth. In this chapter we will address the pessimism of the classical economists, followed in Chapter 4 by the worries of macroeconomists during the Great Depression in the 1930s. Then in Chapter 5 we will discuss the "limits to growth" model introduced in the 1970s, which has since been updated, but still contends that "business as usual" is an unsustainable path for humankind.

We begin with a brief review of mercantilism, a body of ideas and practices before the classical period of Adam Smith, Thomas Malthus, and David Ricardo.

MERCANTILISM

Mercantilism is the label given to the conventional wisdom and economic policies of the period covering roughly 1500–1750 AD, the two and a half centuries prior to the Industrial Revolution.[1] This era saw the rise of the nation state, with increased international competition in trade and colonization. Underlying the economic policies was a zero-sum view of the world: the notion that one nation could gain only at the expense of another nation. In particular, if the total wealth of the world was fixed, then nations would necessarily be in competition, and often at war, to increase their individual wealth.[2]

Moreover, the mercantilist writers narrowly interpreted wealth to be gold, and to a lesser extent silver and other precious metals. The power of the nation state to fund armies and navies for waging war and establishing colonies was directly related to the state treasury's stock of gold. If a nation did not have direct access to gold—for example, gold mines at home or abroad in its

---

[1] Mercantilism is most closely associated with England. For example, France was more inward-looking, emphasizing the regulation of domestic industry. To illustrate, Ekelund and Hébert (1990: 49) note that "in 1666 French Minister Colbert issued a rule that the fabrics woven in Dijon contain no more nor less than 1,408 threads. Penalties for those weavers who strayed from this standard were severe."

Spain focused more on monopolizing trade with its overseas colonies. This required maintaining a strong navy, especially for shipping the gold extracted from these lands. In the Netherlands, there was less regulation of economic activity and freer trade, with the exception of the Dutch East India Company which monopolized commerce with the East Indies. See Ekelund and Hébert (1990: Chapter 3) and Brue and Grant (2007: Chapter 2).

[2] In present times nonrenewable resources, such as fossil fuels, are increasingly recognized as limited, with exhaustible supplies on the planet. Is a similar zero-sum view of the world warranted? Are nations in conflict as they compete for these finite resources?

colonies (as Spain did in the Americas, plundering gold and silver from the Incas and Aztecs), then it was still possible to accumulate gold by running a balance of trade surplus. By exporting more goods and services than it imported, a nation could demand payment for its export surplus in gold. Consequently, policies were implemented to ensure a favorable trade balance. Governments were heavily involved in regulating domestic commerce and international trade, with manufacturing guilds, state-sanctioned monopolies, and trade barriers, especially import duties on manufactured goods.

The mercantilist writers favored population growth. Larger populations directly added to national power through larger armies and navies. Abundant labor would keep wages down, enhancing a nation's competitiveness in international trade. Any surplus population could be used to colonize overseas lands. Consistent with the goal of export surpluses, colonies were seen as both a source of raw materials and a market for the high value-added manufactured goods.

CLASSICAL ECONOMISTS AND ECONOMIC GROWTH

The classical period of economic thought covers roughly a century, from the publication of Adam Smith's *Inquiry into the Nature and Causes of the Wealth of Nations* in 1776, through Thomas Malthus and David Ricardo in the first decades of the nineteenth century, up to the death of John Stuart Mill, considered to be the last major classical economist, in 1873.

ADAM SMITH

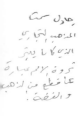

In his great work, commonly referred to as *The Wealth of Nations,* Adam Smith (1723–90) argued against the mercantilist static zero-sum view of the world, where wealth was narrowly defined as the stocks of gold and silver in the state treasury and one nation could gain only at the expense of another nation. Smith saw the wealth of a nation in the ability to produce goods and services and generate income, which would improve the standard of living. Moreover, a balance of trade surplus was not necessarily "good," nor a balance of trade deficit "bad." Trade was mutually beneficial.

Perhaps most revolutionary was Smith's concept of the **invisible hand**. That is, the government need not, and indeed should not, intervene to regulate the economy. Rather, there is a natural order embodied in competition. In a market economy, individuals pursuing self-interest would advance the public good.[3] For example, entrepreneurs and businessmen in the pursuit of profits would seek to produce those goods and services that would be in demand, that is, that the public would want to buy. And competition would require firms to produce those goods as efficiently (cheaply) as possible. To quote from one of Smith's famous passages:

> It is not from the benevolence of the butcher, the brewer, or the baker, that we expect our dinner, but from their regard to their own interest . . . by directing that industry in such a manner as its produce may be of the greatest value, he intends only his own gain, and he is in this, as in many other cases, led by an invisible hand to promote an end which was no part of his intention. (Cited in Viner 1927: 209)

Smith put forth a dynamic theory of growth based on the division of labor and specialization in trade. The division of labor occurs when the production of a good or service is broken down

---

[3] Smith acknowledged that the government still had a role, albeit limited, in the economy, by providing public goods such as national defense and roads, as well as administering justice and issuing the currency. In addition, government should support education for better citizens and more productive workers and public health measures to control disease. See Viner (1927: 222–228).

into distinct stages, with workers assigned to different stages of the production. With the division of labor, individual workers would focus on a particular task, using the appropriate tools and thus becoming more proficient, and perhaps even innovative. Adam Smith provided the example of a pin factory, which also reflects specialization in production:

> One man draws out the wire, another straights it, a third cuts it, a fourth points it, a fifth grinds it at the top for receiving the head; to make the head requires two or three distinct operations; to put it on, is a peculiar business, to whiten the pins is another; it is even a trade by itself to put them into the paper. (Cited in Brue and Grant 2007: 66)

Smith noted that each individual, working alone, would not be able to make even 20 pins a day, but with division of labor, ten workers could make over 40,000 pins in a day—or an average of over 4,000 each.

Specialization in trade refers to businesses producing particular goods (e.g., pins or hats) and individuals specializing in occupations (e.g., doctors, lawyers, and bankers). Even within a trade there may be further specialization (e.g., commercial law, corporate law, and criminal law). Here too, by specializing, businesses and individuals become more efficient and innovative. The variety, quality, and quantity of goods and services increase.

As another example, consider the division of labor and specialization that occur at a university. The administration is broken down into divisions or offices (e.g., academics, admissions, athletics, registrar, residential life, student affairs). Within the divisions there may be further specialization (e.g., the disciplines or departments of English, history, music, and economics within the academic division). Indeed, within each department, there will be further specialization (e.g., within economics there will not only be microeconomists, macroeconomists, and econometricians, but fields such as industrial organization, economic development, mathematical economics, and economic history). Such division of labor and specialization not only is more efficient, but also produces a higher quality of education. Consider the alternative model of universities with general employees, each one charged with recruiting, admitting, housing, feeding, teaching, and coaching a handful of students.

International trade

For Smith the key to realizing the efficiencies from the division of labor and specialization in trade was the extent of the market. The larger the market and the greater the demands to be served, the greater the opportunities for specialization and economies of scale in production. In the small markets of villages and towns there will be less specialization (e.g., if served by any doctor, it would be a general practitioner). And among even smaller, more dispersed rural populations, individuals have to be even more self-sufficient, capable in many tasks, from growing food to making clothes and building their own shelter.

The extent of the market is limited physically and politically. Geographical boundaries, such as mountains and oceans, can separate markets. Advances in transportation can reduce the geographical boundaries, however, and as populations grow and cities develop, markets can be linked. Political boundaries reflect nation states. If friendly relations prevail, then international trade can overcome the political boundaries and also extend the market. The most extreme form would be globalization, where increasingly in the twenty-first century with the technological advances in transportation and telecommunications promoting greater international integration, and the

59

conversion of the former command economies and the reorientation of inward-looking developing economies to more open systems, the relevant market is the world.

Smith showed that international trade would benefit all nations, that is, trade is a positive-sum game, in contrast to the mercantilists who emphasized balance of trade surpluses as a means of acquiring gold. For Smith, the path to economic growth can be illustrated simply as follows:

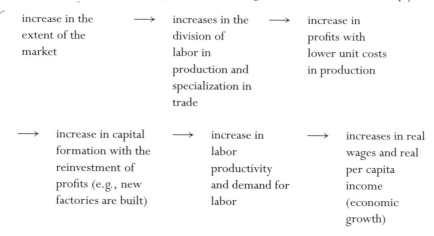

increase in the extent of the market $\longrightarrow$ increases in the division of labor in production and specialization in trade $\longrightarrow$ increase in profits with lower unit costs in production

$\longrightarrow$ increase in capital formation with the reinvestment of profits (e.g., new factories are built) $\longrightarrow$ increase in labor productivity and demand for labor $\longrightarrow$ increases in real wages and real per capita income (economic growth)

International trade not only widened the extent of the market but also, consistent with Smith's emphasis on competition, forced firms to produce goods in demand at the lowest costs possible.

Gains from international specialization

We can illustrate the gains from trade, realized with a more efficient allocation of the world's resources, using a simple two-country example. We will employ the **labor theory of value**, where we can reduce the costs of production of a good into the labor hours required for production.[4]

Consider two countries, England and Spain, and two goods, wine (W) and cloth (C), with the labor requirements of production for a unit of each good given below. The labor requirements per unit of output are the reciprocals of labor productivity. To illustrate:

	Labor hours required per unit of production		
	Wine (W)	Cloth (C)	Opportunity costs
England	5 hours	8 hours	$1\ W = \frac{5}{8}\ C$ or $\frac{8}{5}\ W = 1\ C$
Spain	3 hours	9 hours	$1\ W = \frac{1}{3}\ C$ or $3\ W = 1\ C$

We will also assume **constant costs of production**: no matter how much of a good has been produced in a given period of time, the labor hours required to produce another unit of the good remain constant. Further, we assume no qualitative differences in the wine or cloth produced in the two countries.

The labor costs per unit of a good produced might differ between the two countries due to differences in climate or geography (i.e., natural advantages in production), technology, labor

---

[4] The labor theory of value is a useful simplification to illustrate the basis for and gains from trade. The contribution of physical capital to production could be reduced to the labor hours embodied in the production of that physical capital.

skills, and physical capital stocks. In this example, England has the **absolute advantage** in the production of cloth (8 hours versus 9 hours of labor required per unit of cloth), while Spain has the absolute advantage in the production of wine (3 hours versus 5 hours of labor per unit of wine produced). Absolute advantage is indicated here by lower labor costs.

In **autarky**, nations are self-sufficient and do not engage in international trade. Consequently, the internal exchange ratios (i.e., the **barter terms of trade**) reflect the opportunity costs within the nation. For example, with 5 hours of labor, England can produce one unit of wine, 1W, or five eights of a unit of cloth, $\frac{5}{8}$C. Thus the opportunity cost in England of producing 1W is $\frac{5}{8}$C. Alternatively, the opportunity cost of producing 1C is $\frac{8}{5}$W, since both 1C and $\frac{8}{5}$W embody or require 8 hours of labor. For Spain, the opportunity costs are: $1W = \frac{1}{3}C$ or $1C = 3W$.

We see, then, that England has the lower opportunity cost for producing cloth, since $\frac{8}{5}W <$ 3W; while Spain has the lower opportunity cost for producing wine, with $\frac{1}{3}C < \frac{5}{8}C$. David Ricardo later pointed out that the basis for trade is not absolute advantage (lower resource cost, here fewer labor hours required to produce a unit of output), but **comparative advantage**, reflected in lower opportunity costs. Here England has the comparative advantage in cloth production and Spain has the comparative advantage in wine production.[5]

Consequently, with trade between the two countries, we would expect England to see the advantage of increasing its production of cloth, shifting labor and resources away from wine production, and shipping cloth to Spain as long as it would receive more than $\frac{8}{5}$W per unit of cloth exported.[6] Moreover, Spain would import cloth from England if it could pay anything less than 3W per unit of cloth. An **international terms of trade** will emerge, that is, a common world price, that falls between these opportunity costs. In turn, with international trade, Spain will

---

[5] David Ricardo made this key distinction in his extension of Smith's arguments for trade. Indeed, a nation could have an absolute advantage in both goods compared to another nation, but as long as the opportunity costs differed between the nations, comparative advantages would exist and there would be a basis for trade. For example, assume the following labor hours required per unit of wine and cloth produced:

	Labor hours required per unit of production		
	Wine (W)	Cloth (C)	Opportunity costs
England	2 hours	3 hours	$1W = \frac{2}{3}C$ or $\frac{3}{2}W = 1C$
Spain	3 hours	9 hours	$1W = \frac{1}{3}C$ or $3W = 1C$

Here England has the absolute advantage in both wine and cloth production, a comparative advantage (lower opportunity cost) in cloth, and a comparative disadvantage in wine. Spain has absolute disadvantages in both goods, but a comparative advantage in wine production. Trade would be still mutually beneficial with the international terms of trade falling between: $\frac{3}{2}W < 1C < 3W$.

Alternatively, suppose the labor costs were the following:

	Labor hours required per unit of production		
	Wine (W)	Cloth (C)	Opportunity costs
England	2 hours	6 hours	$1W = \frac{1}{3}C$ or $3W = 1C$
Spain	3 hours	9 hours	$1W = \frac{1}{3}C$ or $3W = 1C$

Now England has the absolute advantages in both goods, but there is no comparative advantage (the opportunity costs in the two countries for the goods are equal) and no basis for trade.

[6] We are ignoring trade barriers and transportation costs in this example. The actual international terms of trade will reflect not just the opportunity costs of production, which set the boundaries for the common world price, but relative demands in the two nations, which reflect tastes and preferences, population sizes, and national incomes. As noted in the illustration for purchasing power parity conversions for national incomes, when countries engage in international trade, there will be common world prices for the traded goods and services (aside from any qualitative differences in the products).

61

shift labor and resources into the production of wine, the good Spain can produce for a lower opportunity cost than England.

Suppose that the international terms of trade settle at $1C = 2W$, that is, one unit of cloth exchanges for two units of wine. To illustrate the gains from trade, note that England could produce 1W directly for 5 hours of labor. England could acquire 1W with only 4 hours of labor, however, through international trade. That is, England could produce $\frac{1}{2}C$ with 4 hours of labor and trade the $\frac{1}{2}C$ for 1W, saving 1 hour of labor per unit of wine imported and consumed. Conversely, Spain could directly produce $\frac{1}{2}C$ with 4.5 hours of labor, or could indirectly produce half a unit of cloth by using 3 hours of labor to produce 1W and trade for $\frac{1}{2}C$, saving 1.5 hours of labor. In short, with trade both nations can consume more than they could produce directly. Consequently, the world gains. Allowing nations to produce more of the goods in which they have comparative advantages (lower opportunity costs) and less of the goods in which they have higher opportunity costs or comparative disadvantages permits a more efficient allocation of the world's resources.

Production and consumption possibilities boundaries

To illustrate the aggregate gains from international specialization and trade, we can use production and consumption possibilities boundaries. The **production possibilities boundary** (PPB) for a nation indicates the combinations of goods that the nation could produce using all of its resources efficiently and completely, that is, with the existing technologies and full employment of the resources. The **consumption possibilities boundary** (CPB) for a nation indicates the combinations of goods that the nation can consume, given its PPB and the international terms of trade. In autarky, a nation's CPB coincides with its PPB.

Returning to our example of England and Spain producing wine and cloth, and assuming the labor theory of value with constant costs of production, we can derive the PPB and CPB for each nation if we are given the number of labor hours available in each nation for production. Suppose that England has 800 labor hours and Spain has 630 labor hours available per period. England can produce a maximum of 160 units of wine ($160W = 800$ hours/5 hours per unit of wine) if no cloth were produced. Alternatively, England could produce a maximum of 100 units of cloth if no wine were produced. Assuming constant costs of production, England's PPB is illustrated in Figure 3.1 by the line ab. Spain could produce a maximum of 210W if it allocated all of its labor to wine production or a maximum of 70 units of cloth if it produced no wine during the period. Spain's PPB is illustrated by the line $b'a'$ in Figure 3.1. Note that the slopes of the PPBs reflect the opportunity costs in the nations: for England, $\Delta W/\Delta C = -\frac{8}{5}$ and for Spain, $\Delta W/\Delta C = -3$.

From the PPBs we can easily derive the CPBs. Given the assumed international terms of trade of $2W = 1C$, then at the extreme, England could specialize in the production of cloth, producing 100C and exporting the 100C for 200W. England's CPB is given by the dashed line bd in Figure 3.1. Similarly, Spain could completely specialize in wine, the good it has the lower opportunity cost for producing, and trade the 210W produced for 105C. Spain's CPB is given by the dashed line $b'd'$. Note that the slopes of the CPBs for England and Spain are equal, $\Delta W/\Delta C = -2$, reflecting the international terms of trade or common world price ratio.

Assume that before trade (i.e., in autarky) England is producing and consuming 80W and 50C, each requiring 400 labor hours, or a total of 800 labor hours (see point e on England's PPB). Assume Spain in autarky is producing and consuming 90W and 40C, requiring 270 and 360 labor hours respectively of the 630 total labor hours available (see point e' on Spain's PPB).

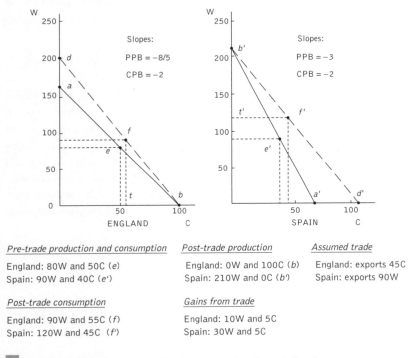

Unit labor costs

	Wine (W)	Cloth (C)	Opportunity costs
England	5 hours	8 hours	$1W = \frac{5}{8}C$ or $\frac{8}{5}W = 1C$
Spain	3 hours	9 hours	$1W = \frac{1}{3}C$ or $3W = 1C$

Assume international terms of trade (ITT) are: $1W = \frac{1}{2}C$ or $1C = 2W$.

Given England has 800 hours of labor and Spain has 630 hours of labor available, and assuming constant costs of production, the production possibilities boundaries (PPBs) of the nations are:

Slopes:
PPB = −8/5
CPB = −2

Slopes:
PPB = −3
CPB = −2

ENGLAND C

SPAIN C

Pre-trade production and consumption

England: 80W and 50C (e)
Spain: 90W and 40C (e')

Post-trade production

England: 0W and 100C (b)
Spain: 210W and 0C (b')

Assumed trade

England: exports 45C
Spain: exports 90W

Post-trade consumption

England: 90W and 55C (f)
Spain: 120W and 45C (f')

Gains from trade

England: 10W and 5C
Spain: 30W and 5C

Figure 3.1 *Gains from trade and international specialization*

With trade, under the assumption of constant costs of production with two nations of comparable size, nations will completely specialize in production. Consequently, with trade, England shifts its labor and resources to specialize in cloth production (see point b on England's PPB) and Spain shifts its labor and resources to specialize in wine production (see point b' on Spain's PPB).[7]

Suppose, for example, England exports 45C in return for imports of 90W. England's trade triangle is here btf, that is, bt exports of cloth for ft imports of wine. With trade, then, England ends up consuming 55C (100C produced less 45C exported) and 90W, all imported from Spain (see point f on England's CPB). England's gains from trade are indicated by the differences between its post-trade and pre-trade consumptions: here 5C (or 55C–50C) and 10W (or 90W–80W).

Similarly, Spain imports 45C for exports of 90W: a trade triangle b't'f' which is equivalent in size to England's with b't' of wine exports for t'f' of cloth imports. Spain's post-trade consumption (indicated by point f' on Spain's CPB) is 120W (210W produced less 90W exported) and 45C, all imported from England. Spain's gains from trade in this example are 30W and 5C.

[7]In practice, with increasing opportunity costs and strictly concave PPBs, countries would not completely specialize.

With the same labor, just reallocated more efficiently, the world has increased the total output of wine and cloth produced by 40W and 10C, which is the sum of the gains from trade for England and Spain. Thus, while before trade both nations were producing on their respective PPBs, using their labor fully and efficiently, the world was not producing on the global PPB (see Figure 3.2). The world PPB, the boundary $B'FB$, is an aggregation of the individual nations' PPBs. Without trade, the individual nations are producing in autarky and the combined output falls within the world PPB (see point E), with a total of 170W and 90C. By engaging in trade and producing more of the goods in which the nations have the lower opportunity costs (here England specializing in cloth and Spain in wine), the world's labor and resources are allocated more efficiently, allowing for greater aggregate production (see point F on the world PPB).

Income distribution

In sum, there are strong theoretical arguments for free trade and international specialization. Nations engaging in trade win by being able to consume beyond their PPBs. In practice, however, not all in the nations might win. Here in this simple example we have assumed full employment of labor (and implicitly full employment of resources) and constant costs of production. Increasing opportunity costs and strictly concave PPBs are more realistic if not all resources are equally well suited for both types of production. With increasing opportunity costs, complete specialization in production with the opening of trade would not likely occur. As nations shift resources from their comparative disadvantage to their comparative advantage industries with international trade,

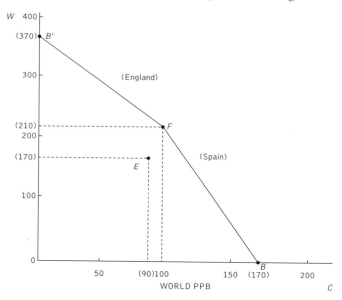

Pre-trade: autarky (both nations self-sufficient)   Post-trade: international specialization

World production: 170W and 90C (E)   World production: 210 W and 100C(F)
England: 80W and 50C   England: 0W and 100C
Spain: 90W and 40C   Spain: 210W and 0 C

Gains from international specialization: 40W and 10C

Figure 3.2 World production possibilities boundary

the labor (and resources) released from the former may not be readily absorbed into the latter. For example, with trade, as England reduces the production of wine and steps up the production of cloth for export, the labor (and resources) released from wine production might not have the skills to be employed in the cloth industry. Moreover, the vineyards and wine presses that had been producing wine in England are no longer in demand. Since England satisfies its demand for wine with imports from Spain, the owners of these resources used to produce wine would suffer declines in income with international trade.

In general, factors (labor and the owners of the capital and natural resources) employed in the comparative disadvantage industries experience income losses with international trade and will therefore lobby for trade barriers. Since nations engaging in trade are able to consume beyond their PPBs, however, it is possible to compensate those resources in the contracting comparative disadvantage industries so that all labor and owners of resources gain from trade. The United States, for example, offers trade adjustment assistance for the labor displaced by foreign competition to compensate for the income lost while that labor is retraining or relocating to gain employment in the expanding comparative advantage industries.

For Adam Smith, international trade would widen the extent of the market, which allows for greater division of labor and specialization. With advances in transportation overcoming geographical boundaries and linking together markets that are increasing in size with population growth and with improved international relations breaking down political boundaries, international trade would promote economic growth.

Limits to growth

Smith nevertheless envisioned limits to economic growth. First, rising per capita incomes and improvements in the standard of living would lead to growth of populations. The higher incomes would lower death rates and increase birth rates as health and living conditions improved. The increases in population and labor supply would then push down real wages, reducing per capita incomes. As we will see, Malthus elaborated on this limit to economic growth. Second, Smith believed that the rate of profits would decline in the course of economic growth with greater competition in the market and increased difficulty in finding new profitable investments. Decreased profits then would reduce the physical capital formation and also depress real wages. As we will discuss, Ricardo elaborated on this limit to economic growth.

In the long run, Smith and the classical economists envisioned a stationary state, with zero economic growth and zero population growth at an average per capita income at the subsistence level.[8] Technological progress could only postpone the arrival of this stationary state, not eliminate its inevitability. Still, Smith was relatively optimistic compared to Malthus and Ricardo, the classical economists who followed.

UTOPIAN SCHOOL

Before discussing Thomas Malthus and his famous "law of population," we should mention the utopian school of the late eighteenth century. The utopian philosophers were optimistic about the future. They argued that through reason humans could achieve a state of harmony and even immortality—a virtual utopia. In 1793, the French philosopher, Marquis de Condorcet, wrote

---

[8] Subsistence-level income for a population corresponds to the level of per capita income where the crude rate of natural increase is zero, that is, the crude birth rate equals the crude death rate. Note that this is an average, with a distribution of incomes around the subsistence level.

of such a rational age where all inequalities of wealth, of education, and of opportunity would disappear. The world would be bountiful without stint. There would be no limits on the span of life, and men would recognize their obligations to future generations.[9] Also writing in 1793, the English philosopher, William Godwin, in his *Political Justice*, envisioned a future of complete equality, a classless society. Indeed, Godwin predicted that "There would be no war, no crime, no administration of justice, as it is called, and no government. Besides this there would be no disease, anguish, melancholy, or resentment" (cited in Heilbroner 1999: 77).

THOMAS MALTHUS

Thomas Malthus (1766–1834) did not share the optimism of the utopians. In fact, the full title of his famous first essay, published anonymously in 1798, was *An Essay on the Principle of Population as It Affects the Future Improvement of Society with Remarks on the Speculations of Mr. Godwin, M. Condorcet, and Other Writers*. Malthus needed only two postulates to "prove" the unattainability of the utopia envisioned by Godwin and Condorcet.

Malthus noted, first, that food is necessary for the existence of man; and second, that passion between the sexes is necessary and will remain nearly in its present state. Malthus then observed that population, when unchecked, goes on increasing in a geometric ratio. On the other hand, Malthus speculated that the means of subsistence could increase only in an arithmetic ratio. Therefore, Malthus predicted that the rate of population growth will have a tendency to outstrip food supply, which will yield misery and vice.

At the time Malthus wrote his first essay, he did not know whether England's population was rising or falling in size. In the late eighteenth century England was undergoing the Industrial Revolution, but the first experimental censuses in England only took place in 1801 and 1811. He used the example of the Americas, where populations appeared to be naturally doubling in each generation, or in 25 years, an implied annual crude rate of natural increase of 2.75 percent. Malthus also noted that even higher population growth rates were possible. In contrast to the potential for accelerating population growth, Malthus pointed to limited growth in the means of subsistence, the food supply, due to the finite amount of cultivable land and diminishing returns to labor working against possible advances in agricultural technology.

Reflected in the postulates underlying his theory, Malthus maintained that man is not only a social being, with the ability to reason, as emphasized by the utopian philosophers, but also a biological being, requiring food and desiring procreation. We can illustrate Malthus's theory that population, when unchecked, grows geometrically (or exponentially), while the food supply grows arithmetically, with the following example. Let N equal a 25-year period, roughly the length of a generation.

Time period:	1	2	3	4	5	...	10	...	N
Population:	2	4	8	16	32	...	1024	...	2^N
Means of subsistence:	10	20	30	40	50	...	100	...	$10N$
Population/Means of subsistence:	0.2	0.2	0.27	0.4	0.64	...	10.24	...	$2^N/10N$

We can see that the ratio of population to means of subsistence is accelerating.

---

[9] Condorcet favored a wide distribution of income, social security, and universally free education for men and women. Population would increase as a result of these beneficial reforms, but the food supply would increase even more rapidly; if not, then Condorcet favored birth control to limit population growth (see Brue and Grant 2007: 86).

Checks to population growth

Only checks to population growth would keep population from increasing indefinitely and overwhelming the means of subsistence. The checks would operate through increases in the death rate or decreases in the birth rate. **Positive checks** operated through the death rate through "vice," such as with wars and murder, or violence that humans inflict on themselves, and "misery," from disease, natural disasters, and famine, that arise from the laws of nature. **Preventative checks** operated through the birth rate. Here Malthus labeled as "vice" decreases in the birth rate from immoral relations, meaning "unnatural passions" (e.g., prostitution), and "arts to conceal consequences of irregular unions" (i.e., birth control). The second preventative check Malthus called "moral restraint," by which he meant postponement of marriage until a family can be adequately supported and the practice of abstinence outside of marriage.[10]

For Malthus, the only acceptable means of limiting births, and, for that matter, checking population growth, was moral restraint. Malthus was against birth control, which he believed permitted sexual gratification freely and thus reduced the drive to self-improvement and industry.[11] Malthus was against welfare for a similar reason. He felt that "poor laws" encouraged indolence and raised the level of the weakest members of society at the expense of others. If individuals knew they could count on parish relief and social welfare, they would lose their motivation to work and improve their own condition.

In the first edition of his essay, Malthus predicted that famine would be the ultimate check to population growth.

> Famine seems to be the last, the most dreadful resource of nature. The power of population is so superior to the power of earth to provide subsistence. . .that premature death must in some shape or other visit the human race. The vices of mankind are active and able ministers of depopulation. . .But should they fail in this war of extermination; sickly seasons, epidemics, pestilence, and plague advance in terrific array and sweep off their thousands and tens of thousands. Should success still be incomplete, gigantic, inevitable famine stalks in the rear, and with one mighty blow, levels the population with the food of the world. (Cited in Heilbroner 1999: 90).

Food shortages, even famines, were not uncommon in the centuries before the Industrial Revolution:[12]

> Between 1600 and 1800, France recorded twenty-six major famines, plus uncountable smaller, local shortages. In Florence, harvests were insufficient one out of every four years. In 1696, nearly a third of Finland's population starved to death. . .In China and India, famines in 1555 and 1596 killed millions . . . Even in nonfamine years, much of the population lived in a state of nutritional purgatory. Physical stunting was endemic. (Roberts 2008: 14)

[10]Malthus added "moral restraint" as a second preventative check in the second edition of his *Essay on the Principles of Population*. Moreover, Malthus practiced what he preached. He married at age 39, shortly after securing a job as a college professor, and with his wife of 11 years younger had only three children.

[11]In an ironic twist, many self-proclaimed neo-Malthusians have agreed with Malthus's predictions while advocating birth control. Malthus (1927: 13) writes: "A promiscuous intercourse to such a degree as to prevent the birth of children seems to lower, in the most marked manner, the dignity of human nature."

[12]We might note that famines and mass starvation have occured even in the twentieth century: for example, in China in 1960–61 with the "Great Leap Forward," when an estimated 30 million perished, and Bangladesh in the 1970s, as well as elsewhere in the developing world, particularly in sub-Saharan Africa, with natural disasters and war.

67

Moreover, the pessimism of Malthus about food supplies keeping pace with population growth might have been warranted. Roberts (2008: 16) describes:

> As land expansions reached their limits and food prices rose (between 1750 and 1800, European wheat prices nearly tripled), producers redoubled their efforts to increase productivity with whatever new technology or input might help raise yields.
>
> But despite impressive results—between 1600 and 1860, English wheat yields tripled—it still wasn't enough. . . . Life expectancy remained low; in 1880, the very peak of the British empire, the average Englishman could expect to live forty years.

There were seven editions in all of Malthus's great work, *An Essay on the Principles of Population*; and in the later editions Malthus allowed that vice and misery were the primary checks in ancient and primitive societies, whereas moral restraint could predominate in modern civilizations. With the continual refinement of his theory—and partially in response to criticism from Godwin and other utopian writers—Malthus acknowledged greater possibilities for moral restraint. Nevertheless, in contrast to the classless society advocated by the utopians, Malthus favored a system of private property, including the accompanying economic inequality and social class structure, provided there were opportunities for upward mobility.

In fact, Malthus became an ardent supporter of universal education, which could engender enlightened self-interest—in particular, moral restraint. With the rise in the standard of living, parents might opt for smaller families, primarily by postponing marriage and childbearing until a family could be adequately supported. Social and economic mobility could in turn be promoted through reduced fertility. In the end, however, Malthus still had a rather pessimistic view of the majority of the human race and of their ability to exercise moral restraint to limit fertility and check population growth.

Malthusian model

The basic mechanism underlying the Malthusian theory can be outlined as follows. Begin with a population at a subsistence level of income (consistent with the long-run stationary state envisioned by the classical writers) and zero economic growth and zero population growth—not only $dy/y = dY/Y - dP/P = 0$, but also $dY/Y = dP/P = 0$. Suppose now that there is an increase in output, for example due to a favorable harvest with good weather or the technological progress in agriculture, so $(dY/Y)' > 0$. With the rise in per capita incomes, the crude death rate would fall (as average health and nutrition increased) and the crude birth rate would rise (as the improved standard of living would allow for earlier marriages and the improved health and nutrition would enhance fecundity, or the biological capacity to bear children). Consequently, the population growth rate would increase and eventually exceed the growth rate in income, $(dP/P)' > (dY/Y)' > 0$, until per capita income was driven back to the subsistence level, with again $dY/Y = dP/P = 0$.

In a cynical summary of the Malthusian model, Clark (2007: 5) states:

> In the Malthusian economy before 1800 economic policy was turned on its head: vice now was virtue then, and virtue vice. Those scourages of failed modern states—war, violence, disorder, harvest failures, collapsed public infrastructures, bad sanitation—were friends of mankind before 1800. They reduced population pressures and increased material living

standards. In contrast policies beloved of the World Bank and the United Nations today—peace, stability, order, public health, transfers to the poor—were the enemies of prosperity. They generated the population growth that impoverished societies.

Also Malthus noted, and Ricardo elaborated, that a rise in population would increase the demand for food and require greater use of existing farmland (with diminishing returns to labor) and the extension of farming to marginal land (with lower soil fertility). Thus, accompanying this process of population growth would be higher food prices, which would reduce real wages and real income per capita.

In sum, for Malthus, the ultimate check to population growth was the food supply, due to limited land and diminishing returns to labor. Malthus did not anticipate the growth in agricultural productivity due to advances in technology that were to follow. Nor did Malthus foresee the declines in birth rates that accompanied economic development with the demographic transition. Though the declines in fertility did not reflect moral restraint as much as birth control, also enhanced by technological advances in contraception.

Nevertheless, might Malthusian concerns still be warranted? As observed by the World Bank (2007: 8):

> Agriculture has been largely successful in meeting the world's effective demand for food. Yet more than 800 million people remain food insecure, and agriculture has left a huge environmental footprint. And the future is increasingly uncertain.
>
> Models predict that food prices in global markets may reverse their long-term downward trend, creating rising uncertainties about global food security. Climate change, environmental degradation, rising competition for land and water, higher energy prices, and doubts about future adoption rates for new technologies all present huge challenges and risks that make predictions difficult.

We will discuss agriculture and the world food supply in Chapter 13.

DAVID RICARDO

We turn now to another great classical economist, David Ricardo (1772–1823), a good friend of Malthus. Although sometimes differing with Malthus over questions of economic policy (e.g., Ricardo opposed the protection of English corn farmers through import tariffs), he shared Malthus's conclusion of a stationary state for the economy in the long run.

Malthus's theory of population growth was generally accepted by the classical economists, including Ricardo. Ricardo is perhaps best known for his elaboration of the theory of trade. That is, comparative advantages (lower opportunity costs) form the basis for trade, not absolute advantages (lower resource costs), as Adam Smith had assumed. Ricardo contributed much more, however, to the development of economic theory, refining the concept of the stationary state, the long-run equilibrium characterized by zero economic growth and zero population growth with average income at subsistence level.

Diminishing returns to labor

Ricardo maintained that continual economic growth was not possible due to the diminishing returns to labor with an ultimately finite supply of land and declining rates of profit. Ricardo incorporated the distribution of income into his analysis, disaggregating national income earned in the production of national output into wages (returns to labor), profits (returns to capitalists, e.g., the owners of factories), and rent (returns to property owners, e.g., owners of farmland). See Box 3.1 for a discussion of economic rent.

BOX 3.1: ECONOMIC RENT

The surplus earnings received by factors of production beyond what is necessary to have the use of those factors is known as **economic rent**. To illustrate, consider the market for a natural resource, such as farmland. The demand for a resource is derived from the demand for the goods and services produced using that resource. So the demand for farmland is derived from the demand for food. The demand curve for farmland, D_R, indicating the inverse relationship between the quantity demanded (in acres) during a period of time and the unit price of using or renting an acre of farmland, P_R, is given below in Figure B3.1. The supply curve of farmland, S_R, depicting the direct relationship between the quantity of farmland supplied per period of time and the unit price of the farmland, is ultimately fixed for a given area (e.g., a nation). Thus there is an upper limit per period of time on the land available for cultivation, indicated by the vertical or perfectly inelastic region of the supply curve.

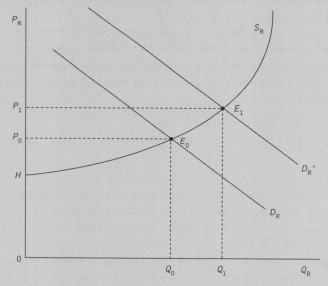

Total payments received by landowners = $TR_0 = P_0 \cdot Q_0$

$$= \text{area } HE_0Q_00 \quad + \quad \text{area } P_0E_0H$$
$$\text{(transfer earnings)} \ + \ \text{(economic rent)}$$

With an increase in demand for land from D_R to D'_R, total payments received by landowners increase to $TR_1 = P_1 \cdot Q_1$, with the share of economic rent (area P_1E_1H) rising in the total receipts.

Figure B3.1: *Market for farmland*

In a competitive market, the equilibrium price matches the demand and supply for the resource, the market-clearing price of P_0. The quantity of the resource transacted during the period, here the acres of land under cultivation, is given by Q_0. The total payments received by the owners of the land equal $TR_0 = P_0 \cdot Q_0$, represented by the area of the rectangle $P_0 E_0 Q_0 0$. The total payments can be broken down into **transfer earnings**, or the payments necessary to have the use of the resource, indicated by the supply price of the resource and, in the aggregate, the area under the supply curve up to the market quantity transacted. Here the area $HE_0 Q_0 0$ represents the transfer earnings. Economic rent, the additional payments received, is indicated by the area $P_0 HE_0$.

Given that the most productive or fertile land would be farmed first, the owners of this land would receive economic rents, given the market-clearing price of P_0. In fact, the owners or suppliers of all the farmland up to the last unit or acre farmed would receive economic rent. On the Q_0th unit of land, all the payment received, equal to the market price, would be transfer earnings. There would be no economic rent on the Q_0th marginal unit. We can see that as the demand for farmland increases with population growth and the demand for food (from D_R to D'_R), the share of economic rent in total payments to landowners increases.

As in the Malthusian model, when real wages rise above a subsistence level, population growth occurs as death rates fall and birth rates rise. The greater population increases the demand for food, requiring either existing farmland to be cultivated more intensively by applying more labor (and other inputs), or bringing additional land under cultivation, likely to be of lower fertility than the land currently being farmed. The former refers to the "intensive margin" and the latter the "extensive margin." Both would occasion **diminishing returns to labor**, reflected in decreasing marginal products of labor. Thus, in expanding the rate of food production, the marginal cost and the supply price of food would increase, which would reduce the real wages earned by labor.

As the production of food increased, the economic rents of the owners of the more fertile farmland would rise. With diminishing returns to labor as food production increases to meet the growth in population, the gains in national output and income will be decreasing. The share of national income received by landowners will be rising, however, with increasing economic rents on the more productive lands. The real wage rate can only be reduced to subsistence level; and the total real wages paid will still increase with growth in the labor force. The share of profits in national income will eventually get squeezed to the point where the level of profits is just sufficient to replace the capital stock wearing out. Capital accumulation ceases and the capital–labor ratio is constant—as are labor productivity and per capita real income. A stationary state will be reached with no economic growth or population growth and zero economic profits and subsistence wages.

We can illustrate with Figure 3.3. The aggregate production function is given by $Y = A \cdot F(K, L, R)$ relating real national output (Y) to the index of technology (A), the levels of physical capital (K), labor (L), and natural resources (R, here farmland). Ricardo assumed that labor and capital were used in a fixed proportion or ratio, and that the supply of land available for cultivation was fixed, $R = R_0$.[13] The aggregate production function as drawn is strictly concave, exhibiting diminishing returns to labor (and capital) from the beginning.

---

[13] Technological change embodied in better seeds and fertilizers and improved cultivation techniques may allow for double-cropping if the time for growing crops can be reduced or extended into less favorable seasons of the year. If so, then the effective supply of land is increased.

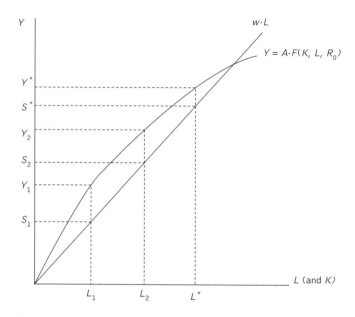

Figure 3.3 *Illustration of the long-run stationary state*

Y = real national output, including agricultural production (subject to diminishing returns to labor) and manufacturing: $Y = A \cdot F(K, L, R_0)$.
A = index of technology
L = labor
K = physical capital
R = natural resources (including land): R_0 is the fixed supply of land.
w = real subsistence wage per worker
S = total wage payments: $S = w \cdot L$

Let w be the subsistence-level real wage. The ray from the origin, $w \cdot L$, gives the total wages earned by labor if paid the subsistence real wage. We are implicitly assuming that the share of labor in the total population is constant.

If we begin with, say, L_1 units of labor in the economy, then the output produced, both manufactured and agricultural goods, and income earned is equal to Y_1. The subsistence wages that must be paid would be S_1. The difference in national income between Y_1 and S_1 would be distributed between capitalists earning profits and landowners receiving rent. If the profits were reinvested in additional capital, then the demand for labor would rise, real wages would rise, and population and labor supply would increase. Suppose the labor supply grows to L_2, resulting in production of real national output of Y_2. With the population growth the demand for food increases, requiring existing farmland to be cultivated more intensively and perhaps expansion to land of inferior fertility. (Recalling the discussion of effective factors of production from Chapter 1, here the index of the quality of natural resources, q_R, would decline with the use of less fertile farm land.) Consequently, the marginal cost of producing food and the price of food increases, pushing down real wages again to the subsistence level, w.

Nevertheless, there might still be sufficient profits from the national income of Y_2, after wages (S_2) and rent have been taken out, for reinvestment and more physical capital accumulation. So economic growth might continue for a while. We can see in Figure 3.3 that as the labor force grows and the economy moves out on the short-run aggregate production function, the gap between national income and subsistence wages required $(Y - S = Y - w \cdot L)$ is shrinking. Eventually, however, with the increasingly diminishing returns to labor as more of the available land is being used and the rising share of rents received by landowners in national income, economic profits would be reduced to zero.[14] Capitalists could only replace the physical capital wearing out each period, so growth in the physical capital stock would be zero, matching the growth in the labor force (and population), with subsistence wages. We illustrate this long-run equilibrium stationary state in Figure 3.3 with Y^*, S^*, and L^*.

Note that technological progress, here indicated by an increase in A, the index of technology, would rotate the aggregate production upwards, allowing greater output for a given amount of labor, raising per capita income and generating economic growth. Nevertheless, classical economists generally believed that in the long run diminishing returns to labor with a finite supply of land and zero economic profits would yield a stationary state. Underlying this pessimistic conclusion was Malthus's population theory, where any increase in per capita income above the subsistence would unleash population growth until per capita income was driven back down to the subsistence level. And, if unchecked, population growth would eventually outpace the means of subsistence, manifested in famine and ensuring the stationary state.

SAY'S LAW

Before turning to John Stuart Mill's more optimistic vision of the stationary state, we should note that as far as macroeconomics was concerned, the classical economists did not worry about aggregate demand, in particular, the insufficiency of aggregate demand to purchase the national output produced at full employment of labor. Classical economists generally assumed **Say's law**, that is, that "supply creates its own demand," meaning that if a dollar's worth of output is produced then the dollar's worth of income generated will be used to purchase that output. There would never be any deficiency in aggregate demand. Interestingly enough, Thomas Malthus argued that aggregate demand might fall short of aggregate supply, resulting in unemployment.[15] While Malthus's arguments for the importance of aggregate demand did not carry the day in his time, a century later, the great British economist, John Maynard Keynes, referred back to Malthus when he put forth his revolutionary theory of macroeconomics.

JOHN STUART MILL

We conclude our discussion of classical theories of economic growth with John Stuart Mill (1806–73). In contrast to the dismal view of the stationary state portrayed above, with zero

---

[14]**Economic profits** are the difference between a firm's total revenues and total costs of production, including the opportunity costs of the capital invested. With zero economic profits, the condition characterizing the long-run equilibrium in competitive markets, firms have no incentive to invest in additional capital or diminish the capital used for production. Rather they will continue to replace the capital that depreciates to maintain their capital stocks.

[15]Say's law is named after the French economist, Jean-Baptiste Say (1767–1832) who held that full-employment national output would be maintained. Malthus noted, however, that investment could fall short of saving as capitalists seek to accumulate wealth. Thus aggregate demand would not meet aggregate supply at full employment. In times of acute economic distress, Malthus recommended government spending on public works (see Brue and Grant 2007: 94). A century later macroeconomists returned to this notion of insufficient aggregate demand during the Great Depression, as we will discuss in the next chapter.

population and economic growth, Mill argued that a stationary state could be a period of enlightenment. He suggested:

> It is scarcely necessary to remark that a stationary condition of capital and population implies no stationary state of human improvement. There would be as much scope as ever for all kinds of mental culture, and moral and social progress; as much room for improving the Art of Living, and much more likelihood of its being improved when minds ceased to be engrossed by the art of getting on.[16]

This optimistic view of Mill, however, did not prevail over the classical emphasis on economic growth and the negative perception of a stationary state. It should be added, though, that Mill's stationary state would be at a higher average level of income than subsistence. That is, although there would still be zero economic growth and zero population growth, Mill believed the distribution of income would be more equal and individuals would be more responsible in consumption (see Brue and Grant 2007: 144).[17]

We should also note that Mill expanded on Smith's view of the role of the government in the economy. Mill allowed for government intervention in the market to protect consumers from unsafe products and workers from unsafe conditions, preserve the environment, promote education, and regulate natural monopolies (see Ekelund and Hébert 1990: 189; Brue and Grant 2007: 145).[18] We will discuss such market failures in Chapter 14.

CONCLUSION

The perception is still prevalent today that the quality of life is measured by per capita consumption. Therefore economic growth that makes possible increasing per capita consumption is economic progress. Indeed, as noted in Chapter 1, economic growth over the past two centuries has substantially reduced poverty and greatly increased the standard of living.

In Chapter 5, however, echoing classical concerns, we discuss possible limits to growth due to natural resource constraints with the arguable inevitability of a long-run equilibrium of zero output and population growth. But first, in the next chapter, we will see that in the twentieth century, during the decade of the Great Depression, macroeconomists also worried about economic stagnation. In contrast to Malthus and the classical economists, the concern was not with unchecked population growth, but with insufficient population growth.

---

[16] This quote is drawn from Mill's *Principles of Political Economy* (1848). See Panarchy: A Gateway to Selected Documents and Web Sites (http://www.panarchy.org/mill/stationary.1848.html).

[17] Mill also favored a tax on bequests to redistribute wealth (Ekelund and Hébert 1990: 187–188). And Mill asserted:

> I know not why it should be a matter of congratulation that persons who are already richer than any one needs to be, should have doubled their means of consuming things which give little or no pleasure except as representative of wealth . . . (Panarchy, op. cit)

We will see this theme reflected later in Veblen's theory of conspicuous consumption (discussed in Chapter 15).

[18] Mill's *Principles of Political Economy* was widely read and used as an economics text for over a half-century. Mill helped develop the concepts of supply and demand in the analysis of the market mechanism.

KEY TERMS

absolute advantage

barter terms of trade

constant costs of production

diminishing returns to labor

economic rent

invisible hand

positive checks to population growth

production possibilities boundary

specialization in trade

autarky

comparative advantage

consumption possibilities boundary

economic profits

international terms of trade

labor theory of value

preventative checks to population growth

Say's law

transfer earnings

QUESTIONS

1. Take two countries, France and Italy, and two goods, cheese and wool, with the following unit labor costs:

Labor hours per unit of output		
	Cheese (C)	Wool (W)
France	4 hours	12 hours
Italy	3 hours	6 hours

Assume constant costs of production.

(a) Determine the absolute and comparative advantages in the production of cheese and wool.

(b) If the international terms of trade were $1C = 0.4W$ (or $1W = 2.5C$), determine the gains from trade (per unit of the export good traded) for France and Italy.

(c) If France has 900 hours of labor and Italy has 600 hours of labor available each day, sketch the production possibilities boundaries for the two countries. What are the slopes of the production possibilities boundaries? Given the international terms of trade of $1C = 0.4W$, sketch the consumption possibilities boundaries of the two countries. What are the slopes of the consumption possibilities boundaries?

(d) If in autarky, France were producing (and consuming) 100 units of cheese, how much wool could it produce? If in autarky, Italy were producing (and consuming) 96 units of cheese, how much wool could it produce?

(e) Given the autarkic or pre-trade productions and consumptions, and assuming complete specialization in production with trade, suppose France exports half of its comparative advantage good. Find the gains from trade for France and Italy.

(f) How would the above analysis change if the international terms of trade were instead $1W = 2.4C$?

(g) When would trade not take place between the two countries? Why not?

2. If France experienced advances in technology which halved its unit labor costs of the two goods to 2 hours (from 4 hours) in cheese production and to 6 hours (from 12 hours) in wool production, repeat Question 1 parts (a) through (e). What do you conclude about technological progress, the gains from trade, and the standard of living, as measured by final consumption per hour of labor?

3. Discuss what you think is the weakest link in Malthus's theory of population. Can his theory of population be disproved? Discuss why or why not.

4. According to Malthus and Ricardo, could population growth and labor force growth continue in the long run? Discuss why or why not.

5. Discuss whether Mill's optimistic view of the stationary state has appeal or is even realistic.

REFERENCES

Brue, Stanley and Randy Grant. 2007. *The Evolution of Economic Thought*, 7th edition. Mason, OH: Thomson South-Western.

Clark, Gregory. 2007. *A Farewell to Alms: A Brief Economic History of the World*. Princeton, NJ: Princeton University Press.

Ekelund, Robert and Robert Hébert. 1990. *A History of Economic Theory and Method*, 3rd edition. New York: McGraw-Hill.

Heilbroner, Robert. 1999. *The Worldly Philosophers: The Lives, Times, and Ideas of the Great Economic Thinkers*, 7th edition. New York: Simon and Schuster.

Malthus, Thomas Robert. 1927. *An Essay on Population*, Vol. 1. London: Dent.

Roberts, Paul. 2008. *The End of Food*. Boston: Houghton Mifflin.

Viner, Jacob. 1927. "Adam Smith and Laissez Faire," *Journal of Political Economy*, 35(2): 198–232.

World Bank. 2007. *World Development Report 2008: Agriculture for Development*. Washington, DC: World Bank.

Chapter 4

Macroeconomics and the great depression

By the latter half of the nineteenth century there was compelling evidence that the pessimism of the classical economists was unwarranted. Beginning around the Industrial Revolution, the nations of Europe and the United States generally experienced long-run economic growth and rising per capita incomes. Clark (2007: 193) argues:

> Around 1800, in northwestern Europe and North America, man's long sojourn in the Malthusian world ended. The iron link between population and living standards, through which any increase in population caused an immediate decline in wages, was decisively broken. Between 1770 and 1860, for example, English population tripled. Yet real incomes, instead of plummeting, rose.

Moreover, food prices declined with the cultivation of the North American prairies and advances in transportation with steamships and railroads connecting markets. For example, the opening of the Suez Canal in 1869 significantly shortened the shipping route between Europe and the East. Roberts (2008: 17) states:

> What staved off Malthusian specter. . .was globalism. . .the emergence of an international food system, built on railways, shipping routes, and new preservation technologies . . .and free trade. . .that began to connect the starving demand centers in Europe with distant suppliers in Australia, Argentina, and especially the US—countries that not only possessed surplus land and small populations, but that also were just then undergoing industrial transformations of their food production.

International trade expanded, allowing for greater efficiencies in production, with nations producing according to their comparative advantages. Capital moved freely in large volumes between countries, not only for foreign direct investment, but also for financing balance of trade deficits. Among the industrializing nations the gold standard served to promote exchange rate stability and confidence in the international monetary system.

Substantial technological progress in both agriculture and manufacturing increased labor productivities. Real wages were rising with the increased demand for labor in manufacturing. Furthermore, profit rates did not appear to be declining, as the classical economists feared. Population growth was not a concern. As populations became more urban and economies more industrial, real per capita incomes increased and birth rates declined. Rising consumer aspirations, universal education, and child labor laws, which diminished the opportunities for children to work off the farm, all reduced the advantages of large families. Greater possibilities for international migration meant that any population pressures within a nation could be relieved by emigration.

Thus the classical vision of a stationary state gave way to neoclassical optimism. During the the neoclassical period in economics, roughly covering the last half of the nineteenth century up through World War I, attention shifted more to microeconomics. The leading economists of the time, including Alfred Marshall, Wilfredo Pareto, and Leon Walras, developed the theory of consumer behavior (now that households had wages above subsistence level and discretionary income), the theory of the firm (with optimal rules for the allocation of resources), and analyses of competitive markets, general equilibrium, and income distribution.

In this chapter we begin with a brief review of the period preceeding World War I, sometimes referred to as the initial era of globalization. The decade following the devastation from World War I, with the lack of international coordination in restoring the gold standard, will then be addressed. The focus of the chapter, however, will be on the Great Depression and the concerns of economists with the stagnation of the 1930s.

THE GOLD STANDARD ERA

The **gold standard** prevailed as the system of international finance for the last quarter of the nineteenth century up until World War I. Under this fixed exchange rate system, nations were to abide by "rules of the game" with clear guidelines for monetary policy.[1]

The rules of the game

Under the gold standard, each nation defined a **par value** or gold price for its currency. For example, $20.67 was equal to one ounce of gold in the US and £4.25 was equal to one ounce of gold in the UK. From these par values, official exchange rates were derived. In this case, £1.00 = $4.866 = $(20.67/4.25). A small range of fluctuation around these official values was allowed, consistent with the shipping costs of gold. Nations were obliged to defend these par values, as national money supplies were backed by gold.

In theory, balance of payments disequilibria would be corrected by gold flows that would alter national money supplies, internal prices and incomes. To illustrate, a nation with a balance of payments deficit, for example due to a large merchandise trade deficit, would lose gold. The nation's money supply would fall, pushing up interest rates, which would attract foreign capital. Higher interest rates would reduce interest-sensitive expenditures and aggregate demand, pushing down wages and prices and incomes, which would improve the nation's international competitiveness and restore the balance of payments equilibrium. A nation with a balance of payments surplus, in contrast, would gain gold, which would increase its domestic money supply, income, and prices. The expansion of the domestic economy would correct the balance of payments surplus. In short, under the gold standard, a nation's money supply was tied to its external balance (the balance of payments condition) and nations were committed to maintaining the par values of their currencies and allowing gold flows to restore equilibria.

---

[1] Dunn and Ingram (1996: Chapter 19) provide a good overview of the theory and history of the gold standard.

The historical experience

During the reign of the gold standard, London was the financial capital of the world. The pound sterling was a key currency, widely accepted as an international medium of exchange and store of value. England was a major world trader and shipping power. Rather than accumulate gold, as the mercantilists favored, England used its export surplus for foreign investment. In fact, England was a major source of long-term capital for the rest of the world.[2] As a result England was able to maintain a current account surplus, despite a deteriorating merchandise trade balance.[3]

The decades before World War I witnessed significant economic growth in the industrializing nations, albeit periodically interrupted by recessions.[4] The adoption of mass production in manufacturing, the decline in food prices with the greater agricultural production from the Americas, and improved transportation all contributed to generally rising real incomes. Moreover, it was a period of relatively free trade, where nations reaped the benefits of international specialization. It was also a period of international factor mobility, with capital and labor movements based on perceived returns.[5]

In particular, short-term financial capital moved freely in response to interest rate differentials, serving more than gold flows as an equilibrating mechanism for balance of payments disequilibria. That capital moved so easily reflected confidence in the system, especially in the par values established for national currencies. For example, if England experienced a balance of payments deficit, perhaps due to its heavy foreign investment exceeding its current account surplus, then rather than losing gold which would reduce the British money supply and contract the domestic economy, the Bank of England would raise its interest rate. The substantial inflows of foreign capital would fairly quickly restore the British balance of payments, reducing the need for a contraction in British economic activity and incomes.

Economic historians cite the *de facto* harmonization of the major economies during the gold standard. National incomes and price levels tended to move in parallel, so that large balance of payments disequilibria were avoided. That this liberal period of economic growth with free trade and minimal government regulation was also characterized by political stability and democratic governance added to the aura of the gold standard. Historians also note that the successful growth and development of the industrializing nations, the so-called "core" countries of England, Western Europe, the US and Canada, under the gold standard was not always shared with the developing

---

[2] Kenwood and Lougheed (1992: 26–28) note that between 1870 and 1914, approximately 4 percent of Britain's national income was invested overseas, mostly in other European countries, but also in the US, Canada, Argentina, South Africa, Australia and New Zealand. During the nineteenth century, France, Germany, and the United States also significantly invested abroad. Much of the foreign investment was in transportation infrastructure, e.g., railroads and canals.

[3] The **current account** in the balance of payments account consists of the balance of trade (the difference between exports and imports of goods and services), net income flows (the difference between factor incomes received from the rest of the world and factor incomes paid to the rest of the world) and net transfers (transfers received less transfers paid to the rest of the world). A current account imbalance must be offset by a corresponding imbalance in the sum of the **capital account** (foreign investment in the nation less the nation's investment abroad) and the **official settlements account** (the nation's official claims on the rest of the world less foreign official claims on the nation's economy). A balance of payments surplus (deficit) is indicated by a net surplus (deficit) on the combined current and capital account balances. Note that, in balance of payments accounting, the capital account is now known as the financial account.

[4] For example, in the US, there were 16 recessions with declining real national output between 1854 and 1919. The longest lasted nearly $5\frac{1}{2}$ years, from October 1873 to March 1879. The average contraction was for 22 months. After World War I there were three more recessions in the 1920s, with an average duration of 15 months, before the Great Depression from August 1929 to March 1933. See National Bureau of Economic Research, "US Business Cycle Expansions and Contractions," at http://www.nber.org.

[5] See Kenwood and Lougheed (1992: Chapters 4–5) for a good overview of the movement of nations, especially Great Britain, toward freer trade.

nations. The stability of the core might have been to some degree at the expense of instability of the "periphery," that is, in the less developed nations of Latin America, Asia, and Africa. These nations, relying on primary products for the bulk of their exports, were subject to volatility in export revenues and international capital flows, which made it difficult to maintain stable exchange rates and sustain imports and domestic investment.

For example, in prosperous times when the industrial nation economies were growing, export revenues of developing nations would surge. These periphery nations would experience significant capital inflows, as the recipients of foreign investment, which also promoted expansion of their economies. Should a major industrial nation experience a balance of payments deficit, however, and subsequently raise interest rates to address the excess supply of its currency on the foreign exchange market, not only would the developing nations' exports fall with the contraction of the industrial economy, but also capital flows would be reversed. International capital would flow to the industrial nation with the higher interest rate, leaving the periphery nations with balance of payments deficits, resulting in depreciations in their currencies and contractions in their economies.

The vulnerability of the developing nations was most in evidence under colonialism. Kenwood and Lougheed (1992: 142) cite the "colony grabbing" that began in the 1880s when:

> Africa was divided among the European powers, [and] British control was extended over Burma and Malaya. France consolidated its Indo-Chinese empire. Even the United States was not free from this desire for political and economic expansion. The Philippine Islands were seized during a war with Spain, a republic was established in Hawaii, and political intervention occurred in Mexico, Costa Rica, Dominica, Colombia, and Nicaragua.

Nevertheless, the gold standard era is widely seen as a period of rising prosperity. Between 1870 and 1913, the average real per capita income in Western Europe, the United States, Canada, Australia, New Zealand, and Japan nearly doubled, from $2,700 to $5,300 (in 2005 PPP dollars). The average annual economic growth rate of 1.57 percent was one-and-a-half times the growth rate (1.06 percent) for the preceeding period 1820–70, and ten times the minimal growth rate (0.14 percent) for the period 1500–1820. For the rest of the world, average real per capita income increased, but by only around 40 percent between 1870 and 1913, from $870 to $1,240 (in 2005 PPP dollars). Still, the average annual economic growth rate of 0.82 percent in the periphery was over 13 times the growth rate (0.06 percent) for the period 1820–70, and 40 times that of the near zero rate (0.02 percent) for the period 1500–1820.

So too, population increase accelerated: from an average annual growth rate of 0.86 percent for 1820–70 to 1.07 percent for 1870–1913 in the industrializing economies of Western Europe, the US, Canada, Australia, New Zealand and Japan; and from an average annual growth rate of 0.29 percent for 1820–70 to 0.72 percent for 1870–1913 in the rest of the world.[6]

POST-WORLD WAR I RECOVERIES

World War I (1914–18) interrupted this period of rising incomes and increasing international integration. With the exception of the US, most of the industrializing economies experienced

---

[6]These income and population statistics are derived from Maddison (2005: Tables 2 and 3). The real per capita income estimates expressed in 2005 purchasing power parity dollars are derived from Maddison's estimates in 1990 PPP dollars by multiplying the latter by $1.44 = 1.023^{16}$, where 0.023 or 2.3 percent is the average annual inflation rate for the US GDP price deflator for 1990–2005.

difficult recoveries during the 1920s. The "rules of the game" that had coordinated national eco-nomic policies under the gold standard were replaced by more independent policy-making as national autonomies trumped international cooperation.[7]

Lack of international cooperation

Nations experienced differential degrees of inflation during the war, reflecting the differences in the damages to their economies and the economic policies pursued, including the use of price controls occasioned by scarcities of key goods. As a result, the relative price levels underlying the pre-war exchange rates had changed. Although there was a general desire to return to a gold standard at the pre-war parities, those exchange rates for the national currencies would not have reflected the underlying economic conditions prevailing at the end of the war. Consequently a number of the major nations adopted flexible exchange rates after the war, with the goal of moving back to a gold standard.

In 1919, the US became the first industrial nation to return to a gold standard at the pre-war parity of $20.67 to an ounce of gold. This par value actually overvalued the dollar and reduced the real value of gold since the US had itself experienced inflation over the war years.

During the 1920s, the experiences of major economies differed significantly. For example, the UK, having suffered greater destruction to its industrial base and more inflation than the US, floated the pound sterling. Tight monetary and fiscal policies were employed to appreciate the pound back to pre-war parity. Consequently, the British economy suffered high unemployment during the first half of the the 1920s. Nevertheless, the pound's pre-war par value of £4.25 to an ounce of gold was reestablished in 1925, when Britain returned to the gold standard. The pound, however, was generally considered to be overvalued at this par value and Britain had to maintain austere economic policies as a result.

Following the war, France also floated its currency, the franc, which sharply depreciated due to the expansionary policies France followed. In 1928, France returned to the gold standard, setting a par value that effectively undervalued the franc, giving France a competitive advantage in international trade.

Germany, defeated in World War I and facing heavy reparations, experienced a hyperinflation in the early 1920s. The German mark became virtually worthless, before a change in administration and monetary reform issued a new mark in late 1923, which stabilized the economy.

The United States, as noted, the first economy to return to the gold standard, was increasingly the dominant economic power in the 1920s. The US ran large balance of payments surpluses, which led to offsetting inflows of gold. In turn, the gold flows should have increased the US money supply, reducing the interest rate while increasing the price level and real national income—the expansionary economic adjustments needed to restore equilibrium in the US balance of payments. Instead, the US Federal Reserve sterilized the gold inflows with offsetting contractionary mone-tary policy, preventing these internal economic adjustments. Increasingly then, during the 1920s, the United States accumulated official gold. So did France with its undervalued franc. In con-trast, the UK, with an overvalued pound, ran balance of payments deficits and lost gold, which, as noted, required the continuation of its tight economic policies.

---

[7]Dunn and Ingram (1996) also provide a good overview of the history of the interwar period, when nations attempted to restore the gold standard. With the rise in national autonomies and varying adherence to the expected balance of payments adjustments and then severe economic declines with the depression in the 1930s, the gold standard was ultimately abandoned, well before the hostilities of the Second World War.

By the end of the decade a general overproduction of agricultural goods on the world market had arisen due to the development of alternative sources of food supply. In particular, the agricultural production from nations in Latin America, which had not experienced the conflict of the world war, was augmented by the return to normal production of the developed nations after the war. As Kenwood and Lougheed (1992: 164) explain:

> Technological progress was particularly rapid in agriculture during the interwar years. In temperate latitudes improvements continued to be made in the breeding of plants and animals, and the use of artificial fertilizers became widespread. Mechanized agriculture was also spreading, with improvements in the efficiency of tractors and the introduction of a growing range of ancillary equipment. Many new developments were also evident in tropical and sub-tropical agriculture. Particularly important were the selective breeding of plants, the increased use of fertilizers, the greater attention paid to the control of plant diseases and pests, and the growing use of selective weed-killers.

Kenwood and Lougheed also note the expansion in mining with advances in technology and increased mechanization. As a result, over the 1920s, a general surplus in primary products emerged on the world market, resulting in price declines. In fact, Calomiris (1993: 69) cites the period 1921–29 in the United States as one of "an unusual rate of loss for banks due to the agricultural depression of the 1920s."

In the United States an investment and construction boom during the decade led to excess capacity in manufacturing. As Romer (1993: 37) relates:

> The United States slipped into recession in mid-1929 because of tight domestic monetary policy aimed at stemming speculation on the US stock market. The Great Depression started in earnest when the stock market crash in the United States caused consumers and firms to become nervous and therefore to stop buying irreversible durable goods.

Optimism turned to pessimism with the downturn in economic activity. The US stock market crash in October 1929 led to panic and a tremendous loss in financial wealth. Banks failed. Consumer and business confidence plummeted. Aggregate demand fell sharply and the US economy entered a steep decline, devolving into the Great Depression, which spread to the other industrialized nations.[8]

THE GREAT DEPRESSION

The downturn in the US economy in late 1929 was severe. Real national output declined by more than a quarter, from $976 billion (expressed in chained (2005) dollars) in 1929 to $716 billion in 1933, the depth of the Great Depression. The annual unemployment rate soared from 3.2 percent

---

[8] The *Journal of Economic Perspectives* (Spring 1993) issue contained a Symposium on the Great Depression with four articles by Romer, Margo, Calomiris, and Temin. As Romer (1993) notes, while severe economic contraction was experienced across the world, save apparently the Soviet Union, the Great Depression began in the United States and it was the US economy that suffered the sharpest and deepest decline in real national output.

to 24.9 percent over the same period.[9] Contrary to the theory of competitive markets, real wages of production workers did not decline, and in fact increased on net as the unemployment rate rose.[10] Per capita real personal disposable income in the United States, however, fell from $6,500 in 1929 to $4,790 in 1933.

The fall in real national output was accompanied by deflation, with a cumulative decline in the aggregate price level of approximately 25 percent from 1929 through 1933. Moreover, real gross private domestic investment collapsed, declining from $101 billion in 1929 to $13 billion in 1932. In an attempt to preserve domestic employment, nations erected trade barriers. For example, the Smoot–Hawley Tariff Act of 1930 set the highest tariff rates in US history, with the average import tax on dutiable goods exceeding 50 percent by 1933. This further contributed to the contraction in international trade, reducing global output with the reallocation of resources away from comparative advantage industries.

With their portfolios of nonperforming loans, banks were vulnerable. Anxious depositors withdrew their savings, when posible, but with the fractional reserve banking system, not all of them could do so. Subsequently, banks failed in unprecedented numbers, and many families lost their savings. Furthermore, in the face of declining deposits and the poor economy, the remaining banks sharply pulled back lending.

In 1931 the UK abandoned the gold standard, inducing panic in the foreign exchange market and a run on US gold reserves. This forced the Federal Reserve to adopt tighter monetary policy in the depressed US economy, in what Temin (1993: 96) calls "one of the most memorable acts of misguided monetary policy in history." Finally, in 1933 the United States devalued the dollar to $35 to an ounce of gold (from the pre-war parity price of $20.67). With the accompanying expansionary monetary policy the US economy recovered, and real gross domestic product increased by over 40 percent from 1933 to 1937. Other nations followed with devaluations of their currencies in attempts to remain internationally competitive. The abandonment of the gold standard, erection of trade barriers, and competitive devaluations were all too tangible further evidence of the lack of international economic coordination that had defined the post-war period.[11] The monetary discipline required by the fixed exchange rate system proved to be too difficult to bear, and indeed too restrictive for the weak economies. Temin (1993: 92) states, "The single best predictor of how severe the Depression was in different countries is how long they stayed on gold. The gold standard was the Midas touch that paralyzed the world economy."

---

[9] The income and expenditure statistics for the US economy are from the Bureau of Economic Analysis (http://www.bea.gov, accessed December 22, 2011). Real incomes and expenditures are expressed in billions of chained (2005) dollars. The unemployment rates are from Council of Economic Advisers (1983: Table B-29) and Margo (1993: 43, Table 1).

[10] Margo (1993: 43, Table 1) presents a real wage index (1940 = 100) for average hourly earnings of US production workers in manufacturing which shows an increase from 69.4 in 1929 to 83.2 in 1931 (as the unemployment rate increased from 3.2 percent to 15.9 percent), before dropping to 79.5 in 1933. The overall rise in the real wage index reflected the downward rigidity in nominal wages and the price deflation, much of the latter unexpected. The real wage index rose to 84.3 in 1934 with economic growth in the US economy, but then fell back some in 1935–36 (as the unemployment rate declined from 21.7 percent to 16.9 percent), before increasing to 85.5 in 1937 and then to 93.9 in 1938, the year of the sharp recession (when the US unemployment rate increased to 19.0 percent from 14.3 percent in 1937). As Margo notes, there is no comprehensive macroeconomic theory that can adequately explain the relative stability, much less the rise, in real wages over the 1930s.

[11] As discussed earlier, under the gold standard, countries with balance of payments deficits were to contract their money supplies. Expansionary monetary policy could not be used to address the weak domestic economy. Temin (1993) provides a good account of how the economic misfortunes of nations were linked under the fixed exchange rate system. In brief, a fall in aggregate demand which reduces real income and thus imports in one nation will have foreign repercussions, reducing in turn the exports and real income of trading partners. Moreover, weak economies reduce foreign investment. See also Calomiris (1993) for a discussion of monetary policy in the 1930s.

In fact, in the United States during the depression years, not only was monetary policy contractionary, constrained by adherence to the gold standard, but so also was fiscal policy, in a misguided attempt to balance the federal budget in a reeling economy.[12]

By 1937, real GDP in the US economy had grown to $1,072 billion (exceeding by 10 percent the 1929 level). Even real gross private domestic investment had recovered to the level of 1929. The unemployment rate, however, had only dropped to 14.3 percent. Then US economic policy again tightened:

> In 1937, after four years of very rapid growth but with the economy still far from fully recovered, both fiscal and monetary policy turned sharply contractionary: the veterans' bonus program of the previous year was discontinued, Social Security taxes were collected for the first time, and the Federal Reserve doubled reserve requirements. (Council of Economic Advisers 2010: 149–150)[13]

Consequently, in 1938 the US economy fell into a sharp recession. Real GDP dropped by 3.4 percent, led by a plunge of a third in real investment expenditures. Pessimism returned.

MACROECONOMIC CONCERNS

In 1937 John Maynard Keynes (1883–1946), the great British economist whose book, *The General Theory of Employment, Interest and Money* (1936), would transform macroeconomic theory and policy, had cautioned:

> We know much more securely than we know almost any other social or economic factor relating to the future, that in the place of steady and indeed steeply rising level of population which we experienced for a great number of decades, we shall be faced in a very short time with a stationary or a declining level. (Keynes 1937: 13)

In the US and Western Europe birth rates had been declining since the mid-nineteenth century and by the 1930s had reached replacement level. Ironically, given the earlier concern of the classical economists with unchecked population growth and diminishing returns to labor, the macroeconomists in the 1930s with the Great Depression were concerned with insufficient population growth.

In his presidential address to the American Economic Association at the end of 1938, Alvin Hansen (1939: 2, 11) warned:

> We are in the midst of a drastic decline in the rate of population growth. . .and it behooves us as economists to take cognizance of the significance of this revolutionary change in our economic life.

---

[12] In his introductory chapter on Keynesian economics, Richard Froyen (2009: 70) notes that the Hoover administration implemented a large income tax increase in 1932 and when Franklin Roosevelt ran for the presidency in 1932, "he attacked Hoover for failing to balance the budget and argued for *cuts* in government spending." Although, it should be noted that earlier Hoover had responded to the stock market crash of 1929 with a "package of public works, spending and tax cuts [that] amounted to less than 0.5% of GDP." See "Briefing Lessons of the 1930s," *The Economist* (December 10, 2011), page 76. In contrasting this with the Obama administration's response to the Great Recession of 2008–2009 with a fiscal stimulus in 2009 and 2010 equivalent to about 2.3 percent of GDP, this article hastens to add that "Hoover's entire budget covered only about 2.5% of GDP; Mr. Obama's takes 25% of GDP and runs a deficit of 10%."

[13] As will be discussed in Chapter 6, economists have attempted to learn from the policy mistakes of the Great Depression. See Council of Economic Advisers (2010: 159–180), which provides the Obama administration's economic analysis and proposals following the Great Recession.

> [The] combined effect of the decline in population growth, together with the failure of any really important innovations of a magnitude sufficient to absorb large capital outlays, weighs very heavily as an explanation for the failure of the recent recovery to reach full employment.

Macroeconomists attributed the economic stagnation of the 1930s to insufficient aggregate demand, in large part, a reflection of low population growth. Keynes rejected Say's law of the classical economists—"supply creates its own demand"—arguing that aggregate demand could fall short of the level needed to purchase the aggregate output produced at full employment. That is, unlike the classical presumption that the economy would maintain full employment of labor (and capital), Keynes maintained—as clearly evidenced by the high unemployment rates during the Great Depression—that an economy could come to an equilibrium well below full employment. Keynes put forth an elaborate theory of aggregate demand.

A simple Keynesian model

To illustrate Keynes's general theory, we will begin with a simple macroeconomic model. In Chapter 6, we will develop a more complete Keynesian model of the economy. To begin, desired aggregate expenditures on real national output can be disaggregated into expenditures by households (real personal consumption expenditures, C), by firms (real gross private domestic investment expenditures, I), by the government (real government consumption and investment expenditures, G), and by the rest of the world (real exports of goods and services, X), less those expenditures on imported goods and services (M). That is,

$$A = C + I + G + X - M = Y^D,$$

where A is desired aggregate expenditures on real national output (aggregate demand Y^D).

The aggregate supply of real national output, Y^S, reflects the productive capacity of the nation, in turn a function of the labor force, capital stock, available natural resources, technology, and the institutional environment, including government regulations. **Full-employment real national output** (or **potential national output**), Y_f, would be produced if the economy were operating at full employment, that is, with no cyclical unemployment and the normal rate of utilization of the physical capital stock. An economy could come to an equilibrium below full employment, where $Y^D = Y^S < Y_f$.[14]

Particularly important for the economy reaching full employment was the adequacy of investment spending. Real gross private domestic investment (I) can be disaggregated into fixed investment, reflecting the purchase of capital goods, and inventory investment, indicated by the change in business inventories of intermediate, semi-finished and finished goods over the period. Fixed investment, in turn, consists of business or nonresidential fixed investment, comprising business purchases of new capital goods (i.e., machinery, equipment, and buildings), and residential fixed investment, or the value of the residential construction over the period. Government purchases of goods and services, G, can be disaggregated into consumption or current expenditures, G_C (e.g., salaries of government workers and military expenditures) and investment or capital

---

[14] Conversely, an economy could operate in the short run beyond full employment, $Y^D = Y^S > Y_f$, with no cyclical unemployment and below average frictional and structural unemployment. Doing so, however, leads to a rise in the inflation rate. Business cycles and the types of unemployment will be discussed in greater detail in Chapter 6. Briefly, cyclical unemployment refers to job losses due to insufficient aggregate demand. Frictional unemployment refers to the natural turnover of the labor force and job searches, while structural unemployment results when there is a mismatch between the labor skills of the unemployed and the requirements for the open jobs.

expenditures, G_I, including government spending on the economic infrastructure (e.g., highways, schools, government buildings). Gross domestic investment, GDI, the sum of private and public investment, (GDI $= I + G_I$), is important not only for aggregate demand, but also for aggregate supply as the resulting capital formation adds to the productive capacity of the economy—given that gross fixed investment exceeds the depreciation of the physical capital stock, so net fixed investment is positive.

In general, if the national output produced over the period generates income where saving (gross domestic saving by households, firms, and the government) exceeds investment (gross domestic investment by firms and the government), then desired spending on national output would fall short of the output produced and the economy would operate below full employment.[15]

Physical capital formation

Gross domestic investment—in particular, business fixed investment—reflects the demand for physical capital (K). Business fixed investment and residential fixed investment depend on business confidence and consumer confidence, which affect aggregate demand. Consumer spending, except perhaps during wartime, tends to account for the largest component of aggregate demand. Keynes argued that the growth in consumer and investment spending is driven by population growth (the number of consumers), growth in per capita incomes (spending per consumer), and technological change, which determines the capital–output ratio (K/Y). *Ceteris paribus*, the higher the capital–output ratio, the higher would be the demand for capital and the need for investment.

Keynes maintained that apart from technological progress (often embodied in new capital goods, inducing businesses to invest in to stay competitive) and an improved standard of living (with increased consumer spending), the demand for capital would increase more or less in proportion to population. With population growth, businesses are more optimistic and thus willing to invest in new plants, equipment, and machinery to increase the productive capacity of the economy to meet the expected increases in aggregate demand driven by consumer spending. With no population growth, or population decline, businesses would be less confident, even reluctant, to invest in new capital. Therefore, if population trends were down—as they were in the US and other industrialized nations in the 1930s due to the long-term secular declines in birth rates and the reduced net in-migration from tighter immigration policies—then not only would the growth

---

[15] In an open economy, any difference between gross domestic investment and gross domestic saving would be covered by foreign savings. A nation will invest more than it saves, equivalently consuming more final goods and services than it produces, when it runs a current account deficit and relies on foreign savings to fill the gap. The basic macroeconomic identity states that $C+I+G+X-M = Y = C+S+T+R+F$, where S is private saving (both personal and business), T net taxes (tax revenues less government transfers), R net transfers to the rest of the world and F net factor payments to the rest of the world. The left-hand side gives desired aggregate expenditures on real national output—the components of aggregate demand. The right-hand side gives the allocation or uses of the income generated in the production of real national output. Alternatively, we can show that in equilibrium, $I+G+X-M = Y-C = S+T+R+F$, or expenditures on national output other than personal consumption (on the left) must equal income generated but not used for expenditures on national output (on the right). Breaking up government purchases of goods and services, G, into government consumption, G_C, and government investment or capital expenditures, G_I (so $G = G_C + G_I$), and rearranging to solve for gross domestic investment, GDI, the sum of private and public investment $(I+G_I)$, in equilibrium we must have: GDI $= I+G_I = S+(T-G_C)+(M-X+R+F)$. The government current budget balance, $T-G_C$, indicates government or public savings (if positive), or a government deficit (if negative). Gross domestic saving, GDS, is the sum of gross private saving (S) and the government current budget balance: GDS $= S + (T - G_C)$. The current account balance is given by $X-M-R-F$, so here $M-X+R+F$ indicates a current account deficit (if positive) and net foreign savings (NFS) available to the nation. In equilibrium then, GDI $= (I + G_I) = $ GDS $+$ NFS $= S + (T - G_C) + (M - X + R + F)$. If GDI $>$ GDS, then the nation's investment exceeds the savings and the nation has a current account deficit (NFS > 0), meaning the rest of the world is acquiring net claims on the nation's economy, reflected in the foreign savings invested in that nation. On the other hand, an excess of gross domestic saving over investment would be reflected in a current account surplus for the nation (NFS < 0), meaning the nation is acquiring net claims on the rest of the world.

in consumer spending be depressed, but so also would the growth in the demand for capital and investment spending.

Moreover, Keynes noted that as economies developed and per capita incomes increased, the share of expenditures on services increased. Services (e.g., education, health care, entertainment) tend to be labor-intensive, and in some cases human capital intensive—not physical capital intensive like manufacturing. This shift in the composition of aggregate demand also tended to depress the derived demand for physical capital, and thus the need for investment.

Thus, in the face of declining population growth, to boost aggregate demand Keynes recommended a redistribution of income from those with lower propensities to consume (i.e., higher-income households) to those with higher propensities to consume (i.e., lower-income households). Also, Keynes (1937: 17) advocated lower interest rates (with expansionary monetary policy) to stimulate investment directly and encourage firms to shift to more capital-intensive methods of production:

> With a stationary population we shall, I argue, be absolutely dependent for the maintenance of prosperity and civil peace on policies of increasing consumption by a more equal distribution of incomes and of forcing down the rate of interest. . .[otherwise we will have] a chronic tendency towards the under-employment of resources.

Demand-management fiscal policy

Keynes is perhaps best known for his advocacy of government spending to stimulate an economy mired in a depression. Contrary to conventional wisdom that the government should set a good example and seek to balance its budget during lean times—just as households might have to pull back their consumption—Keynes argued that the government should run budget deficits, adopting a countercycle stance. Increasing government spending, or reducing tax rates, would increase aggregate demand and induce consumer and business spending. Conversely, according to demand-management policy, during expansions when the economy threatens to overheat and inflation is a concern, the fiscal and monetary policy-makers should adopt tighter policies, cutting government spending, raising tax rates, and increasing interest rates to cool off and stabilize the economy.

As mentioned, in the US during the Great Depression, the government actually increased tax rates to counter the deterioration in the government budget balance due to the declining tax base as national income fell. Moreover, the monetary policy was fairly tight. Keynes prescription of aggressive government spending really was not adopted.[16] Under President Franklin Roosevelt, the federal government did implement some public works programs to increase employment. Social security was introduced to provide for old age welfare. Further, the establishment of the Securities and Exchange Commission to regulate the stock market and the Federal Deposit Insurance Commission to insure bank deposits did bolster investor and consumer confidence. Nevertheless, the fiscal initiatives undertaken in the 1930s were generally too modest to turn the economy around. And, as noted earlier, economic policy became tighter in 1937, even with double-digit unemployment, which sent the US economy into recession in 1938. In a real sense,

[16] The heyday of Keynesian economics came in the 1960s, well after Keynes had died. In the US, however, fiscal policy-makers have tended to favor expansionary policies, erring on the side of maintaining full employment. Sensitive to the voting public, rarely have the president and Congress adopted tighter fiscal policies, for example cutting government spending and raising taxes to address inflation. Thus it usually falls to the monetary authorities, the Federal Reserve, to tighten up the money supply and raise interest rates to deal with inflation.

it was the mandated fiscal stimulus from the national defense spending brought on by World War II that finally recharged the US economy.

Economic stagnation

The use of such demand-management policies, however, was more for short-run stabilization. The concern of macroeconomists in the 1930s was with long-term stagnation.

In his presidential address to the American Economic Association at the end of 1938, Hansen attributed economic growth to population growth, the discovery and development of new territories and natural resources, and technological progress. The decline in the growth rate of population would reduce the growth rate in the number of consumers, directly reducing aggregate demand. Furthermore, the long-term decline in US fertility rates had aged the population. (As we will discuss in detail in a later chapter, declining fertility results in an older population and eventually an increase in the elderly burden of dependency.) The aging of the population shifted the composition of household expenditures away from capital-intensive industries, in particular, housing (residential fixed investment) and consumer durables (e.g., appliances, furniture, and automobiles), toward labor-intensive services, especially health care and nursing homes. This, too, contributed to the decrease in the growth of the demand for physical capital, thus the fall in gross domestic fixed investment spending.

Hansen did not hold out much hope either for the second source for economic growth. The discovery of new territory and development of natural resources would require investment to extend the infrastructure (e.g., the transportation system and power generation) to utilize this natural capital. Hansen observed, however, that few new lands remained to be "discovered" (an echo of the classical concern with cultivable land as a limit to growth). And Hansen discounted the role of foreign direct investment, which was not surprising given the increased protectionism of the 1930s. In sum, Hansen's address reflected the dismal outlook of macroeconomists in the decade. There seemed to be no easy fixes to the economic stagnation.

CAPITAL INTENSITY

Before turning to technological progress as the key to economic growth, we should distinguish between capital widening and capital deepening. We've discussed the importance of population growth for consumption, and indirectly, for investment. As Keynes and Hansen noted, the demand for capital could increase for a given rate of national output if the capital–output ratio increased, i.e., if the aggregate production of goods and services became more capital-intensive.

Economic efficiency

Consider a firm seeking to maximize profits. In the long run, where all the factors of production are variable, the firm would seek the least-cost (or economically efficient) combinations of factors for producing the selected levels of output. Using just a two-factor production function, and assuming the firm is a perfect competitor (price-taker) in the factor markets and the output market, we can illustrate the firm's constrained optimization problem.[17]

---

[17]Using calculus, we can derive the optimal condition for the cost-minimizing combination of capital and labor. Given the total revenues of the firm, reflecting the selected level of output, Q_0, and associated unit price, P_0, then to maximize profits, the firm seeks to minimize the total costs of production.

The objective function to maximize is

$$\Pi = TR - TC$$

subject to the constraint

$$Q_0 = Q = Q(K, L)$$

where Π is the profits of the firm, $TR = P_0 \cdot Q_0$ the total revenues of the firm (P_0 is the unit price of the firm's output, set by the market and exogenous to the firm, and Q_0 the selected output of the firm), $TC = w_0 \cdot L + r_0 \cdot K$ is the total costs of the firm (w_0 is the wage rate (user cost of labor), set by the market and exogenous to the firm, L the labor employed by the firm, r_0 the interest rate (user cost of capital), set by the market and exogenous to the firm, and K the physical capital stock of the firm), and $Q = F(K, L)$ is the firm's long-run production function.

With the selected level of output, Q_0, and associated unit price, P_0, setting the firm's total revenues, the goal of maximizing profits reduces to minimizing the total costs of producing this output. The firm can vary the factor proportions, that is, the capital–labor ratio, according to the production function to find the economically efficient combination of capital and labor, given the market prices for capital and labor. Figure 4.1 illustrates. The firm's **isocost line**, representing all the combinations of capital and labor with the same total cost, here TC_0, is given by the line CC. The firm's **isoquant**, representing all the technically efficient combinations of capital and labor for producing a given level of output, is indicated by the curve Q_0. By **technical efficiency**, we mean that no more of any factor is used than necessary to produce a given level of output—or, in other words, the marginal products of the factors are always positive. The firm's cost-minimizing and **economically efficient** combination of capital and labor, K_0 and L_0, respectively, for producing the output Q_0, is found at the tangency of the isocost line CC with the selected isoquant, Q_0.

This point of tangency, E_0, indicates the lowest isocost line the firm can attain for producing the selected output of Q_0. At this point of tangency, the slope of the isocost line, equal to the (negative) ratio of the user cost of labor to the user cost of capital ($-w_0/r_0$), equals the slope of the isoquant, known as the **marginal rate of factor substitution**, MRFS, which is equal to the (negative) ratio of the marginal product of labor, $Q_L = \partial Q/\partial L$, to the marginal product of capital, $Q_K = \partial Q/\partial K$. That is, at the cost-minimizing combination of factors, $w_0/r_0 = Q_L/Q_K$,

---

We set up the Lagrangian function,

$$G(K, L, \lambda) = w_0 \cdot L + r_0 \cdot K + \lambda \cdot [Q_0 - Q(K, L)]$$

The first-order conditions are:

$$\partial G/\partial K = r_0 - \lambda \cdot Q_K = 0$$

where $Q_K = \partial Q/\partial K$ is the marginal product of capital;

$$\partial G/\partial L = w_0 - \lambda \cdot Q_L = 0$$

where $Q_L = \partial Q/\partial L$ is the marginal product of labor;

$$\partial G/\partial \lambda = Q_0 - Q(K, L) = 0$$

that is, the output constraint is satisfied. From the first two conditions, we can write $Q_K/r_0 = 1/\lambda = Q_L/w_0$. Thus, the condition for the cost-minimizing combination of capital and labor for producing a given level of output is that the marginal products per dollar spent on capital and labor are equal. Alternatively, the condition can be written as MRFS $= -Q_L/Q_K = -w_0/r_0$, or the marginal rate of factor substitution, given by the negative of the ratio of the marginal product of labor to the marginal product of capital, is equal to the negative of the ratio of the user cost of labor to the user cost of capital. Graphically, the isoquant representing the output Q_0 is tangent to the lowest isocost line, representing the minimum total cost.

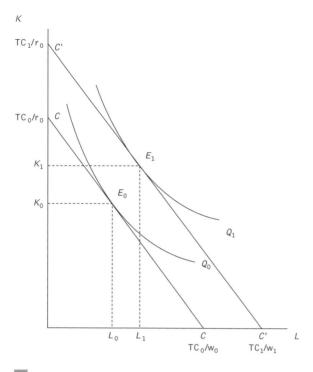

Figure 4.1 *Cost-minimizing combination of capital (K) and labor (L)*

The firm seeks to minimize its total cost: $TC = w_0 \cdot L + r_0 \cdot K$, subject to producing the selected level of output, $Q_0 = Q = Q(K, L)$. At the cost-minimizing combination, indicated by the point of tangency, E_0, the ratio of the marginal products of labor to capital, MP_L/MP_K, equals the ratio of the unit prices of labor to capital, w/r.

An increase in the selected level of output from Q_0 to Q_1, will increase the required quantities of labor and capital.

or the rate at which the firm can substitute labor for capital in the market, w_0/r_0 (the ratio of user costs), is equal to the rate at which the firm can substitute labor for capital in producing the selected level of output, Q_L/Q_K (the ratio of marginal products). Rewriting this expression, we derive the more familiar condition for cost-minimization, $Q_L/w_0 = Q_K/r_0$, or the marginal products per dollar spent by the firm are equal.

An increase in the selected rate of output, from Q_0 to Q_1, indicated by movement to a higher isoquant, *ceteris paribus*, would require an increase in expenditures on the factors of production. Figure 4.1 illustrates the new cost-minimizing combination of factors, K_1 and L_1, at the point of tangency of the new isoquant, Q_1, and isocost line, $C'C'$. If this increase in output is met with proportional increases in capital and labor, leaving the capital–labor ratio constant ($K_1/L_1 = K_0/L_0$), then we have **capital widening**. That is, if the growth rate in the capital stock equals the growth rate in labor, then capital widening occurs.

Capital deepening

Capital deepening refers to an increase in the capital–labor ratio, and that the capital stock is growing faster than labor. To illustrate for this firm, refer to Figure 4.2, and begin with the firm

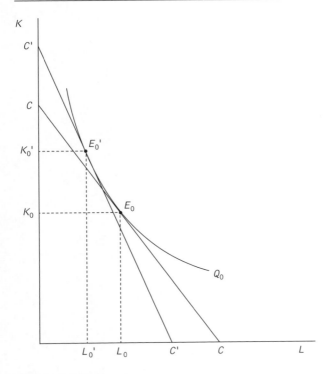

Figure 4.2 *Capital deepening with an increase in wage–rental ratio*

An increase in the wage–rental ratio will result in the firm shifting to a more capital intensive method of production: $K_0'/L_0' > K_0/L_0$.

in equilibrium at E_0. Capital deepening could occur if the firm shifted to a more capital-intensive method of production. For example, an increase in the ratio of the user cost of labor to the user cost of capital, w/r, also known as the wage–rental ratio, would yield steeper isocost lines. For the given output, the firm would substitute away from the relatively more expensive labor and shift to a more capital-intensive method of production. See the new isocost line, $C'C'$, in Figure 4.2, and the tangency with the original isoquant Q_0 at point E_0'. Note that at the new cost-minimizing combination of capital and labor, the capital–labor ratio is higher, $K_0'/L_0' > K_0/L_0$, consistent with capital deepening. This capital deepening also increases the capital output ratio, K/Q, as $K_0'/Q_0 > K_0/Q_0$, and would, *ceteris paribus*, increase the demand for capital and thus investment expenditures.

Recall that Keynes recommended a decrease in the interest rate through expansionary monetary policy to stimulate investment and capital formation. So, too, a declining rate of population growth and labor force growth would put upward pressure on wages, *ceteris paribus*. Either lower interest rates or higher wage rates would raise the ratio of the user cost of labor to the user cost of capital and encourage a more capital-intensive method of production. But recall also that a declining rate of population growth and an aging of the population would tend to reduce the growth rates in capital-intensive goods (e.g., housing and consumer durables) and thus diminish the growth rate in the demand for capital.

An alternative way to promote capital deepening is through the adoption of more capital-intensive technology (e.g., with labor-saving technological change). See Figure 4.3 for an

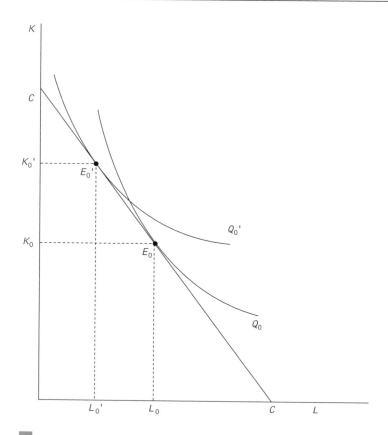

Figure 4.3 *Capital deepening with capital-intensive technology*

Assume $Q_0 = Q'_0$, where $Q = Q(K, L)$ is the initial technology and $Q' = Q'(K, L)$ is the new, more capital-intensive technology. A shift to a more capital-intensive technology (reflected in flatter isoquants, e.g., Q') results in a more capital-intensive method of production: $K'_0/L'_0 > K_0/L_0$.

illustration. The more capital-intensive technology is reflected in a rotation of the isoquant mapping, giving a flatter set of isoquants. Compare Q'_0 (the more capital-intensive technology) with Q_0 (the original technology). If we assume that the firm's output is the same for the two isoquants ($Q'_0 = Q_0$), then we see that the new cost-minimizing combination of capital and labor, $K'_0/L'_0 > K_0/L_0$, has resulted in capital deepening. Note that this capital-intensive technology may well increase the capital–output ratio, boosting capital formation and investment spending. For numerical examples of capital widening and capital deepening for a firm, see Box 4.1.

BOX 4.1: CAPITAL DEEPENING AND CAPITAL WIDENING

Assume a firm with a production function $Q = A \cdot K^\alpha L^\beta$ ($0 < \alpha, \beta < 1$). Let $A = 1.0$ (index of technology), $\alpha = 0.4$ and $\beta = 0.6$ (i.e., the production function is characterized by constant returns to scale). Exogenous to the firm are the market user costs of labor

($w_0 = \$10$) and capital ($r_0 = \$2$). The firm seeks to maximize profits by finding the cost-minimizing combination of K and L for producing the output $Q_0 = 100$, that is, to minimize total cost

$$TC = w_0 \cdot L + r_0 \cdot K = 10L + 2K$$

subject to the output constraint

$$Q = Q_0 = 100 = K^{0.4} L^{0.6} = K^{\alpha} L^{\beta}$$

The Lagrangian function is

$$G(K, L, \lambda) = 10L + 2K + \lambda \cdot (100 - K^{0.4} L^{0.6})$$

where the Lagrange multiplier is the marginal cost of output $\lambda = \delta TC/\delta Q$. The first-order conditions are:

$$\delta G/\delta K = 2 - 0.4\lambda K^{-0.6} L^{0.6} = 0 \quad (r_0 - \delta Q/\delta K = 0)$$

$$\delta G/\delta L = 10 - 0.6\lambda K^{0.4} L^{-0.4} = 0 \quad (w_0 - \delta Q/\delta L = 0)$$

$$\delta G/\delta \lambda = 100 - K^{0.4} L^{0.6} = 0 \quad \text{(output constraint is met)}$$

From the first two conditions we can write

$$2/(0.4 K^{-0.6} L^{0.6}) = \lambda = 10/(0.6 K^{0.4} L^{-0.4})$$

Rearranging gives

$$(0.4 K^{-0.6} L^{0.6})/2 = 1/\lambda = (0.6 K^{0.4} L^{-0.4})/10$$

or the condition for profit-maximization:

$$\frac{\delta Q/\delta K}{r_0} = \frac{MP_K}{r_0} = \frac{MP_L}{w_0} = \frac{\delta Q/\delta L}{w_0}$$

Using this optimal condition, we can express L in terms of K. Here, $L = 0.3K$. Substituting into the output constraint, we can solve for the optimal K and then L:

$$100 = K^{0.4}(0.3K)^{0.6},$$

so

$$K = 100/0.3^{0.6} = 205.9 = K_0 \quad \text{and} \quad L_0 = 0.3K_0 = 61.8$$

The optimal combination of capital and labor for producing $Q_0 = 100$ is then:

$$K_0 = 205.9 \quad \text{and} \quad L_0 = 61.8$$

The capital–labor ratio is

$$(K/L)_0 = 3.33$$

The capital–output ratio is

$$(K/Q)_0 = 2.059 \approx 2.06$$

Output per unit of labor is

$$(Q/L)_0 = 1.62$$

The total cost of production is

$$TC_0 = \$2 \cdot (205.9) + \$10 \cdot (61.8) = \$1029.8$$

Comparative statics

In each of the following cases only one change in made with respect to this base scenario.

Case 1. An increase in the selected level of output to $Q_1 = 120$ ($TC_1 = \$1235.2$)
Now the optimal combination of capital and labor is $K_1 = 247.1$ and $L_1 = 74.1$. The capital–labor ratio remains the same:

$$(K/L)_1 = 247.1/74.1 = 3.33 = (K/L)_0$$

The capital–output ratio remains the same:

$$(K/Q)_1 = 247.1/120 = 2.06 = (K/Q)_0$$

Output per unit of labor remains the same:

$$(Q/L)_1 = 120/74.1 = 1.62 = (Q/L)_0$$

The increase in output, Q, increases the demand for capital, resulting in capital widening, but the K/L and K/Q ratios remain constant. Note that if the production function had been characterized by increasing (decreasing) returns to scale, where $\alpha + \beta > 1$ ($\alpha + \beta < 1$), then the increase in output would result in decreases (increases) in the capital–output and labor–output ratios.

Case 2. A decrease in the user cost of capital to $r' = 1.5$ ($TC_2 = \$918.1$)
Now the optimal combination of capital and labor is $K_2 = 244.7$ and $L_2 = 55.1$. The capital–labor ratio increases to

$$(K/L)_2 = 244.7/55.1 = 4.44 \quad \text{(from } (K/L)_0 = 3.33)$$

The capital–output ratio increases to

$$(K/Q)_2 = 244.7/100 = 2.45 \quad \text{(from } (K/Q)_0 = 2.06)$$

Output per unit of labor increases to

$$(Q/L)_2 = 100/55.1 = 1.82 \quad \text{(from } (Q/L)_0 = 1.62)$$

The decrease in the user cost of capital, r, increases the wage–rental ratio, w/r, and results in capital deepening with increases in K/L and K/Q. The optimal labor decreases.

Case 3. A change in technology to a more capital-intensive production process, with an increase in α to $\alpha' = 0.45$, and a decrease in β to $\beta' = 0.55$ ($TC_3 = \$965.0$)
Note we still have constant returns to scale ($\alpha' + \beta' = 1$). Now the optimal combination of capital and labor is $K_3 = 217.0$ and $L_3 = 53.1$. The capital–labor ratio increases:

$$(K/L)_3 = 217.0/53.1 = 4.09 \quad \text{(from } (K/L)_0 = 3.33)$$

The capital–output ratio increases:

$(K/Q)_3 = 217.0/100 = 2.17$ (from $(K/Q)_0 = 2.06$)

Output per unit of labor increases:

$(Q/L)_3 = 100/53.1 = 1.88$ (from $(Q/L)_0 = 1.62$)

With adoption of a more capital-intensive production process, capital deepening occurs as the K/L ratio rises, as does the K/Q ratio. The optimal labor decreases.

Case 4. An increase in the index of technology to $A' = 1.2$ ($TC_4 = \$858.2$))

Now the optimal combination of capital and labor is $K_4 = 171.6$ and $L_4 = 51.5$. The capital–labor ratio remains the same:

$(K/L)_4 = (171.6/51.5) = 3.33 = (K/L)_0$

The capital–output ratio decreases:

$(K/Q)_4 = (171.6/100) = 1.72$ (from $(K/Q)_0 = 2.06$)

Output per unit of labor increases:

$(Q/L)_4 = (100/51.5) = 1.94$ (from $(Q/L)_0 = 1.62$)

With neutral technical change, the absolute productivities of K and L increase, but there is no change in the K/L ratio.

If we move from the firm to the aggregate economy, we can generalize. To promote investment spending, a key component in aggregate demand, lower interest rates and technological change that increase the capital–output ratio are recommended. In an economy where the growth of consumption spending may be declining with the growth in population, increasing investment spending takes on added importance. Moreover, there is an extra multiplier effect from increased investment spending. An increase in fixed investment spending directly increases aggregate demand and the production of real national output. The increase in real national output, for a given capital–output ratio, increases the demand for capital. The greater demand for capital then requires additional investment, further boosting aggregate demand.[18]

Technological progress

As noted earlier, much of technological progress may be embodied in the new capital goods, increasing the quality of the physical capital, which contributes to economic growth. To stay competitive, firms may have to invest in this new capital, stimulating investment and aggregate demand.

Clearly technological progress, whether neutral, labor-saving, or embodied in new capital goods, is important for economic growth. **Neutral technical change** results in a inward shift in isoquants, allowing outputs to be produced with lower levels of factors, but does not alter the

---

[18]There can be too much investment resulting in excess capacity (as in the 1920s), which can then depress profits (returns on investment), discourage new investment spending, and reduce aggregate demand. Recall that macroeconomists believed that a growing population with increasing demand for output was important for economic growth.

economically efficient capital–labor ratios.[19] (Case 4 in Box 4.1 illustrates neutral technological progress.)

As Hansen (1939: 10) remarked, "The problem of our generation is, above all, the problem of inadequate private investment outlets. . .We need an acceleration in the rate of technological progress. . .and development of new industries." Hansen was not very optimistic, however, about this source of economic growth either. Over the 1930s gross private domestic fixed investment expenditures had not only been depressed, but also volatile. From 14.4 percent of GDP in 1929 and 12.0 percent of GDP in 1930, private domestic fixed investment expenditures in the US economy collapsed over the next three years to 5.6 percent of GDP in 1933, rising to 10.4 percent of GDP by 1937, dropping to 8.9 percent of GDP in 1938, a year of recession, before rebounding some to 9.9 percent of GDP in 1939, still well below the 12.0 percent at the beginning of the decade.[20] As underlying reasons for lagging investment, Hansen cited low business profits that limited funding for the research and development important for technological progress. He added that the growth of labor unions might restrict the adoption of labor-saving, capital-using technologies. And, the increased incidence of imperfect competition with monopolies and oligopolies with their entry barriers to markets might stifle competition and innovation.

CONCLUSION

The macroeconomists in the 1930s were pessimistic about economic growth. While sharing some of the same concerns with the earlier classical economists, including natural resource constraints and diminishing profits, the macroeconomists of the 1930s differed in one important way. The classical stationary state was due in large part to unchecked population growth and diminishing returns to labor. The economic stagnation in the 1930s was due in large part to insufficient population growth and shortfalls in investment.

The concerns with declining population growth and economic stagnation in the 1930s were real. Fertility rates in the US had steadily fallen over the past several decades to reach replacement levels. The predictions of demographers were more of the same. Keynes's prescription of sharply increased government spending, with the deliberate running of large government budget deficits, to stimulate the economy, was never implemented. World War II changed that, requiring massive increases in government spending. Between 1939 and 1944 real national output in the US nearly doubled. Over the same period, the share of government spending in national output increased from 16 percent to 48 percent (with 90 percent of this for national defense). The baby boom that followed World War II sharply increased population growth and revitalized the US economy.

We will see in the next chapter that the classical economists' worries in the nineteenth century about "overpopulation," and the macroeconomists' worries in the 1930s about "underpopulation" both became relevant in the debate over limits to growth that emerged over the last quarter of the twentieth century.

---

[19]Note that neutral technical change or neutral technological progress, indicated by an increase in the index of technology, A, in the production function $Q = A \cdot Q(K, L)$, would allow the firm to produce the same level of output for less capital and labor. The firm's isoquant mapping would shift in toward the origin. That is, for any selected level of output, Q_0, neutral technical change would reduce the required capital and labor, but leave the optimal capital–labor ratio unchanged. The capital–output and labor–output ratios, however, would decline proportionately with neutral technical progress.

[20]These shares of gross private domestic fixed investment in gross domestic product are from the Bureau of Economic Analysis (http://www.bea.gov), Table 1.1.10, accessed December 22, 2011.

KEY TERMS

capital account

capital widening

economic efficiency

gold standard

isoquant

neutral technical change

par value

capital deepening

current account

full employment real national output

isocost line

marginal rate of factor substitution

official settlements account

technical efficiency

QUESTIONS

1. Given a firm with a production function, $Q = A \cdot K^\alpha L^\beta$ ($0 < \alpha, \beta < 1$), let $A = 1.0$ (index of technology), $\alpha = 0.5$ and $\beta = 0.7$ (i.e., the production function has increasing returns to scale). Exogenous to the firm are the market user costs of labor ($w_0 = 10$) and capital ($r_0 = 2$).

   (a) Find the cost-minimizing combination of K and L for producing the output $Q_0 = 100$.

   (b) Determine the optimal capital–labor ratio, $(K/L)_0$, and associated capital–output ratio, $(K/Q)_0$, and output per unit of labor, $(Q/L)_0$.

   (c) Determine the effects of the following independent changes, *ceteris paribus*, on the firm's cost-minimizing combinations of K and L and on the firm's optimal capital–labor and associated capital–output ratio and output per unit of labor:

      (i) an increase in the selected level of output to $Q_1 = 120$;

      (ii) a decrease in the user cost of capital to $r' = 1.5$;

      (iii) a change in technology to a more capital-intensive production process with an increase in α to $\alpha' = 0.6$ and a decrease in β to $\beta' = 0.6$;

      (iv) an increase in the index of technology to $A' = 1.2$ (neutral technical change).

2. Repeat Question 1 assuming the production function is now characterized by decreasing returns to scale: $Q = A \cdot K^\alpha L^\beta$ ($0 < \alpha, \beta < 1$) where $A = 1.0$ (index of technology), $\alpha = 0.3$ and $\beta = 0.5$.

3. Discuss the implications for labor (employment and real wages) if firms shift to more capital-intensive methods of production.

4. Do you think the US would have returned to healthy economic growth in the 1940s if not for the increased defense spending required by World War II? Discuss.

5. Have we learned any economic lessons from the Great Depression? Discuss.

REFERENCES

Calomiris, Charles. 1993. "Financial Factors in the Great Depression," *Journal of Economic Perspectives*, 7(2): 61–86.

Council of Economic Advisers. 1983. *Economic Report of the President 1983*. Washington, DC: United States Government. http://www.presidency.ucsb.edu/economic_reports/1983.pdf.

Council of Economic Advisers. 2010. *Economic Report of the President 2010*. Washington, DC: United States Government: 137–180.

Dunn, Robert and James Ingram. 1996. *International Economics*, 4th edition. New York: Wiley: 431–445.

Froyen, Richard. 2009. *Macroeconomics: Theories and Policies*, 9th edition. Upper Saddle River, NJ: Pearson Prentice Hall: Chapters 5–8.

Hansen, Alvin. 1939. "Economic Progress and Declining Population Growth," *American Economic Review*, 29(1, Part I): 1–15.

Kenwood, A.G., and A.L. Lougheed. 1992. *The Growth of the International Economy; 1820-1990*, 3rd edition, New York: Routledge: 60–92.

Keynes, John Maynard. 1937. "Some Economic Consequences of a Declining Population," *Eugenics Review* 29(1): 13–17.

Maddison, Angus. 2005. *Growth and Interaction in the World Economy: The Roots of Modernity*. Washington, DC: AEI Press.

Margo, Robert. 1993. "Employment and Unemployment in the 1930s," *Journal of Economic Perspectives*, 7(2): 41–60.

Roberts, Paul. 2008. *The End of Food*. Boston: Houghton Mifflin.

Romer, Christina. 1993. "The Nation in Depression," *Journal of Economic Perspectives*, 7(2): 19–40.

Temin, Peter. 1993. "Transmission of the Great Depression," *Journal of Economic Perspectives*, 7(2): 87–102.

Chapter 5

Limits to growth

Toward the end of World War II, the leaders of the allied industrial nations, especially the United States and United Kingdom, recognized the need to plan for a new international economic system. Intended to undergird this new order was international cooperation, as lessons had been learned from the discord of independent monetary policies and damaging protectionism of the interwar period. Clear rules of the game for exchange rates and balance of payments adjustments were to be established as well as a system for liberalizing trade.

In July 1944, an international conference was held at Bretton Woods, New Hampshire, where the International Monetary Fund (IMF) and the International Bank for Reconstruction and Development (World Bank) were created. In 1947, a third institution, the General Agreement on Tariffs and Trade (GATT), began in Geneva, Switzerland, to provide a framework for nations to liberalize trade.

Moreover, in the years immediately following the end of hostilities increasing attention was paid to the less developed nations of the world. As Pomfret (1992: 14) observes:

> Only in designing a world economic order to follow the Second World War and in considering the situation of countries which would be making their own economic policies for the first time, did expressions like the underdeveloped countries and the Third World come into use. Once the subject was identified, there arose a separate field of economics known as "development economics."

In 1950 per capita real gross domestic products in the industrialized nations (i.e., Western Europe, the US, Canada, Australia, New Zealand, and Japan) averaged $5,300 (in 2005 PPP dollars). The average per capita income in the rest of the world was estimated to be $1,240, with an even greater diversity in incomes across these countries. The corresponding average annual economic growth rates for the 1913–50 period, which encompassed two world wars and a depression, had been 1.17 percent for these developed nations and 0.65 percent for the developing nations. These economic growth rates were significantly lower than the 1.57 percent and 0.82 percent, respectively, for the preceding period from 1870–1913. While reduced population growth had accompanied the declining economic growth in the industrialized countries (from an annual average increase in population of 1.07 percent for 1870–1913 to 0.78 percent for 1913–50), increased population growth had occurred in the rest of the world (from an annual average increase of 0.72 percent for 1870–1913 to 0.98 percent for 1913–1950).[1]

---

[1] These statistics are derived from Maddison (2005: Tables 2 and 3). Maddison presents per capita incomes in 1990 international or PPP dollars. To convert to 2005 PPP dollars, the 1990 estimates were multiplied by $1.44 = 1.023^{16}$, where 2.3 percent is the average annual increase in the US price deflator for GDP for 1990–2005.

INTERNATIONAL INSTITUTIONS FOR THE NEW WORLD ORDER

The IMF was charged with monitoring a code of conduct for exchange rate practices and assisting in balance of payments adjustments. The Bretton Woods system, as it became known, was a gold exchange standard. The US had the strongest economy following World War II, just as it did after World War I. Consequently, the US dollar was declared to be the only currency tied directly to gold (at $35 to an ounce of gold). All other countries that were members of the IMF were to establish par values for their currencies expressed in terms of the US dollar. From these relative par values, bilateral exchange rates were derived. The US committed to converting outstanding dollars presented by foreign central banks into gold at $35 an ounce. Other nations were obliged to maintain their par values within a narrow range. The IMF maintained a reserve of currencies that member nations could borrow to support their par values in the case of balance of payments deficits. Unlike a fixed exchange rate system, however, a nation could change or adjust its par value in the case of a fundamental disequilibrium, which meant a chronic balance of payments imbalance, usually a deficit. Thus, as in a gold standard, there were clear "rules of the game" under the Bretton Woods system of adjustable pegs.

The World Bank was designed to channel financial capital to nations for rebuilding and developing their economies. Its attention in its early years was focused on the reconstruction of the war-torn economies of Europe and Japan. In these nations, with educated populations and skilled labor forces, the overwhelming need was to rebuild the economic infrastructure and invest in new plant, equipment and machinery. The US, with the Marshall Plan and the Dodge Plan, respectively, assisted in the reconstruction of the European and Japanese economies. The economic development of the low-income nations of Africa, Asia, and Latin America, was thus relatively unattended—primarily because of the preoccupation with restoring the European and Japanese economies, a concern made all the more important with the onset of the Cold War. Moreover, it was believed that restarting the main engines of the global economy and expanding international trade and investment would also advance the less developed countries (LDCs). Thus, despite requests for assistance, the LDCs received little foreign aid—at least until the mid-1950s, when the strategic significance of these nations was recognized.

GATT provided a system for nations to reduce trade barriers. Underlying it were the principles of **reciprocity** and **most favored nation**. The former served as the basic rationale for trade liberalization. If one nation lowered its trade barriers to a second nation, that second nation should reciprocate, reducing its trade barriers to the first nation—a quid pro quo. Most favored nation status was to be enjoyed by all the members of GATT, whereby trade concessions granted to any other nation would be extended to all other member nations. When trade disputes arose between nations, GATT offered a mechanism for resolving differences. Thus, nations would not have to resort to protectionism and trade wars could be prevented.

In short, the leaders of the free world intended to create a new international economic order that promoted cooperation and mutually beneficial trade and economic growth. The post-World War II era, however, also saw the emergence of the Cold War, with the rise of the Soviet Union and the spread of communism. In fact, the so-called **First World** or the West (particularly the US, the UK, and France) often competed with the so-called **Second World** or the East (the Soviet Union and its allies in Eastern Europe) for support in the **Third World** (the developing nations in the rest of the world). For the West, foreign aid seemed to be a good investment in the containment of communism. Aid was intended to promote economically viable and politically stable countries, oriented toward free markets and democracy. So, too, the Soviet Union employed military and economic aid to bolster its client states. The World Bank increasingly became instrumental in providing loans to the developing nations of Asia, Africa, the Middle East, and Latin America, where there was an abundance of labor from the rapid population growth associated with the sharp declines in mortality rates, but a scarcity of capital. In addition to funding for capital projects, the World Bank provided policy advice and technical assistance to the developing nations. Official multilateral aid was also channeled through the United Nations.

In general the post-war decades of the 1950s and 1960s saw significant economic growth, along with many developing nations, particularly in Africa, gaining their independence. Maddison labels the 1950–73 era the "golden age," when world per capita income grew at an average annual rate of nearly 3 percent. For the West (the US, Canada, Western Europe, Australia, New Zealand, and Japan), the economic growth rate averaged 3.72 percent a year between 1950 and 1973. For the rest of the world, the annual average increase was lower, but a still impressive 2.83 percent. By 1973 average per capita incomes were nearly $18,900 in the West and $3,000 in the rest of the world. Reflecting the baby booms in the industrialized economies and the demographic transitions of the developing economies, the average annual population growth rates had increased from 0.78 percent (for 1913–50) to 1.05 percent (for 1950–73) in the West and from 0.98 percent to 2.15 percent in the rest of the world (Maddison 2005).

INTERNATIONAL FINANCE, TRADE, AND AID

During the 1960s, the US had experienced strong growth with expansionary fiscal policies, including defense spending for the Vietnam War and social spending for the domestic "war on poverty." As the unemployment rate fell, inflation rose. US balance of payments deficits grew, reflecting heavy investment abroad, which put pressure on official gold reserves held by the US. In 1971, President Nixon suspended the US pledge to convert dollars into gold, effectively ending the gold exchange standard. In the years following, many countries allowed their currencies to float, albeit with various degrees of management. A number of Western European nations, however, established a joint float against the dollar, setting adjustable exchange rates between their currencies. (Over time this exchange rate system would expand and evolve into the European Monetary Union with the adoption of a common currency, the euro, in 1999.) In the mid-1970s, the IMF recognized that there were no longer any set rules of the game for exchange rate practices, and essentially allowed member nations the autonomy to adopt any exchange rate mechanism, save pegging to gold, as long as they did not manipulate their exchange rates to gain unfair competitive advantages.

Over the 1950s and 1960s, GATT had sponsored several rounds of multilateral trade negotiations where trade barriers, especially tariffs, were reduced. International trade grew faster than national outputs, reflecting the growing openness of economies. Nevertheless, the most heavily protected sectors in international trade remained agriculture and labor-intensive manufactures, areas where the less developed economies tended to have the comparative advantages.

Overall official aid from the developed to the developing economies in real terms was only marginally increased over the 1960s; and in terms of per capita receipts, official development assistance declined. As a share of the gross national incomes of the developed economies, official development assistance fell from 0.51 percent in 1960 to 0.34 percent in 1970, both well under the recommended target of 1.0 percent.[2] The impact of the World Bank had grown with the

---

[2] These statistics refer to official development assistance from the nations of the Organisation of Economic Co-operation and Development (OECD), which then included the US, Canada, Japan, Australia, New Zealand, and the Western European nations of Italy, the UK, Austria, Belgium, Finland, the Netherlands, France, Germany, Sweden, and Norway. In 1960, 1965, and 1970,

increased amounts of capital that were directed to the LDCs, with the emphasis on infrastructure and large-scale capital projects. While the developing economies were growing and per capita incomes were rising across Asia, Africa, and Latin America, the numbers of extremely poor in these areas were also increasing. Rapid population growth in the developing nations, in some cases annual growth rates exceeding 3 percent, caused alarm and led to increased attention to birth control programs in the 1960s.

STAGFLATION IN THE 1970S

In contrast with the general growth in national outputs and expansion of international trade over the 1950s and 1960s, the decade of the 1970s witnessed economic turbulence. Poor harvests across the world in the early 1970s led to shortfalls and rising prices for agricultural commodities. In late 1973 sharp increases in oil prices triggered by the embargo of the Organization of Petroleum Exporting Countries (OPEC) produced stagflation (a combination of rising unemployment and inflation) in the oil-importing nations and massive transfers of income to the oil-exporting nations. As will be discussed below, the origins of the external debt crisis in the 1980s can be found in these higher oil prices and the subsequent economic policies adopted by both the developed and developing nations.

By the early 1970s, however, the superpower competition for allies in the developing world was waning—in part, a reflection of the general disenchantment with the Vietnam War and the diminished position of the US in the international economy. Emboldened by the success of OPEC in raising oil prices, the LDCs lobbied for a new international economic order, whereby they would exert greater influence in setting the international rules of the game—rules they believed had been dictated by the developed countries that controlled the IMF, World Bank, and GATT. At the First International Population Conference at Bucharest, Romania, in 1974, the developing nations argued that economic development, not birth control programs, was required for curbing rapid population growth. And more effective and reliable aid and preferential treatment in trade, finance, and investment were sought for fostering economic development. In particular, the developed countries were encouraged to contribute 0.7 percent of their gross national incomes for official development assistance, which was actually less than the 1.0 percent target set in the 1960s, but still significantly greater than the existing aid flows. While the demands of the developing nations for a new order were not heeded, in general, there was a reorientation in development policy in the 1970s—away from an emphasis on physical capital formation, industrialization, and economic growth and toward human capital formation, rural development, and basic needs. Moreover, there was a shift from bilateral to multilateral aid, which was seen to be more effective in promoting economic development than the often tied and conditional assistance given by donor governments.

In 1972, a book entitled *The Limits to Growth: A Report for the Club of Rome's Project on the Predicament of Mankind* (Meadows et al. 1972) was published, the culmination of an ambitious effort by a group of researchers at Massachusetts Institute of Technology to develop a large computer model to simulate world population growth, food production, industrial output, resource depletion,

---

the OECD nations gave $16.4, $20.2, and $18.2 billion (in 1980 constant dollars) respectively in official development assistance, representing 0.51 percent, 0.49 percent, and 0.34 percent of their gross national incomes. Between 1960 and 1970, however, the average annual population growth rates in the low- and middle-income economies of Asia, Africa, the Middle East, and Latin America, were 2.3 percent and 2.6 percent, respectively. See World Bank (1984: Tables 18 and 19).

and pollution emissions. This book and the underlying world model generated considerable controversy.[3]

ECONOMIC MODELS

Before discussing this simulation model, we should review the concept of economic models. **Economic models** are logically consistent frameworks for explaining economic behavior. A formal economic model consists of equations and variables. There are two types of variables: **endogenous variables** (to be explained within the model, e.g., dependent variables) and **exogenous variables** (considered as given, e.g., independent variables). There are three basic types of equations: **behavioral equations** (expressing hypothesized relationships among variables); **identities** (accepted facts or definitions); and **equilibrium conditions** (defining the solution to the model or the conditions yielding a balanced state in the system). For example, the basic model of a market has demand and supply equations (behavioral equations, where the endogenous quantities demanded and supplied are functions of the endogenous price, as well as other exogenous factors such as income and input costs) and an equilibrium condition where the quantity demanded equals the quantity supplied. In macroeconomics, the most basic aggregate demand-aggregate supply model contains: a behavioral equation for aggregate demand, consisting of consumption, investment, government expenditures and net exports; a behavioral equation for aggregate supply that is a function of technology and the effective factors of production; and an equilibrium condition setting aggregate demand equal to aggregate supply to determine the aggregate price level and real national output.

In a growth model like the Solow model to be developed in Chapter 7, there are behavioral equations for output, saving, and labor supply, and an equilibrium condition where net saving equals net investment. Underlying the model are definitions like changes in the physical capital stock due to net investment flows. Typically assumed to be exogenous are the saving rate and the growth rate of the labor force. We can derive growth paths for national output, capital, and labor, and project the model over time, tracking the steady-state equilibrium. The model can be enriched by adding technological change, natural resources, and qualitative growth in the factors of production.

A **simulation model** is based on logically consistent relationships, expressed in behavioral equations, identities, and equilibrium conditions, with estimated or assumed parameters (quantifying the relationships between the endogenous and exogenous variables). For given values for the exogenous variables the determination of the values of the endogenous variables is illustrated. By varying the given underlying parameters and values of the exogenous variables, different scenarios can be depicted.

THE LIMITS TO GROWTH SIMULATION MODEL

For the *Limits to Growth* model, there were behavioral equations for world population, food production, industrial output, resource depletion, and pollution emission. Based on initial values of the variables in the model and allowing for feedback effects (e.g., between population growth, food

---

[3] The origins of this effort stemmed from a meeting of scientists, economists, humanists, industrialists, educators, and civil servants in Rome in 1968. The Club of Rome was formed as an informal network, united by an "overriding conviction that the major problems facing mankind are of such complexity and are so interrelated that traditional institutions and policies are no longer able to cope with them, nor even to come to grips with their full content."

production and consumption; investment and depreciation of physical capital; resource utilization and environmental change), and after verifying the ability of the model to accurately represent the past, the model was projected over time. The conclusion of the authors in 1972 was that:

> If present growth trends in world population, industrialization, pollution, food production, and resource depletion continue unchanged, the limits to growth on this planet will be reached sometime within the next hundred years. The most probable result will be a rather sudden and uncontrollable decline in both population and industrial capacity. (Meadows et al. 1972: 23)

They continued, however:

> It is possible to alter these growth trends and to establish a condition of ecological and economic stability that is sustainable far into the future. The state of global equilibrium could be designed so that the basic material needs of each person on earth are satisfied and each person has an equal opportunity to realize his individual human potential. (Meadows et al. 1972: 24)

Could this projection, conditional upon present trends, simply be dismissed as "Malthus with a computer"? Recall that Malthus had predicted nearly two centuries earlier that the world population, if unchecked, would tend to outpace the means of subsistence, inevitably dooming the human race to a subsistence level of living. This, of course, has not happened, mainly due to birth control and technological progress, including advances in agricultural productivity.

Since the initial publication of *Limits to Growth,* there have been two revisions. To mark the twentieth anniversary, Meadows et al. (1992) published *Beyond the Limits,* where they suggested that humanity had already exceeded the earth's support capacity—citing unsustainable deforestation, soil loss, depletion of fishing stocks, and global warming as evidence. Twelve years later, *Limits to Growth: The 30-Year Update* (Meadows et al. 2004) was published with a revised computer simulation model known as World3.

For an overview of the model and the major linkages and feedback effects between population, output, resources, and the environment represented, see Figure 5.1. Clearly with such a large, complex model, a computer is needed to solve and then simulate the model. Before simulating into the future, however, the model should be verified. To do this, the authors begin in the past, setting the initial conditions and then seeing whether the model can replicate the trends in the variables up through the present. If successful in "explaining" the past, then the model can credibly be used to extrapolate into the future. The World3 model was initiated for 1900 and carried up to 2000. As the authors are careful to state, the model is intended not to predict the future, but to understand the implications of behavioral tendencies in order to inform and influence human choice.

Four basic scenarios

The basic *Limits to Growth* argument is that natural resources (R) are required to produce output (Y). The demand for output, in turn, reflects population (P) and per capita income (y), which is directly related to per capita consumption of goods and services. From the equation for economic growth, $dy/y = dY/Y - dP/P$, we can solve for the growth rate for output, $dY/Y = dy/y + dP/P$.

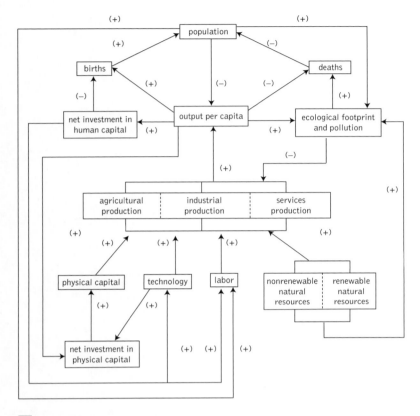

Figure 5.1 *Simplified version of Limits to Growth simulation model*

Some of the linkages in the World3 simulation model are illustrated above, where (+) and (−) indicate positive and negative effects.

This diagram is adapted from Donella Meadows, Jorgen Randers, and Dennis Meadows, Limits to Growth: The 30-Year Update (White River Junction, Vermont: Chelsea Green Publishing Company, 2004): Figures 4-4, 4-5, and 4-6.

Recall from Chapter 2 that carrying capacity was defined as the maximum number of people that can be supported in an area given the available resources, technology, and resource utilization rate. **Ecological footprint** refers to the "total burden humankind places on earth," and can be measured as the land area that would be required to provide the resources for the production of goods and services and absorb the wastes generated by the population. Specifically, the ecological footprint in the World3 model is the sum of three components: the arable land used for crop production, the urban land used for industrial infrastructure, and the amount of absorption land that is required to neutralize the emissions of pollutants.[4]

[4]See Meadows et al. (2004: 138, 293). The authors refer to the work of Mathis Wackernagel et al. (2002: 9266) who defined the ecological footprint as "the area of biologically productive land and water required to produce the resources consumed and to assimilate the wastes generated by humanity, under the predominant management and production practices in any given year." Moreover, Wackernagel et al. (2002: 9268) measure the rapidly increasing ecological footprint:

For each year since 1961, we compare humanity's demand for natural capital to the earth's biological productivity. The calculation provides evidence that human activities have exceeded the biosphere's capacity since the 1980s. This overshoot can

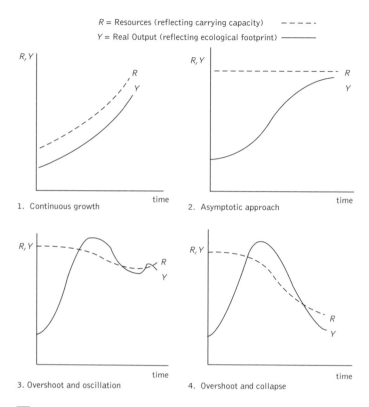

R = Resources (reflecting carrying capacity) ----

Y = Real Output (reflecting ecological footprint) ———

1. Continuous growth

2. Asymptotic approach

3. Overshoot and oscillation

4. Overshoot and collapse

Figure 5.2 *Four scenarios in the long run*

There are four basic future scenarios in the World3 simulation model.

If we then consider the human population and the planet Earth, and let *Y*, the output of goods and services, represent the ecological footprint (i.e., total demands on resources) and *R*, the natural resources, represent the carrying capacity of the world, there are basically four long-run scenarios, reflecting the trends in *Y* and *R* (see Figure 5.2).

Scenario 1, with continuous growth, might have seemed feasible two centuries ago, when there was little population pressure on natural resources or pollution. Some still argue that technology will continue to advance, increasing the carrying capacity so that there are no limits to growth, since there are no limits to human ingenuity and technological progress.

Scenario 2, the asymptotic approach, reflects a logistic curve for output and recognizes that the world is finite, especially the nonrenewable natural resources and the ability of the environment to absorb the wastes generated by humans. While technology can increase the means of subsistence (e.g., improving agricultural yields and reducing the natural resource inputs per unit of output), exponential growth—either in population or per capita consumption—cannot continue in the long run with a closed system like the planet Earth.

---

be expressed as the extent to which human area demand exceeds nature's supply; whereas humanity's load corresponded to 70% of the biosphere's capacity in 1961, this percentage grew to 120% by 1999. In other words, 20% overshoot means that it would require 1.2 earths, or one earth for 1.2 years, to regenerate what humanity used in 1999.

The authors of World3 maintain that the global society is currently above its carrying capacity, that is, the ecological footprint has exceeded the carrying capacity, and therefore one of the following two scenarios is likely.

In Scenario 3, the ecological footprint, indicated by the output of goods and services, with the related demands on natural resources, as sources of inputs, and the environment, as a sink for the waste, has overshot the carrying capacity. This overshoot is manifested in environmental deterioration (e.g., deforestation, desertification, soil erosion, depletion of fish, and global warming). If the damage is not irreversible, then it is possible to recover. Recovery, however, will involve new modes of behavior, including greater conservation. In short, "business as usual" is no longer sustainable.

Finally, Scenario 4 depicts overshoot and collapse. As in Scenario 3, the ecological footprint exceeds the carrying capacity, but there has been irreversible damage. The result will be long-run declines in the carrying capacity and output produced, implying a reduced population and/or reduced consumption per capita.

A key "conflict" inherent in World3 is that between technological progress, which can reduce the amount of natural resources needed per unit of output produced, and the supplies of the effective natural resources remaining. As noted, nonrenewable resources will be depleted with use, and renewable resources are limited in the amounts available for production in any period of time. Recall the classical economists' concern with diminishing returns to labor and rising marginal cost of food production as additional, less fertile land was brought under cultivation. Another conflict, though, exists at the other end of the cycle, between the production and consumption of goods and services and the ability of the environment to assimilate the resulting emissions and wastes.

Future worlds

We might begin with the baseline reference for World3. The size of the world population in 2000 was 6 billion, and the authors estimated that more than 70 percent of the total stocks of nonrenewable resources were remaining. Nevertheless, continuing with "business as usual" or the current trends, within a few decades economic growth would cease and industrial output would decline—mainly due to the accelerating costs of finding, extracting, and processing nonrenewable resources that reduce the ability to invest in the industrial physical capital needed for the production of output.

Recall that Ricardo had anticipated a squeeze on profits with the rising share of rents in national incomes as land became more valuable. That is, increased production of food required existing lands under cultivation to be farmed more intensively and marginal and less fertile lands to be brought under cultivation. In Ricardo's model, the decline in profits reduced the ability of capitalists (factory owners) to invest in new capital beyond replacing the depreciated capital, leading to an eventual stationary state.

In this baseline scenario for World3, population peaks around the year 2030 and then declines due to rising mortality from insufficient food production (hints of Malthus's ultimate check to population growth). The lack of health services contributes to the decline in human welfare.[5] In

---

[5] The authors of World3 use the United Nations Development Programme's Human Development Index (at the time calculated as a weighted average of life expectancy at birth, adult literacy and school enrolment rates, and per capita gross national incomes in PPP dollars) to measure human welfare. In Chapter 11 we will discuss the Human Development Index and its recent revision.

short, in the World3 model, continuing current trends in resource use lead to the "overshoot and collapse" outcome.

Even when the authors of World3 doubled the amounts of nonrenewable resources and allowed for technological progress in harvesting these resources, the "overshoot and collapse" outcome is only postponed. Human population and output would increase even more before declining due to overwhelming pollution, falling land productivity and deteriorating health. *A fortiori*, Meadows et al. (2004: 150) acknowledge:

> World3 has no war, no labor strikes, no corruption, no drug addiction, no crime, no terrorism. Its simulated population does its best to solve perceived problems, undistracted by struggles over political power or ethnic intolerance or by corruption. Since it lacks many social limits, World3 does paint an overly optimistic picture of future options.

There are numerous other scenarios set forth by permutations of World3, but the basic message remains that current trends in production, resource use, and emissions are unsustainable. For example, in another scenario, replacement level fertility is attained in 2002, although population momentum is still present, which results in world population peaking at 7.5 billion in 2040. The reduced population growth allows for increased per capita consumption and greater life expectancy. The greater per capita output, however, still yields accelerating pollution and collapse. Even if, along with replacement level fertility in 2002, a cap is placed on industrial output at an average that is 10 percent higher than in 2000, the model projects a deterioration in human welfare due to greater pollution. Here the stress on resources occurs in agriculture with a decline in food per capita before some recovery near the end of the century—albeit at a lower level than the peak in the early part of the century.

Since the global economy has already overshot the carrying capacity, according to the authors of World3, reaching zero population growth and zero economic growth will not be enough. Continued technological progress to curb pollution, increase natural resource yields, and conserve on natural resources will be required. There is a sustainable equilibrium, however, in World3 with around 8 billion people (likely to be well under the future size of the world's population once stabilized). Zero population growth is combined with constant output per person (i.e., industrial growth is zero), but with continued technological progress to abate pollution, conserve on resources, and increase productivity. This stationary state, with constant per capita consumption, is nevertheless compatible with continued development and improvement in the quality of life. (Recall the classical economist John Stuart Mill's vision of a stationary state with "as much scope as ever for all kinds of mental culture, and moral and social progress.")

We might remember that *Limits to Growth: The 30-Year Update* was published in 2004, before the heightened awareness of global warming. Indeed, the global concern now appears to be more with the deterioration of the environment from climate change than with physical limits to nonrenewable natural resources. Despite the consensus in the scientific community on climate change and the predominant role played by humans over the last two centuries, there are still skeptics about any limits to growth.

A STEADY-STATE ECONOMY

Another work in the 1970s that addressed limits to growth was Herman Daly's *Steady-State Economics: The Economics of Biophysical Equilibrium and Moral Growth*. Daly (1977: 2) begins by saying that:

a steady-state economy is a necessary and desirable future state of affairs and that its attainment requires quite major changes in values, as well as radical, but nonrevolutionary, institutional reforms. Once we have replaced the basic premise of "more is better" with the much sounder axiom that "enough is best," the social and technical problems of moving to a steady state become solvable, perhaps even trivial.

Daly modernizes the Malthusian specter of unchecked population growth outpacing the means of subsistence. The ultimate limit to economic growth, according to Daly, is the supply of low entropy. **Entropy** is a measure of the energy that is no longer capable of being converted into work. Daly invokes the first and second laws of thermodynamics to support his thesis. First, neither matter nor energy can be created or destroyed. Second, energy cannot be recycled and matter can be recycled only at less than 100 percent efficiency.

The use of resources to produce goods and services involves the return to nature of high-entropy matter (with decreased potential for energy conversion into work). And, the ability of the environment to absorb and recycle the wastes is limited. Thus Daly (1977: 17) proposes a steady-state economy defined as:

> an economy with constant stocks of people and artifacts, maintained at some desired, sufficient levels by low rates of maintenance "throughput," that is by the lowest feasible flows of matter and energy from the first stage of production (depletion of low entropy materials from the environment) to the last stage of consumption (pollution of the environment with high entropy wastes and exotic materials).

Continued economic growth, coupled with population growth, requires increased energy and resources to supply the greater stocks of people and artifacts. While technological change may increase the outputs attained for given inputs of energy and resources and even increase the ability of the environment to absorb wastes, it cannot eliminate the rise in entropy.

Daly argues that we need to turn away from the modern and unsustainable addiction to economic growth. Moreover, once we withdraw the hollow promise of more growth as a solution to poverty, we must confront the gross inequities in the distribution of income and wealth. Thus, Daly sets forth a framework for a steady-state economy.

Institutions for a steady-state economy

Daly's blueprint for a steady-state economy combines "macrostability," by setting absolute bounds for population size, resource use, income and wealth, with "microvariability," by allowing for resource allocations within these bounds to be determined by the market mechanism. Three institutions define his steady-state economy. To stabilize population, marketable birth licenses would be issued. Consistent with zero population growth in the long run, each woman would be given licenses for 2.1 births, divisible into units of 0.1 births. Those who desired additional children could purchase deciles of births in the market from those women not using their full quotas.

To stabilize the stocks on renewable natural resources and to reduce the use of nonrenewable resources, quotas would be set and depletion licenses would be auctioned off by the government.

109

The utilization of renewable resources would be held to rates consistent with their long-run sustainability (e.g., the regeneration of forests and maintenance of fishing stocks). Restricting access to nonrenewable resources would drive up the market prices of the depletion licenses, encouraging conservation and the substitution of renewable resources (e.g., wind or solar energy for fossil fuels). The government would capture the quota rents or the revenues from the sale of the depletion licenses. Limiting the use of resources should reduce pollution and the return of high-entropy matter to the environment.

Limiting the use of resources would also restrain the production of goods and services and the generation of real income for the present population. To address poverty and the issue of equity, Daly proposes minimum and maximum limits to individual income and a maximum limit on individual wealth. Income above the maximum would be taxed at 100 percent and redistributed to those below the minimum. Revenues from the auctioning of the depletion quotas could also be used, if needed, for the required income transfers.

Clearly, Daly's steady-state economy would involve a larger role for the government and the loss of individual freedoms in reproduction, the earning of income, and the accumulation of wealth. Enforcement would be a problem—especially with unlicensed births and undeclared income. Daly's steady-state economy would require fundamental changes in attitudes. While economic growth would be zero, economic development could continue. Reducing the resources needed to attain a given level of satisfaction or, alternatively, deriving more satisfaction from a given utilization of resources would constitute economic development. More enlightened use of leisure time would substitute for greater consumption of goods.

Given the present international disparities in per capita incomes and resource utilization, Daly (1977: 148) argues that the developed countries should be the first to adopt the steady-state economy:

> It is absolutely a waste of time as well as morally backward to preach steady-state doctrines to underdeveloped countries before the overdeveloped countries have taken any measure to reduce their own population growth or the growth of their per capita resource consumption.

It is easy to dismiss Daly as an alarmist. Like Meadows et al., the authors of the World3 model, Daly warns of limits to growth in the global economy due to resource constraints and increased pollution. While the developed economies have reduced their population growth—in fact all except the US have below replacement-level fertility—there are no signs of voluntarily reduced per capita consumptions.

In sum, Daly's entropy thesis directly addresses the fundamental question of whether economic growth can continue indefinitely. And Daly offered a model of a steady-state economy which, while arguably draconian, did provide a blueprint for a more sustainable development.

NO LIMITS TO GROWTH

Not surprisingly, at the time, there was strong opposition to the *Limits to Growth* model and Daly's steady-state economics—and this remains so today. Opponents argue that the potential for humans to advance science and technology is unlimited. Moreover, qualitative improvements in the effective factors of production can compensate for any depletion of nonrenewable natural resources. Indeed, accepting any stationary state would reduce, if not undermine, the incentives to develop these very technologies and realize the qualitative improvements in the factors of production necessary for continued economic growth.

Similarly, relying on human ingenuity and unbounded technological progress, many economists and other social scientists discount possible environmental thresholds—as reflected in the capacity of the natural environment to absorb the wastes generated by economic activity and still provide the necessary services for human existence, such as clean air to breathe, water to drink, and land to grow food. As qualitative growth in labor will continue with human capital formation and physical capital will improve with embodied technological progress, gains in the inherent productivity of natural resources will be realized and will offset any declines in the quantities of the same resources. Effective natural resources will continue to increase and economic growth can be sustained in the long run.

These critics pointed to the long-run declines in the real prices of natural resources over the last part of the twentieth century as evidence of the market mechanism addressing any relative scarcities of resources and inducing the development and use of substitutes. The market mechanism reflects scarcity with relative price increases, which induces actions to both conserve and develop new products. Indeed, even that nonrenewable resources are becoming scarcer is contested. According to Clive Cook (2005: 19):

> Natural resources are not running out, if you measure effective supply in relation to demand. The reason is that scarcity raises prices, which spurs innovation; new sources are found, the efficiency of extraction goes up, existing supplies are used more economically, and substitutes are invented. In 1970, global reserves of copper were estimated at 280 m tons; during the next 30 years about 270 m tons were consumed. Where did estimated reserves of copper stand at the turn of the century? Not at 10 m tons, but at 340 m tons. Available supplies have surged, and, it so happens, demand per unit of economic activity has been falling: copper is being replaced in many of its main industrial applications by other materials (notably, fibre-optic cable instead of copper wire for telecommunications).
>
> . . .The same is true for other key minerals. Reserves of bauxite in 1970 were 5.3 billion tons; the amount consumed between 1970 and 2000 was around 3 billion tons; reserves by the end of the century stood at 25 billion tons. Or take energy. Oil reserves in 1970: 580 billion barrels. Oil consumed between 1970 and the turn of the century: 690 billion barrels. Oil reserves in 2000: 1,050 billion barrels. And so on.

We will present evidence on natural resource and primary commodity prices, as well as on climate change and environmental deterioration, in later chapters. We now briefly illustrate how the market mechanism addresses scarcity, before returning to an overview of economic growth in the world over the last decades of the twentieth century.

MARKET MECHANISM AND PRICE SIGNALS

In perfect competition many buyers and many sellers, none with any market power, exchange commodities. Prices serve to equilibrate the demands and supplies. The market is self-regulating, with prices changing in response to disequilibria. In particular, an excess demand for or shortage of a commodity would induce a price increase until a new price is reached where the intents of buyers and sellers are again matched. An excess supply or surplus of a commodity, in contrast, would induce a price decrease until a new equilibrium or balance is restored.

Consider the markets for two goods that are substitutes, such as home heating oil (h) and solar heat (s); see Figure 5.3. These two sources of energy are not perfect substitutes. For example, the initial investment in the solar panels and distribution system may be greater; and for solar heating you will need at least some sun during the day. Home heating oil, in a sense, then, may be more convenient and initially require less of an investment.

The inverse relationship between the quantity demanded of the commodity and its own price reflects the **law of demand**, which is illustrated by the downward-sloping demand curve. The market demand curve for a commodity is drawn holding constant determinants such as the number of demanders, the average income of the demanders, tastes and preferences, and prices of related goods (e.g., substitutes and complements). The positive relationship between the quantity supplied of the commodity and its own price reflects the **law of supply**, which is captured by the upward-sloping supply curve. The market supply curve for a commodity is drawn holding constant determinants such as technology used in the production of the commodity, the prices of the inputs used, the number of suppliers, and government regulations, taxes, and subsidies.

The initial equilibria in the two markets are given by the points E_0, with P_0 and Q_0 as the market equilibrium prices and quantities transacted during the period. An increase in the market equilibrium price can be due to an increase in the demand, a decrease in the supply, or a combination of both. Suppose that in the market for home heating oil the supply decreases from S_h to S_h' (e.g., with higher input costs, perhaps due to higher petroleum prices). Clearly the market-clearing price would rise, from P_0 to P_1, indicative of the excess demand or shortage, while the quantity transacted would fall. The competitive market automatically adjusts, however, as the initial shortage of $Q_0 - Q^{s'} = FE_0$, results in a rise in the market price, which then reduces the quantity demanded (indicated by the movement along the demand curve from E_0 to E_1) and increases the quantity supplied (indicated by the movement along the new supply curve from F to E_1) until the market is back in equilibrium. Not only does this market for home heating oil adjust, but so also would the related market for solar heat. The rise in the price of home heating oil, *ceteris paribus*, would increase the demand for solar heat, a substitute, (from D_s to D_s'), creating an excess demand for solar heat ($Q^{d'} - Q_0 = E_0G$) and pushing up the market-clearing price for solar heat. Thus, the market system is self-regulating, automatically and efficiently adjusting to disequilibria. Furthermore, if the increased revenues generated greater profits in the solar heating market, additional resources would be allocated to this market (as new firms would enter and existing firms may expand by investing more capital).

So, an increase in the relative or real price of a commodity over time, (i.e., adjusted for inflation or the general rise in the average price level), would indicate relative scarcity of the commodity. If nonrenewable natural resources are becoming increasingly scarce as they are depleted, then we would expect to find the real prices of these nonrenewable resources rising over time, as the demands for the resources increase with population and economic growth and the supplies shrink.

DEBT PROBLEMS OF THE 1980S

From the end of World War II to the early 1970s, most capital flows to the developing nations consisted of official loans (directly from developed country governments or channeled through

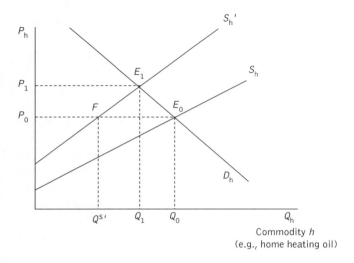

Commodity h
(e.g., home heating oil)

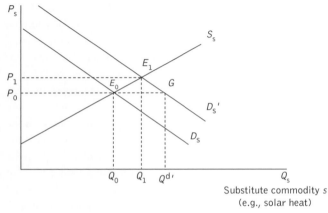

Substitute commodity s
(e.g., solar heat)

Figure 5.3 *Market adjustments*

An increase in the market price of commodity h with a fall in its supply from S_h to S_h' will increase the demand for a substitute commodity s from D_s to D_s'.

multilateral agencies such as the World Bank), short-term trade credit from foreign exporters (often guaranteed by the same developed country governments), and foreign direct investment (which, unlike official loans and trade credit, did not add to the external debt of the developing nations).[6] As noted, in the 1950s the LDCs also began to receive substantial amounts of foreign aid, which reduced their current account deficits and the need for offsetting surpluses in their capital and official settlements accounts. Even so, problems with repayment of debt did arise, and the Paris Club was set up by the developed countries in 1956 for the purpose of rescheduling debts to official creditors.

The OPEC price hikes in late 1973 marked the beginning of the sharp increase in private commercial bank lending to the developing nations. The international price of a barrel of petroleum

---

[6]This account of the debt crises is drawn from Hess and Ross (1997: 473–484).

quadrupled, from under $3 in late 1972 to nearly $12 by the end of 1973. With the higher prices and the short-run inelastic demand for oil, the oil-exporting nations reaped large current account surpluses, significant portions of which were deposited in Western banks. The banks then extended loans to developing nations to finance the higher current account deficits brought on by the escalating oil-import bills.

This **recycling of petrodollars** seemed to be mutually advantageous. The OPEC nations did not want to bear the risk of lending directly to the LDC oil importers, preferring the safe returns on their funds deposited in Western banks. These banks, flush with deposits, were willing to make loans to the developing countries at rates of interest that were generally higher than could be earned on domestic lending. The LDC governments were eager to borrow in order to finance the import surpluses needed to keep their economies growing. Moreover, despite the higher rates of interest on the private loans, there were fewer conditions attached than on official loans. And inflation discounted the nominal rates charged, making the real rates of interest quite low, even negative at times. The developing nations also counted on continued growth in export revenues to service their expanding debts.[7]

By the second half of the 1970s the international economy had recovered from the stagflation induced by the oil price shocks. The developed nations had followed the lead of the US in adopting expansionary policies to deal with the rise in unemployment. For the most part, the oil-importing LDCs, with the financing of their current account deficits, had been able to maintain their economic growth. Inflation, however, remained a concern. In an attempt to protect their real returns from unanticipated inflation, commercial banks began to charge variable rates of interest on their new loans.

In retrospect, the banks might not have paid enough attention to the creditworthiness of the borrowing LDC governments and to the projects funded by the loans. The developing nations, in turn, may not always have used the loans in the most productive ways, that is, to increase their future capacity for repayment. Then, in 1979, with the Iranian revolution and the fall of the shah of Iran, came panic buying to stockpile oil, a second round of oil price hikes, and another burst of inflation. The surging current account deficits required renewed commercial bank lending.

In contrast to the oil price shocks in 1973–74, where the policy emphasis in the developed countries had been to restore employment levels, the priority now was to rein in inflation. In particular, the US, under its newly appointed chairman of the Federal Reserve, Paul Volcker, implemented contractionary monetary policy. Initially the tighter credit boosted the already elevated nominal interest rates. Interest-sensitive sectors such as construction, capital goods, and consumer durables were hit hard. A recession ensued. The deflationary monetary policy, however, contrasted with the expansionary fiscal policy package of tax cuts and increased defense spending set in motion in 1981 by the new Reagan administration. Federal budget deficits grew, which pushed up the demand for credit. Real interest rates in the US rose sharply, as the decline in nominal interest rates lagged behind the reduction in the inflation rate (from the tight monetary policy). The high real interest rates attracted foreign capital, and as the US capital account surplus grew, the dollar appreciated. The stronger dollar hurt the competitiveness of the US; consequently the US current account sharply deteriorated into large deficits.

---

[7]We should also note that not all developing countries received commercial bank lending. The poorer countries continued to rely on foreign aid and official lending. Some of the wealthier Arab OPEC nations did increase substantially the aid given to oil-importing developing economies, especially to other Arab states.

The severe recession of 1981–82 in the US spread to other industrialized nations, which were then forced to adopt tighter monetary policies to stem the outflow of savings to the US. On several fronts the less developed economies—especially the highly indebted nations—were adversely affected.

First, the international rise in interest rates in the late 1970s and early 1980s directly increased the debt burdens of the LDCs. Not only did the new loans carry the higher rates of interest, but also variable rates on existing loans were adjusted upward. Second, the appreciation of the dollar directly increased the burden of the debt denominated in dollars—since more of the currency of the developing nations would be required to pay off each appreciated dollar of foreign debt. Third, the recession in the developed economies reduced the demands for exports from the LDCs. A rise in protectionism in the US and Europe further limited developing nation exports. Fourth, the reversal of the run-up in primary product prices from the early 1970s accelerated with the international recession. For many of the poorer developing economies, primary products accounted for the bulk of their export revenues. And, after 1981, oil prices began to fall, a reflection of both lower demands and increased supplies of oil in the world market. The oil exporters were left in a vulnerable position, especially nations such as Mexico that had accumulated large foreign debt even as their export revenues were booming.

Mexico's announcement in August 1982, after a 30 percent devaluation of the peso in February of that year, that it could not service its debt was a shot heard around the financial world. At the time, Mexico's external debt exceeded $85 billion (approximately equal to half its GDP), and included large loans from some major US banks. Soon the realization set in that other highly indebted developing nations, including Brazil, Argentina, Chile, and Venezuela, were in similar predicaments. The US responded with official loans to Mexico for balance of payments support. The IMF also extended credit and encouraged reluctant commercial banks to make new loans to Mexico, all conditional upon reform of Mexico's economy.

After 1982, however, voluntary commercial bank lending to developing nations was sharply scaled back. Earlier, when developing nations were unable to meet their debt service payments on time, commercial banks would roll over the loans, usually at higher rates of interest, in effect covering the interest and principal due on the old debt with new lending. This allowed the debtor nations to avoid defaulting and kept the loans as performing assets on the balance sheets of commercial banks. Meanwhile, the debt of the developing nations mushroomed. Some nations slipped into arrears, forcing numerous debt reschedulings, or postponements of the payments due on the outstanding debt.[8]

Without new lending, the indebted nations were unable to cover their current account deficits. For numerous of the LDCs, **capital flight** also contributed to their balance of payments difficulties. Especially in Latin America, savings were shifted abroad, not only to take advantage of the high real interest rates in the US and other developed countries, but also in anticipation of devaluations in the domestic currencies. With weak current account balances, often a reflection of overvalued domestic currencies, and insufficient official reserve assets to cover the balance of payments deficits, debtor nations turned to the IMF. As with Mexico, the IMF did extend credit to the developing nations, and even persuaded reluctant commercial banks to make additional

---

[8] Regional differences in the debt of the developing nations should be noted. The greatest exposure of the Western commercial banks was in Latin America, where much of the debt had been incurred on market terms. In sub-Saharan Africa, the other region heavily burdened by foreign debt, most of the loans were official, held by multilateral institutions and governments, usually on softer terms (i.e., concessional interest rates and more generous repayment schedules). In the Middle East and North Africa, the decline in oil prices that began in the early 1980s led to a reversal of the current account surpluses of the oil-producing nations. Asian nations, with generally more prudent economic policies, had largely avoided severe debt problems.

loans. Such assistance, however, was to be conditional upon the recipient nations' taking the IMF medicine.

The IMF medicine

The standard prescription of the IMF, consistent with prevailing economic theory, was devaluation, tighter monetary and fiscal policies, and a greater reliance on the market mechanism. Devaluation was recommended in order to redress overvalued currencies and improve international competitiveness. Fiscal discipline was needed to improve government budget balances and, hopefully, generate public saving. Tighter monetary policy was in order to keep inflation down (and real exchange rates from appreciating) and stimulate saving (with positive real interest rates and through a repatriation of capital from abroad).

An important component of the orthodox stabilization policy involved a shift to more market-oriented policies and private enterprise. Import barriers were to be reduced and exports encouraged. Inefficient and heavily subsidized state-owned enterprises were to be privatized. Price controls were to be dismantled so that resource allocations would respond to market-determined prices. Subsidies for consumption, such as agricultural pricing policies that held down the price of food in urban areas, were to be eliminated. The underlying premise was that the adoption of such measures would not only resolve the balance of payments deficits, but also create an environment conducive to sustained economic growth and debt reduction.

To reduce foreign indebtedness, a nation has to generate current account surpluses. For most developing nations, especially in the 1980s, foreign aid could not be counted on to produce current account surpluses. The primary options for improving the current account were expanding exports and curbing imports. Recall that a current account surplus means that the nation is a net saver over the period. To realize positive net private saving, for a given national income, personal and business saving must exceed gross private domestic investment. Tighter monetary policies that boost the real rate of interest should encourage saving and discourage investment.

If real national income is declining from the austerity measures, however, the ability to save will be hampered. Moreover, given the existing low capital–labor ratios in developing economies, reducing investment and physical capital formation diminishes the potential for future growth. On the public side, given the underdeveloped tax systems and the demands for government expenditures—from education to the infrastructure to national defense—realizing a surplus in the government budget is difficult.

The IMF medicine proved tough to swallow for the developing economies. Imposing austerity measures consistent with economic tightening in nations with low average incomes and prevailing poverty was, to say the least, politically challenging. Urban riots were sparked by the policy reforms required for IMF assistance. During recessions and periods of structural adjustment, the poor may suffer disproportionately. With little wealth to draw on, the poor are more vulnerable to income losses and cutbacks in government services. For the severely indebted nations, the economic consequences were dramatic.

For all the developing nations (i.e., the low- and middle-income economies) the average growth rates for gross domestic product, private and government consumption, gross domestic investment, and merchandise imports significantly declined over the 1980s, especially for the severely indebted nations. The reduced levels of imports (almost certainly including imports of the capital goods, intermediate goods, and raw materials needed for production and development projects) and the fall in investment needed to maintain and expand the physical capital stock not only contributed to the declines in real per capita incomes, but also reduced the potential for economic growth. Despite the adjustments undertaken and the deterioration in economic performance, the debt burden of the developing world increased.[9]

UNEVEN GROWTH IN THE 1990S

In the 1990s, there was considerable diversity across the world in terms of economic growth. For example, the US slipped into a brief recession at the beginning of the decade. Then, with greater fiscal discipline and the information technology revolution, the US experienced a decade-long economic expansion, one with steady, albeit moderate growth, low unemployment, subdued inflation, and improving federal government budget balances. Despite this "golden economy," the large US current account deficits continued, indicating a nation chronically consuming beyond its means. With the dissolution of the Soviet Union at the end of the 1980s, the subsequent transformations of formerly command economies and communist states into more market-oriented economies and democratic states proved to be difficult. For the developing economies, especially for the rapidly growing East Asian nations, foreign capital flows resumed. In a retrospective of the 1990s, the World Bank (2005: 9) summarized:

> In reality the 1990s was favorable for developing countries, even if not every country found ways to benefit. Exports from developing countries as a group grew much faster than in previous decades. Real interest rates were lower. Debt obligations claimed fewer resources, and foreign direct investment and financial flows to developing nations were much larger.

Two of the five disappointments over the decade noted by the World Bank (2005: 31–32) were the "length, depth, and variance" of the recessions of the transition economies of Eastern Europe and the former Soviet Union and the "severity and intensity" of the financial crises in East Asia.[10] We turn now to these two signal developments.

The collapse of the Soviet system and difficult economic transitions

By the late 1970s the economic inefficiencies and the low standards of living characterizing the command economies had became more obvious.[11] In 1986 Mikhail Gorbachev assumed power

---

[9] From 1980 to 1990, public and publicly guaranteed external debt in the low-income economies increased from $100 billion (12.3 percent of gross domestic products) to $340 billion (38.2 percent of GDPs). For the middle-income developing nations, the increase was from $281 billion (12.1 percent of GDPs) in 1980 to $774 billion (22.0 percent of GDPs) in 1990. These statistics are from World Bank (2000: Tables 4.2, 4.16, and 4.18; 2002: Tables 4.2, 4.16, and 4.18). Public and publicly guaranteed external debt comprises long-term external obligations of public debtors, including the national government, and the external obligations of private debtors that are guaranteed for repayment by a public entity. Total external debt also includes private nonguaranteed long-term debt, use of IMF credit, and short-term debt (with an original maturity of less than 1 year), and interest in arrears on long-term debt.

[10] The three other disappointments cited by the World Bank were Argentina's financial and economic implosion following its currency crisis, the general lagging economic performance of the Latin American region, and the continued economic stagnation of sub-Saharan Africa. With respect to Latin America, Rozenwurcel (2007) offers a good account of the "dismal long-run performance" of Latin American economies in the post-World War II era, regardless of whether the prevailing development strategy was inward-looking industrialization or the more outward-oriented, "market friendly" approach recommended by the World Bank in the 1990s. The World Bank (2005) also discusses "three pleasant surprises" during the decade: the rapid economic growth of China, India, and Vietnam; the continued progress in social indicators such as education and health care that were somewhat independent of economic circumstances; and the resilience of the world to the economic shocks that took place.

[11] This brief account of the collapse of the Soviet Union is largely drawn from Hess and Ross (1997: 541–542). The following description of the economic transitions draws on World Bank (2005: 200–206).

Table 5.1 *Average annual real GDP growth rates*

	1970–80	1980–90	1990–2000	2000–10
World	3.6%	3.3%	2.9%	2.7%
Low-income economies	4.3%	4.5%	3.0%	5.5%
Lower middle-income economies	5.1%	4.0%	3.8%	6.3%
Upper middle-income economies	5.9%	1.7%	3.9%	6.5%
High-income economies	3.2%	3.3%	2.7%	1.8%
By region: low- and middle-income economies				
East Asia and Pacific	6.9%	7.5%	8.5%	9.4%
Europe & Central Asia	5.4%	2.1%	−1.8%	5.4%
Latin America & Caribbean	5.4%	1.7%	3.2%	3.8%
Middle East & N. Africa	…	2.0%	3.8%	4.7%
South Asia	3.5%	5.6%	5.5%	7.4%
Sub-Saharan Africa	3.8%	1.6%	2.5%	5.0%

Note: Over the years, nations shift into different income classes, for example, from low-income to lower middle-income economies or from upper middle-income to high-income economies, so the aggregate averages by income groups may not be strictly comparable sets of countries over the decades. For example, rapid economic growth elevated China from a lower middle-income economy to an upper middle-income economy by the end of the first decade of the twenty-first century.

Sources: 1970–80, World Bank (1995: Table 4.2); 1980–90, World Bank (2003: Table 4.1); 1990–2010, World Bank (2012: Table 4.1).

in the Soviet Union and initiated reforms intended to increase political dialogue (*glasnost*) and restructure the command economy (*perestroika*). Economic change was not easy. Some prices were freed to rise to market levels and some private, for-profit cooperatives began offering services. Nevertheless, large state enterprises continued to dominate the planned Soviet economy.

In the early 1990s the communist systems of Eastern Europe and the Soviet Union began to unravel. With the collapse of the Berlin Wall in November 1989, East Germany (the German Democratic Republic) began the process of reunification with West Germany (the Federal Republic of Germany). Concurrently, other nations of Eastern Europe, including Hungary, Romania, Poland, and Bulgaria and Czechoslovakia, asserted their economic and political independence from Moscow.

In autumn 1991, the three Baltic republics, Estonia, Latvia, and Lithuania, declared their independence. By the end of the year, the Soviet Union had formally disbanded. Russia and the other 11 republics (minus these three Baltic states) became a loose economic and political federation called the Commonwealth of Independent States (CIS).

The 1990s proved to be challenging for the nations of Eastern Europe and Central Asia as they sought to liberalize their political systems and economies. Firms had to learn to determine how much and how best to produce their goods and services—decisions that had essentially been made before by the central authorities. Growth rates in real national outputs were negative and physical capital formation declined (refer back to Table 1.5). As formerly controlled prices were freed up, inflation soared and eroded the purchasing power of private savings. The incidence of extreme poverty (the percentage of people living on less than $1.25 per day in 2005 PPP dollars) in Europe and Central Asia increased from 1.5 percent in 1987 to 1.9 percent in 1990 and then to 3.8 percent in 1999 (World Bank 2012: Table 2.8).

118

Developing new tax administrations took time, while heavy demand for government spending, especially with the rising unemployment, resulted in large fiscal deficits. Even so, public spending on education, health care, and social welfare suffered. The World Bank (2005: 33) captures the difficult transitions as follows:

> Not even the most pessimistic observers in 1990 foresaw that the *typical* transition recession would be substantially larger than the Great Depression in the United States and that the time taken to recovery would be more than twice as long as for the defeated countries after World War II.

There was also marked variation across the transition economies. The World Bank cites a U-shaped relationship between the depth of the economic declines and the countries' proximity to Europe (measured by the distance from Brussels).[12] Nevertheless, the transition economies did engage strong economic growth in the following decade, and several of these nations even joined the European Union.

Ironically, the other region of the developing world that experienced profound economic shocks in the 1990s, although much briefer, was rapidly growing East Asia. The sharp recessions here, however, reflected financial crises.

East Asian currency crisis

In less than a year, East Asia was transformed from the world's fastest-growing region into a severe recession due to a currency crisis that began in summer 1997, set off by Thailand's devaluation of its currency, the baht.[13] The origins of the crisis might be traced back to the early 1990s. Expansionary US monetary policy intended to pull the US economy out of the recession of 1990–91 resulted in low interest rates in the US. This, coupled with sluggish growth in Europe and Japan, led international investors to seek higher returns in the rapidly growing Asian economies (especially Thailand, Malaysia, Indonesia, and South Korea). The subsequent heavy foreign investment (both direct and portfolio through mutual funds and loans) and inflows of capital to these nations that were pegging their currencies to the US dollar significantly improved their capital accounts, resulting in balance of payments surpluses. The resulting upward pressure on the exchange values of these currencies (incipient appreciation) required intervention by their central banks supplying (selling) their own currencies in the foreign exchange markets. This foreign exchange intervention, in turn, increased the domestic money supplies and inflation rates. While the nominal exchanges rates remained constant and pegged to the US dollar, the real exchange rates appreciated, undermining the international competitiveness of these nations and worsening their trade balances and current accounts.

The massive increases in bank credit in these Asian nations, often used for speculative investments in commercial and residential properties (malls, offices, apartment complexes), combined

---

[12] The World Bank (2005: 200–201) notes the much greater declines in national outputs and slower recoveries in the countries of the Commonwealth of Independent States (Armenia, Azerbaijan, Belarus, Georgia, Kazakhstan, the Kyrgyz Republic, Moldova, the Russian Federation, Tajikistan, Turkmenistan, Ukraine, and Uzbekistan) than in the Central and Southeastern European countries (Albania, Bosnia and Herzegovina, Bulgaria, Croatia, the Czech Republic, Estonia, Hungary, Latvia, Lithuania, the Former Yugoslav Republic of Macedonia, Poland, Romania, the Slovak Republic and Slovenia).

[13] It should be noted there were other currency crises during the decade, including Mexico (1994–95), Russia (1998), and Brazil (1999). Then early in the next decade, Turkey (2001) and Argentina (2001–02) experienced currency collapses. For a concise summary of these crises, as well as a useful discussion of international capital flows, see Pugel (2009: 511–542). See also World Bank (2005: 242–251).

with substantial borrowing by domestic corporations from foreign banks and growth in the stock markets to create economic booms. Importantly, the borrowing of dollars from foreign lenders was not hedged, since these Asian currencies were assumed to be stable, pegged as they were to the dollar. In retrospect, in the mid-1990s the classic warning signs of a balance of payments crisis were forming: slowing export growth for these countries with the real appreciation of their currencies resulted in current account deficits financed by short-term capital inflows, rapid domestic credit growth, rampant speculation in real estate, and rising domestic inflation rates.

In early 1997 foreign investors became nervous about the sustainability of Thailand's surging economy, especially about Thailand's ability to repay its outstanding loans. Investors began withdrawing funds from the capital markets in Thailand, unleashing a run on the baht. Thailand's central bank was then forced to intervene in the foreign exchange market, selling off dollars (official reserve assets for Thailand) to soak up the excess supply of baht. This mandated tighter monetary policy reduced the Thai money supply, pushing up interest rates, which in turn drove down stock prices and land values. The following sharp declines in wealth and exposed vulnerability of the outstanding loans accelerated the capital flight from Thailand. Soon Thailand's central bank ran low on reserves and in July stopped defending the baht, which then sharply depreciated (from 25 baht to the dollar to 40 baht to the dollar by November). The depreciation of the baht increased the debt burden of Thailand, in particular, the loans in dollars that had been taken out by private businesses in Thailand. As so often happens, fear is contagious and panic spread to surrounding nations perceived to be similarly overextended. Malaysia, South Korea, and Indonesia also had pegged their currencies to the dollar and experienced heavy foreign capital inflows, resulting in increased inflation and real appreciation of their currencies. With the ensuing capital flight from these economies came runs on the Malaysian ringgit, Korean won, and Indonesian rupiah, and sharp depreciations.

These nations also turned to the IMF for help. As noted, the standard IMF medicine in a balance of payments crisis is tighter monetary and fiscal policy, which further contracted these vulnerable economies. From average annual GDP growth rates between 7 and 9 percent for 1990–97, these four nations underwent severe recessions in 1998.[14] Nevertheless, these economies soon recovered and began growing again in 1999. *The Economist* argued that "The International Monetary Fund, which failed miserably to foresee the crisis, deserves some credit. Its emphasis on tight fiscal and monetary policies was controversial, but its advocacy of a swift disposal of bad debts was spot on."[15]

Policy reforms included the shift to more flexible exchange rates and better supervision of banking systems.[16] The World Bank (2005: 246) observed that the currency crises illustrated the theoretical impossibility of the monetary trinity. That is, a country can attain no more than two

[14]Between 1990 and 1997, the average annual GDP growth rates were: Thailand (7.4 percent), South Korea (7.2 percent), Malaysia (8.6 percent), and Indonesia (7.5 percent). In 1998, their real GDP declined: by 9.4 percent in Thailand, 6.6 percent in South Korea, 6.6 percent in Malaysia, and 13.2 percent in Indonesia. See World Bank (1999: Table 4.1; 2000: Tables 1.1 and 4a).

[15]See "The Lost (Half) Decade," *The Economist* (July 4, 2002).

[16]For contemporary accounts of the East Asian currency crisis, see IMF Staff (1998) and Lipsky (1998). For an analysis of the financial reforms in Asia following the currency crises, see Ziegler (2003: 4), who notes:

For much of the region, the crisis destroyed wealth on a massive scale and sent absolute poverty shooting up. In the banking system, corporate loans equivalent to around half a year's GDP went bad—a destruction of savings on a scale more usually associated with a full-scale war.

of the following: an open capital account balance allowing free mobility of international capital, a targeted exchange rate, and an independent monetary policy.[17]

Lessons from the 1990s

In drawing lessons from the last decade of the twentieth century, the World Bank (2005: 11–12), while concluding that there is no "one size fits all" policy formula for economic growth, nevertheless identified four common characteristics of successful economies: rapid physical capital accumulation, efficient resource allocation, technological progress, and a sharing of benefits from the growth. Only 18 developing economies were cited by the Bank, however, as successfully sustaining growth over the last two decades of the twentieth century.[18] Four of these were the East Asian nations of Thailand, South Korea, Malaysia, and Indonesia. While quite diverse in geography, history, culture, and political-economic systems, these 18 developing nations shared relatively high investment rates, low external debt ratios, low inflation rates, stable real exchange rates, and more open economies.

In his review of the World Bank study, Rodrik (2006: 974) summarized: "While lessons drawn by proponents and skeptics differ, it is fair to say that nobody really believes in the Washington Consensus anymore." By the Washington Consensus, Rodrik means the policy package of fiscal and monetary discipline, financial and trade liberalization, competitive real exchange rates, privatization and greater reliance on the market mechanism—all the components of the IMF medicine recommended to developing nations with balance of payments deficits and consistent with theory for promoting economic growth. Reflecting the World Bank's findings, Rodrik advocates that nations identify the particular constraints to growth (e.g., inadequate economic infrastructure, insufficient private investment, low human capital, poor civil administration, or corruption), and then develop policies to address the market failures or government failures. He also recommends attention to building effective institutions for administration, resource allocation, and social welfare.

CONCLUSION

According to the World Bank (2005: 243), "The 1990s will be remembered as a decade of macroeconomic crises and turbulence in emerging markets." Indeed, the last decade of the twentieth century was one of uneven growth across regions of the world, not unlike the earlier two decades. For the period 1973–2001, Maddison (2005: 10) estimates average annual growth rates in real per capita incomes of 1.95 percent for the developed nations of Western Europe, the US, Canada,

---

South Korea, in particular, bounced back quickly, with a consolidation of banks, a write-down of much of the nonperforming loans, and return of foreign direct investment. In several of these nations, political upheaval and changes in governments followed the economic turbulence.

[17] As the World Bank (2005: 246–248) illustrates, seven of the top ten recipients of private foreign capital during the 1990s suffered financial crises (Mexico, Thailand, South Korea, Indonesia, Malaysia, Russia, and Brazil). The three exceptions (China, India, and Chile) all imposed restrictions on international capital inflows.

[18] See World Bank (2005: 80–90). The 18 nations, covering some 60 percent of the world population, are: China, Vietnam, South Korea (at the time still considered a developing economy), Malaysia, Lao PDR, Thailand, Indonesia, India, Bangladesh, Sri Lanka, Bhutan, Nepal, Tunisia, Egypt, Lesotho, Botswana, Mauritius, and Chile. To be included, a nation had to have an average annual per capita GDP growth rate higher than that of the US (1.7 percent) in the 1990s and at least 1.0 percent in the 1980s. The World Bank (2005: 92) also noted that the sustained growth of these nations "was accompanied by wide improvements in social indicators and access to expanding public services." Using the criterion of exceeding the US economic growth rate of 1.0 percent for 2000–10, all 18 nations would still qualify.

Australia, New Zealand and Japan and 1.75 percent for the rest of the world. But, as just discussed, these averages do not reflect the diversity of experience.

Table 5.1 provides a summary of the growth rates in national outputs for the last four decades. The low growth rates for the upper middle-income economies in the 1980s, in part, reflect the debt problems of the Latin America nations. The difficulties of the transition economies of Europe and Central Asia in the 1990s are evidenced with the negative average annual growth rate for real GDP. The relatively strong growth for the lower middle-income economies and upper middle-income economies for the first decade of the twenty-first century largely reflects India and China, respectively.

In general, economic growth picked up for the developing nations in the new decade of the 2000s, especially for these transition economies. In 2008, however, a severe recession hit the US, induced by implosion in the housing and capital markets. This first decade of the twenty-first century, which may well be remembered as a decade of macroeconomic crises and financial turbulence in the developed countries, will be addressed in the next chapter.

KEY TERMS

behavioral equation	capital flight
ecological footprint	economic model
endogenous variable	entropy
equilibrium condition	exogenous variable
First World	identity
law of demand	law of supply
most favored nation	reciprocity
recycling of petrodollars	Second World
simulation model	Third World

QUESTIONS

1. In the *Limits to Growth* World3 simulation model, which of the four scenarios illustrated in Figure 5.2 do you think is the most likely in the future? Explain why.

2. Daly argues that a steady-state economy is a "necessary and desirable state of affairs." Do you agree? Discuss.

3. Daly outlines three institutions for a steady-state economy. Would all three be necessary? That is, could a steady-state economy be attained otherwise or with only one or two of these institutions? Discuss.

4. Discuss why the concern with limits to growth keeps recurring through history—from the classical economists, to the macroeconomists in the 1930s, to the World3 simulation model and Daly's steady state economics.

5. Is the IMF medicine necessary for developing nations with balance of payments crises? Discuss.

REFERENCES

Cook, Clive. 2005. "A Survey of Corporate Social Responsibility," *The Economist*, January 22.

Daly, Herman. 1977. *Steady-State Economics: The Economics of Biophysical equilibrium and Moral Growth*. San Francisco: W.H. Freeman.

Hess, Peter and Clark Ross. 1997. *Economic Development: Theories, Evidence, and Policies*. Fort Worth, TX: Dryden Press.

IMF Staff. 1998. "The Asian Crisis; Causes and Cures," *Finance and Development*, 35(2): 18–21.

Lipsky, John. 1998. "Asia's Crisis: A Market Perspective," *Finance and Development*. 35(2): 10–13.

Maddison, Angus. 2005. *Growth and Interaction in the World Economy: The Roots of Modernity*. Washington, DC: AEI Press.

Meadows, Donella, Dennis Meadows, Jørgen Randers, and William Behrens III. 1972. *The Limits to Growth: A Report for the Club of Rome's Project on the Predicament of Mankind*. London: Earth Island.

Meadows, Donella, Dennis Meadows, and Jørgen Randers. 1992. *Beyond the Limits: Confronting Global Collapse, Envisioning a Sustainable Future*. Post Mills, VT: Chelsea Green.

Meadows, Donella, Jørgen Randers, and Dennis Meadows. 2004. *The Limits to Growth: The 30-Year Update*. White River Junction, VT: Chelsea Green.

Pomfret, Richard. 1992. *Diverse Paths of Development*. New York: Prentice Hall.

Pugel, Thomas. 2009. "International Lending and Financial Crises," in *International Economics*, 14th edition. New York: McGraw-Hill Irwin: 511–542.

Rodrik, Dani. 2006. "Goodbye Washington Consensus, Hello Washington Confusion? A Review of the World Bank's *Economic Growth in the 1990s: Lessons from a Decade of Reform*," *Journal of Economic Literature*, 44(4): 973–987.

Rozenwurcel, Guillermo. 2007. "Why Have All Development Strategies Failed in Latin America?" in George Mavrotas and Anthony Shorrocks (eds), *Advancing Development: Core Themes in Global Economics*. New York: Palgrave Macmillan: 457-475.

Wakernagel, Mathis, Niels Schulz, Diana Deumling, Alejandro Callejas Linares, Martin Jenkins, Valerie Kapos, Chad Monfreda, Jonathan Loh, Norman Meyers, Richard Norgaard, and Jørgen Randers. 2002. "Tracking the Ecological Overshoot of the Human Economy," *Proceedings of the National Academy of Sciences of the USA*, 99(14): 9266–9271

World Bank. 1984. *World Development Report 1984: Recovery or Relapse in the World Economy?* Washington, D.C.: World Bank.

World Bank. 1995. *World Development Report 1995: Workers in an Integrating World*. Washington, D.C.: World Bank.

World Bank. 1999. *World Development Indicators 1999*. Washington, DC: World Bank.

World Bank. 2000. *World Development Indicators 2000*. Washington, DC: World Bank.

World Bank. 2002. *World Development Indicators 2002*. Washington, DC: World Bank.

World Bank. 2003. *World Development Indicators 2003*. Washington, DC: World Bank.

World Bank. 2005. *Economic Growth in the 1990s: Learning from a Decade of Reform*. Washington, DC: World Bank.

World Bank. 2012. *World Development Indicators 2012*. Washington, DC: World Bank.

Ziegler, Dominic. 2003. "The Weakest Link: A Survey of Asian Finance," *The Economist*, February 8.

Part III
Macroeconomic models

Chapter 6

Macroeconomic fluctuations

Compared to the 1990s, growth rates in real national output were higher for the low- and middle-income economies over the first 7 years of the opening decade of the twenty-first century. Moreover, the diversity of experience in the developing economies in the earlier decade, ranging from average annual growth rate in real gross domestic product (1990–2000) in the East Asian and Pacific nations of 8.5 percent to −1.8 percent in the transition economies of Europe and Central Asia, narrowed. The spread between the average annual growth rates in real GDP for 2000–07 ranged from 9.0 percent for East Asia and the Pacific economies to 3.6 percent for the nations of Latin America and the Caribbean. The average annual growth rate in real GDP for the high-income economies, however, was slightly lower: 2.7 percent for 1990–2000 and 2.4 percent for 2000–07.

As illustrated in Table 6.1, accompanying the higher output growth in the developing economies was greater physical capital formation. Even the lowest average annual growth rate in gross capital formation (or gross domestic investment) for these nations (4.7 percent for Latin America and the Caribbean) was more than twice that for the high-income economies (2.1 percent for 2000–07). Furthermore, the low- and middle-income nations, especially in Asia, realized more rapid growth in trade, reaping the efficiencies gained through international specialization.

In 2008 a financial crisis enveloped the United States economy, spread to other high-income economies, and led to a decline in global output of 1.9 percent in 2009. As seen in Table 6.1, real GDP fell by 3.3 percent in 2009 in the high-income economies. The downturn in the high-income economies reduced developing economies' exports, private capital inflows, commodity prices, and workers' remittances. Growth in international trade, which had slowed to 3 percent in 2008, declined by an estimated 12 percent in 2009. Collectively, real GDP fell by 5.8 percent in Europe and Central Asia and 1.9 percent in Latin America and the Caribbean, and in all other regions, except South Asia, the growth rate of output declined. The World Bank projected that additional 64 million people in the developing economies would be living in extreme poverty by the end of 2010 due to the global recession (see World Bank 2010: 217).

In 2010, however, output growth returned to the high-income economies. The economies of Europe and Central Asia and Latin America and the Caribbean recovered strongly and the other developing regions experienced higher growth—in part with the rebound in international trade.

In this chapter we will address short-run macroeconomic fluctuations. An aggregate demand–aggregate supply model will be developed to explain the determination of real national output and the aggregate price level. This first decade of the twenty-first century will be reviewed, in particular the financial crisis in the US that led to the Great Recession. We begin, however, with the long-run trend in economic growth in the United States.

Table 6.1 *Growth in aggregate expenditures, 2000–07*

	Average annual growth rate (2000–07)								
	Pers. Cons.	Govt. Cons.	Gross capital formation	Exports	Imports	2000–07 GDP	2008 GDP	2009 GDP	2010 GDP
WORLD ($11,066)	2.9%	2.6%	3.7%	7.1%	6.6%	3.2%	1.7%	−1.9%	4.2%
Sub-Saharan Africa ($2,148)	4.9%	4.9%	8.0%	...	8.4%	5.1%	5.1%	1.7%	4.8%
Mid. East & N. Africa ($8,068)	5.2%	3.5%	7.2%	7.6%	10.0%	4.5%	5.5%	3.4%	4.3%
Europe & Cen. Asia ($13,396)	7.4%	3.1%	10.5%	8.8%	12.9%	6.1%	4.1%	−5.8%	5.7%
South Asia ($3,124)	5.7%	4.2%	13.9%	14.5%	17.4%	7.3%	5.6%	8.1%	8.1%
India ($3,400)	6.0%	3.4%	15.1%	15.7%	19.4%	7.8%	6.1%	9.1%	8.8%
East Asia & Pacific ($6,657)	7.0%	8.5%	12.0%	17.3%	14.1%	9.0%	8.0%	7.4%	9.7%
China ($7,640)	7.8%	9.1%	13.4%	24.4%	18.6%	10.3%	8.4%	9.1%	10.4%
Lat. Amer. & Carib. ($10,926)	3.8%	2.7%	4.7%	6.2%	7.1%	3.6%	4.3%	−1.9%	6.2%
High-Income Econ. ($37,317)	2.4%	2.2%	2.1%	5.1%	5.3%	2.4%	0.5%	−3.3%	3.1%
US ($47,310)	3.0%	2.5%	2.5%	3.4%	5.2%	2.6%	0.4%	−2.6%	3.0%

Notes: Per capita gross national incomes for 2010 in PPP dollars are listed in parentheses. Revised figures for the US economy show the growth rates in real GDP for 2008 and 2009 to be −0.3% and −3.5%, respectively (see www.bea.gov). This would reduce somewhat the averages for the high-income economies and world in 2008 and 2009.

Personal consumption is the market value of all goods and services purchased by households. It excludes purchases of dwellings, but includes imputed rent for owner-occupied dwellings.

Government consumption includes all government current expenditures for goods and services (including compensation of employees). Also included are most expenditures on national defense and security, except for military expenditures with potentially wider public use that are part of government capital formation.

Gross capital formation (gross domestic investment) is outlays on additions to fixed assets of the economy (including land improvements); plant, equipment, and machinery; and construction (roads, railways, schools, buildings, etc.) and the net changes in inventories (goods held to meet temporary or unexpected fluctuations in production or sales, and work in progress).

Exports and imports of goods and services are the value of all goods and other market services provided to or received from the rest of the world. They exclude compensation of employees and investment income.

Source: World Bank (2009: Tables 4.1 and 4.9; 2010: Table 1.1; 2011: Table 1.1; 2012: Table 1.1).

ECONOMIC GROWTH

As discussed in Chapter 1, per capita income can be disaggregated into labor productivity and aggregate labor force participation, $y = Y/P = (Y/L) \cdot (L/P)$, where y is per capita real national output (per capita real national income), Y is real national output (real national income), P population and L labor force. The economic growth rate can be written as $dy/y = d(Y/L)/(Y/L) + d(L/P)/(L/P)$. Consequently, economic growth will occur with increases in labor productivity, $d(Y/L)/(Y/L) > 0$, and increases in the aggregate labor force participation rate, $d(L/P)/(L/P) > 0$. A rising share of the population in the labor force may reflect the demographic dividend that accompanies the declines in fertility rates during the demographic transition. While there may be upper bounds (usually below 60 percent) on the share of the labor force in the total population, growth in labor productivity is not limited. Furthermore, declines in the youth burden of dependency (the ratio of the population under age 15 to the population in the labor force aged 15–64) make possible more saving and investment in capital formation that increase labor productivity.

Economic growth in United States

We focus on the US, the third most populous nation and by far the largest economy in the world.[1] Overall, US real GDP per capita nearly tripled from approximately $15,600 in 1960 to over $43,700 in 2007, before the recession hit and reduced per capita GDP to $41,300 in 2009. (See the upper panel in Figure 6.1 for the chart from the *Survey of Current Business* of the trend in real GDP per capita, which shows the sharp downturn in the Great Recession from December 2007 to June 2009.) Entering into 2012, real GDP per capita in the US had not returned to the 2007 level. Over time, US economic growth has reflected higher labor productivity with technological progress and human and physical capital deepening, as well as a rising share of the labor force in the total population.

As we know, the growth rate in per capita real GDP is equal to the difference between the growth rates in real GDP and population. Variations in the growth rate in real per capita GDP for the US over the past half-century have primarily been due to variations in the growth rate of real GDP. Periodically, recessions with declines in real national output have interrupted growth in the economy. (See the lower panel in Figure 6.1 for the *Survey of Current Business* chart of the quarterly percentage changes in real GDP.)

In Table 6.2, along with real GDP per capita (Y/P), are annual averages for labor productivity (Y/L), the share of the labor force in total population (L/P), the growth rates in real GDP (GY) and inflation (measured by the percentage change in the price deflator for GDP), and the unemployment rate (measured as the percentage of the civilian labor force unemployed) for the last five decades. The general increase in labor productivity over time periodically would be reversed, usually during recession years (e.g., 1970, 1974–75, 1980, 1982, 1991, 2001, and 2008–09). During recessions firms may initially hoard labor, reluctant to lay off workers until the economic downturn is recognized, so that labor productivity may decline as output falls faster than employment. Conversely, during an economic recovery, firms may postpone hiring workers until convinced the economy is growing again. Thus, growth in labor productivity will rise as the economy recovers from a recession as output expands faster than employment.

Also contributing to economic growth has been the rise in the share of the population in the labor force, with the baby boom generation (those individuals born between 1946 and 1964) coming of labor force age and increasing female labor force participation. In the 1990s, however, the growth in the share of the population in the labor force began to level off, and since 2000 the labor force has stabilized at around 50 percent of the total population.

Finally, we can see that inflation and unemployment rates have varied over the years. The 1970s stand out as the decade for high inflation; in fact, the high inflation was accompanied by higher

---

[1] As the saying goes, "When the United States sneezes, the rest of the world catches a cold." In 2010, for example, the US gross national income of $14.6 trillion accounted for roughly 23 percent of the estimated world output of $62.5 trillion. China and Japan, with national outputs of $5.7 trillion and $5.3 trillion, were next, accounting for approximately 9 percent and 8 percent of the world output, respectively. Expressed in PPP dollars, however, world output in 2010 was estimated to be $76.3 trillion, with US accounting for roughly 19 percent, followed by China with slightly over 13 percent and Japan with almost 6 percent (World Bank 2012: Table 1.1).

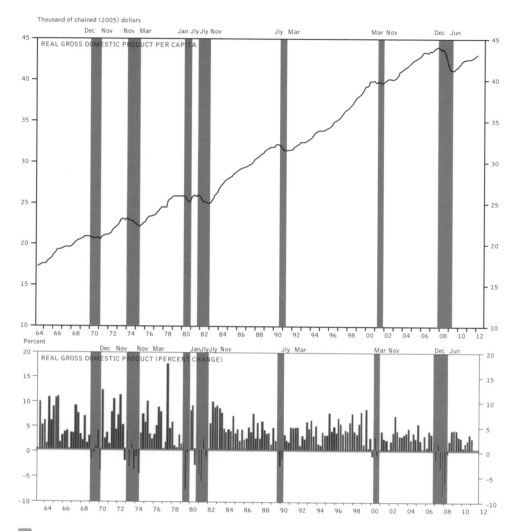

Figure 6.1 *US real GDP: per capita and quarterly growth rates All series are seasonally adjusted at annual rates. The percent changes in real gross domestic product are based on quarter-to-quarter changes. The shaded areas mark the beginning and end of recessions as determined by the Business Cycle Dating Committee of the National Bureau of Economic Research.*

Note: These charts are from US Bureau of Economic Analysis, Survey of Current Business (May 2012), page D-57. http://www.bea.gov/scb/pdf/2012/05%20May/D%20pages/ 0512dpg_d.pdf

unemployment, especially during the recession of 1974–75. Part of the increase in the unemployment rate over the decade, however, reflected a rise in frictional unemployment with the entrance of the baby boomers into labor force.[2] (In Chapter 10 we will discuss the profound impacts of the

---

[2]**Frictional unemployment** refers to the natural turnover in the labor force due to job leavers, new entrants, and reentrants. Some frictional unemployment is inevitable since it usually takes time for individuals to find employment once they begin searching. **Structural unemployment** refers to a misalignment between the skills of the unemployed and the skills required

Table 6.2 *US economic performance*

(a) Annual averages over the decades

Annual averages	1960–69	1970–79	1980–89	1990–99	2000–09
Y/P	$18,200	$23,200	$28,200	$34,300	$41,600
Y/L	$47,100	$53,600	$58,200	$68,900	$82,500
L/P	0.386	0.433	0.484	0.498	0.505
GY	4.4%	3.3%	3.1%	3.2%	1.7%
INF	2.4%	6.6%	4.8%	2.3%	2.4%
UNP	4.8%	6.2%	7.3%	5.8%	5.5%

Y is real GDP (in billions of chained 2005 dollars), P is population, L is labor force, Y/P is real GDP per capita, Y/L is real GDP per member of the labor force, L/P is the percentage of of the population in the labor force, GY is the percentage change in real GDP, INF is the percentage change in the implicit price deflator for GDP, UNP is the civilian unemployment rate. Decade averages are derived with data from Bureau of Economic Analysis (www.bea.gov) and the *Economic Report of the President*.

(b) Estimated annual averages, 1960–2010

Simple regression results: T = time $(1960 = 0, \ldots, 2010 = 51$; sample size: $n = 51)$

		Average annual growth rates	
$\ln(Y/P) = 2.804 + 0.0204T$ (0.011) (0.0004)	$R^2 = 0.985$	Y/P	2.04%
$\ln(Y/L) = 3.753 + 0.0139T$ (0.012) (0.0004)	$R^2 = 0.959$	Y/L	1.39%
$\ln(L/P) = -0.948 + 0.0065T$ (0.012) (0.0004)	$R^2 = 0.844$	L/P	0.65%

(The standard errors are given in the parentheses under the estimated coefficients.)

baby boom generation on the US economy.) This inflationary recession was largely attributed to supply-side shocks from sharp increases in the price of oil.

To find the trend growth rates in per capita real GDP, labor productivity, and aggregate labor force participation, we can use simple regression analysis.[3] Regressing the natural logarithms of real GDP per capita, $\ln(Y/P)$, labor productivity, $\ln(Y/L)$, and aggregate labor force participation rate, $\ln(L/P)$, on time (T, in years) for the US economy for the 51-year period from 1960 through 2010, yields the trend growth rates. The derived average annual growth rates in real GDP per capita, labor productivity, and aggregate labor force participation for this half century are

---

for the jobs that are open. Over time, some industries will be expanding due to positive economic profits and others will be contracting. The labor laid off from the latter will not necessarily be absorbed into the former if the job skills or employment locations are different. **Cyclical unemployment** refers to job losses due to insufficient aggregate demand. When the economy goes into a recession, the decline in production will reduce the demand for labor, resulting in cyclical unemployment. Cyclical unemployment, unlike frictional or structural unemployment, can be reduced to zero.

[3] In Chapter 8 we will discuss the fundamentals of basic regression analysis. A brief review of derivatives of natural exponential and natural logarithmic functions, however, might be helpful at this point. In general, if: $\ln y(t) = x(t)$, then $y(t) = e^{x(t)}$, where ln refers to the natural logarithm and e is the base of the natural logarithm. The derivative of this natural exponential function, $y(t) = e^{x(t)}$, with respect to t is $dy/dt = e^{x(t)} \cdot (dx/dt) = x'(t) \cdot e^{x(t)}$. That is, the derivative of the natural exponential function is equal to the original function times the derivative of the exponent. Therefore, if $\ln y(t) = a + rt$ (here $x(t) = a + rt$), then $y(t) = e^{a+rt} = e^a \cdot e^{rt} = y(0)e^{rt}$, where $y(0) = e^a$. The derivative of this natural exponential function, $y(t) = e^{a+rt}$, with respect to t is $dy/dt = r \cdot e^{a+rt}$. The growth rate of y is then $(dy/dt)/y = r$.

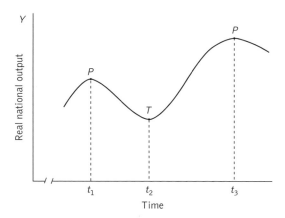

Figure 6.2 *Stylized business cycle*

A business cycle is illustrated by the movement of the economy from one peak (P) to the next. Here after reaching a peak or upper turning point at time t_1, the economy turns down. Real national output (Y) declines until the trough (T) or lower turning point at t_2. After which the economy recovers, with real national output rising until the next peak at t_3. A rise in real national output is known as an expansion (here from t_2 to t_3). A decline in real national output is known as a contraction or, if prolonged, a recession.

respectively 2.04 percent, 1.39 percent, and 0.65 percent—as shown by the estimated coefficients for time in the respective simple regressions. We can see that the growth rate for per capita real GDP is equal to the sum of the growth rates for labor productivity and aggregate labor force participation. As noted, however, these trend growth rates mask considerable annual changes. To explain variations in real national output we will present a macroeconomic model of aggregate demand and aggregate supply. But first we give an overview of business cycles, the periodic fluctuations in economic activity.

BUSINESS CYCLES

Growth in real national output in the long run is largely driven by technological progress and increases in the effective factors of production. The growth in real national output over time, however, is not constant and is occasionally interrupted with periods of economic decline. These fluctuations in GDP growth are known as the **business cycle** (see Figure 6.2 for a stylized graph).

Economic expansion refers to a rise in real national output, while **economic contraction** refers to a fall in real national output. The upper turning point, when the expansion ceases, is called the **peak**. The lower turning point, when the contraction bottoms out and the economy begins to recover, is called the **trough**. The conventional definition of a **recession** is two successive quarters or 6 months of falling real national output. In the US, the official determination of when exactly a recession began and ended is made after the fact by the National Bureau of Economic Research (NBER).[4]

---

[4]The National Bureau of Economic Research, founded in 1920, is a "private, nonprofit, nonpartisan research organization dedicated to promoting a greater understanding of how the economy works" (see http://www.nber.org).

The length of business cycles, that is, the period between peaks in economic activity, varies.[5] In fact, as noted by the NBER, a recession, formally the period between a peak and a trough may include a short period of expansion followed by further contraction. Similarly, an expansion may be briefly interrupted by a contraction. So, too, the amplitude and range between the peak and trough of business cycles vary. In the US economy, the most recent recession began in December 2007 (when the US unemployment rate was 5.0 percent) and lasted 18 months, until recovery began in June 2009 (by which time the unemployment rate had nearly doubled to 9.5 percent).[6] Despite the recession ending in June 2009, the US unemployment rate continued to rise for several months to 10.0 percent in October 2009.

In fact, the unemployment rate is a lagging indicator of the state of the economy. With a recession, the unemployment rate does not usually peak sometime until after the economic recovery has begun. When the economy begins to decline, initially employers may not lay off workers, hoping the downturn will be brief. As the recession goes on, layoffs follow. Then, at the other end of the cycle, as the economy begins to recover, employers may hold off on rehiring, preferring to extend the hours of their smaller workforces, until convinced the economy is growing again. Another reason for the lagging measure of the official unemployment rate is **discouraged workers**, individuals who are out of work, willing and able to work, but have given up looking for work due to the perceived poor job prospects. Discouraged workers are not officially counted as unemployed. During a recession, if unemployed workers give up looking for work, then, *ceteris paribus*, the unemployment rate would fall. Later, when the economy recovers, discouraged workers may begin looking for jobs, reentering the labor force. Given the likely lag between starting their searches and securing employment, the reentrance of discouraged workers, *ceteris paribus*, will increase the unemployment rate—even as the economy is growing.

While no two business cycles are the same, there are some common features. Foremost is that investment spending tends to be relatively volatile. Except in times of war, swings in business fixed investment and residential fixed investment, and to some extent expenditures on consumer durables, tend to account disproportionately for fluctuations in aggregate demand. Consumer expenditures on services and nondurables, in contrast, tend to be more stable. Shocks to the economy, however, can come from the demand side and the supply side.

Keynesian economists believe demand shocks with shifts in business and consumer confidence are prominent. Indeed, we find bubble economies with periods of euphoria and rising asset prices leading to overconsumption and excessive investment that eventually are pierced by corrections, even overcorrections, with collapsing asset prices and steep cutbacks in investment and spending. In short, the economy moves from boom to bust. Supply-side shocks, emphasized by real business cycle theorists, include sharp swings in energy prices and rapid advances in technology, such as the information technology revolution that began in the 1990s.[7] In addition, regime changes, for example the transition to market economies of the former socialist nations in the 1990s, or

---

[5] Ibid. Since 1945 there have been 11 business cycles in the US economy. The average duration of the contractions (peak to trough) has been 11 months. The average length of the expansion (from previous trough to peak) has been 59 months. Before the most recent recession, from December 2007 to June 2009, the previous expansion had been 73 months, well short of the record expansion of 120 months from March 1991 to March 2001.

[6] The other severe recession in the post-World War II era lasted 16 months, from July 1981 to October 1982. The unemployment rate, however, continued to rise until December 1982, when it reached 10.8 percent of the US labor force (compared to 7.2 percent in July 1981, when the recession began). The two recessions in between were milder, lasting 8 months each: from July 1990 to March 1991 (with the unemployment rate increasing from 5.4 percent in July 1990 to 7.7 percent in June 1992, 15 months after the recovery began) and from March 2001 to November 2001 (with the unemployment rate rising from 4.3 percent in March 2001 to 6.0 percent in April 2002, 5 months after the recovery).

[7] For a review of real business cycle theory, see Stadler (1994).

responses to terrorism requiring new security measures, and even significant shifts in environmental, health, and safety regulations that affect the aggregate production function, may affect economic growth. Climate change and the attendant measures adopted to mitigate may well bring on some supply-side shocks.

The economic costs associated with unemployment can be measured by the loss of output and income that would have been produced by those unemployed. Moreover, especially as the duration of unemployment increases, the labor skills of unemployed may atrophy, like an athlete out of practice. The social costs, however, are also profound. A recent study found a loss of an average of 1.5 years of life expectancy for an employee who loses his job at the age of 40. Increased rates of alcoholism, smoking, drug abuse, and depression are also associated with higher unemployment (see Pfeffer 2010).[8] Increases in crime rates, suicide rates, and child abuse have been linked to rises in unemployment rates.

What causes fluctuations in economic activity? The three primary macroeconomic goals are full employment (meaning a national unemployment rate of near 5 percent), price stability (meaning an inflation rate of less than 2 percent), and healthy real national output growth (usually between 3 and 4 percent annually). Why can we not maintain full employment, price stability and steady output growth?

To understand the relationship between growth in real national output, inflation, and unemployment, a model of the economy is needed. Below we set forth a fairly simple model of aggregate demand and aggregate supply.

AGGREGATE SUPPLY

The aggregate supply function relates the quantity of real national output produced (usually represented on the horizontal axis) to the average price level (represented on the vertical axis). The short-run aggregate supply curve (Y^S) is drawn holding constant the supply curves of the primary factors of production, as well as technology, the nation's foreign exchange rate, government regulation and taxes, and the institutional environment.[9]

Microeconomic foundations

In microeconomics, labor is typically assumed to be a variable factor of production in the short run; the physical capital stocks of the firms, as well as technology, are assumed to be fixed. For the

---

[8]In this last recession, the long-term unemployed found it increasingly difficult to regain work. Employers often were reluctant to hire those who had been unemployed for longer than 6 months, believing these individuals were not only "rusty," but somehow diminished by their extended unemployment. The Bureau of Labor Statistics compiles the mean (and median) duration of unemployment, or the average number of consecutive weeks of unemployment for those out of work. Not only does the loss of income increase with the duration of unemployment (as unemployment benefits, which only provide a proportion of wages lost, may run out), but also the health care of families may suffer as the unemployed workers lose their health insurance. To illustrate the severity of the recent Great Recession of 2008–09, the **mean duration of unemployment** in 2009, the year when real GDP declined by 3.5 percent, was 24.4 weeks. In 2010, the year when the economy began to grow again, the mean duration of unemployment actually increased to 33.0 weeks, which again illustrates how the unemployment rate is a lagging indicator of the state of the economy. In 2011, the mean duration actually rose further to 39.3 weeks. In the previous severe recession, in 1982 when real GDP in the US economy fell by 1.9 percent, the mean duration of unemployment was 15.6 weeks; and in the next year of recovery, it rose to 20.0 weeks, before declining to 18.2 weeks in 1984. These statistics on the mean duration of unemployment are from Council of Economic Advisers (2012: Table B-44).

[9]Much of this discussion of the aggregate supply and demand curves as well as the following simple macroeconomic model is from Hess (2010).

individual firm, the short-run marginal cost curve, drawn holding input prices constant, eventually slopes upward due to diminishing returns to labor.

If **perfect competition** in the output market prevails, then the individual firms are price-takers, facing perfectly elastic demand curves given by the equilibrium market price. If imperfect competition prevails, then firms are price-setters, facing downwardly sloping individual demand curves for their outputs. Imperfect competition and entry barriers, however, may result in less than perfectly flexible prices. For example, oligopolists may set prices based on a markup of average costs and refrain from frequent price changes, especially price cutting, for a variety of reasons, including menu costs (the costs of actually changing the listed or posted prices and notifying customers) and uncertain reactions of rivals (whether or not rival firms would match any price changes).

In the labor market, labor supply reflects the summation of the individual workers' labor supply curves. The market labor demand is an aggregation of the individual firms' labor demand curves. In a competitive labor market the common wage adjusts to equilibrate labor supply and demand. Individual firms employing that labor are wage-takers, with perfectly elastic labor supply curves at the market wage. Institutional rigidities such as union contracts, minimum wages, and efficiency wages can result in wages set above market-clearing levels. Changes in labor demand will affect market-clearing wages, but not necessarily the institutionally set wages.

Derivation of the short-run aggregate supply curve

To derive the short-run aggregate supply curve we begin with a short-run aggregate production function. As noted, in the short run, technology is given and physical capital is assumed to be fixed. In addition, we will assume that the natural resources available for production are also fixed in supply. Labor is the variable factor of production. The general short-run production function for an economy can then be written as $Y = A \cdot F(K, L, R)$, where Y is real national output, A an index of technology ($A = A_0$), K physical capital stock ($K = K_0$), L physical labor, and R represents natural resources ($R = R_0$). Note here that technology is neutral and we are abstracting from effective factors of production, that is to say, we do not include quality indices for the physical factors. Later, when we consider growth models, we will return to effective capital, labor, and natural resources. If we assume diminishing returns to labor from the outset, then the graph of the short-run aggregate production function is strictly concave (see Figure 6.3). That is, real national output produced rises with the labor employed at a diminishing rate. The slope of the short-run production function is the **marginal product of labor**, $dY/dL = \text{MPL}$.

Labor market

Comparing marginal benefit with marginal cost, the decision rule for firms in the short run for the profit-maximizing level of labor to employ is to hire up to the point where the **marginal revenue product of labor** (MRPL) equals the **marginal factor cost of labor** (MFCL). If we assume that firms are perfect competitors in the output market (i.e., price-takers) and perfect competitors in the labor market (i.e., wage-takers), then the general condition becomes $\text{MRPL} = P_0 \cdot \text{MPL} = w_0 = \text{MFCL}$, where P_0 is the market price of output (exogenous to the firm), MPL the marginal physical product of labor, and w_0 the market wage (exogenous to the firm).

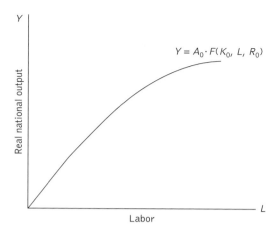

Y

Real national output

$Y = A_0 \cdot F(K_0, L, R_0)$

L

Labor

Figure 6.3 *Short-run aggregate production function*

The short run aggregate production function, $Y = A \cdot F(K, L, R)$, illustrates the relationship between real national output (Y) and the physical labor force employed (L). Held constant are: the index of technology (A), physical capital stock (K), and natural resources (R).

The labor demand curve for a firm is its MRPL curve, which shows the relationship between the quantity of labor demanded and the marginal revenue product of labor (the benefit to the firm of another unit of labor). Due to diminishing returns to labor, the MRPL curve has negative slope. The quantity of labor employed is found where the MRPL equals the wage or the marginal factor cost of that labor (the cost to the firm of another unit of labor). The higher the money wage the firm has to pay, the higher would be the required MRPL. Consequently, the quantity of labor demanded by the firm is inversely related to the money wage. The MRPL curve is drawn for a given price level (P_0) and given levels of technology, physical capital, and natural resources. (See Figure 6.4 (upper panel) for an illustration for an individual firm i, a perfect competitor (wage-taker) in the labor market. For the market wage, w_0, and price level, P_0, the firm would demand and employ L_{i0} units of labor.)

The labor demand curve for the economy is the aggregation of all the firms' labor demand curves. Derived from the short-run aggregate production function, the aggregate labor demand curve is drawn for given technology, physical capital stock, natural resources, and aggregate price level.

The labor supply curve for an individual represents her willingness to work at given wages. For the individual's labor–leisure preferences, the quantity supplied of labor is determined by the expected real wage, or the money wage divided by the expected price level. For a given expected price level, an individual's labor supply curve rises with the money wage, as the incentive to work increases (as does the opportunity cost of leisure). (See Figure 6.4 (lower panel) for an illustration for an individual j. For the market wage, w_0, and the individual's expected price level, P_0^e, the quantity of labor supplied by the individual is L_{j0}.)

The labor supply curve for the economy is the aggregation of the individual labor supply curves of the population. The aggregate labor supply curve, showing the relationship between the total quantity of labor supplied in the economy and the money wage rate, is drawn for given population of labor force years, their underlying labor–leisure preferences, and the expected price level (P_0^e).

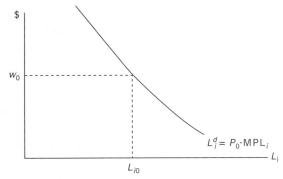

Firm *i* (a perfect competitor in the labor market)

The quantity demanded of labor by firm *i* (a wage-taker) is where MRPL = w_0. The firm's labor demand curve is drawn holding constant the firm's technology, capital stock, and natural resources, as well as the price of the firm's output (P_0).

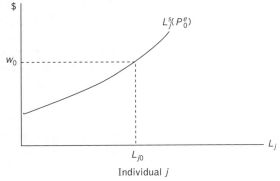

Individual *j*

The quantity of labor supplied by individual *j* is directly related to the money wage, given the individual's expected price level (P^e) and labor–leisure preferences.

Figure 6.4 *Firm's labor demand and individual's labor supply*

How labor supply determines the expected price level is important for the derivation of the aggregate supply curve. If we assume **perfect information**, known as the classical case, then the expected price level would always equal the actual price level (i.e., $P^e_t = P_t$ in any period t).

If instead we assume that labor supply does not have as good information as labor demand and uses previous periods' price levels to form an expectation of the price level, i.e., $P^e_t = f(P_{t-1}, P_{t-2}, \ldots)$, then the Keynesian hypothesis of **adaptive expectations** is relevant. That is, an asymmetry of information may characterize the labor market. The demanders of labor (i.e., the firms) know what the price level for real national output is in the current period. The suppliers of labor (i.e., the workers), however, have agreed to work for wages based on what they expect the price level to be in the current period, which is based on the known past price levels. If workers adjust their expectation of the current price level, then the labor supply curve would shift. For example, an increase in the expected price level would decrease (shift up) the labor supply curve as workers would demand a higher money wage for any quantity of labor supplied.

A third assumption about information is the new classical hypothesis of **rational expectations**, whereby labor supply uses all the available information about the economy, including anticipated economic policies, to forecast the price level based on expected aggregate demand.

Labor market equilibrium

To derive the short-run aggregate supply curve for the economy, Y^S, which shows the relationship between the quantity of real national output produced and supplied and the aggregate price level, we use the labor market and the short-run aggregate production function. In general the labor market is given by the following equations:

$$L^D = \text{MRPL} = P \cdot \text{MPL} = L^D(w) \quad \text{(labor demand)}$$
$$L^S = L^S(w/P^e) \qquad\qquad\qquad \text{(labor supply)}$$
$$L^D(w) = L^S(w) \qquad\qquad\qquad \text{(labor market equilibrium)}.$$

We begin in equilibrium with the market-clearing money wage of w_0 and aggregate employment of L_0 (see Figure 6.5). As noted, the labor demand curve, L^D, is drawn for a given aggregate price level, P_0, as well as given technology, capital stock, and natural resources. The labor supply curve, L^S, is drawn for a given expected price level, P_0^e, as well as a given labor force, that is, population of labor force age and labor force participation rates. Assume initially that $P_0^e = P_0$, that is, labor supply and labor demand are using the actual price level. This level of employment (L_0) in the aggregate production function would produce real national output of Y_0. One point on the aggregate supply curve, Y^S, is given by Y_0 and P_0.

If the price level were to rise to P_1, labor demand would increase to $P_1 \cdot \text{MPL}$ (from $P_0 \cdot \text{MPL}$) as firms adjust to the higher price of output. If we assume perfect information, the labor demand and labor supply curves would both shift up proportionally with the increase in the price level. The money wage would rise proportionally to w_1, maintaining the real wage: $w_1/P_1 = w_0/P_0$. Consequently, the level of employment would remain at L_0 and real national output supplied would still be Y_0. Therefore, the classical short-run aggregate supply curve, Y^S, is vertical at Y_0, which corresponds to full employment, in the sense of no involuntary unemployment.

If we assume instead asymmetric information, then labor supply, using adaptive expectations, would not realize that the price level is higher until the next period when price expectations would be adjusted. Consequently, the excess demand for labor at the initial money wage, w_0, pushes the money wage up to w_1'. Employment rises because firms are willing to hire more workers since the marginal revenue product of labor has increased and workers respond to the higher money wage by supplying more labor as the expected real wage has increased. The actual real wage, however, has decreased: $w_1'/P_1 < w_0/P_0$. The increase in employment to L_1 increases the real national output produced and supplied to Y_1. The short-run aggregate supply curve under Keynesian adaptive expectations is upward-sloping. See the movement along the $Y^{S'}$ curve from E_0 to E'_1.

Finally, under the new classical assumption of rational expectations, if labor supply is able to anticipate the increase in the price level to P_1, that is, using all the information on the economy to forecast correctly the higher price level, then the short-run aggregate supply curve would shift up with the increase in the aggregate price from $Y^{S'}$ to $Y^{S''}$, maintaining in effect the vertical classical short-run aggregate supply curve at Y_0. If labor supply is unable to forecast accurately the increase in the price level, however, then the Keynesian outcome of an increase in the quantity of labor supplied and output produced (here the movement from E_0 to E'_1 along the $Y^{S'}$ curve with the rise in the price level) would hold until the next period when labor supply would recognize that

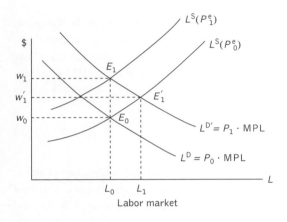

Labor market

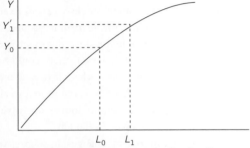

Short-run aggregate production function

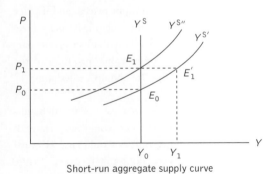

Short-run aggregate supply curve

Figure 6.5 *Derivation of short-run aggregate supply curve*

The effect of an increase in the aggregate price level on the labor market equilibrium and aggregate quantity of real national output supplied depends on price expectations held by labor supply. Under the classical assumption of perfect information, the aggregate supply curve is perfectly inelastic. Under the Keynesian assumption of adaptive expectations, the aggregate supply curve is upward-sloping. Under the new classical assumption of rational expectations, the aggregate supply curve will shift up with the increase in the aggregate price level to maintain the same quantity of real national output supplied.

the aggregate price level had increased and with rational expectations would adjust (indicated here by the $Y^{S''}$ curve and return to Y_0).

Asymmetry of information is more likely to characterize the labor market, so the Keynesian assumption of adaptive expectations seems more relevant for the analysis. In part, firms, the demanders of labor, are setting the prices of output, while workers, the suppliers of labor, may only perceive the changes in prices with a lag—and even then be unable to respond if locked into set wage contracts. Consequently, the short-run aggregate supply curve, Y^S, is upward-sloping (see the $Y^{S'}$ curve in Figure 6.5).

Shifts in the short-run aggregate supply curve

The short-run aggregate supply curve, Y^S, is drawn holding constant technology, capital stock, natural resources, the labor force and the expected price level held by labor supply. Also held constant are the foreign exchange rate, government regulations (e.g., environmental, health, and safety regulations), and taxes on labor and business. Over time the short-run aggregate supply curve would shift right with technological progress, additions to the capital stocks with net fixed investment, growth in the labor force, and, if forthcoming, increases in available natural resources. Increases in the expected price level held by labor supply, however, would reduce the short-run aggregate supply, shifting the curve to the left. Over any period of time, however, there could be declines in the supply curves of the factors of production (e.g., discouraged workers dropping out of the labor force and depreciation of physical capital exceeding gross fixed investment in a weak economy). Depreciation in the home currency would make imported inputs more expensive, raising the cost of production and shifting the aggregate supply curve up or to the left.

Movement along the short-run aggregate supply curve will reflect changes in aggregate demand. Many factor prices, especially wages, are set by either explicit or implicit contracts in the short run. In any case, output prices are usually more flexible than input prices, and if price expectations held by the suppliers of the factors are slower to adjust than the aggregate price level (consistent with adaptive expectations), then changes in output and prices will affect profit margins and the incentive to produce. Thus, in addition to the declining marginal products of the variable factors as production increases, profit incentives may account for the upward-sloping Y^S curve.

For example, with a general economic expansion there would be increases in the demands for factors. Tighter labor markets would bring higher wages, interest rates would increase with greater demand for credit, and market-clearing prices for natural resources would rise. Upward pressures on factor prices intensify as the economy moves rightward along the Y^S curve. While increases in factor prices will shift up their short-run cost curves, firms would nevertheless be willing to supply more output as long as the marginal revenues from their outputs rise more than their marginal costs of production, that is, when the upward shift in their marginal revenue curves with the increase in demand more than compensates for the upward shift in their marginal cost curves with the higher factor prices. (See Figure 6.6, where expansion in the economy with increases in the aggregate price level for national output and input prices induces an increase in the quantity of output supplied by firm i.)

In sum, increases in some market-clearing factor prices during the course of an economic expansion are consistent with rightward movements along the Y^S curve. Given that not all factor prices rise as fast as output prices—due to excess factor supplies and fixed factor price contracts for the period and adaptive expectations—increases in aggregate demand will be accompanied

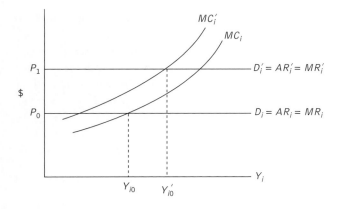

Figure 6.6 *Increase in quantity supplied by a firm*

Firm i is a perfect competitor (a price-taker) in the output market and factor markets. With growth in the economy, the marginal cost curve for the firm shifts up with increases in the market-clearing prices of the factors of production (labor, capital, and natural resources). As long as the firm's demand curve for its output, given by the average revenue curve (equal to the market price of the firm's output and the firm's marginal revenue curve), shifts up more than the firm's marginal cost curve, the profit-maximizing level of output for the firm will increase (here from Y_{i0} to Y_{i0}').

by increases in real output, employment, some factor prices, and the aggregate price level. The underlying factor supply curves, however, reflect the price expectations held by the suppliers of the factors. When these price expectations change the factor supply curves would shift, which, in turn, would shift the Y^S curve.

To determine the equilibrium real national output and aggregate price level, we need to add aggregate demand.

AGGREGATE DEMAND

The aggregate demand (Y^D) curve relates the quantity demanded of real national output to the aggregate price level. Recall that $Y^D = C + I + G + X - M$. Three generally accepted reasons are given for the inverse relationship between the aggregate quantity demanded of real national output and the aggregate price level. The **interest rate effect** considers the impact of a change in the price level on the money market equilibrium. For a given nominal money supply, a higher price level results in an excess demand for liquidity, as the purchasing power of money balances falls. The interest rate would rise, which would decrease desired interest-sensitive expenditures (the business and residential fixed investment and spending on consumer durables financed with credit) and thus the quantity demanded of real national output. The **wealth effect** captures the impact of a change in the aggregate price level on the purchasing power of given nominal wealth (e.g., holdings of stocks, bonds, bank balances and other assets). The **international competitiveness effect** reflects the impact of a change in the aggregate price level on net exports, for a given set of nominal exchange rates or the foreign exchange value of the home currency. For example, a higher domestic price level tends to decrease exports and increase imports of goods and services, reducing the quantity demanded of real national output.

141

The aggregate demand curve is derived holding constant **autonomous expenditures** on real national output, that is, those expenditures independent of the price level and real national income. Fiscal policy with changes in government expenditures and tax rates (reflected in changes in autonomous expenditures) and monetary policy (with discretionary changes in the nominal money supply) would shift the Y^D curve. A depreciation in the home currency would tend to improve the nation's trade balance and increase aggregate demand, shifting the Y^D curve to the right.

The equilibrium real national output, Y_0, and aggregate price level, P_0, are found at the intersection of the aggregate demand, Y^D, and aggregate supply, Y^S, curves. (See Figure 6.7 for the macroeconomic equilibrium.)

Potential output and the natural rate of output

An important concept in the aggregate demand-aggregate supply model is **potential national output** (or **full-employment national output**), which may be defined as the level of real national output produced with average rates of frictional and structural unemployment (i.e., consistent with the underlying population growth, labor force participation rates, and skill composition of the labor force) and the normal rate of utilization of the nation's physical capital stock. At the potential rate of national output, Y_f, there is no cyclical unemployment.

The **natural rate of output**, Y_n, is the rate of real national output produced when the economy is operating at the **natural rate of unemployment**, or the unemployment rate consistent with general equilibrium in the aggregate labor market. The market-clearing real wage and employment reflect the real factors underlying the labor market: explicitly, on the supply side, the population aged 16 and older and their labor–leisure preferences; and on the demand side, technology, the physical capital stock, and available natural resources. At the natural rate of unemployment, the real wage rate is constant and the price expectations held by the suppliers of labor are accurate.

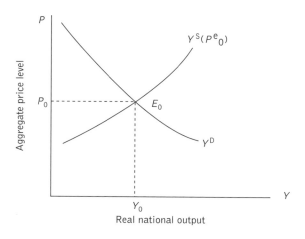

Figure 6.7 *Equilibrium real national output and aggregate price level*

The equilibrium real national output, Y_0, and aggregate price level, P_0, are given by the intersection of the aggregate demand and aggregate supply curves. If price expectations are accurate, i.e., $P_0^e = P_0$, then real national output equals the natural rate of output, $Y_0 = Y_n$.

As noted, a key issue is the extent to which factor prices are free to adjust to market disequilibria. Downward adjustment in factor prices with excess supplies of the factors may be hindered by institutional constraints and contractual obligations. Over any year, however, many factor contracts will expire, and depending on the current condition of the economy, the factor prices stipulated in new contracts may adjust.

A simple linear model for aggregate demand and aggregate supply is offered below to illustrate the difference between demand-pull and cost-push inflation, and to account for observed changes in the aggregate price level and real national output over time. In particular, deflation (in terms of an annual decrease in the aggregate price level) has been absent for the US economy for over 60 years. The last year the aggregate price level (the implicit price deflator for GDP) declined for the US economy was 1949 (and then by only 0.2 percent). Even over the Great Recession of 2008–09, when the unemployment rate reached 10 percent, the aggregate price level did not decline.[10] This model will also explain how a severe recession may not be accompanied by deflation.

A SIMPLE MODEL OF AGGREGATE DEMAND AND AGGREGATE SUPPLY

For simplicity in solving, a linear specification for the aggregate demand (Y^D) and aggregate supply (Y^S) schedules is assumed.[11] Here the aggregate demand and aggregate supply schedules are written in terms of the aggregate demand price (P^D) and aggregate supply price (P^S) dependent on the level of real national output demanded and supplied, respectively. The equations of the model are:

$$P^D = D_0 \cdot (1 + d) - f \cdot Y \tag{6.6.1}$$

$$P^S = S_0 \cdot (1 - s) + \beta \cdot (P_{-1} - P^e_{-1}) + h \cdot Y \tag{6.6.2}$$

$$P^D(Y) = P^S(Y) \tag{6.6.3}$$

The key endogenous variables are: P^D, the aggregate demand price (i.e., the aggregate price level associated with a given quantity of real national output demanded); P^S, the aggregate supply price (i.e., the aggregate price level associated with a given quantity of real national output produced and supplied); and Y, real national output (real national income). The exogenous variables are: D_0, the initial aggregate demand price intercept, reflecting desired autonomous expenditures on real national output ($D_0 > 0$); d, the annual growth rate in the aggregate demand price due to desired autonomous expenditures on real national output; f, the sensitivity of the aggregate demand price to real national output ($\partial P^D / \partial Y = -f < 0$); S_0, the initial aggregate supply price intercept for real national output ($S_0 > 0$); s, the annual growth rate in the aggregate supply price due to supply-side influences, including technological progress, growth in the factors of production, and government regulation; β, the adaptations parameter for unexpected changes in the aggregate price level ($\beta \geq 0$); h, the sensitivity of the aggregate supply price to real national output

---

[10] Real GDP fell by 1.8 percent in the first quarter of 2008, grew by 1.3 percent in the second quarter, before declining again over the next four quarters. Estimates of the annual growth rates for real GDP for the US economy for the four quarters from the third quarter of 2008 through the second quarter of 2009 are respectively −3.7, −8.9, −6.7, and −0.7 percent, yet the corresponding implicit price deflator over these four quarters is estimated to have slightly increased from 109.16 to 109.59. The implicit price deflator for the first quarter of 2008 was 107.59. These statistics are from the Bureau of Economic Analysis, http://www.bea.gov (accessed June 15, 2012).

[11] The linear specification for the short-run aggregate supply curve and the aggregate demand curve is made for the convenience of solving the system mathematically. Actually, the price elasticity of the Y^S curve would decline as the production of real national output increases due to diminishing returns to labor and increases in market-clearing factor prices, making the Y^S curve increasingly steep.

$(\partial P^S/\partial Y = h > 0)$; P_{-1}, the actual aggregate price level from the previous year; and P^e_{-1}, the expected aggregate price level from the previous year.

Equation (1) states that the aggregate demand price, P^D, is inversely related to the aggregate quantity demanded of real national output (Y). The inverse relationship reflects the interest rate, wealth, and international competitiveness effects. Here the aggregate demand price is assumed to change with autonomous expenditures on real national output (D_0), which, in turn, are assumed to increase at the annual rate of d, due to, for example, population growth and increases in wealth, government expenditures, exports, and the money supply. A negative demand shock (e.g., with a fall in personal wealth or business confidence) would be reflected in a decrease in d, and if severe enough, a negative d.

Equation (2) states that the aggregate supply price, P^S, is directly related to the quantity of real national output. Due to diminishing returns to labor and rising market-clearing factor prices as real national output increases, the aggregate supply price rises with the production of national output.

The term S_0 captures the minimum aggregate supply price at the beginning of the period. Over any year, changes in technology, labor supply, the physical capital stock, and the supply of available natural resources, as well as changes in government regulations, taxes, and the institutional environment, would shift the aggregate supply curve. Here this effect of changes in the real determinants of aggregate supply on the aggregate supply price is captured by the term $1 - s$, where the parameter s captures the growth rate in aggregate supply due to these structural factors. Supply-side shocks would be reflected in a change in s. Negative supply-side shocks, for example, with severe weather or higher import prices from a depreciation of the home currency or exogenous hikes in energy prices, would result in a decline in s, or if severe enough, even a negative s. Favorable supply-side shocks, for example, with accelerated technological progress or heavy immigration of labor, would be reflected in an increase in the value of s.

The aggregate supply equation also allows for changes in price expectations. The term $\beta \cdot (P_{-1} - P^e_{-1})$, $\beta \geq 0$, reflects any adjustment in the current aggregate supply price due to an error in price expectations held by factor suppliers from the previous year. Here we are using a simple form of adaptive expectations.[12] For example, if factor suppliers underestimated the aggregate price level in the previous year, $P^e_{-1} < P_{-1}$, then in the current year they would attempt to catch up by demanding higher factor supply prices, which, in turn, would result in a vertical shift up in the Y^S curve. The ability of factor suppliers to realize higher supply prices, however, depends in part on whether they are bound by contracts extending into the current year. For example, labor may be operating under a multi-year contract with a fixed schedule for wages. Flexibility is gained, however, if the labor contracts incorporate cost-of-living adjustments.

---

[12] A term $\alpha \cdot d \cdot D_0$, where α is a recognition parameter for changes in aggregate demand, could be added to the Y^S schedule, giving $P^S = S_0 \cdot (1 - s) + \alpha \cdot d \cdot D_0 + \beta \cdot (P_{-1} - P^e_{-1}) + h \cdot Y$. Consistent with the hypothesis of rational expectations, this term would allow for changes in the aggregate supply price due to anticipation by suppliers of factors of the change in aggregate demand. In the current period (e.g., a year), the value of the parameter α can vary between 0 (no recognition of the change in aggregate demand or an inability to change factor supply prices in the period due to fixed contracts) to 1 (a complete recognition of the change in aggregate demand with perfectly flexible factor supply prices giving an ability to respond fully to the change in aggregate demand—as with the rational expectations).

Solow (1997: 231) observes, however: "In the short-run part of macroeconomics, the rational expectations hypothesis seems to have little to recommend it. In that context, I suggest that expectations are best handled ad hoc, that is in a common sense way." Solow's approach is taken in the simple model presented here. It is difficult to reconcile the hypothesis of rational expectations with the observed annual changes in real national output and the aggregate price level—especially when there is a decrease in aggregate demand.

The distinction between movements along the curves and shifts in the curves is important. With changes in real national output and income (Y), the economy moves along the aggregate demand and supply curves. Changes in the underlying exogenous factors, here D_0, d, or f for aggregate demand and S_0, s, β, P_{-1}, P^e_{-1} or h for aggregate supply, will result in shifts in the curves.

Equation (3) is the equilibrium condition, which states that macroeconomic equilibrium will be found at the level of real national output (real national income) where the aggregate demand price equals the aggregate supply price.

At the beginning of the year, $d = 0$ and $s = 0$, before any adjustment due to incorrect price expectations from the previous year, the initial equilibrium level of real national output is $Y_0 = (D_0 - S_0)/(f + h)$.

Over a year, however, with $d \neq 0$ and $s \neq 0$, (usually $d > 0$, with growth in aggregate demand from increases in D_0, and $s > 0$, with growth in aggregate supply from technological progress, increases in the labor force and physical capital stock), and incorporating any adjustment for errors in price expectations, $\beta \cdot (P_{-1} - P^e_{-1})$, the new equilibrium level of real national output at the end of the year would be Y_1, where

$$Y_1 = [D_0 \cdot (1 + d) - S_0 \cdot (1 - s) - \beta \cdot (P_{-1} - P^e_{-1})]/(f + h)$$

From this general result, specific comparative static experiments can be illustrated.

CHANGES IN NATIONAL OUTPUT AND THE AGGREGATE PRICE LEVEL

In general there are two explanations for an increase in the equilibrium aggregate price level: demand-pull inflation and cost-push inflation. With **demand-pull inflation**, increases in aggregate demand (Y^D) exceed increases in aggregate supply (Y^S), or, in general, $\Delta Y^D > \Delta Y^S \geq 0$. In the case of demand-pull inflation, equilibrium real national output increases. In contrast, with **cost-push inflation**, decreases in aggregate supply dominate decreases in aggregate demand, $\Delta Y^S < \Delta Y^D \leq 0$. Cost-push inflation is accompanied by a fall in equilibrium real national output.

To illustrate, refer to Figure 6.8. Begin in equilibrium at E_0 with Y_0 and P_0, and consider an increase in aggregate demand from Y^D to $Y^{D\prime}$ (see the upper panel). For simplicity we will hold the aggregate supply curve constant. An increase in aggregate demand, *ceteris paribus*, would increase the price level, real national output, and employment. With such demand-pull inflation, we find the traditional tradeoff between inflation and unemployment.

To illustrate cost-push inflation, we will also take the simplest case, where there is a fall in the aggregate supply curve from Y^S to $Y^{S\prime}$, holding constant the aggregate demand curve (see the lower panel in Figure 6.8). A decrease in aggregate supply, *ceteris paribus*, would increase the aggregate price level, but reduce real national output and employment. With such cost-push inflation, we find both inflation and higher unemployment. An inflationary recession with declining real national output and rising aggregate price level is known as **stagflation**.

As noted, full employment and price stability are fundamental macroeconomic objectives. The adverse consequences of unemployment fall primarily on those individuals out of work and their families. The effects of inflation tend to be more diffuse. Inflation affects the distribution of income, in particular, reducing the real income of those living on relatively fixed nominal incomes, likely to be lower-income households and retirees. In Chapter 7, other consequences of inflation (e.g., on the incentives to save, efficiency of resource allocation, and speculative activity) will be discussed.

145

Demand-pull inflation: $\Delta P > 0$ when $\Delta Y^D > \Delta Y^S \geq 0$
(assume here $\Delta Y^S = 0$)

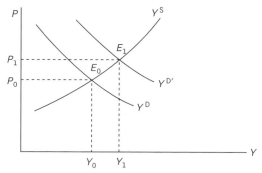

Cost-push inflation: $\Delta P > 0$ when $\Delta Y^S < \Delta Y^D \leq 0$
(assume here $\Delta Y^D = 0$)

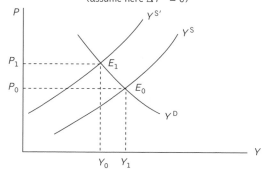

Figure 6.8 *Demand-pull and cost-push inflation*

We will now use the model to illustrate annual fluctuations in real national output and the aggregate price level. As we will discuss, the short-run performance of a national economy can have longer-run implications.

An increase in aggregate demand

Consider first an increase in aggregate demand, reflected in a rise in the aggregate demand price at any level of real national output, $d > 0$. (Refer to Figure 6.9, with an initial equilibrium of Y_0 and P_0. Note that, if price expectations were accurate, $P^e = P$, then Y_0 would be the natural rate of output, $Y_0 = Y_n$. We are not assuming, however, that the initial equilibrium is at the natural rate of output.) The consequence of a given increase in aggregate demand for equilibrium real national output and the aggregate price level depends on aggregate supply. In this simple model, shifts in the supply curve occur with the natural growth in the short-run aggregate supply and changes in price expectations. The natural growth in aggregate supply ($s > 0$) would shift the Y^S curve to the right over the period. To the extent, however, that labor supply and other suppliers of factors are adjusting to unexpected increases in the aggregate price level from the previous period ($\beta > 0$ and, say, $P^e_{-1} < P_{-1}$), the aggregate supply curve shifts to the left.

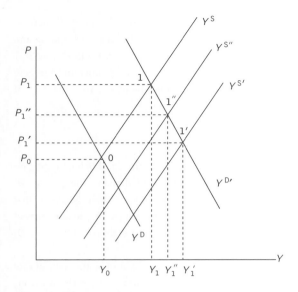

Figure 6.9 *An increase in aggregate demand*

An increase in aggregate demand will usually result in increases in real national output and the aggregate price level. Here:

$Y^{D'} = Y^D$ curve after the initial increase in desired autonomous expenditures $(d > 0)$

$Y^{S'} = Y^S$ curve after the natural increase in supply-side factors $(s > 0)$

$Y^{S''} = Y^S$ curve after the natural increase in supply-side factors $(s > 0)$ and adjustment for incorrect price expectations from the previous year $[\beta \cdot (P_{-1} - P^e_{-1})] > 0$.

Note: If $P^e_{-1} > P_{-1}$, then $Y^{S''}$ would lie to the right of $Y^{S'}$.

To illustrate, begin by ignoring price expectations, that is, assuming $\beta = 0$, and holding constant aggregate supply $(s = 0)$. Then with the growth in aggregate demand $(d > 0)$ we clearly find an increase in the equilibrium levels of real national output and the aggregate price level, consistent with demand-pull inflation. The new equilibrium level of income, Y_1, would be at the intersection of the $Y^{D'}$ and Y^S curves at point 1 with $Y_1 > Y_0$. The aggregate price level would rise to P_1.

If we allow for natural growth in aggregate supply $(s > 0)$, then the increase in real national output will be greater and the rise in the aggregate price level will be less. In fact, the net impact on the aggregate price level will depend on the relative increase in aggregate demand versus aggregate supply. Usually we observe an increase in both Y and P, consistent with demand-pull inflation. In this case, the new equilibrium level of income is Y'_1, found at the intersection of the $Y^{D'}$ and $Y^{S'}$ curves at point $1'$, with $Y'_1 > Y_1$. The demand pull inflation is moderated, with the new equilibrium price level of P'_1, where $P_0 < P'_1 < P_1$. (In Figure 6.9 refer to the $Y^{D'}$ and $Y^{S'}$ curves with the equilibrium Y'_1 and P'_1.)

Finally, in the most comprehensive scenario we allow for adjustment in price expectations. Here, assuming adaptive expectations, labor and other factor suppliers do not recognize current changes in the aggregate price level or are unable to change their factor supplies due to fixed contracts for the year. In the next year, however, at least some factor suppliers will adjust their price expectations. Consequently, the changes in real national output and the aggregate price level

147

over the year depend on: the growth in aggregate demand (with $d > 0$ resulting in Y increasing and P increasing); the growth in aggregate supply (with $s > 0$ resulting in Y increasing and P decreasing); and the adjustment to the previous period's price misperception (with $P^e_{-1} < P_{-1}$ and $\beta > 0$ resulting in Y decreasing and P increasing). In this case, the new equilibrium aggregate price level (P''_1) would be higher and the rise in national output would be less.[13] (See point $1''$ at the intersection of the $Y^{D'}$ and $Y^{S''}$ curves with the equilibrium Y''_1 and P''_1.)

A decrease in aggregate demand

A decrease in aggregate demand, *ceteris paribus*, would result in a fall in the equilibrium aggregate price level. That is, holding constant the Y^S curve, a fall in aggregate demand (here $d < 0$) would also reduce the equilibrium level of real national output. It is not very likely, however, that the Y^S curve would remain constant over the year. In this model, only under previously correct expectations ($P^e_{-1} = P_{-1}$) and no natural growth or decline in aggregate supply (i.e., $s = 0$) would the Y^S curve remain constant.

Refer to Figure 6.10, with initial equilibrium of Y_0 and P_0, where Y_0 would be the natural rate of output if price expectations at the beginning of the period were accurate. As in the previous example, we are not assuming that the economy necessarily begins the year at the natural rate of output. With a fall in aggregate demand ($d < 0$), the Y^D curve shifts to the left and for a given Y^S curve, Y decreases and P decreases, illustrating demand-pull deflation. (See point 1 at the intersection of the $Y^{D'}$ and Y^S curves with the equilibrium Y_1 and P_1.)

As discussed in Chapter 4, the aggregate price level did fall during the Great Depression; but as noted earlier in this chapter, deflation has been rare for the US economy since then. Indeed, a fall in aggregate demand would likely be accompanied by a fall in aggregate supply, especially if the negative demand shock were large. The aggregate supply would decrease ($s < 0$) during the year of declining aggregate demand with discouraged workers leaving the labor force, businesses not replacing their depreciated physical capital, and failed firms with large economic losses leaving the market. The decrease in the aggregate supply curve would add to the decline in real national output, but would offset partially or exactly, or possibly even reverse, the fall in the aggregate price level with the decrease in aggregate demand. That is, before any adjustment of aggregate supply for incorrect past price expectations, the new equilibrium level of real national income would be Y'_1 and P'_1, at point $1'$, the intersection of the $Y^{D'}$ and $Y^{S'}$ curves, with $Y'_1 < Y_1 < Y_0$ and, here, $P_1 < P'_1 < P_0$. In Figure 6.10 a partial offset is illustrated and the deflation is modified.

When we consider price expectations, however, the fall in equilibrium real national output would likely be greater and the aggregate price level may actually increase. That is, if from the previous year because of an underestimation of the aggregate price level, $P^e_{-1} < P_{-1}$, *ceteris paribus*, the aggregate supply curve would shift up and to the left in this year—even with the (unanticipated) drop in aggregate demand during the year. If, as likely with the recession and declining real national output, the growth rate in the aggregate supply price were negative ($s < 0$), then the decrease in the aggregate supply curve from the upward adjustment in price expectations, with $\beta \cdot (P_{-1} - P^e_{-1}) > 0$, would be enhanced. The net effect, then, of the greater decrease in aggregate supply and the decrease in aggregate demand would be a greater decline in real national output but a rise in the aggregate price level ($P''_1 > P_0$). Here, in this most comprehensive

---

[13]Note that if $P_{-1} < P^e_{-1}$, then the $Y^{S''}$ curve would lie to the right of $Y^{S'}$ and $Y''_1 > Y'_1$ and $P''_1 < P'_1$. Other possibilities include a larger adjustment in $Y^{S'}$ due to a greater underestimation of last year's price level, so that the $Y^{S''}$ curve lies to the left of the Y^S curve, reducing Y''_1 to below Y_1 and raising P''_1 above P_1.

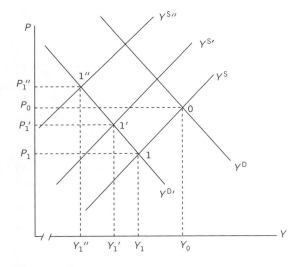

Figure 6.10 *A decrease in aggregate demand*

A decrease in aggregate demand will result in a decrease in real national output and an increase in the aggregate price level when aggregate supply falls more. Here:

$Y^{D\prime} = Y^D$ *curve after the initial decrease in desired autonomous expenditures (d < 0)*

$Y^{S\prime} = Y^S$ *curve after the natural decrease in supply-side factors (s < 0)*

$Y^{S\prime\prime} = Y^S$ *curve after the natural decrease in supply-side factors (s < 0) and adjustment for incorrect price expectations from the previous year* $[\beta \cdot (P_{-1} - P^e_{-1})] > 0$.

Note: If $P^e_{-1} > P_{-1}$, *then* $Y^{S\prime\prime}$ *would lie to the right of* $Y^{S\prime}$.

scenario, the new equilibrium real income is Y''_1 and P''_1, found at point $1''$, the intersection of the $Y^{D\prime}$ and $Y^{S\prime\prime}$ curves, where $Y''_1 < Y'_1 < Y_1 < Y_0$ and $P''_1 > P_0$. As before, the outcomes depend on the relative magnitudes of the changes: in aggregate demand ($d < 0$), and aggregate supply ($s < 0$) and price expectations (with $\beta \cdot (P_{-1} - P^e_{-1}) > 0$).[14,15]

In fact, such inflationary recessions have been observed in the US economy. Since 1960 annual real GDP for the US economy has declined in seven years: −0.6 percent in 1974, −0.2 percent in 1975, −0.3 percent in 1980, −1.9 percent in 1982, −0.2 percent in 1991, −0.3 percent in 2008, and −3.5 percent in 2009. These recessions, however, were accompanied not by deflation,

---

[14] With a significant downturn in the economy, it may be that factor suppliers overestimate the price level, in which case in the next period the Y^S curve would shift right.

[15] If we had assumed rational expectations ($\alpha = 1$ and $P^e_{-1} = P_{-1}$), then the fall in aggregate demand would be matched by an increase in aggregate supply, leaving real national output unchanged and the aggregate price level reduced, *ceteris paribus*. Although if aggregate supply is decreasing ($s < 0$) during the year of declining aggregate demand, then real national output would fall and the decrease in the aggregate price level would be modified, but unlikely reversed. As noted, annual deflation is not common in the US economy, a stylized fact that is not accounted for under the hypothesis of rational expectations.

This is not to deny that economic agents might attempt to use all the economic information to forecast the price level, as under the rational expectations hypothesis. Rather, a combination of errors in forecasting due to delays in accurate information on the economy being available, misperceptions, institutionally set prices for some factors, and sluggish adjustment to changes in the aggregate price level means that the offsetting changes in aggregate supply to changes in aggregate demand envisioned under rational expectations that return the economy to the natural rate of output are unlikely to prevail in practice.

Moreover, Akerlof (2007) emphasizes the importance of incorporating norms in explaining human behavior, pointing to the observed downward inflexibility in money wages and resistance of customers to increases in product prices as evidence undermining the rational expectations hypothesis.

but by inflation—and in four out of the seven recession years by above-average inflation. The corresponding percentage changes in the implicit price deflator for GDP were 9.1, 9.5, 9.1, 6.1, 3.5, 2.2 and 1.1 percent, respectively. For the aggregate price level not to have declined during these recessions implies that any declines in aggregate demand over these years were offset by declines in aggregate supply.[16]

Over an extended period, deflation is rare for the industrial economies. For example, over the first decade of the twenty-first century, the only economy to experience deflation was Japan, with an average annual growth rate in its GDP implicit deflator of -1.1 percent for 2000–10.[17] In the previous period 1990–2000, no nation experienced declines in the aggregate price level over the decade, although a number of economies were plagued with triple-digit inflation. (Recall Table 1.5, where a number of the nations with negative output growth over the 1990s had such high inflation.)

A decrease in aggregate supply

A fall in aggregate supply, with a leftward shift in the Y^S curve, reduces the equilibrium level of real national output and increases the aggregate price level, *ceteris paribus*. In the simple model illustrated here, a fall in aggregate supply could reflect $s < 0$, with decreases in the supply curves for the factors of production (e.g., declines in the labor supply with heavy emigration or prolonged low fertility, decreases in the physical capital stock with the devastation of war or natural disasters, and decreases in natural resources due to mismanagement, pollution, or again, natural disasters). Also, leftward shifts in the Y^S curve could reflect: increased taxes or tighter government regulation or, as noted earlier, depreciation in the domestic currency. By itself, a fall in aggregate supply would produce stagflation. An upward adjustment in price expectations would also shift the aggregate supply curve to the left, contributing to cost-push inflation.

For example, as discussed in Chapter 5, the stagflation of 1974–75 is attributed in large part to sharply higher oil prices induced by the OPEC oil embargo in late 1973. This leftward shift in the Y^S curve ($s < 0$) dominated any decline in aggregate demand (e.g., due to increased expenditures on oil imports and declines in consumer and business confidence). If subsequently

---

[16]For the 51-year period 1960–2010, the simple correlation coefficient for the inflation rate (measured by the percentage change in the implicit price deflator for GDP) between the current and previous years is 0.89. In comparison, the simple correlation coefficient between successive years for the growth rate in real GDP is 0.29. Inflation momentum appears to have been more prevalent than output growth momentum over this period.

Moreover, for this period of 51 years, the average annual growth rate in real GDP was 3.1 percent, while the average inflation rate (measured by the percentage change in the implicit price deflator for GDP) was 3.6 percent. The simple correlation coefficient between the average annual growth rate in real GDP and the average inflation rate is -0.22, which is statistically insignificant but more consistent with cost-push inflation than demand-pull inflation. Data for the regression analysis of the US economy are from the Bureau of Economic Analysis, National Income and Product Accounts Tables (www.bea.gov), accessed January 16, 2012. In Chapter 8 we will discuss how to test economic theory, and provide a review of some basic statistics such as the simple correlation coefficient.

In 2009, however, several industrial economies did experience deflation during their recessions. These countries are (with the percentage changes in the GDP implicit price deflators and real national outputs in 2009, respectively) : Canada (-2.1 and -2.5 percent), Ireland (-3.2 and -7.1 percent), Japan (-0.9 and -5.2 percent), the Netherlands (-0.3 and -4.0 percent), Norway (-4.0 and -1.6 percent), and Singapore (-1.8 and -1.3 percent). These statistics are from World Bank (2011: Table 4.a).

[17]These data are from the World Bank (2012: Tables 4.1 and 4.16). Japan has experienced prolonged economic stagnation. The average annual growth rate for Japan's real GDP for 2000–10 was 0.9 percent. For the previous period 1990–2000, the average annual growth rates for Japan's GDP implicit price deflator and its real GDP were 0.0 percent and 1.0 percent, respectively. The devastating earthquake that struck the northeastern coast of Japan in March 2011 not only resulted in thousands of deaths and the nuclear disaster at Fukushima, but also hurt the Japanese economy. The Council of Economic Advisers (2012: 129) cites an IMF estimate that Japan's real GDP fell by 0.9 percent in 2011, after increasing by 4.0 percent in 2010.

price expectations were adjusted upward, the inflation would build upon itself, especially when aggregate demand recovered—as occurred in the latter half of the 1970s.

An increase in aggregate supply

Increases in aggregate supply with rightward shifts in the Y^S curve likely reflect technological progress, physical capital formation, growth in the labor force, and improved efficiencies in the economy. *Ceteris paribus*, an increase in aggregate supply would yield increased national output and a fall in the aggregate price level, or deflationary output growth. To reiterate, deflation in the US economy rarely happens, which implies that increases in aggregate demand regularly exceed growth in aggregate supply.

We conclude this chapter with a discussion of the recent "Great Recession," drawing lessons from this severe demand shock to the US economy. Then, in the next chapter, we turn to the long-run trends and growth models.

THE GREAT RECESSION

After a brief recession in 2001, the US economy resumed growth, albeit initially modest. The income tax cuts in 2001 and again in 2003, combined with the greater defense spending on the wars in Afghanistan and Iraq, increased expenditures for homeland security and expansion of Medicare benefits, helped turn the federal government budget surpluses realized in 1998–2001 back into deficits. The already low US personal saving rates fell even further, averaging 2.8 percent of disposable income for 2000–07.[18] With the rebound in the stock market and appreciation of housing, however, personal wealth rose, which bolstered consumer spending. In addition, monetary policy in the early part of the new decade was quite accommodating, with the federal funds rate dropping from an annual average of 6.2 percent in 2000 to 1.1 percent in 2003.[19] Fueling a real estate boom was aggressive lending to households for new home purchases. Real residential fixed investment increased by a third from 2000 to 2005 (from 4.5 percent to 6.1 percent of GDP).[20]

The US economic expansion picked up, with real GDP growth rising from 1.8 percent in 2002 to 3.5 percent in 2004, before slowing to 3.1 percent in 2005 and then down to a 1.9 percent increase in 2007. Inflation, while moderate, rose steadily from 1.6 percent in 2002 to 3.3 percent in 2005, due in part to sharply higher oil prices, before declining to a 2.9 percent rate in 2007 with the slowing economy.[21] Accompanying the government budget deficits and low

---

[18] The personal saving rate, the share of personal saving in disposable income, began to decline in the US during the second half of the 1980s, from the average annual rates of 8.3 percent in the 1960s and 9.6 percent in the 1970s. During the decade of the 1990s, the personal saving rate averaged only 5.5 percent of disposable income.

The macroeconomic data for this discussion of the Great Recession are from Council of Economic Advisers (2010), especially historical averages in earlier decades, and from the Bureau of Economic Analysis, especially for the post-2000 period. For the latter, see http://www.bea.gov (accessed June 15, 2012).

[19] The prime rate of interest, the lending rate charged by commercial banks to their most creditworthy corporate borrowers, similarly fell over the first part of the decade, from an average of 9.2 percent in 2000 to 4.1 percent in 2003. While the Federal Reserve began to push up interest rates after 2003, with the federal funds rate (the interbank lending rate for reserves) rising to 5.0 percent in 2007 (from an average of 1.1 percent in 2003), the earlier easy monetary policy contributed significantly to the housing boom. See Council of Economic Advisers (2010: Table B-73) for data on interest rates.

[20] Total mortgage debt outstanding (for nonfarm properties) in the US increased from $6.7 trillion in 2000 to $12.0 trillion in 2005 and then continued to rise to $14.4 trillion in 2007 (Council of Economic Advisers 2010: Table B-75).

[21] The inflation rate here refers to the annual percentage change in the implicit price deflator for GDP. The average annual world price per barrel of petroleum (in 2005 dollars) increased from $32 to $66 between 2000 and 2007, and then to $83 in 2008, before declining to $56 with the recession and drop in global demand in 2009 (see World Bank 2012: Table 6.5). Factors

private saving rates, the current account deficits continued, with the US increasingly dependent on foreign savings, especially from Asian central banks, that were accumulating US government securities.[22] As noted by the Council of Economic Advisers (2010: 110), "by 2005 and 2006, the United States was borrowing nearly 2 percent of world GDP."

All booms must end, however, and bubbles eventually burst. The realization that housing prices were inflated and that the so-called sub-prime mortgage loans for the purchase of many of the homes were no longer viable sent the housing sector into a tailspin. This, in turn, eroded the values of the derived mortgage-backed securities.[23]

In 2006, real residential fixed investment in the US economy fell by 7.3 percent, followed by a decline of 18.7 percent in 2007. The US economy slid into recession at the end of 2007. A wider financial crisis soon followed. In September 2008, the failure of a large investment bank, Lehman Brothers, revealed the vulnerability of numerous other major financial institutions to the excessive risks that had been undertaken. Threatened with a financial implosion, the Federal Reserve rapidly injected liquidity into the system. Confidence, however, was shaken, and households and businesses cut back on their spending. The stock market dropped precipitously, further diminishing the wealth of consumers who were already reeling from the depreciation in their home values, a primary source of net worth.[24] Real consumer spending fell by 0.6 percent in 2008 and another 1.9 percent in 2009.

As real national income and output in the US declined, the unemployment rate rose from 6.2 percent in September 2008 to 10.0 percent by October 2009. Reminiscent of the contagion among the East Asian economies with their collapsing currencies, recession spread to other high-income nations with overextended economies and vulnerable financial systems. With the economic contractions in the developed nations, international trade fell, transmitting the recession worldwide. As observed in *The Economist* (Economics Team 2010: 18):

> First, the effects of the recession were unevenly spread. In countries such as America, Spain or Ireland, the bursting of housing bubbles caused construction to slump, with the loss of many jobs. . ... By contrast, in exporting countries such as Germany or Japan the damage was done mainly by the collapse of global trade, which proved more temporary.

Unlike previous global recessions, however, where economic declines in the developed nations not only spread to, but were sharper in, the developing nations, this time many developing nations,

---

contributing to the rise in world oil prices were the turmoil in the Middle East with the war in Iraq, tighter OPEC supplies, and, in the US, the disruption in oil refining with Hurricane Katrina in 2005. In 2008, speculation in the world oil market drove the spot price to over $140 a barrel in July, even though by then the US was well into recession. As discussed, significantly higher oil prices lead to leftward shifts in the aggregate supply curve, and *ceteris paribus*, stagflation.

[22] O'Sullivan (2011: 13) ties the earlier Asian financial crisis to the bubble economies in the US and Europe. Citing the perceived lesson from this 1998 crisis for developing economies to build up international reserves to reduce their vulnerability to capital flight, he notes how the savings of the emerging economies, especially China and other Asian nations running large current account surpluses, financed the consumption binge in the US and other developed economies. In particular, O'Sullivan argues:

The surge in demand for safe and liquid assets in dollars, euros and pounds pushed down long-term borrowing costs. The savings of the emerging world allowed the rich world to spend too freely, one of the deeper causes of the wave of crises that has afflicted the rich world since 2007. America's financial markets met the global demand for "safe" dollar assets by repackaging the mortgages of marginal borrowers as bonds, which turned sour. But the resulting financial crisis hit mainly the rich world rather than emerging markets.

[23] See Lewis (2011) for a colorful account of the dishonesty, incompetence, and greed underlying the sub-prime housing crisis, which morphed into the financial crisis triggering the Great Recession.

[24] As noted by the Council of Economic Advisers (2010: 42), "All told, household and nonprofit net worth declined 20 percent between December 2007 and December 2008." The *Economic Report of the President 2010*, in particular, Chapters 1–3, provides a good account of the Great Recession and the policy measures undertaken.

especially in South Asia and East Asia, continued growing. As seen earlier in Table 6.1, on average, only in Europe and Central Asia and in Latin America and the Caribbean did real outputs decline in 2009. Moreover, in marked contrast to the Great Depression, not only was countercyclical economic policy more aggressive, but also the major developed nations coordinated their actions and did not resort to protectionist measures to preserve employment.[25] In the United States, the Obama administration, soon after taking office in early 2009, implemented a large fiscal stimulus, a combination of increased spending and tax cuts, including relief to the automobile industry. In pushing the federal funds rate to near zero, the Federal Reserve pumped additional reserves into the banking system. Other central banks undertook similar expansionary policies and cooperated not only with lines of credit for support of currencies, but also with additional reserves for the IMF. Concerns with the soaring budget deficits and mushrooming national debts restrained even more aggressive fiscal policies.

The recession in the US was deep. Real GDP fell by 0.3 percent in 2008 and by 3.5 percent in 2009, the sharpest annual decline since the Great Depression. However, consistent with the simple macroeconomic model offered earlier, the significant fall in aggregate demand did not result in deflation. The implicit price deflator for GDP in the US rose by 2.2 percent in 2008 and by another 1.1 percent in 2009. While the US economy slowly began to recover by mid-2009, unemployment rates remained high.

Recession in Europe

Financial crises not only can spread to other economies, especially with the global capital markets, but also tend to produce sharper and deeper recessions. In Europe, a number of economies were hard hit. The economic interdependencies were greatest within the euro zone, with the 17 nations that had adopted the euro as a common currency and are linked together in a monetary union. See Box 6.1 for a brief history of the European Union (EU) and the euro zone.

BOX 6.1: THE EUROPEAN UNION AND THE EURO ZONE

The origins of the European Union (EU) date back to 1957, with the formation of the European Community by West Germany, France, Italy, Belgium, the Netherlands, and Luxembourg as a **customs union**, that is, a **free trade area** with common external trade barriers. The European Community subsequently evolved into a **common market**, that is, a customs union with free mobility of capital and labor, along the way instituting common policies for agriculture, energy, and transportation. By the mid-1980s, six more nations had become members: Denmark, Ireland and the United Kingdom in 1973, Greece in 1981, and Portugal and Spain in 1986. In 1995 Austria, Finland, and Sweden joined. Then a major expansion took place in 2004 with eight former socialist economies of Eastern Europe (Czech Republic, Estonia, Hungary, Latvia, Lithuania, Poland, Slovakia, and Slovenia) and two Mediterranean islands (Cyprus and Malta). The European Union, as it came to be known, increased to its present size of 27 nations in 2007 when Bulgaria and Romania joined. Concerns

---

[25] For a brief comparison of the Great Recession that began in the US in late 2007 with the Great Depression of the 1930s, see "There could be trouble ahead: Briefing Lessons of the 1930s," *The Economist* (December 10, 2011): 76–78.

expressed with the recent expansions included the required transfers from the wealthier economies to the relatively poorer former transition economies and security issues, since membership in the EU usually resulted in joining the North Atlantic Treaty Organization (NATO), the Western security alliance. For good overviews of the European Union, see Peet (2007) and Rennie (2008).

The European Monetary Union (EMU), or the euro zone, is a subset of the EU. Ten nations (Denmark, Sweden, the UK, Bulgaria, Czech Republic, Hungary, Latvia, Lithuania, Poland, and Romania) are not members. The origins of the EMU go back to 1979 with the formation of the European Monetary System, initially created like a regional Bretton Woods system with adjustable exchange rates. In 1991 with the signing of the Maastricht Treaty, countries began to move towards a **monetary union** with one currency and a common central bank. In a monetary union, member nations give up their monetary independence and there is a singular monetary policy. The overriding goal of the European Central Bank was to be price stability, since low inflation is important for international competitiveness and efficient resource allocation.

To join the EMU, nations had to meet convergence criteria, including: federal budget deficits under 3 percent and national debts of less than 60 percent of GDP; inflation rates within 1.5 percentage points of the three lowest members; and long-term interest rates within 2 percentage points of the three lowest members. On January 1, 1999, 11 nations joined the EMU, adopting the euro as the common currency and handing over monetary policy to the European Central Bank. Within 3 years, their national currencies were replaced by euro coins and banknotes. The EMU has since increased to 17 members.

Perhaps the primary advantage of a common currency is the greater integration of trade and finance as foreign exchange conversion costs are eliminated. Up until the recent financial crises, the EMU was generally viewed as successful. While the EU likely increased trade between the member nations and collectively enhanced the influence of these nations in the international economy, the EMU also contributed to low inflation. The euro itself became the second key currency in the world, after the US dollar, accounting for roughly a quarter of the total international foreign exchange reserves.

A disadvantage for a nation of a common currency, however, in addition to not having an independent monetary policy, is not being able to devalue the national currency in case of a chronic deficit in the balance of payments. Thus, fiscal policy has to be relied on to address any internal and external imbalances.

There have been recurrent tensions in the EU. For one, because of stricter labor regulations and more generous social programs, high unemployment rates have characterized many of the Western European nations, even in the 1990s. Moreover, the low fertility rates in Europe have resulted in rising elderly burdens of dependency, adding to the fiscal stresses. The influx of immigrants, many from less developed nations, while countering the aging of the populations and bolstering the labor forces, has often been met by resistance, if not animosity. Finally, Russia views the incorporation of many of the former socialist economies of Eastern Europe into the EU, and even more so into NATO, as eroding its influence in the region.

Whether the EMU will remain intact after the economic crises of the Great Recession and the future of the euro and economic integration in Europe remain open questions in the second decade of the twenty-first century.

In particular, several nations, the so-called PIIGS of Portugal, Ireland, Italy, Greece and Spain, came under scrutiny with their perceived inability to service their national debts.[26] Profligate fiscal policies and generous entitlement programs had sharply increased their national debts—in the cases of Greece and Italy, central government debt neared or exceeded their national incomes even before the recession. Western banks holding much of these sovereign debts were exposed to pressures on their balance sheets. Financing the even larger budget deficits now with their reeling economies would be difficult, if not highly unlikely, without incurring sharply higher interest costs to account for the palpable risks of default.

Foremost among the problem economies was Greece. Rescue packages for Greece entailed the writeoff of half of the national debt coming due by private creditors, who were required to accept "safer" government bonds at a discount, as well as the infusion of funds into European banks and supporting purchases by the European Financial Stability Fund and the European Central Bank of new bonds issued by the Greek government. In addition, the IMF extended credit. Portugal and Ireland also received assistance. Spain, twice as large an economy as those of Greece, Portugal and Ireland combined, and facing its own housing crisis, needed support too. Yet, the stronger economies, especially Germany, were reluctant to "bail out" the spendthrift weaker nations, namely the PIIGS, without the latter adopting tighter fiscal policies. Consistent with the IMF medicine were the austerity measures to deal with the balance of payments problems. The United Kingdom, not a member of the euro zone, but with its own debt problems, aggressively adopted such measures on its own.

As encountered in the US, there was a conflict between tighter fiscal policies to address the long-term debt problems (which will be exacerbated by heavy demands for social support with the aging of the populations) and the short-run need to bolster weak economies. (Recall the premature tightening of fiscal and monetary policies in the US in 1937, which reversed the recovery from the Great Depression and plunged the US economy into a sharp recession in 1938.) Already the fiscal tightening is hurting. For example, in Greece, sharp cutbacks in public spending contributed to a health care crisis.[27] Still, with the reeling Greek economy and a history of tax evasion, large budget deficits continue, despite austerity measures.

The recessions in Europe were steep. The average decline in real national outputs in 2009 was 5.6 percent for the EU nations, following a year of an average of only 1.5 percent growth.[28]

---

[26] For an overview of the economic woes of the European Union, in particular the euro zone countries, and the implications for the US, see Council of Economic Advisers (2012: 131–139).

[27] See Daley (2011), who reports:

Greece used to have an extensive public health care system that pretty much ensured that everybody was covered for everything. But in the last two years, the nation's creditors have pushed hard for dramatic savings to cut back the deficit. These measures are taking a brutal toll on the system and on the country's growing numbers of poor and unemployed who cannot afford the new fees and co-payments instituted at public hospitals as part of the far-reaching austerity drive.

Violent protests spilled into the streets of Athens and other cities across Greece in response to the forced austerity measures, which resulted in large public sector layoffs of labor, sharp cuts in the minimum wage and pensions, higher taxes, and reduced government spending—all of which portended a continued recession. Ultimately the government fell, elections were held, and a new government came to power.

[28] These statistics on real GDP growth are simple averages, not weighted by population shares, as reported in Tables 1.1 and 1.6 of World Bank (2010, 2011, 2012). There are differences within the EU: for the 17 nations in the euro zone, the average growth rates for GDP were 0.9 percent, −4.8 percent, and 1.7 percent in 2008, 2009, and 2010, compared to the average for ten EU members that did not adopt the euro of 2.1 percent, −7.0 percent, and 1.9 percent. To illustrate further the diversity of experience, within the EU, real GDP declined in every nation, except Poland, in 2009, with the contractions ranging from only 1.0 percent in Cyprus to 14.1, 15.0, and 18.0 percent in the three Baltic economies of Estonia, Lithuania, and Latvia, respectively.

155

Moreover, unlike the US economy that began to grow after 2009, for many of these nations, renewed recessions were possible.[29] Indeed, the recovery of the US itself was hampered by the economic turmoil in Europe.

Lessons from the Great Recession

Hopefully economic insight was gained with the Great Recession, so that future bubbles and the subsequent painful contractions can be avoided. Concerning the lessons that might be learned, the Council of Economic Advisers (2010: 25) suggests that:

> For too many years, America's growth and prosperity were fed by a boom in consumer spending stemming from rising asset prices and easy credit. The Federal Government had likewise been living beyond its means, resulting in large and growing budget deficits. And our regulatory system had failed to keep up with financial innovation, allowing risky practices to endanger the system and the economy.

American consumers seem to have learned a lesson. In an attempt to rebuild wealth, personal saving rates have risen since 2008 to over 5 percent of disposable income, albeit well below the levels of the 1960s and 1970s. Unfortunately, the increased thriftiness of American consumers has hindered the economic recovery. With the adoption of greater austerity measures to deal with public debt, the economic recoveries of many of the European economies were even more tentative.

The expansionary fiscal policy the government implemented to deal with the recession, however, sharply increased the US federal government deficit to 10 percent of GDP in 2009. With the looming retirements of the baby boom generation and the attendant demands on the social security and Medicare systems, the national debt is projected to accelerate, unless fiscal reforms are enacted. In addition to higher taxes and reduced spending, necessary consequences of the nation's earlier living beyond its means, there may be significant changes in these entitlement programs. Europe, with its older populations, faces even more daunting fiscal reform challenges. In Chapter 10 we will address the consequences of an aging population. As a result of the tighter fiscal policies and greater government regulation of the financial system, the future economic growth of the United States and Europe may well be reduced.

After the severe recessions in the developed nations, renewed growth in the world economy was seen to depend on the robust emerging economies, led by China and India. O'Sullivan (2011: 24), however, urged caution:

> The biggest emerging markets, with their huge foreign-exchange reserves, appear to be almost crisis-proof (at least outside of eastern Europe) in contrast to the seemingly crisis-prone rich world. But setbacks in making the shift from poor to rich are inevitable. Indeed a lesson of recent economic history is that countries and regions that ride out a crisis well are all the more vulnerable to the next one. Hubris leads to policy mistakes, as the developed world has proved so devastatingly.

We should note that most other developed economies outside of the US and Europe experienced recessions. In particular, Japan, whose economy has been stagnant over the last two decades, suffered declines in real national output of 0.7 percent in 2008 and 5.2 percent in 2009. With a public debt exceeding national income, Japan has long been hard pressed to recharge its economy. On the other hand, Australia and South Korea were able to maintain positive, if reduced, output growth rates in 2008 and 2009. South Korea, moreover, had a robust 6.2 percent increase in its real GDP in 2010.

[29]The Council of Economic Advisers (2012: 137) cites IMF estimates that the economies of the euro zone grew only 1.6 percent in 2011, with recession likely in 2012.

CONCLUSION

Short-run fluctuations in the growth of national output, reflected in the business cycle, can have longer-run implications. Often periods of rapid economic growth end with sharp recessions. During recessions the decline in business investment and reduced physical capital formation can reduce the subsequent growth potential of the economy. With the decline in investment the introduction of new technology embodied in capital goods may also be delayed. Businesses that shut down due to the decline in aggregate demand may not reopen when the economy recovers. Individuals losing their jobs may suffer permanent loss of income—if not rehired for the same positions and subsequent employment is at lower wages. Moreover, there may be a loss in workers' human capital, particularly job-specific skills, with prolonged unemployment. The fall in tax revenues with the decline in national income may reduce public spending on the infrastructure, research and development, and education, all of which can reduce the future growth of the economy. In the next chapter we will address longer-run sources of economic growth.

KEY TERMS

adaptive expectations	autonomous expenditures
business cycle	cost-push inflation
common market	customs union
cyclical unemployment	demand-pull inflation
discouraged workers	economic contraction
economic expansion	free trade area
frictional unemployment	interest rate effect
international competitiveness effect	marginal factor cost of labor
marginal product of labor	marginal revenue product of labor
mean duration of unemployment	monetary union
natural rate of output	natural rate of unemployment
peak	perfect competition
perfect information	potential national output
rational expectations	recession
stagflation	structural unemployment
trough	wealth effect

QUESTIONS

1. Assume the following linear aggregate demand-aggregate supply model:

    $$P^D = D_0 \cdot (1 + d) - fY \quad \text{(aggregate demand schedule)}$$
    $$P^S = S_0 \cdot (1 - s) + \beta \cdot (P_{-1} - P^e_{-1}) + hY \quad \text{(short-run aggregate supply schedule)}$$
    $$P^D(Y) = P^S(Y) \quad \text{(equilibrium condition)}$$

    where P^D is the aggregate demand price (i.e., the aggregate price level associated with a given quantity of real national output demanded), P^S the aggregate supply price (i.e., the aggregate price level associated with a given quantity of real national output produced and supplied), Y real national output and real national income, P_{-1} the actual price level from the previous year, and P^e_{-1} the expected price level from the previous year. Assume initially that $D_0 = 5$, $d = 0$, $f = 0.004$, $S_0 = 0.8$, $s = 0$, $h = 0.002$, and $P_{-1} = P^e_{-1}$.

(a) Plot the aggregate demand and aggregate supply curves on a large graph, using scales for the axes of $1.9 < P < 2.6$ and $650 < Y < 750$.

(b) Find the initial equilibrium real national output (Y_0) and aggregate price level (P_0) algebraically and graphically.

2. Find the new equilibrium real national output (Y_1) and aggregate price level (P_1) when $d = 0.03$, $s = 0.02$, and $\beta = 1$, with $P^e_{-1} = 2.15 < 2.20 = P_{-1}$. (Give your answers to two decimal places.)

(a) Plot the new aggregate demand and aggregate supply curves on the same graph as the initial curves.

(b) Determine whether there has been demand-pull or cost-push inflation in period 1. Explain.

(c) Determine the growth rate in real national output and inflation rate in period 1.

3. Return to the initial equilibrium and find the new equilibrium real national output (Y_1) and aggregate price level (P_1) when $d = -0.015$, $s = -0.01$, $\beta = 1$, and $P^e_{-1} = 2.15 < 2.20 = P_{-1}$. (Give your answers to two decimal places.)

(a) Plot the new aggregate demand and aggregate supply curves on a new large graph together with the initial curves.

(b) Determine whether there has been demand-pull or cost-push inflation in period 1. Explain.

(c) Determine the growth rate in real national output and inflation rate in period 1.

4. Do you think lessons really have been learned from the Great Recession? Discuss, noting the implications for economic growth in the future.

5. Will the euro zone prevail? Discuss.

REFERENCES

Akerlof, George. 2007. "The Missing Motivation in Macroeconomics," *American Economic Review*, 97(1): 5–36.

Daley, Suzanne. 2011. "Fiscal Crisis Takes Toll on Health of Greeks," *New York Times*, December 26.

Economics Team. 2010. "How to Grow: A Special Report on the World Economy," *The Economist*, October 9.

Council of Economic Advisers. 2010. *Economic Report of the President 2010*. Washington, DC: United States Government.

Council of Economic Advisers. 2012. *Economic Report of the President 2012*. Washington, DC: United States Government.

Hess, Peter. 2010. "A More Realistic Aggregate Demand-Aggregate Supply Model for Use in Introductory Economics Classes," *Australasian Journal of Economics Education*, 7(2): 13–35.

Lewis, Michael. 2011. *The Big Short: Inside the Doomsday Machine*. New York: W.W. Norton.

O'Sullivan, John. 2011. "A Game of Catch-up: Special Report: The World Economy," *The Economist*, September 24.

Peet, John. 2007. "Fit at 50? A Special Report on the European Union," *The Economist*, March 17.

Pfeffer, Jeffrey. 2010. "Laying Off the Layoffs," *Newsweek*, February 15: 32–37.

Rennie, David. 2008. "In the Nick of Time: A Special Report on EU Enlargement," *The Economist*, May 31.

Solow, Robert. 1997. "Is There a Core of Usable Macroeconomics We Should All Believe In?," *American Economic Review*, 87(2): 230–232.

Stadler, George. 1994. "Real Business Cycles," *Journal of Economic Literature*, 32(4): 1750–1783.

World Bank. 2009. *World Development Indicators 2009*. Washington, DC: World Bank.

World Bank. 2010. *World Development Indicators 2010*. Washington, DC: World Bank.

World Bank. 2011. *World Development Indicators 2011*. Washington, DC: World Bank.

World Bank. 2012. *World Development Indicators 2012*. Washington, DC: World Bank.

Chapter 7

Growth models

Growth models explain long-run trends or potential growth paths in the economy. In the long run, over a decade or more, supply-side factors, such as technological progress and gains in efficiency, as well as increases in the effective factors of production, largely explain economic growth. In the short run, annually or over periods of several years, however, demand-side factors, such as changes in spending with shifts in consumer and business confidence and variations in exports and government expenditures, are important and largely account for the business cycle. As discussed in the previous chapter, however, short-run fluctuations in economic activity, especially investment spending, can have longer-run consequences for physical capital formation and technological change. Below we set forth the basic neoclassical growth model. Then we extend the model to incorporate technological progress, natural resources, and qualitative changes in the factors of production. We discuss the implications of the growth models for convergence in per capita incomes between the developing and developed economies.

SIMPLIFYING ASSUMPTIONS

A number of simplifying assumptions are commonly made in setting forth aggregate growth models. First, we abstract from inflation and changes in the aggregate price level, to model growth in real national output, driven by the supplies of the effective factors of production and technological change. Second, a closed economy is usually assumed with full-employment macroeconomic equilibrium always holding. So, we are no longer concerned with business cycles and fluctuations in aggregate demand. We also assume that the share of the labor force in population is constant. This implies that the labor force is growing at the same rate as the population, consistent with a stable population with constant labor force participation rates. Making this assumption allows us to focus on labor productivity and directly relate economic growth to labor productivity growth. As we will see, there are other simplifying assumptions in growth models. In this sense, then, the growth models are not as rich or detailed as the short-run aggregate demand–aggregate supply models. On the other hand, growth models allow for a more careful analysis of long-run trends and the underlying determinants of economic growth.

We begin with a basic version of the Solow growth model, also known as the **neoclassical growth model** (see Solow 1956).[1] In this model, there is no technological change or qualitative change in the factors of production. There are just two primary factors of production, physical capital and labor.

---

[1] Solow won the Nobel Prize in Economics in 1987 primarily for his work in economic growth theory.

A BASIC SOLOW GROWTH MODEL

In this simple Solow model there are four equations. The key endogenous variables of real income (Y), physical capital (K), labor (L), real net investment (I) and real net saving (S) are functions of time, denoted by the variable t:

(S1) $\quad Y(t) \quad = \quad F[K(t), L(t)] \quad$ (aggregate production function)
(S2) $\quad I(t) \quad = \quad S(t) \quad$ (macroeconomic equilibrium condition)
(S3) $\quad S(t) \quad = \quad s \cdot Y(t) \quad$ (net savings function)
(S4) $\quad L(t) \quad = \quad L(0)e^{nt} \quad$ (labor supply function)

To facilitate the derivations, we will drop the formal time notation. Nevertheless, we should remember that in dynamic models, like this growth model, the endogenous variables are measured over time. When we want to indicate a variable for a particular period of time, we will use subscripts, for example Y_0 for the initial value of Y, that is, for period $t = 0$, and Y_1 for the value of Y for period $t = 1$.

Equation (S1) depicts the aggregate production function in general form, where real national output, Y, is a function of physical capital, K, and labor, L. Constant returns to scale are assumed, which means that multiplying each of the factors by a scalar c would multiply output by $c^1 = c$. That is, $c \cdot Y = F(cK, cL)$. An important feature of this Solow model, constant returns to scale allow us to write the aggregate production function in its intensive form, $y = f(k)$, where output per unit of labor, $y = Y/L$, is a function of the capital–labor ratio, $k = K/L$.

To show this, let $c = 1/L$; then $cY = (1/L)Y = Y/L = y = F(cK, cL) = F(K/L, L/L) = f(k, 1) = f(k)$. (Here we use y here to indicate output per unit of labor (Y/L) or labor productivity, instead of our usual output per capita ($y = Y/P$). As noted, in growth models the focus is on output per unit of labor, not output per capita. If the labor force is assumed to be a constant share of the population, then increases in labor productivity will yield increases in per capita income and economic growth.)

With constant returns to scale for the original production function, the **intensive production function**, $y = f(k)$, exhibits diminishing returns to capital intensity, that is, $dy/dk = f'(k) > 0$, and $d^2y/dk^2 = d(dy/dk)/dk = f''(k) < 0$, which means that output per unit of labor, y, rises with the capital–labor ratio, k, at a diminishing rate. (See Box 7.1 for the derivation of the intensive production function as well as a specific example of a production function with constant returns to scale.)

BOX 7.1: AN INTENSIVE PRODUCTION FUNCTION

The production function, $Y = A \cdot K^\alpha L^{1-\alpha}$, where $0 < \alpha < 1$, and A is an index of neutral technical change), is characterized by constant returns to scale. As such, we can write this production function in its intensive form as $y = A \cdot k^\alpha$.

To illustrate, begin with the production function, $Y = A \cdot K^\alpha L^{1-\alpha}$. Multiplying each of the two factors of production by the constant c will also multiply output by the constant c. That is, $A \cdot (cK)^\alpha(cL)^{1-\alpha} = c^{\alpha + (1-\alpha)} A \cdot (K)^\alpha(L)^{1-\alpha} = c^1 \cdot A \cdot (K)^\alpha(L)^{1-\alpha} = c \cdot Y$. Letting $c = 1/L$ gives: $Y/L = (1/L) \cdot A \cdot (K)^\alpha(L)^{1-\alpha} = A \cdot (K)^\alpha(L)^{-\alpha} = A \cdot (K/L)^\alpha$ or $y = A \cdot (k)^\alpha$, where $y = Y/L$ and $k = K/L$.

161

For example: let $A = 1$ and $\alpha = 0.4$, so the Cobb-Douglas production function is: $Y = K^{0.4}L^{0.6}$. Dividing through by L gives: $Y/L = K^{0.4}L^{0.6}/L = K^{0.4}L^{-0.4} = (K/L)^{0.4}$ or $y = k^{0.4}$. Output per unit of labor, or the average product of labor, increases with the capital-labor ratio: $dy/dk = 0.4k^{-0.6} > 0$, but at a diminishing rate: $d(dy/dk)/dk = -0.24k^{-1.6} < 0$, indicating diminishing returns to capital intensity. Plotting $y = k^{0.4}$ shows a strictly concave intensive production function, with diminishing returns to capital intensity from the outset.

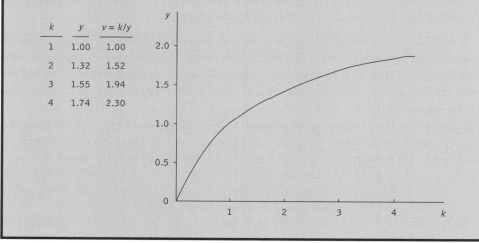

k	y	$v = k/y$
1	1.00	1.00
2	1.32	1.52
3	1.55	1.94
4	1.74	2.30

Equation (S2) represents the macroeconomic equilibrium. We are abstracting from depreciation of the capital stock, so S and I refer to net saving and net investment, respectively. Recall that, in the macroeconomic model, general equilibrium is defined by the condition $C + I + G + X - M = Y$, that is, desired aggregate expenditures on real national output (personal consumption (C), investment (I), government expenditures (G), and net exports ($X - M$)) equal the real national output produced. Moreover, the national income generated can be used for personal consumption, savings (S), net taxes (T), net transfers to the rest of the world (R), and net factor payments to the rest of the world (F): $Y = C + S + T + R + F$. Therefore, in equilibrium we have:

$$C + I + G + X - M = Y = C + S + T + R + F.$$

If, as is traditional in simple growth models like this, we assume no government ($G = 0$ and $T = 0$) and no foreign trade ($X = 0$ and $M = 0$), transfers ($R = 0$), or international factor mobility ($F = 0$), then this basic equilibrium condition reduces to $C + I = Y = C + S$. Subtracting C throughout gives: $I = Y - C = S$ or, here, $I(t) = S(t)$. That is, in macroeconomic equilibrium, with no government or foreign trade, all income not used for personal consumption is saved, $Y - C = S$.[2] The savings are made available to firms for investing in capital goods, so that all final output that is not consumption goods and services will be capital goods,

---

[2] The growth model could be extended to allow for public investment and foreign savings. As noted in Chapter 4,

$I + G_I$	=	$S + (T - G_C)$	+	$(M - X + R + F)$
gross domestic	=	gross domestic	+	deficit on current
investment		saving		account balance (if +)
(GDI)	=	(GDS)	+	(net foreign saving)

$I = Y - C$. Growth models hold that macroeconomic equilibrium always prevails, so net savings equal net investment, as represented in equation (S2). Moreover, the net investment forthcoming in any period (i.e., gross fixed investment less the capital depreciation) will yield the change in the physical capital stock, $I = dK$.

Equation (S3) represents the savings function, $S(t) = s \cdot Y(t)$, where we assume net savings are a constant fraction, s, of real national income. In theory, the incentive to save depends on the after-tax real return to saving, in turn, a function of the interest rate. The national saving rate would also be affected by the burden of dependency and the level and distribution of per capita income. In this model, however, the saving rate is exogenous.

Equation (S4) gives the supply of labor, $L(t) = L(0)e^{nt}$. The supply of labor is assumed to be growing at a continuous annual rate of n, expressed as a decimal (e.g. $n = .02$ for two percent growth). That is, differentiating both sides of equation (S4) with respect to time and then dividing through by $L(t)$, we can derive the natural growth rate of labor, n:

$$dL(t)/dt = nL(0)e^{nt} \quad \text{and} \quad dL(t)/L(t) = n.$$

The growth rate of labor supply reflects the population growth rate, in turn equal to the crude rate of natural increase and the net migration rate, as well as labor force participation rates. In this model, the natural growth rate of labor supply is exogenous and assumed to be constant.

The endogenous variables in the Solow model are Y, K, L, S, and I. The exogenous variables are the saving rate, s, and the natural growth rate in the labor force, n. The key variable in the Solow model, however, is the capital–labor ratio, $k = K/L$. Recall that, with the assumption of constant returns to scale for the production function, output per unit of labor, y, rises with the capital–labor ratio, k, at a diminishing rate.

STEADY-STATE EQUILIBRIUM

Steady-state equilibrium in this basic Solow model is defined by a constant capital–labor ratio, $dk = 0$, and thus a constant output per unit of labor, $dy = 0$. To derive the steady-state condition, we can differentiate the capital–labor ratio and then substitute in the conditions of the model. We will drop the time notation for simplicity. Beginning with $k = K/L$ and differentiating both sides, we get:

$$dk = [dK \cdot L - K \cdot dL]/L^2 = dK/L - (K/L) \cdot (dL/L)$$

By definition, $dK = I$, that is, the annual change in the capital stock is equal to the net investment over the year. Macroeconomic equilibrium requires $I = S$, as in equation (S2), and net saving is a fixed share of national income, $S = sY$, as in equation (S3). Finally, labor supply is growing continuously at the annual rate of n, that is, $dL/L = n$, as derived from equation (S4).

where $T - G_C$ is the current government budget balance, GDI $= I + G_I$ is gross domestic investment, GDS $= S + (T - G_C)$ is gross domestic saving, and G_I and G_C are government investment (capital expenditures) and government consumption (current expenditures) respectively.

Gross capital formation can exceed gross domestic saving if the nation runs a current account deficit. Conversely, the nation is a net saver, with GDS exceeding GDI, when it runs a current account surplus. To derive the change in the physical capital stocks, however, capital consumption would have to be subtracted from GDI. In market economies, most of the physical capital formation is private and financed through private domestic saving, so the typical assumption underlying growth models of no government, foreign trade, aid, or international factor mobility is analytically convenient. For developing economies and for command economies, government capital formation, especially for the economic infrastructure (the transportation and communications networks and public utilities) can be significant. Moreover, developing nations, especially early on, rely on foreign savings to augment their domestic saving to allow for greater domestic investment.

Substituting these conditions in the expression for the change in the capital–labor ratio, we find:

$$dk = sY/L - kn = sy - nk,$$

where $y = Y/L = f(K/L) = f(k)$. We have derived the **fundamental equation of the Solow model**, $dk = sy - nk$, which describes the change in the capital–labor ratio as equal to the difference between the net savings forthcoming per unit of labor, $sy = sY/L = S/L$, and the net investment required per unit of labor to maintain the capital–labor ratio given the natural growth rate of labor supply, $nk = nK/L = I/L$.

As noted, in steady-state equilibrium, the capital–labor ratio, $k = K/L$, is constant, therefore $dk = sy - nk = 0$. For steady-state equilibrium then, $sy = nk$, or the savings per unit of labor forthcoming, sy, must equal the investment per unit of labor required to maintain the capital–labor ratio given the natural growth rate in the labor force, nk. (Note that this condition reflects the macroeconomic equilibrium, $S = I$. To show this, we write $S/L = sY/L = sy = nk = nK/L = dK/L = I/L$. Multiplying through by L, gives $S = I$.)

The required net investment to maintain the capital–labor ratio depends on the growth rate in labor, n. To illustrate with a simple example, suppose the capital–labor ratio were equal to 40 (e.g., \$40 of capital per worker or 40 units of capital per unit of labor). If the labor force were growing at an annual rate of 3 percent ($n = 0.03$), then the physical capital stock would also have to grow at 3 percent to maintain the capital–labor ratio of 40. Let $K_0 = 800$, $L_0 = 20$, and $n = 0.03$. Then initially $k_0 = K_0/L_0 = 800/20 = 40$. Over the year, the labor supply will increase by 3 percent to $L_1 = (1 + n) \cdot L_0 = (1 + 0.03) \cdot 20 = 20.6$. The required increase in the capital stock will also be 3 percent: $K_1 = (1 + n) \cdot K_0 = 1.03 \cdot 800 = 824$. The change in the capital stock is $dK = K_1 - K_0 = 824 - 800 = 24 = I$. Therefore, for this macroeconomic equilibrium, the saving forthcoming, S, must equal the required investment of 24 to maintain the capital–labor ratio of $k = 40 = 824/20.6 = 800/20$.

We can illustrate the Solow model graphically. In Figure 7.1 we plot sy, the net saving per unit of labor forthcoming, and nk, the net investment per unit of labor required to maintain the capital–labor ratio, against the capital–labor ratio. The net saving per unit of labor curve is strictly concave, like the intensive production function, $y = f(k)$, since we are multiplying output and income per unit of labor, which increases at a diminishing rate with the capital–labor ratio, by a constant saving rate, $0 < s < 1$. The required net investment per unit of labor curve, nk, is a ray from the origin with a slope equal to the natural growth rate of the labor force.

The steady-state equilibrium capital–labor ratio, k_0^*, is found graphically where the saving and investment curves intersect. (See point E_0, where $sy_0^* = nk_0^*$ and $y_0^* = f(k_0^*)$). The model is dynamically stable, since any departure from this steady-state equilibrium capital–labor ratio would be corrected. For example, consider a capital–labor ratio, k', that is less than the steady-state equilibrium, k_0^*. At k' the saving per unit of labor forthcoming (F') would exceed the required net investment (G') to maintain the capital–labor ratio k'. The excess supply of saving, indicated by the gap $F'G'$, would drive down the interest rate, or the user cost of capital, and stimulate investment. Firms would shift to more capital-intensive methods of production. The capital–labor ratio would then rise, which increases the income and saving per unit of labor (the movement from F' to E_0 along the saving curve), but at a slower rate than the required investment per unit of labor (the movement from G' to E_0 along the investment curve) until the excess saving is eliminated and the steady-state equilibrium capital–labor ratio is reached at k_0^*.

Conversely, a capital–labor ratio, k'', that is greater than the steady-state equilibrium, k_0^*, would generate saving per unit of labor forthcoming (F'') that falls short of the required net

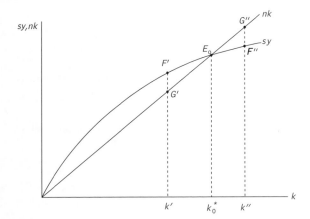

Figure 7.1 *Steady-state equilibrium in a basic Solow model*

In steady-state equilibrium, net saving per unit of labor forthcoming (sy) is equal to the required net investment per unit of labor (nk). Here at the equilibrium point, E_0, with the capital-labor ratio of k_0^*, this condition is met: $sy_0^* = nk_0^*$, where $y_0^* = f(k_0^*)$. In steady-state equilibrium in this basic Solow growth model, capital stock, labor, and output are all growing at the rate $s/v = n$. Consequently, the capital-labor ratio (k) and output per unit of labor (y) are constant.

investment (G'') to maintain the capital–labor ratio k''. The shortage of saving, indicated by the gap $G''F''$, would drive up the interest rate and reduce investment. Firms would shift to more labor-intensive methods of production, conserving on the more expensive capital. The capital–labor ratio would fall, which decreases the income and saving per unit of labor (the movement from F'' to E_0 along the saving curve), but at a slower rate than the declining required investment per unit of labor (the movement from G'' to E_0 along the investment curve) until the shortage of saving is eliminated and the steady-state equilibrium capital–labor ratio is reached at k_0^*.

At the steady-state equilibrium capital–labor ratio k_0^*, where d$k = 0$, output per unit of labor, y_0^*, is constant, where $y_0^* = f(k_0^*)$. Thus, in the basic Solow model with no technological progress or qualitative change in the factors of production, economic growth is zero. Real national output, the capital stock, and labor supply are all growing at the same rate, given by n, the natural growth rate of the labor supply. That is, in steady-state equilibrium in this most basic growth model, d$Y/Y = $ d$K/K = $ d$L/L = n$. The steady-state equilibrium growth paths are $Y(t) = Y(0)e^{nt}$, $K(t) = K(0)e^{nt}$, and $L(t) = L(0)e^{nt}$.

Moreover, this growth rate for output, capital, and labor, is equal to the saving rate divided by the capital–output ratio, $v = K/Y$. Beginning with the condition for steady-state equilibrium, d$k = sy - nk = 0$ or $sy = nk$, we can divide through by the capital–labor ratio, k, to get $sy/k = n$ or $s(Y/L)/(K/L) = s(Y/K) = s/(K/Y) = s/v = n$. In turn, the steady-state equilibrium capital–output ratio, v^*, is equal to the ratio of the saving rate to the natural growth rate of labor supply, s/n.

Illustration of steady-state equilibrium

Given a specific aggregate production function, we can solve for the steady-state equilibrium capital–labor ratio. Consider the following basic Solow model:

(S1) $Y = K^\alpha L^{1-\alpha}$

(S2) $I = S$
(S3) $S = sY$
(S4) $L = L_0 e^{nt}$

As shown earlier, this production function, $Y = K^\alpha L^{1-\alpha}$, is characterized by constant returns to scale. Multiplying through by $1/L$, we can write the production function in intensive form as $Y/L = K^\alpha L^{1-\alpha}/L$ or $y = K^\alpha L^{-\alpha}$ and $y = k^\alpha$, where $y = Y/L$ and $k = K/L$.

To derive the fundamental equation of the basic Solow model, we differentiate the capital–labor ratio and then substitute in the conditions of the model:

$$dk = (dK \cdot L - K \cdot dL)/L^2 = dK/L - (K/L) \cdot (dL/L)$$
$$= sY/L - kn$$
$$= sy - nk$$

since $dK = I = S = sY$ and $dL/L = n$. In steady-state equilibrium, the capital–labor ratio is constant, so $dk = 0$. Thus $dk = sy - nk = 0$ and

$$sk^\alpha - nk = 0$$
$$sk^\alpha = nk$$
$$s/n = k^{1-\alpha}$$

Solving for the steady-state equilibrium capital–labor ratio by raising both sides of the equation to the power of $(1/1-\alpha)$ gives $k^* = (s/n)^{1/(1-\alpha)}$. The steady-state equilibrium output per unit of labor is $y^* = (k^*)^\alpha = (s/n)^{\alpha/(1-\alpha)}$. In sum, the steady-state equilibrium capital–labor ratio and output per unit of labor are directly related to the saving rate (s) and inversely related to the natural growth rate of labor (n).

Changes in steady-state equilibrium

As seen, the steady-state capital–labor ratio depends on the given values of the net saving rate, s, and natural growth rate of labor, n. Any change in the net saving rate or natural growth rate of labor will lead to a new steady-state equilibrium.

For example, consider an increase in the net saving rate from s to s' (see Figure 7.2). The saving curve would rotate in a counterclockwise direction, since at any capital–labor ratio and income per unit of labor, saving per unit of labor forthcoming would be higher. At the original steady-state equilibrium capital–labor ratio of k_0^*, there would now be excess saving (indicated by the gap $F'E_0$). Consequently, the fall in interest rate would prompt greater investment and adoption of more capital-intensive methods of production. The capital–labor ratio would rise to a new steady-state equilibrium at E_1 with k_1^*, where $s' \cdot y_1^* = n \cdot k_1^*$. As the capital–labor ratio increased from k_0^* to k_1^*, income per unit of labor would rise and there would be economic growth. But, in the new steady-state equilibrium, as in the initial one, economic growth would be zero. Nevertheless, income per unit of labor (and income per capita) is higher in the new steady-state equilibrium: $y_1^* = f(k_1)^* > y_0^* = f(k_0)^*$. Here the increase in the saving rate, from s to s', is reflected in an increase in the capital–output ratio from $v_0^* = k_0^*/y_0^*$ to $v_1^* = k_1^*/y_1^*$.

A fall in the natural growth rate of labor, from n to n', would also raise the steady-state equilibrium capital–labor ratio and output per unit of labor (see Figure 7.3, where the decrease in the natural growth rate of labor rotates the investment ray in a clockwise direction, increasing the

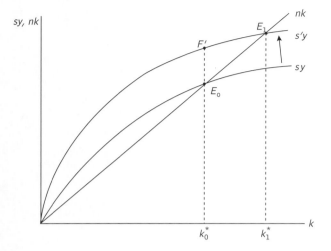

Figure 7.2 *Increase in saving rate*

An increase in the net saving rate from s to s′ will result in a counter-clockwise rotation of the net saving curve. At the initial equilibrium, E_0, there will be a surplus of saving. The capital-labor ratio will increase from k_0^* to k_1^*. Economic growth will occur until the new steady-state equilibrium is reached at E_1.

steady-state equilibrium capital–labor ratio from k_0^* to k_1^*). Here too, economic growth would be temporary—only occurring between the steady-state equilibria.

We can see, however, that one reason for the higher per capita incomes in the more developed economies might be their higher saving rates and lower natural growth rates than in less developed economies. Giving the likely upper limits to the saving rate and lower limits to the natural growth rate of labor, however, these gains in per capita income are bounded.

Moreover, to explain sustained economic growth, we need to extend the basic Solow model where steady-state equilibrium is characterized by zero economic growth. That is, the capital stock, labor force, and output are all growing at the rate of n, the natural growth rate of labor supply: $dK/K = dL/L = dY/Y = n$. Thus the capital–labor ratio is constant, $dk = 0$, as is output per unit of labor, $dy = 0$. To extend the model, we begin by incorporating technological progress. Before doing this, we should introduce convergence theory.

CONVERGENCE THEORY

Convergence theory predicts that poor countries should grow faster than rich countries. Consequently, the per capita gaps in income should diminish over time. The simplest case is known as unconditional convergence.

Unconditional convergence

Given the constant returns to scale production function, $Y = K^{\alpha}L^{1-\alpha}$, or, in intensive form, $y = k^{\alpha}$, the steady-state equilibrium capital–labor ratio and output per unit of labor are given by $k^* = (s/n)^{1/(1-\alpha)}$ and $y^* = (s/n)^{\alpha/(1-\alpha)}$. If two countries, 1 and 2, have this same production function, and the same saving rate ($s_1 = s_2$) and natural growth rate in the labor force ($n_1 = n_2$),

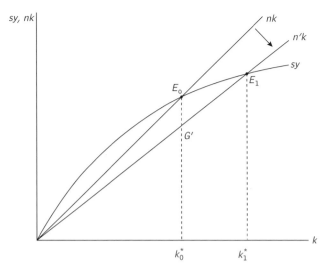

Figure 7.3 *Decrease in natural growth rate of the labor force*

A decrease in the natural growth rate of labor from n to n' will result in a clockwise rotation of the net investment ray. At the initial equilibrium, E_0, there will be a surplus of saving. The capital-labor ratio will increase from k_0^* to k_1^*. Economic growth will occur until the new steady-state equilibrium is reached at E_1.

and if both countries are initially below the steady-state equilibrium capital–labor ratio of k^*, but $k_1 < k_2$, then the countries will converge to the same steady-state equilibrium k^* and y^*. Country 1, however, will grow more since it has further to go (see Figure 7.4). **Unconditional convergence** illustrates the simplest, but also the least relevant form of convergence in per capita incomes in the basic Solow model.

Conditional convergence

Conditional convergence allows for different initial saving rates and natural growth rates of labor, though we will still assume the two countries have the same production function. Suppose that country 2 begins with a higher capital–labor ratio and higher output per unit of labor in steady-state equilibrium than country 1. For example, country 2 may have a higher saving rate, $s_2 > s_1$, or its natural growth rate of labor supply might be lower, $n_2 < n_1$. Both conditions are depicted in Figure 7.5.

   If we open the model to allow for international factor mobility, we will see a convergence in the saving rates and natural growth rates of the labor forces, thus in the capital–labor ratios and per capita incomes in the two countries.[3]

   With a higher capital–labor ratio, country 2 is **capital-abundant**. The marginal product of capital, and consequently the interest rate and the return to capital, would be lower in country 2 than in country 1. Conversely, country 1 would be considered **labor-abundant**, and with

---

[3] Opening the model to allow for international trade, aid, and factor mobility, and including the government gives us the most comprehensive analysis. Thus the condition characterizing macroeconomic equilibrium becomes $I + G_I = S + (T - G_C) + (M - X + R + F)$.

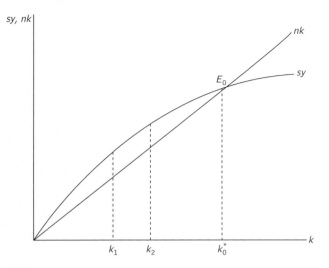

Figure 7.4 *Unconditional convergence*

Two countries, 1 and 2, with the same production function, $y = f(k)$, same saving rate, s, and same natural growth rate in the labor force, n, will converge to the same steady-state equilibrium, k_0^*. Assume that both countries are initially below this steady-state equilibrium, and that $k_1 < k_2 < k_0^*$. Therefore, country 1 has the lower per capita income, $y_1 < y_2 < y_0^*$, where $y_0^* = f(k_0^*)$. Country 1 would then grow faster than country 2 as they both converge to the steady-state equilibrium at k_0^*.

a lower marginal product of labor, the wage rate or return to labor would be lower than in country 2.

Allowing international factor mobility, labor would migrate from country 1 to country 2, where the returns to labor are higher.[4] The natural growth rate of labor supply would fall in country 1 but rise in country 2 until the differential disappeared: $n_1' = n_2'$. Similarly, with international investment, on net, capital would flow from country 2 to country 1, seeking a higher return, enhancing the domestic saving rate in country 1 and reducing the saving rate in country 2 until the two saving rates converged: $s_1' = s_2'$. Therefore, with international mobility, where factors flow to where their returns are higher, the net saving rates and natural growth rates of the labor forces of the two countries would tend to converge until per capita incomes were equal. This illustrates conditional convergence in the basic Solow model. Important underlying assumptions are identical production functions, homogeneous capital and labor, and free movement of the factors between countries.

In fact, on net, labor does emigrate from poorer or less developed countries and capital does flow in the opposite direction from the richer, developed countries. That we do not always see convergence in per capita incomes around the world over time suggests that this most basic Solow model is limited and needs to be made more realistic. We will begin by adding technological progress.

---

[4] Key underlying assumptions are that there are no qualitative differences in the factors of production between the two countries and that diminishing returns apply to both capital and labor.

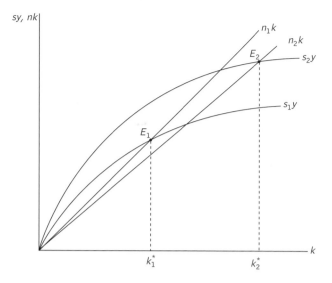

Figure 7.5 *Conditional convergence with international factor mobility*

Assume two countries, 1 and 2, have the same production function, $y = f(k)$, and that there are no qualitative differences in the capital and labor between the two countries. Country 1, however, has the higher natural growth rate in labor, $n_1 > n_2$, but country 2 has the higher saving rate, $s_2 > s_1$. Consequently, country 1 has the lower initial equilibrium capital labor ratio, $k_1^* < k_2^*$, and per capita income, $y_1^* < y_2^*$. With international factor mobility, on net labor will migrate to country 2 and savings (capital) will flow to country 1, until the natural growth rates of labor are equal ($n_1' = n_2'$) and the saving rates are equal ($s_1' = s_2'$). Thus, the steady-state equilibrium capital-labor ratios and per capita incomes converge.

Adding technological progress

To incorporate technological progress, we will include an index of neutral technological change with the production function. Moreover, we will assume that this index, A, increases at an annual rate of g: $A(t) = A(0)e^{gt}$. The Solow model becomes:

(S1) $Y(t) = A(t) \cdot [K(t)]^{\alpha}[L(t)]^{1-\alpha} = A(0)e^{gt} \cdot [K(t)]^{\alpha}[L(t)]^{1-\alpha}$
(S2) $I(t) = S(t)$
(S3) $S(t) = s \cdot Y(t)$
(S4) $L(t) = L(0)e^{nt}$

Proceeding as before, we simplify by dropping the time notation for the endogenous variables and convert the aggregate production function, still characterized by constant returns to scale, into the intensive form by multiplying through by $1/L$:

$$Y/L = A(0)e^{gt} \cdot K^{\alpha}L^{1-\alpha}/L$$
$$y = A(0)e^{gt} \cdot k^{\alpha}$$

Using the fundamental equation of the Solow model, which describes the change in the capital–labor ratio, $dk = sy - nk$, we can write $dk = s \cdot A(0)e^{gt} \cdot k^{\alpha} - nk$. If we set this equal to zero, consistent with a steady-state equilibrium condition of a constant capital–labor ratio, and then

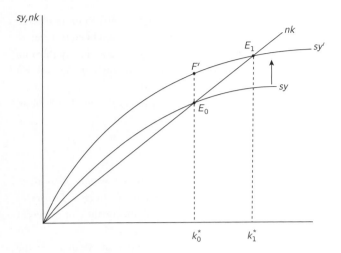

Figure 7.6 *Steady-state equilibrium with technological progress*

Over time with neutral technological progress, A(t) increases and the net saving curve rotates counter-clockwise, increasing the steady-state equilibrium capital-labor ratio and output per unit of labor.

solve for k, we find that $k = [s \cdot A(0)^{gt}/n]^{1/(1-\alpha)}$. Note, however, that k is no longer solely a function of the exogenous variables, s and n, but now dependent on time, as the index of technology is increasing at an annual rate of g. Therefore, the capital–labor ratio is no longer constant in steady-state equilibrium.

Returning to the fundamental equation, $dk = sy - nk = 0$, we see that the net saving per unit of labor forthcoming is increasing over time with the capital–labor ratio and income per unit of labor: $sy = s \cdot A(0)e^{gt} \cdot k^{\alpha}$. Graphically the net saving curve is rotating counterclockwise with increases in technology, which, for the given net investment ray, increases the equilibrium capital–labor ratio and income per unit of labor over time. With continuous technological progress, the steady-state equilibrium is now characterized by economic growth (see Figure 7.6).

With a rising capital–labor ratio and a moving steady-state equilibrium, we need to derive the growth rate in labor productivity or income per unit of labor directly from the intensive production function, $y = A(0)e^{gt} \cdot k^{\alpha}$. Differentiating both sides gives:

$$dy = g \cdot A(0)e^{gt} \cdot k^{\alpha} + \alpha \cdot A(0)e^{gt} \cdot k^{\alpha-1}dk.$$

Dividing through by $y = A(0)e^{gt} \cdot k^{\alpha}$ to obtain the growth rate in labor productivity, dy/y, we get $dy/y = g + \alpha \cdot (dk/k)$. That is, the growth rate in income per unit of labor is equal to the sum of the growth rate in technology (g) and the product of the partial output elasticity of capital (α) with the growth rate in the capital–labor ratio (dk/k).[5] Since $dk = sy - nk$, we can also write the growth rate in labor productivity as $dy/y = g + \alpha \cdot [(sy - nk)/k]$.

Here $sy - nk$ represents the excess saving that results from the rise in income per unit of labor at any capital–labor ratio with continuous technological progress (see $F'E_0$ in Figure 7.6). The

---

[5] Recall that, given the production function, $Y = A \cdot K^{\alpha}L^{1-\alpha}$, totally differentiating gives $dY = dA \cdot K^{\alpha}L^{1-\alpha} + A \cdot \alpha \cdot K^{\alpha-1}L^{1-\alpha}dK + A \cdot (1-\alpha) \cdot K^{\alpha-1}L^{\alpha}dL$. Dividing through by Y, gives $dY/Y = dA/A + \alpha \cdot dK/K + (1-\alpha) \cdot dL/L$. Taking the partial derivative of the growth rate of output, dY/Y, with respect to the growth rate of capital, dK/K, yields the partial output elasticity of capital: $\partial(dY/Y)/\partial(dK/K) = \alpha$. Similarly, the partial output elasticity of labor equals $1 - \alpha$.

surplus saving exerts downward pressure on the interest rate, encouraging shifts to more capital-intensive production methods and additional investment. The steady-state equilibrium capital–labor ratio is increasing over time. Note that, consistent with the macroeconomic equilibrium $I = S$, we are assuming that the surplus saving will be invested in additional capital goods and that there will be sufficient demand for the greater national output produced.

Next, we extend the model to incorporate qualitative change in physical capital and labor, consistent with the notion of effective factors of production.

Qualitative change in capital and labor

In addition to incorporating technological progress, we can extend the Solow model to allow for qualitative change in physical capital and labor. Recall the concept of effective factors of production, where the physical factors are multiplied by indices of the quality or inherent productivity of the factors.

Define the effective physical capital stock for time t, $\underline{K}(t)$, as the product of an index of the quality of the physical capital stock, $q_K(t)$, and the quantity of the physical capital stock, $K(t)$. That is, $\underline{K}(t) = q_K(t) \cdot K(t)$. Increases in the physical capital stock reflect positive net fixed investment. Increases in the quality of the capital often reflect technological advances, since much of new technology is embodied in the newest capital goods (e.g., more energy-efficient machines and faster computers). So, too, the newest intermediate goods may embody the most recent technologies (e.g., maintenance-free batteries, more durable tires, higher-yielding seeds, and improved fertilizers).

Endogenous growth theory maintains that there may be increasing returns to investment in capital goods that embody the latest technologies.[6] That is, not only will the effective capital stock increase with the index of the quality of capital, but also the new capital goods may stimulate human capital formation, as labor may be required to learn new skills in order to use the improved capital. For example, with advances in computer software that allow for more efficient processing of information, users may need to learn new spreadsheet applications. The gains in knowledge can be passed along to other users, in effect increasing the average quality of labor.

Moreover, we can define effective labor for time t, $\underline{L}(t)$, as the product of an index of the quality of labor, $q_L(t)$, and the physical labor force, $L(t)$. That is, $\underline{L}(t) = q_L(t) \cdot L(t)$. The index of the quality or inherent productivity of a unit of labor reflects the average level of human capital, in turn a function of the education, nutrition, health, and experience of the labor force. As noted above, technological progress, some of which is embodied in the latest generation of physical capital, can improve labor productivity (e.g., the use of cell phones and email can improve communications).

Below we will assume that the indices of the quality of capital and labor are growing at annual rates of j and m, respectively. Therefore, we can write:

$$\underline{K}(t) = q_K(t) \cdot K(t) = e^{jt} \cdot K(t) \quad \text{and} \quad \underline{L}(t) = q_L(t) \cdot L(t) = e^{mt} \cdot L(t)$$

Incorporating the effective factors of production along with neutral technical change, assumed to be growing continuously at an annual rate of g, gives an aggregate production function of $Y(t) = A(t)[\underline{K}(t)]^{\alpha}[\underline{L}(t)]^{1-\alpha} = A(0)e^{gt}[e^{jt} \cdot K(t)]^{\alpha}[e^{mt} \cdot L(t)]^{1-\alpha}$. Simplifying, we have $Y = A(0)e^{gt} \cdot e^{\alpha jt} \cdot e^{(1-\alpha)mt} \cdot K^{\alpha}L^{1-\alpha}$ or $Y = A(0)e^{\theta t} \cdot K^{\alpha}L^{1-\alpha}$, where $\theta = g + \alpha j + (1-\alpha)m$. Here θ represents the

---

[6] A good introduction to endogenous growth theory can be found in the *Journal of Economic Perspectives* (Winter 1994), with articles by Romer, Grossman and Helpman, Solow, and Pack. Pack (1994: 56–57) discusses a very simple endogenous growth model, $Y = A \cdot K$, where K is both physical and human capital. With this production function, there are no diminishing returns to capital, since $dY/dK = A$.

growth rate in total factor productivity, that is, the growth rate in output not attributable to growth in the physical factors of production. The growth rate in total factor productivity in this model is equal to the sum of the growth rate in neutral technical progress and the weighted growth rates in the qualities of capital and labor, where the weights reflect the partial output elasticities of effective capital and effective labor, α and $1 - \alpha$, respectively.

The extended version of the Solow model now becomes:

$$\begin{aligned}
\text{(S1)} \quad Y &= A(0)e^{\theta t}K^{\alpha}L^{1-\alpha}, \quad \text{where } \theta = g + \alpha j + (1 - \alpha)m \\
\text{(S2)} \quad I &= S \\
\text{(S3)} \quad S &= sY \\
\text{(S4)} \quad L &= L(0)e^{nt}
\end{aligned}$$

Note that the aggregate production function is still characterized by constant returns to scale. Therefore we can multiply both sides by $1/L$ and convert to the intensive form $y = A(0)e^{\theta t}k^{\alpha}$, where $y = Y/L$ and $k = K/L$. To derive the growth rate in output per unit of labor, $\mathrm{d}y/y$, we need to differentiate this intensive production function and then divide through by output per unit of labor, y:

$$\mathrm{d}y = \theta A(0)e^{\theta t}k^{\alpha} + A(0)e^{\theta t}\alpha k^{\alpha-1}\mathrm{d}k$$

$$\mathrm{d}y/y = \theta + \alpha \cdot (\mathrm{d}k/k) = \theta + \alpha \cdot [(sy - nk)/k]$$

Thus the growth rate in labor productivity or output per unit of labor, $\mathrm{d}y/y$, is equal to the sum of the growth rate in total factor productivity, θ, and a term representing the contribution of capital deepening, $\alpha \cdot (\mathrm{d}k/k) = \alpha \cdot [(sy - nk)/k]$. The contribution of capital deepening reflects the excess of net savings over the net investment required to maintain the capital–labor ratio for the given natural growth rate in the labor force.

Recall the steady-state condition in the most basic version of the Solow model introduced at the outset, where in steady-state equilibrium, in the absence of technological progress, steady-state equilibrium was defined by a constant capital–labor ratio, $\mathrm{d}k = sy - nk = 0$. Now allowing for neutral technical change and qualitative improvements in capital and labor, the growth rate in total factor productivity will increase output per unit of labor for a given capital–labor ratio, thus increasing saving per unit of labor forthcoming above the required net investment, leading to increases in the capital–labor ratio and additional economic growth.

In steady-state equilibrium in this enhanced Solow model we would find not only economic growth but also the growth rate in output per unit of labor rising over time. As we will discuss later, in practice we do not find steadily rising economic growth. In fact, not only do the economic growth rates for a nation vary over time, but periodically we also find negative economic growth, even negative output growth. The latter was conveyed with the short-run aggregate demand–aggregate supply model presented in the previous chapter, where short-run fluctuations in real national output correspond to the business cycle.

Furthermore, the economic growth rate, given by the difference in the growth rates of real output and population, also equals the sum of the growth rates in labor productivity and the share of the labor force in total population. Demographic factors, notably the demographic dividend that comes with the fertility transition, will affect economic growth, controlling for the growth rate in labor productivity (the focus of the growth models).

To summarize from the Solow growth model, differences in output per unit of labor, and more generally per capita incomes across nations, may reflects differences in the national saving rates (s) and differences in natural growth rates of labor (n), as well as differences in the initial levels of technology $A(0)$. Differences in the growth rates of labor productivity across nations may also reflect differences in the growth rates of neutral technical change and the growth rates of the qualities of capital and labor. Differences in economic growth rates may also reflect differences in the growth rates of the shares of the labor force in population.

INCORPORATING NATURAL RESOURCES

Usually the Solow model includes just two of the primary factors of production, physical capital and labor. When considering sustainable development, however, natural resources should also be included. Let $\underline{R}(t) = q_R(t) \cdot R(t)$ be the effective natural resources available for use in production at time t, where $R(t)$ is the natural resources available at time t and $q_R(t)$ is an index of the quality or inherent productivity of the available natural resources at time t.

We will assume that natural resources are, on net, being depleted each period or year—that is, $R(t) = R(0)e^{-ut}$, where $R(0)$ is the initial quantity of natural resources available for production and u is the annual depletion rate in natural resources.

For example, nonrenewable resources, such as minerals and fossil fuels, will be depleted as they are used. Even if we are not aware of all the stocks or deposits of nonrenewable resources at present, the global supplies are nevertheless finite. In the short run, renewable resources, such as farmland, forests, and fishing stocks, can (but should not) be used beyond their sustainable rates (e.g., fishing beyond the regeneration capacities of the fish stocks, net deforestation, and overgrazing of pastures resulting in desertification). Other renewable resources, such as solar and wind energy, depend on nature, and are limited in the amounts available during any given period.

Changes in effective natural resources

In this model the overall stock of natural resources is assumed to be diminishing at the rate u. Although the growth rate of natural resources available and utilized may be positive or zero over a given period, for the world in the long run the growth rate is negative. That is, the discovery of new sources or reserves could dominate the depletion of nonrenewable resources so that it appears that nonrenewable resources are increasing (so that $u < 0$), at least for a while. Furthermore, advances in technology may allow the increased harnessing of renewable resources, such as solar, wind, and tidal energies. Reforestation or the recovery of fishing stocks could outpace the depletion of mineral reserves, although forests, fishing stocks, and minerals, of course, are not perfect substitutes in production. In the long run, however, we assume $dR/R = -u =< 0$.

In addition, we will assume $q_R(t) = e^{ht}$—that is, the index of the quality of the natural resources (e.g., fertility of the soil, richness of the mineral deposits) increases at the annual rate of h. Note that, with environmental deterioration (e.g., soil erosion), $h < 0$. Careful management of resources may enhance the productivity of natural resources—for example, fertilization can enhance the fertility of farm land. Advances in technology may increase the natural productivity of minerals or better capture the available solar and wind energy, so that $h > 0$. On the other hand, with increased demand for food, less fertile farmland may be cultivated or existing land cultivated more intensely, so that the average productivity of land declines—as in Ricardo's model. Fishing stocks may be depleted so that the average size of the fish caught declines, and forests may be harvested faster so the average tree felled yields less lumber. In these cases, $h < 0$

and the index of the quality of natural resources declines. In sum, effective natural resources can be written as $\underline{R}(t) = e^{ht}R(t) = e^{ht}R(0)e^{-ut}$.

We might add that a nation could increase the supply of natural resources available for its production of goods and services at the expense of other nations. Recall the mercantilist zero-sum view where the world's wealth (narrowly defined as the stock of gold) was fixed and a nation could only increase its holdings of gold if other nations decreased their shares. For the planet, though, the stocks of nonrenewable resources, such as fossil fuels and gold deposits, are finite, thus exhaustible. While the possibility in the future of securing additional natural resources from other planets cannot be ruled out, we assume that natural resources are limited.[7] *A fortiori*, considering environmental thresholds, manifested in the ability of planet Earth to absorb the wastes generated by human activity, reinforces the assumption of natural resource depletion.

ENHANCED SOLOW MODEL

Incorporating effective natural resources, along with effective physical capital and effective labor and neutral technological progress, the enhanced Solow model becomes:

$$
\begin{array}{llll}
\text{(S1)} & Y(t) & = & A(t) \cdot [\underline{K}(t)]^{\alpha}[\underline{L}(t)]^{\beta}[\underline{R}(t)]^{\gamma} \\
\text{(S2)} & I(t) & = & S(t) \quad \text{(macroeconomic equilibrium condition)} \\
\text{(S3)} & S(t) & = & sY(t) \quad \text{(s = saving rate)} \\
\text{(S4)} & L(t) & = & L(0)e^{nt} \quad \text{(n = natural growth rate of the labor force)} \\
\text{(S5)} & R(t) & = & R(0)e^{-ut} \quad \text{(u = rate of depletion of natural resources)}
\end{array}
$$

In equation (S1), we have:

$A(t) = A(0)e^{gt}$ (g = rate of neutral technological change)

$\underline{K}(t) = e^{jt}K(t)$ (j = rate of growth of the quality of capital)

$\underline{L}(t) = e^{mt}L(t)$ (m = rate of growth of the quality of labor)

$\underline{R}(t) = e^{ht}R(t)$ (h = rate of growth of the quality of natural resources)

As before, with technological change and qualitative change in the factors of production, the steady-state equilibrium will be characterized by a changing capital–labor ratio. Consequently, we have to derive the growth rate in labor productivity directly. We begin by simplifying the production function, which no longer assumes constant returns to scale. That is, the sum of α, β, and γ, the partial output elasticities with respect to capital, labor and natural resources, respectively, is not restricted to equal one.[8] We have

$$
Y = A(t) \cdot [\underline{K}(t)]^{\alpha}[\underline{L}(t)]^{\beta}[\underline{R}(t)]^{\gamma} = A(0)e^{gt}[e^{jt}K]^{\alpha}[e^{mt}L]^{\beta}[e^{ht}R]^{\gamma} = A(0)e^{\theta t}K^{\alpha}L^{\beta}R^{\gamma}
$$

where $\theta = g + \alpha \cdot j + \beta \cdot m + \gamma \cdot h$ is the comprehensive growth rate of total factor productivity. Totally differentiating both sides, and dividing through by Y, we can show that:

$$
dY/Y = \theta + \alpha \cdot (dK/K) + \beta \cdot (dL/L) + \gamma \cdot (dR/R)
$$

---

[7] In fact, in 2012, Planetary Resources, a joint venture of film-maker James Cameron (*Titanic* and *Avatar*) and Larry Page and Eric Schmidt (from Google) was announced to mine asteroids "near" Earth for valuable resources. Whether this venture is feasible and how far in the future it might take place remains uncertain.

[8] If constant returns to scale do characterize the production function, that is, if $\alpha + \beta + \gamma = 1$, then the growth rate in labor productivity can be written as $dy/y = \theta + \alpha \cdot [(sy - nk)/k] - \gamma \cdot (n + u)$.

175

Using the conditions of the model ($dK = I = S = sY$, $dL/L = n$, and $dR/R = -u$) and subtracting $dL/L = n$ from both sides, we write:

$$dy/y = dY/Y - dL/L = \theta + \alpha \cdot (sY/K) + \beta n - \gamma u - n$$

which, after adding and subtracting αn, converting sY/K to sy/k, and combining like terms, can be simplified to:

$$dy/y = \theta + \alpha \cdot [(sy - nk)/k] - (1 - \alpha - \beta) \cdot n - \gamma u$$

For economic growth from rising labor productivity to occur over time ($dy/y > 0$) requires $\theta + \alpha \cdot [(sy - nk)/k] > (1 - \alpha - \beta) \cdot n + \gamma u$. In words, for long-run economic growth, the forces of neutral technical change, qualitative improvements in physical capital, labor, and natural resources, and physical capital deepening must dominate natural resource depletion and diminishing returns to labor.

Rearranging the simplified equation for dy/y to isolate the natural resource effect on labor productivity growth, captured by the term $-\gamma(u - h)$, we can write:

$$dy/y = (g + \alpha j + \beta m) + \alpha \cdot [(sy - nk)/k] - (1 - \alpha - \beta) \cdot n - \gamma(u - h)$$

The effect on the growth rate of labor productivity of an increase in the partial output elasticity of natural resources (γ) is derived as $\partial(dy/y)/\partial\gamma = h - u$, which may be positive, negative or zero, depending on whether the qualitative growth rate in the productivity of the natural resources (h) exceeds, falls short of, or equals the depletion rate of the natural resources (u).

In general, the growth rate in labor productivity, dy/y, depends on

$$dy/y = \overset{+\ \ +\ \ +\ \ +\ \ +\ \ +\ \ ?\ \ -\ \ -}{f(g,\ j,\ m,\ h,\ s,\ \alpha,\ \beta,\ \gamma,\ n,\ u)}$$

That is, the growth rate in labor productivity (and economic growth) is directly related to the growth rate in technology (g), physical capital deepening ($dk = sy - nk$), qualitative improvements in the primary factors of production (j, m, and h), and the partial output elasticities of capital and labor (α and β). The growth rate in labor productivity depends inversely on the natural growth rate of the labor force (n) and the rate of depletion of natural resources (u).

POLICY IMPLICATIONS FOR ECONOMIC GROWTH

From the general equation for the determinants of labor productivity growth we can derive the instruments for promoting economic growth. As suggested, technological progress and increases in the effective physical capital and natural capital to labor ratios, along with human capital formation, will promote economic growth.

Saving rate

In the most basic Solow model, steady-state equilibrium was defined by a constant capital–labor ratio and zero economic growth. An increase in the net saving rate would only generate temporary growth until the new higher steady-state equilibrium capital–labor ratio was attained. Incorporating technological change and qualitative improvement in the factors of production, however, yields steady-state equilibrium with capital deepening, which continually raises labor productivity. Increases in the saving rate will augment this physical capital deepening. There are upper limits to the net saving rate and, unless the greater saving flows into productive investment (assumed to be the case in growth models), higher saving rates can actually reduce aggregate demand and output growth in the short run.

Nevertheless, policies to increase the saving rate center on increasing the expected after-tax real return to saving, $rr_s^e = (1 - t_s) \cdot r_s - \text{INF}^e$, where t_s is the tax rate on income earned from saving (e.g., interest, dividends, or capital gains), r_s the nominal return to saving (e.g., nominal interest rate on saving deposits), and INF^e the expected inflation rate. Keeping inflation low is important for ensuring a positive after-tax real return to saving. For example, even if the nominal return to saving were adjusted to the rate of inflation, so that the expected real return to saving, $r_s - \text{INF}^e$, were constant, higher inflation can reduce the expected after-tax real return and so discourage saving, hence the supply of funds for physical capital formation.

Consider the following example. Suppose that nominal rates of interest were indexed or adjusted to the actual rate of inflation (INF). Let $r_s = 0.06$ and $\text{INF} = 0.02$ initially, and $t_s = 0.25$ (or 25 percent). The before-tax and after-tax real returns are respectively $r_s - \text{INF} = 0.06 - 0.02 = 0.04$, or 4 percent, and $rr_s = (1 - 0.25) \cdot 0.06 - 0.02 = 0.025$, or 2.5 percent. If the inflation rate increases by 8 percentage points to 10 percent, $\text{INF}' = 0.10$, and the nominal rate of interest on saving is adjusted upward by 8 percentage points to 14 percent, $r_s' = 0.14$, then the before-tax real return is still 4 percent ($r_s' - \text{INF}' = 0.14 - 0.10$). The after-tax real return, however, is reduced from 2.5 percent to 0.5 percent, since $rr_s' = (1 - t_s) \cdot r_s' - \text{INF}' = (1 - 0.25) \cdot 0.14 - 0.10 = 0.005$. Ceteris paribus, then, even with adjustable nominal interest rates, inflation can discourage saving when tax liabilities are based on nominal, not real, incomes.[9]

Measures to increase private saving and the supply of loanable funds for investment include keeping inflation low to ensure positive after-tax real returns on saving and lowering tax rates on income earned from saving. In particular, investment tax credits can subsidize private capital formation, increasing the productive capacity of the economy.

The government can increase public saving by running budget surpluses, an excess of tax revenues over government transfer payments and current expenditures on goods and services. Budget surpluses contribute to the supply of loanable funds. Lower budget deficits reduce the government's demand for credit, making it less expensive for business fixed investment.

Inflation

High rates of inflation can hinder economic growth in other ways than discouraging saving. First, nations with relatively high inflation are less internationally competitive, so they export less and import more, hurting not only their trade balances but also their output growth and employment.[10]

Second, as noted earlier, with high rates of inflation, relative prices in the domestic markets are harder to discern, which may impede the efficient allocation of resources. For example, if the

---

[9] If tax liabilities were based on real income, rather than nominal income, the expected after-tax real return to saving would be $rr_s^e = (1 - t_s) \cdot (r_s - \text{INF}^e)$. Then higher inflation with a nominal interest rate indexed to the inflation rate would not reduce the after-tax real return to saving.

[10] A country's international competitiveness depends on its **real exchange rate**, rer, or the nominal exchange rate, er (the domestic currency price of a unit of foreign exchange), adjusted for the relative price level. Let P_d be the domestic price index for internationally traded goods and services and P_f the foreign price index for internationally traded goods and services. Then $rer = er \cdot (P_f / P_d)$. A real depreciation in the domestic currency, indicated by a rise in rer, makes the nation more competitive internationally. A real depreciation can result from either a nominal depreciation (an increase in er) or relative inflation in the rest of the world (an increase in P_f / P_d). Conversely, a nation with relatively high inflation, resulting in a decrease in (P_f / P_d), would experience a real appreciation in its currency. That is, for a given nominal exchange rate, the real exchange rate would fall, reducing the nation's international competitiveness.

overall inflation rate were 2 percent and the price of good i increases by 4 percent while the price of good j increases by 1 percent, perhaps reflecting an increase in the demand for good i from a shift in tastes and preferences, then additional resources would likely be reallocated from the production of good j to good i. If instead the overall inflation rate were 20 percent, and the price of good i increased by 22 percent and the price of good j increased "only" by 19 percent, while the absolute difference in the two prices is the same 3 percent, the relative price signals may be harder to discern.[11]

Third, high rates of inflation may encourage speculative activity by individuals seeking to profit from even higher expected prices (e.g., for real estate, stocks, bonds), which may generate a bubble economy. Speculators trying to anticipate relative future prices detract from more productive activity of actually producing goods and services for consumption.

Finally, as we illustrated in Chapter 6, under adaptive expectations, inflation can build on itself as factor suppliers recognize the past price increases and adjust their price expectations upwards, shifting the labor supply and aggregate supply curves back, reducing equilibrium real national output, *ceteris paribus*.

Labor force growth

In the growth models, reductions in the natural growth rate of the labor force lead to a higher steady-state capital–labor ratio and per capita income. We noted the demographic dividend that accompanies the initial declines in fertility, reducing the share of youth in the population and increasing the share of the population in the labor force years, at least for a few decades. Eventually, though, the dividend expires, with the rise in the share of the elderly in the population resulting in an increased burden of dependency. In fact, the prolonged fertility rates below replacement level in Europe and Japan have led to concerns with labor shortages and economic stagnation. (Recall the angst expressed by the macroeconomists during the Great Depression with the low rates of population growth in the industrialized economies contributing to insufficient demand for national outputs.) Growth models, by assuming macroeconomic equilibrium, do not address shortfalls in aggregate demand.

Technological progress

Perhaps the keys to sustained economic growth are technological progress and qualitative improvement in the factors of production. Resources devoted to research and development can increase the probability of technological progress. Basic research into science and technology is a public good, as many can benefit from the knowledge created. Tax credits and subsidies are therefore warranted. The patent system provides incentives for invention and innovation, giving the inventor a monopoly on the new product or process for a number of years. The high-income nations are more likely to have the scientists and engineers for the creation of new knowledge, which extends the frontiers of technology. The low- and middle-income nations can benefit from the technologies developed, but need to have access to these technologies and the skilled labor to fully employ them. The growth of the Internet has significantly increased the dissemination of knowledge.

As noted, much of the technological progress is embodied in new capital and intermediate goods, improving the quality or inherent productivity of these inputs. International trade,

---

[11] Perhaps an analogy would be that is is far easier to carry on a conversation in a quiet library than at a boisterous party where, to be heard, you must raise your voice, which only adds to the general din.

immigration, and investment are conduits for transferring goods and services embodying new technologies as well as capital, skilled labor, and expertise.

As O'Sullivan (2011: 24) notes:

> The broad economic logic suggests more of the world economy's gains should come from convergence by emerging markets than from the rich world pushing ahead. Each innovation adds less to rich world prosperity than the adoption of an established technology does to a poor country.

This productivity enhancing diffusion of technology can be illustrated by a world production function, $Y = A \cdot F(\underline{K}, \underline{L}, \underline{R})$, where an increase in A, the index of neutral technical change, could reflect not just innovation and new technologies developed by the advanced nations, but the adoption of better, but already existing, technologies by developing nations.

Entrepreneurship should be encouraged. **Entrepreneurs** seek out profitable opportunities by starting, organizing, and operating business ventures. Business creation is a key to economic growth. Laws and regulations that make it easier to start a business and generate capital, and that protect private property and enforce contracts, promote an environment conducive to investment and economic growth.

Underlying technological progress, entrepreneurship, and the development of a skilled and productive labor force is education. Beginning even before primary school, ensuring adequate nutrition and health care for children lays the groundwork for human capital formation. Demanding curricula and good teachers in schools with well-equipped classrooms are important investments for human capital. Education increases the knowledge and skills in a population, and an informed and engaged population can promote democracy and political stability.

In the growth models, limits to growth were evident in the finite stocks of nonrenewable resources, as well as the bounded availability of renewable resources for use in any given period. Consequently, continued efforts are warranted to increase the efficiency with which natural resources are harvested. For example, fishing nets and practices can be improved so that unintended fish are not swept up in the haul. Sustainable forestry should be adopted with clear-cutting of timber replaced by selective harvesting, careful management and reforestation. Conservation and recycling of products should be encouraged. Technological change can reduce the reliance on nonrenewables; for example, fiber optics replacing copper wiring and lighter-weight composites replacing steel in automobiles. More fuel-efficient automobiles and energy-efficient buildings and machinery are important for conserving scarce resources. Policies and measures for more efficient uses of natural resources and better stewardship of the environment will be addressed further when we turn to sustainable development.

Before returning to convergence theory and looking at the recent evidence for the developing economies, a brief assessment of growth models might be in order. In particular, having addressed some of the insights of the growth models presented in this chapter, we should be aware of their limitations.

Assessment of growth models

The limitations of growth models for developing policy largely reflect their underlying simplifying assumptions, which were necessary to be able to solve the models. First, the focus is on the supply-side and long-run trends. The major sources of growth are technological change and increases in the effective factors of production. Steady-state or long-run equilibrium paths are derived for output per unit of labor. Aggregate demand, however, is subsumed as in Say's law, where supply creates its own demand. Yet, as we know, business cycles occur with fluctuations around long-run trends. In particular, insufficient aggregate demand in the short run can have longer-run implications when the reduced capital formation and research and development lower possible future economic growth.

Furthermore, the underlying parameters (e.g., the saving rate, natural growth rate of the labor force, and growth rates of neutral technical change and the qualities of capital, labor, and natural resources) change over time, if not year by year. Allowing for such changes, while adding realism, would make the models considerably more complex and harder to tract. Large-scale simulation models, such as the World3 model discussed in Chapter 5, do incorporate this additional realism and complexity, but at the price of requiring computer programs for solutions.

Notwithstanding their limitations, growth models do allow us to better understand the phenomenon of economic growth. We conclude this chapter by revisiting convergence theory, assessing some recent evidence on whether the developing nations are closing the gaps in per capita income with the high-income economies.

CONVERGENCE THEORY REVISITED

As discussed earlier, the most basic version of the Solow model (i.e., without technological change or qualitative improvement in the factors of production) predicts convergence in per capita incomes. In the case of unconditional convergence, two countries with the same production functions, net saving rates, and natural growth rates in labor would converge to the same steady-state equilibrium capital–labor ratio and output per unit of labor. With conditional convergence, two countries with the same production function, but different saving and natural growth rates, would converge if international factor mobility were allowed and labor migrated to the higher-wage, capital-abundant country, while capital flowed to the labor-abundant country until factor returns equalized.

When we allow for different production functions, technological progress, and qualitative differences in the factors, as more likely prevails across countries, we may find divergence in per capita incomes. Recall that the steady-state equilibrium in a Solow growth model, with continuous neutral technological change and qualitative growth in the primary factors of production, is characterized by economic growth, with both continuous total factor productivity increases and capital deepening. Two countries, then, with different rates of technological progress or different qualitative growth rates in their capital, labor, and natural resources, may well experience different steady-state equilibrium growth rates in labor productivity and per capita income. In addition, countries at different points in the demographic transition will experience different changes in the shares of their populations in the labor forces. The demographic dividends for economic growth from declining fertility will eventually be spent, though, and sustained lower fertility rates will yield older populations with higher elderly burdens of dependency.

Increasing returns to investment

There may well be increasing returns to investment in human and physical capital, as opposed to diminishing returns. With factor mobility, whether within or across nations, both poverty traps and growth poles may coexist, generating divergence in per capita incomes. Consider the **brain drain**, the emigration of skilled labor and human capital from developing nations to developed nations. If diminishing returns apply to skilled labor, which is relatively scarce in low-income economies, but relatively abundant in high-income economies, then the returns to that labor should be higher in the low-income nations. Yet physicians, nurses, engineers, and other highly educated workers emigrate from the less developed to the developed economies—albeit in numbers less than desired by the potential emigrants due to restrictive immigration policies. For example, using data from the 2008 American Community Survey, Gibson and McKenzie (2011: 112) find that migrants from developing countries account for 47 percent, 36 percent, and 35 percent, respectively, of those with doctorates working as computer software engineers, medical scientists, and engineers in the United States.

The reason, contrary to the theory of diminishing returns, is that some factors of production may be **complementary.** The productivity of skilled labor is greater when working with other skilled labor and technologically advanced capital. Gibson and McKenzie (2011: 111) also estimate that 79 percent of working migrants to the United States from developing countries who have a bachelor's degree or higher are employed in occupations where the majority of workers have post-secondary education. These shares rise to 90 percent of those with at least a master's degree and to 96 percent of those with a doctorate.

For instance, a nurse may be sorely needed in a poor country with few skilled nurses in the population, yet because of limited medical facilities, supplies, and physicians, that nurse's productivity and the real wage she could earn would be lower in that poor country than in a rich country with abundant complementary resources for health care. Thus, the poor country, having incurred the cost of training the nurse, may well lose that investment when that nurse migrates to a wealthier nation. As a result, poverty traps in developing economies may be created, where low-skilled laborers, working with little capital, concentrate and low labor productivities and per capita incomes are perpetuated. Meanwhile, in developed economies, productive employment is generated for the immigrants.

To some extent, the loss in income from the emigration of skilled labor will be offset by remittances sent back to families in the countries of origin. Such transfers are a significant source of income and foreign exchange for developing nations with heavy out-migration. Furthermore, the emigration of educated labor may actually increase human capital formation in the originating economies if more individuals are induced to seek additional schooling to enhance their prospects for emigration. Since not all, and likely only a minority, of these individuals will be able to emigrate, there could be a net gain in human capital in the developing nations. Finally, the remittances received by the families of emigrants may be used, in part, to fund more education.

Clemens (2011: 84) estimated that "the emigration of less than 5 percent of the population of poor regions would bring global gains exceeding the gains from the total elimination of all policy barriers to merchandise trade and all barriers to capital flows." This calculation reflects the higher productivity of labor in the developed economies. While such a reallocation of labor could result in aggregate gains for world output, it may well be resisted by the developed nations. Five percent of the 6 billion people of the low- and middle-income economies would be 300 million immigrants, exceeding by half the 200 million population currently living outside their native countries. Moreover, to the extent emigration from the developing areas is dominated by the more educated and skilled labor, the income gaps between the developed and developing economies could widen.

Finally, we tend to find foreign direct investment flowing in the largest volumes not to the less developed nations where capital, technical expertise, and skilled labor are relatively scarce, but primarily between developed economies. On a second order is the foreign investment in the faster-growing middle-income economies. An exception, however, may be the foreign direct investment attracted to developing nations abundant in natural resources. In all cases, foreign direct investment is driven by profitable opportunities, which are far fewer in poor countries beset by political-economic instability, weak governments, corruption, inadequate infrastructure, and little human capital.

Agglomeration

Cities or urban concentrations of business and commerce also reflect the phenomenon of increasing returns to investment—at least up to a point—with the gains from **agglomeration**. As noted by the World Bank (2000: 125-126):

> Goods and services are often produced most efficiently in densely populated areas that provide access to a pool of skilled labor, a network of complementary firms that act as suppliers, and a critical mass of customers. For this reason sustained economic growth is always accompanied by urbanization.
> . . .Agglomeration increases the productivity of a wide array of economic activities in urban areas. Productivity rises with city size, so much so that a typical firm will see its productivity climb 5 to 10 percent if city size and the scale of local industry double.

Industrial parks are another example of the concentration of business investment. Building a factory does not make sense if there is not a reliable infrastructure of power, transportation, and communication in place. So, industrial parks and research centers develop where a number of like businesses operate. The Internet is a good example of increasing returns as the potential productivity of any one user will be higher the more users there are.

This is not to imply, however, that bigger is always better. Just as firms can become too big and experience diseconomies of scale with rising long-run average cost of production, so cities can become too big, too fast. Indeed, for many developing economies, urban populations are growing beyond the capacities of the cities to provide adequate shelter, essential public services, and productive employment. Fueled by rural migration as well as natural population growth, shanty towns and slums proliferate within the urban areas. Congestion, crime, environmental deterioration, stress, and informal economic activities mushroom.

Less developed economies

From a global perspective, considering environmental thresholds and finite supplies of natural resources, there may well be limits to growth, as addressed in Chapter 5. What is increasingly evident, though, is that when factors are complementary (e.g., skilled labor and advanced machinery), there may be significant increasing returns, which can lead to growing divergence in labor productivities and per capita incomes across economies.

Nevertheless, less developed countries and low-income economies can make progress and per capita incomes may converge. Although it tends to be the high-income nations with an abundance of scientists and engineers and the resources to advance knowledge and create new technologies, the less developed nations can benefit from these advances. To do so, these less developed nations need to invest in their populations, beginning with quality primary education and health care.

They need to develop literate populations and skilled labor forces that can use the technologies created. Indeed, there may be advantages from being latecomers in the sense that less developed nations do not incur the expenses of creating the technologies but can select the most appropriate of the technologies that are available. For example, rather than investing heavily in the traditional infrastructure required for traditional phones, developing countries can directly adopt cell phones. Similarly, rather than invest in coal-fired power plants, developing economies may be better off investing in renewable and cleaner energy, such as solar and wind.

Developing nations with political-economic stability, sound institutions, and literate populations may well attract foreign direct investment that brings in needed international expertise, capital, and new technologies. One of the advantages of more open economies and increased participation in international trade is greater access to foreign technologies, whether embodied in the goods and services imported or transferred through foreign direct investment.

China and India, the two demographic billionaires, are examples of poor countries that have experienced rapid economic growth over the past quarter century. Fifty years ago South Korea, now considered a developed country, was one of the poorest, most densely population nations in the world. O'Sullivan (2011: 3) begins his overview of the state of world economy as follows:

> A "great convergence" in living standards is under way as poorer countries speedily adopt the technology, know-how and policies that made the West rich. China and India are the biggest and fastest-growing of the catch-up countries, but the emerging market boom has spread to embrace Latin America and Africa, too.

Recent evidence on convergence between the less developed regions of the world and the high-income economies is provided in Table 7.1. The higher economic growth rates do indicate convergence. In the period 2000–10, the average annual growth rate in GDP per capita in East Asia and the Pacific (dominated by China), has been extraordinary at over 8 percent. South Asia, dominated by India, has also experienced rapid growth. The high growth rate for Europe and Central Asia, mainly the transition economies, reflects in large part their recoveries from the difficult decade of the 1990s, when they were transforming their economic and political systems. In fact, all of the developing regions, even sub-Saharan Africa, grew significantly faster than the high-income economies during the past decade—although, as discussed in Chapter 6, the high-income economies experienced sharp recessions at the end of the decade which trimmed their average growth rates.

Even so, the gaps in per capita income remain large. It would take 205 years from 2010 for sub-Saharan Africa's average income to converge to the average income of the high-income economies under the average annual economic growth rates for 2000–10. At this point (in 2215), the average income (in PPP dollars) in sub-Saharan Africa and the high-income economies would be nearly $355,000. Needless to say, these are not expected projections for economic growth, only illustrative.

Income distribution revisited

As stated in Chapter 1, economic growth has improved the average material standard of living and has significantly reduced absolute poverty. Faster growth in the low- and middle-income economies will close the income gaps with the high-income economies, implying that the world

Table 7.1 *Recent evidence on convergence: economic growth rates*

Low- and middle income economies (2010 GNI/POP)	Average annual growth rates (%), 2000–10		
	GDP	POP	GDP/POP
East Asia & Pacific ($6,623)	9.4%	0.8%	8.6%
Europe & Central Asia ($13,200)	5.4%	0.2%	5.2%
Latin America & Caribbean ($10,951)	3.8%	1.2%	2.6%
Middle East & North Africa ($7,851)	4.7%	1.8%	2.9%
South Asia ($3,028)	7.4%	1.5%	5.9%
Sub-Saharan Africa ($2,108)	5.0%	2.5%	2.5%
High-income economies ($37,183)	1.8%	0.7%	1.1%
United States ($47,020)	*1.9%*	*0.9%*	*1.0%*

Notes: The average annual growth rate in per capita gross domestic product (GDP/POP) is equal to the difference between the average annual growth rates in GDP and population.

Gross national income per capita (GNI/POP) in 2010 is expressed in internationally comparable or PPP dollars, where an international dollar has the same purchasing power over output as a US dollar does in the United States.

Source: World Bank (2012: Tables 1 and 4).

income distribution is becoming more equal. But as Bourguignon and Morrison (2002) point out, to measure income inequality in the world, we need to consider not only differences in average incomes across countries, but also income disparities within countries. In fact, income distribution across the world's population is substantially less equal than indicated by income the gaps between countries.

We have noted that economic data extending back over time are limited, especially the further back the analysis goes and the poorer the populations considered. Nevertheless, in a careful study, Bourguignon and Morrison (2002: 733) estimated that over the period from 1820 to 1992:

> the mean income of the world population increased by a factor of 7.6. The mean income of the bottom 20 percent increased only by a factor of slightly more than 3, and that of the bottom 60 percent by about 4, and that of the top decile by almost 10. At the same time, however, the extreme poverty headcount fell from 84 percent of the world population in 1820 to 24 percent in 1992.

The authors conclude that world income inequality significantly worsened from 1820 to 1992, largely due to growing gaps between countries and regions. In fact, they estimated that within-country inequality was halved from 80 percent or more of world inequality in 1820 to 40 percent by 1950.

Over the last half of the twentieth century, the accelerated economic growth in Asia contributed to decreasing income inequality across regions of the world, while the lagging performance of Africa, along with its rapid population growth, increased world income inequality. In the last two decades, though, the evidence is that income inequality has increased within countries. China's explosive growth, which dramatically reduced the incidence of extreme poverty, has been accompanied by growing income inequality, particularly between urban and rural areas and between the more and less educated. The transitions in the former socialist economies of

Eastern Europe and the Soviet Union in the 1990s increased not only income inequality, but also the incidence of poverty in this region.

Even in the rich countries, the income distribution has deteriorated. Milanovic (2011: 8) notes that "between the mid-1980s and the mid-2000s, inequality rose in 16 out of 20 rich OECD countries." While the severe recessions from the financial crises in the high-income economies at the end of the decade may have narrowed the across-country income gaps, the rise in poverty and erosion of the middle classes likely exacerbated the income inequality in these rich countries. Among the rich nations, the United States has become one of the most unequal (see Box 7.2).

BOX 7.2: INCOME INEQUALITY IN THE UNITED STATES

In a comprehensive study the Congressional Budget Office (2011: 3) found that household income distribution in the United States grew significantly less equal over the past three decades. Between 1979 and 2007, the average real household income (after federal taxes and transfers) for the richest 1 percent of the population increased by 275 percent. For the others in the top quintile (i.e., the 81st through the 99th percentile), the increase in average real income was 65 percent. For the middle 60 percent (or second third, and fourth quintiles), the gain was just under 40 percent; while for the poorest 20 percent of the population (the bottom quintile), average real income rose by only about 18 percent. Consequently, the share of household income after transfers and federal taxes going to the top 1 percent had more than doubled, from 8 percent in 1979 to 17 percent in 2007; and for the top quintile, the share rose from 43 percent to 53 percent. In contrast, the share of household income received by the bottom quintile declined from 7 percent to 5 percent.

As noted, the household incomes in the study are measured after federal taxes and transfers (state taxes are not incorporated), and the progressivity of the US tax and transfer system reduces the inequity in market incomes. Over this period, however, the equalizing effects of the taxes and transfers were reduced. In part, regressive payroll taxes on labor (for social security and Medicare) rose relative to the progressive income taxes. Also transfers became less progressive, in part, with increased Medicare benefits that are relatively independent of income. The Congressional Budget Office (CBO) reports that households in the bottom quintile received more than 50 percent of the transfer payments in 1979, but closer to 35 percent in 2007.

With respect to the underlying causes of the growing inequity in US household income distribution, the CBO cites increased wage inequality between educated, highly skilled workers, who benefited disproportionately from technological progress (e.g., in information technology and advanced manufacturing), and the less educated, lower-skilled workers suffering job displacement. Also decreases in the real minimum wage, increased foreign competition in basic manufacturing, and declines in unionization contributed to the growing wage gaps. According to the CBO (2011: 18) the sharply higher labor incomes for the top 1 percent, while most evident for superstars (in sports and entertainment) and in the salaries of major corporate executives, more reflected the high earners in the financial, legal, and medical professions.

The period of the study ended in 2007, just before the Great Recession and the ensuing rise in unemployment and loss in personal wealth with the collapse in housing values. Berg and Ostry (2011: 13) observe that:

> the increase in US income inequality in recent decades is strikingly similar to the increase that occurred in the 1920s. In both cases, there was a boom in the financial sector, poor people borrowed a lot, and a huge financial crisis ensued.

The ongoing intense lobbying by corporate interests for favorable legislation, as well as the concentrated wealth that disproportionately funds political campaigns, pays off—whether in favorable tax treatment for capital gains, subsidies for special interests, or loopholes in government regulations. Milanovic (2011: 9) observes a political reality:

> The rich wield a disproportionate influence over policy because they are politically more active and contribute more to politicians than their less affluent counterparts... political systems [in these democratic societies] have moved closer to "one dollar, one vote," from the more traditional "one person, one vote" model.

> The "Occupy" movement that arose in the United States in 2011 reflected the growing inequities in US society between the 1 percent at the top and the other 99 percent. The growing inequality and rise in social tensions is not limited to the US and the developed economies. *Time* magazine's Person of the Year for 2011 was the Protestor. Rick Stengel (2011) opened his essay with:

> History often emerges only in retrospect. Events become significant only when looked back upon. No one could have known that when a Tunisian fruit vendor set himself on fire in a public square in a town barely on the map, he would spark protests that would bring down dictators in Tunisia, Egypt, and Libya and rattle regimes in Syria, Yemen and Bahrain. Or that that spirit of dissent would spur Mexicans to rise up against the terror of drug cartels, Greeks to march against unaccountable leaders, Americans to occupy public spaces to protest income inequality, and Russians to marshal themselves against a corrupt autocracy.

Stengel's essay introduced a longer article by Andersen on the protest movements that erupted across the world in 2011. Andersen (2011: 61) notes:

> It's remarkable how much the protest vanguards share. Everywhere they are disproportionately young, middle class, and educated... All over the world, the protestors share a belief that their countries' political systems and economies have grown dysfunctional and corrupt—sham democracies rigged to favor the rich and powerful and prevent significant change.

Aside from the loss of social capital that growing income inequality might bring, Berg and Ostry (2011) find that high income inequality can hinder economic growth. Unequal societies may be less politically stable, which itself can discourage productive investment and make it difficult to implement effective economic policy, particularly if tighter fiscal measures are required to address growing public debt. In addition, the poor likely have less access to education and credit, both of which can promote entrepreneurship and increase income.

The answer to damaging income inequality is not simply a redistribution of income with higher taxes on the wealthier transferred to the lower classes. Moreover, the goal is not complete income equality, even if possible, since incentives are important. The solution is to promote socioeconomic mobility. As Milanovic (2011: 7) summarizes, "widespread education has become the secret to growth. And broadly accessible education is difficult to achieve unless a society has a relatively even income distribution."

CONCLUSION

The relationship between economic growth, poverty, and income distribution is complicated. Economic growth will increase the average levels of income and consumption and will tend to reduce absolute poverty. The degree to which the economic growth alleviates poverty, however, depends on the type of development a nation pursues, including the extent to which economic opportunities are shared and investments in human capital made. Even so, increased income inequality may accompany economic growth. The degree to which this is addressed reflects a nation's institutions and priorities.

While the regional averages suggest the low- and middle-income economies are growing faster than the high-income economies, this is not to say that all nations within these developing regions also are advancing. Nor does this imply that all within the nations are prospering.

In the final third of the book, we discuss sustainable development and the implications for economic growth. As will be argued, sustainable development for the world will not be possible unless the welfare of the poor in all nations becomes a higher priority. Underlying effective policy is insightful theory informed by the evidence. In the next chapter, we address how economic theories are tested, using empirical models for the determinants of economic growth.

KEY TERMS

agglomeration	brain drain
capital-abundant	complementary factor
conditional convergence	endogenous growth theory
entrepreneurs	fundamental equation of the Solow model
growth rate in total factor productivity	intensive production function
labor-abundant	neoclassical growth model
real exchange rate	steady-state equilibrium
unconditional convergence	

QUESTIONS

1. Given the following basic Solow growth model:

$$(S1) \quad Y(t) = [K(t)]^{0.4}[L(t)]^{0.6}$$
$$(S2) \quad I(t) = S(t)$$
$$(S3) \quad S(t) = 0.10Y(t)$$
$$(S4) \quad L(t) = 30e^{0.02t}$$

(a) Derive the fundamental equation of this growth model.

(b) Plot the net saving and required net investment per unit of labor curves for the following values of the capital–labor ratio: $k = 0, 5, 10, 15, 20$, and 25. Solve graphically for the steady-state equilibrium capital–labor ratio, k_0^*.

(c) Solve mathematically for the steady-state equilibrium capital–labor ratio, k_0^*, output per unit of labor, y_0^*, and capital–output ratio, v_0^*. (Round off your answers to two decimal places.)

(d) Determine the levels of real national output, physical capital, and labor at time $t = 3$, that is, $Y(3)$, $K(3)$, and $L(3)$.

(e) Suppose that after $t = 3$, the natural growth rate of the labor force decreases to $n = 0.015$. Find the new steady-state equilibrium capital–labor ratio, k_1^*, output per unit of labor, y_1^*, and capital-output ratio, v_1^*. Discuss the transition to the new steady-state equilibrium.

(f) Suppose instead that after $t = 3$ the saving rate decreases to $s = 0.08$. Find the new steady-state equilibrium capital–labor ratio, k_2^*, output per unit of labor, y_2^*, and capital-output ratio, v_2^*. Discuss the transition to the new steady-state equilibrium.

2. Assume the following Solow growth model with neutral technological progress and effective capital and effective labor:

(S1) $Y(t) = 2e^{0.015t}[\underline{K}(t)]^{0.4}[\underline{L}(t)]^{0.6}$, where $\underline{K}(t) = e^{0.01t}K(t)$ and $\underline{L}(t) = e^{0.012t}L(t)$

(S2) $I(t) = S(t)$

(S3) $S(t) = 0.10Y(t)$

(S4) $L(t) = 30e^{0.02t}$

(a) Derive the equation for the growth rate for real national output per unit of labor, d_y/y.

(b) Given an initial value of the capital–labor of $k(0) = 46.4515$, find the equilibrium values for output per unit of labor at $t = 0, 1$, and 2, that is, $y(0)$, $y(1)$, and $y(2)$. What is happening to the growth rate in output per unit of labor over time? Explain why. (Round off your calculations to four decimal places.)

3. If the natural growth rate in the basic Solow model were negative, $n < 0$, could there be a steady-state equilibrium? Discuss, and illustrate if possible. How would your answer change if neutral technical change at an annual rate of g were allowed?

4. Assume the following Solow model that includes effective natural resources, $\underline{R}(t)$:

(S1) $Y(t) = 2e^{0.015t}[\underline{K}(t)]^{0.3}[\underline{L}(t)]^{0.6}[\underline{R}(t)]^{0.1}$, where

$\underline{K}(t) = e^{0.01t}K(t)$, $\underline{L}(t) = e^{0.012t}L(t)$, and $\underline{R}(t) = e^{0.002t}R(t)$

(S2) $I(t) = S(t)$

(S3) $S(t) = 0.10Y(t)$

(S4) $L(t) = 30e^{0.02t}$

(S5) $R(t) = 100e^{-0.005t}$

(a) Derive the equation for the growth rate for real national output per unit of labor, d_y/y, where $y = Y/L$.

(b) Contrast this with the equation for the growth rate in labor productivity from the Solow model in Question 2. Discuss the insights from incorporating effective natural resources in the growth model.

REFERENCES

Andersen, Kurt. 2011. "The Protester," *Time*, December 26.

Berg, Andrew and Jonathan Ostry. 2011. "Equality and Efficiency: Is There a Trade-off between the Two or Do They Go Hand in Hand?" *Finance & Development*, 48(3): 12–15.

Bourguignon, Francois and Christian Morrison. 2002. "Inequality among World Citizens: 1820–1992," *American Economic Review*, 92(4): 727–744.

Clemens, Michael. 2011. "Economics and Emigration: Trillion Dollar Bills on the Sidewalk?" *Journal of Economic Perspectives*, 25(3): 83–106.

Congressional Budget Office. 2011. *Trends in the Distribution of Household Income between 1979 and 2007*. Washington, DC: Congress of the United States.

Gibson, John and David McKenzie. 2011. "Eight Questions about the Brain Drain," *Journal of Economic Perspectives*, 25(3): 107–128.

Grossman, Gene and Elhanan Helpman. 1994. "Endogenous Innovation in the Theory of Growth," *Journal of Economic Perspectives*, 8(1): 23–44.

Milanovic, Branko. 2011. "More or Less: Income Inequality Has Risen over the Past Quarter-Century Instead of Falling as Expected," *Finance & Development*, 48(3): 7–11.

O'Sullivan, John. 2011. "A Game of Catch-up: Special Report: The World Economy," *The Economist*, September 24.

Pack, Howard. 1994. "Endogenous Growth Theory: Intellectual Appeal and Empirical Shortcomings," *Journal of Economic Perspectives*, 8(1): 55–72.

Romer, Paul. 1994. "The Origins of Endogenous Growth," *Journal of Economic Perspectives*, 8(1): 3–2.

Solow, Robert. 1956. "A Contribution to the Theory of Economic Growth," *Quarterly Journal of Economics*, 70(1): 65–94.

Solow, Robert. 1994. "Perspectives on Growth Theory," *Journal of Economic Perspectives*, 8(1): 45–54.

Stengel, Rick. 2011. "2011 Person of the Year," *Time*, December 26.

World Bank. 2000. "Dynamic Cities as Engines of Growth," in *World Development Report 1999/2000: Entering the 21st Century*. New York: Oxford University Press: 125–138.

World Bank. 2012. *World Development Report 2012: Gender Equality and Development*. Washington, DC: World Bank.

Chapter 8

Empirical analysis

We have discussed various models of economic growth, beginning with the classical economists' concept in the early nineteenth century of a long-run stationary state. Depression in the industrialized economies during the 1930s renewed the interest in macroeconomic models. The World3 simulation model, initiated in the early 1970s, addressed natural resource constraints and environmental limits to growth and the linkages between population, food supply, industrial output, resource use, and pollution.

A theoretical model of aggregate demand and aggregate supply was offered in Chapter 6 to explain short-run changes in real national output and inflation. The more dynamic growth models in Chapter 7 focused on the sources of long-run growth in labor productivity, in particular, technological progress and qualitative changes in the primary factors of production. Each approach or model provided some insight into economic growth.

In this chapter we turn to empirical analysis and how economic theory can be tested. While there are several approaches to testing economic theory, including randomized evaluations, micro-level surveys, and case studies, the emphasis here will be on regression analysis, in particular, cross-country multiple regressions for economic growth.

THEORY, EVIDENCE, AND POLICY

In social science, knowledge is organized systematically: theories are formulated and then confronted with evidence, after which policies are developed. Models embody the theories, which refer to the hypothesized relationships among the phenomena of interest. Data are collected and analyzed to assess whether the predictions derived from the theories are confirmed. When theories are supported by the evidence, informed policies of how to attain given objectives can be devised.

In the natural sciences, such as physics, chemistry, and biology, often theories can be tested under controlled laboratory environments, where relationships of interest can be isolated and carefully examined. In the social sciences, such as economics, sociology, and political science, however, opportunities for controlled laboratory experimentation are more limited.[1] Therefore, to test their theories social scientists rely on uncontrolled experiments, collecting evidence based on observations of actual events. Human behavior, subject to free will, is less bound by universal laws than the natural elements in chemistry or gravity in physics. Nevertheless, economists seek

---

[1] Behavioral economics and experimental economics are rapidly growing fields on interest. Drawing on the insights from psychology and sociology, observations of human behavior under controlled experiments can be used to test specific hypotheses. Simulations of markets and randomized evaluations of incentives are examples of this mode of inquiry. For a good introduction to randomized evaluations, see Cohen and Easterly (2009).

to develop theories of human behavior, in particular, how populations decide which goods and services to produce, and how the goods and services are produced and distributed. Moreover, economists are interested in **rational behavior** that is consistent with achieving the objective (e.g., profit maximization for firms and utility maximization for households).

Unlike mathematics, where theorems (propositions provable on the basis of explicit assumptions) can be disproved by finding a single counterexample, in the social sciences even well-accepted theories will at times be at variance with observed behavior. In the social sciences, theories or organized explanations of reality cannot be proven, only confirmed or supported. Counterexamples may be found to even the most accepted theories in the social sciences. For example, in economics the theoretical law of demand which describes the inverse relationship between the quantities demanded and prices of a good may not hold for "snob" goods, where, at least up to a point, the higher the price of the good, the more desirable it becomes as an indicator of status.

Testing economic theory

In general there are four stages to empirical analysis in economics. The first is **specification**, where economic theory is used to construct a model to explain the behavior of interest. The hypothesized relationships between the endogenous variables (to be explained) and the exogenous variables (assumed to be independent and determined by factors outside the model) are set forth with the behavioral equations, identities, and equilibrium conditions. Where possible, functional forms can be adopted to represent economic theory, for example, aggregate production functions that are nonlinear to capture diminishing returns to factors of production in the short run or constant returns to scale in the long run. The expected signs of influence should be clearly identified, for example, output rises with labor at a diminishing rate in the short run. Expected limits on parameters should also be set forth (e.g., the saving rate should be between zero and one).

The second stage is **estimation**. Here we use econometrics and data to estimate the model, essentially quantifying the hypothesized relationships. In this chapter, multiple regression analysis is employed to identify significant relationships between the endogenous variable (e.g., the economic growth rate) and exogenous variables (e.g., net saving rate, growth rate in exports). To illustrate the principles of regression analysis, we will use the most basic technique known as ordinary least squares.

With respect to the data or evidence, there are two basic ways to organize the sample of observations on the variables. Longitudinal data sets are time series, where the observations extend over a period of time. For example, we could estimate the determinants of economic growth for a country over a period of years, where we have annual observations for all of the variables in the model. With cross-sectional data sets the observations of the variables are for a specific period of time. For instance, we could take a cross-section of countries and look at the determinants of economic growth for a given year or for a given n-year period.

The third stage is **verification**. Here we assess the estimated model. Are the estimated relationships consistent with theory and statistically significant according to accepted criteria? How "strong" are the results? Was the most appropriate method of estimation used?

The last stage is **application**. If the model is verified, that is, if the hypothesized relationships are supported by the evidence, then what are the policy implications? For example, if human capital formation is important for economic growth, then policies promoting investment in education, training, health, and nutrition can be developed. We should note that the first three stages are more **positive economics**, establishing what is. The formulation of policy—what to do to achieve given objectives—while it should be supported by established theory, is more normative. For example, to increase economic growth, should we use investment tax credits for business or invest in vocational training for future workers? Estimated macroeconomic models may be used for **forecasting**, that is, predicting future values for the dependent variables based on assumed values of the independent variables.

Before developing and testing an empirical model for the determinants of economic growth, we review some fundamentals of statistics. Then we present the theory and method of basic regression analysis.

REVIEW OF DESCRIPTIVE STATISTICS

We begin with a sample of observations, a subset of the universe of possible observations, for a selected variable, X. Let X_t be the tth observation of the variable X ($t = 1, \ldots, n$, where n is the sample size).

The arithmetic **mean** of the variable, $\bar{X}$, is the average of the values of the variable in the sample:

$$\bar{X} = \frac{1}{n} \sum_{t=1}^{n} X_t$$

The **variance** of the variable, S_X^2, is a measure of the distribution of the values of the variable around its mean:

$$S_X^2 = \frac{1}{n-1} \sum_{t=1}^{n} [X_t - \bar{X}]^2$$

The **degrees of freedom** for a statistic refer to the number of free or linearly independent observations in the sample used in the calculation. Here the degrees of freedom are equal to $n-1$. In calculating the sample variance, we use up one observation from the sample of size n when the mean is computed; since if we know the sample mean and the other $n-1$ observations, we could determine the nth observation. For example, if the first two observations of a variable, X, in a sample of size 3 ($n = 3$) are $X_1 = 4$ and $X_2 = 10$, and we know the sample mean is $\bar{X} = 5$, then we can infer that the third observation, X_3, is equal to 1, since $5 = (4 + 10 + X_3)/3$.

The **standard deviation** of the sample, S_X, is the square root of the sample variance, and indicates the "average" deviation from the sample mean: $S_X = \sqrt{S_X^2}$. In general, if the sample standard deviation is as large as or larger than the sample mean of a variable, then the values of that variable can be considered relatively dispersed.

To illustrate, consider the following simple example of a sample of five ($n = 5$) observations of a variable X. Let $X_1 = 10$, $X_2 = 20$, $X_3 = 30$, $X_4 = 40$, $X_5 = 50$. Then

$$\bar{X} = \frac{1}{5} \sum_{t=1}^{5} X_t = \frac{1}{5}(10 + 20 + 30 + 40 + 50) = \frac{1}{5} \cdot 150 = 30$$

$$S_X^2 = \frac{1}{4} \sum_{t=1}^{5} [X_t - \bar{X}]$$

$$= \frac{1}{4}[(10 - 30)^2 + (20 - 30)^2 + (30 - 30)^2 + (40 - 30)^2 + (50 - 30)^2]$$

$$= \frac{1}{4}[(-20)^2 + (-10)^2 + 0^2 + 10^2 + 20^2] = 250$$

$$S_X = \sqrt{S_X^2} = \sqrt{250} = 15.8$$

The **covariance** of a sample of observations on two variables, X and Y, is a measure that quantifies how much the values of the two variables vary together. The covariance of X and Y, $Cov_{X,Y}$ or $Cov(X, Y)$, is given by:

$$Cov_{X,Y} = \frac{1}{n-1} \sum_{t=1}^{n} (X_t - \bar{X}) \cdot (Y_t - \bar{Y})$$

If the covariance is positive (negative), then larger than average values of one variable are associated with larger (smaller) than average values of the other variable. If the covariance equals zero, then the values of the two variables appear to be unrelated, as would be the case for two random variables. A **random variable** is one whose values are determined by probability or a **stochastic** process, such as the flip of a coin or the roll of a pair of dice.

To illustrate, consider the following ordered pairs for two variables, X and Y:

observation	X_t	Y_t
1	10	2
2	20	4
3	30	8
4	40	16
5	50	32

The means and standard deviations for the variables are: $\bar{X} = 30$, $\bar{Y} = 12.4$ and $S_X = 15.8$, $S_Y = 12.2$. The sample covariance is:

$$Cov_{X,Y} = \frac{1}{4}[(-20)(-10.4) + (-10)(-8.4) + 0 \cdot (-4.4) + 10 \cdot 3.6 + 20 \cdot 19.6] = 180$$

Here it appears that the two variables are positively related. The problem with the variance as an indicator of the relationship between two variables, however, is the sensitivity to the scale of measurement. To illustrate, if we define $A = X/100$ and $B = Y/100$, that is, express the variables X and Y in decimals or hundredths of units, then the covariance is divided by 10,000: $Cov_{A,B} = 0.0180$, which does appear close to zero.

A standardized measure of the relationship between two variables is the **correlation coefficient**. The sample correlation coefficient, $r_{X,Y}$, is equal to the ratio of the sample covariance to the product of the sample standard deviations of the two variables:

$$r_{X,Y} = \frac{Cov_{X,Y}}{S_X \cdot S_Y}$$

$r_{X,Y}$ lies between -1 and $+1$.

The correlation coefficient measures the strength of the linear relationship between two variables and is independent of the units in which the two variables are measured. If the sample correlation coefficient, $r_{X,Y} = -1$, then the two variables are perfectly negatively correlated. A plot of the sample ordered pairs would lie on a straight line with a negative slope. If $r_{X,Y} = +1$, then the two variables are perfectly positively correlated and the sample ordered pairs would lie on a positively-sloped line. If $r_{X,Y} = 0$, then the two variables are not linearly correlated. In this example, the sample correlation coefficient is $r_{X,Y} = Cov_{X,Y}/S_X \cdot S_Y = 180/(15.8) \cdot (12.2) = 0.934$, which indicates a strong positive correlation.

193

Two points should be emphasized. First, the correlation coefficient indicates the strength of the linear relationship between two variables. The variables might be highly correlated, but not linearly. In the simple example $Y = 2^{0.1X}$, the relationship between the two variables actually is nonlinear. (You might recall that Malthus observed that unchecked population growth increases geometrically (e.g., $2, 4, 8, 16, 32, \ldots, 2^x$), while he speculated that the means of subsistence could grow only arithmetically (e.g., $10, 20, 30, 40, 50 \ldots 10x$, where x is the time period).)

Second, correlation is not the same as causality. Finding a high degree of correlation between two variables, a value of $r_{X,Y}$ close to -1 or $+1$, does not necessarily indicate a cause-and-effect relationship or dependency between the two variables. There may be a spurious correlation. For instance, the populations of India and China have both increased significantly over the past 50 years, but there is no causality or deterministic relationship between the two variables. The population growth in each country reflects the underlying economic development, culture, and population policies. Both nations are undergoing demographic transitions, and China is much further along than India. Both populations might be adversely affected in the future by climate change.

To establish causality between variables or phenomena of interest, theories have to be developed. A deterministic relationship is hypothesized and a model is constructed to convey that relationship. Recall the first stage in testing economic theory, specification of a model. With this review of descriptive statistics, we can illustrate the testing of economic theory, beginning with the mechanics of simple regression analysis.

SIMPLE REGRESSION ANALYSIS

In **simple regression analysis** the behavior of a dependent variable, say Y, depends on one independent or explanatory variable, say X. Moreover, we specify a linear relationship: $Y_t = a + bX_t + u_t$, $t = 1, \ldots, n$, where Y_t is the tth observation on the dependent variable, X_t the tth observation on the independent or explanatory variable, u_t the tth value of the error term (unobserved), and a and b are unknown regression parameters to be estimated. The value of a indicates the intercept of the population regression line, or the expected value of the dependent variable, Y, when the independent variable, X, equals zero. The value of the coefficient b indicates the marginal effect on the dependent variable of a unit change in the independent variable, here $b = dY/dX$.[2] The variable u is the **error term** or disturbance term, and represents the combined impact of factors other than the included independent variable X that could affect the dependent variable Y.

The regression model consists of a set of assumptions about the relationship between the variables, that is, the hypothesized dependency of Y on X, and assumptions about the error term, u. The theoretical relationship between Y and X, whether direct or indirect, will be reflected in the expected sign of b, positive or negative. Here we also assume a linear specification between X and Y, although this is not as restrictive as it might appear.[3]

---

[2] Actually the coefficient b, the population regression parameter, represents the instantaneous change in the dependent variable associated with an infinitesimal change in the independent variable, $b = dY/dX$. Practically speaking, and here with a linear model, we can speak of a unit change in the independent variable.

[3] Nonlinear relationships can be modeled—for example, the independent variable X may be the square or square root or the natural logarithm of another variable, say Z, that is, $X = Z^2$, $X = \sqrt{Z}$, or $X = \ln(Z)$.

The error term

The error term is included in the econometric model since the model's specification is recognized as imperfect. Even if all the variables were measured accurately and the theoretical relationship mathematically correct, that is, Y is a linear function only of the variable X, the error term would still be required since there is a random element in any model in the social sciences. Human behavior, subject to free will, is not perfectly predictable. Moreover, an error term is necessary to allow for measurement error, incorrect specification of the relationship between X and Y, and other possible influences on the dependent variable besides X. Thus, in theory, for every value of X_t, there is a probability distribution for the values of Y_t, for $t = 1, \ldots, n$.

A simple example might help. Suppose it should take a trained worker exactly 1 hour to assemble 10 units of output. We might find, however, a distribution of output for any sample of n labor hours, likely centered on a mean of 10, even for the same worker, due to swings in concentration or energy, or simply with biorhythms. In contrast, the formula for the temperature conversion from Celsius (C) to Fahrenheit (F) is deterministic, F = 32 + 1.8C. There is no random error. It is always true that $10°$C is exactly $50°$F.

In sum, the error term represents three basic concerns. One is incomplete specification of the model due to omitted explanatory variables or incorrect functional forms. The former is especially likely in simple regression models with only one explanatory variable. The relationship between X and Y may be nonlinear or there may be a lagged influence of X on Y (e.g., $Y_t = a + bX_{t-1}$). The second reason for including an error term is inexact measurement of the dependent variable. The explanatory variable is assumed here to be measured exactly.[4] The dependent variable to be explained, Y, is inevitably measured with some error. For example, estimates of gross domestic product are based not on a comprehensive recording of every transaction of final goods and services, but on a sample of sales. The third reason, already noted, is the randomness of human behavior.

Assumptions on the error term

There are five standard assumptions about the error term in simple regression analysis. First, the error term, u_t, is assumed to be **normally distributed** for each observation ($t = 1, \ldots, n$) on the dependent variable (Y_t) in the sample. That is the distribution of values for the error term is shaped like a bell curve, symmetric around the mean value, μ, where

$$\mu = \sum_{t=1}^{n} p(u_t) \cdot u_t$$

in which $p(u_t)$ is the probability of the value u_t occurring (see Figure 8.1). The area under a normal curve, indicating the sum of the probabilities of the values of the error terms, is equal to one.

The second standard assumption is that the mean of the probability distribution of error terms equals zero, $\mu = 0$.[5] On net, the error terms cancel out.

Third is the assumption of **homoscedasticity**, which means the variance of the error term, σ_u^2, is constant. Every error term, $u_t, t = 1, \ldots, n$, has the same variance. See Figure 8.2,

---

[4] This is not to imply that there are no measurement errors for the explanatory variable. Instead, for our purposes here with simple empirical analysis, the standard assumption of exact measurement of the explanatory variable(s) will be made. More advanced econometrics would allow for measurement errors in the explanatory variable(s).

[5] The expected value of the error term is zero: $E(u_t) = \sum_{t=1}^{n} u_t \cdot p(u_t) = \bar{u} = \mu = 0$, where $p(u_t)$ is the probability of a certain value of u occurring in the sample of size n. The expected value of this random variable, u, is the mean of the variable, μ.

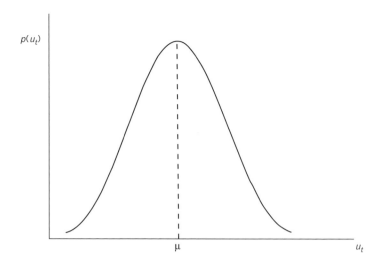

Figure 8.1 *Normal distribution for the error term, u_t*

The error term is normally distributed around a mean of zero ($\mu = 0$) with a constant variance, σ_u^2. That is, $u_t \sim N(0, \sigma_u^2)$, where $\mu = \sum_{t=1}^{n} p(t) \cdot u(t) = 0$ and $p(u_t) =$ probability of $u(t), t = 1 \ldots n$.

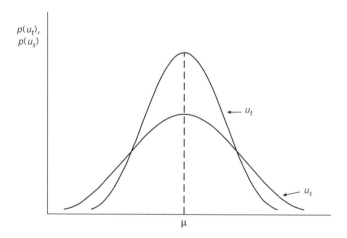

■ **Figure 8.2** *Homoscedasticity of the error term*

Under homoscedasticity, the variance of the error term is constant, i.e., $(\sigma_u^2)_t = (\sigma_u^2)_s = (\sigma_u^2)$ for $t = 1 \ldots n$ and $s = 1 \ldots n$, $t \neq s$. This rules out the possibility of heteroscedasticity, where the variances of the error terms vary, illustrated above with $(\sigma_u^2)_t < (\sigma_u^2)_s$.

where two normal distributions, for u_t and u_s, $s = 1, \ldots, n$, have the same mean, μ, but are characterized by different variances. Here $(\sigma_u^2)_s > (\sigma_u^2)_t$. The assumption of a constant variance for a distribution of error terms may more likely be violated, a condition known as **heteroscedasticity**, in cross-sectional samples, especially if the values of the dependent variable vary significantly in size. For example, if the dependent variable were gross national income and the sample included countries of very different population sizes, say China and Costa Rica, respectively in 2010 with populations of 1.34 billion and 4.7 million and estimated gross national incomes of $10,222 billion (PPP dollars) and $53 billion (PPP dollars), then the assumption of a constant variance might not hold. For one, larger measurement errors in the dependent variable would be more likely for China. To standardize across countries of vastly different sizes, the dependent variable might be per capita income, with China and Costa Rica in 2010 having per capita purchasing power parity-adjusted gross national incomes of $7,640 and $11,270, respectively (World Bank 2012: Tables 1.1 and 2.1).

The first three assumptions about the error term can be concisely written as:

$$u_t \sim N(0, \sigma_u^2), t = 1, \ldots, n$$

That is, the error term is normally distributed with a mean of zero and a constant variance. For each value of the independent variable, X_t, in the sample, the disturbance term is assumed to be normally distributed around zero. Recall the underlying model, $Y_t = a + bX_t + u_t (t = 1, \ldots, n)$. We can consider each value of the random or stochastic error term to be the result of a large number of small causes, each producing a small deviation of the dependent variable, Y_t, from what it otherwise would be if the relation were deterministic or exactly determined by the explanatory variable, X_t. The assumption of homoscedasticity or constant variance rules out the possibility that the dispersion or distribution of the error terms would vary systematically with the independent variable, X_t, or any other factor not included in the model.

Intuitively, even if there is only one set of observations on the dependent and independent variables in the sample available, that is, the historical record, theoretically, for the given values of the independent variable (X_t), a range of outcomes (values for any Y_t) could have been possible due to the error terms (u_t). The error terms, however, are not observed, so in order to estimate a relationship, here between Y and X, we have to make assumptions about the likely properties of these error terms, such as normally distributed around a mean of zero with a constant variance.

The fourth assumption about the error terms is called **nonautocorrelation**. That is, the error terms are assumed to be independent of each other. Formally, the covariance between any two error terms, u_t and u_s, equals zero: $\text{Cov}(u_t, u_s) = 0, t \neq s, t = 1, \ldots, n, s = 1, \ldots, n$. This assumption is most likely to be violated in time series analysis where there may be cyclical influences or carry-over effects from one period to the next. For example, if the dependent variable were the annual growth rate in real per capita national income for a country over a sample of years, and the independent variable were the net savings rate, then an economic shock in one year (e.g., a fall in consumer confidence resulting in a recession) would likely affect the growth rate of per capita income in subsequent years.

The fifth assumption underlying this simple regression model is that the independent variable, X, is assumed to be nonstochastic, with values that are exogenous. That is, the values of the independent variable are given and assumed to be fixed over any sample. Formally, the explanatory variable is independent of the error term, so $\text{Cov}(X_t, u_t) = 0$. Therefore, the randomness associated with the values of the dependent variable, Y, is due to the error term, not to the independent explanatory variable, X. The deterministic influence on Y_t reflects $a + bX_t$. The stochastic or random influence reflects the error term, u_t.

These are the assumptions underlying this simple regression model. We now need to come up with a process for estimating the parameters, a and b, that define the deterministic part of the model, that is, the hypothesized relationship between the independent or explanatory variable, X, and the dependent variable, Y. The method we use, ordinary least squares, is the most basic technique in simple regression analysis.

197

ESTIMATION OF A SIMPLE REGRESSION MODEL

We begin with the specified model, $Y_t = a + bX_t + u_t$, which is hypothesized to describe the relationship between a dependent variable, Y, that we seek to explain, and an independent variable, X, that influences the behavior of this dependent variable. An error term, u, is included to capture any specification error in the model as well as random influences on the dependent variable. We seek to estimate the values of the parameters, a and b, which are unknown, but capture the hypothesized deterministic influences on the dependent variable.

We make the standard assumptions about the error terms: normally distributed with a mean of zero and constant variance, independent of each other and independent of the explanatory variable. It follows that the values of the dependent variable then are also normally distributed, reflecting the error terms, around a mean given by the deterministic part of the model, $a + bX_t$, with a constant variance given by the variance of the error term, σ_u^2. That is, $Y_t \sim N(a + bX_t, \sigma_u^2)$.

The **population regression line**, $Y_t = a + bX_t$, represents the hypothesized true relationship between Y and X. As noted, the values of the error term, u_t ($t = 1, \ldots, n$), are unobserved. We use the observed values of the dependent and independent variables to come up with estimates of the population parameters, a and b, denoted by $\hat{a}$ and $\hat{b}$.

The **sample regression line** is given by the equation, $\hat{Y}_t = \hat{a} + \hat{b}X_t$, which is the estimate of the unknown population regression line. The unobserved values for the error term can be estimated by the residuals or prediction errors from the sample regression line.

The **prediction error** for observation t is given by $\hat{u}_t = Y_t - \hat{Y}_t = Y_t - \hat{a} - \hat{b}X_t (t = 1, \ldots, n)$. By examining the prediction errors, we can assess the validity of the assumptions made about the behavior of the error term.

The ordinary least squares criterion

The estimates of the values for the parameters, $\hat{a}$ and $\hat{b}$, are derived using the **ordinary least squares** (OLS) criterion. That is, we find the values of a and b that minimize the sum of the squares of the prediction errors (SSE):

$$\text{minimize SSE} = \sum_{t=1}^{n} (\hat{u}_t)^2 = \sum_{t=1}^{n} (Y_t - \hat{Y}_t)^2 = \sum_{t=1}^{n} (Y_t - \hat{a} - \hat{b}X_t)^2$$

This is a classic optimization problem, here with two endogenous variables, $\hat{a}$ and $\hat{b}$, the estimates of the unknown population parameters, a and b. The first-order conditions are:

$$\partial \text{SSE}/\partial \hat{a} = -2 \sum_{t=1}^{n} (Y_t - \hat{a} - \hat{b}X_t) = 0$$

$$\partial \text{SSE}/\partial \hat{b} = -2 \sum_{t=1}^{n} (Y_t - \hat{a} - \hat{b}X_t) \cdot X_t = 0$$

Solving simultaneously for $\hat{b}$ and $\hat{a}$, we find:

$$\hat{b} = \frac{\text{Cov}(X_t, Y_t)}{S_X^2}, \quad \hat{a} = \bar{Y} - \hat{b}\bar{X}$$

where $\bar{Y}$ and $\bar{X}$ are the sample means of Y and X and S_X^2 is the sample variance of X.

Graphically, in simple regression analysis, a line is fitted through a scatter plot of data points, representing the ordered pairs of the observations on the independent and dependent variables,

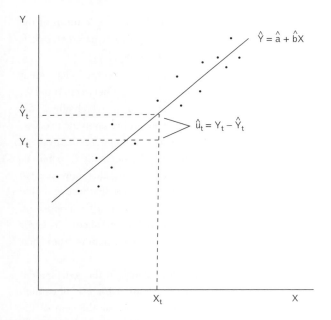

Figure 8.3 *Scatter diagram for simple regression model*

The scatter diagram is a plot of the ordered pairs of observations of the dependent variable, Y, and independent variable, X. The line of best fit is given by: $\hat{Y} = \hat{a} + \hat{b}X$. The residual for any observation t, (t = 1 ... n), $\hat{u}_t$, is the difference between the observed value of the dependent variable, Y_t, and the predicted value, $\hat{Y}_t = \hat{a} + \hat{b}X$, obtained from the line of best fit. That is: $\hat{u}_t = Y_t - \hat{Y}_t$.

(X_t, Y_t). This **line of best fit** minimizes the sum of the distances of these points to the line. See Figure 8.3 for an example of a **scatter diagram**. The observed values of X_t and Y_t are plotted $(t = 1, \ldots, n)$. For any X_t, the predicted value of Y_t, $\hat{Y}_t$, is found on the sample regression line, $\hat{Y}_t = \hat{a} + \hat{b}X_t$, or the line of best fit, where $\hat{a}$ is the vertical intercept and $\hat{b}$ is the slope. For any observation $t = 1, \ldots, n$, the predicted value for Y (i.e., $\hat{Y}_t$, derived from the sample regression line) may differ from the actual observed value of Y (i.e., Y_t). This difference is the prediction error or **residual**, u_t (i.e., $\hat{u}_t = Y_t - \hat{Y}_t$), which may be positive or negative. (In Figure 8.3, for observation t, $\hat{u}_t < 0$.)

There are sampling distributions associated with both $\hat{a}$ and $\hat{b}$, the OLS estimators of the population parameters. Focusing on $\hat{b}$, which reflects the hypothesized influence of the explanatory variable X on the dependent variable Y:

$$\hat{b} \sim N(b, \hat{s}_{\hat{b}}^2), \quad \text{where } \hat{s}_{\hat{b}}^2 = \frac{\hat{\sigma}_u^2}{\sum_{t=1}^{n} (X_t - \bar{X})^2}$$

Here, $\hat{s}_{\hat{b}}^2$ is the sample standard error of the estimate for b, and $\hat{\sigma}_u^2$ is the sample variance of the error term:[6]

$$\hat{\sigma}_u^2 = \frac{1}{n-2} \sum_{t=1}^{n} (\hat{u}_t - 0)^2 = \frac{1}{n-2} \sum_{t=1}^{n} (\hat{u}_t)^2 = \frac{1}{n-2} \sum_{t=1}^{n} (Y_t - \hat{Y}_t)^2$$

---

[6] We divide by $n - 2$ because two degrees of freedom are lost in calculating the estimates of a and b.

Recall that the mean of the error term is assumed to be zero. So, too, the sample mean of the prediction errors is equal to zero. In sum, $\hat{b}$, the estimate for the population parameter b, is normally distributed with a mean of b (the true value), and a constant variance, $\hat{s}^2_{\hat{b}}$.

Intuitively, $\hat{b}$ has a sampling distribution. For a given a set of observations on the independent variable, X, the value for b depends not only on the deterministic relationship between Y and X, but also on the outcomes or unobserved values of the random error term, u, which affects the observed values of the dependent variable, Y. Theoretically, if we repeated the sampling process, then for the same set of X_t values, we could observe, except by coincidence, a new set of Y_t values, due to the random nature of the error term, u_t, which is assumed to be normally distributed. Thus, the estimated values for a and b could be different in each sample. In practice, however, we only have one history, so only one set of observations is used. But we realize that history could have been different and, given the underlying theoretical model hypothesized in the population regression line, $Y_t = a + bX_t$, that the Y values are influenced by random disturbances, the error terms. Consequently the calculated values of $\hat{a}$ and $\hat{b}$ are just one possible outcome from their sampling distributions.

Focusing on the estimated value for b, the marginal impact of a change in the independent variable on the dependent variable, $b = dY/dX$, the sampling distribution for $\hat{b}$ is illustrated in Figure 8.4. As noted, the area under the normal curve is equal to one, or the sum of the probabilities of the values of the variable b occurring. Within one standard deviation, $\hat{s}_{\hat{b}}$, on either side of the mean, here b, roughly 68 percent of the area under the normal curve is found. Within two standard deviations of the mean, 95 percent of the area under the normal curve is found.

Hypothesis testing

In the model, the independent variable X is hypothesized to be a determinant or explanatory influence on Y, the dependent variable. Therefore, we expect the coefficient b, which captures this influence, to be statistically significant. We set up the **null hypothesis**, H_0, which states that X is not an influence on Y, that is, that the true value of the parameter b is zero.[7] The **alternative hypothesis**, H_a, implies that X is a significant influence on Y, that is, that the true value of b is not zero. Thus

$$H_0 : b = 0$$

$$H_a : b \neq 0$$

Clearly we would like to be able to reject the null hypothesis, otherwise we would not have selected X as an explanatory influence on Y. The test statistic is $t = (\hat{b} - b)/\hat{s}_{\hat{b}}$ and is called the **t-ratio**, which follows a t-distribution, with $n - 2$ degrees of freedom. The t-distribution is similar to a normal distribution for "large" samples, usually meaning samples of size 30 or more. Under the null hypothesis, $b = 0$, the test statistic in the **t-test** reduces to $t = \hat{b}/\hat{s}_{\hat{b}} \sim t_{n-2}$; that is, the t-ratio is the estimated coefficient, b, divided by the standard deviation of its sampling distribution, known as the **standard error**. There are t-tables in statistics texts that provide the values of the t-ratio for which the null hypothesis can be rejected at standard levels of significance.

---

[7] Here we are using a **two–tail test** of significance for an estimated parameter. A **one–tail test** would be a null hypothesis of H_0: $b \leq 0$ (or $b \geq 0$), with the alternative hypothesis of H_a: $b > 0$ (or $b < 0$). If there is a strong presumption that the influence of X on Y is positive (or negative), then a one-tail test might be appropriate. Some researchers prefer the more conservative two-tail test illustrated in this chapter.

The calculated t-ratio and its level of statistical significance, along with the estimate $\hat{b}$, will also be presented as part of the output from any statistical software program for regression analysis. For example, in simple regression analysis with a sample size of 30, the probability of finding a $\hat{b}$ that lies at least two standard deviations away from the mean of 0, that is, consistent with the null hypothesis $b = 0$, is approximately 5 percent. In other words, if the absolute value of the calculated t-ratio is 2 or greater, the probability that the null hypothesis is true is only 5 percent.

There are two types of errors in hypothesis testing. The **Type I error** is rejecting a true null hypothesis. The probability of this error is indicated by the selected level of significance. The standard levels of statistical significance are 10, 5, and 1 percent. If the calculated t ratio for the estimated parameter, b, is so large that the chances of finding a t-ratio this large and having the null hypothesis be true is less than 10, 5, or 1 percent respectively, then we say that the value of b is respectively "marginally significantly," "significantly," or "very significantly" different from zero. The exact values for the critical t-ratios depend on the sample size, as well as the selected level of significance. For example, in a sample size of 30 with a simple regression model, the critical values of the t-ratio for the null hypothesis, H_0: $b = 0$, are 1.70, 2.05, and 2.75 for the significance levels of 10 percent, 5 percent, and 1 percent, respectively.

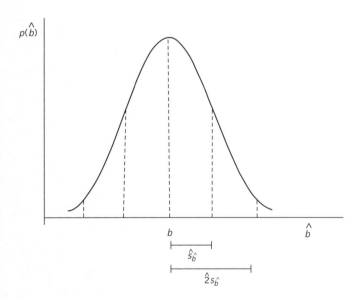

Figure 8.4 *Sampling distribution for estimate of b*

The estimate, $\hat{b}$, for the population parameter, b, has a sampling distribution.

$$\hat{b} \sim N\left(b, \hat{\sigma}_u^2 / \left[\sum_{t=1}^{n}(X_t - \bar{X})^2\right]\right) \quad \text{or} \quad \hat{b} \sim N(b, \hat{s}_{\hat{b}}^2)$$

where $\hat{s}_{\hat{b}}$ is the sample standard error of the estimate for $\hat{b}$, and $\hat{\sigma}_u^2$ is the sample estimate for the b variance of the error term.

$$\hat{\sigma}_u^2 = [1/(n-2)]\sum_{t=1}^{n}(\hat{u}_t - 0)^2 = [1/(n-2)]\sum_{t=1}^{n}(\hat{u}_t)^2 = [1/(n-2)]\sum_{t=1}^{n}(Y_t - \hat{Y}_t)^2$$

A **Type II error** is failing to reject a false null hypothesis. It is important to remember that we can never empirically prove (or disprove) a theory in the social sciences. We can confirm theories that are supported by the evidence; for example, in simple regression analysis, rejecting a null hypothesis at the 5 percent level of significance.

Goodness of fit

A statistic that indicates the explanatory power of a regression model is the coefficient of determination, R^2. To derive this statistic, we note that for any observation t in the sample ($t = 1, \ldots, n$), we can write:

$$(Y_t - \bar{Y}) = (\hat{Y}_t - \bar{Y}) + (Y_t - \hat{Y})$$

total	=	explained	+	unexplained
deviation		deviation		deviation
from mean		from mean		from mean

The unexplained deviation is the residual or prediction error. We can show, consistent with the OLS criterion of minimizing the sum of the squared prediction errors, that squaring both sides and summing over all observations yields

$$\sum_{t=1}^{n}(Y_t - \bar{Y})^2 = \sum_{t=1}^{n}(\hat{Y}_t - \bar{Y})^2 + \sum_{t=1}^{n}(Y_t - \hat{Y})^2$$

total sum	=	regression sum	+	error sum
of squares		of squares		of squares
(SST)		(SSR)		(SSE)

That is, $\text{SST} = \text{SSR} + \text{SSE}$. Dividing through by SST gives

$$1 = \frac{\text{SSR}}{\text{SST}} + \frac{\text{SSE}}{\text{SST}}$$

Rearranging to solve for R^2, we have

$$R^2 = \frac{\text{SSR}}{\text{SST}} = 1 - \frac{\text{SSE}}{\text{SST}}, \quad 0 \leq R^2 \leq 1$$

R^2, the **coefficient of determination**, is the ratio of the explained variation (SSR) to the total variation (SST) of the dependent variable, Y. The explained variation, in turn, is the variation in Y accounted for by the regression equation. In a simple regression (with only one explanatory variable), the coefficient of determination is equal to the simple correlation coefficient squared: $R^2 = r_{X,Y}^2$.

Before turning to multiple regression analysis, where we allow for more than one explanatory variable, an example of simple regression will be given.

Illustration of simple regression

In Chapter 6 we developed a simple macroeconomic model of aggregate demand and aggregate supply to explain the determination of real national output and the aggregate price level. In particular, the theoretical model provided insight into short-run fluctuations in real national income.

In Chapter 7 the basic neoclassical growth model was extended to include technological progress, natural resources, and qualitative changes in these primary factors of production. Here we gained insight into longer-run trends in economic growth. The theoretical models provide the foundation for empirical analysis, where we confront the hypothesized relationships with evidence, that is, we test the theory.

To illustrate simple regression analysis with an example, return to the growth model of the previous chapter, where a reduced-form general equation for the economic growth rate was derived. In particular, we showed the growth rate in per capita income is directly related to the net saving rate in the economy. There were other important determinants, but in simple regression analysis there is only one explanatory variable.

The simple regression model is then: $GYP_t = b_0 + b_1 SY_t + u_t$, where GYP_t is the average annual growth rate in real gross domestic product per capita in country t, SY_t the average annual net national saving rate in country t, and u_t the error term. We make the usual assumptions about the error term, that u_t is normally distributed around a mean of zero with a constant variance. And the error terms are assumed to be independent of each other and independent of the explanatory variable, here the net national saving rate.

To test this hypothesis derived from the theoretical growth model, we collect data on developing economies. Using the 10-year period from 2000 through 2009, we collect data for low- and middle-income economies from the World Bank's *World Development Indicators*. We have 64 developing economies in the final sample. The countries included and the variables used with data sources are listed in the data appendix at the end of the chapter.

Formally, the dependent variable, GYP, is derived as the difference between the average annual growth rates in real gross domestic product (GY) and population (GP) for the period 2000–09. The explanatory variable, SY, is represented by the average annual net national saving rate for 2000, 2003, and 2006. Net national saving is equal to gross national saving less the consumption of fixed capital. The share of net national saving in gross national income is the net saving rate.

Using OLS the estimated simple regression equation is:

$$\hat{GYP} = 3.54 + 0.056\,SY, \quad R^2 = 0.045$$
$$\phantom{\hat{GYP} = }{\scriptstyle(0.45)} {\scriptstyle(0.033)}$$

The estimated standard errors of the coefficients are provided in parentheses below the estimated coefficients. The null hypothesis is that the net saving rate is not a statistically important determinant of economic growth, that is, the true value of the coefficient representing this influence is zero ($H_0: b_1 = 0$).[8] We would like to be able to reject this null hypothesis with a high degree of confidence. The alternative hypothesis is: $H_a: b_1 \neq 0$. The calculated t-ratio for the explanatory variable, however, is only 1.70 (i.e., $t_{SY} = 0.056/0.033 = 1.70$), which is only marginally significant, that is, at the 10 percent level of significance. Here, the estimated value of b_1 lies only 1.70 standard deviations away from a value of 0, the true value under the null hypothesis. The chances of obtaining an estimate for b_1 this far from zero and having the null hypothesis be true is a little under 10 percent, which is considered only marginally significant. In fact, with an R^2 of 0.045, indicating that only 4.5 percent of the variation in the economic growth rate for this sample of 64 less developed countries for 2000–09 is accounted for by variation in the net saving rate, the model does not have much explanatory power. Nevertheless, the interpretation of this

---

[8] Since we hypothesize that the economic growth rate is positively related to the net saving rate, we could have used a one-tail test with $H_0: b_1 \leq 0$ and the alternative hypothesis, $H_a: b_1 > 0$. The more conservative approach, and the one we will adopt, is a two-tail test, where $H_a: b_1 \neq 0$.

estimation would be that a one percentage point increase in the average net national saving rate, *ceteris paribus*, is associated with an increase of 0.056 percentage points in the average economic growth rate for 2000–09 in this sample of 64 less developed economies. Clearly the model is underspecified and there are other important determinants of economic growth that need to be included in the regression. To do so, we turn to multiple regression analysis.

MULTIPLE REGRESSION ANALYSIS

Multiple regression analysis allows for the influence of multiple determinants of the dependent variable. That is, there is more than one explanatory variable included in the multiple regression. While we can no longer graphically represent the regression model with a simple scatter diagram for observations on the dependent and independent variables and an estimated line of best fit, extending the analysis to multiple dimensions with an estimated multivariable equation is mathematically straightforward.

The basic model

In general, we begin with a hypothesized behavioral relationship between a dependent variable, Y, and K independent variables, $X_1, X_2, \ldots, X_K$:

$$Y_t = b_0 + b_1 X_{1t} + b_2 X_{2t} + \cdots + b_K X_{Kt} + u_t, \quad t = 1, \ldots, n$$

where Y_t is the tth observation on the dependent variable, X_{kt} the tth observation on the kth explanatory variable ($k = 1, \ldots, K$), u_t the tth value of the error term (unobserved), b_k the coefficient of the kth explanatory variable, and b_0 a constant term. Note that the first of the two subscripts on the independent variables, X_{kt}, corresponds to the number of the independent variable ($k = 1, \ldots, K$) and the second subscript corresponds to the observation number ($t = 1, \ldots, n$, where n is the sample size). The coefficients of the independent variables, b_k, are the unknown regression parameters that represent the marginal influences on the dependent variable, Y. That is, $b_k = \partial \mathrm{E}(Y_t)/\partial X_{kt}$, where the expected value of the dependent variable, $\mathrm{E}(Y_t)$, for any observation reflects the hypothesized relationship determined by the independent variables, X_{kt}, outside of any random influences from the error term, u_t. The constant term, b_0, indicates the expected value of the dependent variable if all the explanatory variables were set equal to zero.

As with simple regression analysis, in addition to the hypothesized behavioral relationships captured by the equation above, the regression model includes assumptions about the unobserved error terms, u_t. Recall that the error terms pick up errors in measurement of the dependent variable, specification errors in the hypothesized relationship with the independent variables, omitted influences on the dependent variable, and random disturbances, including the variation in human behavior. In addition, there are assumptions about the explanatory variables, which are still assumed to be measured without error.

Underlying assumptions

The first set of assumptions about the error terms is familiar from the simple regression model and can be written concisely as:

$$u_t \sim N(0, \sigma_u^2), \quad t = 1, \ldots, n$$

That is, the error terms are normally distributed with a mean of zero and constant variance.

Secondly, the error terms are independent:

$$\text{Cov}(u_t, u_s) = 0, \quad t = 1, \ldots, n; s = 1, \ldots, n; t \neq s$$

Thirdly, the explanatory variables are nonstochastic and independent of the error term:

$$\text{Cov}(X_{kt}, u_t) = 0, \quad t = 1, \ldots, n; k = 1, \ldots, K$$

This means that the deterministic influences on the dependent variable (due to the X_k variables) can be separated from the random or stochastic influences (from the error terms, u).

Fourthly, there is no exact linear relationship between any of the explanatory variables:

$$X_j \neq \sum_{k=1}^{K-1} \beta_k X_k$$

where X_j is not one of the other $K-1$ explanatory variables. That is, **perfect multicollinearity** is ruled out. We cannot write any one of the K independent variables, say X_j, as a linear combination of the other $K-1$ independent variables. If we could, we would have perfect multicollinearity and the model could not be estimated. Intuitively, if one of the independent variables were equal to a linear combination of one, two, or more of the other independent variables, that independent variable would not add any explanatory power to the model, since its influence on the dependent variable would be exactly captured by the other related independent variables. A very simple example would be not including as explanatory variables in a regression both an interest rate measured in percentage points, say X_1, and the same interest rate measured in decimals, say X_2, since $X_1 = 100X_2$.

Perfect multicollinearity would be a fatal specification error in a multiple regression model. Often, however, a high degree of multicollinearity exists when there are multiple independent variables, which can make it difficult to discern the separate influences of the independent variables on the dependent variable. Formally, multicollinearity increases the standard errors of the estimated regression coefficients, thereby deflating the estimated t-ratios and increasing the probability of failing to reject the null hypothesis of no statistically significant influence on the dependent variable.

The final assumption is necessary to ensure there are sufficient degrees of freedom to estimate the model:

$$n > K + 1$$

The number of observations (n) must exceed the number of coefficients to be estimated ($K + 1$). The coefficients to be estimated are the b_k and the constant term, b_0. In general, the larger the sample is the better. There may be tradeoffs, however, between the sample size and the accuracy or comparability of the observations. For example, in time series analysis, say for the growth rate in real national output per capita for a nation, the period for accurate or reliable macroeconomic data might be limited, extending back only so many years in time. In the US, comprehensive national income data only began to be collected and published after the 1920s. So, too, for a cross-section of developing economies, some nations may not have reliable macroeconomic data for the period of interest, whether due to lack of funds for data collection or crises in the nations, with civil war or political turmoil.

Ordinary least squares estimation

Given the above specification, the dependent variable, Y, is normally distributed around its expected value with a constant variance:

$$Y_t \sim N(b_0 + b_1 X_{1t} + b_2 X_{2t} + \cdots + b_K X_{Kt}, \sigma_u^2), \quad t = 1, \ldots, n$$

The distribution of Y_t is centered on the expected value of Y_t, $E(Y_t)$, which is given by the deterministic part of the model, $b_0 + b_1 X_{1t} + b_2 X_{2t} + \cdots + b_K X_{Kt}$. The variance of the distribution is given by the constant variance of the error terms, σ_u^2, which captures the stochastic or random influences on the dependent variable.

The OLS technique for estimating the unknown population parameters, b_k ($k = 1, \ldots, K$) and the constant term, b_0, is an extension of the simple regression model. For any observation $t = 1, \ldots, n$, the actual value of Y_t can be decomposed into the fitted or estimated value, $\hat{Y}_t$, and the residual, $\hat{u}_t$. Recall that $\hat{u}_t = Y_t - \hat{Y}_t$ is the prediction error, which is the estimate of the unobserved error term, where

$$\hat{Y}_t = \hat{b}_0 + \hat{b}_1 X_{1t} + \hat{b}_2 X_{2t} + \cdots + \hat{b}_K X_{Kt}$$

The OLS criterion is to find the values of $\hat{b}_0, \hat{b}_1, \ldots, \hat{b}_K$ that minimize the sum of the squared prediction errors (SSE):

$$\text{minimize SSE} = \text{minimize} \sum_{t=1}^{n} (Y_t - \hat{Y}_t)^2 = \text{minimize} \sum_{t=1}^{n} \hat{u}_t^2$$

For this optimization, we set forth the first-order conditions:

$$\partial \text{SSE}/\partial b_0 = -2 \sum_{t=1}^{n} (Y_t - \hat{b}_0 - \hat{b}_1 X_{1t} - \cdots - \hat{b}_K X_{Kt}) = 0$$

$$\partial \text{SSE}/\partial b_1 = -2 \sum_{t=1}^{n} (Y_t - \hat{b}_0 - \hat{b}_1 X_{1t} - \cdots - \hat{b}_K X_{Kt}) \cdot X_{1t} = 0$$

$$\vdots$$

$$\partial \text{SSE}/\partial b_K = -2 \sum_{t=1}^{n} (Y_t - \hat{b}_0 - \hat{b}_1 X_{1t} - \cdots - \hat{b}_K X_{Kt}) \cdot X_{Kt} = 0$$

Solving these $K + 1$ equations simultaneously yields the OLS estimates $\hat{b}_0, \hat{b}_1, \ldots, \hat{b}_K$. Each of the estimates $\hat{b}_k$ is normally distributed around the unknown true value, b_k, with a constant variance, given by $s_{\hat{b}_k}^2$.

This is similar to the distribution of the estimated coefficient for the single explanatory variable in a simple regression, except that the calculation of the estimates is more complex, involving observations on not only this explanatory variable and the dependent variable, Y, but also on all the other $K - 1$ explanatory variables in the regression model. While the math is more difficult (the estimates can be obtained from a computer software program such as SAS), hypothesis testing is straightforward.

Hypothesis tests

As before, we can test for the statistical significance of the explanatory variables. Each of the estimated coefficients, $\hat{b}_k$ ($k = 1, \ldots, K$), has a sampling distribution. For each of the K explanatory variables, as well as the constant term, we set up the null hypothesis H_0: $b_k = 0$, which implies $\partial E(Y_t)/\partial X_{kt} = 0$, that is, the kth explanatory variable does not have a statistically significant influence on the dependent variable. The alternative hypothesis is H_a: $b_k \neq 0$. The test statistic is again the t-ratio

$$\frac{\hat{b}_k}{\hat{s}_{b_k}} \sim t_{n-K-1}$$

which is distributed with $n - K - 1$ degrees of freedom. Generally for 30 or more degrees of freedom, the t statistic is normally distributed.

Recall the coefficient of determination, R^2, measures the percentage of the variation in the dependent variable over the sample of observations accounted for, or explained, by the explanatory variable. In multiple regression, with more than one explanatory variable, a standardized measure of the goodness of fit is the **adjusted coefficient of determination**, or the **adjusted R-squared**, written as $\bar{R}^2$ and calculated as $\bar{R}^2 = R^2 - [K/(n - K - 1)] \cdot [1 - R^2]$.

The adjusted R^2 is used to control for the number of explanatory variables that are included in the regression equation. Adding explanatory variables can only increase the percentage of the variation in the dependent variable accounted for in the model. Thus, to better compare explanatory power or goodness of fit, across models with different numbers of observations and explanatory variables, the adjusted R^2 is the proper statistic. While the adjusted R^2 cannot exceed 1, it could actually be negative; and it is always less than the R^2. Adding an irrelevant explanatory variable to the regression would significantly reduce the adjusted R^2.

To test for the goodness of fit for the entire model, we use the **F-test**. Here the null hypothesis is H_0: $b_1 = b_2 = \cdots = b_K = 0$. If true, then none of the coefficients are statistically different from zero. The model would have no significant explanatory power and the behavior of the dependent variable, Y, would be random. The alternative hypothesis for the F-test is H_a: at least one of the $b_k \neq 0$, $k = 1, \ldots, K$.

Dummy variables

Some influences on a dependent variable may be hard to quantify—for example, institutional factors, political coups, and geography. Some explanatory variables may be attributes, conditions, or states. For instance, in explaining wage rates in a given occupation, gender and race should be controlled for and represented in the model. In a time series model explaining the Dow Jones Industrial Average, whether it was a presidential election year or not might be influential.

A **dummy variable** is a variable that takes on the value of 1 or 0, depending on whether or not a designated condition or attribute characterizes that observation in the sample. Unlike an explanatory variable that can be measured continuously, such as income, a dummy variable is like a light switch—either on or off. For example, in a cross-section of countries a nation is either in sub-Saharan Africa, in which case the dummy variable, say DA, would be set equal to 1 for that observation; if not, then DA $= 0$. Dummy variables can be used to shift the intercept or constant term in a regression equation and to alter the partial regression coefficients, that is, the estimated influences of the explanatory variables on the dependent variable.[9]

Consider the simple regression model $Y_t = b_0 + b_1 X_t + u_t$, where $t = 1, \ldots, n$.

---

[9]Levine and Renelt (1992: 949) discount the use of continent or regional dummy variables in cross-country regressions as "suggesting the importance of omitted variables."

If we want to distinguish among the observations as having a certain characteristic, attribute, or condition, we could use a dummy variable, D_t, where $D_t = 1$ if observation t possesses the attribute or condition, and $D_t = 0$ if observation t does not possess the attribute or condition. Adding the dummy variable, D_t, to the regression means $Y_t = b_0 + b_1 X_t + b_2 D_t + u_t$ when observation t has that attribute ($D_t = 1$). The regression equation becomes $Y_t = (b_0 + b_2) + b_1 X_t + u_t$. If observation t does not have that attribute ($D_t = 0$), the regression equation is simply $Y_t = b_0 + b_1 X_t + u_t$. In effect, the constant term may be different depending on whether the observation is characterized by the condition represented by the dummy variable.

Figure 8.5 illustrates the population regression lines $E(Y_t) = (b_0 + b_2) + b_1 X_t$ (where $D_t = 1$) and $E(Y_t) = b_0 + b_1 X_t$ (where $D_t = 0$), and we assume $b_2 > 0$. The population regression lines will be estimated by the line of best fit, $\hat{Y}_t = \hat{b}_0 + \hat{b}_1 X_t + \hat{b}_2 D_t$. Like any regression coefficient, the coefficient of the dummy variable, here $\hat{b}_2$, can be tested for statistical significance, with the null hypothesis H_0: $b_2 = 0$.

Dummy variables can also be used to alter the slope coefficients, or the estimated influence of an explanatory variable on the dependent variable. Consider the model $Y_t = b_0 + b_1 X_t + b_2 D_t + b_3 Z_t + u_t$ ($t = 1, \ldots, n$), where $Z_t = D_t X_t$ and $D_t = 1$ ($D_t = 0$) if observation t has (does not have) that attribute. Consequently, the population regression lines are $E(Y_t) = (b_0 + b_2) + (b_1 + b_3) X_t$ (when $D_t = 1$) and $E(Y_t) = b_0 + b_1 X_t$ (when $D_t = 0$). In the illustration in Figure 8.6, b_2 and b_3 are assumed to be positive. The population regression lines are estimated by the sample regression line $\hat{Y}_t = \hat{b}_0 + \hat{b}_1 X_t + \hat{b}_2 D_t + \hat{b}_3 Z_t$. As before, the normal tests of hypotheses can be used.

Note that, whenever a slope dummy is used, an intercept dummy should also be included. Otherwise, the two population regression equations are constrained to having the same intercept, albeit different slopes.

To illustrate the use of a dummy variable, we can return to the simple regression for the growth rate of real GDP per capita, GYP, against the net national saving rate, SY, which was estimated for a cross-section of 64 low- and middle-income countries for the period 2000–09.

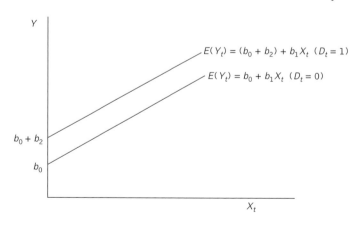

Figure 8.5 *Illustration of intercept dummy variable*

The population regression lines, E(Y_t), are estimated by the sample regression:

$$\hat{Y}_t = \hat{b}_0 + \hat{b}_1 X_t + \hat{b}_2 D_t$$

where $D_t = 1$ if the condition is present for that observation (0 otherwise). Here for illustration, we hypothesize $b_2 > 0$.

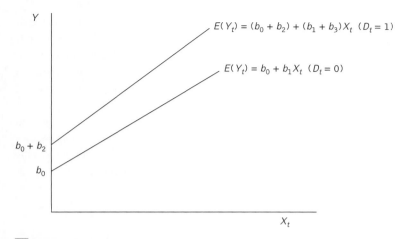

Figure 8.6 *Illustration of intercept and slope dummy variables*

The population regression lines, $E(Y_t)$, are estimated by the sample regression:

$$\hat{Y}_t = \hat{b}_0 + \hat{b}_1 X_t + \hat{b}_2 D_t + \hat{b}_3 Z_t$$

where $Z_t = D_t \cdot X_t$ and $D_t = 1$ if the condition is present for that observation (0 otherwise). Here for illustration we hypothesize $b_2 > 0$ and $b_3 > 0$.

Landlocked countries, that is, nations without any coast, may be hampered in generating economic growth. This geographical disadvantage of no seaports may well increase the transportation cost of engaging in international trade. Moreover, nations without direct access to the ocean are not able to reap the natural resources in the ocean, such as fish, fossil fuels, and minerals. Collier (2007: 57) identifies being "landlocked with bad neighbors" as one of the poverty traps facing the least developed nations: "Being both resource-scarce and landlocked, along with having neighbors who either do not have opportunities or do not take them, pretty well condemns a country to the slow lane." Landlocked nations are more dependent on the infrastructure, especially transportation networks, of neighboring nations. If these adjoining countries are also poor, with little in the way of economic growth, then the opportunities for trade and development in the landlocked nation are reduced.

To test for the hypothesized disadvantage of landlocked countries, we add a dummy variable, DL, to the regression model, where DL = 1 (0 otherwise) if the nation is landlocked. There are 13 nations in the sample of 64 that are landlocked. Here we are using an intercept dummy. The estimated regression model is:

$$\hat{\text{GYP}} = 3.17 + 0.067\,\text{SY} + 1.27\,\text{DL}, \quad R^2 = 0.096, \bar{R}^2 = 0.067$$
$$\underset{***}{(0.48)} \quad \underset{**}{(0.033)} \quad \underset{*}{(0.68)}$$

Here the explanatory power of the model has increased, but only 7 percent of the variation in the average growth rate of real GDP per capita is explained by variation in the average net national saving rate. The asterisks under the estimated standard errors in the parentheses indicate the threshold levels of statistical significance: $*$, $**$, and $***$ indicate statistical significance at the 10, 5, and 1 percent levels, respectively. The saving rate is significant at the 5 percent level, with a calculated t-ratio of 2.0, and we can reject the null hypothesis of no influence with a fairly high degree of confidence. The intercept dummy is only marginally significant, with an estimated coefficient of 1.27 and t-ratio equal to 1.9.

Contrary to theory, however, being a landlocked country, *ceteris paribus*, increases the economic growth rate, here by approximately 1.27 percentage points annually on average. Moreover, including this intercept dummy increases the estimated coefficient (from the earlier simple regression estimate of 0.056) and the statistical significance of the net saving rate. Now an increase of one percentage point in the average annual net national saving rate would increase the predicted average annual growth rate in real gross domestic product per capita by 0.07 percentage points.[10]

Clearly the model is underspecified. There are important determinants of economic growth that have been omitted from the analysis. Indeed, simple regressions, limited to one explanatory variable, are unlikely ever to explain sufficiently the behavior of a dependent variable, especially one as complex as economic growth. Thus, we turn to a multiple regression model.

EMPIRICAL DETERMINANTS OF ECONOMIC GROWTH

Recall the first stage in testing economic theory, the specification of a model to explain the behavior of a variable of interest. To explain fluctuations in real national output, we draw on the aggregate demand–aggregate supply model in Chapter 6, which explicitly incorporates demand-side influences on output growth, such as domestic investment spending and exports. To account for longer-run trends in economic growth, the extended Solow growth model in Chapter 7 is important for deriving the supply-side influences on economic growth, that is, the longer-run determinants such as technological progress and changes in the effective factors of production.

With respect to the supply-side factors, we began in the extended Solow model with an aggregate production function, $Y = A(t) \cdot [\underline{K}(t)]^{\alpha}[\underline{L}(t)]^{\beta}[\underline{R}(t)]^{\gamma} = A(0)e^{gt}[e^{jt}K]^{\alpha}[e^{mt}L]^{\beta}[e^{ht}R]^{\gamma} = A(0)e^{\theta t}K^{\alpha}L^{\beta}R^{\gamma}$, where $\theta = g + \alpha j + \beta m + \gamma h$ denotes the comprehensive growth rate of total factor productivity. Then differentiating, incorporating the condition for macroeconomic equilibrium (net savings equals net investment) and the assumptions about the growth rates in the effective factors of production, we derived an equation for the growth rate in labor productivity.

Economic growth, however, is equal to the sum of the growth rate in labor productivity and the growth rate in the aggregate labor force participation rate, $n - p$, where the growth rate in the population (dP/P) is given by p. The economic growth rate, or the growth rate in output per capita, is then equal to $\theta + \alpha \cdot (sy/k) + \beta n - \gamma u - p$. In general, we can state that, *ceteris paribus*, the rate of economic growth is directly related to the net saving rate (s), the rate of neutral technical change (g), the rates of growth in the quality of the primary factors of capital, labor, and natural resources $(j, m,$ and h, respectively) and the natural growth rate of the labor force (n). The rate of economic growth is inversely related to the rate of depletion of natural resources (u) and the rate of population growth (p).

In growth models a macroeconomic equilibrium is always assumed, that is, net national saving is matched by net domestic investment. This need not be the case in practice, however, as an excess of saving over investment could result in a fall in real national output. Conversely, an excess of desired investment over saving would tend to increase real national output. In short, we cannot assume that aggregate demand always equals aggregate supply at full employment. The importance of aggregate demand was illustrated in the aggregate demand–aggregate supply model of Chapter 6. Over any year, real national output is determined by both aggregate supply and

---

[10]When a slope dummy for a landlocked country was also included, the results were insignificant. The intercept dummy no longer was statistically significant, and the interaction term, the product of the dummy variable and the net national saving rate, was insignificant.

aggregate demand. We modeled aggregate demand simply as: $P^D = D_0(1 + d) - fY$, where P^d was the aggregate demand price, or the aggregate price level associated with a given quantity of real national output demanded (Y). The term D_0 captured the influence of desired real autonomous expenditures on real national output, assumed to grow at an annual rate d. Real autonomous expenditures, independent of the level of real income (Y), depend on real wealth, foreign demand for the nation's exports, business confidence in investment spending, and other exogenous factors. Demand shifts, reflected in changes in real autonomous expenditures, can have significant consequences for the growth of real national output, and should be included in a model of economic growth.

AN EMPIRICAL MODEL FOR THE DETERMINANTS OF ECONOMIC GROWTH

In testing economic theory, a major challenge is selecting appropriate measures of the theoretical influences (e.g., technology, the quality of the factors of production, and even the use of natural resources), and then finding comparable data for the variables included in the model. Often proxies or substitute measures have to be used for the theoretical influences, and the lack of data may result in the omission of important influences.

To illustrate, we return to the model for economic growth, which we estimated using OLS for a sample of 64 developing economies for the period 2000–09. We hypothesize that

$$\text{GYP} = f(\overset{+}{SY}, \overset{-}{NY}, \overset{?}{YPO}, \overset{+}{LFP}, \overset{+}{FYL}, \overset{+}{GI}, \overset{+}{GX}, \overset{-}{DL})$$

where GYP is the average annual growth rate in real GDP per capita for 2000–09; SY the average annual net national saving rate for 2000, 2003, and 2006; NY the average annual rate of depletion of natural resources for 2000, 2003, and 2006; YPO the real gross national income per capita in PPP dollars in 2000 (US $= 100$); LFP the ratio of the population aged 15–64 to the total population in 2000; FYL the female youth literacy rate for 2000; GI the average annual growth rate in gross domestic investment for 2000–09; GX the average annual growth rate in real exports of goods and services for 2000–09; and DL a dummy variable equal to 1 if the nation is landlocked (and 0 otherwise). The measurement of these variables and the data sources are given in the data appendix to this chapter.

Drawing on the underlying theoretical models, the economic growth rate is hypothesized to be directly related to: the net saving rate (SY), which indicates the potential rate of physical capital formation; the share of the population aged 15–64 (LFP), which reflects the age structure of the population and would capture the potential demographic dividend from lower fertility; and the female youth literacy rate (FYL), a proxy for human capital formation and the quality of the labor force.

The economic growth rate, however, is hypothesized to be inversely related to the natural resource depletion rate (NY). Recall from the enhanced growth model in Chapter 7, where depletion of natural resources, indicated by a negative growth rate in the natural resources available for production, would reduce the growth rate in real national output per laborer. To capture this influence in the empirical model, we use a measure of natural resource rents for minerals and energy (fossil fuels) as a share of national incomes. Strictly speaking, this is not the physical depletion rate, which depends on the estimated stocks of the nonrenewable resources ultimately available. This measure, however, does reflect the relative dependence of national output on nonrenewable natural resources. (In Chapter 12 we will discuss the so-called "natural resource curse," where nations richly endowed with minerals or fossil fuels may fail to develop sound institutions for governance and resource allocation and may be unusually plagued by corruption and conflict, all of which impairs economic growth and development. Moreover, such nations are also vulnerable to the Dutch disease, a distorted type of development defined by an overreliance on natural resource exports.)

To test for convergence theory, that is, that lower-income economies would tend to grow faster, we include the per capita income at the beginning of the period of analysis (YP0), expressed in PPP dollars, as a share of US per capita income. While the most basic growth model implies convergence in per capita incomes, more comprehensive models which allow for differential technological change and qualitative differences in the factors of production suggest that divergence in per capita incomes may be as likely, if not more likely. Thus, the hypothesized influence of the initial per capita income is *a priori* indeterminate.

The growth rate in gross domestic investment (GI), largely driven by business confidence, is a demand-side factor, here indicative of the growth in autonomous expenditures on real national output. As noted, in the growth models a macroeconomic equilibrium of net saving equal to net investment is assumed. In any given year, however, for an economy, desired saving need not match desired investment, so indicators of aggregate demand are important to include in an empirical model for economic growth. Another important component of aggregate demand is exports, so we include the average annual growth of exports of goods and services (GX). More open economies tend to be more successful in generating economic growth, in part because of the more efficient allocation of resources when production is driven by comparative advantages, but also with the dynamic efficiencies encouraged by international competition. Moreover, the increased capability to import, realized from greater export revenues, allows for greater access to foreign technologies embodied in the imported goods and services.[11]

As mentioned, technological change is difficult to quantify and data on the growth rate in technology are accordingly not available. Likewise, comparable data for qualitative change in physical capital, labor, and natural resources are hard to find. Here we use the female youth literacy rate (FYL) as a proxy for human capital and the quality of labor in the economy. Theoretically, the influences of technological progress and qualitative changes in the factors of production are included in the term for the growth rate in total factor productivity. In the empirical model, the growth rate in total factor productivity is captured by the growth in output not accounted for by growth in the physical factors of production. The error term in this equation for economic growth also picks up other influences, such as price expectations, government regulations, and the institutional environment, that are not explicitly included in the model, also due to difficulties in quantifying these factors and the attendant data constraints.[12]

The sample

Before discussing the results of this OLS regression for the average annual growth rate in real GDP per capita over 2000–09 for this sample of 64 low- and middle-income economies, we should comment on the characteristics of the nations included. As listed in the data appendix, the

---

[11] Levine and Renelt (1992: 957) dismiss the use of demand-side factors like export growth to explain economic growth rates, because of the GDP identity, $GDP \equiv C + I + G + X - M$. In a macroeconomic model of aggregate demand and aggregate supply, however, exports and investment are important demand-side determinants of output, ones that are largely driven by foreign incomes and domestic business confidence, respectively.

[12] For a good review of the literature on cross-country regressions for economic growth, see Temple (1999). For a good discussion of technological change, see Weil (2009).

numbers of nations in each of the major geographical regions of the developing world are: East Asia and the Pacific (8); Europe and Central Asia (14); Latin America and the Caribbean (18); Middle East and North Africa (7); South Asia (3); and sub-Saharan Africa (14). Refer to Table 8.1 and the descriptive statistics for the sample.

First we note the considerable diversity of experience, captured by the range between the maximum and minimum values for variables. As noted earlier, if the mean of a variable is less than the standard deviation, then the values for that variable are fairly dispersed. For example, the distributions of values for the share of the population aged 15–64 (LFP) and the female youth literacy rate (FYL) are relatively tight, in contrast to the widely dispersed average annual growth rates for natural resource depletion (NY). The range of initial per capita incomes in PPP dollars (as a percentage of US per capita GDP in 2000) goes from 1.52 for Tanzania (roughly \$520) to 35.3 for Argentina (roughly \$12,050). The average economic growth rate for this sample of 64 developing nations is 4.14 percent, with a range from −1.4 percent for Côte d'Ivoire to 10.5 percent for Armenia.

The regression results

The estimated multiple regression equation for the average economic growth rate for the 64 low- and middle-income economies for the 2000–09 period is as follows:

$$\hat{GYP} = -10.71 + \underset{(0.017)}{0.060}\, SY - \underset{(0.015)}{0.029}\, NY - \underset{(0.022)}{0.066}\, YP0 + \underset{(0.033)}{0.179}\, LFP + \underset{(0.010)}{0.019}\, FYL$$
$$\underset{(1.62)}{}\quad *** \qquad *** \qquad * \qquad ** \qquad ** \qquad *$$

$$+ \underset{(0.031)}{0.262}\, GI + \underset{(0.029)}{0.081}\, GX + \underset{(0.35)}{1.18}\, DL, \quad \bar{R}^2 = 0.807, F = 33.98$$
$$*** \qquad *** \qquad ***$$

Underneath the estimated coefficients are the estimated standard errors. Statistical significance for rejecting the null hypothesis that the coefficient for a given explanatory variable is actually zero, i.e., that there is no influence on the dependent variable, is indicated by the asterisks under the estimated standard errors, with meanings as given earlier in the chapter. Thus, with a degree of confidence

Table 8.1 *Sample statistics*

	Mean	Standard deviation	Minimum	Maximum
GYP	4.14	2.23	−1.4 (Côte d'Ivoire)	10.5 (Armenia)
SY	10.74	8.35	−15.2 (Lebanon)	37.6 (China)
NY	5.91	9.61	0 (15 nations)	42.2 (Iran)
YP0	13.65	8.23	1.52 (Tanzania)	35.3 (Argentina)
LFP	60.52	5.70	48.3 (Uganda)	69.6 (Russian Federation)
FYL	87.34	16.80	40 (Bangladesh)	100 (13 nations)
GI	7.73	4.60	−0.4 (Syria)	18.8 (Belarus)
GX	6.96	4.67	−7.6 (Lao PDR)	20.2 (China)

GYP = average annual growth rate in real gross domestic product per capita for 2000–09. SY = average annual net national saving rate for 2000, 2003, and 2006. NY = average annual rate of depletion of natural resources for 2000, 2003, and 2006. YP0 = real gross national income per capita in PPP-adjusted dollars in 2000 (US = 100). LFP = ratio of the population aged 15–64 to the total population in 2000. FYL = female youth literacy rate for 2000. GI = average annual growth rate in gross domestic investment for 2000–09. GX = average annual growth rate in real exports of goods and services for 2000–09.

of 90, 95, or 99 percent we can reject the null hypothesis in favor of the alternative hypothesis that this independent variable has a statistically significant influence on the dependent variable.

In this regression, all of the estimated coefficients are statistically significant, with signs in accordance with the underlying theory. Interpreting these coefficients and rounding to the nearest hundredth, we can state, *ceteris paribus*, that the effect on the predicted growth rate of real GDP per capita of:

- a one percentage point increase in the average net saving rate (SY) is an increase of 0.06 percentage points.
- a one percentage point increase ratio of natural resource rents in national income (NY, a measure of the nonrenewable natural resource depletion rate) is a decrease of 0.03 percentage points.
- a one percentage point increase in the ratio of the nation's initial gross national income per capita to the that of the US (YP0) is a decrease of 0.07 percentage points. (Note that this result supports the convergence theory of the basic Solow growth model, that is, that lower-income nations tend to grow faster, closing the gaps with higher-income economies.)
- a one percentage point increase in the ratio of the population aged 15–64 in the total population (LFP, a measure of the share of the economically active population) is an increase of 0.18 percentage points. (Note that this is consistent with the demographic dividend for economic growth that accompanies lower fertility rates.)
- a one percentage point in the female youth literacy rate (FYL) is an increase of 0.02 percentage points.
- a one percentage point increase in the average growth rate of gross domestic investment (GI) is an increase of 0.26 percentage points.
- a one percentage point increase in the average growth rate of exports of goods and services (GX) is an increase of 0.08 percentage points.

Finally, controlling for the above influences, a landlocked nation (DL = 1), would have a predicted average annual growth rate in real per capita GDP for 2000–09 that is 1.18 percentage points higher. Again, this finding is contrary to theory and warrants additional study.

A measure of the goodness of fit of the estimated regression equation is provided by the adjusted R^2 of 0.807, which indicates that nearly 81 percent of the variation in the average annual growth rate in real GDP per capita for 2000–09 in this sample of 64 low- and middle-income economies is explained or accounted for by the variation in these independent variables. Not surprisingly, the associated F-statistic is so strong that we can reject the null hypothesis that all the regression coefficients are equal to zero at the 1 percent level of significance.

Sensitivity tests

Levine and Renelt (1992) argue that cross-country regressions with the multitude of explanatory variables included in the different studies are suspect. That is, the reported results for the determinants of economic growth are fragile and sensitive to even slight alterations in the sets of included variables. In general, Ross and Levine find that only the share of investment in GDP is robust, or a consistently significant influence over different regressions.[13] Soludo and Kim (2003: 33, 46) concur, concluding:

> Our ideas about why nations prosper and others stagnate remain largely fickle and contentious.
>
> ... since income growth is a result of a complicated process of economic development, it is almost impossible to specify an explicit causal mechanism from determinants to growth. Furthermore, there is probably a feedback effect from growth to its determinants, and thus the direction of causality is not clear.

When doing empirical analysis it is essential to begin with a sound theoretical model. Here, the empirical model for the determinants of economic growth was derived from the extended Solow growth model in Chapter 7 and the aggregate demand–aggregate supply model in Chapter 6. The variables were clearly defined and the sample was limited to the low- and middle-income economies for which a complete data set could be assembled (described in the data appendix). Nevertheless, when doing cross-country regressions, it is good practice to do sensitivity analysis to verify the robustness of the estimations. In particular, it is important to check for influential observations—countries whose inclusion in the sample significantly alters one or more estimated coefficients. In some cases, one or a few countries may significantly bias estimated coefficients, resulting in possibly misleading interpretations.

The initial sample for this regression analysis actually included 67 low- and middle-income economies. From the first regression run, Chad was identified as an influential observation, one whose inclusion in the sample significantly inflated the estimated coefficients for GX, in particular, but also for NY. Then in the reduced sample of 66 nations, first Mauritania and then Madagascar, like Chad, sub-Saharan African economies, were identified as influential observations. Including Mauritania in the sample significantly deflated the estimated coefficient for GI, while also inflating that for GX. Including Madagascar in the sample would significantly deflate the estimated impact of GI, but inflate those for LFP and the dummy DL. For the final sample of 64 nations, there were no influential observations remaining, so the multiple regression results reported above are deemed to be robust.

This is not to say that these estimations are free from all concerns. These results are conditional upon the accuracy of the assumptions underlying the OLS method of estimation. There well may be better—albeit more complicated—methods of estimation; for example, simultaneous systems that incorporate the likely endogeneity of some of the assumed independent explanatory variables, such as the net saving rate and the growth rate in gross domestic investment. Moreover, finding statistically significant results does not prove anything. As noted at the outset, in the social sciences, dealing with human behavior and free will, we cannot prove theories. We can only test hypotheses and confirm or refute the underlying theories. Multiple tests are needed, with different samples, and perhaps different specifications of the economic model, before any theory would be generally accepted.

Nevertheless, these regression results for this cross-section of countries can be considered strong (with an adjusted R^2 of nearly 81 percent), and, with the exception of the landlocked dummy, consistent with theory (with all the included determinants statistically significant,

---

[13] Levine and Renelt (1992) in their regression samples include developed (high-income) economies with less developed (low- and middle-income) economies, which is a questionable practice given the significantly different production functions (i.e., more advanced technologies) and institutional conditions in the former.

although the female youth literary rate and the natural resource depletion rate variables are only marginally so). Still, there are omitted variables or important factors that are not included in the regression model. We have already noted the omission of direct measures for technological progress and qualitative changes in physical capital and natural resources, and the imperfect proxies for human capital formation (the female youth literacy rate) and natural resource depletion rate (the estimated share of mineral and fossil fuel energy rents in national income).[14] Data limitations and the difficulty in quantifying these influences explain their omission. Economists are always seeking better measures and more accurate data for economic phenomena, such as technological progress and the institutional environment.

Cross-country regressions are useful for identifying trends or common determinants of economic growth. And identifying those countries that are outliers can lead to interesting case studies to explore the reasons for the extraordinary performance. For example, the nations with the largest positive prediction errors, $GYP - G\hat{Y}P$, indicating better than predicted economic growth rates in this sample are Tajikistan (+2.2 percent) and Ukraine (+2.0 percent), two former socialist economies. The top two underperformers, with the largest negative prediction errors, in the sample are Côte d'Ivoire (−2.2 percent) and Kenya (−1.7 percent), two sub-Saharan African economies. Reasons for the significantly better (or worse) than predicted economic growth rates may be uncovered in case studies with in-depth analysis of these outlier nations, where the particular historical, political, cultural, as well as economic circumstances, can be discerned. Insights into policy can be gained by accounting for such unusual performances.

POLICY IMPLICATIONS

If theories are well supported by the evidence, that is, subject to repeated tests, like the one illustrated in this multiple regression analysis, then informed policies can be derived. From the results of this model, increasing the net saving rate, the growth rates in gross domestic investment and exports, the share of the population aged 15–64, and the female youth literacy rate, will promote economic growth. Increased reliance on nonrenewable natural resources, reflected in the ratio of resource rents for fossil fuels and minerals in national income, however, is associated with lower economic growth. Finally, lower-income nations, *ceteris paribus*, do appear to grow faster, consistent with convergence theory. In addition to these qualitative insights, we have estimated the quantitative impacts, that is, the statistically significant coefficients of the explanatory variables.

After identifying the key determinants of economic growth, policies to promote or enhance these drivers can be developed. One useful framework offered some two decades ago by the World Bank is the "market-friendly strategy" of development.

---

[14] The World Bank (2009: 195) altered the measurement for natural resource rents from minerals and energy to one based on a change in real wealth, which estimates depletion rates as the ratio between the total value of the natural resource (the present value of current and future rents from resource extractions) and the remaining lifetime reserve. As a sensitivity test, the correlation coefficient between the 2009 share of natural resource rents for minerals and energy in gross national income (using the new methodology) and the NY variable used here (the average annual rates of depletion for minerals and energy for 2000, 2003, and 2006) was equal to 0.92. Replacing the NY variable with the new measure for the 2009 share of natural resource rents in the multiple regression model slightly improved the estimates. In particular, the estimated coefficient for natural resource rents nearly doubled (from −0.029 to −0.052) and became statistically significant at the 5 percent level, while the estimated coefficients for the other explanatory variables were virtually unchanged.

MARKET-FRIENDLY STRATEGY OF DEVELOPMENT

The World Bank (1991) introduced a **market-friendly strategy** for economic growth and development. The four major components of the market-friendly strategy are a stable economy, competitive domestic markets, investments in human capital, and integration with the international economy.[15]

Macroeconomic stability

One of the primary responsibilities of the government is to maintain a stable economy. A strong, independent central bank is needed, not only to exercise control over the money supply, but also to supervise the banking system. Sound fiscal and monetary policies are crucial for macroeconomic stability. Fiscal discipline is reflected in generally balanced budgets, although Keynesian demand management fiscal policies would produce budget deficits during recessions, and should yield budget surpluses during expansions. To be avoided are chronically large government budget deficits that have to be financed either by borrowing in the bond market, resulting in higher interest rates and a crowding out of private domestic investment, or by borrowing from the central bank, in which case the money supply is expanded. Frequently, in developing economies, the second option is used, and the monetization of the government budget deficits results in inflation.

Monetary discipline in controlling inflation is important not only for avoiding a deterioration in the position of those with relatively fixed nominal incomes (including a decline in the real wages of unskilled labor), but also for keeping real interest rates positive and encouraging saving. Further, unchecked inflation can trigger an inflation–depreciation cycle. The trade balance worsens as the domestic currency appreciates in real terms. The capital account may also weaken if there is capital flight in anticipation of continuing depreciation (or devaluation). Monetary discipline becomes easier when there is fiscal discipline.

Exercising fiscal discipline, however, is difficult in developing economies. The demands for government expenditures are great: from providing public education for rapidly increasing school-age populations, to investing in the infrastructure, to securing the national defense. Thus, in addition to economy in government spending, a comprehensive system of taxation on incomes, property, and sales needs to be implemented. Trade barriers, if initially relied on to generate revenues, as well as to protect young domestic industries, should take the form of tariffs, rather than quotas. As the nation establishes a domestic tax system and moves toward freer trade, the tariffs would be phased out.

Competitive domestic markets

The government is also involved in the next component of the market-friendly strategy—the promotion of competitive domestic markets. Here, establishing a sound institutional environment is important. There should be fair and efficient legislative and judicial processes. Property rights should be well defined and laws should be understood and respected. Regulations to protect the environment and promote health and safety in the workplace and in the consumption of the goods and services produced should be transparent, cost-effective, and consistently enforced. A competent and honest civil service is needed to administer efficiently the functions of the public sector.

---

[15] This discussion is drawn from Hess and Ross (1997: 523–531).

Because of the inherent efficiencies in the allocation of resources—in the absence of externalities—the market mechanism should be relied on whenever possible. Interest rates, wage rates, and exchange rates should be set in the market, free to respond to changes in demand and supply conditions. Interest rate ceilings and overvalued official exchange rates result in scarcities of credit and foreign exchange respectively, and encourage unproductive, if privately profitable, rent-seeking.

The government should promote competition through antitrust action to break up monopolies and oligopolies that restrain commerce. International trade and competition from foreign producers helps to achieve the same effect—particularly when domestic markets are too small to support many producers. There should be straightforward and streamlined procedures for forming businesses, as well as for the dissolution of bankrupt businesses.

State-owned enterprises, when inefficient and unprofitable—as is frequently the case—should be privatized. There may even be a greater role in developing economies for private enterprise in the operation of public utilities, where substantial economies of scale make market competition less feasible. Regulation could be used to encourage efficiency and innovation. For example, private firms could bid on the government contracts to supply water or electricity to a given population at set user charges. Rather than regulate the rate of return earned by the private companies, the government could set standards of service. In many cases, the governments of the developing economies may have to make the initial investments in the public utility infrastructure, but private enterprise could be relied on to provide the actual services.

As will be discussed in Chapter 14, the government also provides public goods such as national defense, courts, police protection, and highways. Because of the positive externalities, basic research, geared to the needs of the developing economy, might also be subsidized. The World Bank (1991: 92) notes how "A strong central system of metrology, norms, standards, testing, and quality control helps an economy to upgrade and diffuse technology. . .[and that] standards should conform to international specifications."

Investments in human capital

Human capital formation builds a solid foundation for sustained economic development. Investments in nutrition, health, and education accumulate in a virtuous cycle of improvements in the quality and quantity of life. To begin, adequate nutrition and child care should be ensured. Well-nourished and healthy children have more success in school—eventually producing a better educated and more productive labor force. Economic mobility increases and average wages rise. Parents have fewer children, but invest more in each child. Family planning programs to assist couples in controlling their fertility should be available. The reduced youth burden of dependency permits greater saving and additional gains in physical and human capital deepening. The returns to investments in population quality are bolstered by the more competitive domestic markets and greater opportunities for entrepreneurship.

In any case, special attention should be given to improving the educational and economic opportunities afforded to females. The extent of the many contributions women make to development—as caregivers, workers, managers, entrepreneurs, and community leaders—has only recently been fully appreciated. As will be discussed in Chapter 10, a key to lowering the high fertility rates in developing economies is increased female education.

A responsibility often assumed by governments has been the alleviation of poverty—in the short run through transfers and direct provision for basic needs, and in the long run through investments in human capital. In addition to more equitable access to education and health care services, the average quality of life in developing economies could be improved by public invest-ments in clean water supplies and sanitation systems. Foreign aid could help with funding of the infrastructure, and nongovernmental organizations could assist in the delivery of these essential services to rural and poor urban communities.

Literate and healthy labor forces should bolster the developing nations' comparative advantages in labor-intensive manufacturing—a basis for rapid growth through the expansion of manufac-tured exports that has been effectively employed by East Asian economies, including South Korea, Taiwan, and China.

International integration

International trade is an extension of the market mechanism across national borders. As illus-trated in the simple model of trade in Chapter 3, there are efficiency gains from international specialization realized in increased global output. Nations producing according to their compar-ative advantages and engaging in trade are able to consume beyond their production possibilities boundaries. National incomes and employments rise.

Furthermore, there are dynamic gains from trade and international competition—including the attention to product quality, cost efficiencies, and innovation. The gains from international factor mobility were also noted in the discussion of convergence theory in Chapter 7. Allowing factors to flow to their most productive uses, regardless of national borders, increases global out-put and employment. Restrictions on international migration limit significantly the flows of labor; however, capital is more mobile. Foreign direct investment can involve the transfer of skilled labor, as well as physical capital. So, too, foreign portfolio investment is increasing, serving to improve developing country access to international financial capital.

The World Bank (1991: 14) observed that "The key to global development has been the diffusion of technological progress. New technology has allowed resources to be used more pro-ductively, causing incomes to rise and the quality of life to improve." Technology transfers can occur through: merchandise trade (new technologies embodied in the imported intermediate, capital, and consumer goods); trade in services (the direct licensing of new technologies and the hiring of foreign consultants); international investment (the knowledge conveyed by the expatriate management of the foreign subsidiaries of transnational corporations); foreign aid (technical and program assistance); and the return of native students and workers from other nations.

In sum, the market-friendly strategy of development is based on: sustained human capital formation; a stable economy with disciplined fiscal and monetary policies; competitive domes-tic markets driven by private enterprise, enhanced by productive public investment in the infrastructure, complemented by the efficient provision of public goods, and grounded in fair, effective legislative and judicial systems; and an outward orientation through liberalized trade and investment policies.

COMPREHENSIVE DEVELOPMENT FRAMEWORK

A decade after promoting its market-friendly strategy, the World Bank (2000: 13–30) added a more holistic approach known as the **Comprehensive Development Framework**. This strategy has four dimensions.

The structural dimension emphasizes the development of sound institutions, governmental, judicial, and financial, for administering government, enforcing laws, and allocating resources.

Honest, effective government in a system that upholds property rights while also providing social safety nets is essential. The human dimension, much like in the market-friendly strategy, builds on investment in the population. Quality universal primary education forms the base of the educational pyramid, with strong secondary and tertiary systems above. So, too, comprehensive health care, with an emphasis on child care and family planning, forms the base of the public health pyramid. The physical dimension encompasses: the economic infrastructure (transportation systems, communications networks, and public utilities for essential services, including water, waste disposal, electricity); the social infrastructure (cultural and historical sites, museums, and libraries); and the natural environment, to ensure sustainable development. In particular, measures should be in place to safeguard and preserve indigenous cultures. The fourth dimension is sectoral, which included attention to integrated rural development as well as strong urban management.

The World Bank (2000) stressed the need for collaboration or partnerships between government, business, civil society, nongovernmental organizations, and international aid agencies in carrying forth this Comprehensive Development Framework. Hall and Jones (1997), in a summary of their empirical work on the levels of per capita income across countries, emphasize the economic environment. Institutions such as a strong judiciary system that upholds contracts and secure property rights, open economies, and government policies that promote private enterprise, entrepreneurship, and investment are important for the physical and human capital formation, which, along with technological progress, generate economic growth. In contrast, corruption, which acts as a tax on economic activity, and rent-seeking, a nonproductive—if potentially privately profitable—diversion of resources, undermine economic growth.

Interestingly, Hall and Jones find that distance from the Equator is the "strongest predictor of long-term economic success." That is, more temperate climates are more conducive to economic growth. Underlying reasons are the greater incidence of endemic diseases, such as malaria and dengue fever, in tropical areas and the hotter weather during the summer, also which can reduce labor productivity. Unfortunately, location is not subject to more effective policy formulation or institution building. And with the expected global warming and attendant climate change, the geographical disadvantage of tropical economies will be exacerbated.

CONCLUSION

As is clear, many factors are important for economic growth and development. There is no universal formula, much less a silver bullet, to ensure growth. The less developed nations of the world have yet to complete their demographic transitions—even those that have attained replacement-level fertility—therefore some population growth is guaranteed for the next few decades at least. Furthermore, the relatively, if not absolutely, low levels of living found in the developing countries argue for continued economic growth with increases in per capita consumption of goods and services. For the developed or high-income economies, most have maintained fertility rates well below replacement level and, having largely depleted any population momentum, are close to zero crude rates of natural increase. These nations face significant depopulation even if their fertility rates rise back to replacement level, unless immigration is increased. The seemingly universal desire for higher material consumption, however, implies that even in the high-income countries greater per capita consumption may continue to be sought, requiring further growth in national outputs. In the final chapter, we will revisit this consumption drive.

We turn now from economic growth back to population growth. In Chapter 9 population dynamics and formal demography are presented. Measures of mortality and fertility, the age–sex structure of populations, and population projections are presented. Then, in Chapter 10, models of mortality and fertility transitions are discussed.

KEY TERMS

adjusted coefficient of determination	alternative hypothesis
application	coefficient of determination
comprehensive development framework	correlation coefficient
covariance	degrees of freedom
dummy variable	error term
estimation	F-test
forecasting	heteroscedasticity
homoscedasticity	line of best fit
market-friendly strategy	mean
multiple regression analysis	nonautocorrelation
normal distribution	null hypothesis
one-tail test	ordinary least squares
perfect multicollinearity	population regression line
positive economics	prediction error
random variable	rational behavior
residual	scatter diagram
sample regression line	simple regression analysis
specification	standard deviation
standard error	stochastic
t-ratio	t-test
two-tail test	Type I error
Type II error	variance
verification	

QUESTIONS

1. Observations on the average annual growth rates for real GDP (GY) and population (GP) for the period 2000–10 for the following six developing countries are available:

Country	GY	GP
Algeria	5.4%	1.5%
Bolivia	4.1%	1.8%
Chad	9.0%	3.1%
Kazakhstan	8.3%	0.9%
Nepal	3.8%	2.1%
Vietnam	7.5%	1.1%

    (a) Find the means, standard deviations, and variances for GY and GP.
    (b) Find the covariance and simple correlation coefficient for GY and GP.

221

(c) Plot these six ordered pairs on a scatter diagram with GY on the vertical axis and GP on the horizontal axis. With a ruler, sketch as best you can a "line of best fit" for these observations and estimate its slope and vertical intercept. Discuss whether correlation implies causation here.

2. The multiple regression results for determinants of the economic growth rate for the sample of 64 low- and middle income economies for the 2000–08 period are as follows:

$$\hat{GYP} = -13.05 + 0.086\,SY - 0.047\,NY - 0.067\,YP0 + 0.204\,LFP + 0.030\,FYL$$
$$\quad\;\; (2.00) \quad\;\; (.021) \qquad (.018) \qquad (.027) \qquad\;\; (.043) \qquad\;\; (.013)$$
$$\qquad\quad *** \qquad\;\;\; *** \qquad\;\;\; ** \qquad\;\;\;\; ** \qquad\;\;\;\; *** \qquad\;\;\; **$$

$$\quad + 0.173\,GI + 0.109\,GX + 1.45\,DL \qquad\qquad \overline{R}^2 = 0.729, F = 23.58$$
$$\quad\;\;\; (.030) \qquad (.023) \qquad (.42) \qquad\qquad\qquad\qquad\qquad\qquad\quad ***$$
$$\qquad\;\;\; *** \qquad\;\;\; *** \qquad\;\; ***$$

where GYP is the average annual growth rate in real GDP per capita for 2000–08; SY the average annual net national saving rate for 2000, 2003, and 2006; NY the average annual rate of depletion of natural resources for 2000, 2003, and 2006; YP0 the real gross national income per capita in PPP dollars in 2000 (US = 100); LFP the ratio of the population aged 15–64 to the total population in 2000; FYL the female youth literacy rate for 2000; GI the average annual growth rate in gross domestic investment for 2000–08; GX the average annual growth rate in real exports of goods and services for 2000–08; and DL a dummy variable for a landlocked country.

(a) Discuss why each of the explanatory variables (SY, NY, YP0, LFP, FYL, GI, and GX) is included as a theoretical influence in this regression for the growth rate in real GDP per capita.

(b) Discuss what additional theoretical influences should be included in a regression for the growth rate of real GDP. How might you measure or quantify these influences?

(c) Interpret the coefficients of all the significant explanatory variables, that is, the marginal effect of each explanatory variable on the dependent variable.

(d) Compare these estimation results for the 2000–08 period with the results in the chapter for the 2000–09 period for the same 64 low- and middle-income economies.

DATA APPENDIX

The low- and middle-income economies in the sample are listed below by region:

East Asia and the Pacific	Cambodia, China, Indonesia, Lao PDR, Malaysia, Philippines, Thailand, Vietnam
Europe and Central Asia	Albania, Armenia, Belarus, Bulgaria, Croatia, Latvia, Lithuania, Moldova, Poland, Romania, Russian Federation, Tajikistan, Turkey, Ukraine
Latin America and the Caribbean	Argentina, Bolivia, Brazil, Chile, Colombia, Costa Rica, Dominican Republic, Ecuador, El Salvador, Guatemala, Honduras, Mexico, Nicaragua, Panama, Paraguay, Peru, Uruguay, Venezuela

Middle East and North Africa	Egypt, Iran, Jordan, Lebanon, Morocco, Syria, Tunisia
South Asia	Bangladesh, India, Pakistan
Sub-Saharan Africa	Botswana, Cameroon, Côte d'Ivoire, Ethiopia, Kenya, Mali, Mauritius, Namibia, Senegal, South Africa, Swaziland, Sudan, Tanzania, Uganda

The variables are listed below used with definitions and data sources. The World Bank's *World Development Indicators* is abbreviated as WDI, with the edition noted. The World Bank's *World Development Report* is abbreviated as WDR, with the edition noted.

GYP = GY–GP is the average annual growth rate in real gross domestic product per capita for 2000–09. GY is the average annual growth rate in real GDP for 2000–09 and GP is the average annual growth rate in population for 2000–09 (WDI 2011: Table 4.1; WDR 2011: Tables 1 and 6).

SY is the average annual net national saving rate for 2000, 2003, and 2006. The net national saving rate is the ratio of net national saving (calculated as gross national saving less physical capital consumption) in national income. Gross national saving, in turn, is calculated as gross national income less public and private consumption plus net transfers. The net national saving rates for three years in the period, 2000, 2003, and 2006, are averaged to obtain SY (Table 3.15 in WDI 2002, 2005, and 2008).

NY is the average annual rate of depletion of natural resources for 2000, 2003, and 2006. The natural resource depletion rate is measured as the mineral and energy rates of depletion as a share of gross national income. Mineral and energy depletion are unit resource rents (the difference between world prices and the average unit extraction costs, including a normal return on capital) multiplied by the physical quantities extracted. The minerals included are tin, gold, lead, zinc, iron, copper, nickel, silver, bauxite, and phosphate. The energies included are coal, crude oil, and natural gas. The depletion rates for three years in the period, 2000, 2003, and 2006, are averaged to obtain NY (Table 3.15 in WDI 2002, 2005, and 2008).

YP0 is the index of real gross national income per capita in purchasing power parity-adjusted dollars in 2000 (US = 100). Gross national income is the income earned by residents of a nation in the production of final goods and services. Purchasing power parity per capita income is expressed in international dollars, which have the same purchasing power as a US dollar has in the United States. YP0 is calculated as the ratio of the nation's per capita gross national income in 2000 to the US gross national income of $34,100 in 2000 in PPP dollars (WDI 2002: Table 1.1).

LFP is the ratio of the population aged 15–64 to the total population in 2000. The total population (mid-year estimates) includes all residents who are present, regardless of legal status or citizenship, except for refugees not permanently settled. The population of ages 15–64 is a proxy for the potential labor force (WDI 2002: Table 2.1).

FYL is the youth female literacy rate for 2000. This is the percentage of females aged 15–24 who can, with understanding, read and write a short, simple statement about their everyday life (WDI 2002: Table 2.14).

GI is the average annual growth rate in real gross domestic investment for 2000–09. Gross domestic investment is also known as gross capital formation and includes mainly outlays on the fixed assets of an economy, encompassing expenditures on land improvements; plant, machinery and equipment; and construction of roads, schools, and buildings (WDI 2011: Table 4.9).

223

GX is the average annual growth rate in real exports of goods and services for 2000–2009. Exports are the value of all goods and market services provided to the rest of the world. They include the value of merchandise, freight, insurance, transport, travel, royalties, license fees, and other services (communication, construction, financial, information, business, personal and government). They exclude compensation of employees and investment income (WDI 2011: Table 4.9).

REFERENCES

Cohen, Jessica and William Easterly. 2009. "Introduction: Thinking Big versus Thinking Small," in Jessica Cohen and William Easterly (eds), *What Works in Development? Thinking Big and Thinking Small*. Washington, DC: Brookings Institution: 1–23.

Collier, Paul. 2007. *The Bottom Billion: Why the Poorest Countries Are Failing and What Can Be Done About It*. New York: Oxford University Press.

Hall, Robert and Charles Jones. 1997. "What Have We Learned from Recent Empirical Growth Research?" *American Economic Review*, 87(2): 173–177.

Hess, Peter and Clark Ross. 1997. *Economic Development: Theories, Evidence, and Policies*. Fort Worth, TX: Dryden Press: 523–531.

Levine, Ross and David Renelt. 1992. "A Sensitivity Analysis of Cross-Country Growth Regressions," *American Economic Review* 82(4): 942–963.

Soludo, Charles and Jongil Kim. 2003, "Sources of Aggregate Growth in Developing Regions: Still More Questions than Answers?" in Gary McMahon and Lyn Squire (eds), *Explaining Growth: A Global Research Project*. New York: Palgrave Macmillan.

Temple, Jonathan. 1999. "The New Growth Evidence," *Journal of Economic Literature*, 37(1): 112–156.

Weil, David. 2009. "The Cutting Edge of Technology," in *Economic Growth*, 2nd edition. Boston: Pearson Addison Wesley: 244–272.

World Bank, 1991. *World Development Report 1991: The Challenge of Development*. New York: Oxford University Press.

World Bank. 2000. "Introduction: New Directions in Development Thinking," in *World Development Report 1999/2000: Entering the 21st Century*, New York: Oxford University Press: 13–30.

World Bank. 2009. *World Development Indicators 2009*. Washington, DC: World Bank.

World Bank. 2012. *World Bank Development Indicators 2012*. Washington, DC: World Bank.

Part IV
Demography

Chapter 9

Population dynamics

In 1994, the demographer Wolfgang Lutz (1994: 34) asserted three major certainties. First, the world's population would continue to grow. He speculated that by 2030 the population would have increased by at least 50 percent. In 1994, the world population was approximately 5.6 billion, so this would imply an average annual population growth rate over the next 36 years of around 1.1 percent, which is lower than the actual annual rates of 1.4 percent for 1990–2000 and 1.2 percent for 2000–10. Second, developing nations would account for a greater share of the world population. Lutz predicted that by 2030 the contemporary developing nations would hold between 85 and 87 percent of the world's population. In 1994 the low- and middle-income nations already accounted for 85 percent of the world population. Over time, with economic growth, some low- and middle-income nations will become high-income nations; for example, South Korea was an upper middle-income economy in 1994 and has since become a high-income economy. So this prediction might be harder to measure. What will certainly happen is that the shares of the world's population from sub-Saharan Africa, South Asia, the Middle East, and North Africa will rise. Third, Lutz predicted that all populations will become older. This is very likely, given the trends in fertility rates. The percentage of the world population aged 60 or over may increase from under 10 percent in the mid-1990s to over 15 percent by 2030.[1]

Population projections, however, are exercises rife with uncertainty. The uncertainty arises from the difficulty in predicting human behavior, subject to free will, and the inability to forecast changes in the human and natural environments. (Recall Malthus's positive checks (through increases in the death rate) and preventative checks (through decreases in the birth rate) to population growth.) Even so, projections for the world population are easier than for national or subnational populations since the world population is closed, that is, not affected by immigration or emigration. For example, in the late 1930s demographers Warren Thompson and Pascal Whelpton projected the population of the United States forward, reflecting the low US fertility and net emigration of the Great Depression decade. Their estimates for the US population size for 1980 ranged from 134 million to 158 million. The US population in 1980, however, was almost 228 million, over 40 percent greater than the upper estimate. The much higher actual population than projected reflected in large part the post-World War II baby boom and the return to significant immigration (see Haub 1987: 31).

---

[1] The United Nations Secretariat (1999: 3) in *The World at Six Billion* observes: The median age increased from 23.5 years in 1950 to 26.4 years in 1999. By 2050, the median age is projected to reach 37.8 years. The number of people in the world aged 60 or older will also rise from the current one-of-ten persons to two-of-nine by 2050. Currently around one-of-five persons in the developed countries are aged 60 or older; in 2050 nearly one-of-every three persons will be aged 60 or older.

What are the present trends in the world's population? Demographers are constantly reassessing the evidence on fertility and mortality to develop more reliable projections. In this chapter we will discuss measures of mortality and fertility. Then we will show how population projections are made, gaining insights into the value, as well as the limitations, of such exercises.

MEASURES OF MORTALITY

There are numerous measures of mortality, differing on the basis of the assumptions, units of analysis, and applications. The most basic measure, the crude death rate (CDR), has already been discussed. Recall from Chapter 2 that the crude death rate is used in calculating the crude rate of natural increase and the population growth rate. To measure the crude death rate we divide the number of deaths to a population over a year (*D*) by the mid-year population (*P*):

$$\text{CDR} = \frac{\text{Deaths}}{\text{Mid-year population}} = \frac{D}{P}$$

Assuming that the deaths, as well as births and immigration and emigration, in the area under consideration occur at a uniform rate over the year, the mid-year population P can be found as the simple average of the beginning and end-of year populations. The CDR is usually expressed per thousand mid-year population.

The crude death rate is "crude" in that it is not adjusted for the age or sex structure of the population. Therefore, comparing the CDRs for two populations of different age and sex structures can be misleading for drawing inferences about relative mortality levels. For example, in 2010, both India, a lower middle-income nation, and the US had a crude death rate of 8 (per thousand). Higher incomes do improve the average standard of living, with the attendant gains in education and nutrition, better shelter, and greater access to health care, and thus do tend to reduce mortality rates. The crude death rate, however, may not reflect this improvement in the standard of living, although age-specific death rates would.

Age-specific death rates

The **age-specific death rate** (ASDR$_x$) measures the deaths to the population of a given age x (D_x) per thousand mid-year population of that age (P_x). For any year,

$$\text{ASDR}_x = \frac{\text{Deaths to population of age } x}{\text{Mid-year population of age } x} = \frac{D_x}{P_x}$$

Age-specific death rates, also known as age-specific mortality rates, like the crude death rate, are usually expressed per thousand mid-year population. Across populations, there is a common pattern to age-specific death rates. The graph of the age-specific death rates by age resembles a fish hook or an elongated "J." Usually age-specific death rates are presented for 5- or 10-year age intervals after the first year of life. In general, the age-specific death rate is relatively high for the first year of life, but then quickly declines through childhood, before slowly rising through adolescence and early adulthood. The rate of increase in mortality picks up, but the initially high age-specific death rates found in the first year of life are not reached again until middle age. Thereafter, the rise in mortality rates accelerates with age.

While there is a common pattern to the age-specific death rates, we should note that, in general, mortality rates are lower for females than males, especially in more developed economies.

In poor countries, however, where maternal mortality rates are high and gender discrimination is prevalent and manifested in lower access to education, health care, and nutrition for females, mortality rates for females may be equal to or even greater than for males. With economic development, however, age-specific mortality rates decline across all ages for both males and females.

The crude death rate is the weighted average of age-specific death rates, where the weights are the percentages of the population in each age interval (P_x/P):

$$\text{CDR} = \sum_{x=0}^{\omega} (D_x/P_x) \cdot (P_x/P) = \sum_{x=0}^{\omega} \text{ASDR}_x \cdot (P_x/P)$$

where ω is the life span of the population or the maximum age that humans could attain under optimal conditions. A working definition of **life span** might be the age beyond which less than 0.1 percent of the initial population lives. Clearly the crude death rate is sensitive to the age and sex composition of the population. In fact, it is possible for one population to have uniformly lower age-specific death rates across all ages than a second population, yet have a higher crude death rate.

Table 9.1 gives the age-specific death rates for the US female populations in 1980 and 2008. Due to improvements in the standard of living and health care, age-specific death rates have declined over time. In this table we see the uniformly lower death rates for all ages in 2008. Low fertility rates, however, have contributed to the aging of the US population, reflected in a rise in the median age, from 31.3 years in 1980 to 38.1 years in 2008, and in the decrease in the share of the female population under age 15 (from 21.6 percent in 1980 to 19.4 percent in 2008) and increase in the share of the female population aged 65 and over (from 13.1 percent in 1980 to 14.5 percent in 2008). With the aging of the population, the crude death rate has increased, despite the lower age-specific death rates, from 7.85 in 1980 to 8.08 in 2008.

To compare mortality conditions across populations in different countries or over time, we could use particular age-specific death rates. A widely used measure of mortality conditions, sensitive to the average standard of living, access to health care, and environmental conditions, is the **infant mortality rate** (IMR). In any year, the infant mortality rate is calculated as:

$$\text{IMR} = \frac{\text{Deaths occurring to infants under age 1}}{\text{Number of live births}}$$

The infant mortality rate is usually expressed per thousand live births, so if IMR $= 60$, then out of every thousand live births in the year, sixty infants died before their first birthdays. The infant mortality rate is sometimes broken down into neonatal mortality, occurring during the first month of life, and post-neonatal mortality, between the second and 12th months. Neonatal mortality reflects more biological and genetic factors, such as congenital diseases, premature deliveries, and complications during delivery. Post-neonatal mortality is related more to the standard of living (adequacy of shelter and nutrition, as well as access to health care).

A more comprehensive measure of child mortality is the **under-five mortality rate** (U5MR), which is the probability that a newborn would die before reaching her fifth birthday, if subject to current age-specific death rates. Both the infant mortality and under-five mortality rates are independent of the age distributions of the populations and thus are useful measures for comparing mortality conditions across countries. As indicated in Table 9.2, there are significant

Table 9.1 *Selected statistics on US mortality*

	1980		2008		
	ASDR	% Pop	ASDR	% Pop	
under age 1	11.42	1.4%	5.88	1.4%	
1–4	0.55	5.5%	0.25	5.3%	
5–14	0.24	14.7%	0.12	12.7%	
15–24	0.58	**18.1%**	0.40	13.4%	Baby boom generation,
25–34	0.76	**16.1%**	0.63	13.0%	born 1946–64, was
35–44	1.59	11.2%	1.35	13.7%	aged 16–34 in 1980 and
45–54	4.13	10.1%	3.18	**14.6%**	aged 44–62 in 2008.
55–64	9.34	9.9%	6.69	**11.3%**	
65–74	21.45	7.6%	16.23	7.0%	
75–84	54.40	4.2%	43.16	5.0%	
85 +	147.47	1.3%	125.36	2.5%	
All ages	7.85	100%	8.08	100%	
Total female population		116.49 million		154.14 million	
Median age		31.3 years		38.1 years	

$CDR_{1980} = 0.014 \times 11.42 + 0.055 \times 0.55 + \cdots + 0.013 \times 147.47 = 7.85$
$CDR_{2008} = 0.014 \times 5.88 + 0.053 \times 0.25 + \cdots + 0.025 \times 125.36 = 8.08$

Note: Age-specific death rates (ASDRs) for US female population (number of deaths per 1,000 population in age group)
From: US Department of Commerce, *Statistical Abstract of the United States 2012* (Table 110 for death rates); *Statistical Abstract of the United States 2010* (Tables 7, 10 for population by age).
Average expectation of life in years in US, 2008

Life expectancy	Total	White		Black	
		Male	Female	Male	Female
at birth	78.0	75.9	80.8	70.9	77.4
at age 20	58.9	56.8	61.4	52.6	58.7
at age 40	40.0	38.1	42.1	34.5	39.6
at age 60	22.6	21.0	24.0	18.7	22.7
at age 80	8.8	7.9	9.3	7.8	9.5

From: http://www.census.gov/compendia/statab/2012/Tables/12s015.pdf (Table 105).

differences in the infant and under-five mortality rates across countries. We do see that these mortality rates, on average, have declined between 1990 and 2010, continuing the trends of the last few decades.

In addition to the averages for the groups of nations classified by income class, we give the range of the values for these mortality rates. The diversity in experience across national populations is striking. For example, the lowest infant mortality rate in 2010 was 2, found in Finland, Japan, Singapore, Slovenia, and Sweden. The highest IMR was 112 in the Democratic Republic of Congo, where one out of every nine newborns would not live to her first birthday. Finland, Japan, Norway, Singapore, Slovenia, and Sweden had the lowest under-five mortality rates of 3, or not much higher than their infant mortality rates, indicating the very low mortality to children between the ages of 1 and 5; and Somalia, a failed state on the east coast of Africa, had the highest U5MR of 180—nearly one-fifth of newborns did not survive to their fifth birthdays.

Table 9.2 *Selected statistics on mortality*

	ECONOMIES BY INCOME CLASSIFICATION							
	WORLD	Low	Lower Middle	India	Upper Middle	China	High	US
Crude death rate, 2010 Max. 17 (Guinea-Bissau) Min. 1 (United Arab Emirates)	8	11	8	8	7	7	8	8
Infant mortality rate, 1990	62	103	78	81	39	38	10	9
2010 Max. 112 (Congo Dem. Rep.) Min. 2 (Finland, Japan, Singapore, Slovenia, Sweden)	41	70	50	48	17	16	5	7
Under-five mortality rate 1990	90	165	113	115	49	48	12	11
2010 Max. 180 (Somalia) Min. 3 (Finland, Japan, Norway, Singapore, Slovenia, Sweden)	58	108	69	63	20	18	6	8
Life expectancy at birth (years) 1990	65	53	59	58	69	69	75	75
2010 Max. 83 (Japan) Min. 47 (Lesotho, Sierra Leone)	70	59	65	65	73	73	80	78
% of population in 2010 Aged 0–14 Max. 49% (Niger) Min. 13% (Japan, Qatar)	27%	39%	32%	31%	22%	19%	17%	20%
Aged 65+ Max. 23% (Japan) Min. 0% (United Arab Emirates)	8%	4%	5%	5%	8%	8%	16%	13%
GNI per capita (PPP dollars) 2010 Max. $58,570 (Norway) Min. $320 (Congo Dem. Rep.)	$11,066	$1,307	$3,632	$3,400	$9,970	$7,640	$37,317	$47,310

Table 9.2 *continued*

	ECONOMIES BY REGION						
	Sub-Saharan Africa	Middle East & N. Africa	Europe & Central Asia	South Asia	East Asia & Pacific	Latin America & Caribbean	High Income Economies
Crude Death Rate:							
2010	13	5	11	8	7	6	8
Infant Mortality Rate:							
1990	105	56	42	86	42	43	10
2010	76	27	19	52	20	18	5
Under-Five Mortality Rate:							
1990	175	74	51	120	56	54	12
2010	121	34	23	67	24	23	6
Life Expectancy at Birth (yrs.)							
1990	50	64	68	59	68	68	75
2010	54	72	71	65	72	74	80
% of Population in 2010							
Aged 0–14:	42%	31%	19%	32%	22%	28%	17%
Aged 65+:	3%	5%	11%	5%	7%	7%	16%
GNI per capita (PPP$)							
2010	$2,148	$8,068	$13,396	$3,124	$6,657	$10,926	$37,317

Notes: Crude death rate is the number of deaths occurring during the year per 1,000 population at mid-year.

Infant mortality rate is the number of infants dying before reaching age 1 per 1000 live births in a given year.

Under-five mortality rate is the probability that a newborn baby will die before reaching age 5, if subject to current age-specific mortality rates. The probability is expressed as a rate per 1,000.

Life expectancy at birth is the number of years a newborn baby would live if prevailing patterns of mortality at the time of its birth were to stay the same throughout its life.

Source: World Bank (2012: Tables 1.1, 2.1, and 2.23).

To illustrate the sensitivity of the crude death rates to age distributions, we noted that the lower middle- and high-income economies in 2010 had the same average crude death rate of 8 per thousand. Yet, at 69 per thousand, the average under-five mortality rate was over 11 times greater in the lower middle-income economies. As measures of mortality, crude death rates are biased downwards with the younger populations in less developed economies. The shares of the populations under 15 years of age in 2010 averaged 32 percent and 17 percent for the lower middle-income and high-income nations, respectively.

Life expectancy

A more comprehensive measure of mortality is the **life expectancy at birth**, e_0, which is derived from a life table. Life expectancy at birth, a hypothetical measure, indicates the average number of years a newborn would live if subject to the prevailing age-specific death rates. We can also measure the life expectancy at any other age, e_x. We will discuss below how life tables are developed and life expectancies for a population are derived. Referring to Table 9.2, we can see the gaps in life expectancies at birth across countries, indicating differences in the standards of living, access to health care, and environmental conditions. As reflected in the lower infant mortality and under-five mortality rates, life expectancies at birth have increased across the world over the past two decades, and indeed over the past half century.

There are, however, some exceptions to the improving mortality conditions found in most countries, in particular, in those nations severely afflicted with AIDS. In the southern part of sub-Saharan Africa, the incidence of AIDS has been so high that life expectancies have declined over the last two decades in several of these nations.[2] For example, in Zimbabwe, a poor sub-Saharan African country with a repressive dictator, the life expectancy at birth declined from 61 years in 1990 to 50 years in 2010.[3]

In sum, there are numerous measures of mortality. The crude death rate is the most general and is used to determine the crude rate of natural increase and the population growth rate. The crude death rate is not a good indicator for comparing mortality across populations with different age–sex compositions. Infant and child mortality rates and life expectancies at birth are better indicators of mortality. Returning to Table 9.2, where we present the various mortality rates for developing nations grouped by region and for the high-income economies, we again see the diversity of conditions across the world. In general, mortality rates are highest in the poorer nations of sub-Saharan Africa and South Asia. Outside of sub-Saharan Africa, the highest crude death rate is for Europe and Central Asia, which reflects the older populations in that region. We might note that in Europe and Central Asia, the gap in the life expectancies at birth between females (75 years) and males (66 years) in 2010 is the largest in the world (World Bank 2012: Table 1.5).[4] In the next chapter we will address the epidemiological transition and the changing causes of mortality and morbidity.

LIFE TABLES

A **life table** is a statistical device for summarizing the mortality experience of a population. Underlying this device is the concept of a **cohort**, which consists of a group of individuals who have experienced the same significant demographic event during a specified brief period of time, usually a year, and who may be identified as a group at successive later dates on the basis of this common experience. For example, individuals in a nation born in 1950 would be a birth cohort. Students graduating from college in the class of 2012 would be another cohort.

A life table displays the life history of a hypothetical cohort of individuals as a group gradually diminished by death. That is, the life table is computed on the basis of a synthetic cohort by taking age-specific mortality rates for a given population for a year, rather than waiting for an actual birth cohort to experience mortality over its life span. A life table may be based on single-year age groups or abridged, with single-year data aggregated into five- or ten-year age intervals. Life tables may be for both sexes combined, or more appropriately for a single sex, since male and female age-specific death rates differ.

---

[2] All of the nations in the southern cone of sub-Saharan Africa have exceptionally high incidences of HIV, which causes AIDS. Incidences in 2009 as a percentage of the population aged 15–49 were: Botswana (24.8 percent), Lesotho (23.6 percent), Namibia (13.1 percent), South Africa (17.8 percent), Swaziland (25.9 percent), Zambia (13.5 percent), and Zimbabwe (14.3 percent). The average incidence of HIV for all of sub-Saharan Africa in 2009 was 5.5 percent of the total population aged 15–49, compared to a world average of 0.8 percent (World Bank 2012: Table 2.22).

[3] The other countries with declines in life expectancies at birth from 1990 to 2010 are: Botswana (from 64 to 53 years), Lesotho (from 59 to 47 years), South Africa (from 62 to 52 years), and Swaziland (from 59 to 48 years). Only in Namibia (from 61 to 62 years) and Zambia (from 47 and 48 years) did life expectancies increase over these two decades (World Bank 2012: Table 2.23).

[4] The region with the next largest gap is Latin America and the Caribbean, with female and male life expectancies at birth of 77 and 71 years, respectively. In 2010 the differential in Russia, with over a third of the population of the low- and middle-income economies of Europe and Central Asia, was 12 years. During the difficult economic transition and political turmoil of the 1990s, health conditions seriously deteriorated in Russia, especially for males with the high incidence of alcoholism.

Table 9.3 *Abridged life tables for the United States: 1996*

Age interval	Proportion dying	Of 100,000 born alive		Stationary population		Average remaining lifetime
Period of life between two exact ages stated in years, race, and sex	Proportion of persons alive at beginning of age interval dying during interval	Number living at beginning of age interval	Number dying during age interval	In the age interval	In this and all subsequent age intervals	Average number of years of life remaining at beginning of age interval
(1)	(2)	(3)	(4)	(5)	(6)	(7)
x to $x+n$	$_nq_x$	l_x	$_nd_x$	$_nL_x$	T_x	e_x^o
ALL RACES						
0–1	0.00732	100,000	732	99,370	7,611,825	76.1
1–5	0.00151	99,268	150	396,721	7,512,455	75.7
5–10	0.00097	99,118	96	495,329	7,115,734	71.8
10–15	0.00118	99,022	117	494,883	6,620,405	66.9
15–20	0.00390	98,905	386	493,650	6,125,522	61.9
20–25	0.00506	98,519	499	491,372	5,631,872	57.2
25–30	0.00544	98,020	533	488,766	5,140,500	52.4
30–35	0.00710	97,487	692	485,746	4,651,734	47.7
35–40	0.00944	96,795	914	481,820	4,165,988	43.0
40–45	0.01283	95,881	1,230	476,549	3,684,168	38.4
45–50	0.01801	94,651	1,705	469,305	3,207,619	33.9
50–55	0.02733	92,946	2,540	458,779	2,738,314	29.5
55–60	0.04177	90,406	3,776	443,132	2,279,535	25.2
60–65	0.06649	86,630	5,760	419,530	1,836,403	21.2
65–70	0.09663	80,870	7,814	385,659	1,416,873	17.5
70–75	0.14556	73,056	10,634	339,620	1,031,214	14.1
75–80	0.21060	62,422	13,146	280,047	691,594	11.1
80–85	0.31754	49,276	15,647	207,474	411,547	8.4
85 and over	1.00000	33,629	33,629	204,073	204,073	6.1
MALE						
0–1	0.00802	100,000	802	99,307	7,305,955	73.1
1–5	0.00167	99,198	166	396,407	7,206,648	72.6
5–10	0.00111	99,032	110	494,860	6,810,241	68.8
10–15	0.00142	98,922	140	494,355	6,315,381	63.8
15–20	0.00552	98,782	545	492,690	5,821,026	58.9
20–25	0.00755	98,237	742	489,370	5,328,336	54.2
25–30	0.00774	97,495	755	485,567	4,838,966	49.6
30–35	0.00994	96,740	962	481,323	4,353,399	45.0
35–40	0.01281	95,778	1,227	475,977	3,872,076	40.4
40–45	0.01714	94,551	1,621	468,983	3,396,099	35.9
45–50	0.02348	92,930	2,182	459,601	2,927,116	31.5
50–55	0.03465	90,748	3,144	446,380	2,467,515	27.2
55–60	0.05276	87,604	4,622	427,115	2,021,135	23.1
60–65	0.08395	82,982	6,966	398,394	1,594,020	19.2
65–70	0.12205	76,016	9,278	357,755	1,195,626	15.7
70–75	0.18255	66,738	12,183	303,928	837,871	12.6
75–80	0.25936	54,555	14,149	237,528	533,943	9.8
80–85	0.38255	40,406	15,457	162,498	296,415	7.3
85 and over	1.00000	24,949	24,949	133,917	133,917	5.4

Table 9.3 *continued*

Age interval	Proportion dying	Of 100,000 born alive		Stationary population		Average remaining lifetime
Period of life between two exact ages stated in years, race, and sex	Proportion of persons alive at beginning of age interval dying during interval	Number living at beginning of age interval	Number dying during age interval	In the age interval	In this and all subsequent age intervals	Average number of years of life remaining at beginning of age interval
(1)	(2)	(3)	(4)	(5)	(6)	(7)
x to $x+n$	$_n q_x$	l_x	$_n d_x$	$_n L_x$	T_x	e_x^0
FEMALE						
0–1	0.00659	100,000	659	99,435	7,907,507	79.1
1–5	0.00135	99,341	134	397,043	7,808,072	78.6
5–10	0.00083	99,207	82	495,812	7,411,029	74.7
10–15	0.00093	99,125	92	495,426	6,915,217	69.8
15–20	0.00220	99,033	218	494,654	6,419,791	64.8
20–25	0.00242	98,815	239	493,488	5,925,137	60.0
25–30	0.00311	98,576	307	492,128	5,431,649	55.1
30–35	0.00430	98,269	423	490,336	4,939,521	50.3
35–40	0.00608	97,846	595	487,848	4,449,185	45.5
40–45	0.00858	97,251	834	484,325	3,961,337	40.7
45–50	0.01269	96,417	1,224	479,247	3,477,012	36.1
50–55	0.02036	95,193	1,938	471,421	2,997,765	31.5
55–60	0.03150	93,255	2,938	459,363	2,526,344	27.1
60–65	0.05068	90,317	4,577	440,808	2,066,981	22.9
65–70	0.07484	85,740	6,417	413,497	1,626,173	19.0
70–75	0.11607	79,323	9,207	374,780	1,212,676	15.3
75–80	0.17495	70,116	12,267	321,360	837,896	12.0
80–85	0.27721	57,849	16,036	250,275	516,536	8.9
85 and over	1.00000	41,813	41,813	266,261	266,261	6.4

From: Anderson R. N. United States abridged life tables, 1996. *National vital statistic reports,* Vol. 47, No. 13. Hyattsville, Maryland: National Center for Health Statistics. 1998.

To illustrate, see Table 9.3, where abridged life tables for the total population, males, and females in the US for 1996 are presented (Anderson, 1998). Since the underlying age-specific death rates for females are uniformly lower, the derived probabilities of dying at each age are higher for males. The age intervals, except for the first two, from 0 to 1 and from 1 to 5 years of age, and the last open interval, 85 years and over, are 5 years in length. These age intervals reflect **exact ages**. While the age intervals appear to be overlapping (0–1, 1–5, 5–10, etc.), exact ages mean a range from the younger age up to, but not including the older age. We could write the age intervals as [0, 1), [1, 5), [5, 10), etc. For example, the age interval 40–45 years, [40, 45), covers from age 40 up to, but not including age 45.

Several important assumptions underlie a life table. First, the original cohort, called the **radix**, indicates the number of births and constitutes the initial population, which will be decreased in number by mortality over the course of its hypothetical life experience. Usually the radix is set equal to 100,000. Second, the population is closed: there is no migration in or emigration from the initial population. The only way to enter this population is to be included in the radix, the initial cohort of births. The only way to exit the population is through death. Third, we assume a fixed schedule of age-specific death rates, from which we will derive the probabilities of dying in the age intervals. The initial cohort of births, the radix, is then survived forward according to these probabilities. Fourth, at each age interval, except the first two, $[0, 1)$, and $[1, 5)$, and the last open interval, 85 and over, we assume that the deaths occurring are evenly distributed over the interval. We will discuss later the assumptions for these other three age intervals.

Construction of a life table

To begin, we should distinguish between central rates and probabilities. A **central rate** measures the ratio of events to a population (e.g., the ratio of deaths over a year to the mid-year population). The crude death rate and age-specific death rates are examples. In contrast, a **probability** measures the ratio of events, such as deaths, to a population at risk, which is usually the initial population or the population at the beginning of the period of analysis. The infant mortality rate and the under-five mortality rates are probabilities. In constructing a life table, the given age-specific deaths rates need to be converted into probabilities of dying within the age intervals.

Let n be the length of the age interval. Denote by $_nM_x$ the age-specific death rate for the population aged x to $x + n$, and by $_nq_x$ the probability of dying between age x and age $x + n$:

$$_nq_x = \frac{n \cdot _nM_x}{1 + (n/2) \cdot _nM_x}$$

Basically we are adding to the mid-point population of age x to $x + n$, which would be in the denominator of a central rate, half of the deaths that occurred to the population initially of age x to $x + n$ over the period to get the initial population of age x to $x + n$. This conversion to a probability is only accurate if deaths are evenly distributed over the age interval.[5]

In Table 9.3 the probabilities of dying, $_nq_x$, are presented in column (2), having been derived from the underlying age-specific death rates, $_nM_x$, given by the ratio of deaths to persons of age x to $x + n$ to the mid-year population of age x to $x + n$. For example, for US females in 1996 the probability of dying between the ages of 40 and 45 is 0.00858 or slightly less than 0.9 percent. The probability of dying for US males in 1996 between the ages of 40 and 45 is 0.01714 or slightly over 1.7 percent.

In column (3) of the life table we find the population surviving to age interval x to $x + n$. The l_x values indicate the number of persons alive at exact age x (i.e., at the beginning of the age interval x) out of the total number of births (the radix, l_0). The next column (4) gives the deaths to the population in the age intervals. That is, $_nd_x$ indicates the number of persons who die within the indicated age interval x to $x + n$ out of the total number of births. The numbers of deaths in the age intervals, in turn, are found by subjecting the initial populations to the respective probabilities of dying:

$$_nd_x = l_x \cdot _nq_x$$

For example, 1,621 deaths would occur to the initial cohort of 100,000 males between the ages of 40 and 45. Of the initial cohort of births, 94,551 would reach age 40 and the probability of dying between the ages of 40 and 45 is 1.714 percent. Consequently, $_5d_{40} = 1,621 = l_{40} \cdot _5q_{40} = 94,551 \cdot 0.01714$. (Note that there may be some rounding error, given that we always round to

---

[5]For the first year of life, or the initial age interval $[0, 1)$, the formula for the probability of dying is given by $_1q_0 = _1M_0/(1 + 0.85 \cdot _1M_0)$, since more of the deaths to infants under age 1 occur nearer birth. For the second age interval, $[1, 5)$, the formula for the probability of dying is $_4q_1 = 4 \cdot _4M_1/(1 + 0.6 \cdot _4M_1)$. For the last open age interval, 85+, the probability of dying is 1.

the nearest whole person. Rounding error is even more likely in abridged life tables aggregated from single-year life tables.)

The population alive at the beginning of the next age interval, $_nl_{x+n}$, is found by subtracting the deaths from the population alive at the beginning of the previous age interval.

$$_nl_{x+n} = {_nl_x} - {_nd_x}$$

As we see in life table for US males in 1996, out of the initial cohort of 100,000 births, 92,930 would reach the age interval 45–50, if subjected to the probabilities of dying prevailing in 1996. That is, $_5l_{45} = 92{,}930 = {_5l_{40}} - {_5d_{40}} = 94{,}551 - 1{,}621$.

The number of person-years lived in any age interval is given in the fifth column. $_nL_x$ represents the number of person-years that would be lived within the indicated age interval x to $x + n$ by the initial cohort. The maximum number of years lived by any individual in an n-year age interval would be clearly n. For the initial cohort of 100,000 births, if there had been no deaths up to and through age interval x to $x + n$, the value of $_5L_x$ would be then 500,000. Realizing that the initial cohort of births will be diminished by deaths before that age interval, and assuming all the deaths occurring in the age interval are evenly distributed, the $_nL_x$ values are calculated:[6]

$$_nL_x = (n/2) \cdot (l_x + l_{x+n})$$

For example, the number of person-years that would be lived by the cohort of males between the ages of 40 and 45 is $_5L_{40} = \frac{5}{2}(l_{40} + l_{45}) = 2.5(94{,}551 + 92{,}930) = 468{,}703$ (which is 99.94 percent of 468,983, the actual life table value; the difference is due to rounding error and the aggregation from single years to 5-year intervals).

The number of person-years lived by this hypothetical cohort from ages x and older are given by the T_x values in column (6). That is, T_x equals the total number of person-years that would be lived after the beginning of the age interval x by the cohort (i.e., in that age interval and all subsequent age intervals). Calculation of the T_x values is straightforward.

$$T_x = {_nL_x} + T_{x+n}$$

To illustrate, the number of person-years lived by this cohort of males from age 40 and older is:

$$T_{40} = 3{,}396{,}099 = {_5L_{40}} + T_{45} = 468{,}983 + 2{,}927{,}116$$

To find the highest T_x value, here T_{85}, required to close the life table and for the calculation of the other T_x values, an approximation is used for the oldest age interval, L_x, here L_{85}. We divide the population living to the oldest age interval, l_{85}, by the age-specific death rate for the oldest age interval, M_{85}: $L_{85} = l_{85}/M_{85}$. In this life table for males, we have $L_{85} = 133{,}917$ (which implies an age-specific death rate for males 85 and older in 1996 of 18.63 per hundred or 18.63 percent). Dividing by the last age-specific death rate, here 0.1863, roughly allows for an average of 5.4 years lived before dying for the population surviving to age 85.

The last and most comprehensive measure of mortality derived from the life table is the life expectancies, found in the last column. Let e_x indicate expectation of life at age x (i.e., the average remaining lifetime in years for a person who survives to the beginning of the indicated age

---

[6]For the first years, since more deaths occur earlier in the age intervals, the formulas are: $_1L_0 = 0.15 l_0 + 0.85 l_1$ and $_4L_1 = 4(0.4 l_1 + 0.6 l_5)$. From the life table for US females in 1996, we find:

$$_1L_0 = 0.15 \cdot 100{,}000 + 0.85 \cdot 99{,}341 = 99{,}440$$

$$_4L_1 = 4(0.4 \cdot 99{,}341 + 0.6 \cdot 99{,}207) = 397{,}042$$

which differ from the figures in Table 9.3 due to rounding error.

interval). These life expectancies are calculated from the T_x and l_x columns as follows:

$$e_x = T_x/l_x$$

For example, the life expectancy for a US male of age 40 in 1996 if subject to the prevailing age-specific deaths rates would be 35.9 years. That is, $e_{40} = 35.9 = T_{40}/l_{40} = 3,396,099/94,551$. As we see from Table 9.3, the life expectancy at birth for US males in 1996 was 73.1 years.

Selected average life expectancies for the US in 2008 are given in Table 9.1. We can see that life expectancies vary by gender and race. In the US, female life expectancies at any age exceed male life expectancies. And, at any age, white life expectancies generally exceed black, reflecting, on average, the lower incomes and education and less access to health care for minorities in the US. We do see, however, that black females at age 80 have a slightly higher life expectancy than their white counterparts.

Survival rates

We can derive **survival rates** for age groups from life tables. For any n-year age group and a T-year time period (where T is a multiple of n), the survival rate for T years is given by:

$$(_nS_x)^T = {}_nL_{x+T}/{}_nL_x$$

For example, from the abridged life table for US females in 1996, the proportion of females aged 40–45 who will survive another 5 years is given by:

$$(_5S_{40})^5 = {}_5L_{45}/{}_5L_{40} = 479,247/484,325 = 0.9895 = 98.95 \text{ percent}$$

For the 20-year survival rate for this age group, we use:

$$(_5S_{40})^{20} = {}_5L_{60}/{}_5L_{40} = 440,808/484,325 = 0.9101 = 91.01 \text{ percent.}$$

If survival from birth to the mid-point of an age interval is desired, then the formula is:

$$(S_0)^{x \text{ to } x+n} = {}_nL_x/(n \cdot l_0)$$

For example, survival from birth to the mid-point of the age interval 45–50, by which age almost all childbearing has ceased, is given by:

$$(S_0)^{45-50} = {}_5L_{45}/(5 \cdot l_0) = 479,247/(5 \cdot 100,000) = 0.9585 = 95.85 \text{ percent.}$$

Uses of a life table

As we discussed, life expectancies at any age can be derived from a life table. A commonly used indicator of mortality conditions in a population is life expectancy at birth, e_0. Independent of the age distributions of populations and applied to a single sex, life expectancies at birth are comprehensive measures of mortality rates across populations. Recall that life tables capture the experience of a hypothetical cohort if exposed to the current age-specific death rates throughout their life spans. Consequently, the derived life expectancies at birth (or any age) are synthetic measures, not actual experiences, giving the consequences of the current mortality rates.

Clearly life insurance companies use life tables to determine the premiums to charge for given death benefits. Knowing the expected number of years an individual would live after purchasing a life insurance policy (and the probabilities the annual premiums would be paid as well as the expected time before the death benefit would be paid out) is crucial for the life insurance policy. So, too, health insurance policies would be based on life tables, where, instead of mortality, morbidity or the incidence of disease would be tracked. The "life" tables calculated would be more sharply defined, not just by sex, but also by health (e.g., smokers versus nonsmokers). Car insurance companies would have "accident" life tables, tabulating the probability of car accidents, differentiated by the age of the driver, with discounts on premiums for safer drivers.

STATIONARY POPULATIONS

A **stationary population** is one whose size and age–sex distribution are constant over time. Therefore, a stationary population has zero population growth. A life table can be interpreted as a stationary population.

As a depiction of a stationary population closed to migration, the l_x values would refer to the number of persons who reach the beginning of the age interval each year (not the number in the original cohort of births surviving to the age interval). The $_nd_x$ values are the number of persons who die each year within the indicated age interval (not the number of deaths occurring between the ages of x and $x + n$ to the initial cohort of births). The $_nL_x$ values measure the number of persons in the population who at any moment are living within the indicated age interval, and the T_x values indicate the number of persons in the population who at any moment are living within the indicated age interval and all higher age intervals. The probabilities of dying, $_nq_x$, and life expectancies at each age, e_x, are the same as in the traditional interpretation of the life table.

For example, from Table 9.3, interpreting the life table for all races as a stationary population, there would be 100,000 births each year (l_0), 95,881 persons becoming 40 each year (l_{40}), and 476,549 persons aged 40–45 ($_5L_{40}$), at any point in time. Each year there would be 1,230 deaths of persons aged 40–45 ($_5d_{40}$). The total population size would be 7,611,825 (T_0), with 3,684,168 in the population aged 40 and older (T_{40}). Note that the life table could be adjusted to correspond to the size of any stationary population with this set of age-specific death rates by scaling up or down the entries. For example, suppose there were 2 million births each year, then multiplying the radix (100,000) and all the other l_x, $_nd_x$, $_nL_x$, and T_x values by 20 would scale up the life table to correspond to the stationary population with 2 million births each year.

Recall that the life expectancy at birth, e_0, is determined by the ratio of the T_0 and l_0 values. In a stationary population, T_0 indicates the population size, constant over time, and l_0 indicates the annual births. Therefore, in a stationary population, the ratio l_0 to T_0 gives the crude birth rate (CBR), which is equal to the crude death rate, since the crude rate of natural increase (CRNI = CBR − CDR) is zero. In sum, the reciprocal of life expectancy at birth in a stationary population is equal to the crude birth rate and crude death rate: $1/e_0 = l_0/T_0 = $ CBR $=$ CDR. In this example, the reciprocal of the life expectancy at birth, 76.1 years, is 0.0131, or 13.1 births and 13.1 deaths per thousand population.

Finally, we observe that, in a stationary population closed to migration, planning for the economic infrastructure (e.g., schools, hospitals, nursing homes), would be much easier, since the sizes of the school-age, potential working, and elderly populations would be constant. Allowing for immigration and emigration, however, would complicate the planning as the movement of migrants would likely affect the age–sex structure and population size over time. Nevertheless, if the global population is to become stationary in the future, then for given per capita consumptions and technologies, the demand for natural resources may more likely stabilize.

FERTILITY

As with mortality, there are a number of measures of fertility, differentiated by controls for the age–sex structure of the population. We can begin by distinguishing fecundity from fertility. **Fecundity** refers to the biological capacity to reproduce or for humans to bear children. **Fertility** refers to the realization of this potential or the actual number of children born.

In general, three factors affect fertility in a population. The first is exposure to the risk of conception, determined by the initiation and frequency of sexual unions, which in turn reflect customs with respect to marriage and sanctions on premarital and extramarital sexual activity. The second is the probability of conception. For a given exposure, the probability of conception would reflect fecundity and the incidence of effective contraception. The third factor affecting fertility is **gestation**, the carrying of the conception to term and successful birth. This, too, reflects fecundity and the health of the mother, including the incidence of miscarriages, as well as the practice of abortion.

Estimates of the biological maximum for fertility vary. If, for example, we start with a woman, marrying at age 16 and remaining fecund and married for 30 years, and if there are no fetal deaths, and if all of her babies are breastfed for one year after birth (breastfeeding acts as a natural contraceptive), then the average birth interval would be approximately 2 years and the woman would have 15 births. If we allowed for longer childbearing (e.g., earlier marriage and fertility beyond the age 45) and no breastfeeding, then the biological maximum might be half as great again. If occasional multiple births are allowed for, then the maximum would be even higher.

All societies, and almost all individuals, are well below these biological maximums. Reasons include reduced exposure to the risk of conception with later marriage, periods of sexual inactivity (e.g., with separation of partners through death, divorce, or migration) and practices which limit conception such as extended breastfeeding and the use of contraception, poor health which impairs fecundity, and unsuccessful gestation due to fetal loss and abortion.

An important concept in demography is **natural fertility**, or the fertility in a population with passive decision-making about childbearing. That is, if individuals exercised no personal discretion over the number and spacing of their children, but simply followed the prevailing social customs and traditions, then the fertility would be natural. There would be no conscious or deliberate use of birth control. Even then natural fertility would be below the biological maximums due to the social practices that evolved to limit or space fertility, including marriage traditions, breastfeeding, and sanctions against extramarital unions. Natural fertility rates, usually not observed or recorded, will vary across societies for these reasons as well as for differences in health and environment conditions. Actual fertility rates, usually recorded, will also differ across populations due to underlying differences in natural fertility as well as differences in the prevalence and effectiveness of birth control.

MEASURES OF FERTILITY

The most basic measure of fertility is the crude birth rate. Recall that, for any year, the crude birth rate is the ratio of births to the mid-point population, usually expressed per thousand mid-year population:

$$\text{CBR} = \frac{\text{Births}}{\text{Mid-year population}} = \frac{B}{P}$$

The difference between the crude birth rate and crude death rate is the crude rate of natural increase, which is used in the calculation of the population growth rate. Like the CDR, the CBR is affected by the age–sex composition of a population. Thus for comparing fertility across populations, the CBR is not the best measure. A more precise measure is the **general fertility rate**, GFR, where the denominator is the population of females aged 15–49, FP_{15-49}, corresponding to the usual reproductive period. For any year, the GFR is then

$$GFR = \frac{Births}{Mid\text{-}year\ population\ of\ females\ aged\ 15\text{--}49} = \frac{B}{FP_{15-49}}$$

In fact, the CBR can be written in terms of the GFR, as follows:

$$CBR = \frac{B}{FP_{15-49}} \cdot \frac{FP_{15-49}}{P} = GFR \cdot \frac{FP_{15-49}}{P}$$

which clearly shows that the CBR is affected by the age–sex distribution of the population. In particular, the CBR will rise (fall) for a given GFR as the share of females of childbearing years in the total population rises (falls).

As with mortality, there are age-specific fertility rates. Let $ASBR_x$ represent the **age-specific birth rate** or age-specific fertility rate for age x, where for any year,

$$ASBR_x = \frac{Births\ to\ women\ of\ age\ x}{Mid\text{-}year\ population\ of\ females\ of\ age\ x} = \frac{B_x}{FP_x}$$

The age-specific fertility rate for females between the ages of 15 through 19, $ASBR_{15-19}$, is known as the **adolescent fertility rate**. Adolescent fertility may be one of the greatest obstacles to female socioeconomic mobility. A girl having children as a teenager usually forecloses her opportunity for further education. Moreover, teenage mothers are usually less able, financially and emotionally, to care for their children. Their children, in turn, are disadvantaged, which tends to perpetuate poverty.

Total fertility rate

The total fertility rate, TFR, measures the average number of children that would be born alive to a woman if she were to live through the childbearing years and bear children according to the prevailing age-specific fertility rates. Like life expectancy at birth, the total fertility rate is a hypothetical or synthetic measure based on an assumed experience of a representative female. The total fertility rate provides a summary indicator of the consequences of a given set of age-specific fertility rates. In fact, the total fertility rate is the summation of the age-specific fertility rates ($ASBR_x$). For n-year age intervals, usually $n = 5$, the total fertility rate is equal to:

$$TFR = n \cdot \sum_{x=\alpha}^{\beta} ASBR_x$$

where α and β are the age limits for childbearing. Menarche indicates the earliest age for childbearing (here α) and menopause signals the latest age for childbearing (here β). The total fertility rate provides a useful indicator of fertility across populations since, like life expectancy at birth, it is independent of the age–sex distribution of the population.

If each generation of parents is having just enough children to replace themselves, then we have **replacement-level fertility**. For high-income or developed economies, a total fertility rate of slightly more than 2, or between 2.05 and 2.1, indicates replacement-level fertility. A TFR slightly greater than 2 would be required simply because not all women survive from birth through the childbearing years as assumed by the total fertility rate.[7] For example, from the life table for US females in 1996 (Table 9.3) we derived the survival rate from birth through age interval 45–49 as 95.85 percent, $(S_0)^{45-50} = {}_5L_{45}/(5 \cdot l_0) = 479,247/500,000 = 0.9585$. Consequently the replacement level TFR for the US would be near 2.1.

For low-income and developing economies replacement-level fertility may imply a total fertility rate between 2.3 and 2.5. For example, from a life table for India for females in 2008, the derived survival rate for females from birth through the age interval 45–50 is 0.847 or 84.7 percent.[8] For populations with even higher mortality, the replacement-level fertility would be even greater.

If maintained, then in the long run replacement-level fertility will result in a crude rate of natural increase of zero. We will see, however, that reaching replacement-level fertility does not result in a zero crude rate of natural increase in the short run, indeed for quite some time, due to the phenomenon of population momentum.

Table 9.4 illustrates the common pattern of age-specific fertility rates by age. Three sets of age-specific fertility rates are shown: for Panama in 1960, and for the United States in 1960 and 2000. We see that peak fertility occurs in the twenties. For example, the age-specific fertility rate of 258.1 for 20–24-year-olds in the US in 1960 means that there were on average 258 births over the year per thousand women aged 20–24. The age-specific fertility rates in 1960 for Panama (a developing economy) are uniformly higher than for the US (a few years after the peak of the baby boom). And, in comparing the uniformly higher age-specific fertility rates for the US in 1960 with 2000, we do notice a shift rightward in the peak fertility in the latter year, indicating the general rise in the age of marriage and delay in childbearing in the US over the past few decades.

Table 9.5 provides selected statistics on fertility for the nations grouped by per capita incomes and then by region. We see differences across the income groups, with, in general, fertility rates declining with income. The averages, however, mask the diversity across nations, as indicated by the ranges for the measures. We note that the average total fertility rates are below replacement level for the high-income and upper middle-income economies. In fact, in 2010, 63 nations, including all the developed economies of Western Europe, Canada, Japan, and Australia, most of the former socialist economics of Eastern Europe and republics of the former Soviet Union, and numerous developing economies (e.g., Brazil, China, Cuba, Iran, Thailand, and Trinidad and Tobago) had TFRs of 2.1 or less. As shown earlier in Table 2.4, 15 nations had negative crude rates of natural increase in 2010—mostly the former socialist economies of Eastern Europe and republics of the former Soviet Union, but also Germany, Italy, and Japan. As will be discussed in the next chapter, China's low total fertility rate of 1.6 in 2010 reflects an authoritarian birth control policy. The US, with a TFR of 2.1, has replacement-level fertility, but its adolescent fertility rate is nearly twice as high as the average for high-income economies.

High fertility is reflected in young populations. From the earlier Table 9.2 on mortality, we can note that the share of populations under age 15 in the low-income nations averages 39 percent in 2010, more than twice the average of 17 percent for the high-income economies. On the other hand, the shares of the elderly population aged 65 and older in the totals average 16 percent in the high-income economies and only 4 percent in the low-income economies.

---

[7] Another more technical reason why replacement-level fertility is not a total fertility rate of exactly 2.0 is that the sex ratio at birth, or male babies per 100 female babies born, exceeds 100, and is usually around 105 or 106 in developed economies.

[8] See World Health Organization (WHO) life tables for WHO member states at http://www.who.int/healthinfo/statistics/mortality_life_tables/en/.

Table 9.4 *Age-specific birth rates and the total fertility rate (TFR)*

Age interval	Panama (1960) $ASBR_x$	United States (1960) $ASBR_x$	United States (2000) $ASBR_x$
15–19	138.9	90.2	49.4
20–24	308.1	258.1	112.3
25–29	289.9	197.4	121.4
30–34	198.6	112.7	94.1
35–39	129.1	56.2	40.4
40–44	41.2	15.5	7.9
45–49	8.6	0.9	0.5
$TFR = 5 \cdot \sum_{15-19}^{45-49} ASBR_x$	5.6	3.7	2.1

Notes:

$$ASBR_x = \frac{\text{Births to women in age interval } x \text{ during the year}}{\text{Population of women in age interval } x \text{ at mid-year}}$$

The age-specific birth rates ($ASBR_x$) are expressed per thousand women of age interval x:
The age interval 15–19 also includes the fertility of younger age intervals.
The total fertility rate (TFR) is expressed as the number of children per woman.

Sources: Shryock and Siegel (1975: 473), for Panama and US 1960 birth rates; US Department of Commerce, Bureau of the Census, *Statistical Abstract of the United States 2002* (122nd edition), 2002, p. 60, for US 2000 birth rates.

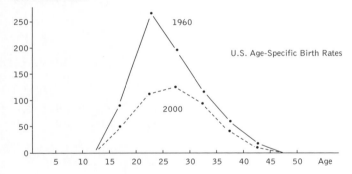

The use of contraception increases with income (and education), accounting for, in large part, the declines in fertility with economic growth. The percentages of pregnant women receiving prenatal care and births attended by skilled health staff also rise with income. In 2008, on average, one in 39 women in the low-income economies were likely to die in a pregnancy or childbirth over their lifetimes—one hundred times the rate for women in high-income economies. The much greater incidence of maternal mortality reflects not just lower incomes and inferior public health care, but the higher fertility rates in the low-income nations.

Perusing the fertility statistics from Table 9.5 also reveals significant differences across the regions of the developing world. Note that the average crude birth rates in 2010 for Europe and Central Asia and for East Asia and the Pacific are respectively 15 and 14 (per thousand population), although the total fertility rate in the former region is slightly lower, reflecting an older population. The average adolescent fertility rate in Latin America and Caribbean is twice that in the Middle East and North Africa, despite its significantly lower total fertility rate. The relatively poor health care afforded to women (reflected in percentages of pregnant women receiving prenatal care and

243

births attended by skilled health staff) in sub-Saharan Africa and South Asia is evidenced by high maternal mortality. In short, fertility is influenced not just by income, but also by culture and public policy.

Gross and net reproduction rates

Other measures of fertility include the gross reproduction rate and net reproduction rate. The former modifies the total fertility rate by including only daughters born. That is, the **gross reproduction rate** (GRR) is the average number of daughters born to a woman if she lived through the childbearing years and were subject to the age-specific birth rates currently prevailing. For any year,

$$\text{GRR} = n \cdot \sum_{x=\alpha}^{\beta} \frac{\text{Female births to women of age } x}{\text{Mid-year population of females of age } x} = \sum_{x=\alpha}^{\beta} \text{ASBR}_x^f$$

Table 9.5 *Selected statistics on fertility*

	WORLD	Low	Lower Middle	India	Upper Middle	China	High	US
			ECONOMIES BY INCOME CLASSIFICATION					
Crude birth rate, 2010	20	33	24	22	14	12	12	14
Max. 49 (Niger)								
Min. 8 (Germany)								
Adolescent fertility rate, 2010	53	94	68	79	29	9	18	33
Max. 199 (Niger)								
Min. 1 (N. Korea)								
Total fertility rate, 1990	3.2	5.7	4.2	3.9	2.6	2.3	1.8	2.1
2010	2.5	4.1	2.9	2.6	1.8	1.6	1.8	2.1
Max. 7.1 (Niger)								
Min. 1.1 (Bosnia and Herzegovina)								
Contraceptive prevalence rate, 2005–10	62%	34%	50%	54%	81%	85%	...	79%
Max. 88% (Norway)								
Min. 5% (Chad)								
% pregnant women with prenatal care, 2005–10	84%	69%	78%	75%	94%	92%	...	...
Max. 100% (10 countries)								
Min. 26% (Somalia)								
% births attended by staff, 2005–10	66%	44%	57%	53%	98%	99%	...	...
Max. 100% (32 nations)								
Min. 6% (Ethiopia)								
Lifetime maternal mortality risk, 2008	140	39	100	140	880	1,500	3,900	2,100
Max. 11 (Afghanistan)								
Min. 31,800 (Greece)								

■ **Table 9.5** continued

	ECONOMIES BY REGION						
	Sub-Saharan Africa	Middle East & N. Africa	Europe & Central Asia	South Asia	East Asia & Pacific	Latin America & Caribbean	High Income Economies
Crude birth rate, 2010	37	23	15	23	14	19	12
Adolescent fertility rate, 2010	108	37	27	73	19	72	18
Total fertility rate, 1990	6.2	4.9	2.3	4.2	2.6	3.2	1.8
2010	4.9	2.7	1.8	2.7	1.8	2.2	1.8
Contraceptive prevalence rate, 2005-10	22%	62%	69%	51%	78%	75%	...
% Pregnant women with prenatal care, 2005-10	74%	85%	...	71%	92%	97%	...
% births attended by staff, 2005-10	46%	81%	98%	48%	91%	90%	...
Lifetime maternal mortality risk, 2008	31	380	1,700	110	580	480	3,900

Notes: Crude birth rate is the number of births occurring during the year per 1,000 population at mid-year.

Adolescent fertility rate is the number of births per 1000 women aged 15–19.

Total fertility rate is the number of children that would be born to a woman if she were to live to the end of the childbearing years and bear children in accordance with current age-specific fertility rates.

Contraceptive prevalence rate is the percentage of women aged 15–49 married or in union who are practicing, or whose sexual partners are practicing, any form of contraception.

Pregnant women receiving prenatal care is the percentage attended to at least once during pregnancy by skilled health personnel for reasons related to pregnancy. Data are for the most recent year available.

Births attended by skilled health staff are the percentage of deliveries attended by personnel trained to give the necessary care to women during pregnancy, labor, and post-partum; to conduct deliveries on their own; and to care for newborns. Data are for the most recent year available.

Lifetime risk of maternal death is the probability (expressed as one in the number of women likely to die due to a maternal cause) that a 15-year-old girl will eventually die due to a maternal cause, if throughout her lifetime she experiences the maternal death risk and overall fertility and mortality rates of the specified year for a given population.

Source: World Bank (2012: Tables 2.1 and 2.19).

where ASBR_x^f is the female age-specific birth rate at age x. An approximation of the GRR is the product of the TFR and the share of total births that are female:

$$\mathrm{GRR} \approx \mathrm{TFR} \cdot \frac{\text{Female births}}{\text{Total births}}$$

Since the sex ratio at birth may vary with the age of the mother, this is only an approximation.

Like the TFR, the GRR assumes that the representative female lives through the childbearing years, surviving through age interval 45–49. A more precise measure of fertility that incorporates the survival rates of the females is the **net reproduction rate** (NRR). The NRR measures the average number of daughters born per woman and surviving to the age of their mothers, given the current age-specific birth rates and survival rates. For any year,

$$\mathrm{NRR} = n \cdot \sum_{x=\alpha}^{\beta} (\mathrm{ASBR}_x^f) \cdot (S_0)^{x \text{ to } x+n}$$

where $(S_0)^{x \text{ to } x+n} = {}_nL_x/(n \cdot l_0)$ is the survival rate for females from birth to age interval x to $x+n$. Replacement-level fertility in any population would be a net reproduction rate of exactly one, NRR $= 1.0$. This means that the women of each generation are just replacing themselves with their daughters, or the average woman is being survived by one daughter. A NRR greater than (less than) 1 indicates above (below) replacement-level fertility, which if maintained would result in a positive (negative) crude rate of natural increase.

To illustrate the various demographic statistics, Table 9.6 compares measures for Japan and India. Although the crude death rates for 2005–10 are similar for the two countries, India has a much higher crude birth rate and consequently higher crude rate of natural increase. India had net out-migration, while Japan had net in-migration, over the period. The estimated population growth rates for India and Japan for 2005–10 were 1.43 percent and 0.02 percent, respectively, with implied doubling times of 48 years and 3,465 years. With a total fertility rate of 2.73, India was still a half a child above replacement-level fertility, while Japan with a TFR of 1.32 was well below replacement-level fertility, which if maintained would result in depopulation. The corresponding net reproduction rates are slightly less than half of the total fertility rates since the natural sex ratio at birth, that is, the ratio of male to female births, is usually around 1.05. Japan, a high income economy, had the highest female life expectancy at birth in the world 2005–10 at 86.1 years, more than 20 years greater than India's.

To illustrate the sensitivity of the crude birth rate to the age distribution, compare the Netherlands with Iran. As shown in Table 9.7, although having nearly identical total fertility rates in 2010, Iran's crude birth rate is half as high (17.7) compared to that of the Netherlands (11.3), which reflects Iran's younger population. Females between the ages of 15 and 49 make up 30.5 percent of the population in Iran, but only 23.1 percent in the Netherlands. A high-income European nation, Netherlands has maintained below replacement-level fertility over the past few decades. In fact, the total fertility rate in Netherlands in 1980 was 1.6. (In the next chapter, we will discuss trends in European fertility.) Iran, a Middle Eastern nation with a per capita income (in PPP dollars) in 2010 of $11,500, which is only about a quarter of that of the Netherlands, has nevertheless experienced one of the most dramatic declines in fertility in the world. As recently as 1980, Iran's total fertility rate was 6.7. This fertility rate steadily fell to 4.8 in 1990, to 2.6 in 2000, and to 1.7 in 2010.[9] Roudi-Fahmi and Kent (2007: 10) refer to "a veritable contraceptive revolution in North Africa and Iran in the 1990s." In this region of the world, strong cultural traditions of early marriage and large families have been eroded in recent decades by education, especially for females, delayed marriage, and increased adoption of family planning. In fact, the contraceptive prevalence rate in Iran (79 percent of married women aged 15–49 in 2005–10) exceeded that of Netherlands (69 percent).[10]

Period and cohort measures of fertility

A period measure of fertility is affected not only by the decisions of the women with respect to desired family size, but also by the timing of the fertility and the spacing of children. The CBR, GFR, ASBRs, TFR, GRR, and NRR are all period measures which can be influenced by varying socioeconomic conditions, since each is calculated for a specific period in time or a selected year.

---

[9] The historical data on the total fertility rates for 1980 and 2000 come from World Bank (2012: Table 2.17). For 1990 and 2010, the total fertility rates are from World Bank (2012: Table 2.19).

[10] Roudi-Fahmi and Kent (2007) provide a good overview of population trends in this region of the world. The contraceptive prevalence rates for 2005–10 are from World Bank (2012: Table 2.19).

Table 9.6 *Selected demographic statistics: India and Japan, 2005–10*

	India	Japan
Crude birth rate (CBR)	23.1	8.6
Crude death rate (CDR)	8.3	8.8
Net migration rate (NMR)	−0.5	0.4
Population growth rate	14.3	0.2
($r_t = CBR_t - CDR_t + NMR_t$)	(1.43%)	(0.02%)
Population doubling time (years)	48	3,465
Total fertility rate	2.73	1.32
Net reproduction rate	1.17	0.64
Female life expectancy at birth (years)	65.7	86.1

Source: United nations, department of economic and social affairs, *World Population Prospects, the 2010 Revision* (http://esa.un.org/wpp/unpp/panel_population.htm).

Table 9.7 *Selected demographic statistics: Netherlands and Iran, 2005–10*

	Netherlands	Iran
Crude birth rate	11.3	17.7
Total fertility rate	1.74	1.77
Net reproduction rate	0.84	0.82
Female life expectancy at birth (years)	82.2	73.9
Share of female population aged 15–49	23.1%	30.5%
Median age, 2010 (years)	40.7	27.1

Source: United Nations, Department of Economic and Social Affairs, *World Population Prospects, the 2010 Revision* (http://esa.un.org/wpp/unpp/panel_population.htm).

In contrast, a cohort measure records the historical experience of a given population, covering many years or the entire life span. A cohort measure of fertility is **children ever born** (CEB), defined as the average number of children ever born alive to a woman after the completion of her childbearing years. Recall that the TFR is based on a synthetic cohort, not the record of completed fertility for an actual cohort. As such, the TFR may vary over time due to the timing of births with changes in the age of marriage and variable economic conditions.

A widely cited example is from Japan. The TFR in Japan dropped sharply from 2.0 in 1965 to 1.5 in 1966, before recovering to 2.0 again in 1967. Why was there this one-year decline of 25 percent in the TFR? In Japanese culture, 1966 was a "Year of the Fiery Horse," which was widely believed to be inauspicious for daughters to be born. According to superstition, girls born in the Year of the Fiery Horse, occurring once every 60 years, have a tendency to murder their husbands. Thus, it appears that in 1966, parents delayed childbearing to avoid having a daughter who might be difficult to marry off. Sixty years before, in 1906, without the benefit of modern contraception, the Japanese birth rate also took a one-year dip (Weeks 1996: 154).[11] Clearly,

---

[11] Weeks also notes that in the Chinese calendar the Years of the Dragon (e.g., 1976, 1988, 2000) are auspicious and have resulted in upticks in fertility rates. Hanson (2012) notes that the ratio of girl to boy babies born in 1966 in Japan hit a historic low, implying the selective use of abortion. Japan's baby boom after World War II was short-lived (1947–49) but intense, with the total fertility rate exceeding 4. By the mid-1950s, Japanese fertility had fallen to near replacement level. While a baby

using the TFR for a Year of the Fiery Horse would not be a good indicator of completed fertility in cultures subscribing to this belief.

AGE–SEX STRUCTURE OF A POPULATION

As discussed, the age–sex structure of a population can affect the crude measures of fertility and mortality, as well as migration. Age-specific death, birth, and net migration rates vary between the sexes and across age intervals. So, too, we find different propensities for saving and committing crime across age intervals, so aggregate saving rates and crime rates are affected by the age distribution of the populations.

Population pyramids

Population pyramids are a widely used method for graphically illustrating the age–sex structure of a population. The vertical axis represents age (or age intervals) and the horizontal axis, with males on the left and females on the right, measures the sizes (or percentages) of the populations in that age interval. Figure 9.1 shows examples of the three basic shapes of the population pyramid.[12]

The population pyramid for Nigeria, a resource-rich, sub-Saharan African nation, in 2010, is **expansive**, indeed shaped like a pyramid. The high rates of fertility in Nigeria yield a "young population," with a high percentage of the population under age 15, reflected in the wide base to the population pyramid. Fertility in Nigeria has always been well above replacement level.

The second basic shape for a population pyramid is illustrated by the United States in 2010, with more of a rectangular shape, like the side of a house. With a fairly uniform age distribution, until narrowing at the older ages, the US population pyramid is approaching a **stationary** shape. The bulge in the 45–64 age intervals reflects the post-World War II baby boom cohorts born between 1946 and 1964. The profound effects of the baby boom generation on the US population and economy will be discussed in Chapter 10. The United States is relatively open to immigration, which also affects the age–sex structure of the population. If a total fertility rate of 2.1 is maintained, the US population, outside of net migration, will eventually assume a constant stationary shape.

The third basic shape for a population pyramid is **constrictive**, as illustrated by Italy in 2010. In Italy, fertility has been well below replacement level (TFR < 2.1) for several decades, reflected in the narrower base and low percentage of the population under age 15. A constrictive population pyramid may be likened to a cupcake. Italy also experienced a post-World War II baby boom, albeit with a delay. The peak total fertility rate for Italy of 2.5 occurred in the second half of the 1960s, versus a peak total fertility rate for the US of 3.7 in the latter half of the 1950s; see the three extended bars for the 35–49 age intervals in the 2010 population pyramid for Italy. By the end of the 1970s, however, Italy's TFR had declined to under 2, where it has remained. The US TFR

boomlet, or echo of the earlier brief baby boom, took place in Japan in 1971–74, Japanese total fertility rates have remained low, resulting in an aging population, rising elderly burden of dependency, and potential depopulation.

[12] The US Census Bureau website (http://www.census.gov/population/international) provides a wealth of international demographic data, including population pyramids for countries. See the International Data Base and scroll down to Population Pyramid Graph under the Select Report window. You can then choose your country and year for the population pyramid. The population pyramids for 2010 for Nigeria, United States, and Italy in Figure 9.1 and for China and Germany in Figure 9.2 are from this web site. See http://www.census.gov/population/international/data/idb/informationGateway.php.

fell below 2 in the second half of the 1970s, but then rebounded to replacement level. Note that between 1980 and 2010, Nigeria's population increased by 120 percent, while Italy's did not even grown by 10 percent. If fertility rates remain below replacement level, then Italy faces future depopulation, barring offsetting inflows of immigrants.

Dependency rates

To quantify the age composition of a population, dependency rates are used. The **youth burden of dependency** (YBD) is the ratio of the population under age 15 to the population aged 15–64. The **elderly burden of dependency** (EBD) is the ratio of the population 65 and older to the population aged 15–64. The total **burden of dependency** (BD) is the sum of the youth and elderly burdens, and gives in a rough sense the ratio of net consumers (dependants) to net producers (workers) in a population:

$$BD = YBD + EBD = \frac{\text{Pop } (0-14)}{\text{Pop } (15-64)} + \frac{\text{Pop } (65+)}{\text{Pop } (15-64)} = \frac{\text{Pop } (0-14) + \text{Pop } (65+)}{\text{Pop } (15-64)}$$

Usually the burdens of dependency are expressed per hundred population aged 15–64.

For nations with high fertility and expansive population pyramids, the youth burdens of dependency will be high (e.g., 70 or more children under age 15 per hundred population in the prime labor force years). Consequently, the demands on households for feeding, clothing, and caring for these young dependents are significant, as are the social welfare expenditures for education. Often found in low-income nations, high youth burdens of dependency hinder the ability to generate savings for the investment needed for the human and physical capital deepening important for economic growth. Moreover, low per capita incomes and high youth burdens of dependency constrain the income tax revenues which could have been used for public spending on education and health care as well as the physical infrastructure (e.g., transportation and communications networks, public utilities providing power, water, and sanitation) important for improving labor productivities.

On the other hand, nations with low fertility rates, especially if below replacement levels, will have relatively high elderly burdens of dependency (e.g., 20 or more seniors aged 65 years or older per hundred population in the prime labor force years). For these nations with older populations, the burden on the economy will be in providing for social security and health care for the elderly. Moreover, after retirement, individuals begin to dissave, drawing down their wealth to cover their consumption since they are no longer earning income. Just as high youth burdens of dependency can depress savings and investment, so too can high elderly burdens of dependency. Recall the concerns of the macroeconomists in the 1930s with the low rates of population growth and aging of the populations in the industrialized or developed nations.

For the three countries depicted in Figure 9.1, the burdens of dependency for 2010 are given in Table 9.8. Nigeria has nearly 80 children under age 15 for every hundred population of labor force age. For Italy, the youth burden of dependency is 21 children for every hundred population in the prime working years. Because of its prolonged low fertility, however, Italy's elderly burden of dependency, 30 persons aged 65 years or older per hundred persons aged 15–64, is greater than its youth burden of dependency. The US's overall burden of dependency is slightly lower than Italy's, although the composition is quite different, reflecting the younger US population.

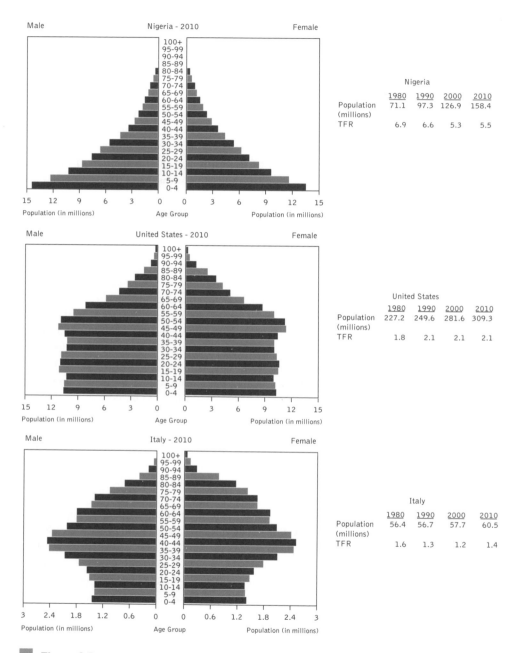

Figure 9.1 *Population pyramids in 2010*

*From: For Population Pyramids: US Census Bureau, http://www.census.gov/ipc/www/idb/ coun-
try.php. For Population statistics and total fertility rates: World Bank, World Development
Indicators 2002 (Tables 2.1, 2.17), World Development Indicators 2012 (Tables 2.1, 2.19).*

Table 9.8 *Selected statistics on age distribution, 2010*

	Nigeria	United States	Italy
% population aged 0–14	43	20	14
% population aged 15–64	54	67	66
% population aged 65+	3	13	20
Youth burden of dependency	79.6	29.9	21.2
Elderly burden of dependency	5.6	19.4	30.3
Total burden of dependency	85.2	49.3	51.5
Share of labor force in population	31.8%	50.9%	41.5%
Population momentum in 2000	1.5	1.2	0.9

Notes: Population momentum is an estimate of the ratio of the future population size once stabilized, i.e., with a crude rate of natural increase of zero, to the initial population size in 2000, if the population had attained a replacement level fertility in 2000 and had then maintained this rate of fertility.

Sources: World Bank (2000: Table 2.2; 2012: Tables 2.1 and 2.2).

Demographic dividend

We noted in Chapter 1 how, for a given average product of labor (Y/L), per capita income (Y/P) would rise with a rise in the share of the population in the labor force (L/P). That is, $y = (Y/P) = (Y/L) \cdot (L/P)$. With economic development, birth rates tend to decline and nations can experience a demographic dividend for economic growth. The decline in fertility, *ceteris paribus*, will reduce the youth burden of dependency, freeing up resources that would have been used to provide for the children who would have been born had fertility rates not declined. Thus, additional productive investment in human and physical capital can be realized. The increases in human and physical capital–labor ratios will increase labor productivities. Per capita incomes will also be higher since the population size will be lower than if fertility rates had been constant.

Moreover, with the fall in fertility the share of the population in the working years, roughly between the ages of 15 and 64, will rise, at least for two decades. This favorable decline in the YBD and rise in (L/P) will accompany falling fertility for several decades, before the elderly burden of dependency begins to rise (although not so much as to offset the lower YBD for some time). And if fertility rates fall to below replacement level, there will be not only a decline in population and labor force growth rates, but eventually depopulation and decreases in labor forces, unless offset by immigration.

The burdens of dependency, however, are rough measures of the "drag" of the age structure of the population on economic growth, since in developing economies, labor force participation may start well before age 15 so that working children are net producers, not net consumers. In developed economies, children tend to stay in school well beyond age 15, and remain net dependants often into their twenties. So, too, not all in the populations in the prime labor force years will be economically active, much less productively employed. On the other hand, individuals may retire before, as well as work beyond, age 65. Nevertheless, the demographic dividend accompanying the transition to lower fertility has been important for economic growth.

Table 9.8 gives the shares of the labor force in population for 2010 for the three nations highlighted. The US has the highest share of the labor force in population at 50.9 percent. Italy, with a 41.5 percent share, has largely exhausted its demographic dividend with its high elderly burden of dependency. Nigeria, on the other hand, will not reap its demographic dividend until its fertility declines. With total fertility rates still above 5, the share of the labor force in Nigeria's population in 2010 was only 31.8 percent.

Population momentum

An important consideration in demography is population momentum. Even if a nation with previous high fertility, evidenced in an expansive population pyramid, attains replacement-level fertility (recall that this is approximately a total fertility rate of 2.1 and exactly a net reproduction rate of 1.0), its population would tend to increase in size for some time before finally stabilizing with a zero crude rate of natural increase. Imagine a truck speeding along a highway. Even if the driver slams on the brakes, the truck will continue forward, skidding for some time down the highway. How long before the truck stops after the brakes are applied depends on how fast the truck was going when the driver hit the brakes.

Population momentum is measured as the ratio of the future population size once it is finally stabilized to the initial population size when replacement-level fertility began. For nations with expansive population pyramids, even if the current generation of parents (i.e., the population in the childbearing years) adopts replacement-level fertility, the future size of the population will be greater since the children already born (who will be surviving to the childbearing years, just replacing their parents), will still exceed in number the older population dying off. That is, for sometime after NRR = 1, the CBR will exceed the CDR, yielding a positive CRNI. The concept of population momentum applies to a closed population. As noted, migration into or from a population will also affect population size for a given CRNI.

Box 9.1 illustrates population momentum with a simple example for a closed female population where the mortality rate is 100 percent once a generation becomes grandparents. Here the population size increases after the onset of replacement-level fertility (NRR = 1) with the third generation (C daughters) for another generation—as the generation of grandparents dying off (generation 2 or the Bs) is smaller than the generation of children born (generation 4 or the Ds). Thus the CBR exceeds the CDR and despite replacement-level fertility, population momentum increases the size of the population from 6 to 8 for another generation until it stabilizes. Here the population momentum is 8/6 = 1.33.

In Table 9.8 we see that Nigeria's population momentum in 2000 was estimated to be 1.5. That is, even if Nigeria had attained replacement-level fertility (NRR = 1) in 2000 and maintained this rate thereafter, its population would continue to grow, increasing by 50 percent above its population size in 2000, before stabilizing likely several generations in the future. The US, despite being at replacement-level fertility in 2000, still has some population momentum (20 percent), largely due to the baby boom generation. The US population will likely continue to increase more than indicated by the population momentum even if replacement-level fertility is maintained because of net immigration. Population momentum can be negative, as illustrated by Italy in 2000. Negative population momentum means that if the fertility rate were to increase to replacement level (NRR = 1) and thereafter be maintained, the size of the population would decrease in the long run before stabilizing. Here, if Italy's net reproduction rate had increased from 0.9 to 1.0 in 2000, the future size of the population in Italy, without regard to migration, would be 10 percent lower, or only 90 percent of the population in 2000.

The importance of understanding the phenomenon of population momentum should be clear. Even if the world were to attain replacement-level fertility tomorrow, the future size of the world's population when growth ceased would likely be nearly half again its present size. While the developed countries are (and have been for some time) below replacement-level fertility, many developing nations are well above replacement-level fertility, so the world is far from attaining a net reproduction rate of unity. We will address the trends in fertility in both the developed and developing nations in the next chapter.

BOX 9.1: Simple Illustration of Population Momentum

The net reproduction rate (NRR) measures the average number of daughters (per woman) that would be born and survive to the age of their mothers, given the current age-specific birth rates and survival rates:

$$NRR = n \cdot \sum_{x=\alpha}^{\beta} f_x \cdot (_n L_x / n \cdot l_0)$$

$$f_x = \text{female age-specific birth rate} = \frac{\text{female births to women of age } x}{\text{mid-point population of women of age } x}$$

$_n L_x / n \cdot l_0$ = survival rate from birth to the mid-point of the age interval x to $x + n$

Example: Consider a female population with no mortality until the grandparent generation, when ASDR = 1,000 (or 100%). Begin with an initial female A, who has two daughters, B and B (NRR = 2.0).

Generation	NRR		Births	Deaths	Population size
1		A			1 (generation 1)
	2.0	/\	2	0	
2		B B			3 (generations 1 and 2)
	2.0	/| |\	4	1 (A)	
3		C C C C			6 (generations 2 and 3)
	1.0	||| ||	4	2 (B,B)	
4		D D D D			8 (generations 3 and 4)
	1.0	||| ||	4	4 (C,C,C,C)	
5		E E E E			8 (generations 4 and 5)

Here, the onset of replacement-level fertility (NRR = 1.0) occurs with generation 3 (each woman C has one daughter, D), but the population size continues to increase for one more generation, since the number of births (D,D,D,D) exceeds the number of deaths (B,B) with the fourth generation, due to population momentum. That is, as long as NRR > 1.0, the generations will increase in size, building population momentum.

Demographic history

Before turning to population projections, however, we should note that population pyramids reflect a nation's demographic history and may have more irregular shapes than the three generic shapes of expansive, stationary, and constrictive. Figure 9.2 illustrates population pyramids for Germany and China in 2010. The Malthusian positive and preventative checks to population growth operating through higher death rates and lower birth rates, respectively, are evident.

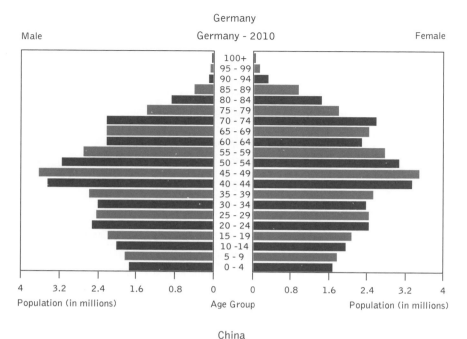

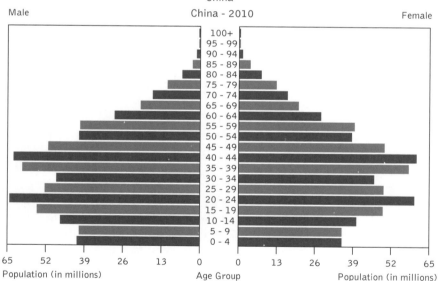

2010	TFR	CBR	CDR	Average annual population growth rates	
				2000–10	2010–20 (projected)
Germany	1.4	8	11	−0.1	−0.2
China	1.6	12	7	0.6	0.3

Figure 9.2 *Population pyramids for Germany and China*

From: World Bank, World Development Indicators 2012 (Tables 2.1, 2.19). For Population Pyramids: US Census Bureau, http://www.census.gov/ipc/www/idb/country/php.

The German population pyramid is basically constrictive, due to maintaining fertility rates well below replacement level over the last four decades. For the cohorts before World War II, who are aged 70 and over in 2010, however, the population pyramid is fairly expansive. The marked imbalance of females over males for the 80 and older population, in addition to the usually higher male death rates, reflect the heavy German male casualties from World War II. Like the United States, Germany experienced a baby boom, although the cohort born right after hostilities ceased, between 1945 and 1950 (aged 60–64 in 2010), was quite small. The German baby boom is evidenced in the bulge in the middle of the population pyramid, the cohorts (aged 40–54 in 2010) born between 1955 and 1970. Fertility rates fell sharply in the 1970s and have remained low, contributing to the aging of the German population and negative population momentum.

For China, the population pyramid in 2010 is also constrictive, but more irregular. Like Germany, China's total fertility rate is well below replacement level; yet, because of China's earlier high fertility, China still has some population momentum. Compare the positive crude rate of natural increase in 2010 for China of 5 (per thousand) with Germany's of −3 (per thousand). We can see an indentation in the Chinese population pyramid for the age group 50–54 in 2010. This largely reflects the famine that accompanied the economic dislocation of China's Great Leap Forward strategy of decentralized industrialization in the late 1950s. An estimated 30 million Chinese perished from the famine between 1958 and 1961. Not only did the mortality rate soar, but also the birth rate plummeted. Chinese fertility rates rebounded in the early 1960s, alarming the government, which feared China would not be able to feed its much greater future population. Consequently China adopted a strict birth control policy, culminating in the "one-child campaign" at the end of the 1970s. In short, the authoritarian government has attempted to impose negative population momentum. The subsequent decline in the fertility rate is evident in the narrowing of the base of the population pyramid. The relative bulge for the birth cohorts of 1980–95 (population aged 15–29 in 2010) reflects the population momentum from earlier baby boom in the 1960s and early 1970s.[13] The most recent birth cohorts, born in 2000–10, represented by the bottom two bars, illustrates the well below replacement-level fertility rates in contemporary China. China's population policy will be discussed in greater detail in Chapter 10.

Aging of a population

Fertility is the main determinant of the age structure of a population, barring unusual volumes of migration concentrated in certain age intervals (e.g., retirees moving to Florida). We can measure the age of a population by the median age (which divides the population in half, so that 50 percent are older and 50 percent younger). And we can measure the mean or average age of the population. More generally, we can measure the percentages of youth (e.g., under age 15) and elderly (65 years and over). High fertility produces a young population, reflected in an expansive population pyramid, a high youth burden of dependency, and low median and average ages. Low fertility produces an old population, reflected in a stationary or constrictive population pyramid, a high elderly burden of dependency, and high median and average ages.

The median age of the US population fell from 30.0 years in 1950 to 28.2 years in 1970, reflecting the baby boom, and then steadily increased to 35.3 years by 2000. The projected median age of the US population in 2050 is 40.0 years.[14] This projection, of course, is contingent upon

---

[13] For a good overview of China's population policy, see Riley (2004).

[14] See United Nations Department of Economic and Social Affairs, "World Population Prospects, the 2010 Revision", http://esa.un.org/wpp/unpp/panel_indicators.htm.

Table 9.9 US aged-to-child ratio, 1940–2010

| Year | Population (thousands) | | ACR |
	Under 16 years	65 years and over	
1940	35,390	9,031	25.5
1970	61,982	20,107	32.4
2000	64,344	35,070	54.5
2010	65,524 (+85%)	40,438 (+348%)	61.7 (+142%)

Source: Council of economic advisers (2012: Table B-34).

assumed future birth, death, and net migration rates. Below we will illustrate how to project a population.

An alternative measure of the age of a population is the **aged-to-child ratio** (ACR), defined as the ratio of the population 65 and older to the population under 16, usually expressed with a base of 100:

$$ACR = 100 \cdot \frac{\text{Population 65 and older}}{\text{Population under 16}}$$

The aged-to-child ratio increased by 142 percent in the United States between 1940 and 2010, as illustrated in Table 9.9.

The impact of mortality on the age of a population is less certain. An improvement in mortality conditions, reflected in increases in life expectancies at all ages, will have conflicting effects on the average age of the population.

First, a general increase in the survival rates will increase the number of old people, as the probability of surviving from birth to old age is greater. This would tend to age the population. For example, from life tables for US females, the survival rates from birth to age interval 65–70 increased from

$$(S_0)^{65-70} = {}_5L_{65}/(5 \cdot l_0) = 388,798/500,000 = 0.778 = 77.8 \text{ percent}$$

in 1974 to

$$(S_0)^{65-70} = {}_5L_{65}/(5 \cdot l_0) = 415,722/500,000 = 0.831 = 83.1 \text{ percent}$$

in 1988.

Second, improved survival rates would tend to increase the average age at death (e.g., the life expectancy at age 65 would rise). Using the same two life tables for US females, life expectancy at age 65 increased from 17.5 years in 1974 to 19.3 years in 1998. So not only do more births survive to age 65, but also the average number of years lived after age 65 increases, which also contributes to an older population.

Yet, with the general improvement in mortality conditions, the number of women from a given cohort surviving through the childbearing years will rise, and, for given age-specific fertility rates, the net reproduction rate will increase, leading to a younger population. That is, the survival rate for females from birth to the age interval 45–50 will increase. From 1974 to 1998, For example, the survival rate for US women from birth through the childbearing years increased from

$$(S_0)^{45-50} = {}_5L_{45}/(5 \cdot l_0) = 468,594/500,000 = 0.937 = 93.7 \text{ percent}$$

in 1974 to

$$(S_0)^{45-50} = {}_5L_{45}/(5 \cdot l_0) = 479,843/500,000 = 0.960 = 96.0 \text{ percent}$$

in 1988.

Thus, the net effect of improved mortality on the age of the population depends. For populations with expansive pyramids, the consequences of the initial declines in mortality are usually a younger population as the initial improvements in health yield the greater increases in survivorship among the young, reflected in lower infant and under-five mortality rates. Consequently, an increased percentage of youths survive to become parents; and, for given age-specific fertility rates, the crude birth rate would rise, contributing to the increasing population growth and younger population. For developed nations with high life expectancies, further improvements in mortality would likely produce an older population, since child mortality rates are already low and a very high percentage of newborn girls survive through the childbearing years.

As we noted with the demographic transition, historically declines in mortality have preceded declines in fertility, so during the period of rapid population growth, the populations have become younger. With the completion of the demographic transition and the return to replacement-level fertility, further advances in health and reductions in mortality rates will likely result in older populations.

Stable populations

A **stable population** is one where the age–sex distribution is constant, so the shape of the population pyramid is unchanging. Consider a population closed to migration. A stable population results when the age-specific fertility and mortality rates have been constant for an extended period of time, usually for several decades. The resulting crude birth and death rates associated with a stable population are known as the intrinsic birth and death rates, $\underline{CBR}$ and $\underline{CDR}$ respectively. The intrinsic crude rate of natural increase, $\underline{CRNI}$, is the difference between the intrinsic crude birth and death rates: $\underline{CRNI} = \underline{CBR} - \underline{CDR}$. If the intrinsic crude rate of natural increase equals zero, then the stable population is also a stationary population with a net reproduction rate equal to 1.

The concept of a stable population provides a useful way to interpret current vital rates without the confounding effects of fluctuating age distributions. If you project a closed population forward assuming constant age-specific birth and death rates, you will eventually get a stable population. For purposes of economic planning (e.g., schools, hospitals, and social security systems) a stable population would have advantages.

POPULATION PROJECTION

In our discussion of population momentum, we alluded to future population sizes. We can extrapolate forward an initial total population, P_0, by simply assuming an annual growth rate, r, as in the formula for a population at time T in the future, $P_T = P_0 e^{rT}$. A richer, albeit considerably more complex, procedure for projecting a population is the **cohort component method**. The required data are an initial population by age categories and assumed age-specific birth, death, and net migration rates. Recall that age-specific death rates differ between males and females. Likewise, age-specific net migration rates differ between males and females. To illustrate the basic method with a simple example, however, we will assume a population of only females that is closed to migration. Using the cohort components method for population projections requires knowledge of matrix multiplication. Box 9.2 provides a brief tutorial on matrix multiplication.

Life table survival rates

To project populations of given age intervals forward, we use survival rates derived from life tables. For example, the population aged $(x + T)$ to $(x + T + n)$ in T years, $(_nP_{x+T})^T$, would be the beginning population aged x to $(x + n)$, $(_nP_x)^0$, times the T-year survival rate, $(_nS_x)^T$. That is, $(_nP_{x+T})^T = (_nS_x)^T \cdot (_nP_x)^0$.

To illustrate, let $(_5P_{30})^0 = 94,000$ be the initial population of females aged 30–34, and from the earlier life table for US females for 1996 we derive the 5-year survival rate for this age group as $(_5S_{30})^5 = _5L_{35}/_5L_{30} = 487,848/490,336 = 0.9949$. The projected population of females aged 35–39 in 5 years is $(_5P_{35})^5 = (_5S_{30})^5 \cdot (_5P_{30})^0 = 0.9949 \cdot 94,000 = 93,523$.

We could do this for all of the 18 age groups of the population, 0–4, 5–9, . . ., 80–84, 85+, or for additional age intervals up to the last open interval (e.g., 100+). For the last age open interval, by definition the probability of dying is 100 percent. Figure 9.3 illustrates a population projection matrix.

Using 18 age intervals, ranging from 0–4 to 85+, the initial population of females is given by the population matrix, **POP**^{0}, with 18 rows and 1 column, or a column vector with 18 elements, the initial populations in each age interval. The population of females by age in 5 years, the length of the age interval and the projection period, is given by **POP**^{5}, the column vector with 18 elements. The population projection matrix, **J**, which contains the survival rates and the fertility factors, has 18 rows and 18 columns.

We will address row 1 which contains the fertility factors shortly. First, we note that surviving forward the initial female population by age over the 5-year projection is quite straightforward. If we were to include males in the population and allow for immigration and emigration, then the task would be more complicated.[15] Nevertheless, we see that the survival rates for each age interval are listed in the diagonal right below the main diagonal of the population projection matrix. See the $(_5S_x)^5$ elements in the (2,1), (3,2), (4,3), etc. positions in the **J** matrix. Multiplying the second through 18th rows of the population projection matrix **J** by the initial population vector **POP**^{0} gives the population surviving through the projection or the population by age in 5 years, **POP**^{5}.

For example, to find the population aged 15–19 in 5 years, $(_5P_{15})^5$, in the (4,1) position in the **POP**^{5} matrix, or the fourth element in this population vector, we multiply row 4 of the **J** matrix, containing zeros except for the 5-year survival rate, $(_5S_{10})^5$, found in the third column of **J**, which corresponds to the initial population of ages 10–14, with the initial population matrix **POP**^{0}, picking up the relevant initial population $(_5P_{10})^0$, found in the third row of **POP**^{0}. That is: $(_5P_{15})^5 = (_5S_{10})^5 \cdot (_5P_{10})^0$. In matrix notation, multiplying the fourth row of the projection matrix by the first (and only) column of the initial population matrix gives the element in the (4,1) position of the final population matrix. If we look at the two population matrices in Figure 9.3, we see that the initial populations in each age interval in **POP**^{0} that survive will slide down one position in the new population matrix, **POP**^{5}. The oldest age group, 85+ years in the initial population matrix, will all die out. Note that the survival rate for this oldest age group is zero, found in the (18, 18) position of the population projection matrix.

---

[15]We would use a separate population projection for males, with male survival rates, age-specific fertility rates for male births, and the population of males by age intervals. For both the female and male populations, over any period of projection, the net migration of females and males would be added to each age interval.

Assumptions:

1. Female population only—closed to migration
2. Fertility only in ages 15-49
3. Probability of survival $= 0$ for last age interval 85+

f_x = female age-specific fertility rate for age group x to $x + n$
$(_nP_{x+T})^T$ = population aged $(x + T)$ to $(x + n + T)$ at time T
$(_nS_x)^T$ = probability of survival for T years for age group x to $(x + n) = (_nL_{x+T}/_nL_x)$

$$
\begin{bmatrix}
0 & 0 & F_1 & F_2 & \cdots & F_8 & 0 & \cdots & 0 & 0 \\
(_5S_0)^5 & 0 & 0 & 0 & \cdots & 0 & 0 & \cdots & 0 & 0 \\
0 & (_5P_5)^5 & 0 & 0 & \cdots & 0 & 0 & \cdots & 0 & 0 \\
0 & 0 & (_5P_{10})^5 & 0 & \cdots & 0 & 0 & \cdots & 0 & 0 \\
\cdot & \cdot & \cdot & \cdot & \cdots & \cdot & \cdot & \cdots & \cdot & \cdot \\
\cdot & \cdot & \cdot & \cdot & \cdots & \cdot & \cdot & \cdots & \cdot & \cdot \\
\cdot & \cdot & \cdot & \cdot & \cdots & \cdot & \cdot & \cdots & \cdot & \cdot \\
0 & 0 & 0 & 0 & \cdots & \cdot & 0 & \cdots & (_5S_{80})^5 & 0
\end{bmatrix}
\begin{bmatrix}
(_5P_0)^0 \\ (_5P_5)^0 \\ (_5P_{10})^0 \\ (_5P_{15})^0 \\ \cdot \\ \cdot \\ \cdot \\ (P_{85})^0
\end{bmatrix}
=
\begin{bmatrix}
(_5P_0)^5 \\ (_5P_5)^5 \\ (_5P_{10})^5 \\ (_5P_{15})^5 \\ \cdot \\ \cdot \\ \cdot \\ (P_{85})^5
\end{bmatrix}
$$

$$J$$
$(18 \times 18 \text{ population projection matrix})$

$$POP^0 \qquad POP^5$$
$(18 \times 1) \qquad (18 \times 1)$

Fertility factors: Initial population:

$F_1 = (_5L_0/2 \cdot l_0) \cdot (_5L_{15}/_5L_{10}) \cdot f_{15}$ 10-14
$F_2 = (_5L_0/2 \cdot l_0) \cdot [f_{15} + (_5L_{20}/_5L_{15}) \cdot f_{20}]$ 15–19
$F_3 = (_5L_0/2 \cdot l_0) \cdot [f_{20} + (_5L_{25}/_5L_{20}) \cdot f_{25}]$ 20–24
$F_4 = (_5L_0/2 \cdot l_0) \cdot [f_{25} + (_5L_{30}/_5L_{25}) \cdot f_{30}]$ 25–29
$F_5 = (_5L_0/2 \cdot l_0) \cdot [f_{30} + (_5L_{35}/_5L_{30}) \cdot f_{35}]$ 30–34
$F_6 = (_5L_0/2 \cdot l_0) \cdot [f_{35} + (_5L_{40}/_5L_{35}) \cdot f_{40}]$ 35–39
$F_7 = (_5L_0/2 \cdot l_0) \cdot [f_{40} + (_5L_{45}/_5L_{40}) \cdot f_{45}]$ 40–44
$F_8 = (_5L_0/2 \cdot l_0) \cdot f_{45}$ 45–49

Figure 9.3 Population projection

Fertility factors

Finding the population aged 0–4 in 5 years, or the births over the projection that survived is considerably more difficult. The element in the first row of the new population matrix, $(_5P_0)^5$, represents this population of surviving births. Let $(\underline{B_0})^5$ represent this population in 5 years of the births that survived over the 5-year population projection.

BOX 9.2: Brief Review of Matrix Algebra

A matrix is a rectangular array of elements (numbers or variables) enclosed in brackets. The number of rows and number of columns in a matrix define the dimension of the matrix. For example, if matrix A contains m rows and n columns, then the dimension of matrix A is m by n, written as $A_{m \times n}$ or $A_{m,n}$.

The elements of a matrix are identified by two subscripts, indicating their position in the matrix, with the first subscript indicating the row and the second subscript indicating the column of that element. For example, a_{ij} is the element in the ith row and jth column of a matrix A of m rows and n columns ($i = 1,\ldots,m$; $j = 1,\ldots,n$):

$$A_{m,n} = \begin{bmatrix} a_{11} & a_{12} & \cdots & a_{1n} \\ a_{21} & a_{22} & \cdots & a_{2n} \\ a_{31} & \cdot & \cdot & \cdots \\ \cdot & & & \\ \cdot & & & \\ a_{m1} & a_{m2} & \cdots & a_{mn} \end{bmatrix}$$

Matrix multiplication

Two matrices can be multiplied together only when the number of columns of the first (lead) matrix equals the number of rows of the second (lag) matrix.

For example, if $A_{m,n}$ and $B_{n,p}$ are two matrices, then the product matrix is $C_{m,p} = A \cdot B$. [Note that we cannot multiply in reverse order, $B \cdot A$, unless $p = m$, that is, the numbers of columns in matrix B equals the number of rows in matrix A.]

The general rule for matrix multiplication, given that the above dimensionality condition is met, is to multiply each element in row i of the lead matrix by the corresponding element in column j of the lag matrix and sum the products to get the (ith, jth) element of the product matrix.

For example, given the matrices A and B, the product matrix is $A \cdot B = C$

$$A_{2\times3} = \begin{bmatrix} a_{11} & a_{12} & a_{13} \\ a_{21} & a_{22} & a_{23} \end{bmatrix} \quad \text{and} \quad B_{3\times1} = \begin{bmatrix} b_{11} \\ b_{21} \\ b_{31} \end{bmatrix}$$

$$A \cdot B = C_{2\times1} = \begin{bmatrix} a_{11}b_{11} + a_{12}b_{21} + a_{13}b_{31} \\ a_{21}b_{11} + a_{22}b_{21} + a_{23}b_{32} \end{bmatrix} = \begin{bmatrix} c_{11} \\ c_{21} \end{bmatrix}$$

[Note how the inner subscripts match.]

$$A_{2\times3} = \begin{bmatrix} 1 & 5 & 0 \\ 2 & 3 & 1 \end{bmatrix} \quad \text{and} \quad B_{3\times1} = \begin{bmatrix} 10 \\ 8 \\ 4 \end{bmatrix}$$

$$A \cdot B = C_{2\times1} = \begin{bmatrix} (1)(10) + (5)(8) + (0)(4) \\ (2)(10) + (3)(8) + (1)(4) \end{bmatrix} = \begin{bmatrix} 50 \\ 48 \end{bmatrix}$$

To obtain the births that occurred over the 5-year interval, $(B_0)^5$, we need to take the average number of females in each age category over the childbearing years 15–49 and multiply by the female age-specific fertility rates, $ASBR_x^f$, denoted here by f_x (recall that we are only dealing with a female population):

$$(B_0)^5 = 5 \sum_{x=15}^{45} \frac{1}{2}\left[(_nP_x)^0 + (_nP_x)^5\right] \cdot f_x$$

For example, the first term, $\frac{1}{2}[(_5P_{15})^0 + (_5P_{15})^5]f_{15}$, gives the average population aged 15–19 over the 5-year interval of the projection (and thus exposed to the ASBR for 15–19-year-olds) times the ASBR for 15–19-year-olds (f_{15}).

Since the population aged $x+5$ to $x+n+5$ in 5 years, $({}_nP_{x+5})^5$, is the initial population aged x to $x+n$, that is, $({}_nP_x)^0$, that survived the 5-year projection, we can express this summation in terms of the initial population. For example, $({}_5P_{15})^5 = ({}_5S_{10})^5 \cdot ({}_5P_{10})^0$ and, in general, $({}_5P_{x+5})^5 = ({}_5S_x)^5 \cdot ({}_5P_x)^0$, so we can expand the summation for the births over the 5-year projection using these survival rates, $({}_5S_x)^5 = {}_5L_{x+5}/{}_5L_x$, to obtain:

$$(B_0)^5 = \frac{5}{2}\{[({}_5S_{10})^5 \cdot f_{15}] \cdot ({}_5P_{10})^0 + [f_{15} + ({}_5S_{15})^5 \cdot f_{20}] \cdot ({}_5P_{15})^0$$
$$+ [f_{20} + ({}_5S_{20})^5 \cdot f_{25}] \cdot ({}_5P_{20})^0 + \cdots + f_{45} \cdot ({}_5P_{45})^0\}$$

Note that we have combined like terms, i.e., the initial populations by age intervals, $({}_5P_x)^0$, and factored the $\frac{1}{2}$ out of the summation, so we have $\frac{5}{2}$ on the outside of the summation in the equation for $(B_0)^5$.

For example, on average, $({}_5P_{20})^0$, the initial population aged 20–24, is exposed to the age-specific fertility rate for 20–24-year-olds, f_{20}, for $2\frac{1}{2}$ years of the projection period, and for those who survive, given by $({}_5S_{20})^5$, to the age-specific fertility rate for 25–29-year-olds, f_{25}, for $2\frac{1}{2}$ years of the projection. The term $\frac{5}{2}[f_{20} + ({}_5S_{20})^5 \cdot f_{25}] \cdot ({}_5P_{20})^0$ gives the births contributed by this initial cohort of 20–24-year-olds over the 5-year projection. Assuming fertility begins with the 15–19 age interval and ends with the 45–49 age interval, females initially 10–14 years old surviving are only exposed to, on average, the youngest age-specific fertility rate, f_{15}, for half of the projection, or $2\frac{1}{2}$ years. And, females initially aged 45–49 would only experience, on average, the last age-specific fertility rate, f_{45}, for $2\frac{1}{2}$ years. Moreover, in the population projection, the 5-year survival rate for those females initially aged 45–49 is not relevant for the births over the projection, since there would be no fertility for females of older ages, that is, in the age intervals 50–54 and above.

Finally, to find the number of surviving births, $(\underline{B_0})^5$, we need to take into consideration the proportion of the births that survive over the projection interval, $(S_0)^{0-5} = ({}_5L_0)/(5 \cdot l_0)$. Therefore the surviving births over the 5-year projection, and the population aged 0–4 in 5 years, $({}_5P_0)^5$, is given by $(\underline{B_0})^5$:

$$(\underline{B_0})^5 = (S_0)^{0-5} \cdot (B_0)^5$$
$$= [({}_5L_0)/(2 \cdot l_0)] \cdot \{[({}_5S_{10})^5 \cdot f_{15}] \cdot ({}_5P_{10})^0 + [f_{15} + ({}_5S_{15})^5 \cdot f_{20}] \cdot ({}_5P_{15})^0$$
$$+ [f_{20} + ({}_5S_{20})^5 \cdot f_{25}] \cdot ({}_5P_{20})^0 + \cdots + f_{45} \cdot ({}_5P_{45})^0\}$$
$$= F_1 \cdot ({}_5P_{10})^0 + F_2 \cdot ({}_5P_{15})^0 + F_3 \cdot ({}_5P_{20})^0 + \cdots + F_8 \cdot ({}_5P_{45})^0$$
$$= ({}_5P_0)^5 = (1, 1) \text{ element in the } \mathbf{POP}^5 \text{ matrix}$$
$$= \text{Population aged 0–4 after the 5-year projection}$$

In this equation for $(\underline{B_0})^5$, we write the relevant age-specific fertility rates for each age group as fertility factors, $F_1, F_2, \ldots, F_8$. For example, the fertility factors for the first two age groups are:

$$F_1 = ({}_5L_0/2 \cdot l_0) \cdot ({}_5L_{15}/{}_5L_{10}) \cdot f_{15}$$

for the initial population aged 10–14 and,

$$F_2 = ({}_5L_0/2 \cdot l_0) \cdot [f_{15} + ({}_5L_{20}/{}_5L_{15}) \cdot f_{20}]$$

for the initial population aged 15–19. In Figure 9.3 the fertility factors for all of the age groups are listed. The fertility factors are found are found in row 1 in the population projection. Multiplying row 1 of the population projection matrix $\mathbf{J}$ by the initial population matrix $\mathbf{POP}^0$ gives the population aged 0–4 in 5 years, $(_5P_0)^5$, the (1,1) element in the new population matrix, $\mathbf{POP}^5$.

A simple example of a population projection is given in Box 9.3. Note that assuming fertility and survival rates remain constant, we project the population forward over subsequent 5-year periods using the population projection matrix and rotating in the new populations after each projection. That is, $\mathbf{POP}^{10} = \mathbf{J} \cdot \mathbf{POP}^5 = \mathbf{J} \cdot \mathbf{J} \cdot \mathbf{POP}^0 = \mathbf{J}^2 \cdot \mathbf{POP}^0$.

As noted, including males and allowing for migration to and from the population make the population projections more complicated. Nevertheless, the underlying process of the cohort components method of population projection should be clear. In this example, the initial population of 3,200 increases to 3,650 after 10 years (a 14.1 percent increase); to 4,226 in the next 10 years (a 15.7 percent increase); and to 5,086 in the third 10-year projection (a decade increase of 20.3 percent); despite the underlying constant age-specific fertility and mortality rates. Eventually, however, the crude rate of natural increase would stabilize, consistent with a stable population.

BOX 9.3: Simple example of a population projection

Given a closed female population with the following:

Age interval	Pop^x	Female age-specific birth rate (f_x)	Survival rates
0–10	800	0	$_{10}L_{10}/_{10}L_0 = 0.95$
10–20	700	0.04	$_{10}L_{20}/_{10}L_{10} = 0.90$
20–30	600	0.12	$_{10}L_{30}/_{10}L_{20} = 0.85$
30–40	500	0.06	$_{10}L_{40}/_{10}L_{30} = 0.70$
40–50	400	0	$_{10}L_{50}/_{10}L_{40} = 0.50$
50+	200	0	Note: $_{10}L_0/2 \cdot l_0 =$
			$10 \cdot (_{10}L_0/10l_0) \cdot 1/2 = 4.5$
	3,200		where $_{10}L_0/10l_0 = 0.90$ is the
			assumed survival rate from birth to
			age interval 0 to 10

The initial 10-year population projection is:

$$
\begin{bmatrix}
0.171 & 0.666 & 0.7695 & 0.27 & 0 & 0 \\
0.95 & 0 & 0 & 0 & 0 & 0 \\
0 & 0.90 & 0 & 0 & 0 & 0 \\
0 & 0 & 0.85 & 0 & 0 & 0 \\
0 & 0 & 0 & 0.70 & 0 & 0 \\
0 & 0 & 0 & 0 & 0.50 & 0
\end{bmatrix}
\begin{bmatrix}
800 \\ 700 \\ 600 \\ 500 \\ 400 \\ 200
\end{bmatrix}
=
\begin{bmatrix}
1200 \\ 760 \\ 630 \\ 510 \\ 350 \\ 200
\end{bmatrix}
$$

$\qquad$ (6 × 6 population projection matrix) $\quad$ Pop^0 $\qquad$ $Pop^{10} = 3650$

To find the fertility factors in row 1:

$F_1 = (_{10}L_0/2l_0) \cdot (_{10}L_{10}/_{10}L_0) \cdot f_{10} = 4.5 \times 0.95 \times 0.04 = 0.171$

$F_2 = (_{10}L_0/2l_0) \cdot [f_{10} + (_{10}L_{20}/_{10}L_{10}) \cdot f_{20}] = 4.5(0.04 + 0.90 \times 0.12) = 0.666$

$$F_3 = (_{10}L_0/2l_0) \cdot [f_{20} + (_{10}L_{30}/_{10}L_{20}) \cdot f_{30}] = 4.5(0.12 + 0.85 \times 0.06) = 0.7695$$

$$F_4 = (_{10}L_0/2l_0) \cdot (f_{30}) = 4.5 \times 0.06 = 0.27$$

Continuing the populations after 20 and 30 years would be:

$$
Pop^{20} = \begin{bmatrix} 1{,}334 \\ 1{,}140 \\ 684 \\ 536 \\ 357 \\ 175 \end{bmatrix} \quad Pop^{30} = \begin{bmatrix} 1{,}658 \\ 1{,}267 \\ 1{,}026 \\ 581 \\ 375 \\ 179 \end{bmatrix}
$$

Total 4,226   Total 5,086

Population forecasts

Finally, we should distinguish between a population projection and forecast. The mathematical process is identical. A **population projection** illustrates the consequences for an initial population of assumed vital rates (age-specific birth, death, and net migration rates). A **population forecast** attempts to predict the vital rates (drawn from some behavioral model) over the course of the future. The forecasted populations can then be used for economic planning.

Forecasting population is very challenging. Current trends may not continue. Reflecting this uncertainty, demographers usually set forth at least three scenarios (low, medium, and high) reflecting expected natural rates of increase and net migration. In general, the smaller the geographic area (e.g., regions, states, or cities), the more net migration is likely to be the main uncertainty about future population. Nations, however, have immigration policies and can better control migrant flows—although, as in the United States, illegal immigration can be significant.

CONCLUSION

Globally, the main uncertainty with respect to the future population is fertility. Key unknowns include when the less developed nations of Asia, Africa, the Middle East, and Latin America will complete their demographic transitions, and whether the developed nations will remain below replacement-level fertility and experience depopulation. On the mortality side, however, there is also uncertainty. Recalling the Malthusian positive checks of disease, war, natural disasters, famine, there may be new pandemics, like HIV/AIDS.[16] Will climate change unleash new diseases or will existing afflictions such as malaria thrive? Indeed, it is easier to record and explain climate change, like population growth, after the fact than to predict the course and future consequences. Since there is a built-in momentum to climate change, due to the accumulation of greenhouse gas emissions in the atmosphere, the global warming the world experiences will depend on present mitigation efforts. In Chapter 12 we will address climate change.

---

[16] Haub (1987: 22) notes the consensus among demographers in the 1980s that AIDS would only have a minimal overall effect on life expectancy, with limited impact on the population growth rate in any one country.

In the next chapter we turn to population transitions, beginning with epidemiological transition and the changing patterns of mortality and morbidity. Then we discuss behavioral models of fertility, followed by population policy. Sustainable development in the world will depend significantly on the future fertility and mortality rates.

KEY TERMS

adolescent fertility rate

age-specific birth rate

burden of dependency

children ever born

cohort component method

elderly burden of dependency

exact ages

fertility

gestation

infant mortality rate

life span

natural fertility

population forecast

population projection

probability

replacement-level fertility

stationary

survival rates

youth burden of dependency

aged-to-child ratio

age-specific death rate

central rate

cohort

constrictive

expansive

fecundity

general fertility rate

gross reproduction rate

life expectancy at birth

life table

net reproduction rate

population momentum

population pyramid

radix

stable population

stationary population

under-five mortality rate

QUESTIONS

1. Calculate the crude death rate for the following population given its age structure and age-specific death rates (ASDRs).

Age interval (years)	% of population	ASDR
0–1	4	30
1–14	35	4
15–44	30	10
45–64	26	40
65 and over	5	120

If the crude birth rate were 50 (births per thousand mid-year population) and the net in-migration rate were −2 (net in-migrants per thousand mid-year population), find the annual population growth rate and estimate the population doubling time.

2. Given the following age-specific births rates (ASBRs), calculate the total fertility rate of the population.

Age interval of mother (years)	ASBR
10–14	2
15–19	120
20–24	230
25–29	200
30–34	150
35–39	80
40–44	10
45–49	1

3. Construct a life table for a hypothetical cohort of armadillos under the following assumptions. The life span of armadillos is 5 years, that is, no armadillo lives beyond its fifth birthday. For each year, including the first year of life, armadillo deaths are evenly distributed over the age interval. There is no migration—this is a closed population. The radix equals 1000. The age-specific death rates for armadillos, $_1M_x$, are:

$$_1M_0 = 0.20, _1M_1 = 0.10, _1M_2 = 0.40, _1M_3 = 0.60$$

so that, for example, $_1M_2$, the age-specific death rate for armadillos aged 2–3, is 400 per thousand. Fill in the life table below. (Round off decimals to three places and show your calculations. However, the l_x and $_1L_x$ columns should not contain fractional armadillos.)

Age x	$_1q_x$	l_x	$_1d_x$	$_1L_x$	T_x	e_x
0–1	—	—	—	—	—	—
1–2	—	—	—	—	—	—
2–3	—	—	—	—	—	—
3–4	—	—	—	—	—	—
4–5	—	—	—	—	—	—

(a) What is the proportion of armadillos aged 2–3 that will survive another 2 years?
(b) What is the chance that an armadillo will survive from birth to the age interval 3–4?

4. Using the information below for the US population in 1970, calculate the following statistics:

(a) crude birth rate;
(b) schedule of age-specific fertility rates;
(c) total fertility rate;
(d) gross reproduction rate;
(e) net reproduction rate.

Round off decimals to four places and show your calculations. Assume the population numbers refer to the mid-point populations.

265

Age x	Females (thousands)	Births to females of age x	From life table (females) $_5L_x$
0–4	8,391		490,648
5–9	9,848		489,242
10–14	10,232	10,468	488,524
15–19	9,477	604,654	487,440
20–24	8,351	1,356,448	485,756
25–29	6,824	957,314	483,797
30–34	5,852	423,672	481,349
35–39	5,711	189,750	477,800
40–44	6,154	54,502	472,430
45–49	6,250	3,398	464,375
50–54	5,735		452,518
55–59	5,229		435,829
60–64	4,610		412,546
65–69	3,873		379,846
70–74	3,132		333,666
75–79	2,282		270,248
80–84	1,406		190,550
85+	970		181,176

Sex ratio of US population (1970) = 94.78
Sex ratio of births in US (1970) = 105.30

5. Given the following two populations, both closed to migration and each consisting of females only, draw the initial population pyramids (here just the right sides). Which of the two populations has the greater potential for further growth? Why?

Age interval	Population A	Population B
0–10	3,500	1,500
10–20	2,500	1,700
20–30	2,000	2,000
30–40	1,000	1,600
40–50	500	1,400
50–60	400	1,000
60+	100	800
Total	10,000	10,000

Using the vital rate information given below, project the two populations forward at 10-year intervals for a total of 60 years. This means six projections for each population. In your calculations for the population projection matrix, round off the fertility factors to the nearest thousandth. Round off the populations in each age group to the nearest integer (whole person).

Fill in the table:

	Population size at time T						
T	0	10	20	30	40	50	60
Population A	—	—	—	—	—	—	—
Population B	—	—	—	—	—	—	—

Age interval	$ASBR_x^f$	$_nL_x$	$l_0 = 100,000$
0–10	0	900,000	
10–20	0.025	882,000	
20–30	0.070	837,900	
30–40	0.026	754,110	
40–50	0	603,288	
50–60	0	452,466	
60+	0	226,233	

$ASBR_x^f$ = female birth rate for women aged x to $x + 10$

(a) Draw the population pyramids for populations A and B at times $T = 30$ and $T = 60$. What do you notice about the age distributions of the two populations over time?

(b) Calculate the net reproduction rate. What do you conclude with respect to the immediate imposition of replacement-level fertility and population growth?

REFERENCES

Anderson, R.N. 1998. "United States Abridged Life Tables,1996," *National Vital Statistics Reports*, Vol. 47, No. 13. Hyattsville, MD: National Center for Health Statistics. 1998.

Council of Economic Advisers. 2012. *Economic Report of the President 2012*. Washington, DC: United States Government.

Hanson, Richard. 2012. "Fiery Horse Hobbles Japan's Fertility Future," *Asia Times*, March 12. http://www.atimes.com/atimes/Japan/GA05Dh02.html

Haub, Carl. 1987. "Understanding Population Projections," *Population Bulletin*, 42(4).

Lutz, Wolfgang. 1994. "The Future of World Population," *Population Bulletin*, 49(1).

Riley, Nancy. 2004. "China's Population: New Trends and Challenges," *Population Bulletin*, 59(2).

Roudi-Fahimi, Farzaneh and Mary Kent. 2007. "Challenges and Opportunities—The Population of the Middle East and North Africa," *Population Bulletin*, 62(2).

Shryock, Henry and Siegel, Jacob. 1975. *The Methods and Materials of Demography*, Vol. 2. Washington, DC: US Bureau of the Census, Department of Commerce.

United Nations Secretariat. 1999. *The World at Six Billion*. New York: Population Division, Department of Economic and Social Affairs, United Nations. http://www.un.org/esa/population/publications/sixbillion/sixbillion.htm.

Weeks, John. 1996. *Population: An Introduction to Concepts and Issues*, 6th edn. Belmont, CA: Wadsworth.

World Bank. 2000. *World Development Indicators 2000*. Washington, DC: World Bank.

World Bank. 2012. *World Development Indicators 2012*. Washington, DC: World Bank.

Chapter 10

Population transitions

The demographic transition, as discussed in Chapter 2, describes the movement of populations from a traditional equilibrium of high mortality and fertility rates to a modern equilibrium of low mortality and fertility rates, both yielding minimal, if not essentially zero, population growth. In between is a disequilibrium transition stage, where declines in mortality precede those in fertility, generating rapid population growth. The developed nations of the world have completed their demographic transitions, attaining high life expectancies and experiencing aging populations with rising elderly burdens of dependency. In fact, the Western European nations, a number of Eastern European nations, Japan, Australia, and Canada have been well below replacement-level fertility for some time, which will result in their depopulation, unless offset by immigration. An increasing number of developing nations, especially in East Asia, are also below replacement-level fertility, but because of past high fertility, still have some population momentum to expend before converging to a zero crude rate of natural increase. The developing nations of Latin America and the Caribbean, the Middle East and North Africa, South Asia, and sub-Saharan Africa, with differential progress in the demographic transition, will face continued population growth for some decades yet.

Accompanying the demographic transition are two related transitions. One, the epidemiological transition, captures the changing patterns of mortality and morbidity with economic development. The second, the fertility transition, accounts for the declines in birth rates that accompany economic development. In this chapter we will discuss both population transitions, not only explaining the trends in human population, but also addressing future concerns.

THE EPIDEMIOLOGICAL TRANSITION

Epidemiology is the study of health in populations, including illness, disease, and epidemics (outbreaks of rapidly spreading contagious diseases). Demographers have put forth a model of the **epidemiological transition** to explain the changing courses of mortality that accompany economic development. Four primary stages have been identified (see Rockett 1999: 8–10).

Four stages

The first stage of the epidemiological transition, the **age of epidemics and famine**, corresponds to the traditional or Malthusian stage of the demographic transition, which has defined most of human existence. Death rates are high and volatile due to epidemics, famine, and violence. With advances in agriculture, however, famines diminished in importance as a major cause of mortality, while diseases became more consequential.[1] As populations clustered in cities with unsanitary conditions, contagious diseases spread more easily. The life expectancy at birth during this stage might have risen to as high as 35–40 years.

The second stage is the **age of receding epidemics**, which corresponds to the first part of the transition stage where death rates are significantly declining while fertility rates remain high. Here humans begin to gain some control over their environment. Average levels of nutrition improve with more reliable food supplies. Populations become more resistant to disease and better able to withstand illness. Later advances in medicine (e.g., a smallpox vaccine at the end of the nineteenth century) and improvements in public health and sanitation further reduce mortality. Life expectancies might have risen to 50 years as infectious and parasitic diseases gradually come under control. Infectious diseases include measles, pneumonia, influenza, cholera, typhus, tetanus, and tuberculosis. Parasitic diseases are transmitted by an external agent, like the bubonic plague by fleas from rodents and malaria by mosquitoes.

The **age of degenerative and man-made diseases** is the third stage of the epidemiological transition, occurring in the latter part of the demographic transition when declining fertility rates begin to catch up to the lower mortality. Further improvements in public health and advances in medicine (vaccines for polio, antibiotics, and spraying for malaria) suppress infectious and parasitic diseases. Individuals live longer to where chronic disorders associated with aging come into force, such as cardiovascular diseases (heart, lungs, and strokes) and cancers. Also afflictions associated with lifestyle become more important (e.g., smoking and pollution). In this stage of the epidemiological transition, life expectancy at birth may exceed 60 years.

The fourth stage is the **age of delayed degenerative diseases**. With further medical breakthroughs, including treatments and even cures that can extend lives in middle and older ages (e.g., heart transplants and chemotherapy), as well as improved diet and lifestyle, life expectancies at birth rise above 70. Deaths occur later as more individuals succumb to degenerative diseases such as Alzheimer's.

For an example of the changing course of mortality with economic development within a nation, see Table 10.1, which lists the leading causes of death for the United States at the beginning and end of the twentieth century. In 1900, the four leading causes of death, accounting for nearly 40 percent of mortality, were pneumonia, tuberculosis, diarrhea and enteritis (inflammation of the intestinal tract), and heart disease. Life expectancy at birth increased from 47 to 77 years between 1900 and 1998. And, by the end of the century, 12.7 percent of the American population was aged 65 years or older, compared to 4.1 percent in 1900. In 1998, the four leading causes of death in the US, accounting for 66 percent of mortality, were heart disease, cancer, stroke, and lung diseases. In fact, heart disease and cancer alone were responsible for over half of these deaths (see Rockett 1999: Table 1).[2]

---

[1] According to Robert Fogel (1994: 382–383):

> famines accounted for less than 4 percent of the premature mortality of Malthus's age, and . . . the excess mortality of the ultra-poor (the bottom fifth of society) accounted for another sixth of premature mortality. About two-thirds of all premature mortality in Malthus's time came from the part of society that Malthus viewed as productive and healthy. Yet by current standards, even persons in the top half of the income distribution in Britain during the 18th century were stunted and wasted, suffered far more extensively from chronic diseases at young adult and middle ages than is true today, and died 30 years sooner than today.

[2] Recent data for 2010 show largely the same pattern for mortality, albeit with some notable exceptions. Heart disease remained first, accounting for 24 percent of all deaths in the US in 2010 (compared with 31 percent in 1998). Alzheimer's

Table 10.1 Top ten causes of death in United States, 1900 and 1998

Cause of death	Percent of all deaths
1900	
1. Pneumonia	12%
2. Tuberculosis	11%
3. Diarrhea and enteritis	8%
4. Heart disease	8%
5. Chronic nephritis	5%
6. Unintentional injury (accidents)	4%
7. Stroke	4%
8. Diseases of early infancy	4%
9. Cancer	4%
10. Diphtheria	2%
1998	
1. Heart disease	31%
2. Cancer	23%
3. Stroke	7%
4. Lung Diseases	5%
5. Pneumonia and influenza	4%
6. Unintentional injury (accidents)	4%
7. Diabetes	3%
8. Suicide	1%
9. Nephritis, kidney diseases	1%
10. Liver diseases	1%

Source: Rockett (1999: Table 1).

A possible fifth stage

There is some speculation that a fifth stage in the epidemiological transition may be unfolding, one characterized by the reemergence of infectious and parasitic diseases with a concentration on younger ages. For example, it is likely that the HIV, which causes AIDS, originated as a pandemic in the late 1970s, although not identified as such until the 1980s. The resurgence of infectious and parasitic diseases reflects not only new diseases (such as AIDS and the Ebola virus) but also the revival of old diseases due to slackened public health efforts at disease control, poverty, and evolution of antibiotic-resistance strains of disease (e.g., severe acute respiratory syndrome (SARS) and avian flu).

With more frequent incursions into rainforests and destruction of animal habitats, new viruses may be released into civilization. The increased mobility of people and international trade of agricultural produce can transmit diseases much faster—within days, if not hours. And always diseases spread more effectively through populations concentrated in urban areas. Future climate change, bringing global warming and more volatile weather, may add to the mortality rates, especially in the poorer nations in the tropics.

disease ranked sixth in 2010, while pneumonia and influenza dropped from fifth to ninth place. See Murphy et al. (2012: Table B), which reports preliminary data for the leading causes of death in the US in 2010. In order, the ten leading causes of death (percentage share of all deaths) are: heart disease (24.1%), cancer (23.3%), lung diseases (5.6%), stroke (5.2%), unintentional injury or accidents (4.8%), Alzheimer's disease (3.4%), diabetes (2.8%), pneumonia and influenza (2.0%), and suicide (1.5%).

Table 10.2 *Top ten causes of death in the world, 2008*

Cause	Death in millions	Percentage of deaths
Low-income countries		
1. Lower respiratory infections	1.05	11.3%
2. Diarrheal diseases	0.76	8.2%
3. HIV/AIDS	0.72	7.8%
4. Ischemic heart disease	0.57	6.1%
5. Malaria	0.48	5.2%
6. Stroke and other cerebrovascular diseases	0.45	4.9%
7. Tuberculosis	0.40	4.3%
8. Prematurity and low birth weight	0.30	3.2%
9. Birth asphyxia and birth trauma	0.27	2.9%
10. Neonatal infections	0.24	2.6%
Middle-income countries		
1. Ischemic heart disease	5.27	13.7%
2. Stroke and other cerebrovascular diseases	4.91	12.8%
3. Chronic obstructive pulmonary disease	2.79	7.2%
4. Lower respiratory infections	2.07	5.4%
5. Diarrheal diseases	1.68	4.4%
6. HIV/AIDS	1.03	2.7%
7. Road traffic accidents	0.94	2.4%
8. Tuberculosis	0.93	2.4%
9. Diabetes mellitus	0.87	2.3%
10. Hypertensive heart disease	0.83	2.2%
High-income countries		
1. Ischemic heart disease	1.42	15.6%
2. Stroke and other cerebrovascular diseases	0.79	8.7%
3. Trachea, bronchus, lung cancers	0.54	5.9%
4. Alzheimer's disease and other dementias	0.37	4.1%
5. Lower respiratory infections	0.35	3.8%
6. Chronic obstructive pulmonary disease	0.32	3.5%
7. Colon and rectum cancers	0.30	3.3%
8. Diabetes mellitus	0.24	2.6%
9. Hypertensive heart disease	0.21	2.3%
10. Breast cancer	0.17	1.9%

Source: adapted from World Health Organization (http://www.who.int.mediacentre/factsheets/fs310/en/index.html), accessed March 17, 2012.

Over 90 percent of the deaths due to infectious and parasitic diseases occur in populations in the less developed countries, where poverty, unsanitary conditions, malnutrition, and inadequate public health programs all contribute to mortality from what often are preventable and treatable diseases. For example, diarrhea remains a major cause of child mortality in poor countries.

To illustrate the pattern of mortality across income, see Table 10.2. While there is considerable overlap—in particular, lower respiratory infections, ischemic heart disease, and stroke and other cerebrovascular diseases are found in the top six in the low-, middle-, and high-income nations—there are also distinct differences. Only for the low-income countries are malaria, and afflictions associated with childbearing (prematurity and low birth weight, birth asphyxia and birth trauma, and neonatal infections) found in the top ten causes of death. Road traffic accidents are in the top ten for only the middle-income nations. Alzheimer's disease and other dementias, and cancers (lung, colon and rectum, and breast) are leading causes of mortality in the high-income nations only. The pattern of disease found in the contemporary high-income nations may be predictive for the low- and middle-income nations as they experience economic growth and development and their populations age.

Improving conditions

As shown in Table 10.3, life expectancies have improved over the last half-century, even in the poorest regions of the world of sub-Saharan Africa and South Asia. As noted in Chapter 9, however, a number of sub-Saharan African nations in the southern cone of Africa experienced sharp declines in life expectancies in the last two decades of the twentieth century, mainly due to the high incidence of HIV/AIDS. In fact, the average female life expectancy at birth for all of sub-Saharan Africa fell from 52 years in 1990 to 47 years in 2000.

In general, the initial increases in life expectancy largely reflect improved child mortality. Life expectancies at birth rise with incomes, albeit at a diminishing rate. There are other factors that affect mortality, such as diet, lifestyle, the environment, and public policy. For example, Japan leads the world in life expectancy, with a female life expectancy at birth of 86 years in 2010, 5 years higher than the United States, despite Japan's significantly lower per capita income.

With respect to the underlying health conditions, we see dramatic differences with income and across the developing world. To begin, adequate nourishment is essential for the development of children. Two common measures of child malnutrition, underweight (low weight for age) and **stunting** (low height for age), are presented in Table 10.4.[3] Severe underweight is more indicative of acute malnutrition, reflecting acute shortages of food as might happen during famines and civil wars. Stunting is more indicative of chronic undernourishment due to poverty. That one fifth of the world's children under age 5 are significantly underweight and nearly a third stunted in the twenty-first century is tragic. Regionally, we see that South Asia is most afflicted, with over 40 percent of the children under age 5 significantly underweight and stunted. Child malnutrition is also endemic in sub-Saharan Africa. Only in Latin America and the Caribbean is the incidence of stunting less than 15 percent. Conversely, the problem of obesity often rises with income. As we will discuss in Chapter 13, obesity may reflect not only overconsumption of food, but also poor diet, lack of exercise, and, less frequently, genetic factors.

Reflecting poor choice is the consumption of tobacco, which may initially rise with income and then decline as populations become more educated. Striking about the prevalence of smoking across incomes and regions of the world are the much higher rates for males. For the world in 2009, over a third of males aged 15 and older smoked—compared with less than 10 percent of females.

The incidence of tuberculosis declines with income, and has been greatly diminished in the high-income economies. In contrast, the prevalence of adult diabetes is more constant across incomes. The onset of adult diabetes is often correlated with obesity.

The sixth Millennium Development Goal (MDG 6) is combating HIV/AIDS, malaria and tuberculosis. The World Bank (2010: 16) noted that, "Worldwide, some 33.4 million people—two-thirds of them in sub-Saharan Africa and most of them women—are living with HIV/AIDS, but the prevalence rate has remained constant since 2000."

---

[3] A third measure of child malnutrition is **wasting** (low weight for height).

Table 10.3 *Trends in mortality: sub-Saharan Africa, South Asia, the United States, Japan, and the World*

	1965	1980	1990	2000	2010
Female life expectancy at birth					
Sub-Saharan Africa ($2,148)	43	49	52	47	55
South Asia ($3,124)	45	54	58	63	67
United States ($47,310)	74	78	80	80	81
Japan ($34,610)	73	79	82	84	86
WORLD ($11,066)	58	64	67	69	72
Infant mortality rate					
Sub-Saharan Africa	157	116	105	91	76
South Asia	147	119	86	73	52
United States	25	13	9	7	7
Japan	18	8	5	4	2
WORLD	91	80	62	54	41

Note: Per capita gross national incomes (in PPP dollars) in 2010 are indicated in the parentheses.

Female life expectancy at birth is the number of years a newborn infant girl would live if prevailing patterns of mortality at the time of her birth were to stay the same throughout her life.

Infant mortality rate is the number of infants dying before reaching 1 year of age, per 1,000 live births in a given year.

From: World Bank (1992: Tables 28 and 32; 1997: Table 2.14; 2002b: Tables 1.5 and 2.20; 2012: Tables 1.1, 1.5, and 2.23).

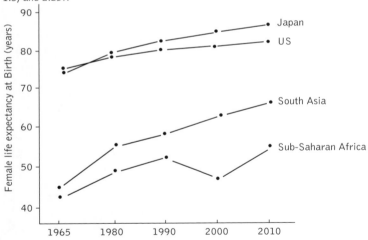

HIV is the precursor to AIDS, an economically devastating disease in that adults in the prime working years are often the most afflicted. Progress in halting the spread of AIDS reflects greater awareness as well as increased, but still insufficient, access to antiretroviral treatment.[4] See Box 10.1 for a case study of Botswana, a small sub-Saharan African nation that has enjoyed remarkable economic growth, but has one of the most HIV-afflicted populations in the world.

[4]Lamptey et al. (2006: 15) cite an estimate of 6.5 million people needing antiretroviral treatment in 2005, but only 1 million with access to it. According to the World Health Organization, in 2010, of an estimated 34 million people living with HIV, at least 15 million were in need of antiretroviral therapy. In the low- and middle-income countries, 6.6 million had access to the therapy (http://www.who.int/hiv/topics/treatment/en).

Table 10.4 *Selected statistics on health conditions*

	ECONOMIES BY INCOME CLASSIFICATION							
	WORLD	Low	Lower middle	India	Upper middle	China	High	US
Prevalence of child malnutrition, 2004–09								
Underweight	21.3%	27.7%	24.0%	43.5%	...	4.5%	...	1.3%
Stunting	31.7%	44.0%	33.1%	47.9%	...	11.7%	...	3.9%
Overweight	6.1%	4.9%	5.9%	1.9%	...	5.9%	...	8.0%
Prevalence of adult smoking, 2009								
Male	37%	28%	32%	26%	46%	51%	34%	33%
Female	8%	4%	4%	4%	7%	2%	21%	25%
Incidence of tuberculosis per 100,000, 2010	128	264	174	185	89	78	14	4
Prevalence of adult diabetes: 2011	8.3%	5.9%	8.0%	9.2%	9.4%	9.0%	7.9%	9.6%
Prevalence of HIV, population 15–49								
1990	0.3%	1.8%	0.3%	0.1%	0.2%	...	0.2%	0.5%
2009	0.8%	2.6%	0.7%	0.3%	0.7%	0.1%	0.3%	0.6%
Access to improved water source, 2010								
Urban	96%	86%	93%	97%	98%	98%	100%	100%
Rural	81%	57%	83%	90%	86%	85%	98%	94%
Access to improved sanitation, 2010								
Urban	79%	47%	66%	58%	82%	74%	100%	99%
Rural	47%	32%	34%	23%	62%	56%	99%	99%
Causes of death, 2005–10								
Communicable disease	27%	58%	38%	37%	11%	7%	7%	6%
Noncommunicable disease	63%	33%	53%	53%	79%	83%	87%	87%
Injuries	9%	9%	9%	10%	10%	10%	6%	7%
Particulate matter concentration, urban-population-weighted, of PM10, micrograms per cubic meter								
1990	79	127	124	110	78	115	37	30
2009	43	56	58	57	43	60	23	18

Table 10.4 *continued*

	ECONOMIES BY REGION						
	Sub-Saharan Africa	Middle East & N. Africa	Europe & Central Asia	South Asia	East Asia & Pacific	Latin America & Caribbean	High Income Economies
Prevalence of child malnutrition, 2004–09							
Underweight	24.7%	6.8%	...	42.5%	8.8%	3.8%	...
Stunting	42.0%	25.0%	...	47.5%	19.0%	14.1%	...
Overweight	7.0%	16.6%	...	1.9%	6.6%	7.2%	...
Prevalence of adult smoking, 2009							
Male	16%	35%	50%	29%	52%	25%	34%
Female	3%	3%	18%	4%	3%	13%	21%
Incidence of tuberculosis per 100,000, 2010	271	42	90	192	123	43	14
Prevalence of adult diabetes, 2011	4.6%	11.6%	7.7%	9.0%	8.3%	10.5%	7.9%
Prevalence of HIV, population 15–49:							
1990	2.4%	0.1%	0.1%	0.1%	0.1%	0.4%	0.2%
2009	5.5%	0.1%	0.6%	0.3%	0.2%	0.5%	0.3%
Access to improved water source, 2010							
Urban	83%	94%	99%	95%	97%	98%	100%
Rural	49%	81%	91%	88%	84%	81%	98%
Access to improved sanitation, 2010							
Urban	42%	94%	87%	60%	76%	84%	100%
Rural	23%	80%	80%	28%	57%	59%	99%
Causes of death, 2005–10							
Communicable Diseases	65%	19%	6%	39%	13%	16%	7%
Noncommunicable	28%	69%	84%	51%	76%	72%	87%
Diseases Injuries	7%	12%	9%	10%	10%	12%	6%
Particulate matter concentration, urban-population-weighted PM10, micrograms per cubic meter							
1990	119	125	57	130	112	57	37
2009	46	66	23	68	56	30	23

Notes: Prevalence of child malnutrition is the percentage of children under age 5 whose weight for age (underweight) or height for age (stunting) is more than two standard deviations below the median for the international reference population aged 0–59 months.

Prevalence of overweight children is the percentage of children under age 5 whose weight for height is more than two standard deviations above the median for the international reference population of the corresponding age.

Prevalence of smoking is the adjusted and age-standardized prevalence estimate of smoking among adults aged 15 and older.

Incidence of tuberculosis is the estimated number of new tuberculosis cases (pulmonary, smear positive, extrapulmonary) per 100,000 people.

◾ **Table 10.4** *continued*

Note: Continued

Prevalence of diabetes is the percentage of the population aged 20–79 with type 1 or type 2 diabetes.

Prevalence of HIV is the percentage of the population aged 15–49 who are infected with human immunodeficiency virus, which is related to AIDS.

Access to an improved water source is the percentage of the population with reasonable access (i.e., availability of at least 20 liters per person per day from a source within 1 kilometer of the dwelling) to an improved water source, such as piped water into a dwelling, plot or yard; public tap or standpipe; tubewell or borehole; protected dug well or spring; and rainwater collection.

Access to improved sanitation facilities is the percentage of the population with access to at least adequate excreta disposal facilities (private or shared, but not public) that can effectively prevent human, animal, and insect contact with excreta. Improved facilities range from simple but protected pit latrines to flush toilets with a sewerage connection.

Causes of death is the share of all deaths due to the specified underlying cause. Communicable diseases and maternal, perinatal, and nutrition conditions are infectious and parasitic diseases, respiratory infections, and nutritional deficiencies such as underweight and stunting. Noncommunicable diseases are cancer, diabetes mellitus, cardiovascular diseases, and congenital anomalies. Injuries include unintentional and intentional injuries.

Particulate matter concentration, urban-population-weighted, of PM10 in micrograms per cubic meter is fine suspended particulates of less than 10 micrometers in diameter (PM10) that are capable of penetration deep into the respiratory tract and causing severe health damage. Data are urban-population-weighted PM10 levels in residential areas of cities with more than 100,000 residents. The estimates represent the average annual exposure level of the average urban resident to outdoor particulate matter.

Source: World Bank (2011: Table 2.20; 2012: Tables 2.22, 3.5, 3.13, and 3.15).

BOX 10.1: BOTSWANA: ECONOMIC SUCCESS AND DEMOGRAPHIC TRAGEDY

Botswana, a small nation of 2 million in population in the southern cone of sub-Saharan Africa, is noted for its impressive economic growth, political stability, and sound institutions. Botswana is one of the few sub-Saharan African to have engaged economic growth over the past two decades, and its growth rate in per capita income has been among the highest in the world. The average annual growth rate in GDP per capita for sub-Saharan Africa was −0.1 percent over the last decade in the twentieth century, while Botswana's per capita GDP grew at an average annual rate of 3.4 percent.

	Average annual growth rates					
	GDP		*Population*		*GDP per capita*	
	1990–2000	*2000–10*	*1990–2000*	*2000–10*	*1990–2000*	*2000–10*
Low & Middle Income Econ.	3.9%	6.4%	1.6%	1.3%	2.3%	5.1%
Sub-Saharan Africa	2.5%	5.0%	2.6%	2.5%	-0.1%	2.5%
Botswana	5.7%	4.1%	2.3%	1.3%	3.4%	2.8%

Botswana, well endowed with diamonds, has escaped the "natural resource curse," the unfortunate tendency of some developing nations with abundant natural resources, especially minerals and fossil fuels, to be plagued by corruption and political instability. Due to good fortune, a relatively benign colonial experience, and, most importantly, effective political leadership, Botswana has used its mineral wealth to promote development (for a good case study, see Acemoglu et al. 2003).

In the first decade of the twenty-first century, the average annual growth rate in per capita GDP for Botswana fell to 2.8 percent, while the average economic growth rate for sub-Saharan African nations increased to 2.5 percent, due in part to higher world prices for natural resources. Furthermore, while sub-Saharan Africa's average population growth rate only slightly fell from 2.6 percent to 2.5 percent over the two periods, Botswana's declined by a percentage point from 2.3 percent for 1990–2000 to 1.3 percent for 2000–10.

Unfortunately, as found in other nations in southern Africa, Botswana has been ravaged by HIV/AIDS. This disease particularly afflicts young adults, robbing a population of productive workers. In Botswana, an estimated 24.8 percent of its population between the ages of 15 and 49 were affected with HIV in 2009, up from 3.5 percent in 1990. Despite its strong economic growth, resulting in a fairly high per capita income ($13,700 in PPP dollars in 2010), Botswana has seen its life expectancy at birth decline from 64 years in 1990 to 53 years in 2010 (see World Bank 2002a: Table 1; World Bank 2012: Tables 1.1, 2.1, 2.22, 2.23, and 4.1).

In 2002, however, the leaders of Botswana established the first free AIDS program in Africa, delivering antiretroviral therapy to 42,000 Botswanans, or 56 percent of the total who needed it (Lamptey et al. 2006: 14). Nevertheless, the contrast between Botswana's economic success and demographic tragedy is stark. Botswana's future economic growth and, indeed its stability, may be undermined by this horrible disease, a Malthusian population check of the cruelest kind.

Sub-Saharan Africa accounts for 90 percent of estimated nearly 1 million malaria-related deaths in the world, mostly to children under 5.[5] The World Bank (2010: 16) adds: "Children who survive malaria do not escape unharmed. Repeated episodes of fever and anemia take a toll on their mental and physical development." While increased use of insecticide-treated bed nets have helped curb the incidence of malaria, global warming in subtropical regions may well increase the potential spread of this debilitating disease.

The seventh Millennium Development Goal is ensuring environmental sustainability. The Millennium Development Goals will be discussed in greater detail in Chapter 11, when we address sustainable development. Suffice to observe here is that one of the four explicit targets of MDG 7 is halving by 2015 the proportion of people without sustainable access to safe drinking water and basic sanitation. The World Bank (2010: 20) observes that more than 1 billion people in the developing countries do not have adequate access to safe drinking water and over 1.5 billion lack access to adequate sanitation.[6] The incidence of water-borne illnesses such as diarrhea and cholera is directly related to unsafe water and poor sanitation. With rising incomes and better public health measures, environmental conditions improve. Sub-Saharan Africa and South Asia

---

[5] This is an estimate for 2006 from the World Health Organization, which also estimated between 190 and 330 million malaria episodes in that year. See World Bank (2010: 16).

[6] The United Nations Population Fund (2009: 23) notes that every year 2 million children die from diarrheal diseases, largely due to unsafe water and poor sanitation and hygiene.

lag well behind other regions of the world, especially with regard to improved sanitation. While rural populations generally are relatively deprived of these basic necessities, insufficient sanitation can be more of a problem in congested urban slums, where diseases are be more easily transmitted.

Another explicit target under MDG 7 is to significantly improve the lives of at least 100 million slum dwellers by 2020. Related to this concern with urbanization is pollution. Economic growth brings more industry, increased consumption of energy and utilization of automobiles, and, unless accompanied by greater mitigation efforts, more emissions of greenhouse gases, which directly contribute to global warming. As shown in Table 10.4, however, there may be a nonlinear relationship between particulate matter concentration and income. Increased concentrations of particulate matter, which contribute to respiratory illnesses, initially rise with income, urbanization, and industrialization, before public policies to address environmental deterioration are demanded and enacted with higher incomes.

In sum, the developed countries are in the fourth stage of the epidemiological transition, where delayed degenerative diseases are dominant, while most of the less developed countries are dispersed over the second stage (where infectious and parasitic diseases still are prevalent) and third stage (where chronic disorders associated with aging come into force, including heart disease and cancers). Whether a fifth stage comes to pass remains to be seen. Advances in medical technology continue, but pollution, climate change, obesity, and less healthy diets and lifestyles are a growing concern.

Unlike mortality, which to a large extent is beyond the control of individuals, fertility and migration are discretionary behaviors. That is, while individuals can reduce the probability of dying by maintaining good health and nutrition, everyone will experience death, usually at a time not of their choosing. The decision to migrate or to have a child, however, is subject to individual control. Migration, reflecting a redistribution of population, can be a significant component of population growth for specific geographical areas—cities, states, even countries and regions. Migration will be briefly addressed at the end of this chapter. We now turn to fertility, the main driver of population growth.

THE FERTILITY TRANSITION

The **fertility transition** refers to the shift from the high-fertility regimes that characterize traditional societies to the low-fertility regimes that define modern societies. Recall that in the demographic transition, declines in mortality precede declines in fertility, yielding rapid population growth. The nations of the world are at various points in the fertility transition. Collectively the high-income nations are well below replacement-level fertility and the low- and middle-income nations still roughly half a child above replacement-level fertility. Overall world fertility has significantly decreased over the second half of the twentieth century. Kent and Haub (2005: 5) observe that for the world the average number of children per woman fell from 5.0 around 1950 to 2.7 in 2005.

Net intergenerational wealth flows

With a simple, intuitive theory, John Caldwell (1976) explains the fertility transition in terms of a shift in the **net flow of intergenerational wealth**. The important underlying premise is that rational behavior, that is, behavior consistent with attaining given objectives, must be evaluated in the socioeconomic context.

Caldwell notes that in agrarian societies children are put to work at an early age in the fields and around the household. Even in urban areas of developing economies many children work long hours in sweatshops or odd-jobbing on the streets. Older siblings or grandparents watch after the children too young to work. Moreover, in the absence of social security systems, parents rely on their children for old age support.

Thus, in addition to the universal psychic and emotional satisfaction parents can experience, in traditional societies children, especially sons, are economic assets. With high rates of child mortality, more births are required to ensure the desired number of surviving sons. Under such conditions, where wealth flows on net from children to parents, high fertility is economically rational behavior.

In high-income societies, in contrast, the net flow of wealth is decidedly from parents to children. Children are expensive. Not only are primary and secondary schooling required, but also costly higher education is widely perceived as the key to economic mobility. With affluence, consumer aspirations rise and children would naturally share in the higher standards of living. Children are not expected to generate much income, however; and with social security systems, parents need not depend on their children for old age support. While the emotional and psychic satisfaction derived from children may be just as strong, in modern, industrial societies the economic advantages of children are usually far outweighed by the costs. Lower fertility then is economically rational behavior.

To illustrate, in the US, for a middle-income family (earning between $57,600 and $99,730), the estimated cost of raising a child born in 2010 through the age of 17 is $227,000. Factoring in expected inflation, the estimated cost rises to $287,000. Even recognizing economies of scale in childrearing (e.g., children can share bedrooms and toys), and that there is likely a wide range around the average, the expenses incurred for shelter, food, clothing, basic amenities, public schooling and health care are substantial—and these are all before college.[7]

Caldwell argues that the small-family norm is largely a Western phenomenon, one that nevertheless can be transmitted to developing economies. Education and the popular media, both heavily influenced by Western culture, are the means of transmission. In less developed countries the school curriculum, texts, and instruction are typically based on the Western model. Advertising and entertainment on television and radio and in magazines promote the Western lifestyle. The elite, urban, educated women will be the first in the developing economies to limit fertility. Their examples are emulated by other women as education and economic mobility increase and rising consumer aspirations conflict with large families.

In sum, when net flows of wealth from children to parents (as in traditional societies and developing economies) changes to one from parents to children (as in Western societies and developed economies), then economically rational behavior shifts from high fertility to low fertility. Accompanying the demographic transition, according to Caldwell, is a wealth transition. To complement Caldwell's insights and to more formally model discretionary fertility, we draw on consumer theory.

---

[7]For families earning less than $57,600 per year, the expected average cost totals $163,000 (in 2010 dollars). For family incomes over $99,730, the estimated average totals $377,000. See United States Department of Agriculture, "A Child Born in 2010 Will Cost $226,920 to Raise according to USDA Report" (http://www.usda.gov/wps/portal/usda/usdahome?contentid=2011/06/0241.xml&contentidonly=true). The full report, *Expenditures on Children by Families, 2010*, is available at http://www.cnpp.usda.gov/Publications/CRC/crc2010.pdf.

THE DEMAND FOR CHILDREN

The seminal application of the utility-maximization framework to the analysis of the demand for children is associated with Gary Becker (see Becker 1960).[8] The decision to have children implies a substantial commitment of resources for their upbringing—with the opportunity costs being expenditures and discretionary time that would enhance the parent's own standard of living.

Formally, consider a representative couple at the beginning of their planning horizon, when they contemplate their family size and lifestyle choices. They seek to maximize their lifetime utility or satisfaction derived from their children and other goods and services. Their objective function is to:

$$\text{maximize } U = U(\overset{+}{C}, \overset{+}{X}, \overset{+}{Q}, \overset{+}{R}),$$

where U is the lifetime total utility of the couple, C the number of children, X represents quantities of other goods and services unrelated to childrearing, Q is expenditures per child or "quality of children," and R represents status (i.e., perceived relative standing in society). The plus signs over the arguments C, X, Q, and R indicate the positive marginal utilities associated with children ($U_C = \partial U/\partial C$), consumption ($U_X = \partial U/\partial X$), expenditures on children ($U_Q = \partial U/\partial Q$), and status ($U_R = \partial U/\partial R$). That is, we assume that children are a source of satisfaction (the so-called "joys of parenting"), as well as necessary to preserve family lines. Increases in the consumption of goods and services unrelated to children (X) improve the material standard of living and so increase the total utility of the couple. By the "quality" of children, Becker meant expenditures per child, or the intensity of resource commitment to each child, not a moral judgment on the inherent worth of the child. An increase in Q indicates "child-deepening." Better provision for their children adds to the utility of the representative couple.

As Caldwell observed, developing economies children may be put to work at an early age, and so generate income for their parents. Children may also be a source of old-age security. Here we regard Q then as "net expenditures per child," or average expenditures on children less the average income earned by the children.[9] The desired quality of children is influenced by the social reference group with which the parents identify. For example, poor parents in a developing economy may typically expect their children to attend only a few years of primary school before beginning work and contributing to the family's income. With economic development, parents' aspirations for their children rise (e.g., ensuring more education per child), while their expectations of income generation from the child fall—consistent with an increase in child quality.

Status (R) is included as an argument in the utility function. Individuals may derive satisfaction from more than just the absolute consumption of goods and services; individuals may measure their consumption against that of some reference group. Attaining or exceeding some aspired-to standard of performance may add to total utility.

Here relative status is measured by the ratios of the individual couple's consumption of goods and services and the quantity and quality of their children to standards associated with the relevant social reference group. By the **social reference group** we mean that segment of the population that influences the behavior of this representative couple. In traditional societies the relevant social

---

[8] Although initially receiving mixed reviews, Becker's analysis stimulated much research in the economics of fertility. In 1992 he was awarded the Nobel Prize in Economics for his innovative applications of economic theory to human behavior. Becker's initial focus was on fertility in developed countries. The model presented here is a modified version of Becker's basic theory and is drawn from Hess and Ross (1997: 193–199) and Hess (1988).

[9] In traditional societies, Q might be quite small, even negative, for some couples, in which case the economically rational behavior would be to have as many children as possible, consistent with the health of the mother and children.

reference group might be the older generation of parents. In more modern societies, individuals may seek to emulate the behavior of their peers or even identify with a higher socioeconomic class. With opportunities for socioeconomic mobility, individuals may well aspire to improve their perceived relative standing in the population. For example, considering family size, the economist Leibenstein (1975: 22) noted:

> To a considerable degree people take their cues about the correct number of children from others in the same social status. Something like a "bandwagon effect" occurs. Thus, if most households are having between 2 and 3 children, that fact influences the desired number.

We will assume that this behavior extends also to the consumption of goods and services (X^*) and investment in children (Q^*). Let X^*, C^*, and Q^* be those standards for achievement. Status, R, is then a function of relative performance: $R = R(C/C^*, X/X^*, Q/Q^*)$. Thus the representative couple seeks to maximize its total lifetime utility subject to its total lifetime income or permanent income, $Q \cdot C + P \cdot X = I$, where I is permanent income and P is a price index of goods and services unrelated to childrearing. **Permanent income** is an estimate of the discounted future income of the couple based on their education, labor force participation, job prospects, and financial wealth. Total expenditures on children are given by $Q \cdot C$, while total expenditures on other goods and services are equal to $P \cdot X$.

In sum, the demand for children reflects a constrained optimization:

$$\text{maximize} \quad U = U(\overset{+}{C}, \overset{+}{X}, \overset{+}{Q}, \overset{+}{R} [\overset{+}{C/C^*}, \overset{+}{X/X^*}, \overset{+}{Q/Q^*}])$$

$$\text{subject to} \quad I = Q \cdot C + P \cdot X.$$

Further, we will assume that the desired quality of children is predetermined by the parents and equal to the quality standard associated with the relevant social reference group, $Q = Q^*$, reflecting the parents' expectations of, and aspirations for, their children. Consequently, the utility function can be rewritten as $U = U(C, X, Q^*, R[C/C^*, X/X^*])$. This simplification seems realistic and allows for graphical illustration.[10]

Also assumed to be given are permanent income (projected by the couple) and the price index for other goods and services (exogenously set by the market). Thus, a couple seeks to choose the combination of family size or number of children (C) and other consumption (X) that maximizes their total utility (U), given their permanent income (I), their desired quality of children (Q^*), and the price index for other goods and services (P).

Constrained optimization

We can show this constrained optimization by setting up the Lagrangian function and deriving the first-order conditions. The Lagrangian function is

$$G(C, X, \lambda) = U(C, X, Q^*, R[C/C^*, X/X^*]) + \lambda \cdot (I - Q^* \cdot C - P \cdot X)$$

The first-order conditions, required to find the critical points, are found by partially differentiating the Lagrangian function G with respect to the choice variables, C and X. Recall that the desired

---

[10] Alternatively, we could assume that the desired quality of children (Q) is simultaneously determined with the quantity of children (C) and other goods and services (X), which would require a three-dimensional graph for illustration, while not affecting the key insights from the model.

quality, Q^*, net expenditures per child, as well as the permanent income, I, are predetermined by the couple. We have:

$$\partial G/\partial C = U_C + U_R \cdot R_C \cdot (1/C^*) - \lambda \cdot Q^* = 0$$
$$\partial G/\partial X = U_X + U_R \cdot R_X \cdot (1/X^*) - \lambda \cdot P = 0$$
$$\partial G/\partial \lambda = I - Q^* \cdot C - P \cdot X = 0$$

The third first-order condition ensures that the lifetime income constraint is satisfied. Rearranging the first two conditions, we can derive the decision rule for utility maximization:

$$\frac{U_C + U_R \cdot R_C \cdot (1/C^*)}{Q^*} = \frac{MU_C}{Q^*} = \lambda = \frac{MU_X}{P} = \frac{U_X + U_R \cdot R_X \cdot (1/X^*)}{P}$$

That is, at the optimal combination of family size and material standard of living, the marginal utility of children per dollar is equal to the marginal utility of other goods and services per dollar. The marginal utilities for children and goods, MU_C and MU_X, are made up of the satisfaction gained from the absolute consumption, U_C and U_X, and the additional satisfaction gained from enhanced relative status, $U_R \cdot R_C \cdot (1/C^*)$ and $U_R \cdot R_X \cdot (1/X^*)$, where $R_C = \partial R/\partial C$ and $R_X = \partial R/\partial X$. This additional satisfaction from relative status is discounted, however, by the social reference group standards, C^* and X^*. The higher the standards set, the harder it is to realize this satisfaction. The marginal utilities per dollar for children and other goods are, in turn, equal to λ, which represents the marginal utility of income.[11]

Consider the representative couple at the outset of their planning process, when choices about family size and lifestyle are first contemplated. Based on their education and labor skills, perception of the job prospects, and financial wealth, the couple will project their permanent income. Within this income constraint and given their aspirations for the quality of their children (here Q^*), the couple will etch plans for the number of children and their lifetime consumption of other goods and services. These initial plans, likely to be tentative, are not made in a vacuum. The couple's choices are influenced by the benchmark performance of a social reference group.

In traditional, agrarian societies with limited educational opportunities and restricted economic mobility, high fertility can be easily perpetuated. There are social pressures to conform to the conventional behavior. Alternative role models, especially in remote villages, are few, if present at all. The expected life pattern is well established. Minimal education, marriage at a young age, early and frequent childbearing, the primary responsibility for the maintenance of the family, as well as expectations for contributing to the income of the household (e.g., working in the fields), confront the typical young woman.

With economic development and the structural change of urbanization and industrialization, the cohesiveness of such high-fertility regimes tends to break down. Increased opportunities for education, improved health, and access to family planning programs, along with better employment opportunities, yield new options. Fertility behavior becomes more discretionary and the demand for children falls.

---

[11] The optimal value of λ, the Lagrangian multiplier, represents the partial derivative of the optimal utility with respect to the income constraint, $\lambda = \partial U/\partial I$, which is the marginal utility of income.

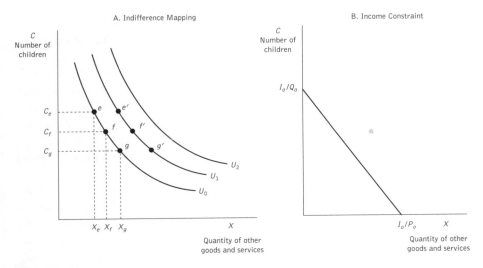

A. Indifference Mapping   B. Income Constraint

Figure 10.1 *Indifference mapping and income constraint*

(A) Three indifference curves in the indifference mapping of the couple are depicted. Each indifference curve represents the combinations of children (C) and other goods and services (X) yielding the same utility. Indifference curves further from the origin indicate higher levels of utility. The indifference curves are drawn holding constant the couple's tastes and preferences. (B) The income constraint of the couple represents the combinations of children (C) and other goods and services (X) that have the same cost. The income constraint is drawn holding constant the couple's permanent income (I), desired quality of children (Q), and the price index for other goods and services.

Indifference mapping and income constraints

We can illustrate this constrained optimization problem with indifference curves and a budget line. Returning to the utility function, **indifference curves** can be derived that show the combinations of the number of children and consumption of other goods and services yielding the same total utilities. For example, in Figure 10.1(a) the representative couple is indifferent between any two combinations of C and X on the indifference curve U_0. The combinations of children and other goods represented by points e, f, and g all yield the same total utility (U_0). As we move out from the origin to higher indifference curves (such as U_1 and U_2), the total utilities rise. Therefore, while the couple is indifferent between combinations e', f', and g' on indifference curve U_1, any combination on U_1 is preferred to any combination on U_0, a lower indifference curve.

The indifference curves are negatively sloped and convex to the origin. The negative slope indicates the tradeoff between family size and other consumption. Given that additional children or other goods always contribute to total utility (formally, the marginal utilities of C and X are assumed to be always positive), then along an indifference curve, a couple would be willing to have fewer children only if their consumption of other goods increased.

The slope of an indifference curve, called the **marginal rate of substitution**, indicates the rate at which a couple is willing to trade off or substitute children for other goods.[12] The

---

[12] If we take the utility function, $U = U(C, X, Q^*, R[C/C^*, X/X^*])$ and totally differentiate, we find, $dU = U_C dC + U_X dX + U_{Q^*} dQ^* + U_R \cdot R_C(dC/C^*) + U_R \cdot R_X(dX/X^*)$. Along an indifference curve, total utility is constant ($dU = 0$) and the quality standard for children is predetermined ($dQ^* = 0$). Solving this total differential for dC/dX gives the slope of the indifference

hypothesis of diminishing marginal utility accounts for the strict convexity of the curves. As increasing amounts of other goods are consumed (i.e., as X rises), the additional satisfaction received from the consumption of another unit of X decreases (i.e., the marginal utility of X falls). Conversely, as the number of children declines, the willingness to reduce further family size decreases. Therefore, as a couple moves down and to the right along an indifference curve, the quantity of other goods required to replace each child increases. The slope of the indifference curve becomes flatter. In Figure 10.1(a), in moving from combinations e to f to g along indifference curve U_0, the decrease in the number of children is equal (i.e., $C_e - C_f = C_f - C_g$), but the increase in other goods required to maintain the total utility of the parents is rising ($X_g - X_f > X_f - X_e$).

A set of indifference curves, called an **indifference mapping**, is drawn for given tastes and preferences of the couple. A change in tastes and preferences would rotate the indifference curves. For example, an increase in consumer aspirations or a shift in tastes in favor of smaller families would rotate the indifference curves in a clockwise fashion (the indifference curves would become steeper). The couple would be more willing to "give up" children (accept a smaller family size) for a given increase in the consumption of other goods and services.

The maximization of total utility is constrained by permanent income. The **income constraint**, plotted in Figure 10.1(b), represents all the combinations of children and other goods the couple can afford given the permanent income ($I = I_0$), the predetermined quality of children ($Q_0 = Q^*$), and the price index for other goods ($P = P_0$). At one extreme, if all income were devoted to children, the maximum number of children would be I_0/Q_0. At the other extreme, if there were no children, the maximum quantity of other goods would be I_0/P_0. The slope of the income constraint is equal to the negative of the ratio of the price index to the quality of children ($-P_0/Q_0$). An increase in permanent income would shift the income constraint out to the right in a parallel fashion. A change in the desired quality of children (expenditures per child) or in the price index for other goods would affect the slope of the income constraint.

The maximization of total utility of the couple occurs at the tangency of the income constraint with the highest indifference curve. In Figure 10.2 the income constraint BB is tangent to the indifference curve U_0 at point e_0, giving an optimal combination of children and other goods of C_0 and X_0. An increase in permanent income, *ceteris paribus*, would shift the income constraint out to the right in a parallel fashion, allowing the couple to attain greater consumption levels. If children (C) and other goods (X) are "normal", that is, have positive income elasticities, then the increase in income results in increases in the demands for children and other goods. (See the increase from C_0 to C_1 and from X_0 to X_1 in Figure 10.2.) Thus, the widely observed negative correlation between fertility and income must be due to other factors, such as changes in tastes and preferences and relative increases in the desired quality of children.

ECONOMIC DEVELOPMENT AND DECLINING FAMILY SIZE

With economic development there are factors which contribute to the decline in the demand for children even as incomes rise. In particular, with gains in education the economic mobility of

---

curve, known as the marginal rate of substitution, MRS, which equals:

$$\frac{dC}{dX} = \text{MRS} = -\frac{U_X + U_R \cdot R_X \cdot (1/X*)}{U_C + U_R \cdot R_C \cdot (1/C*)}$$

and gives the rate at which the couple is willing to trade off family size for material standard of living.

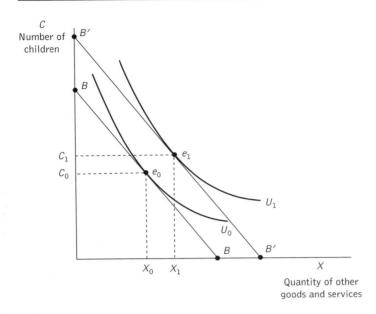

Figure 10.2 *Utility-maximizing demand for children*

The utility-maximizing combination of children and other goods and services is found at the tangency of the income constraint and the highest indifference curve that can be reached, here U_0. At this combination, C_0 and X_0, the marginal rate of substitution of children for other goods and services is equal to the negative ratio of the price index (P_0) to the desired quality of children (Q_0). That is, $MRS = -P_0/Q_0$.

An increase in income allows the couple to increase their utility, moving to a tangency with a higher indifference curve.

females is enhanced. Women are more likely to postpone marriage and participate in the labor force as the wages they could earn rise with their education. As the opportunity cost of a woman's time increases, child care, a time-intensive activity, becomes more expensive. Consequently, the time spent by more educated women on childrearing becomes more valuable—which can be modeled as an increase in the quality of children (here a rise in Q^*).

Also, as individuals become more educated, their appreciation for the value of schooling and their aspirations for their children rise. Couples decide to spend more on each child—an investment in human capital that makes more economic sense as child survival rates increase with economic development. In short, with education couples become more inclined to substitute "quality" for "quantity" of children (also in this model indicated by an increase in Q^*).

With the gains in income that accompany economic development, consumer aspirations may be stimulated. In order to afford an improved lifestyle, couples may have to limit family size. This shift in tastes and preferences in favor of higher consumption standards and smaller families is reflected in a rotation of the indifference mapping in a clockwise manner; that is, at any combination of children and other goods, the slope of the relevant indifference curve becomes steeper. There is an increased willingness to trade off children for other goods (reflected here in an increase in X^*). Finally, as smaller families become more accepted and prevalent for the social reference group (here a decrease in C^*), the representative couple is more comfortable in demanding fewer children.

Kinsella and Phillips (2005: 24) observe that, "increasingly, people are choosing not to have children, reflecting lower marriage rates and cultural changes that make childlessness more socially acceptable." The incidence of childlessness among women aged 40–44 in the US rose from 10 percent in 1980 to 19 percent in 2000. In Europe, and increasingly in Latin America and Southeast Asia, women without children are common. They note, however, that not all childlessness is voluntary. Poor health, infecundity, and not having a suitable partner for bringing children into the world will account for some women never having children.

In Figure 10.3 we summarize the effects of economic development on the demand for children. At low levels of development the representative couple's utility-maximizing combination of children and other goods is given by C_0 and X_0, respectively. (See point e_0, where the indifference curve U_0 is tangent to the income constraint BB.) As incomes rise with economic development, the income constraint shifts out to the right. The shift, however, is not parallel, since there is a relative increase in the desired quality of children compared to the price index for other goods. (The slope of the new income constraint is flatter. With economic development, consumer goods may become relatively plentiful, moderating the rise in P.) The new utility-maximizing combination for the couple based on the increase in income and the relative rise in the desired quality of children would be at point e_1. But the change in tastes and preferences in favor of higher consumption standards and smaller families rotates the indifference mapping in a clockwise manner. (Compare the indifference curves U_1' and U_1.) As a result, the new utility-maximizing combination of children and other goods becomes C_1' and X_1', represented by point e_1' at the tangency of the income constraint $B'B'$ with the indifference curve U_1'. In sum, with economic development the demand for children declines.

Returning to the constrained utility-maximization model, we can write the reduced form equation for the demand for children as:

$$C^d = C^d(\overset{+}{I},\ \overset{?}{P},\ \overset{-}{Q}{}^*,\ \overset{-}{X}{}^*,\ \overset{+}{C}{}^*)$$

where the signs over the arguments indicate the hypothesized influence of those variables on the demand for children.[13] The ambiguity with respect to the influence of the price level for goods and services unrelated to children (P) reflects the substitution and income effects. The former indicates an increase in the price level would induce a substitution away from these goods and services (X), thus increase the demand for children. The income effect works the other way. An increase in the price level reduces real income (I/P), and, given children are "normal goods," would reduce the demand for children. With economic growth and development, incomes rise, *ceteris paribus*, increasing the demand for children. It is likely that the growth in income exceeds the growth in the desired quality of children, which, in turn, exceeds the growth in the price level. That is, the income constraint shifts out, but becomes flatter. The increase in real income raises the demand for children, while increases in the desired quality of children (Q^*) and consumer aspirations (X^*) reduce the demand for children. The latter effects dominate. And declines in the social reference group standard for family size, C^*, contribute to reducing the representative couple's demand for children.

---

[13] If we invoke the implicit function theorem, then from the first-order conditions, the optimal values for C and X can theoretically be written as functions of the predetermined or exogenous variables in the system. To invoke the implicit function theorem, the first-order conditions must have continuous partial derivatives with respect to each of the variables in the system.

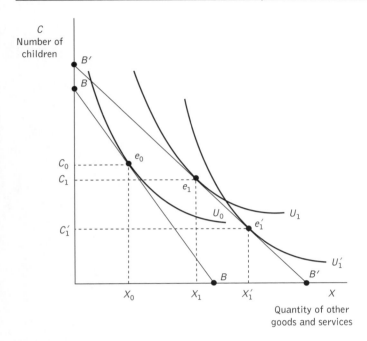

Figure 10.3 *Decrease in demand for children with economic development*

With economic development, the couple's income rises, as do their desired quality of children and the general price level. Also, the couple's tastes and preferences change in favor of other goods and services and smaller family sizes. As a result, economic development tends to reduce the demand for children. Here the utility-maximizing number of children declines from C_0 to C_1'.

As we will see, a decrease in the demand for children, by itself, need not translate into lower fertility. Before extending the model to consider "supply-side" fertility factors and the practice of birth control, we can illustrate sub-optimal equilibria for a representative couple.

Non-utility-maximizing equilibrium

The above analysis assumed that the representative couple were able to realize their optimal demand for children. In practice, however, there may be suboptimal equilibria reflecting either excess fertility or insufficient fertility. To illustrate, refer to Figure 10.4.

First consider an equilibrium where the couple has more than their optimal number of children, $C_a > C_1$, placing them on a lower indifference curve, U_0, than the utility-maximizing curve, U_1. (See point a, where the income constraint cuts the indifference curve, U_0.) Such excess fertility could reflect a natural fertility regime, where couples do not exercise individual discretion over their childbearing, or a failure to use effective birth control due prohibitive costs or lack of knowledge.

A second suboptimal outcome is where the couple is not able to have as many children as they desire, $C_b < C_1$, again resulting in a lower than optimal utility, $U_0 < U_1$. (See point b, where the income constraint cuts the indifference curve, U_0.) This smaller than optimal family size might reflect supply constraints such as impaired fecundity or reduced exposure to the risk of conception or mandatory birth control as under an authoritarian population policy. Later in the chapter we will discuss China's coercive birth control policy.

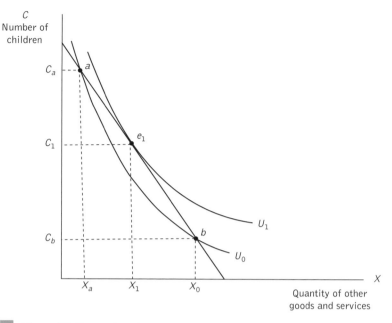

Figure 10.4 *Supply influences on the number of children*

It is possible that the couple is not maximizing their utility. The couple might have an excess number of children, here C_a, due to an inability to control their fertility. Or the couple may not have as many children as they desire, here C_b, due to health problems or mandatory birth control.

DEMAND FOR BIRTH CONTROL

The representative couple's demand for children, by itself, may not determine their actual fertility. We need to include supply-side factors as well as the costs of birth control.

Returning to this representative couple, given their demand for children, C^d, derived from the utility-maximizing model, their demand for births, B^d, would be directly related to expected child mortality, M^e. That is, if child mortality rates were high, then to achieve a given desired family size, extra births may be necessary as replacement fertility. In high-income societies, in contrast, child mortality, however, would be minimal. Most parents would fully expect their children to survive. In general though, we can write:

$$B^d = B^d(\overset{+}{C^d}, \overset{+}{M^e})$$

The potential supply of children, B^s, is directly related to exposure to the risk of conception (E) and fecundity (H). The former is determined by marriage customs and sanctions on sexual unions outside of marriage. Fecundity, the ability to have children, reflects the health of the couple, especially the woman. On the supply side then, let

$$B^s = B^s(\overset{+}{E}, \overset{+}{H})$$

The cumulative or lifetime fertility of the representative couple, then, is a weighted average of the demand and supply of births, where the weight is an index of the practice of birth control. That is,

$$F = k \cdot B^d + (1 - k) \cdot B^s,$$

where F is the cumulative or lifetime fertility of the representative couple, and k is the index of the use of birth control ($0 \leq k \leq 1$). If $k = 0$, then a natural fertility regime prevails, with no individual discretionary control over fertility. If, at the other extreme, $k = 1$, then there is a perfect birth control regime, where actual fertility equals the demand for births. The value of k, in turn, will be determined by the costs of using birth control, both monetary and psychic.

Monetary costs are the direct expenditures for contraception (e.g., pills, intrauterine devices (IUDs), condoms) and abortion, including visits to doctors and pharmacies to secure the services and prescriptions. Psychic costs are the emotional stress of using birth control. The practice of contraception (especially the more modern techniques) may be an innovative behavior in traditional societies, and thus meet with the disapproval of authority figures—from parents of couples desiring many grandchildren, from husbands whose self-esteem may be tied to their number of sons, and from churches for moral reasons. Moreover, any new behavior carries with it uncertainty and risk. Women with minimal education may be fearful of the reported (and often exaggerated) side-effects of modern contraception. Visits to a doctor may evoke apprehension. Women may be anxious about even discussing sexual practices. Where illegal or back-alley abortions are the primary means of birth control, the fears are clearly credible. Indeed, one of the benefits of education is an increased awareness of, and receptivity to, new types of behavior. Educated individuals feel more in control of their lives and are more able to practice effective contraception.

A reduced-form expression for the cumulative fertility of the representative couple is given by:

$$F = F(\overset{+}{I}, \overset{?}{P}, \overset{-}{Q}{}^{*}, \overset{-}{X}{}^{*}, \overset{+}{C}{}^{*}, \overset{+}{M}{}^{e}, \overset{+}{E}, \overset{+}{H}, \overset{-}{k})$$

As discussed, with economic development the demand for children falls.

Rising real income per capita is accompanied by greater aspirations of parents for their children (Q^{*} increases) and for their own consumption (X^{*} increases). Tastes change in favor of smaller families (with decreases in C^{*}), as parents substitute quality for quantity of children and the desire and ability to realize a higher material standard of living conflict with large families. Also, with economic development, child survival rates improve (M^{e} decreases), further reducing the demand for births to insure a given desired family size.

In low-income economies with inadequate health care and poor nutrition the incidences of sterility and miscarriage are high. On the supply side, fecundity would increase with economic development as health and nutrition improve and incidences of disease diminish, which would enhance the natural supply of children. Natural exposure to the risk of conception may well decrease with economic development if the average ages at marriage and usual onset of child-bearing rise with more education and better employment prospects. Exposure may also decrease with the separation of couples, for example, the migration of males to urban areas, or even out of the country, for employment. If, however, the practice of breastfeeding, prevalent in traditional societies, is reduced with modern sector employment, then exposure to the risk of conception may well increase. Without greater individual control over fertility, an increase in natural fertility translates into higher birth rates.

Fertility rates do decline with economic development as increasingly the lower demand for children will dominate the potential supply. With economic development, the costs of contraception fall. Family planning programs increase the availability of modern contraceptive techniques (reducing the direct costs) and, by providing information and encouragement, lend legitimacy to the practice of modern contraception (reducing the psychic costs). Therefore the greater practice of birth control (an increase in k) to realize the reduced number of births desired brings down birth rates.[14]

Evidence on the determinants of fertility

In Table 10.5 selected statistics on determinants of fertility are given for nations grouped by income and region. First we note that fertility, as measured by the total fertility rate, does decline with income, although as explained above, not because children are "inferior goods." Fertility rates and child mortality rates are directly related. With economic development and improved survival rates for children, replacement-level fertility declines. Fewer births would be necessary to achieve a given desired family size (e.g., two surviving sons). Not surprisingly, we find total fertility rates higher in those nations with higher infant mortality.

The primary reasons for the lower fertility that accompanies economic development are the decline in the demand for children and the increased use of effective contraception. The average contraceptive prevalence rates for the period 2005–10 range from 34 percent in the low-income economies to 81 percent in the upper middle-income economies (a reflection of China's 85 percent rate). Gains in female education increase the opportunity cost of childrearing and the ability and willingness to use effective contraception. So, too, urbanization increases the cost of childrearing, as shelter is more expensive and opportunities for children to work are fewer than in rural areas.

Fertility rates, however, are determined not just by socioeconomic factors, but by cultural influences. For example, the average total fertility rates for South Asia and for the Middle East and North Africa in 2010 are identical, although child survival rates, per capita income, female literacy, and urbanization are significantly higher in the latter region.

We turn now to modern trends in fertility, beginning with the US. An interesting explanation for the post-World War II baby boom is provided by Easterlin's theory of relative economic status.

POST-WORLD WAR II TRENDS

After World War II the US and other industrialized countries experienced "baby booms." With a growing economy and underlying demographic factors, the US total fertility rate increased to over 3.5 children per woman by the mid-1950s.

The US baby boom

In part, the rise in US birth rates reflected the increased proportions of women of childbearing age, a consequence of the population momentum that had built up before the replacement-level fertility in the 1930s. Second, with the relatively prosperous times, the average age at marriage and proportions remaining single fell. There were shorter intervals between marriage and first and subsequent births. In addition, some catch-up in desired family size occurred with older women

---

[14]There are, however, other points in the life cycle where contraception is used even though fertility is short of the demand for children. Contraception may be used to avoid unwanted fertility (e.g., outside of marital unions), to postpone the first birth, or to increase the interval between births. At the International Conference on Population and Development in Cairo in 1994, the underlying themes were promoting reproductive health and empowering females (see United Nations Population Fund and Population Reference Bureau 2009). This report noted that while the Cairo Consensus called for universal access to modern methods of contraception, more than 200 million women across the world have an "unmet need" for contraception, that is, they would like to delay their next pregnancy by at least 2 years or stop childbearing entirely, but are not using a modern method of contraception.

Table 10.5 *Selected statistics on determinants of fertility*

	Total fertility rate 2010	Infant mortality rate 2010	Contraceptive prevalence rate 2005–10	Female youth literacy rate 2005–10	Share of urban population 2010
WORLD ($11,066)	2.5	41	62%	87%	51%
Low-income economies ($1,307)	4.1	70	34%	68%	28%
Lower middle-income economies ($3,632)	2.9	50	50%	79%	39%
India ($3,400)	2.6	48	54%	74%	30%
Upper middle-income economies ($9,970)	1.8	17	81%	99%	57%
China ($7,640)	1.6	16	85%	99%	45%
High-income economies ($37,317)	1.8	5	...	99%	78%
United States ($47,310)	2.1	7	79%	...	82%
LOW & UPPER MIDDLE-INCOME ECONOMIES					
Sub-Saharan Africa ($2,148)	4.9	76	22%	67%	37%
Middle East & North Africa ($8,068)	2.7	27	62%	87%	58%
Europe & Central Asia ($13,396)	1.8	19	69%	99%	64%
South Asia ($3,124)	2.7	52	51%	72%	30%
East Asia & Pacific ($6,657)	1.8	20	78%	99%	46%
Latin America & Caribbean ($10,926)	2.2	18	75%	97%	79%

Notes: Per capita gross national incomes for 2010 in PPP dollars are listed in next to the country classification or region.

Total fertility rate is the number of children that would be born to a woman if she were to live to the end of her childbearing years and bear children in accordance with current age-specific fertility rates.

Infant mortality rate is number of infants dying before reaching 1 year of age per 1,000 live births in a given year.

Contraceptive prevalence rate is the percentage of women married or in union aged 15–49 who are practicing any form of contraception.

Female youth literacy rate is the percentage of females aged 15–24 who can, with understanding, both read and write a short, simple statement about everyday life.

Share of urban population is the percentage of the total population living in urban areas. Note, there is no consistent and universally accepted standard for distinguishing urban from rural.

Source: World Bank (2012: Tables 1.1, 2.14, 2.19, 2.23, and 3.13).

who had postponed childbearing during the depression years. In short, after the Great Depression and World War II, couples were marrying more and starting families earlier, and many older mothers were having a third or fourth child.

After the war, employment opportunities were abundant for the smaller cohorts born during the 1930s. Accompanying the growing population was a construction boom, with housing and schools, hospitals and libraries. Along with housing, the demands for consumer durables, including furniture and appliances, as well as toys, increased. Demands for teachers and pediatricians and the attendant service industries also accelerated. With increased ownership of automobiles and expansion of the population to suburbs, larger families were more affordable.

By the mid-1960s, however, the baby boom was over. Fertility rates began to decline sharply, falling below replacement level by the mid-1970s. The baby boom was followed by the "baby

Table 10.6 *US post-World War II trends*

Period	Total fertility rate	Crude birth rate	Crude death rate	Net migration rate	Population growth rate
1950–55	3.45	24.3	9.5	1.4	1.62
1955–60	3.71	24.3	9.4	2.1	1.70
1960–65	3.31	21.8	9.4	1.3	1.36
1965–70	2.55	17.7	9.5	1.6	0.98
1970–75	2.02	15.7	9.2	2.5	0.90
1975–80	1.79	15.1	8.6	3.1	0.96
1980–85	1.80	15.5	8.7	2.8	0.96
1985–90	1.89	15.7	8.8	3.1	0.99
1990–95	1.99	15.3	8.7	3.4	1.00
1995–2000	1.96	14.2	8.6	6.2	1.18
2000–05	2.04	14.1	8.5	4.3	0.99
2005–10	2.07	14.0	8.3	3.3	0.89

Notes: The total fertility rate is expressed as births per woman.

The crude birth rate (CBR), crude death rate (CDR), and net migration rate (NMR) are expressed per thousand mid-point populations.

The population growth rate, equal to CBR − CDR + NMR, is expressed in percentage points.

Source: Population Division of the Department of Economic and Social Affairs of the United Nations, *World Population Prospects: The 2010 Revision* (http://esa.un.org/unpd/wpp/index.htm), accessed June 19, 2012.

bust." With greater opportunities for females, women increasingly enrolled in colleges and participated in the labor force. Marriage and childbearing were postponed. With more education, the wages women could earn rose, and the opportunity cost of childrearing, measured by the income lost by not working, increased. Modern contraception, including the birth control pill, IUD, and sterilization, gave women more control over their reproduction. And, with greater sexual freedom, unions before marriage became more common—contrary to Malthus's recommendation of "moral restraint"—increasing the demand for contraception.

We can see from Table 10.6 the sharp increase in the total fertility rate after World War II. The post-war fertility rate in the US peaked in the late 1950s. The **baby boom generation**, the large cohorts born between 1946 and 1964, experienced greater competition from the beginning—in elementary school classrooms in the 1950s, in applying for colleges in the 1960s, when entering the labor force in the 1970s, and then when buying their first homes in the 1980s. The greater economic pressure prompted more couples to work and both earn income.

The consequences of the baby boom generation for the US economy have been and will continue to be profound. For example, the 1970s were a turbulent time for the US economy, with periodic stagflation. Nevertheless, over the decade US employment grew by 25.5 percent, from 78.7 million to 98.8 million. The labor force grew even faster, by 26.8 percent, from 82.8 million to 105.0 million, largely due to the entrance of baby boomers into the labor market as well as the continued increase in female labor participation, including the reentrance into the labor force of the mothers of the baby boomers. Despite the impressive job creation, the unemployment rate in the US increased by nearly a percentage point, from 4.9 percent in 1970 to 5.8 percent in 1979.

With the baby bust in the decade after the baby boom (i.e., the cohorts born between 1965 and 1977), labeled **Generation X**, we found excess capacity in some school systems. American businesses reoriented to the changing demographics. Smaller families and higher gasoline prices induced the shift to smaller, more fuel-efficient automobiles. Appealing to an older audience, Disney added Epcot Center to the Magic Kingdom and Touchstone Pictures to the traditional fare of family films.

As noted, the total fertility rate in the US had fallen below 2 in the early 1970s, stabilized and then even increased back to above 2 by the 1990s, due, in part, to the relatively high fertility rates of immigrants to the US. In general, immigrants from less developed to more developed countries have higher fertility rates for some time until fully assimilated into the culture of the developed country.[15]

The number of births, however, continued to fluctuate, with the baby bust of 1965–77 followed by a baby boomlet, the so-called **Generation Y**, covering the cohorts born between 1978 and 1995.[16] Largely the offspring of the baby boomers, reflecting some delayed fertility, Generation Y is renewing the demands for schools, teachers, pediatricians, and entertainment. For example, in 2000 there were approximately 52 million students enrolled in elementary and secondary schools in the US, the largest number ever (see Kent and Mather 2002: 31). Because of the population momentum from the earlier baby boom, the cohorts born between 1978 and 1995 are relatively large, despite the maintenance of low fertility rates.

Recently the US total fertility rate has risen, albeit marginally, from 1.96 (1995–2000) to 2.07 (2005–10), even as the crude birth rate fell, from 14.2 to 14.0, as shown in Table 10.6. Will the US maintain replacement-level fertility or revert to below replacement-level fertility as other developed countries have maintained now for over a quarter century? Or might US fertility rates fluctuate over time with generations?

Easterlin's relative economic status

One theory suggesting a cyclical movement in fertility rates was put forth by Richard Easterlin (see Easterlin 1968; Macunovich 2002). The key to explaining fertility, according to Easterlin, is **relative economic status**. Determined by comparing present employment and income prospects with consumption aspirations, a rise in relative economic status would prompt higher fertility. In contrast, if consumption aspirations, a function of upbringing formed largely during childhood and early adolescence, were greater than income prospects, couples would likely opt for smaller family sizes. The relative size of cohorts—for example, the baby boom generation, followed by the baby bust, Generation X (born 1965–77), and then the baby boomlet, Generation Y (born 1978–95)—could affect relative economic status. Individuals born in a cohort smaller than the

[15] Kent and Haub (2005: 10–11) observe that in 2004 it was the relatively high total fertility rate of 2.82 for Hispanic women that kept the overall US fertility near replacement level. Black, Asian, and white total fertility rates in 2004 were respectively 2.01, 1.90, and 1.85. In 2008, the TFRs were little changed: Hispanic (2.96), black (2.15), Asian (1.92), and white (1.86). See Jacobsen and Mather (2010: 11).

[16] Generation Y is also known as the Millennials. See Scott Keeter and Paul Taylor, "The Millennials" (http://pewresearch.org/pubs/1437/millennials-profile), written in 2009. The age intervals attached to the various generations, except for the well-defined baby boom generation, may differ somewhat across scholars. For example, Keeter and Taylor refer to the Millennials as the cohorts born from 1981 to 2000, and Generation X as the cohorts born from 1965 to 1980.

For an interesting study, see Carlson (2009). Carlson identifies seven generations in the twentieth century: New Wonders (born 1871–89), one fourth of whom were immigrants; Hard Timers (born 1890–1908), who fought in World War I, experienced the Great Depression, and largely became grandparents of the baby boomers; Good Warriors (born 1909–28), who fought in World War II and have been labeled the Greatest Generation by Tom Brokaw; Lucky Few (born 1929–45), a smaller generation, who, with favorable job opportunities after World War II, married earlier and largely are the parents of baby boomers; Baby Boomers (born 1946–64); Generation X (born 1965–82), the baby bust cohorts who delayed marriage and childbearing; New Boomers (born 1983–2001), who are also known as Generation Y and the Millennials.

preceding one would encounter less competition for jobs and earn higher incomes, which might encourage them to marry earlier and have more children.

For example, the cohorts born in the 1920s and 1930s were smaller than earlier cohorts, due to the long-term decline in US fertility rates. Combined with the lower immigration to the US in the 1930s, these smaller cohorts were in a favorable position in the expanding job market following World War II. Moreover, these birth cohorts of the 1920s and 1930s grew up during the depression and then war years, so their consumer aspirations were modest. Thus, according to the theory of relative economic status, it is not surprising that these same cohorts produced the baby boom.

Their children, the baby boomers born during 1946–64, in contrast, grew up in relatively prosperous times (the 1950s and 1960s), especially the "front-enders" (cohorts born in 1946–57), had fairly high consumption aspirations, but, with the large size of the cohorts, experienced tighter job markets and less economic mobility than expected. Thus the baby boomers responded by delaying marriage and reducing fertility. The baby bust cohorts, born between 1965 and 1977, began entering the prime childbearing years (20–34 years of age) in the mid-1980s. Consistent with Easterlin's theory, with the trend towards later marriage and childbearing, the US total fertility rate did rebound a bit beginning in the latter half of 1980s.

The baby boomlet or baby boom echo (the cohorts born between 1978 and 1995) reflects to a considerable extent the fertility, often delayed, of the baby boomers. This relatively large cohort of the children of the baby boomers might have grown up in relatively affluent conditions (especially during the 1990s), but find their income prospects somewhat dampened. This Generation Y, beginning to enter their prime childbearing years at the turn of the century, might respond with lower fertility. The US total fertility rate, however, slightly increased over the first decade of the twenty-first century. Will fertility subsequently drop back to well below replacement level? Even if Generation Y maintains the current replacement-level fertility, there would be another echo effect with an increase in the total number of births due to the larger size of this generation.

Needless to say, migration will also affect the population size and distribution and the national fertility and mortality rates. We will discuss the determinants of migration later in this chapter. We can see from Table 10.6, however, that net migration rates into the US are significant and have fluctuated over the post-World War II period. For 2005–10, net migration accounted for over a third of the US population growth. In fact, as Kent and Haub (2005: 10) note, "The United States receives about half of the world's international immigrants, a remarkable fact considering that the United States accounts for just 5 percent of world population."

In short, barring offsetting swings in immigration or unusual economic conditions, Easterlin's theory would suggest a series of fertility swings, with relatively high and low fertility rates with alternating generations, driven by relative economic status. In any case, US population will almost certainly not only increase for the next few decades, but become significantly older.

AGING OF THE US POPULATION

The US population in 2040 may be more than 20 percent greater than in 2010, with a fifth aged 65 and older, as illustrated in Table 10.7. Recall from Chapter 9 that the primary determinant of the age of a population is fertility. Low fertility produces older populations. Improvements in mortality, reflected in greater life expectancies, will also contribute to the aging of the US

Table 10.7 *US population by age group in millions (and percent)*

	Total	0–14	15–64	65+	80+
1950	157.8	42.6 (27.0%)	102.2 (64.7%)	13.0 (8.3%)	1.8 (1.1%)
1980	229.8	51.9 (22.6%)	152.0 (66.1%)	25.9 (11.3%)	5.2 (2.3%)
2010	310.4	62.3 (20.1%)	207.5 (66.9%)	40.5 (13.0%)	11.8 (3.8%)
2040	383.5	72.0 (18.8%)	231.2 (60.3%)	80.2 (20.9%)	27.4 (7.1%)

Source: World Population Prospects: The 2010 Revision. The population for 2040 is projected.

population. Migration, however, has partially offset the aging of the US population, as immigrants tend to be younger, and at least initially have higher fertility, than the average.

The movement of the baby boomers through the life cycle, as just discussed, has profoundly affected the US economy. The oldest baby boomers are beginning to retire, drawing on the social security system, rather than paying into the system. In fact, the severe recession in 2008–09 appears to have accelerated the retirement of those baby boomers who lost their jobs. Whether these families have saved enough to fund their retirements is unclear. Recent research by the Federal Reserve shows that the net worth of the median US family declined from $126,400 in 2007 to $77,300 in 2010, with the decline in housing prices accounting for three-fourths of this loss in wealth (Applebaum 2012).

The percentage of the US population 65 or over increased from 8.3 percent in 1950 to 13.0 percent in 2010 and is projected to rise to 20.9 percent by 2040. The share of the 80 and older population, with the attendant heavy demands on the health care system, will increase from 1.1 percent in 1950 to 3.8 percent in 2010 and a projected 7.0 percent in 2040. Given the pay-as-you-go nature of social security and, to a large extent, Medicare, the elderly burden of dependency on the working population will be significantly higher. In the 1960s there were nearly four workers for every social security retiree, but by 2030 there may be only two workers for every retiree (Weeks 2008: 347).

In 1970, spending on social security and Medicare accounted for 4 percent of US gross domestic product. In 2000, their combined total was 6 percent. If not reformed, social security and Medicare are projected to total 12 percent of GDP by 2030, with Medicare outlays by that point exceeding social security expenses (Jacobsen et al. 2011: 14). Reforms in social security and Medicare are inevitable, but politically challenging. Key issues include: increasing the eligibility age for full social security retirement benefits (from the current, phased-in 66 to 67 years of age), increasing the social insurance tax rate, and increasing the income limits subject to the social security tax.[17] Taxing labor, however, discourages employment. In fact, at the end of 2010, the US Congress passed another fiscal stimulus plan to boost employment, including a one-year reduction in the payroll tax to 4.2 percent (from 6.2 percent on employees). This payroll tax cut was eventually extended a second year in 2012. The federal government replaced the revenue lost to social security from this temporary stimulus so that the trust fund would not be diminished.

---

[17] The social security tax withheld from employees during the year 2010 was 6.2 percent of the first $106,800 of each employee's taxable earnings. The employee's earnings in excess of $106,800 were not subject to the social security tax. In addition to the social security tax, the entire amount of each employee's taxable earnings was subject to the Medicare tax of 1.45 percent. Both the social security tax and the Medicare tax must be matched by the employer. This means the employer must remit to the federal government 12.4 percent of each employee's first $106,800 in wages plus 2.9 percent of each employee's total wages. Self-employed individuals are responsible for paying both the employee and the employer portions of the social security tax and the Medicare tax.

Concerns with an aging population

There are fundamental issues to be addressed on health care and the quality of life for older people. Advances in medicine and health technology have been phenomenal. In many cases, though, the majority of lifetime health care expenses are concentrated in the last year or two of life, when the medicine and technology to keep people alive are present, but the diminishing quality of life is a concern. Greater reliance on palliative and hospice care makes sense, and arguably in the future there may be careful consideration of euthanasia.

In addition to the expected demands on the government budget, there are social concerns with an aging population. One is the possible reduced vitality of the population. To the extent that older people are more conservative and resistant to change, there may be less innovation and a stifling of creative energy in society. With an older population seniority may become more prevalent, where the older cohorts dominate decision-making and resource allocations. For example, the powerful AARP (formerly the American Association of Retired Persons) is an influential lobbyist. In the US the elderly poverty rate has generally declined over the last few decades, in large part to more generous social security benefits, while the youth poverty rate has remained persistently high.[18]

Will aging societies lead to greater generational conflicts? When budgets become tight, spending for elderly support (e.g., for social security and health care) may be pitted against investing in youth, through education, primary health care, and nutrition. Another dynamic is the growing heterogeneity of societies, which could be embraced for the greater diversity, but is resisted by older, established native populations. Jacobsen et al. (2011) speculate on the possible emergence of a "new generation gap," in the US, between an older, majority white population and increasingly racially mixed younger generations, in part due to the heavy immigration of younger Hispanics and their higher fertility.

Generational conflicts, however, need not be. Several years ago *The Economist* asked: "At what point does an ageing mind become a liability and not an asset?" The answer depends on what the mind is asked to do. If the task requires a wealth of knowledge and experiences, then the elders have what it takes. On the other hand, if the job needs sharp and fast thinking, then youth has the advantage.[19] Perhaps this complementarity of insights, from seniors and juniors, or elderly and youth, holds the key.

In short, the challenge of an older population will be in incorporating the elderly into the economy, polity, and society in a productive and meaningful way. Kinsella and Phillips (2005: 32–34) refer to "successful aging," meaning being actively engaged with life, which will be increasingly possible for the elderly with improving health, and "productive aging," meaning the ability to contribute directly and indirectly to the common good.

---

[18] Poverty rates among the elderly have declined sharply over the past 50 years. US Census Bureau data show that the fraction of Americans aged 65 and over with incomes below the poverty rate declined from 35.2 percent in 1959 to 9.9 percent in 2000, where it stabilized, even remaining under 10 percent through the 2008–09 recession. In contrast, for the US population under 18 years of age, the poverty rate declined from 27.3 percent in 1959 to only 16.2 percent in 2000, and then increased again, especially with the Great Recession, from 18.0 percent in 2007 to 22.0 percent in 2010. The poverty rate for all Americans declined over the same period at a much slower rate, from 22.4 percent in 1959 to 11.3 percent in 2000, before trending up and then increasing from 12.5 percent in 2007 to 15.1 percent in 2010. See http://www.census.gov/hhes/www/poverty/data/historical/people.html.

The expansion of the social security program has contributed significantly to lower poverty among older Americans; in 2002, social security benefits were 83 percent of income for Americans over age 65 in the bottom income quintile. There is concern, however, that increasing earnings inequality among today's workers, higher divorce rates, the erosion of defined benefit pension plans, and a lower social security replacement rate could raise poverty rates among the elderly in the future. See Toder (2005).

[19] *The Economist* (February 18, 2006): 66.

LESSONS FROM EUROPE

Western European nations generally preceded the US in the first demographic transition and may have entered a second demographic transition, one characterized by fertility that has remained significantly below replacement level. Without increases in immigration, these European nations face future depopulation.

The so-called second demographic transition began in Europe in mid-1960s, with the decline in fertility from slightly above to slightly below replacement level.[20] The underlying attitude characterizing this transition has been one of "individualism," here meaning personal choice free from convention and traditional roles with respect to family formation. The adult couple became the focal point, rather than family and children. Traditionally, marriage initiated cohabitation and regular sexual union, with fertility usually closely following. Increasingly, regular sexual union and cohabitation came first, with sometimes delayed fertility and then perhaps marriage. In an interesting twist on the Malthusian notion of moral restraint with delayed marriage and limited childbearing, in Western Europe in the latter part of the twentieth century, the rise in mean age of marriage and increased incidence of nonmarriage reflected birth control in "unofficial" unions—which for Malthus amounted to "vice."

That is, with the greater availability of effective contraception over the 1960s and then liberalization of abortion in the 1970s, couples increasingly were able to exercise control over fertility before marital union. And with liberalization of divorce laws, marriage became less important as an institution. Accordingly consensual unions and cohabitation became more accepted, as was childbearing within such unions.[21] Also, within this discretionary fertility regime, couples adopted sterilization to avoid unwanted births once the desired family size was attained. (Note that the use of sterilization as contraception implies that parents are confident about their children's survival.) Moreover, childlessness is no longer regarded as unusual, but as a socially acceptable option for couples. (In the earlier model of fertility, C^*, the family size standard of the social reference group includes zero.)

The second demographic transition of sustained below replacement-level fertility began in Western and Northern Europe, followed with lag in Southern Europe and then Eastern Europe. In Table 10.8, where vital rates in Europe are compared with those in the US, we see the continual decline in the total fertility rates after the post-World War II baby booms to well below replacement levels. In contrast, as we noted earlier, the total fertility rate in the US, which dipped below 2 in the late 1970s, recovered a bit to replacement level by the 1990s. With more population momentum from a larger baby boom and higher total fertility rates, the crude rate of natural increase in the US was 0.57 percent for 2005–10, compared to 0.10 percent in Western Europe, 0.25 percent in Northern Europe, 0.06 percent in Southern Europe, and −0.28 percent in Eastern Europe.

Kent and Haub (2005: 9–11), however, note differences across Europe.

> Cohabitation—either as a prelude to or substitute for marriage—has increased in Europe, but it is much more common in northern than in southern Europe, and varies by country.

---

[20] See van de Kaa (1987) and Bianchi and Spain (1996: 39), who observe that "Fertility in many European countries has declined since the 1970s, despite policies designed to promote childbearing, including subsidized maternity leave and family allowances for each child."

[21] In the US more than half of births to mothers under 30 are outside of marriage (see Deparle and Tavernise 2012). For all mothers in the US in 2009, nearly 60 percent were married when they had children. For college graduates, 92 percent are married before giving birth, compared with 43 percent of women with high school diplomas.

Table 10.8 Vital rates, Europe and the United States

	Western Europe	Northern Europe	Southern Europe	Eastern Europe	United States
Total fertility rate					
1950–55	2.42	2.33	2.64	2.82	3.45
1975–80	1.66	1.80	2.26	2.07	1.79
2005–10	1.63	1.83	1.43	1.40	2.07
Life expectancy at birth, female					
1950–55	70.1	71.4	65.4	67.0	71.7
1975–80	76.5	76.2	75.8	73.4	77.0
2005–10	83.0	81.5	82.6	75.3	80.5
Crude birth rate					
1950–55	17.4	16.6	21.1	25.8	24.3
1975–80	11.8	12.8	16.0	16.5	15.1
2005–10	10.4	12.2	10.2	10.8	14.0
Crude death rate					
1950–55	11.4	11.2	10.6	10.3	9.5
1975–80	11.1	11.4	9.2	10.3	8.6
2005–10	9.4	9.7	9.6	13.6	8.3
Net migration rate					
1950–55	0.7	−1.4	−2.0	−0.7	1.4
1975–80	0.8	0.6	1.0	0.2	3.1
2005–10	1.8	3.5	5.9	0.8	3.3
Population growth rate					
1950–55	0.67%	0.40%	0.85%	1.48%	1.62%
1975–80	0.15%	0.20%	0.78%	0.64%	0.96%
2005–10	0.28%	0.59%	0.65%	-0.20%	0.89%

Notes: Western Europe includes: Austria, Belgium, France, Germany, Liechtenstein, Luxembourg, Monaco, Netherlands, and Switzerland.

Northern Europe includes: Channel Islands, Denmark, Estonia, Faeroe Islands, Finland, Iceland, Isle of Man, Latvia, Lithuania, Norway, Sweden, and United Kingdom.

Southern Europe includes: Albania, Andorra, Bosnia and Herzegovina, Croatia, Gibraltar, Greece, Holy See, Italy, Malta, Montenegro, Portugal, San Marino, Serbia, Slovenia, Spain, and the former Yugoslav Republic of Macedonia.

Eastern Europe includes: Belarus, Bulgaria, Czech Republic, Hungary, Poland, Republic of Moldova, Romania, Russian Federation, Slovakia, and Ukraine.

Source: World Population Prospects: The 2010 Revision, accessed March 17, 2012.

. . . In Italy, most births occur within marriage and marriage is often delayed because young people cannot find a secure job. . . . In Sweden, by contrast, cohabitation is common and just over one-half of babies are born to unmarried parents. Sweden's TFR was 1.7 in 2004, relatively high for Europe.

Eastern Europe presents a different situation because of severe economic shocks the region has suffered in the transition from centrally planned to market economies. Fertility has plummeted in the region, although out-of-wedlock births are common and effective contraceptives are less available than elsewhere in Europe. Many women rely on abortion to prevent unwanted births. The region has among the world's highest abortion rates.

Concerns with inflows of immigrants (especially from developing nations) often resulted in tightening of immigration laws in Western Europe (to protect employment and to reduce drain on social welfare systems). Although younger migrants with their initially higher fertility would counter the aging of the European population and could even reverse the future depopulation. There is no clear trend in the net migration rates in Europe, however, and in the US, historically a more open country, immigration policy remains controversial.

Will European fertility rates remain well below replacement level and bring depopulation and economic stagnation? Will the aging of the European populations reduce the creative energy in the nations or increase generational conflict? Will immigration laws be liberalized? Will populations stabilize?

That European nations are concerned with their low fertility is reflected in Germany's recent attempts to support childbearing. In 2010, Germany's crude birth rate of 8 was the lowest in the world, and combined with its crude death rate of 11, yielded a crude rate of natural increase of -3. As reported by Haub and Gribble (2011: 11):

To try to increase the birth rate, the government gives 184 euros monthly for the first and second child, 190 euros for the third, and 215 for the fourth until each child turns 18 (or 25 if still pursuing an education). Maternity leave spans 14 weeks, six weeks prior to the birth and eight weeks afterward—with a minimum benefit paid of 13 euros per day. Finally, a monthly minimum of 300 euros is allocated for care of a newborn but can rise to 1,800 euros or 67 percent of one's prior salary. This is paid for 14 months with the stipulation that one parent must use the benefit for two months, a feature that ensures that fathers will take part in child care.[22]

We should note that other developed nations outside of Europe are concerned about prolonged below replacement-level fertility. In 2008, for example, Japan's total fertility rate of 1.3 was down from 1.5 in 1990, but then rose to 1.4 in 2009 and 2010.[23] The total fertility rate in South Korea, a nation that went from one of the poorest in the world in the early 1960s to a developed, high-income economy in the twenty-first century, aided by a demographic dividend from lower fertility, saw its total fertility rate fall from 1.6 in 1990 to 1.2 in 2008, rise to 1.3 in 2009, and then decline back to 1.2 in 2010. In fact, South Korea has initiated a five-year plan to encourage childbearing, with a target total fertility rate of 1.7 for 2030.[24]

We turn now to China, the most populous nation in the world and still a developing nation. China's fertility is also well below replacement level, not as a matter of popular choice, but due to state policy.

---

[22] Haub and Gribble (2011: 11) also note that if the German total fertility rate remains at 1.4 children and annual immigration at 100,000, in 2060 the population in Germany would decline to under 65 million (from 82 million in 2010), with over a third of the population aged 65 or older.

[23] The statistics on the total fertility rates for Japan and South Korea are from Table 2.19 of World Bank (2010, 2011, 2012).

[24] See Banyan (2010). Included in the pro-fertility plan are increased maternity benefits up to 40 percent of salaries, more liberal hours of work for mothers, and state funded school fees for second children. See also Bremner et al. (2010: 7), who note that the total fertility rate in South Korea reached a "historic global low of 1.08 in 2005."

CHINA'S POPULATION

With an estimated population of 1.34 billion in 2010, China has one out of every five people in the world. On the other hand, China has only 7 percent of the world's arable land, with very limited, if any, potential for increasing the land under cultivation.

Rapid population growth in China began in the 1930s with sharp declines in mortality.[25] After the rise to power of Mao Zedong and the establishment of the communist People's Republic in 1949, China implemented a massive public campaign to control diseases and provide basic health care to the population largely through the proliferation of barefoot doctors (paramedics with additional training in preventative medicine) and the expansion of rural medical facilities. Birth rates remained high, due in part to a cultural predisposition to large families bolstered by strong son preference. Into the 1950s, fertility averaged over six children per woman.

In the early 1950s the first birth control measures, including the legalization of abortion, were adopted. By the latter half of the decade, birth rates were declining. With the economic dislocation in 1958–60 of the "Great Leap Forward" (a failed development strategy of industrial decentralization), followed by crop failures and famine in 1960–61 (from which an estimated 30 million Chinese perished), the crude birth rate (CBR) fell to under 20 (births per thousand population). China then experienced a brief baby boom. The CBR doubled in one year, peaking at 44 in 1963. Consequently, the government launched another attempt at birth control, which did moderate fertility but was undermined by the chaos of the Cultural Revolution of 1966–76 (an attempt to reeducate the population and establish a new socialist China). The CBR remained above 33 for the rest of the 1960s.

In 1970, with a crude rate of natural increase of 26 (per thousand), China's leaders recognized the need, even urgency, to rein in population growth. An inability to feed China's rapidly expanding population was forecast. The Marriage Law of 1950, which had set a minimum legal age of marriage of 18 for women and 20 for men, was tightened to 23 and 25 years of age for women and men in rural areas, and to 25 and 28 years of age in urban areas.[26] The CBR fell over the 1970s from 34 to 18, but even this decline was deemed insufficient given the scarcity of agricultural land and the prospect of continued population increase. So, in 1979 China instituted the "one-child campaign" in an attempt to reverse population momentum.[27]

Birth licenses

The key feature of the new population policy was a system of birth licenses. Consistent with central planning, the state would set a target fertility rate, which was translated into birth quotas at the local level. Licenses for authorized pregnancies were distributed. Unlicensed couples were expected to use effective contraception. Birth control was available free of charge. IUDs became popular among younger couples, and sterilization was relied on by older couples who had completed their families. Unauthorized pregnancies were to be terminated by abortion.

---

[25] From 1930 to 1950 the crude death rate (CDR) in China was halved, from over 40 to under 20 (deaths per thousand population). By the mid-1960s the CDR had declined to under 10. This reduction in the Chinese CDR is comparable to the decline in the CDR in the United States over the period from 1800 to 1970 (see Tien 1983: 5). Tien provides a good account of the population history of China after the Communist Revolution, from which the historical summary given here is drawn.

[26] As Tien (1983: 20–22) relates, premarital fertility is rare in China, so raising the legal age of marriage would have effectively reduced exposure to the risk of conception. Moreover, permission to marry was not usually granted to a couple by the local authorities unless their combined ages exceeded 50 years.

[27] The total fertility rate (TFR) fell from 5.8 in 1970 to 2.2 in 1980, where it more or less stabilized. The 1992 TFR was also 2.2 (see Kalish 1993: 5). The Chinese TFR since has declined further to below 2.

Constant propaganda promoted the "one child" norm, a policy that was not popular, particularly given the traditional son preference. Economic incentives and disincentives have also been used to compel socially responsible reproduction. "Only" children received free medical care and school tuition. Preferential treatment in housing and old age pensions were to be provided to couples who limited their childbearing to one. Income penalties and discrimination in housing, schooling, and employment have been used to punish couples who do not conform.

The aggressive population control measures did dramatically reduce fertility. Despite low per capita incomes and a predominantly rural population, China succeeded in lowering the total fertility rate from 6 to replacement level over the decade of the 1970s (Tien 1983: 20).[28] China's population policy, viewed by many as coercive and harsh, was justified by proponents as necessary for the nation's economic survival. A comprehensive "one-child norm" was deemed the most equitable way to distribute the burden and ensure sustainable development. As noted, China's total fertility rate fell below 2 in the 1990s, where it has remained.

Future concerns

Nevertheless, because of the population momentum from the previous high fertility, and some slippage in the one-child policy, China still faces the real prospect of its population reaching nearly 1.4 billion before stabilizing.

We can see the history and projected future of Chinese population policy in its population pyramids. Figure 10.5 shows the population pyramid for China in 2000 and the projected pyramid for 2040. Up to the 1970s China had an expansive population pyramid (see the bars for the population of ages 30 and older in 2000). The tighter population policies beginning in the 1970s and culminating in the one-child mandate at the end of the decade are evidenced in the narrowing of the bars for ages below 30. By the 1990 China had reached replacement-level fertility. The wide bar for 10–14-year-olds in 2000 largely reflects population momentum. Nevertheless the consequences of the authoritarian birth control policy are reflected in the emerging constrictive population pyramid.

The one-child policy, an attempt to move well below replacement-level fertility and reduce the final size of the population, has dramatically effected the nation's age distribution. China's extraordinary rates of economic growth over the past three decades have been enhanced by the declines in fertility. This demographic dividend, however, will be exhausted over the next generation. As illustrated by the projected population pyramid for 2040, the continuation of below replacement-level fertility will produce a much older population. The share of the Chinese

---

[28] Tien et al. (1992: 11) observe that the total fertility rate did not fall below 2.5 births in rural areas, although it dropped to 1.2 births in urban areas. In the late 1980s, couples in the rural areas were generally permitted to have a second child, if the first had been a girl. From the outset ethnic minorities were granted special dispensation for second, and even third, births. Even so, the sex ratios at birth in China over the past decade have been extraordinarily high. Strictly enforcing the one-child norm has proven to be difficult, especially in rural areas. That traditional son preference remains is evidenced by China's high male–female ratio.

As Riley (2004: 19) notes:

Son preference has a long history in China and is tied to the social and economic roles of males in Chinese families. Family lineage is traced through males, and sons are responsible for caring for their parents in their old age. Marriage practices reflect these traditions. When daughters marry, they leave their birth families to join their husbands' families.

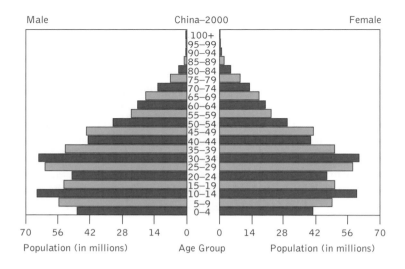

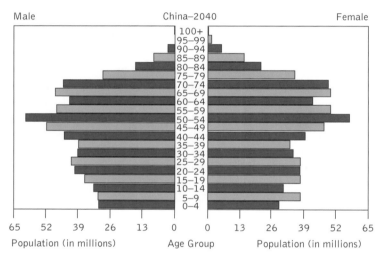

Figure 10.5 *China's population pyramids, 2000 and 2040*

From: US Census Bureau, International Data Base (http://www.census.gov/ipc/country.php)

population of ages 65 and over is projected to increase from 7.0 percent in 2000 to 23.3 percent in 2040.[29]

The rapid aging of the Chinese population may bring a rigid, overly conservative society, where seniority rules and frustrated youth confront blocked upward mobility. Of more immediate concern may be the social implications of generations of one-child families. Single children, lavished with attention and gifts from two sets of grandparents and the beneficiaries of preferential treatment in school, may become spoiled, unaccustomed to sharing and sacrifice and unfamiliar with the normal give-and-take of growing up with siblings. The generations of single children,

---

[29] These shares reflect the medium variant population projection and are from the Population Division of the Department of Economic and Social Affairs of the United Nations Secretariat, *World Population Prospects: The 2010 Revision* (http://esa.un.org/wpp/unpp/panel_indicators.htm).

moreover, will be responsible, directly or indirectly, for the support of the larger generations of grandparents.

Tragic consequences of the one-child population policy have been the increase in selective abortions, female abandonment and even infanticide. With the strong son preference still prevailing, especially in rural China, couples, when limited to one child, often seek to ensure the birth of males. Instead of a sex ratio at birth of 105 or 106 (males per hundred females) typical in general populations, in China we see ratios of 110 and higher. This gender imbalance will yield a marriage squeeze as eligible females will be in relatively short supply—likely a further cause of frustration for the generations of single children.[30]

China's experiment in authoritarian birth control is still unfolding. The implications for the rest of the world of China's striving to cope with its population growth are profound. Will other nations face a similar predicament in the future? In fact, sometime in the twenty-first century India will likely surpass China as the most populous nation. Can China's population policy be replicated? Should it?

We conclude this chapter with a brief overview of migration. While the Earth is a closed system, with the population growth rate equal to the crude rate of natural increase, net migration can significantly affect the population growth rates of individual countries and regions. Moreover, the future distribution of the world population across nations and regions will be influenced by immigration.

MIGRATION

While everyone will be born once and everyone will die once, not everyone will migrate or change residences across political boundaries, whether within a nation or across nations. Individuals, moreover, may migrate more than once, indeed many times. And an individual may reverse her migration, returning to the place or origin, so that her net migration has been zero, although she has migrated twice.

Internal migration, in particular, from rural to urban areas accompanies, even promotes, economic development, as populations shift from primarily agricultural production to manufacturing and services, and cities grow as centers of industry, commerce, and government. Here, the focus will be on international migration, although the underlying motives for migration, whether internal or international, are essentially the same.

The migration decision

We can use a simple model to explain the major factors underlying the decision to migrate (see Lee 1966). First, voluntary and involuntary migration should be distinguished. **Voluntary migration** is movement in response to incentives or net benefits. In contrast, **involuntary migration**, may be forced due to unfortunate circumstances at the place of origin, for example, natural disasters requiring the evacuation of people or civil war resulting in the flight of refugees. Involuntary migration can also be coerced; infamous examples being the slave trade and the relocation of urban residents to the countryside in the late 1970s in Cambodia under the revolutionary Khmer Rouge government.

---

[30]For the first decade of the twenty-first century, the sex ratio at birth in China averaged 120 (males per hundred females), well above even the 108 found in India, another population with a strong preference. See *World Population Prospects: The 2010 Revision*.

As noted, voluntary migration is motivated by the perceived net advantages of moving across a political boundary—whether internal as in a city, county, or state, or international across countries—to a new residence for an extended period. There are positive, negative, and even neutral factors associated with both the origin and destination of the migrant. A major motivation for much migration is the opportunity for better employment (i.e., higher wages and improved working conditions). Also, the place of destination of the migrant may have better educational opportunities and health care, more freedom of expression, greater security, and, in general, prospects for an improved life style. Disadvantages associated with the potential destination of the migrant might include the loss of frequent interaction with old friends as well as the stress of adjusting to new surroundings. Nevertheless, if there are perceived net advantages associated with the destination over the origin, then motivation for migration exists.

There are, however, costs and obstacles to migration. There are the monetary costs of relocation, which are directly related to the distance between the origin and destination. In addition, there are the opportunity costs of the income lost during the move and while securing new employment in the destination. In the case of international migration, the migrant must have permission to enter the destination country, and sometimes permission to emigrate from the home country. All countries now have strict requirements for immigration and obtaining the necessary permits may be difficult, if not almost impossible, for many who would like to move. Illegal immigration is a growing problem, with numerous examples of individuals risking their lives to enter another country.

International migration

Martin and Zurcher (2008: 1) observed that in 2005 the number of international migrants reached an all-time high of 190 million (roughly 3 percent of the world's population). The flows of migrants that year consisted of 62 million moving from developing to developed countries, 61 million moving between developing countries, 53 million moving between developed countries, and 14 million moving from developed to developing countries.

Stylized facts about migration include the selectivity of the migrants and the streams of migration. In general, legal migrants tend to be younger and more educated, often motivated by opportunities for employment. Much migration is for family reunification, as members of a family eventually join the earlier immigrant. When an immigrant community is established, it becomes easier and more familiar for other migrants to follow.

Earlier we discussed the so-called "brain drain," where educated, skilled labor migrates from developing to developed economies, a shift in human capital that contributes to the growing income gaps between the wealthy and poor nations. Partially compensating for this movement of population are the remittances sent back to the developing nations by their emigrants. Martin and Zurcher report that formal remittances of income to developing countries reached $208 billion in 2006.[31] For many developing nations these remittances are a major source of income and foreign exchange.

Some developed nations, such as the United States and Canada, are relatively open, yet still face an excess demand for entry. Other developed nations with below replacement-level fertility and facing depopulation are unlikely to compensate with more open policies. Kent and Haub (2005:18) observe that "Immigration cannot make up for natural population decrease over the long

---

[31] Martin and Zurcher (2008) provide a good overview of the regional patterns in international migration.

term. In most low-fertility countries, immigration would have to rise to politically unacceptable levels to make up for the natural decrease and prevent population decline."

Perhaps, as with population projections, predictions about migration flows will be amiss.

CONCLUSION

Not surprisingly, the future is considerably uncertain. Demographically, the world population is likely to stabilize below 10 billion sometime in the latter half of this century, with almost all of intervening population increase from developing nations. Bremner et al. (2010: 2) note:

> Projections of world population in 2050 currently range from 9.15 billion to 9.51 billion. Considering the 40-year timespan and the uncertainty of demographic trends, those projections are all actually quite close, and for a reason: World population projections have long made the assumption that the TFR will decline to two children or less in developing countries much as it did in the developed countries and that the decline will be continuous and uninterrupted. It is recognized, however, that such a tidy pattern of TFR decline will not take place everywhere and that projections will have to be adjusted. TFR declines have stalled in some countries and have barely begun in others.

After stabilizing, the world population may then decline, if below replacement-level fertility rates found in the contemporary developed nations persist and are adopted by developing nations. The world's population will be older, and how to incorporate effectively the older populations in the societies and economies will be a challenge. Climate change, environmental degradation, and natural resource limitations are other major challenges we face. In short, how to achieve sustainable development will be the paramount issue of the twenty-first century. We turn now to this topic.

KEY TERMS

age of degenerative and man-made diseases
diseases age of epidemics and famine
baby boom generation
epidemiology
Generation X
income constraint
indifference mapping
marginal rate of substitution
permanent income
social reference group
voluntary migration

age of delayed degenerative
age of receding epidemics
epidemiological transition
fertility transition
Generation Y
indifference curve
involuntary migration
net flow of intergenerational wealth
relative economic status
stunting
wasting

305

QUESTIONS

1. Assume the following utility-maximizing model for a representative couple in a developing economy:

    maximize $U = U(C, X)$

    subject to $Q \cdot C + P \cdot X = I$

    where U is the lifetime total utility of the couple, C the number of children, X represents quantities of other goods and services unrelated to childrearing, Q is expenditures per child (desired quality of children), P a price index of goods and services unrelated to childrearing, and I permanent income.

    (a) Assume initially that $I_0 = 100$, $P_0 = 1$ and $Q_0 = 10$. Assume also that the couple is indifferent among the following ten combinations of C and X on one of its indifference curves, U_0:

C	10	9	8	7	6	5	4	3	2	1
X	20	22	26	32	40	52	68	90	115	150

    Using a large graph and graph paper, carefully sketch the couple's indifference curve, U_0, placing C on the vertical axis. Graphically determine the utility-maximizing combination of children and other goods and services.

    (b) Discuss whether the demand for children found in part (a) will necessarily equal the actual fertility of the representative couple.

    (c) Suppose that with economic development, permanent income rises to $I_1 = 330$, the price index for other goods and services doubles, $P_1 = 2$, and a representative couple triple their desired quality of children to $Q_1 = 30$. Assume also that the tastes and preferences of the representative couple change. A different mapping is relevant, and the following combinations of C and X on a new indifference curve U_1' are given below.

C	10	9	8	7	6	5	4	3	2	1
X	77	78	80	84	90	98	108	120	138	160

    On the same graph, sketch the new indifference curve, U_1', and determine the new utility-maximizing combination of children and other goods and services. With economic development and the rise in income, what has happened to the relative preference for children? Specifically, how can you tell?

2. The per capita GNPs (in international dollars) and total fertility rates in 2010 are listed below for four countries.

	2010 per capita GNI	2010 total fertility rate
Bangladesh	$1,810	2.2
Morocco	$4,600	2.3
Mozambique	$930	4.9
Yemen	$2,500	5.2

    (a) Discuss the factors that might explain why Bangladesh and Morocco had nearly identical total fertility rates, but significantly different incomes. Check the World Bank's *World Development Indicators* for evidence supporting your hypotheses.

(b)   Repeat part (a) for Mozambique and Yemen.

(c)   Based on these two pairs of countries, can you draw any conclusions about the determinants of fertility in developing countries? Discuss.

3.   In Iran the median age of the population is projected to increase from 27.1 years in 2010 to 44.6 years in 2040. In Japan the median age of the population is projected to increase from 44.7 years on 2010 to 52.6 years in 2040. These median ages reflect the medium variant population projections from *World Population Prospects: The 2010 Revision*.

(a)   Discuss the underlying cause and likely consequences of the aging of the Iranian population.

(b)   In 2040, the percentages of the populations under age 15 are projected to be 13.6 percent in Iran and 12.8 percent in Japan. Which nation in 2040 do you think will be better able to provide for their elderly? Discuss why.

4.   The table below gives the average annual growth rates for population and net migration for 2005–10 for the Philippines, an East Asian Pacific nation of 93 million with per capita gross national income in 2010 of $3,980 (in PPP dollars), and the United Arab Emirates, a Middle Eastern nation of 8 million with per capita gross national income in 2010 of $50,580 (again in PPP dollars):

	Average annual growth rates (2005–10)	
	Population	Net migration
Philippines	1.73%	-0.28%
United Arab Emirates	12.3%	10.63%

(a)   Determine the average crude rates of natural increase in the two countries for 2005–10.

(b)   What might account for the Philippines having net out-migration over this period?

(c)   What might account for the United Arab Emirates having net in-migration over this period?

5.   The World Health Organization (2008) predicted the following changes in the leading causes of mortality in the world from 2004 to 2030:

- Diarrheal diseases would decline from the 5th leading cause (3.6 percent of all deaths in 2004) to the 23rd leading cause (0.9 percent of all deaths in 2030).
- HIV/AIDS would decline from the 6th leading cause (3.5 percent of all deaths in 2004) to the 10th leading cause (1.8 percent of all deaths in 2030).
- Road traffic accidents would rise from the 9th leading cause (2.2 percent of all deaths in 2004) to the 5th leading cause (3.6 percent of all deaths in 2030).
- Diabetes would rise from the 12th leading cause (1.9 percent of all deaths in 2004) to the 7th leading cause (3.3 percent of all deaths in 2030).
- Malaria would decline from the 13th leading cause (1.7 percent of all deaths in 2004) to the 41st leading cause (0.4 percent of all deaths in 2030).
- Alzheimer's disease and other dementias would rise from the 25th leading cause (0.8 percent of all deaths in 2004) to the 17th leading cause (1.2 percent of all deaths in 2030).

Note that the top four causes of deaths projected for 2030 are the same as actually prevailing in 2004: ischemic heart disease, stroke and other cerebrovascular diseases, chronic obstructive pulmonary disease, and lower respiratory infections (projected collectively to account for 38.7 percent of all deaths worldwide in 2030 versus a collective 34.0 percent in 2004).

(a)　In each case, try to explain the reason for the change in mortality rank and incidence.

(b)　Discuss whether these projections are consistent with the epidemiological transition.

REFERENCES

Acemoglu, Daron, Simon Johnson, and James Robinson. 2003. "An African Success Story: Botswana," in Dani Rodrik (ed.), *In Search of Prosperity: Analytic Narratives on Economic Growth*. Princeton, NJ: Princeton University Press: 80–119.

Applebaum, Binyamin. 2012. "Family Net Worth Drops to Level of Early '90s, Fed Says," *New York Times*, June 11. http://www.nytimes.com/2012/06/12/business/economy/family-net-worth-drops-to-level-of-early-90s-fed-says.html.

Banyan. 2010. "An Exercise in Fertility," *The Economist*, September 16.

Becker, Gary. 1960. "An Economic Analysis of Fertility," in National Bureau of Economic Research, *Demographic and Economic Change in Developed Countries*. Princeton, NJ: Princeton University Press: 209–231.

Bianchi, Suzanne and Daphne Spain. 1996. "Women, Work, and Family in America," *Population Bulletin*, 51(3).

Bremner, Jason, Ashley Frost, Carl Haub, Mark Mather, Karin Ringheim, and Eric Zuehlke. 2010. "World Population Highlights: Key Findings from PRB's 2010 World Population Data Sheet," *Population Bulletin*, 65(2).

Caldwell, John. 1976. "Toward a Restatement of Demographic Transition Theory," *Population and Development Review*, 2(3–4): 321–366.

Carlson, Elwood. 2009. "20th-Century U.S. Generations," *Population Bulletin*, 64(1).

Deparle, Jason and Sabrina Tavernise. 2012. "More Young Mothers Unwed," *Charlotte Observer*, February 19.

Easterlin, Richard. 1968. "An Explanation of the American Baby Boom following World War II," in David Heer (ed.), *Readings on Population*. Englewood Cliffs, NJ: Prentice Hall: 120–156.

Fogel, Robert. 1994. "Economic Growth, Population Theory, and Physiology: The Bearing of Long-Term Processes on the Making of Economic Policy," *American Economic Review*, 84(3): 369–395.

Haub, Carl and James Gribble. 2011. "The World at 7 Billion," *Population Bulletin*, 66(2).

Hess, Peter. 1988. "An Eclectic Model of the Fertility Transition," in *Population Growth and Socioeconomic Progress in Less Developed Countries: Determinants of Fertility Transition*. New York: Praeger: 111–125.

Hess, Peter and Clark Ross. 1997. *Economic Development: Theories, Evidence, and Policies*. Fort Worth, TX: Dryden Press.

Jacobsen, Linda, Mary Kent, Marlene Lee, and Mark Mather. 2011. "America's Aging Population," *Population Bulletin*, 66(1).

Jacobsen, Linda and Mark Mather. 2010. "U.S. Economic and Social Trends Since 2000," *Population Bulletin*, 65(1).

Kalish, Susan. 1993. "In China, the Peak Childbearing Years Have Peaked," *Population Today*, 21(1).

Kent, Mary and Carl Haub. 2005. "Global Demographic Divide," *Population Bulletin*, 60(4).

Kent, Mary and Mark Mather. 2002. "What Drives U.S. Population Growth?" *Population Bulletin*, 57(4).

Kinsella, Kevin, and David Phillips. 2005. "Global Aging: The Challenge of Success," *Population Bulletin*, 60(2).

Lamptey, Peter, Jami Johnson, and Marya Khan. 2006. "The Global Challenge of HIV and AIDS," *Population Bulletin*, 61(1).

Lee, Everett. 1966. "A Theory of Migration," *Demography*, 3(1): 47–57.

Leibenstein, Harvey. 1975. "The Economic Theory of Fertility Decline," *Quarterly Journal of Economics*, 89: 1–31.

Macunovich, Diane. 2002. "Using Economics to Explain U.S. Fertility Trends," in Kent and Mather (2002: 8–9).

Martin, Philip and Gottfried Zurcher. 2008. "Managing Migration: The Global Challenge," *Population Bulletin*, 63(1).

Murphy, S.L., J.Q. Xu, and K.D. Kochanek. 2012 "Deaths: Preliminary Data for 2010," *National Vital Statistics Reports*, 60(4). Hyattsville, MD: National Center for Health Statistics. 2012.

Riley, Nancy. 2004. "China's Population: New Trends and Challenges," *Population Bulletin*, 59(2).

Rockett, Ian. 1999. "Population and Health: An Introduction to Epidemiology," *Population Bulletin*, 54(4).

Tien, H. Yuan. 1983. "China: Demographic Billionaire," *Population Bulletin*, 38(2).

Tien, H. Yuan, with Zhang Tianlu, Ping Yu, Li Jingneng, and Liang Zhongtang. 1992. "China's Demographic Dilemmas," *Population Bulletin*, 47(1).

Toder, Eric. 2005. "What Will Happen to Poverty Rates among Older Americans in the Future and Why?" Urban Institute, http://www.urban.org/uploadedPDF/900893_poverty_rates.pdf.

United Nations Population Fund and Population Reference Bureau. 2009. *Healthy Expectations: Celebrating Achievements of the Cairo Consensus and Highlighting the Urgency for Action*. New York: United Nations Population Fund.

van de Kaa, Dirk. 1987. "Europe's Second Demographic Transition," *Population Bulletin*, 42(1).

Weeks, John. 2008. "Who Will Pay for the Baby Boomers to Retire in the Richer Countries?" in *Population: An Introduction to Concepts and Issues*, 10th edition. Belmont, CA: Thomson Wadsworth: 346–348.

World Bank. 1992. *World Development Report 1992: Development and the Environment*. Washington, DC: World Bank.

World Bank. 1997. *World Development Indicators 1997*. Washington, DC: World Bank.

World Bank. 2002a. *World Development Report 2002: Building Institutions for Markets*. Oxford: Oxford University Press.

World Bank. 2002b. *World Development Indicators 2002*. Washington, DC: World Bank.

World Bank. 2010. *World Development Indicators 2010*. Washington, DC: World Bank.

World Bank. 2011. *World Development Indicators 2011*. Washington, DC: World Bank.

World Bank. 2012. *World Development Indicators 2012*. Washington, DC: World Bank.

World Health Organization. 2008. *World Health Statistics 2008*. Geneva: WHO.

Part V
Sustainable development

Chapter 11

Introduction to sustainable development

Acording to the World Bank (1992: 1), "The achievement of sustained and equitable development remains the greatest challenge facing the human race." Two decades later, the challenge still stands. We now turn to the concept of sustainable development. We begin by distinguishing between growth and development, using the analogy of human beings.

GROWTH AND DEVELOPMENT

To *grow* means "to increase in size by a natural process," and to *develop* means "to realize the potentialities of."[1] Even more intuitively, to grow means to get bigger and expand, while to develop means to get better and evolve.

Consider humans. From conception a human will grow and develop, getting bigger and acquiring more capabilities. But growth, in terms of physical stature, ceases by early adulthood, and in fact human bodies then begin the process of reversing this natural growth in the sense of gradually getting shorter and physically weaker, and with age increasingly more vulnerable to illness and accidents. With clean living, good diet and exercise, however, individuals can ward off this natural decline and maintain, maybe even gain, strength and vigor with age—up to a point. Conversely, with bad habits, poor diets and insufficient exercise, individuals may continue to expand in weight, even becoming obese—an unhealthy growth that accelerates the inevitable decline in the physical body. Nevertheless, physical growth, even the healthiest and most natural kind, is limited. Eventually, even with excellent care, the physical body deteriorates with age.

Human development, on the other hand, need not cease or be reversed. An individual can continue to learn, gain insight, acquire skills, and improve her quality of life, even if physical growth is limited and indeed declines with age. Even if an individual does not die prematurely through illness or accident, and survives to old age, while the human body wears down, the human mind need not diminish. To wit, there is no upper age limit for service on the US Supreme Court.

Having said that, we realize that in many cases there are declines in cognitive skills with senility and Alzheimer's disease. And the decline in physical robustness that does accompany age may well diminish an individual's development. Is there an analogy to economies and societies? Can the global economy continue to grow? Can human societies continue to develop?

---

[1] From *The American Heritage Dictionary*, second college edition.

Nations are not limited by a natural life span. Economic growth over the past two centuries has significantly improved the average standard of living of humans. Nations experiencing the greater economic growth have been more successful in reducing absolute poverty and not only raising life expectancies, but also increasing the quality of the years lived with better health and nutrition, and more education. But can nations grow indefinitely, increasing in population, production of output, and consumption of natural resources? Or are there limits to growth for the nations of the world due to finite supplies of nonrenewable resources and the ability of the environment to absorb the waste generated without degradation? Even before these limits are reached, can economic growth be unhealthy?

Recall from the short-run macroeconomic model how too rapid growth in aggregate demand can lead to inflation, an economic fever signaling a nation straining its productive capacity. High inflation distorts relative price signals, reducing the efficiency of markets in allocating resources. Inflation can build on itself, with expectations of higher prices reducing the labor supply and aggregate supply curves. To the extent all incomes are not indexed to changes in the aggregate price level, inflation affects the distribution of income—usually resulting in a less equitable distribution.

On the other hand, too little growth, especially declines in aggregate demand, can increase unemployment, with an accompanying rise in poverty and social ills. Recall the concerns of the macroeconomists in the 1930s with insufficient aggregate demand and economic stagnation.

In short, while some argue there are, or should be, limits to economic growth, maybe all could agree there are no limits to development. We explore further the argument for limits to growth before turning to the concept of sustainable development.

A basic ecological identity

With population growth and increased per capita consumption, the production of goods and services will require more resources and will generate more wastes for the environment to absorb. A basic ecological identity might be used to illustrate:[2]

$$I = P \cdot A \cdot T$$

where I is environmental impact, P population size, A affluence, and T technology.

Consider the Earth. The environmental impact (I) reflects the Earth as both a supplier of natural resources for the production of goods and services and the sink for the absorption of the wastes generated. Affluence (A) might be measured by per capita consumption of goods and services. Multiplying population size (P) by per capita consumption gives the global demand for output. Technology (T) reflects the state of the knowledge used to produce the goods and services. Here technology captures the environmental requirements per unit of output.

Technological progress can reduce the environmental inputs for a given level of output. With advances in technology the natural resource requirements (e.g., fossil fuel inputs per unit of output) and impacts (e.g., carbon dioxide emissions per unit of output) may decline. So, too, with improved techniques for processing natural resources and absorbing the wastes generated, the environmental impact of human consumption may be reduced. Changes in the production of output (e.g., greater reliance on public transportation or bicycles, shifts away from chemical fertilizers and heavy irrigation to organic fertilizers, no-till farming and drip irrigation) may reduce

---

[2] This equation is known as the **Ehrlich identity**, after Paul Ehrlich, the American population biologist and ecologist, who is perhaps best known for his 1968 work, *The Population Bomb*; see Ehrlich and Holdren (1971). For additional discussion of this identity, see Daily and Ehrlich (1992) and Rogers et al. (2008: 31–32).

the overall environmental impact of given consumptions. Moreover, with economic development, the shares of modern services in national outputs increase, while the shares of the more natural resource-intensive manufacturing and agriculture decline.

Nevertheless, given a finite planet and surrounding environment, is it possible for economic growth to continue indefinitely? Can either population or per capita consumption grow without limits? If there is an upper limit to I, that is, a carrying capacity to this planet, then increases in output $(P \cdot A)$ could not continue indefinitely without sufficient technological progress (a decline in T). Can we count on this? A quarter century ago, this dilemma was recognized in *Our Common Future*, a report by the World Commission on Environment and Development (1987):[3]

> Growth has no set limits in terms of population or resource use beyond which lies ecological disaster. Different limits hold for the use of energy, materials, water, and land. Many of these will manifest themselves in the form of rising costs and diminishing returns, rather than in the form of any sudden loss of a resource base. The accumulation of knowledge and the development of technology can enhance the carrying capacity of the resource base. But ultimate limits there are, and sustainability requires that long before these are reached, the world must ensure equitable access to the constrained resources and reorient technological efforts to relieve the pressure.

Echoing the concern with equitable access, Eadie and Pettiford (2005: 199) note that "both affluence and poverty result in environmental degradation, the former through desire and the latter through necessity." In the developed countries, high incomes permit the consumption of goods and services well beyond those required for meeting basic needs. On the other hand, the poor in developing nations, especially in rural areas, often are forced to "mine" natural capital just to survive, for example, cutting down young trees for fuel wood, farming on fragile hillsides that are eroded with heavy rains, and overgrazing livestock on pastureland. In his classic article, "The Tragedy of the Commons," Garrett Hardin (1968: 1243) discounted the notion that a technical solution, defined as "one that requires a change only in the techniques of the natural sciences, demanding little or nothing in the way of change in human values or ideas or morality," would be sufficient for addressing exploitation of open access resources. In other words, while new technologies will be part of the solution, achieving sustainable development will likely entail new human behaviors too.

Economic development

Unlike economic growth, measured by the percentage change in per capita output, **economic development** cannot be captured by a single indicator. It encompasses more than the rise in average income that accompanies economic growth; also essential are the alleviation of poverty and the formation of human capital reflected in increases in the average levels of education, nutrition, and health. Structural change also characterizes economic development as primarily agrarian and natural resource-dependent economies become more industrialized and diverse, and modern services expand. Institutions for more efficiently allocating resources evolve with economic development. Increased international integration enhances the growth and development of nations.

---

[3] This report is commonly known as the Brundtland Report, after the chair of the commission, Gro Harlem Brundtland, then Prime Minister of Norway.

The quality of life, moreover, clearly extends beyond the material standard of living. Other important dimensions of human welfare are the individual freedoms to participate fully and fairly in the political process and to practice religious beliefs, as well as to be protected from physical harm and discrimination. These basic rights are embodied in the Universal Declaration of Human Rights, adopted by the United Nations General Assembly in December of 1948:

> Article 1. All human beings are born free and equal in dignity and rights.
> Article 18. Everyone has the right to freedom of thought, conscience, and religion.
> Article 25. Everyone has the right to a standard of living adequate for the health and well-being of himself and his family.
> Article 26. Everyone has the right to education.

SUSTAINABLE DEVELOPMENT

The concept of sustainable development adds an important dynamic dimension to economic development. The World Commission on Environment and Development (1987) offered a definition of **sustainable development** that has become widely used:

> Sustainable development is development that meets the needs of the present without compromising the ability of future generations to meet their own needs. It contains within it two key concepts: the concept of "needs," in particular the essential needs of the world's poor, to which overriding priority should be given; and the idea of limitations imposed by the state of technology and social organization on the environment's ability to meet present and future needs.[4]

The first sentence, which is the most frequently cited, establishes the importance of intergenerational equity, at least in terms of the opportunities for maintaining, if not improving, the quality of life. The second sentence, not nearly as well known, emphasizes the need to address current poverty and the notion of limits, for example, as captured by the basic ecological identity, $I = P \cdot A \cdot T$.

Expanding on the poverty dimension of sustainable development, Anand and Sen (2000: 2038) remark:

> The moral obligation underlying sustainability is an injunction to preserve the capacity for future people to be as well off as we are. This has a terribly hollow ring if it is not accompanied by a moral obligation to protect and enhance the well-being of present people who are poor and deprived.

Elaborations on the concept of sustainable development are given in Box 11.1. Despite Bhagwati's (2007) skepticism that "Even God does not know what *sustainable development* means," other useful definitions of sustainable development have been offered. Blewitt (2008) provides the

---

[4] See Rao (2000: 85–87) for a discussion of this definition. Rist (1997) criticizes the Brundtland Report's definition of sustainable development for its vague notion of "needs." That is, how are legitimate basic needs determined and how can the needs and capabilities of future generations be anticipated? Rist concludes, however, that the term "sustainable development" owes its success to its ambiguity. Ecologists interpret sustainable development to mean production within ecological limits, while others see continuing economic growth warranted. In short, Rist argues that the World Commission on Environment and Development, while popularizing the concept, failed to provide clear guidelines and responsibilities for achieving sustainable development.

simplest: "that the future should be a better, healthier, place than the present." The World Bank's (2003) explanation of sustainable development captures some of the noneconomic dimensions, such as assurance of physical security, the exercise of basic civil liberties, and the enjoyment and maintenance of the natural environment. Harris et al. (2001) identify three basic components of sustainable development: economic, environmental, and social. The economic dimension for a nation is maintaining its capacity for producing goods and services. The environmental dimension entails maintaining an environmental equilibrium, both in the source and sink functions provided by natural resources and the environment. The social dimension acknowledges the importance of equity and opportunity.

BOX 11.1: DEFINITIONS OF SUSTAINABLE DEVELOPMENT

Even God does not know what *sustainable development* means. (Bhagwati 2007: 156)

Sustainable development is simple. It is the idea that the future should be a better, healthier, place than the present. (Blewitt 2008: ix)

Sustainable development is about enhancing human well-being through time.

> ...Having the ability and opportunity to shape one's life—which increase with better health, education, and material comfort.
> ...Having a sense of self-worth...enhanced by family and social relationships, inclusiveness, and participation in society.
> ...Enjoying physical security and basic civil and political liberties.
> ...Appreciating the natural environment—breathing fresh air, drinking clean water, living among an abundance of plant and animal species, and not irrevocably undermining the natural processes that produce and renew these features.

(World Bank 2003: 13)

[T]here has been a growing recognition of three essential aspects of sustainable development:

> Economic—An economically sustainable system must be able to produce goods and services on a continuing basis, to maintain manageable levels of government and external debt, and to avoid sectoral imbalances that damage agricultural or industrial production.
> Environmental—An environmentally sustainable system must maintain a stable resource base, avoid overexploitation of renewable resource systems or environmental sink functions and depleting nonrenewable resources only to the extent that investment is made in adequate substitutes. This includes maintenance of biodiversity, atmospheric stability, and other ecosystem functions not ordinarily classed as economic resources.
> Social—A socially sustainable system must achieve fairness in distribution and opportunity, adequate provision of social services, including health and education, gender equity, and political accountability and participation.

(Harris et al. 2001: xxix)

Measures of sustainable development

Not surprisingly, there is no single indicator of sustainable development. Indeed, the United Nations (2007) lists 50 core indicators of sustainable development, along with 46 other indicators.[5] Included by the UN among the core indicators for a nation are: gross domestic product per capita, proportion of the population living below the national poverty line, proportion of the population using an improved sanitation facility, under-five mortality rate, adult literacy rate, carbon dioxide emissions, proportion of marine area protected, investment share of gross domestic product, and the generation of hazardous waste.

As we know, economic growth is measured by the percentage change in real national output per capita. Increases in per capita national incomes, even when expressed in international dollars adjusted for differences in purchasing power parity, however, may provide only limited insight into comparative progress in economic development, especially sustainable development.

The limitations of per capita gross national incomes (or per capita GDP) for comparing the average standards of living across nations are well known. Differences in the distribution of income, in the composition of output, and in the measurement of economic activity across nations will affect the welfare of the hypothetical "representative" resident—even when per capita national incomes are similar. Moreover, economic growth rates may be a misleading indicator of sustainable development. As discussed in Chapter 6, real national outputs are subject to short-run fluctuations in aggregate demands. In particular, declines in aggregate demand can result in periodic recessions that do not reflect longer-run growth prospects. Secondly, a nation may aggressively draw down its natural resources to promote higher economic growth in the short run, although such depletion of natural capital is not sustainable. Third is the fundamental question of whether increases in per capita output and population are compatible with sustainable development. As illustrated by the $I = P \cdot A \cdot T$ identity, in the long run there may be limits to economic growth—at least without continued, and even accelerated, technological progress.

Millennium Development Goals

The Millennium Declaration, adopted by 189 nations in 2000, set forth **Millennium Development Goals** (MDGs) with targets for eradicating poverty and improving the human condition (see Box 11.2). Eight major goals were set forth: eradicating extreme poverty and hunger; achieving universal primary education; promoting gender equity and empowering women; reducing child mortality; improving maternal health; combating HIV/AIDS, malaria, tuberculosis, and other diseases; ensuring environmental sustainability; and developing a global partnership for development. Associated with the eight major goals were 21 targets. Sixty indicators are offered for measuring progress towards the MDGs.[6]

---

[5]In fact, as noted by the UN Division for Sustainable Development, the initial set contained 134 indicators of sustainable development.

[6]You can follow the progress of nations in achieving these Millennium Development Goals and specific targets: see the United Nations Development Programme's MDG Monitor at http://www.mdgmonitor.org. For a list of the 60 indicators, see World Bank (2012a: 18–19). The World Bank (2012b) observed that the MDG targets of halving the incidence of extreme poverty and halving the proportion of people without access to safe drinking water had been met. Moreover, the world appeared to be on track to reach the gender parity in school enrollment and primary school completion goals by 2015. Significantly less progress had been made in other goals, especially halving the proportion of people suffering from hunger, and reducing by two-thirds the under-five child mortality rate and by three-fourths the maternal mortality ratio.

BOX 11.2: MILLENNIUM DEVELOPMENT GOALS AND TARGETS

Goal 1: Eradicate extreme poverty and hunger.

Target 1.A: Halve, between 1990 and 2015, the proportion of people whose income is less than $1 a day.

Target 1.B: Achieve full and productive employment and decent work for all, including women and young people.

Target 1.C: Halve, between 1990 and 2015, the proportion of people who suffer from hunger.

Goal 2: Achieve universal primary education.

Target 2.A: Ensure that, by 2015, children everywhere, boys and girls alike, will be able to complete a full course of primary schooling.

Goal 3: Promote gender equality and empower women.

Target 3.A: Eliminate gender disparity in primary and secondary education, preferably by 2005, and in all levels of education no later than 2015.

Goal 4: Reduce child mortality

Target 4.A: Reduce by two-thirds, between 1990 and 2015, the under-five mortality rate.

Goal 5: Improve maternal health

Target 5.A: Reduce by three-quarters, between 1990 and 2015, the maternal mortality ratio.

Target 5.B: Achieve by 2015 universal access to reproductive health.

Goal 6: Combat HIV/AIDS, malaria, and other diseases.

Target 6.A: Have halted by 2015 and begun to reverse the spread of HIV/AIDS.

Target 6.B: Achieve by 2010 universal access to treatment for HIV/AIDS for all who need it.

Target 6.C: Have halted by 2015 and begun to reverse the incidence of malaria and other major diseases.

Goal 7: Ensure environmental sustainability.

Target 7.A: Integrate the principles of sustainable development into country policies and programs and reverse the loss of environmental resources.

Target 7.B: Reduce biodiversity loss, achieving, by 2010, a significant reduction in rate of loss.

Target 7.C: Halve by 2015 the proportion of the population without sustainable access to safe drinking water and basic sanitation.

Target 7.D: Achieve by 2020 a significant improvement in the lives of at least 100 million slum dwellers.

Goal 8: Develop a global partnership for development.

Target 8.A: Develop further an open, rule-based, predictable, non-discriminatory trading and financial system.

Target 8.B: Address the special needs of least developed countries.

Target 8.C: Address the special needs of landlocked developing countries and small island developing states.

Target 8.D: Deal comprehensively with the debt problems of developing countries.

Target 8.E: In cooperation with pharmaceutical companies, provide access to affordable essential drugs in developing countries.

Target 8.F: In cooperation with the private sector, make available the benefits of new technologies, especially information and communications.

From: United Nations Millennium Development Goals (http://www.un.org/millenniumgoals)

For example, Goal 7 (ensuring environmental sustainability) has four targets: integrating sustainable development principles into national policies; reducing biodiversity loss; halving the proportion of people without access to safe water and adequate sanitation; and improving the lives of urban slum dwellers. Associated are ten specific indicators: proportion of land area covered by forest; carbon dioxide emissions: total, per capita, and per (PPP) dollar of GDP; consumption of ozone-depleting substances; proportion of fish stocks within safe biological limits; proportion of total water resources used; proportion of terrestrial and marine areas protected; proportion of species threatened with extinction; proportion of population using an improved drinking water source; proportion of population using an improved sanitation facility; and proportion of urban population living in slums.

In Chapter 12, where we address natural resources and climate change, statistics on resource use and the environment will be presented for nations grouped by per capita incomes and by geographical region. In this current chapter, however, we will focus on three more comprehensive measures of sustainable development: the **adjusted net saving rate**, the Human Development Index, and an index of youth investment.

COMPREHENSIVE INDICATORS OF SUSTAINABLE DEVELOPMENT

The concept of sustainable development renewed the importance of the "greening" of national income accounts. While net domestic product is measured as gross domestic product less the depreciation of the physical capital stock in a nation, no such adjustment is made for the depletion of natural capital (e.g., the use of nonrenewable resources) or the deterioration of the environment (e.g., with the pollution of the atmosphere).

Adjusted net saving rate

Statistics on "genuine saving" were introduced by the World Bank in its *World Development Indicators 1998*.[7] Now known as the **adjusted net saving rate**, genuine saving was defined by the World Bank (1998: 110) as a "comprehensive measure of a country's rate of saving after accounting for investments in human capital, depreciation of produced assets, and depletion and degradation of the environment." Negative adjusted net saving rates imply unsustainable developments. In particular, the World Bank (2003: 16) suggests that "only if adjusted net savings is positive will intergenerational well-being rise."

The adjusted net saving rate is derived as follows. First, net national saving is found by subtracting the consumption of fixed capital (the estimated loss in the value of the nation's physical capital stock) from gross national savings, which is basically the gross national income not used for private and public consumption. Current public education expenditures are added to net national saving and estimates of natural resource depletion (energy, mineral, and forest) and environmental damage (carbon dioxide and particulate emissions) are subtracted to derive adjusted net national saving. Dividing by gross national income gives the adjusted net saving rate.[8]

The adjusted net saving rates in 2010 for nations, with the usual groupings by incomes and regions, are provided in Tables 11.1a and b. The mean gross national incomes per capita, expressed in PPP dollars, are also given. As we can see, there is no necessary correlation between the adjusted net saving rates and per capita incomes. The high adjusted net saving rates for the lower- and upper middle-income economies largely reflect the corresponding saving rates for India and China. These two demographic billionaires have been among the fastest-growing economies in the world. The near-zero adjusted net saving rate of the United States primarily reflects the low gross national saving rate due to large government budget deficits stemming from the Great Recession. For the last three decades, however, the US has been consuming beyond its means, evidenced by the chronic, large current account deficits in its balance of international payments.

For the developing regions of the world, we see that, on average, sub-Saharan Africa and the Middle East and North Africa had negative adjusted net saving rates in 2010. On average, nations in Europe and Central Asia have low adjusted net saving rates, due in large part to relatively high rates of fossil fuel energy depletion. In contrast, the high adjusted net saving rates for East Asia and the Pacific and for South Asia are due their high gross national saving rates and significantly lower rates of energy depletion.

---

[7] The World Bank (1998) presented genuine domestic saving rates for 1994 (as a percentage of gross national product) for a sample of 22 Latin American and Caribbean nations. The following year it elaborated on the rationale for this "greener" measure of national savings and discussed the data limitations in accurately measuring resource depletion, environmental damage, and human capital formation (World Bank 1999: 115–117). It gave estimates of genuine domestic savings rates for the low-, middle-, and high-income economies for 1997. Later, the World Bank (2002) modified the measure, which previously had begun with gross domestic savings, which were calculated as the difference between gross domestic product and public and private consumptions. Here the initial basis is gross national savings, which are calculated as the difference between gross national income and public and private consumption, plus net current transfers to foreigners. The resulting measure, after subtractions for the consumption of fixed capital, energy, mineral, and net forest depletions, carbon dioxide damage, and the addition of education expenditures is labeled "adjusted net savings." The World Bank (2003) incorporated an estimate for pollution damage from particulate emissions in the measure of adjusted net savings. Then, in 2009, the World Bank modified its estimation of the natural resource depletion rates for energy and mineral resources. See World Bank (2009: 195) for the new measurement methodology, which underlies the statistics presented in Tables 11.1 and 11.2.

[8] For an assessment of the adjusted net saving rate, see Hess (2010a). The following discussion draws on this study.

Table 11.1a *Adjusted net saving rates (by income classification)*

% of GNI in 2010	ECONOMIES BY INCOME CLASSIFICATION							
	WORLD	*Low*	*Lower-middle*	*India*	*Upper-middle*	*China*	*High*	*US*
Gross National Saving	22.5%	24.6%	29.2%	*34.0%*	35.1%	*52.7%*	17.6%	*10.9%*
Less								
Consumption of Fixed Capital	(13.0%)	(7.7%)	(9.8%)	*(9.3%)*	(11.6%)	*(10.8%)*	(13.9%)	*(14.0%)*
Plus								
Education Expenditure	4.2%	2.9%	3.3%	*3.1%*	3.3%	*(1.8%)*	4.6%	*4.8%*
Less								
Energy Depletion	(2.1%)	(1.4%)	(6.0%)	*(2.5%)*	(4.8%)	*(3.7%)*	(0.7%)	*(0.8%)*
Less								
Mineral Depletion	(0.5%)	(1.2%)	(1.2%)	*(1.3%)*	(1.3%)	*(1.4%)*	(0.2%)	*(0.1%)*
Less								
Net Forest Depletion	(0.0%)	(1.2%)	(0.3%)	*(0.5%)*	(0.0%)	*(0.0%)*	(0.0%)	*(0.0%)*
Less								
Carbon Dioxide Damage	(0.4%)	(0.3%)	(0.7%)	*(0.9%)*	(0.7%)	*(1.1%)*	(0.2%)	*(0.3%)*
Less								
Local Pollution	(0.3%)	(0.8%)	(0.7%)	*(0.7%)*	(0.7%)	*(1.2%)*	(0.1%)	*(0.1%)*
Equals								
ADJUSTED NET SAVING	**10.4%**	**15.2%**	**13.8%**	***21.9%***	**19.3%**	***36.3%***	**7.1%**	***0.4%***
2010 GNI per capita (PPP$)	$11,066	$1,307	$3,632	*$3,400*	$9,970	*$7,640*	$37,317	*$47,310*

Adjusted net saving equals net national saving (gross national saving less capital consumption) *plus* current expenditures on education *less* depletion of natural resources *less* damage from emissions (carbon dioxide and particulate).

When there is a discrepancy between the totals for adjusted net saving rates reported for the country groups in World Bank (2012a: Table 4.11) and the sum of the components given, the latter is used here.

Source: World Bank (2012a: Tables 1.1, 4.11)

Table 11.2 presents a list of some of the nations in 2010 with negative adjusted net saving rates. Here we see basically two reasons for negative adjusted net savings in a nation. One is an over-reliance on natural resources (usually fossil fuels), as illustrated by Angola, Guinea, Kazakhstan, Mongolia, Saudi Arabia, Sudan, Syria, Yemen, and Zambia. The second is a low national saving rate, sometimes not even covering the depreciation of physical capital, as with the Dominican Republic, Greece, Portugal, Swaziland, Tajikistan, and also Yemen.[9]

The adjusted net saving rate is listed by the UN as one of the 96 indicators of sustainable development, albeit not one of the 50 core indicators. The adjusted net saving rate,

---

[9] We should note there are a number of other nations with negative adjusted net savings rates in 2010, but the data reported by the World Bank are incomplete, for example, Congo Republic (with energy depletion an estimated 60 percent of its gross national income) and Liberia (with negative gross national savings and net forest depletion of 5 percent of gross national income). Among other nations with missing data, but economies dependent on fossil fuels and likely to have negative adjusted net savings rates in 2010, are Chad, Gabon, Iran, Iraq, Libya, Mauritania, Nigeria, Papua New Guinea, Trinidad and Tobago, and Turkmenistan.

Table 11.1b *Adjusted net saving rates (by region)*

| % of GNI in 2010 | ECONOMIES BY REGION | | | | | | |
	Sub-Saharan Africa	Middle East & N. Africa	Europe & Central Asia	South Asia	East Asia & Pacific	Latin America & Caribbean	High Income Economies
Gross National Saving	18.0%	19.2	23.9%	32.7%	48.4%	20.9%	17.6%
Less							
Consumption of Fixed Capital	(10.9%)	(10.7%)	(12.2%)	(9.2%)	(10.7%)	(12.1%)	(13.9%)
Plus							
Education Expenditure	3.6%	4.3%	3.6%	2.8%	2.2%	4.7%	4.6%
Less							
Energy Depletion	(9.4 %)	(12.4%)	(8.6%)	(2.4%)	(3.8%)	(3.8%)	(0.7%)
Less							
Mineral Depletion	(1.9%)	(0.4%)	(0.8%)	(1.1%)	(1.3%)	(1.6%)	(0.2%)
Less							
Net Forest Depletion	(0.5%)	(0.1%)	(0.0%)	(0.6%)	(0.0%)	(0.0%)	(0.0%)
Less							
Carbon Dioxide Damage	(0.5%)	(0.7%)	(0.8%)	(0.8%)	(1.0%)	(0.3%)	(0.2%)
Less							
Local Pollution	(0.5%)	(0.9%)	(0.4%)	(0.7%)	(1.1%)	(0.4%)	(0.1%)
Equals							
ADJUSTED NET SAVING	−2.1%	−1.7%	4.7%	20.7%	32.7%	7.4%	7.1%
2010 GNI per capita (PPP$)	$2,148	$8,068	$13,396	$3,124	$6,657	$10,926	$37,317

Notes: Gross national saving is calculated as the difference between gross national income and private and government consumption plus net current transfers.

Consumption of fixed capital represents the replacement value of capital used up in the process of production.

Education expenditure is the public current operating expenditures in education, including wages and salaries and excluding capital investment in buildings and equipment. Private expenditures on education are not included.

Estimates of energy and mineral resource depletion are the ratios of the present value of current and future rents from resource extractions and remaining lifetime reserves. For each type of resource and each country, unit resource rents are derived by taking the difference between world prices of the resource and the average unit extraction costs (including a normal return on capital). Unit rents are then multiplied by the physical quantity extracted to arrive at a total rent. To estimate the value of the resource, rents are assumed to be constant over the life of the resource and the present value of the rent flow is calculated using a 4 percent social discount rate.

Energy depletion is the ratio of the value of the stock of energy resources (includes crude oil, natural gas, and coal) to the remaining reserve lifetime (capped at 25 years).

Mineral depletion is the ratio of the value of the stock of mineral resources (includes bauxite, copper, iron, lead, nickel, phosphate, tin, zinc, gold, and silver) to the remaining reserve lifetime (capped at 25 years).

Net forest depletion is calculated as the product of unit resource rents and the excess of roundwood harvest over natural growth.

Carbon dioxide damage is estimated to be $20 per ton of carbon (unit damage in 1995 US dollars) times the tons of carbon emitted.

Local pollution is calculated as the willingness to pay to avoid illness and death (including lung cancer, cardiopulmonary disease, and acute respiratory infections) attributable to particulate emissions.

while an improvement over the net national saving rate as a measure of net capital formation in a nation, is still incomplete. The incorporation of natural capital depletion, pollution damage, and human capital formation is not comprehensive. For example, measures of water depletion, depletion of fishing stocks, and soil erosion and degradation are not included. Nor

Table 11.2 Negative adjusted net saving rates in 2010

Country	Percentage of gross national income					
	Gross national savings	Consumption of fixed capital	Net national savings	Energy depletion	Mineral depletion	Adjusted net national savings
Angola** ($5,410)	17.9%	12.1%	5.8%	35.1%	0.0%	−29.2%
Dominican Rep. ($9,030)	7.5%	11.4%	−3.9%	0.0%	0.2%	−2.6%
Greece** ($27,630)	4.8%	13.6%	−8.8%	0.2%	0.1%	−6.7%
Guinea** ($1,020)	10.5%	8.2%	2.3%	0.0%	12.0%	−10.6%
Kazakhstan* ($10,770)	31.6%	13.3%	18.3%	21.6%	1.8%	−2.3%
Mongolia ($3,670)	29.8%	10.9%	18.9%	17.5%	14.8%	−12.6%
Portugal* ($24,590)	10.8%	18.4%	−7.6%	0.0%	0.1%	−3.1%
Saudi Arabia** ($22,750)	32.5%	12.1%	20.4%	29.1%	0.0%	−3.6%
Sudan** ($2,030)	19.7%	10.3%	9.4%	12.9%	0.0%	−3.6%
Swaziland* ($5,430)	2.7%	10.6%	−7.9%	0.0%	0.0%	−1.4%
Syria** ($5,120)	17.4%	10.6%	6.8%	11.7%	0.1%	−4.8%
Tajikistan ($2,140)	2.6%	8.6%	−6.0%	0.4%	0.4%	−4.3%
Yemen ($2,500)	9.6%	9.7%	−0.1%	14.5%	0.0%	−11.5%
Zambia ($1,380)	25.4%	10.3%	15.1%	0.0%	18.9%	−2.8%

Notes: Figures in parentheses are 2010 per capita incomes in PPP dollars.

Adjusted net saving equals gross national saving less consumption of fixed capital *plus* current expenditures on education *less* depletion of natural resources (energy, mineral, and forest) *less* damage from emissions (carbon dioxide and particulate).

Energy depletion includes crude oil, natural gas, and coal.

Mineral depletion includes bauxite, copper, iron, lead, nickel, phosphate, tin, zinc, gold, and silver.

An asterisk indicates the nation also had a negative adjusted net saving rate in 2009. Two asterisks indicate the nation also had negative adjusted net saving rates in 2008 and 2009.

Source: World Bank (2012a: Table 4.11)

is all pollution accounted for—just pollution damage from carbon dioxide and particulate emissions.

Public expenditures on education are included in adjusted net savings, but a more comprehensive measure of human capital formation would include private expenditures on education as well as other expenditures that add to the stock of human capital in the nation, that is, that improve the average life expectancy with adjustments for the quality of those years. Note that current expenditures on education and for improving health care and nutrition are traditionally counted as consumption in national income accounting, although these outlays do contribute to human capital and therefore are akin to investment.

Data limitations restrict a more comprehensive measurement of adjusted net saving rates. Nevertheless, while incomplete, the adjusted net saving rate is a useful indicator of sustainable development.

The Human Development Index

In the 1990 publication of the first *Human Development Report*, the United Nations Development Programme (UNDP 1990: 10) defined human development as "a process of enlarging people's choices. The most critical ones are to lead a long and healthy life, to be educated and to enjoy a decent standard of living."[10]

The **Human Development Index** (HDI), significantly revised in 2010, and further modified in 2011, by the UNDP, is a geometric average of indices for the life expectancy at birth, education, and the natural logarithm of per capita gross national income in PPP dollars. Ranging from 0 to 1, the HDI indicates a nation's relative progress in achieving the maximums for these key measures of human development. See Box 11.3 for the description of the construction of the HDI. The calculation of the HDIs for India and the US in 2011 is illustrated. Using the natural logarithms for per capita gross national incomes, reflecting the UNDP's assumption of diminishing returns to income in improving human development, significantly discounts the income gaps between nations, which tends to compress the HDI scores. For example, the US per capita gross national income in 2011 was 12 times that of India, yet the relative income indices for the US and India were less than two to one.

BOX 11.3: UNDP HUMAN DEVELOPMENT INDEX

The United Nations Development Programme (UNDP) devised a Human Development Index (HDI) to capture the most important dimensions of economic development. Now included as components, with the observed extreme values for a country, are:

- life expectancy at birth:
    minimum (20.0 years)
    maximum (83.4 years: Japan, 2011)
- combined education index:
    minimum (0)
    maximum (0.978: New Zealand, 2010)
    based on: mean years of schooling:

        minimum (0 years)
        maximum (13.1 years: Czech Republic, 2005)

    and expected years of schooling:
        minimum (0 years)
        maximum (18 years)
- per capita gross national income (in PPP dollars):
    minimum ($100)
    maximum ($107,721: Qatar, 2011)

The HDI can range from 0 to 1 and indicates a nation's relative progress in attaining the maximum levels of performance. The maximum values for life expectancy, mean years of

---

[10] In this inaugural report, the Human Development Index was introduced and scores for 130 countries for 1987 were presented, launching what was to become a widely reported indicator of economic development. Over the years, the HDI has been refined and other indicators of the human condition have been created by the United Nations Development Programme (UNDP). In 2010, on the occasion of the 20th anniversary edition of this report, the UNDP modified the construction of the HDI; see UNDP (2010: 15, 216–217) for a summary of the new methodology. This revised measure, which is more complicated to calculate, will be used for the statistics presented in Table 11.3. See UNDP (2011) for the most recent modifications.

schooling and income reflect actual observed maximum values for nations over the period 1980–2011. The maximum value for expected years of schooling is set independently (18 years). The minimum values for life expectancy (20 years), years of schooling (0 years) and income ($100) are set independently. For the life expectancy and education indices, the scores for a country i are computed according to the formula:

$$\text{index}_i = \frac{\text{value for country } i - \text{minimum value}}{\text{maximum value} - \text{minimum value}}$$

The education index is calculated as geometric mean of the two subcomponents, mean years and expected years of schooling. Mean years of schooling are measured as the average number of years of education received by people aged 25 and older. The expected years of schooling is calculated as the "number of years of schooling that a child of school entrance age can expect to receive if prevailing patterns of age-specific enrolment rates were to stay the same throughout the child's life" (UNDP 2011: 130).

For per capita gross national income, however, the index is calculated using natural logarithms to discount the contribution of higher incomes to human development. The overall HDI is a geometric average of the life expectancy, education, and income indices.

To illustrate the calculation of the HDI, consider India and the United States, with the following values for 2011:

Life expectancy at birth in 2011: India (65.4) and United States (78.5)

$$\text{Life expectancy index} = LI_{India} = (65.4 - 20)/(83.4 - 20) = 0.716$$
$$\text{Life expectancy index} = LI_{US} = (78.5 - 20)/(83.4 - 20) = 0.923$$

Mean years of schooling in 2011: India (4.4) and United States (12.4)

$$\text{Mean years of schooling index} = MY_{India} = (4.4 - 0)/(13.1 - 0) = 0.336$$
$$\text{Mean years of schooling index} = MY_{US} = (12.4 - 0)/(13.1 - 0) = 0.947$$

Expected years of schooling in 2011: India (10.3) and United States (16.0)

$$\text{Expected years of schooling index} = EY_{India} = (10.3 - 0)/(18 - 0) = 0.572$$
$$\text{Expected years of schooling index} = EY_{US} = (16.0 - 0)/(18 - 0) = 0.889$$
$$\text{Education Score}_{India} = (0.336 \cdot 0.572)^{1/2} = 0.438$$
$$\text{Education Score}_{US} = (0.947 \cdot 0.889)^{1/2} = 0.917$$
$$\text{Education index} = EI_{India} = (0.438 - 0)/[0.978 - 0] = 0.448$$
$$\text{Education index} = EI_{US} = (0.918 - 0)/[0.978 - 0] = 0.938$$

Per capita GNI (in PPP dollars) in 2011: India ($3,468) and United States ($43,017)

$$\text{Income index} = II_{India} = [\ln(3,468) - \ln(100)]/[\ln(107,721) - \ln(100)] = 0.508$$
$$\text{Income index} = II_{US} = [\ln(43,017) - \ln(100)]/[\ln(107,721) - \ln(100)] = 0.869$$

The Human Development Indices for India and the United States in 2011 are therefore:

$$HDI_{India} = LI^{1/3} \cdot EI^{1/3} \cdot II^{1/3} = 0.716^{1/3} \cdot 0.448^{1/3} \cdot 0.508^{1/3} = 0.547$$
$$HDI_{US} = LI^{1/3} \cdot EI^{1/3} \cdot II^{1/3} = 0.923^{1/3} \cdot 0.938^{1/3} \cdot 0.869^{1/3} = 0.910$$

Table 11.3 Human Development Index, by region

Country Group	HDI 2011	Life expectancy at birth (years)	Years of schooling Mean	Expected	GNI per capita (PPP$)
Developing economies					
Arab States	0.641	70.5	5.9	10.2	$8,554
East Asia & Pacific	0.671	72.4	7.2	11.7	$6,466
Europe & Central Asia	0.751	71.3	9.7	13.4	$12,004
Lat. America & Carib.	0.731	74.4	7.8	13.6	$10,119
South Asia	0.548	65.9	4.6	9.8	$3,435
Sub-Saharan Africa	0.463	54.4	4.5	9.2	$1,966
Developed economies					
Norway	0.943	81.1	12.6	17.3	$47,557
United States	0.910	78.5	12.4	16.0	$43,017
South Korea	0.897	80.6	11.6	16.9	$28,230
World	0.682	69.8	7.4	11.3	$10,082

Notes: The country grouping differs somewhat from the World Bank's regional classifications. For example, Somalia and Sudan are included here in the Arab states, but as sub-Saharan African nations in the World Bank groupings. Iran is included in South Asia by the UNDP, but in the Middle East & North Africa for the World Bank. Kuwait, Oman, and Saudi Arabia are high-income nations in the World Bank classification.

The Arab states include Algeria, Bahrain, Djibouti, Egypt, Iraq, Jordan, Kuwait, Lebanon, Libya, Morocco, Occupied Palestinian Territories, Oman, Qatar, Saudi Arabia, Somalia, Sudan, Syria, Tunisia, United Arab Emirates, and Yemen.

Source: UNDP (2011: Table 1).

Scores for the HDI in 2011 for developing economies grouped by region and for three developed economies are given in Table 11.3. The wide range of human experience is again evident, from an average HDI in 2011 of 0.463 for sub-Saharan African nations to 0.943 for Norway, which has the highest HDI in 2011 of the 187 nations listed. (The HDI values for the US and South Korea, ranked fourth and 15th, respectively, in 2011 are also presented.) Along with the aggregate score, the underlying components of the HDI are provided. The developing regions of sub-Saharan Africa and, to a lesser extent, South Asia, are lagging behind in life expectancies at birth, years of schooling, and per capita incomes. We are reminded that regional averages can mask the diversity across individual nations—from the wealthiest of the developed nations to the poorest developing nations. Indeed, the nation with the lowest HDI in 2011 is the failed state of the Democratic Republic of the Congo (0.286, which is approximately 60 percent of the average value for sub-Saharan Africa).

From the outset, the HDI has received considerable attention and some criticism. Common points of contention include: the selection and weighting of the individual components of the index; the arbitrary discounting of the contribution of income to human development; the failure to incorporate other dimensions of development, such as the environmental, political, and social; and the need to address inequities within nations.[11]

---

[11] The UNDP (1990: 16) readily acknowledged the limitations of the Human Development Index, in particular, the omission of other relevant economic, social, and political dimensions of the quality of life and "protection against violence, insecurity and discrimination." For early critiques, see Kelley (1991) and McGillivray (1991). Both argue that the HDI adds little insight beyond that provided by the more widely used per capita gross national incomes. Sajar and Najam (1998: 253) also highlight the UNDP's treatment of income, which compresses the HDI scores across countries, resulting in a "falsely equitable picture of the world which in fact is more inequitable than ever." In addition to the earlier measures that had been designed to address some of

The HDI is not listed itself by the United Nations (2007) as an indicator of sustainable development, although a number of its components are, including per capita national income and life expectancy at birth. Nevertheless, increases in the HDI, suggesting an improving human condition, would be consistent with sustainable development. On the occasion of the 20th anniversary of its 1990 *Human Development Report*, the UNDP (2010:101) concluded that "People in most, but not all countries have made steady, long term progress in health and education over recent decades." The UNDP added, however, that the correlation between economic growth and changes in health and education was weak.

We turn now to a third indicator of sustainable development, an index of youth investment, which complements the adjusted net saving rate and HDI.

Index of youth investment

Sustainable development might also be defined as an improvement in each generation's capacity for healthy, satisfying and productive lives.[12] To measure this, an **index of youth investment** (IYI) is offered. For a nation, the IYI is calculated as the geometric average of a quality-adjusted measure of child survivability and a quality-adjusted net enrollment rate in secondary school. Specifically,

$$IYI = [(M \cdot CSR) \cdot (Q \cdot NSE)]^{1/2},$$

where M is an index of health ($0 \leq M \leq 1$), CSR the child survival rate (i.e., the probability that a newborn baby will survive to age 5 if subject to the prevailing age-specific mortality rates, $0 \leq CSR \leq 1$), Q an index of reading, mathematics, and science literacy for 15-year-old students ($0 \leq Q \leq 1$), and NSE the net secondary school enrollment rate ($0 \leq NSE \leq 1$). Box 11.4 describes the components and construction of the IYI variable in greater detail. Basically the geometric average of indices for the health of children under 5 and the education of secondary school-age children is used to measure the nation's investment in youth.

BOX 11.4: THE INDEX OF YOUTH INVESTMENT

The index of youth investment, IYI, is calculated as $IYI = [(M \cdot CSR) \cdot (Q \cdot NSE)]^{1/2}$, where:

M = index of quality of health ($0 \leq M \leq 1$). M is the ratio of the expected years lived in good health to total life expectancy. The latest data on healthy and total life expectancies available are for 2007 and are from World Health Organization, *World Health Statistics 2010* (http://www.who.int).

CSR = child survival rate ($0 \leq CSR \leq 1$). CSR is the probability that a newborn baby will survive to age 5 if subject to the prevailing age-specific mortality rates. The data for the under-five mortality rates for 2009 are from the World Bank (2011: Table 2.22).

---

these concerns (in particular, an inequality-adjusted HDI, reflecting inequalities in health, education, and income; and a gender inequality index, to account for discrimination against females reflected in reproductive health, empowerment, and labor force participation), the UNDP (2010) introduced a multidimensional poverty index to replace the earlier Human Poverty Index and measure deprivation in basic needs.

[12] See Hess (2010b), on which the following discussion draws. The statistics for the IYI, however, are based on the most recent international test scores for 2009.

Q = index of science and mathematics literacy for 15-year old students ($0 \leq Q \leq 1$). Q is the ratio of the sum of the average scores for reading, mathematics, and science literacy on the 2009 Program for International Student Assessment tests to the maximum scores possible. The scores are reported in Fleischman et al. (2010).

NSE = net secondary school enrollment rate in 2009 ($0 \leq$ NSE ≤ 1). NSE is the ratio of total enrollment of children of official secondary school age to the population of children for that age interval. As noted by the World Bank (2011: 83), "The net enrollment ratio excludes over-age and under-age students and more accurately captures the system's coverage and internal efficiency." The data for the net enrollment rates are from World Bank (2011: Table 2.12).

The child survival rate is calculated from the under-five mortality rate, cited by the United Nations Children's Fund (UNICEF 2007b: 2) as "a barometer of child well-being in general and child health in particular." To proxy the quality of health, the ratio of healthy life expectancy (an estimate of the expected number of years lived in good health) to total life expectancy at birth is used to measure M, the index of health.[13]

To capture the investment in education, the net secondary school enrollment rate is multiplied by an index for the average score for 15-year-olds on reading, mathematics, and science components of an internationally standardized test, the Program for International Student Assessment (PISA); see Fleischman et al. (2010).[14] Net, as opposed to gross, secondary school enrollment rates are used in the construction of the IYI indicator for better comparability across countries. Measuring the quality of the education is important, for example, through the use of standardized tests comparable across countries, like the PISA.

As calculated, the IYI can vary between 0 and 1. A perfect score of 1 would mean all the expected years lived were in good health, an under-five mortality rate of zero, a net secondary school enrollment rate of 100 percent, and the maximum scores of 1000 on all three of the PISA reading, mathematics and science tests—absolutely an upper limit. Countries can be ranked according to their IYI scores, but more importantly, sustainable development is indicated by an increase in a country's IYI score over time, implying gains in generational capabilities.

To illustrate, consider Mexico, an upper middle-income economy, in 2009. With an under-five mortality rate of 0.017, yielding a child survival rate of 0.983; ratio of healthy to total life years of expectancy of ($67/76 = 0.882$); a net secondary school enrollment rate of 0.72; and average scores of 425, 419, and 416 on the reading, mathematics, and science standardized tests for an

---

[13] See World Health Organization (2010). The data for life expectancy (how many years a person might be expected to live) and **healthy life expectancy** (how many years they might live in "good" health) are from Table 1 (Mortality and burden of disease) and reflect estimates "based on country life tables, analyses of 135 causes of disability for 17 regions of the world and 69 health surveys in 60 countries."

Whether the fraction of healthy to total years of life expectancy is indeed a good indicator of the quality of health for children may be arguable. Disability-adjusted life years are a standardized measure (expressed per thousand population) of the years of productive life lost to disease and premature death, based on the prevailing morbidity and mortality rates of the population compared to a low-mortality population. The morbidity rates are weighted by the severity of the diseases, ranging from 0 (perfect health) to 1 (death). Were such data available, the index for the quality of child health would include the adverse effects on child development from malnutrition, diarrhea, and diseases such as malaria, tuberculosis, and measles.

[14] PISA assesses 15-year-old student proficiencies in reading, mathematics, and science every 3 years with a system of standardized tests, which focus on the application of knowledge to realistic problems. The maximum score on each of the three areas is 1000. For each country administering the tests, a representative sample of at least 4,500 students aged 15 from a minimum of 150 schools had to sit for the tests. In 2009, the latest year the test was administered, 60 countries participated.

329

educational quality score of 0.420, Mexico's IYI would equal 0.512. Sustainable development for Mexico would be indicated by an increase in its IYI over time.[15]

Comparing the indicators of sustainable development

A comparison of the IYI, the HDI, the adjusted net saving rate (ASY), and, for reference, per capita gross national income (YP) is given for a cross-section of nations. A complete data set for only 38 nations could be assembled for the four indicators. Twenty of these countries are high-income economies, 13 are upper middle-income economies, four are lower middle-income economies, and only one (Kyrgyz Republic) is a low-income economy; thus the range of country experiences is more limited than desirable. In Table 11.4 descriptive statistics for the sample and the simple correlation coefficients are reported for the four indicators. Not surprisingly, the HDI and YP are very highly correlated with each other and also highly correlated with the IYI. The ASY, however, is uncorrelated with these other three indicators.

As indicated by the ratio of the standard deviation to the mean, the dispersion of values for the IYI is slightly greater than for the HDI, the other indicator with range between 0 and 1. In contrast, the dispersion of per capita incomes and adjusted net saving rates are much greater. As noted, per capita national incomes and adjusted net savings are subject to business cycle fluctuations, which may not reflect long-run trends and sustainable development.

With development, the child survival component in the IYI might approach 1, as the under-five mortality rate falls below 5 per thousand and the share of healthy to total life expectancy would be over 90 percent. Even the net secondary school enrollment rate could reach 100 percent. Increasingly, then, with development, the main driver of the IYI score will be the quality of education, Q, as measured by the ratio of the average scores on the reading, mathematics, and science literacy tests to the maximum scores possible.

In Table 11.5 the country scores and ranks for the four indicators are given. Insights can be gained by comparing the per capita income rank with the ranks for the other indicators. For example, the Republic of Korea (South Korea) and Poland rank relatively high in terms of their IYI scores (3rd and 8th, respectively) compared to their per capita incomes (15th and 20th, respectively), indicating these two countries have used their economic growth to invest in their youth. In fact, South Korea, an East Asian economic success story noted for its early and impressive investments in human capital, ranked second in the sample for the schooling quality index (Q).

Conversely, Switzerland and the US rank relatively low in their IYI scores (15th and 17th, respectively) given their per capita incomes (2nd and 3rd highest in the sample, respectively), implying economic growth that has not effectively translated into investment in youth. The relatively poor showing of the US in the IYI reflects its rankings of 14th and 22nd in the quality indices for education and child health and 19th and 20th in the school enrollment and child survival rates, respectively. Moreover, the US ranks 34th in the adjusted net saving rate, largely due to its modest 9.8 percent gross national saving rate, which fell short of the rate of capital consumption, yielding

---

[15] While the calculation of the IYI statistic is straightforward, the supporting databases are still limited. First, only 60 nations participated in the PISA tests in 2009. Given every 3 years, beginning with 2000, the PISA tests seem to be an especially appropriate indicator, emphasizing "the application of knowledge and skills," with scores representing "a 'yield' of learning at age 15, rather than a direct measure of attained curriculum knowledge at a particular grade level" (Fleischman et al. 2010: 4). Moreover, net secondary school enrollment rates are not as available as gross rates, even for high-income economies. Of the nations with PISA scores for 2009, a fourth did not report data for net secondary school enrollment rates. National under-five mortality rates are commonly published. Estimates of healthy life expectancy, however, are more difficult to calculate, and like the PISA test scores, apparently are not available every year. For the IYI calculated here, healthy life expectancy data for the latest year available (2007) were used.

Table 11.4 *Sample statistics for the key indicators*

	Descriptive statistics			
	Mean deviation	Standard	Minimum	Maximum
IYI (Index of youth investment)	0.582	0.076	0.423 (Brazil)	0.689 (Finland)
YP (Per capita gross national income)	$22,418	13,802	2,200 (Kyrgyz Rep.)	55,420 (Norway)
HDI (Human Development Index)	0.791	0.090	0.598 (Kyrgyz Rep.)	0.938 (Norway)
ASY (Adjusted net saving rate)	9.02	7.35	−7.9 (Greece)	28.4 (Panama)
CSR (Child survival rate)	0.988	0.010	0.959 (Indonesia)	0.997 (Finland, Sweden)
NSE (Net secondary enrollment rate)	0.841	0.111	0.52 (Panama)	0.99 (Sweden)
M (Quality of health index)	0.896	0.015	0.864 (Kyrgyz Rep.)	0.923 (Denmark)
Q (Quality of schooling index)	0.455	0.056	0.325 (Kyrgyz Rep.)	0.544 (Finland)

	Correlation coefficients			
	IYI	YP	HDI	ASY
IYI (Index of youth investment)	1.00	0.821 ***	0.857 ***	−0.064
YP (GNI per capita)		1.00	0.922 ***	0.017
HDI (Human development index)			1.00	0.011
ASY (Adjusted net saving rate)				1.00

Notes: Simple correlation coefficients statistically significant at the 1% level and 5% level are indicated by *** and ** respectively.

a negative net national saving rate in 2009, the depth of the Great Recession, when real gross domestic product fell 3.5 percent in the US. In contrast, overachievers in the adjusted net saving rate for 2009 are Thailand, Tunisia, and Panama, ranking 3rd, 7th, and 1st, respectively, in the sample for this measure of sustainable development, compared with 35th, 34th, and 28th ranks in per capita income.

Bearing in mind that sustainable development would be indicated by steady improvements in the IYI and the HDI and continually positive adjusted net saving rates, we can nevertheless assess national performances for a given year. For instance, while in this sample of countries the US ranked 2nd and the Republic of Korea ranked 7th in the HDI, their IYI relative rankings (17th for the US and 3rd for Korea) as well as their relative rankings for the adjusted net savings rate (34th for the US versus 1st for Korea) imply a more sustainable development for Korea. Finally, if we take the average ranking for the IYI, HDI, and ASY indicators, then Norway, followed by Sweden, and then Japan, Republic of Korea, and Finland are at the top, all with uniformly strong performances.

In sum, the three measures discussed are complementary indicators of sustainable development. The adjusted net saving rate incorporates a broader measure of the rate of net capital formation in an economy, although natural depletion, environmental change, and human capital formation are incompletely measured, and social capital formation, difficult to quantify, is not included. Increases in the HDI are indicative of sustainable development, although for the most developed countries the value of the index is close to 1, suggesting little room for improvement.

Table 11.5 Country values for the key indicators

Country	Index of youth investment IYI	Gross national income per capita YP	Human Development Index HDI	Adjusted net saving rate ASY
Finland	.689 (1)	$35,280 (8)	.871 (11)	8.1% (6)
Japan	.688 (2)	$33,440 (10)	.884 (6)	12.1% (7)
Republic of Korea	.678 (3)	$27,240 (15)	.877 (7)	20.0% (1)
Sweden	.668 (4)	$38,050 (6)	.885 (5)	16.0% (6)
France	.661 (5)	$33,950 (9)	.872 (9)	7.0% (23)
Norway	.657 (6)	$55,420 (1)	.938 (1)	12.8% (10)
Spain	.647 (7)	$31,490 (13)	.863 (13)	9.7% (17)
Poland	.646 (8)	$18,290 (20)	.795 (19)	9.7% (17)
United Kingdom	.645 (9)	$35,860 (7)	.849 (16)	2.2% (33)
Italy	.644 (10)	$31,870 (12)	.854 (15)	6.1% (24)
Netherlands	.644 (11)	$39,740 (4)	.890 (4)	11.6% (13)
Denmark	.643 (12)	$38,780 (5)	.866 (12)	10.7% (15)
Slovenia	.642 (13)	$26,470 (17)	.828 (17)	13.6% (9)
Estonia	.641 (14)	$19,120 (19)	.812 (18)	14.4% (8)
Switzerland	.633 (15)	$47,100 (2)	.874 (8)	21.6% (2)
Ireland	.630 (16)	$33,040 (11)	.895 (3)	−1.1% (35)
United States	.624 (17)	$45,640 (3)	.902 (2)	−0.8% (34)
Greece	.621 (18)	$28,800 (14)	.855 (14)	−7.9% (38)
Portugal	.621 (19)	$24,080 (18)	.795 (19)	−1.8% (37)
Israel	.595 (20)	$27,010 (16)	.872 (9)	12.2% (11)
Chile	.576 (21)	$13,420 (25)	.783 (21)	3.2% (30)
Bulgaria	.567 (22)	$13,260 (26)	.743 (27)	6.1% (24)
Azerbaijan	.550 (23)	$9,020 (31)	.713 (30)	5.4% (27)
Kazakhstan	.549 (24)	$10,320 (29)	.714 (29)	−1.2% (36)
Turkey	.546 (25)	$13,500 (24)	.679 (35)	2.9% (32)
Jordan	.531 (26)	$5,730 (36)	.681 (34)	3.0% (31)
Argentina	.525 (27)	$14,090 (22)	.775 (22)	10.6% (16)
Romania	.523 (28)	$14,540 (21)	.767 (23)	18.8% (5)
Uruguay	.513 (29)	$12,900 (27)	.765 (24)	6.1% (24)
Mexico	.512 (30)	$14,020 (23)	.750 (26)	9.1% (20)
Thailand	.511 (31)	$7,640 (35)	.654 (36)	20.5% (3)
Colombia	.505 (32)	$8,600 (32)	.689 (32)	5.4% (28)
Tunisia	.493 (33)	$7,810 (34)	.683 (33)	14.6% (7)
Peru	.475 (34)	$8,120 (33)	.723 (28)	8.6% (21)
Indonesia	.475 (35)	$3,720 (37)	.600 (37)	11.0% (14)
Kyrgyz Republic	.462 (36)	$2,200 (38)	.598 (38)	9.4% (19)
Panama	.458 (37)	$12,180 (28)	.755 (25)	28.4% (1)
Brazil	.423 (38)	$10,160 (30)	.699 (31)	4.6% (29)

Table 11.5 *continued*

IYI Overachievers: $Rank_{YP} - Rank_{IYI} > 0$
Poland (+12), Republic of Korea (+12), Jordan (+10)

IYI Underachievers: $Rank_{YP} - Rank_{IYI} < 0$
United States (−14), Switzerland (−13), Panama (−9)

HDI Overachievers: $Rank_{YP} - Rank_{HDI} > 0$
Republic of Korea (+8), Ireland (+8), Israel (+7)

HDI Underachievers: $Rank_{YP} - Rank_{HDI} < 0$
Turkey (−9), United Kingdom (−9), Denmark (−7)

ASY Overachievers: $Rank_{YP} - Rank_{ASY} > 0$
Thailand (+32), Tunisia (+27), Panama (+27)

ASY Underachievers: $Rank_{YP} - Rank_{ASY} < 0$
United States (−31), United Kingdom (−26), Ireland (−24)

Notes: See Box 11.4 for the data sources for the IYI for 2009. See Table 11.2 for the data sources for YP and ASY for 2009. See UNDP (2010: Table 1) for the data sources for the HDI for 2010.

Moreover, we have noted the data limitations in each of these indicators, and several years, at least, are need to reveal trends. Not adequately captured by any of the three indicators is social capital. Drawing on often eloquent testimony from the poor, a World Bank study (Narayan et al. 2000: 31) cites, in addition to their material deprivation, the vulnerability of the poor to "rudeness, humiliation, and inhumane treatment." Further, the study concludes that "Poor people focus on assets rather than income and link their lack of physical, human, social, and environmental assets to their vulnerability and exposure to risk." The mistreatment of people, whether intolerance of differences, or discrimination by age, race, ethnic group, sexual orientation, or income class, undermines the social capital and indeed the sustainable development of a nation. In another study, the World Bank (2005: 5) summarized:

> Fairer societies offer their citizens more public goods, more social support, and more social capital. Hence they are more capable of sharing the costs and benefits of improving economic policies, and in turn facilitating consensus building and decision making.

CHILD LABOR

The World Bank (2003: 184) states that "ending global poverty is much more than a moral imperative—it is the cornerstone of a sustainable world." Recall the emphasis in the Brundtland Commission's definition of sustainable development on intergenerational equity in opportunities. The World Bank (2006: 10) describes an unfortunate cycle:

> Because basic skills in schools are learned early, the failure to invest in education can greatly increase the costs of pursuing healthy life styles and of working. By the same token, risky behaviors leading to a young man's premature death or a girl's unexpected early pregnancy can significantly lower the returns to schooling. Prolonged unemployment can lead to disinterest in investing in further schooling, possible mental stress, delayed family formation, and negative manifestations of citizenship.

There may be no greater disinvestment in the future or guarantee of intergenerational poverty than the exploitation of children. Perhaps all parents share the desire to see their children enjoy better lives than they themselves have experienced. Yet, across the world, overwhelming poverty has cut short the lives of millions of children and forced many other children prematurely into the labor force, forgoing the chance for schooling and limiting their opportunities for development.

In the extreme, children are sold into indentured labor or trafficked, contrary to Article 4 of the United Nations Universal Declaration of Human Rights: "No one shall be held in slavery or servitude; slavery and the slave trade shall be prohibited in all forms." Moreover, Articles 2 and 6 of the United Nations Convention on the Rights of the Child, enjoin states to "take all appropriate measures to ensure that the child is protected against all forms of discrimination or punishment on the basis of the status, activities, expressed opinions, or beliefs of the child's parents, legal guardians, or family members," and "ensure to the maximum extent possible the survival and development of the child."[16] Child labor, especially the more exploitive types, is not only a violation of human rights, but also a disinvestment in children that perpetuates poverty across generations.[17]

Incidence of child labor

To the international community, the term "child labor" does not encompass all work performed by children under the age of 18 years. The International Labour Office defines child labor more narrowly than economically active children, since those children aged 12 years and older who are working only a few hours a week in permitted light work and those aged 15 years and above whose work is not classified as "hazardous" are excluded.[18]

While accurate and current data on child labor are understandably difficult to collect, the International Labour Office (2010) estimated that in 2008 there were 215 million children aged 5–17 trapped in child labor (down from 222 million in 2004 and 246 million in 2000). Of these children, 115 million were in hazardous work (down from 128 million in 2004 and 171 million in 2000). The majority of child labor is still found in the agricultural sector, usually as unpaid family members. Nearly half of children working also attended school, although in many if not most cases their attendance and performance were likely adversely affected by their working.[19]

The incidence of child labor is greatest in sub-Saharan Africa, with 65 million child laborers (25 percent of children aged 5–17). Over 38 million of these children are in hazardous work.[20]

---

[16] The Convention on the Rights of the Child was initiated in 1989 to protect children under 18 from harm and to ensure their basic human rights to survive, develop their potential, and participate fully in family, cultural, and social life. Over 190 nations have ratified the Convention, more than any human rights treaty in history. The US and Somalia have signed, but not ratified, the Convention.

[17] As Fyfe (2007: 67) states, it is important to remember "the fact that today's developing countries did not invent child labor." Indeed, in his review of the literature on child labor, Basu (1999: 1083) observes:

In different parts of the world, at different stages of history, the laboring child has been a part of economic life. In particular, children have worked in large numbers in factories from the time of the industrial revolution in Europe and from the mid-nineteenth century in America.

[18] According to the International Labour Office (2010: 6), hazardous work by children "is any activity or occupation that, by its nature or type, has or leads to adverse effects on the child's safety, health and moral development." Hazardous work encompasses the worst forms of child labor, including "night work and long hours of work; exposure to physical, psychological or sexual abuse; work underground, underwater, at dangerous altitudes or in confined spaces; work with dangerous machinery, equipment, and tools, or which involves the manual handling or transport of heavy loads; and work in an unhealthy environment which may, for example, expose children to hazardous substances, agents or processes, or to temperatures, noise levels, or vibrations damaging to their health."

[19] For an earlier report, see Frank Hagemann, Yacouba Diallo, Alex Etienne, and Farhad Mehran, *Global Child Labor Trends 2000 to 2004*, (Geneva: International Labour Office, 2006).

[20] The International Labour Office (2010: 43) notes that sub-Saharan Africa is also the region making the least progress on the Millennium Development Goals, in particular universal primary education.

Asia, in particular India and South Asia, has the greatest number of child laborers, nearly 114 million in 2008, with 48 million children aged 5–17 in hazardous work.

Perhaps the keystone of the contemporary international effort to address child labor is the International Programme on the Elimination of Child Labour (IPEC), launched in 1992. The initial focus of IPEC was to eliminate the worst forms of child labor. In particular, International Labour Organization (ILO) Conventions Nos. 138 and 182 set the boundaries on the types of work that are unacceptable under international standards. ILO Convention No. 138 establishes minimum ages at which children can begin work. For example, light work that does not hinder the health or education of the child is permitted after age 12. Hazardous work, however, is prohibited before the age of 18. ILO Convention No. 182 stipulates that any person under 18 is to be protected from employment in the worst forms of child labor, including slavery, debt bondage, forced recruitment in armed conflicts, prostitution, pornography, illicit activities, and work that has adverse effects on the child's safety, health (physical or mental), and moral development.[21]

Eradication of child labor

A vicious cycle of poverty can be perpetuated by child labor. In traditional societies, children, especially sons, are viewed as economic assets.[22] This reality bolsters high fertility, in turn, limiting parental and societal investment in the human capital of their children. Child workers increase the supply of labor, keeping wages low and perpetuating the reliance of poor parents on their children's labor. Children forced to work are often unable to attend school—at least regularly—and are deprived of education and the means to earn better incomes as adults. Poverty, high fertility, and child labor are perpetuated across generations.

The International Labour Office (2006: 20) describes the poverty trap:

> High levels of child labour can be *self-reinforcing*. For example, in a situation of mass poverty, child labour is part of the survival strategy of poor families. . . . Mass child labour acts as a disincentive to employers to invest in labour-saving technology. Moreover, in a society where child labour is the norm the demand for education will be low, and it will be difficult to enforce laws on minimum age and compulsory education. Finally, as child labourers become adults, it is increasingly likely that they in turn will send their children to work rather than school. In a society marked by a high child labour equilibrium, families and whole societies can thus be trapped in a vicious cycle of poverty.

Although it has 19 percent of the world's population of primary school age, sub-Saharan Africa accounts for 47 percent of the world's out-of-school children. The region also suffers from the highest prevalence of HIV/AIDS and of those orphaned by the pandemic. Conflict has also been endemic in some countries, leading to the abuse and exploitation of millions of children.

[21] See http://www.ilo.org/ipec/facts/ILOconventionsonchildlabour/lang--en/index.htm (accessed April 14, 2012). Conventions No. 138 and 182 have been ratified by 161 and 174 nations, respectively. Among the nations that have not ratified Convention No. 138 are Australia, Bangladesh, Canada, India, Iran, Mexico, New Zealand, Saudi Arabia, and the US. With the exception of India, however, these nations have ratified Convention No. 182.

[22] Sons are often preferred by parents as better sources of income and old-age security, since daughters require dowries and after marriage are "lost" to their parents. As described by Gilligan (2003: 65):
Widespread legal and illegal discrimination against women and girls in issues such as property, inheritance, access to justice, education, and health care, all conspire to increase the levels and types of vulnerabilities which create the supply of girls for child labor. It also permits child marriage, limited mobility and control over income, a lack of access to resources, an unequal distribution of household work, drudgery, celebrates boy children at the expense of girls, and offers limited protection from domestic violence.

For an interesting study, see Koolwal (2007), who finds that traditional son preference in Nepal may be modified when opportunities for daughters to earn income increase.

Indentured servitude, one of the most exploitive forms of child labor, is primarily found in South Asia. For a profile of the Kamlari system of indentured child labor in Nepal, see Box 11.5.

BOX 11.5: CHILD LABOR AND THE KAMLARIS OF NEPAL

Nepal is one of the poorest countries in the world, ranking 157th out of 187 countries in the UNDP Human Development Index for 2011. Political instability, civil strife, and lack of a coherent development strategy have hampered socioeconomic progress. As in other South Asian nations, child labor is all too prevalent.[a]

In 2001 the International Labour Organization (ILO) estimated in Nepal there were over 17,000 children employed outside their homes, most under some form of bonded labor. At the time, the ILO estimated that 75 percent of these children were working more than 12 hours per day, 43 percent were working without pay, 15 percent were below the age of 10, and 95 percent did not attend school (see Understanding Children's Work Project 2003: 27).[b]

The Kamaiya tradition

Kamaiyas, under a system existing in Nepal for decades, are agricultural laborers forced to work for landowners to repay debts incurred earlier, sometimes by their parents or grandparents. The overwhelming majority of Kamaiyas are Tharu, an ethnic group indigenous to the Terai, a fertile region of Nepal along the border with India which includes the five western districts of Dang, Banke, Bardiya, Kailali, and Kanchanpur. Until the 1960s, the Tharu were the primary inhabitants of the Terai, in large part due to their natural immunity to malaria. Then malaria eradication along with land reform, intended by the powers in Kathmandu to help integrate the nation, led to hill people moving into the lowlands of the Terai. Many Tharus did not have legal title to their land and were soon displaced, becoming sharecroppers. Meager wages and the exorbitant interest rates charged by the landowners on the small loans taken by the Tharu, whether to buy seed or to pay for medical emergencies, funerals, or weddings, resulted in unsustainable debts, eventually binding the Tharu families to the same landowners. To have any access to land, the Kamaiyas would often have to pledge their children, usually daughters, as working collateral. The bonded children would also be forced to labor for the landowners.[c]

In July 2000, the Nepali parliament declared the practice of Kamaiya and the associated debts of the bonded laborer illegal.[d] Already laws were in existence in Nepal intended to protect children. For example, the 1990 Constitution of Nepal protected the interests of children by conferring on them certain fundamental rights. The 1992 Children's Act ensured their "physical, mental, and intellectual development" and "contained a number of provisions on child labor."[e] Moreover, Nepal had ratified the UN Convention on the Rights of the Child in 1990, ILO Convention 138 in 1997, and ILO Convention 182 in 2002. As Sharma et al. (2001: 9) note, Nepal was even chosen by IPEC as one of the first three countries in which to implement a large-scale Time Bound Program to eliminate the worst forms of child labor, including bonded child labor. Nepal's Child Labor Act of 2000 does not cover family-based work, work in private homes, or work in agriculture—which account for the overwhelming majority of Nepalese child workers (see Understanding Children's Work 2003).

The practice of Kamlari

Ironically there is evidence that the legislation that freed the Kamaiyas actually increased the practice of Kamlari, as destitute parents remained unable to provide for their children. That is, former Kamaiyas are still being pressured by landowners to sell their children to the landowners as laborers as a condition for leasing land. Alternatively, poor families without land may contract their daughters for employment outside their villages.[f]

To illustrate, each January in the Dang district, brokers come to villages to arrange for the purchase of the girls. Parents or guardians are given an average of 5,000 rupees (roughly $65) for the year's contract. There are several indigenous nongovernmental organizations working to free the Kamlaris, by applying social pressure on the owners to release the girls from their contracts. Sometimes, after securing their freedom, the girls return to their homes. Other times, however, the girls go to live with other relatives or guardians or are taken in by children's homes.

Interviews I had with over a dozen former Kamlari girls who had been rescued from their indentured servitude revealed some of the girls had worked for as little as a year, while others had worked for several, and sometimes more than six, years before being rescued.[g] The number of employers the girls had ranged from one to six. Few of the girls attended school while working as a Kamlari. In a typical day, a Kamlari, who lived and worked in the households of their employers, would rise before dawn and begin her work, fetching water, cleaning the house, washing dishes, doing laundry, and frequently cooking. Sometimes the tasks might include feeding cows and cleaning the shed, collecting wood from the forest, and caring for children of the employer. Their days usually ended well after sunset.

Not surprisingly, none of the girls liked being a Kamlari, although most seemed to accept their fate, recognizing the poverty of their parents or guardians. Many of the Kamlaris had lost one or both parents. Others were from broken families. Almost all had brothers and sisters. If their parents had remarried, then the girls often experienced harsh treatment from their stepparents before being sold. The most frequent reason given by the girls for disliking their positions as Kamlaris was not being able to go to school. Also mentioned all too frequently was the ill-treatment suffered, including being scolded and beaten by the employers, insufficient food to eat, and having to sleep on the floor. Most received no money for their work, although their parents or guardians likely received payment for their sale. Some of the girls, however, did report earning a pittance.

In September 2008 it was reported that the Supreme Court of Nepal had struck down the Kamlari system. Although, as with the 2000 legislation outlawing the Kamaiya system, acts of law or decrees do not guarantee the abolition of an ingrained practice. Continued economic development, social vigilance, and improved educational opportunities will be essential.

Notes

a. This case study is drawn from Hess (2009).

b. Bales (2005: Appendix 2) in his ranking of countries for slavery and human trafficking, ranging from 1 (low) to 4 (high), assesses Nepal at 4 in the incidence of slavery, 2 in the flow of human traffic into, and 4 in the flow of human traffic from the country.

c. See United Nations Commission on Human Rights (Geneva, June 2000) at http://www. antislavery.org/archive/submission/submission2000-Nepal.htm and Suman Pradhan, "Nepal: Land Reforms, Key to Social Harmony," http://www.ipsnews.net/news.asp? idnews=34736 (Sept. 15, 2008). Bales (2005: 2) notes that, "Under the most common system of bondage in South Asia, work does not repay the debt. When a person borrows from a landlord, that person, his or her family, and all the work that all of them are capable of is simply *collateral* against the loan. Until the debt is repaid, the money lender owns the family and everything they grow or produce. . .The control of the landlord is total, and if he is unsatisfied with his returns, a child can be taken from the family and sold."

d. As noted on the Government of Nepal's Ministry of Land Reforms and Management website, the eradication of the Kamaiya system meant that "no landlord can employ anybody as Kamaiya, and the debt or sauki has been declared null and void. If anybody wishes to engage an agricultural and household laborer, s/he should be paid the minimum wage and the working hours as laid down by labor law should be maintained" (see http://www.molrm.gov.np/programs.php).

e. See International Labour Organization, "National Legislation and Policies Against Child Labor in Nepal," http://www.ilo.org. Sharma et al. (2001: 13) point out that under the Kamaiya system there were basically two types of child laborers: those who work in or around the village of origin, usually as domestic servants and agricultural laborers, and those who migrate to urban areas and work as domestic servants or in the informal service sector. It should also be noted that bonded child labor in Nepal exists outside of the Kamaiya system, with children found working in hotels, restaurants, brick kilns, stone quarries, and the carpet industry, among other areas. The IPEC estimates that 12,000 Nepalese girls are trafficked each year, with most ending up in brothels in India, and nearly 40 percent trafficked before the age of 14 (Understanding Children's Work Project 2003: 27–28).

f. Bales (2005: 82–83) comments: "the law abolishing Kamaiya was established by decree rather than legislation, and it occurred much more quickly than expected. As a result grassroots organizations in the countryside were not prepared for the harsh reaction of landowners or the resulting tens of thousands of refugees driven from their homes." Sadly, Sharma et al. (2001: 40) also observe: "Although the government has promised to redistribute land to ex-Kamaiya labourers, very few Kamaiyas have been issued with the necessary certification to claim the land."

g. The interviews were conducted in Nepal in the fall of 2008, during my sabbatical from Davidson College. In the interest of disclosure, since 2005, I have served as president of Nepal Orphans Home, a 501(c)(3) public charity, founded by my brother, Michael Hess.

The eradication of child labor, while not an explicit target of the Millennium Development Goals, is promoted indirectly through poverty reduction. Moreover, two of the MDGs set forth in 2000 directly address investment in youth: achieving universal primary education by 2015 (MDG 2) and reducing child mortality by two-thirds between 1990 and 2015 (MDG 4). Unfortunately, trends are not encouraging. As assessed by the UNICEF (2007a), the sub-Saharan African and South Asian regions were not making progress and the Latin America and Caribbean region had made insufficient progress toward MDG 2. The former two regions were also making insufficient progress to achieve MDG 4. The global recession of 2009 further set back progress.[23]

Moreover, one of the indicators for monitoring MDG 5 (improving maternal health) is the adolescent fertility rate. Early fertility can limit the socioeconomic mobility of women, if not lock families into poverty. The incidence of babies of low birth weight and the attendant child development problems increase as the age of the mother falls. Young mothers tend to be less physically, mentally, and economically prepared for children. As a result the quality of child care may suffer.

Eradication of child labor should be an international priority not only for human rights but also for promoting sustainable development. The "solution" to child labor, however, is not to be found simply in legislation prohibiting the practice, but with economic development and universal quality schooling for children and improved wages for adults. While enforcing existing legislation against exploitative or hazardous child labor is important, laws need to be complemented with programs for the rehabilitation of former child workers and opportunities for schooling. Particular attention, with remedial education, counseling, and vocational training should be accorded to former child soldiers, children who were trafficked, and indentured child laborers.

The International Labour Office (2010: 21) cites Brazil as a leader in combating child labor. Brazil joined IPEC in 1992 as one of the original participating countries. A new constitution in the late 1980s made 8 years of education compulsory. An engaged civil society, the media, and a large rural worker's union all mobilized to protect children's rights. In 1996, a conditional cash transfer program designed to keep children in school targeted the rural poor. The incidence of child labor between the ages of 5 and 15 in Brazil fell from 13.6 percent in 1992 to 5.8 percent in 2008.

Investing in children starts from the earliest ages. With respect to health, the UNICEF's GOBI strategy, launched in the early 1980s to improve child survival rates, has proven effective. GOBI encompasses growth monitoring (G) by parents of their children to detect early signs of malnutrition; oral rehydration therapy (O) to combat severe dehydration and even death accompanying diarrhea from unsafe water and unsanitary conditions; promotion of early breastfeeding (B) as the best source of infant nutrition; and immunization of children (I) against the major childhood diseases, including diphtheria, pertussis (whooping cough), tetanus, measles, polio, and tuberculosis. In the 1990s, GOBI was extended to GOBI-FFF to promote food supplementation, family spacing, and female education (see UNICEF 2007b: 31).

---

[23] In mid-2011, only Northern Africa and Eastern Asia were expected to meet MDG 2 (achieving universal primary education) by 2015. The other regions of the developing world listed, sub-Saharan Africa, Southeast Asia, Southern Asia, Western Asia, and Latin America and the Caribbean were making insufficient progress. The Caucasus and Central Asia were assessed to have made no progress. With respect to MDG 4 (reducing child mortality), only Northern Africa, Eastern Asia, and Latin America and Caribbean were on target. See http://www.un.org/millenniumgoals/pdf/(2011E)_MDReport2011_ProgressChart.pdf (accessed April 14, 2012).

With respect to education, the International Labour Office (2010: 78) concluded:

> What is quite clear is that we will not eliminate child labour without free, compulsory and universal education up to the minimum age for entry into employment, nor will we ensure every child is in school unless we eliminate child labour.

In addition to the building of accessible schools staffed by qualified and motivated teachers, increasing the enrollment of poor children may be encouraged by conditional cash transfers—as Brazil has done. As described by the World Bank (2006: 87):

> Introduced in the late 1990s, particularly in Latin America, they provide cash to poor young people conditional on school attendance, and are quickly becoming popular in other parts of the world. Mexico's Oportunidades, the best documented, has increased secondary school attendance rates by 8 percent, the transition to secondary school by nearly 20 percent, and grade attainment by 10 percent, with significantly larger effects for girls than for boys.

In sum, improvements in health and education and decreases in the incidence of child labor promote economic development. Indeed, such investments in youth are a key to sustainable development. The vicious cycle of intergenerational poverty needs to be turned into a virtuous cycle of intergenerational mobility with early investments in child survival and improved education opportunities. Then with increased earnings, delayed marriage and lower fertility, better child care and greater investment in the next generation of children will be realized.

MANAGING ASSETS FOR SUSTAINABLE DEVELOPMENT

The World Bank (2003: 13) states that "Enhancing human well-being on a sustained basis requires that a society manage a portfolio of assets." Five asset types are identified, similar to the four basic types of capital earlier discussed. Human assets include physical labor and skills. Human-made assets consist of the physical capital stocks—the plant, equipment, and machinery used to produce goods and services, and the economic infrastructure (e.g., the transportation and communications networks, government buildings, public utilities, health care facilities, schools, and residential structures). Knowledge assets are the stock of knowledge that exists in the society, as codified in the natural and social sciences and the humanities. Social assets, like social capital, refer to the shared beliefs and institutions that give cohesion to society and facilitate interpersonal cooperation. Natural assets are the nonrenewable and renewable natural resources which provide the raw material inputs for production of goods and services, provide irreplaceable life services such as air, water and land, and absorb the subsequent waste generated.[24]

Human capital formation, especially education, is a key to economic development. Among the contributions of education are the gains in general knowledge and understanding of science and technology. Education and training can lead to the development of specific skills and increase the

---

[24] The World Bank (2003) gives a good overview of the concept of sustainable development, its measurement, and the associated policy implications. In addressing the role played by social capital in sustainable development, the World Bank (2003: 18) discusses the "interpersonal trust and networks. . .and. . .understanding and shared values. . .which facilitate cooperation within and among groups." The contribution of social capital can enhance—and can be enhanced by—the contributions of human, physical, and natural capital. For example, an understanding of ecological systems and awareness of environmental thresholds can engender an identification with the common good and concern for future generations which, in turn, can promote a more efficient use of natural resources and research into and development of more energy-efficient and environmentally sound capital goods.

productivity of labor. Education can promote entrepreneurship, the ability to recognize and pursue profitable business opportunities. Moreover, a more educated population not only promotes economic growth and development, but also enjoys a higher quality of life with increases in the expectation of life that accompanies better health and nutrition practices and with the insights gained through improving the mind. Knowledge can be passed on from one generation to the next, although effort is required in the education to acquire and use that knowledge.

As discussed in Chapter 10, there is a strong inverse relationship between fertility and female education. Since educated women can earn more in the labor force, the opportunity cost of having and rearing children is higher. Educated women are also more willing and able to use effective contraception. Thus, they tend to have fewer children, but invest more in each child born. In short, education can also promote economic growth and development with the demographic dividend realized from lower fertility and greater investment in children.

All of these assets, human, human-made, knowledge, social, and natural, are drawn upon to produce the goods and services consumed by humans. The key question is whether these assets will always be in sufficient supply to produce the goods and services required to maintain, if not improve, human welfare. Moreover, if one or more of these assets become limited, will the ability to meet human needs similarly be limited? To what extent are these assets substitutable?

Weak and strong sustainability

The degree of substitutability among assets will affect the rate of production of goods and services consistent with sustainable development. According to the condition of **weak sustainability**, the total stock of assets or the total capital stock must be maintained, although the composition of the assets can change. This condition implies that substitution across assets can be used to compensate for relative scarcity in one or more assets. This is an implicit assumption underlying the adjusted net saving rate discussed earlier.

The condition of **strong sustainability** is stricter in that the stock of every asset or type of capital must remain intact. Strong sustainability regards the types of capital more as complements in production, with limited substitution possible (see World Bank 2003: 18–19).[25]

Maintaining the aggregate capital stock (weak sustainability) or individual stocks (strong sustainability) intact would be consistent with sustainability for a population of a given size. With population growth the capital stock or stocks would have to increase to maintain the per capita ratios. Furthermore, with rapid population growth and rising youth burdens of dependency, it becomes more difficult to generate the savings for investments in human and physical capital. That said, recall that technological progress is often embodied in the new plant, equipment, and machinery and improves the quality of the capital, which can offset declines in the physical capital stock.

Increases in knowledge assets and advances in technology may well be unlimited with human resources devoted to education and research and development. Indeed, if there are limits to growth due to existing natural resource limits and environmental thresholds, then technological progress offers the best hope for continued growth on this finite planet. Technological progress, however, is not free or guaranteed; there are opportunity costs in the resources devoted to knowledge creation and human capital formation.

---

[25] See also Rao (2000: 88–89) for a discussion of sustainability conditions.

With the more realistic weak sustainability criterion, sustainable development could occur even with declines in the stock of natural capital (e.g., the depletion of nonrenewable resources) if other forms of capital can be substituted. Technological advances (increases in knowledge assets) have reduced the natural resource requirements for much of the output produced (e.g., the substitution of fiber optics for copper in wiring, the substitution of plastics for steel yielding lighter, more fuel-efficient automobiles, and the shift to fluorescent from incandescent light bulbs).

With the more stringent criterion of strong sustainability, depletion of nonrenewable resources, like fossil fuels, would have to be offset by increases in renewable resources, like solar and wind energy. Here too advances in technology can maintain the effective natural capital stock, even if components of that stock decline. In any case, clearly an important consideration for sustainability is the degree of substitutability across capital stocks or assets. Below a simple model is set forth to illustrate.

Efficiency in production

For the purpose of graphical exposition, consider just two types of factors or inputs into production, natural resources and human resources. Natural resources include the land, minerals, forests, energy sources, and waterways required to produce physical capital goods and consumer goods and services, as well as the natural environment that absorbs the waste from human consumption. Human resources include here physical labor, human capital, and social capital.

Using the global economy and a general aggregate production function,

$$Y = A \cdot F(R, H)$$

where Y is gross world output of final goods and services during the period, A an index of technology, R natural resources available for use in production during the period, and H human resources available for use in production during the period, we can plot all the technically efficient combinations of natural and human resources capable of producing a given level of global output, for a given state of technology. The isoquant, Y_0, is illustrated in Figure 11.1. Recall that technically efficient production processes do not use more of any resource than is needed for the level of production. In other words, the marginal products of the resources are always positive. The slope of an isoquant, known as the marginal rate of factor substitution (MRFS, or marginal rate of technical substitution), reflects the degree of resource substitutability. Here the MRFS equals the negative of the ratio of the marginal products: MRFS $= -$MPH$/$MPR.[26] The isoquant mapping represents the set of isoquants, for a given technology, associated with different levels of output.

The optimal or economically efficient combination of resources for producing a given level of output reflects the prices of the resources. Economic efficiency refers to the least-cost combination of resources. The total cost of resources used for production (TC) is given by $TC = P_R \cdot R + P_H \cdot H$, where P_R and P_H are the user costs of a unit of natural resources and human resources, respectively. The user costs refer to the comprehensive opportunity costs, inclusive of the private and public or

---

[26] To derive the slope of an isoquant, begin by totally differentiating the production function, $Y = A \cdot F(R, H)$, holding constant the index of technology, A, to obtain $dY = A \cdot [F_R \cdot dR + F_H \cdot dH]$, where $F_R = \partial F / \partial R = $ MPR and $F_H = \partial F / \partial H = $ MPH, the marginal products of natural and human resources. Since the rate of output is held constant along a given isoquant, $dY = 0$, solving for the slope of the isoquant, dR/dH, gives the marginal rate of factor substitution, MRFS $= dR/dH = -F_H/F_R = -$MPH$/$MPR. Note that, given the condition of technical efficiency, the slope of an isoquant will be negative as long as the marginal products of resources are positive. This negative slope is also intuitive since using less of one resource will require using more of the other resources to maintain the same rate of output.

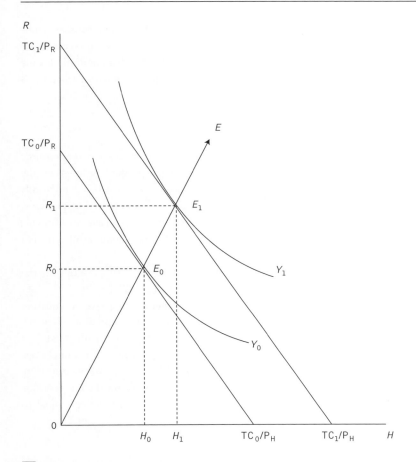

Figure 11.1 *Cost minimizing combination of natural resources (R) and human resources (H)*

The cost minimizing combinations of human and natural resources for producing output Y_0 and Y_1, respectively, are (H_0, R_0) and (H_1, R_1). The output expansion path is given by the ray from the origin, OE.

social costs of the resources. For given user costs, the combinations of natural and human resources that require the same total cost, say TC_0, give an isocost line, also illustrated in Figure 11.1. The slope of the isocost line is equal to $-P_H/P_R$.[27] The isocost mapping is the set of isocost lines, for given user costs of human and natural resources, associated with different total costs.

Consider a production function with smooth, strictly convex isoquants, for example a Cobb–Douglas production function $Y = A \cdot R^{\alpha} H^{\beta}$ ($0 < \alpha, \beta < 1$). If the world seeks to minimize the total cost of producing a selected level of output, Y_0, then we seek the lowest isocost line (closest to the origin) that reaches the isoquant corresponding to the output Y_0. In Figure 11.1 this optimal combination of natural and human resources for producing the output, Y_0, is indicated by the point of tangency, E_0, between the isocost line and isoquant. At this point of tangency, the slopes of the isoquant and isocost line are equal, $\mathrm{MRFS} = -\mathrm{MPH}/\mathrm{MPR} = -P_H/P_R$.

---

[27] To derive the slope of an isocost line, $TC_0 = P_R \cdot R + P_H \cdot H$, we can rewrite the equation as $R = TC_0/P_R - (P_H/P_R) \cdot H$. Then taking the derivate dR/dH gives the expression for the slope of a line in the $R - H$ plane, $dR/dH = -P_H/P_R$.

Intuitively, the marginal rate of factor substitution is the rate at which human resources can be substituted for natural resources to keep the same rate of output. The ratio of resource user costs gives the rate at the resources can be exchanged. Rearranging gives the familiar condition for the least-cost combination of resources, that is, where the marginal product per dollar of resources is equal: $\mathrm{MPR}/P_R = \mathrm{MPH}/P_H$.

Output-expansion path

The **output-expansion path** is the locus of least-cost combinations of resources, given resource prices, for producing varying levels of output. For this Cobb–Douglas production function, the output-expansion path is a ray from the origin.[28] In Figure 11.1 the least-cost or economically efficient combination of resources for producing the higher output, Y_1, is indicated by point E_1, where the MRFS equals the given ratio of user costs. This condition characterizes all of points on the output-expansion path, given here by the ray $0E$, including the two economically efficient combinations illustrated by points E_0 and E_1.

We can illustrate with the Cobb–Douglas production function $Y = A \cdot R^\alpha H^\beta$. Multiplying the inputs of natural resources and human resources by a constant c gives $A \cdot (cR)^\alpha (cH)^\beta = c^{\alpha+\beta} \cdot A \cdot R^\alpha H^\beta = c^{\alpha+\beta} \cdot Y = c^n \cdot Y$ (where $n = \alpha + \beta$ is the degree of homogeneity). To derive the equation for the output-expansion path for Y, return to the condition that defines economic efficiency and characterizes each point or resource combination on the output-expansion path, $\mathrm{MRFS} = \mathrm{MPH}/\mathrm{MPR} = P_H/P_R$. The associated marginal products of natural and human resources are $\mathrm{MPR} = \partial Y/\partial R = \alpha A \cdot R^{\alpha-1} H^\beta$ and $\mathrm{MPH} = \partial Y/\partial H = \beta A \cdot R^\alpha H^{\beta-1}$. Thus, we can write $\beta A \cdot R^\alpha H^{\beta-1}/\alpha A \cdot R^{\alpha-1} H^\beta = \alpha R/\beta H = P_H/P_R$. Solving for R, we obtain the equation for the output-expansion path, $R = (\beta/\alpha) \cdot (P_H/P_R) \cdot H$, which is linear with a slope equal to $(\beta/\alpha) \cdot (P_H/P_R)$.

Elasticity of substitution

Important for sustainability is the degree of substitution between factors of production. The **elasticity of substitution** gives the responsiveness of the optimal factor ratio to a change in the relative factor prices. The elasticity of substitution, ε, between natural and human resources, is defined as:

$$\varepsilon = \frac{\mathrm{d}(R/H)/(R/H)}{\mathrm{d}(P_H/P_R)/(P_H/P_R)}$$

$$\approx \frac{\text{Percentage change in the optimal ratio of natural to human resources}}{\text{Percentage change in the ratio of user costs of human to natural resources}}$$

We expect ε to be positive, that is, a relative decrease in the user cost of human resources would decrease the optimal ratio of natural to human resources. Or, if natural resources became more expensive relative to human resources, then there would be a substitution of human for natural resources. The elasticity of substitution between resources will reflect the production function.

From the equation for the output-expansion path, the elasticity of substitution, ε, can be derived. Important for the concern with weak sustainability is the degree to which resources can

---

[28] For any production function **homogeneous of degree** n, the output-expansion path is a ray from the origin, meaning that, as output increases, the economically efficient ratio of resources used remains the same. An equation, such as a production function, is homogeneous of degree n when multiplying each of the arguments by the scalar c results in a multiplication of the dependent variable by c^n. This Cobb–Douglas production function is homogeneous of degree $n = \alpha + \beta$, where α and β are the partial output elasticities of natural and human resources, respectively.

be substituted for each other. The inclination is to substitute away from relatively scarce resources, indicated by increases in their relative prices. The elasticity of substitution is a standardized measure of the responsiveness of the economically efficient ratio of resources to a change in the relative user costs.

For the Cobb–Douglas production function $Y = A \cdot R^{\alpha} H^{\beta}$, with an output-expansion path of $R = (\beta/\alpha) \cdot (P_H/P_R) \cdot H$, we can find the elasticity of substitution. First, rewriting the output-expansion path as $R/H = (\beta/\alpha) \cdot (P_H/P_R)$, then taking the natural logarithm of both sides, we get $\ln(R/H) = \ln[(\beta/\alpha) \cdot (P_H/P_R)] = \ln(\beta/\alpha) + \ln(P_H/P_R)$. Now differentiating $\ln(R/H)$ with respect to $\ln(P_H/P_R)$, we derive the elasticity of substitution:

$$\varepsilon = \frac{\mathrm{d}\ln(R/H)}{\mathrm{d}\ln(P_H/P_R)} = \frac{\mathrm{d}(R/H)/(R/H)}{\mathrm{d}(P_H/P_R)/(P_H/P_R)} = 1$$

That is, the elasticity of substitution for the Cobb–Douglas production function $Y = A \cdot R^{\alpha} H^{\beta}$ is equal to 1. An n percent increase (decrease) in the ratio of the user costs of human resources to natural resources would induce an n percent increase (decrease) in the optimal ratio of natural to human resources for a given level of output and given state of technology.

For example, a rise in the user cost of natural resources, *ceteris paribus*, reflected in flatter isocost lines, would induce a substitution of human for natural resources and movement along the given isoquant to a new economically efficient combination with a lower natural to human resource ratio. In Figure 11.2, compare the point E'_0, the new optimal combination of resources reflecting the absolute (and relative) increase in the user cost of natural resources, with E_0, the initial optimal combination.

Flexibility in production, reflected in the elasticity of substitution, is clearly important for the weak sustainability condition. The Cobb–Douglas production function, with an elasticity of substitution of 1, exhibits such flexibility.[29] Consider two special and extreme types of production functions.

Fixed-coefficients production function

One of the simplest, but most restrictive production functions is the **fixed-coefficients production function** of the form $Y = A \cdot \min[R/r, H/h]$, where $r = R/Y$ is the natural resource-output ratio, or the fixed share of natural resources in output, and $h = H/Y$ is the human resource-output ratio, or the fixed share of human resources in output.

For each output produced, the input requirements are fixed at $R = rY/A$ and $H = hY/A$. In other words, natural resources and human resources are **perfect complements** in production. There is no input or factor substitution possible. For fixed-coefficients production functions, the isoquants are right-angles, with the only technically efficient input combinations at the corner of each isoquant. For each rate of output there is only one technically efficient combination of resource inputs. Therefore, regardless of the ratio of user costs, there is only one economically efficient input combination for each rate of output.

---

[29] Another commonly used production function is known as the constant elasticity of substitution (CES) production function. Its general form is $Y = A \cdot [uH^{-\rho} + (1-u)R^{-\rho}]^{-n/\rho}$, where u is a distribution parameter ($0 < u < 1$), ρ a substitution parameter ($\rho > -1$ and $\rho \neq 0$), and n a returns to scale parameter ($n > 0$). We can show that the CES production function is, like the earlier Cobb–Douglas production function, homogeneous of degree n. The elasticity of substitution associated with this CES production function is equal to $1/(\rho+1)$, that is, constant, but not equal to unity. For example, if $\rho = 2$, then $\varepsilon = \frac{1}{3}$ and a 10 percent increase in the user cost of human resources relative to the user cost of natural resources would induce a 3.3 percent increase in the optimal natural resource to human resource ratio.

For this fixed-coefficients production function, the output expansion path is given by the equation $R = (r/h) \cdot H$. The elasticity of substitution is equal to zero, $\varepsilon = 0$.

Figure 11.3 illustrates two of the right-angled isoquants for this fixed-coefficients production function, corresponding to outputs of $Y = 1$ and $Y = 2$. The marginal products of natural resources and human resources are zero along the vertical and horizontal portions of the isoquants. The only relevant points on the isoquants are the corner points, corresponding to the technically efficient input combinations. Regardless of the ratio of the user costs of human to natural resources, only one combination of human and natural resources is economically efficient and technically efficient for each level of output. Since no resource substitution is possible, output growth is strictly limited by the growth of the less abundant resource. Note that this

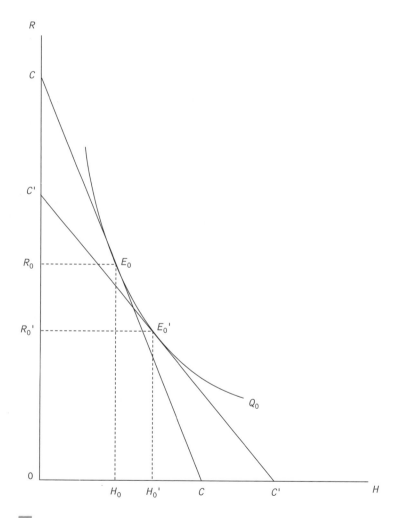

Figure 11.2 *A rise in the user cost of natural resources*

An increase in the user cost of natural resources, P_R, leads to a more human resource-intensive method of production: $R_0'/H_0' < R_0/H_0$. With the higher user cost of natural resources, the isocost line $C'C'$ represents a greater cost of production.

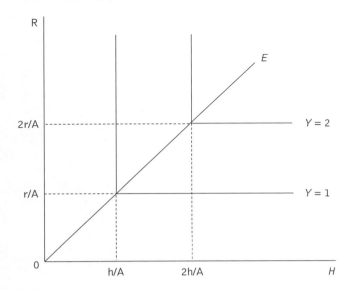

Figure 11.3 *Fixed-coefficients production function*

With the fixed coefficients production function, $Y = A \cdot minimum[R/r, H/h]$, if $Y = 1$, then $R = r/A$ and $H = h/A$. If output doubles to $Y = 2$, then the required inputs double to $R = 2r/A$ and $H = 2h/A$. The equation for the expansion path is $R = (r/h) \cdot H$.

fixed-coefficients production function exhibits constant returns to scale, that is, increasing natural and human resources by n percent would increase output by n percent.

Some production functions might be highly specific, such as the production of nuclear energy or the manufacture of an anti-cancer medicine where the key ingredients are finely calibrated. Or there is no substitute for the air we breathe. Compelling evidence of this is the failed biosphere experiment in the early 1990s, where a self-contained glass ecosystem was built for eight humans to live with no exchange from the outside except for the energy to run their appliances. The fixed supplies of air and water were to be recycled, producing, if possible, the natural services provided by the biosphere. The experiment was halted after one and a half years due to the failure of the human biosphere to replicate nature's cycles for air, water, and crop production (see World Bank 2003: 15).

Linear production function

At the other extreme would be **perfect substitutes** in production. For example, the linear production function, $Y = A \cdot [aR + bH]$. Here the marginal products of natural and human resources are constant, $MPR = dY/dR = aA$, and $MPH = dY/dH = bA$. This production function is also characterized by constant returns to scale and the growth rate of output is equal to the growth rate of the more abundant factor.

Figure 11.4 illustrates. The isoquant corresponding to the output Y_0 is linear, with slope equal to $MRFS = -MPH/MPR = -b/a$. With natural and human resources being perfect substitutes in production, the economically efficient resource combinations would be the corner points, unless the ratio of user costs equaled the marginal rate of factor substitution. That is, if $|MRFS| = MPH/MPR = b/a < P_H/P_R$, the slope of the isocost line, then only natural resources

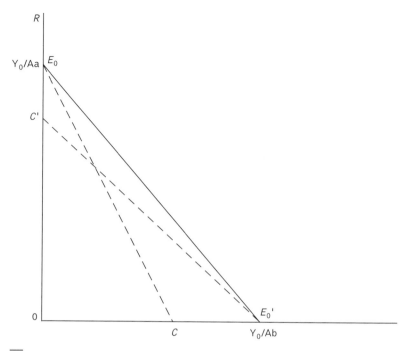

Figure 11.4 *Linear production function*

The linear production function is $Y = A \cdot [aR + bH]$. The slope or marginal rate of resource substitution is equal to $-MPH/MPR = -b/a$. If the slope of the isocost lines, $-P_H/P_R$, is greater in absolute value than $-b/a$, then only natural resources would be used. See point E_0. If the slope of the isocost lines, $-P_H/P_R$, is less in absolute value than $-b/a$, then only human resources would be used. See point E_0'. If the slope of the isocost lines, $-P_H/P_R$, is equal to $-b/a$, then any combination of resources on the isoquant would be economically efficient and could be used.

would be used in production. The economically efficient combination is the point E_0 on the R-axis. If, on the other hand, $|MRFS| = MPH/MPR = b/a > P_H/P_R$, then only human resources would be used in production and the economically efficient point would be E_0', where the isoquant and isocost line have a common point. Finally, if $|MRFS| = MPH/MPR = b/a = P_H/P_R$, then the isoquant coincides with the isocost line and any combination of resources on the isoquant would be economically efficient.

The elasticity of substitution for a linear production function is infinite, $\varepsilon = \infty$. Intuitively, the optimal ratio of resources could change from all natural resources ($R = Y_0/Aa$) and no human resources ($H = 0$), at point E_0, when $MPH/MPR < P_H/P_R$, to only human resources ($H = Y_0/Ab$) with no natural resources ($R = 0$), at point E_0', with only an infinitesimal change in the ratio of user costs such that $MPH/MPR > P_H/P_R$. In fact, the output expansion path is either the vertical axis, $Y = AaR$ (if natural resources are more abundant), or the horizontal axis, $Y = AbH$ (if, instead, human resources are relatively abundant).[30]

---

[30]Note that both the fixed-coefficients production function, $Y = A \cdot \min[R/r, H/h]$, and the linear production function, $Y = A \cdot [aR + bH]$, are homogeneous of degree 1 and characterized by constant returns to scale. To illustrate for the former, scaling up the resources by a factor c scales up output by $c^1 = c$. That is, $A \cdot \min[cR/r, cH/h] = c \cdot A \cdot \min[R/r, H/h] = cY$. For the linear production function, scaling up the resources by a factor c, $A \cdot [acR + bcH] = c \cdot A \cdot [aR + bH] = c \cdot Y$.

In practice, neither of these extreme cases ($\varepsilon = 0$ or $\varepsilon = \infty$) is likely, so there will be some substitution between resources possible with the production of goods and services. Nevertheless, the degree of substitution across resources, or more generally human, physical, and natural assets, is an important consideration for sustainable development. With the market mechanism, prices are signals for the allocation of resources. We expect that an increase in the price of natural resources relative to human resources would induce a substitution away from natural resources and the adoption of more human resource-intensive production processes. Moreover, relative price increases, indicating relative scarcities, would stimulate research to develop goods and services and production processes to conserve on the scarce resources.

CONCLUSION

In sum, in addition to the possibilities for substitution across factors in production, continued technological progress is important for sustainable development. Research and development will likely be induced by relative scarcities. For example, as fossil fuels become scarcer and more expensive, the incentive to develop renewable energy sources such as solar, wind, and tidal increases. A concern, however, is that market prices may not reflect user costs. As we will discuss, if externalities in the production or consumption of a good or service result, the market prices will not accurately reflect opportunity costs. Consequently, there is a case for government intervention in the markets. There is also an ongoing research agenda to develop more flexible production functions (allowing for greater factor substitutions), as well as technical change which allows for greater output from a given set of inputs, or, equivalently, which reduces the input requirements for a given output, in effect shifting the isoquants in toward the origin. Consider hybrid cars that can run on electricity or gasoline.

In Chapter 12 we turn to natural resources. As nonrenewable resources are used and their stocks depleted, their relative prices should rise. Yet, over the last three decades of the twentieth century, real prices of nonrenewable natural resources generally declined. The greater concerns seemed to be with the overuse of renewable resources and the deterioration of the natural environment.

KEY TERMS

adjusted net saving rate	economic development
Ehrlich identity	elasticity of substitution
fixed-coefficients production function	healthy life expectancy
homogeneous of degree n	Human Development Index
index of youth investment	Millennium Development Goals
output-expansion path	perfect complements
perfect substitutes	strong sustainability
sustainable development	weak sustainability

QUESTIONS

1. The statistics for three island nations for 2011 are as follows:

	Madagascar	Sri Lanka	Cuba
Life expectancy at birth (years)	66.7	74.9	79.1
Mean years of schooling	5.2	8.2	9.9
Expected years of schooling	10.7	11.9	17.5
Gross national income per capita (PPP dollars)	824	4,943	5,416

    (a) Calculate the Human Development Index values for the nations.
    (b) Calculate Sri Lanka's Human Development Index not discounting the contribution of income to human development, that is, use gross national income per capita instead of the natural logarithm of gross national income per capita.
    (c) Cuba's HDI rank is 51st among the 187 nations listed by UNDP (2011). Cuba's gross national income per capita rank, however, is 103rd. What insight does this give you into Cuba's economic growth?

2. Recall the Ehrlich identity, $I = P \cdot A \cdot T$, where we measure I as total primary energy produced in the world (million tons of oil equivalent), P is the world population, A is per capita output, and T is the energy intensity of output (measured as primary energy per unit of output). Suppose that the world's primary energy production in 2008 were 12.4 billion metric tons of oil equivalent; the world population was 6.7 billion, per capita world GDP was $10,000 (PPP dollars), and world output per kilogram of oil equivalent was $5.4. (Note that one metric ton is equivalent to 1000 kilograms). Thus, in 2008, $I = 12.4$ billion tons of energy production, $P = 6.7$ billion people, $A = \$10,000$, and $T = 1/5,400$. Further, suppose the carrying capacity of the world is 16 billion tons of energy production ($I' = 16.0$), the world population will eventually stabilize at 9 billion ($P' = 9$), and per capita world GDP will increase to $15,000 ($A' = 15,000$). What will be the implied level of technology (T') needed to keep the world below the carrying capacity?

3. The statistics in Table 11.5 suggest that South Korea is currently more successful in sustainable development than the United States. Discuss. What are the policy implications for the United States?

4. Suppose, for the production function $Y = A \cdot H^\alpha R^\beta (0 < \alpha, \beta < 1)$, that the growth of H (human resources) and R (natural resources) is given by the equations $H(t) = H(0)e^{jt}$ and $R(t) = R(0)e^{ut}$. The growth in neutral technological change is given by $A(t) = A(0)e^{gt}$.

    (a) Determine the growth rate in output, dY/Y.
    (b) Find the equation for the expansion path given the ratio of user costs, $P_H/P_R = 2$.

5. Suppose, for the fixed-coefficients production function $Y = A \cdot \min[H/h, R/r]$, that the growth of H (human resources) and R (natural resources) is given by the equations $H(t) = H(0)e^{jt}$ and $R(t) = R(0)e^{ut}$. The growth in neutral technological change is given by $A(t) = A(0)e^{gt}$. Determine the growth rate in output, dY/Y.

REFERENCES

Anand, Sudhir and Amartya Sen. 2000. "Human Development and Economic Sustainability," *World Development*, 28(12): 2029–2049.

Bales, Kevin. 2005. *Understanding Global Slavery: A Reader*. Berkeley: University of California Press.

Basu, Kausik. 1999. "Child Labor: Cause, Consequence, and Cure with Remarks on International Labor Standards," *Journal of Economic Literature*, 37(3): 1083–1119.

Bhagwati, Jagdish. 2007. *In Defense of Globalization*. New York: Oxford University Press.

Blewitt, John. 2008. *Understanding Sustainable Development*. Sterling, VA: Earthscan.

Daily, Gretchen and Paul Ehrlich. 1992. "Population, Sustainability, and Earth's Carrying Capacity: A Framework for Estimating Population Sizes and Lifestyles that Could Be Sustained without Undermining Future Generations," *BioScience*, 42(10). http://dieoff.org/page112.htm.

Eadie, Pauline and Lloyd Pettiford. 2005. "The Natural Environment," in Jeffrey Haynes (ed.), *Palgrave Advances in Development Studies*. New York: Palgrave Macmillan: 181–200.

Ehrlich, Paul, and John Holdren. 1971. "The Impact of Population Growth," *Science*, 171(3977): 1212–1217.

Fleischman, H.L., P.J. Hopstock, M.P Pelczar, and B.E. Shelley. 2010. *Highlights from PISA 2009: Performance of U.S. 15-Year-Old Students in Reading, Mathematics, and Science Literacy in an International Context*, NCES 2011-004, US Department of Education, National Center for Education Statistics. Washington, DC: U.S. Government Printing Office.

Fyfe, Alec. 2007. *The Worldwide Movement Against Child Labor: Progress and Future Directions*. Geneva: International Labour Office.

Gilligan, B. 2003. *An Analysis of the Determinants of Child Labor in Nepal, the Policy Environment and Response*, Understanding Children's Work (UCW) Project. Rome: University of Rome.

Hardin, Garrett. 1968. "The Tragedy of the Commons," *Science*, 162(3859): 1243–1248.

Harris, Jonathan, Timothy Wise, Kevin Gallagher, and Neva Goodwin (eds). 2001. *A Survey of Sustainable Development: Social and Economic Dimensions*. Washington, DC: Island Press.

Hess, Peter. 2009. "Child Labor and the Kamlaris of Nepal," Davidson College, May 15.

Hess, Peter. 2010a. "Determinants of the Adjusted Net Saving Rate in Developing Economies," *International Review of Applied Economics*, 24(5): 591–608.

Hess, Peter. 2010b. "A Sustainable Development Metric Based on Youth," *International Journal of Sustainable Development & World Ecology*, 17(6): 542–551.

International Labour Office. 2006. *The End of Child Labor: Within Reach*, Report of the Director General. Geneva: International Labour Office.

International Labour Office. 2010. *Accelerating Action against Child Labor*, Global Report under the follow-up to the ILO declaration on Fundamental Principles and Rights at Work. Geneva: International Labour Office.

Kelley, A.C. 1991. "The Human Development Index: 'Handle with Care'," *Population Development Review*, 17(2): 315–324.

Koolwal, Gayatri. 2007. "Son Preference and Child Labor in Nepal: The Household Impact of Sending Girls to Work," *World Development*, 35(5): 881–903.

McGillivray, M. 1991. "The Human Development Index: Yet Another Redundant Composite Development Indicator?" *World Development*, 19(10): 1461–1468.

Narayan, Deepa with Raj Patel, Kai Schafft, Anne Rademacher, and Sarah Koch-Schult. 2000. *Voices of the Poor: Can Anyone Hear Us?* New York: Oxford University Press.

Rao, P.K. 2000. *Sustainable Development: Economics and Policy*. Malden, MA: Blackwell.

Rist, Gilbert. 1997. "The Environment, or the New Nature of Development," in *The History of Development: From Western Origins to Global Faith*. London: Zed Books: 171–196.

351

Rogers, Peter, Kazi Jalal, and John Boyd. 2008. *An Introduction to Sustainable Development.* London: Earthscan.

Sajar, A.D. and A. Najam. 1998. "The Human Development Index: A Critical Review," *Ecological Economics,* 25(3): 249–264.

Sharma, Shiva, Bijendra Basnyat, and Ganesh G.C. 2001. *Nepal: Bonded Labor among Child Workers in the Kamaiya System: A Rapid Assessment.* Geneva: International Labour Organization, International Programme on the Elimination of Child Labour.

Understanding Children's Work Project. 2003. *Understanding Children's Work in Nepal,* Country Report. Rome: University of Rome.

United Nations. 2007. *Indicators of Sustainable Development: Guidelines and Methodologies,* 3rd edition. New York: United Nations.

United Nations Development Programmme. 1990. *Human Development Report 1990.* New York: Oxford University Press for the UNDP.

United Nations Development Programmme. 2010. *Human Development Report 2010: The Real Wealth of Nations.* New York: Palgrave Macmillan for the UNDP.

United Nations Development Programmme. 2011. *Human Development Report 2011: Sustainability and Equity.* New York: Palgrave Macmillan for the UNDP.

UNICEF. 2007a. *Progress for Children: A World Fit for Children Statistical Review,* 6 December. New York: United Nations Children's Fund.

UNICEF. 2007b. *The State of the World's Children 2008: Child Survival.* New York: United Nations Children's Fund.

World Bank. 1992. *World Development Report: Development and the Environment.* New York: Oxford University Press.

World Bank. 1998. *World Development Indicators 1998.* Washington, DC: World Bank.

World Bank. 2002. *World Development Indicators 2002.* Washington, DC: World Bank.

World Bank. 2003. *World Development Report 2003: Sustainable Development in a Dynamic World.* New York: Oxford University Press.

World Bank. 2005. *Economic Growth in the 1990s: Learning from a Decade of Reform.* http://www1.worldbank.org/prem/lessons1990s.

World Bank. 2006. *World Development Report 2007: Development and the Next Generation.* New York: Oxford University Press.

World Bank. 2009. *World Development Indicators 2009.* Washington, DC: World Bank.

World Bank. 2011. *World Development Indicators 2011.* Washington, DC: World Bank.

World Bank. 2012a. *World Development Indicators 2012.* Washington, DC: World Bank.

World Bank. 2012b. *Food Prices, Nutrition, and the Millennium Development Goals: Global Monitoring Report 2012.* Washington, DC: World Bank

World Commission on Environment and Development. 1987. *Report of the World Commission on Environment and Development: Our Common Future.* http://www.un-documents.net/wced-ocf.htm.

World Health Organization. 2010. *World Health Statistics 2010.* Geneva: WHO.

Chapter 12

Natural resources and climate change

The Doomsday Clock is a symbolic clock face created in 1947 by University of Chicago scientists who had participated in the Manhattan Project that developed the first atomic weapons. Published in the *Bulletin of the Atomic Scientists*, the Doomsday Clock indicates how close—in minutes before midnight—the world is to "catastrophic destruction." Historically the main concerns have been with nuclear destruction. More recently climate change and biosecurity with the potential for bioterrorism or misguided research that could unleash dangerous pathogens have been included as threats to humankind.[1]

In 1947, at the beginning of the Cold War, the clock was initially set at seven minutes before midnight. The clock moved to three minutes before midnight in 1949 with the Soviet Union's test of nuclear devices and the commencement of the arms race. In 1953, with the US testing of the hydrogen bomb, followed by the Soviet testing of their hydrogen bomb, the directors of the *Bulletin of the Atomic Scientists* "advanced" the clock to two minutes before midnight. Over time, the clock has been reset according to conflicts or arms treaties or other global developments. For example, in 1963 with the Partial Test Ban Treaty that ended atmospheric nuclear testing, the clock fell back to 12 minutes before midnight. In 1981, with the Soviet invasion of Afghanistan and the heightened tensions between the two military superpowers, the clock moved to four minutes before midnight. With the dissolution of the Soviet Union and the end of the Cold War, followed by the US and Russia agreeing to deep cuts in their nuclear arsenals, the clock was reset to 17 minutes before midnight in 1991—the furthest back in the history of the clock. Then over the decade the clock moved closer to midnight. In 1998, nuclear weapons testing by India and Pakistan shifted the clock to nine minutes before midnight. In 2002 concerns with nuclear terrorism from unaccounted-for nuclear materials brought the clock to seven minutes before midnight.

In 2007, with the apparent deterioration in US–Russian relations, the radical regimes in Iran and North Korea seeking to acquire or actually with nuclear weapons, and for the first time, recognition of compelling evidence of global warming, the clock moved to five minutes before midnight. Then in 2010, the clock fell back one minute to six minutes before midnight, with strategic arms reduction between the US and Russia and hoped-for progress on climate change from the consensus agreement at the Copenhagen conference, where the industrial and developing nations agreed to share the responsibility of reducing carbon emissions and to limit the global temperature increase to 2 °C.

In January of 2012, however, the *Bulletin of the Atomic Scientists* announced the Doomsday Clock had been reset to five minutes before midnight since:

---

[1] See http://www.thebulletin.org/content/doomsday-clock/overview.

The challenges to rid the world of nuclear weapons, harness nuclear power, and meet the nearly inexorable climate disruptions from global warming are complex and interconnected. In the face of such complex problems, it is difficult to see where the capacity lies to address these challenges. Political processes seem wholly inadequate; the potential for nuclear weapons use in regional conflicts in the Middle East, Northeast Asia, and South Asia are alarming; safe nuclear reactor designs need to be developed and built, and more stringent oversight, training, and attention are needed to prevent future disasters; the pace of technological solutions to address climate change may not be adequate to meet the hardships that large-scale disruption of the climate potends.[2]

In this chapter we discuss the importance of natural resources for economic growth and sustainable development. There is increasing evidence of environmental stress, threatening future livelihoods. Extensive resource depletion, global warming and loss of biodiversity may be signs of unsustainable development. Recently, the United Nations Development Programme (UNDP 2010: 102) asserted: "Climate change may be the single factor that makes the future very different from the past, impeding the continuing progress in human development that history would lead us to expect."

GIFTS OF NATURE

Natural resources, sometimes referred to as "gifts of nature," encompass the land, forests, mineral deposits, energy sources, bodies of water, wildlife, and the overall natural environment that supplies the raw materials for the production of goods and provides the services essential for life, including water for drinking, soil for growing food, and air for breathing.[3] In addition, the natural environment provides sinks for the absorption of the wastes generated by humans and other living creatures. Moreover, the natural environment can contribute to the quality of human life, when for recreation we climb the mountains, hike the forests, and swim in the oceans.

Natural resources are a primary factor of production, along with human labor and physical capital. Increases in the quantity or quality of natural resources available to an economy enhance the productive capacity of the nation. Natural resources can be classified as renewable or nonrenewable. As we know, nonrenewable resources have finite stocks—at least for any foreseeable planning horizon. Mineral deposits and reserves of fossil fuels are nonrenewable resources. With renewable resources, in contrast, the stocks can be regenerated through proper use and management— farmland, forests, and fisheries are examples. Some forms of energy (solar, tidal, and wind) are renewable, but their current availability depends on the forces of nature.

The quality of the available resources reflects their intrinsic values in production and consumption. The value of petroleum reserves differs according to costs of accessing the deposits as well as the subsequent costs of refining. The quality of coal varies directly with its carbon content, with anthracite the oldest and most valuable. So, too, soils differ according to their inherent fertility.

Natural resource endowments vary across nations. Extensive mineral deposits (e.g., copper, iron ore, bauxite, diamonds) and significant reserves of petroleum, coal, and natural gas tend to be concentrated in parts of the world. Some nations are endowed with especially fertile lands

[2] Since the initial clock was set at seven minutes before midnight in 1947, the time has been reset 20 times. See http://www.thebulletin.org/content/doomsday-clock/timeline (accessed April 19, 2012).

[3] Some of the discussion of natural resources in this chapter draws on Hess and Ross (1997).

and advantageous climates for the growing of crops. Coastal nations clearly have greater access to the fish and resources in the oceans. Tropical rainforests are found mostly in Latin America; the tropical dry forests are mainly in Africa. The unevenness of natural resource endowments provides a basis for international trade. Indeed, for some nations the export of natural resources has been a leading sector of economic growth. The natural beauty of mountains and seashores gives some countries an advantage in tourism and recreation. As we will discuss below, however, often nations well endowed with fossil fuels or minerals experience little economic growth or development.

Primary factors of production

To use natural resources in the production of goods and services, the factors of human labor and, usually, physical capital have to be applied—to cultivate the land, catch the fish, harvest the forests, and extract the minerals. As discussed in Chapter 11, weak sustainability depends on the substitutability across assets. Physical assets (buildings, equipment, and machinery) are made from natural assets. Raw materials can be processed not only into capital goods, but also into intermediate and final goods. For example, diamonds are mined for use in industry in precision cutting machines and for personal consumption as fine jewelry. Iron ore is used to make steel for automobiles, appliances, and girders for construction. Timber can be cut and processed into lumber for home construction, kitchen tables, and hockey sticks. Fertile farmland can be used to grow cotton, which can be processed into textiles and clothing.

The quality and quantity of natural resources are affected by human behavior. Fertilizers can improve the fertility of the soil. New trees can be planted. On the other hand, overuse, mismanagement, or pollution can decrease the quantity and quality of the natural resource base. Overgrazing can turn a viable pasture into barren scrub land. Air pollution and acid rain can diminish forests. Improper disposal of industrial wastes can poison bodies of water. Such environmental deterioration not only reduces the production possibilities of a nation, but also may directly diminish the quality of life by posing health hazards and impairing esthetic enjoyment.

In the less developed countries the issues of how to manage the natural resources to promote economic growth and development and how to meet the basic needs of their populations for clean water, food, and energy would seem to take precedence over concerns with the environment. But in promoting economic development and addressing their widespread poverty, these nations cannot afford to neglect the environment. A vicious cycle of poverty, rapid population growth, pressure on the natural resource base, and environmental deterioration can be unleashed. Usually it is the poorest in a nation that suffer the most from degradation of the environment—whether from the consumption of unsafe water, the indoor air pollution from cooking over wood fires, or the erosion of soils as fragile lands are overused. At the same time, poverty and population pressures contribute to environmental deterioration—as young trees are cut down for fuel; rivers and streams are used for bathing and washing clothes, even as toilets; pastures are overgrazed; and proper investments in farmland are unaffordable. Furthermore, with economic growth and development come not only greater rates of resource utilization, but also the challenges of properly disposing of the increasing industrial and consumer wastes.

Below we review two natural resource-intensive sectors, mining and forestry. Agriculture and fishing will be addressed in Chapter 13. Two afflictions found in some nations associated with natural resource-intensive growth, the Dutch disease and the "natural resource curse," are also discussed.

NATURAL RESOURCE-INTENSIVE GROWTH

In Table 12.1 the direct contributions of mineral, fossil fuel, and forest rents to gross domestic products are given for nations grouped by per capita income and region. As explained by the World Bank (2011: 187):

> Natural resources give rise to economic rents because they are not produced. For produced goods and services competitive forces expand supply until economic profits are driven to

Table 12.1 *Contribution of natural resources to gross domestic product*

	Percentage of GDP (2010)					
	Total natural resource rents	Oil rents	Natural gas rents	Coal rents	Mineral rents	Forest rents
World	4.0%	1.8%	0.4%	0.8%	0.8%	0.2%
Low-income economies	6.5%	1.2%	1.3%	...	1.8%	2.3%
Lower middle-income economies	11.4%	5.7%	1.2%	2.2%	1.8%	0.6%
India	6.7%	1.0%	0.4%	2.6%	2.1%	0.6%
Upper middle-income economies	9.3%	4.3%	0.8%	2.0%	2.1%	0.2%
China	7.8%	1.5%	0.1%	3.8%	2.2%	0.2%
High-income economies	1.4%	0.6%	0.2%	0.2%	0.3%	0.1%
United States	1.4%	0.7%	0.1%	0.4%	0.1%	0.1%
Low- and middle-income economies						
Sub-Saharan Africa	16.7%	12.0%	0.5%	...	2.8%	1.3%
Mid. East & North Africa	18.7%	14.9%	3.2%	0.0%	0.6%	0.1%
Europe & Central Asia	14.2%	8.9%	2.5%	1.3%	1.2%	0.3%
South Asia	6.2%	0.9%	0.6%	2.3%	1.7%	0.7%
East Asia & Pacific	7.9%	1.7%	0.4%	3.4%	2.1%	0.2%
Latin America & Caribbean	8.0%	4.7%	0.4%	0.1%	2.6%	0.2%
Top three nations	69.3% (Iraq)	69.1% (Iraq)	25.8% (Trinidad & Tobago)	22.9% (Mongolia)	54.2% (Mauritania)	12.5% (Liberia)
	64.1% (Congo Rep.)	61.6% (Congo. Rep.)	24.2% (Turkmenistan)	5.5% (Kazakhstan)	32.2% (Papua NG)	12.0% (Burundi)
	54.7% (Mauritania)	46.4% (Gabon)	18.1% (Uzbekistan)	5.1% (S. Africa)	26.7% (Zambia)	9.5% (Congo DR)

Notes: Estimated natural resource rents are calculated as the difference between the world price of a commodity and the average unit cost of extracting or harvesting the commodity (including a normal return on capital). These unit resource rents are then multiplied by the physical quantities extracted or harvested to determine the rents for each commodity as a share of GDP.

Source: World Bank (2012: Table 3.18).

zero, but natural resources in fixed supply often command returns well in excess of their cost of production. Rents from nonrenewable resources—fossil fuels and minerals—as well as rents from overharvesting of forests indicate the liquidation of a country's capital stock. When countries use such rents to support current consumption rather than invest in new capital to replace what is being used up, they are, in effect, borrowing against their future.

In general, the share of natural resource rents in gross domestic product decline with economic growth, as nations develop their industry and modern service sectors. However, this is not clear in the aggregate statistics for the average shares for total resource rents, which rise from the low- through the upper-middle income economies before declining sharply for the high-income economies. In large part, those nations well endowed with oil and gas reserves have drawn on these nonrenewable resources to fuel their economic growth. To accent the uneven geographical distribution of natural resources, the regional statistics clearly illustrate the relative dependence of the Middle East and North Africa, sub-Saharan Africa, and Europe and Central Asia on natural resource rents. To illustrate the extreme reliance of some economies, the top three nations are given for each natural resource rent. With a few exceptions, common features of these nations listed are conflict, authoritarian governments, and poverty. For example, the three nations with the highest shares of forest rents in GDP, Liberia ($340), Burundi ($400) and the Democratic Republic of the Congo ($320), had the three lowest per capita incomes (in PPP dollars) in the world in 2010.

While generalizations about natural resources—availability, use, and conservation—can be made, it is important to realize that important differences exist across the natural resource-intensive sectors of an economy. For one, mining is a sector based on nonrenewable resources. Forests are renewable and should be managed with sustainability as a goal. The cycles for many trees from seedlings to mature growth cover several decades though, so in the short to medium run, individual tree stands can be considered as nonrenewable. Both sectors, mining and forestry, however, have profound environmental impacts.

Mining

The extraction of minerals is capital-intensive. Most mining activity is large scale—although there may be small operations working on the fringe, prospecting for gold and precious stones. The start-up costs in mining are considerable and include the exploration of mineral reserves and the heavy equipment needed to extract and transport the minerals. Mining has been a leading sector for foreign direct investment in a number of less developed countries. Transnational corporations from the developed countries have the technical expertise, capital equipment, and funds to finance large-scale mining operations. Because mineral deposits can be considered as "gifts of nature," hence state property, national governments have often been involved in the mining sector—either directly through state-owned mining companies and joint ventures with foreign corporations or indirectly through taxation of the revenues generated from mining.

Second, for nations with significant deposits of minerals, especially developing economies, domestic demands will fall far short of production capacities. Consequently, from the outset there may be a heavy reliance on foreign markets. This export orientation of mining has provided additional incentive for governments to get involved—to secure a share of the foreign exchange generated. While many developing nations also rely on cash crops for export revenues, usually a large part of the agricultural produce is for domestic consumption.

Third, mineral deposits can be considered to be nonrenewable. Therefore, an important concern in mining is the appropriate rate of depletion. A factor that tempers the long-run demand for minerals has been the development of synthetic substitutes, such as plastic or fiberglass for steel in automobiles and biofuels for fossil fuels.

Fourth, the extraction of minerals has serious environmental costs, including the improper disposal of wastes and degradation of the landscape. The consequences and government policies to address these negative externalities will be examined in Chapter 14.

All of the above concerns also apply to fossil fuels (oil, natural gas, and coal). These sectors are capital-intensive, given the drilling required for the extraction and the infrastructure necessary for the transmission of these fuels. Nations well endowed with these nonrenewable resources depend on foreign demand and export revenues. Moreover, the consumption of fossil fuels places heavy demands on the environment, especially with the greenhouse gas (GHG) emissions generated.

The importance of these fossil fuels for current energy production, however, cannot be understated. Before turning to forestry, selective statistics on world energy are provided in Table 12.2. In particular, estimates of the proved reserves of oil, natural gas, and coal, along with remaining lifetimes, undermine the premise that these fossil fuels are becoming scarcer. As Table 12.2(a) illustrates, the proved reserves of oil and natural gas have increased over the past two decades by 38 percent and 48 percent, respectively. And, at current rates of utilization, coal reserves should last for at least another century. Nevertheless, the primary concern from using fossil fuels remains global warming and the damage to the environment from GHG emissions.

The three fossil fuels are not perfect substitutes. As Coley (2008) discusses, the most important use of coal is for power plants and the generation of electricity. While relatively abundant, coal, when combusted, is the most environmentally harmful with four main pollutants: carbon dioxide, particulates (a major health risk with inhalation), and sulfur dioxide and nitrogen dioxide (both contributing to acid rain). Oil is highly flammable, easier to store than natural gas, and particularly well suited for transportation, where engine combustion is subject to frequent starts and stops. Natural gas burns more cleanly than oil and can be readily transported through pipelines.

Overwhelmingly, these fossil fuels are concentrated in a relatively few nations. In Table 12.2(b) we see that 60 percent of the oil reserves, 62 percent of natural gas reserves, and 75 percent of coal reserves are held by the top five nations. The natural endowments of Saudi Arabia, Russia, and Iran stand out. We note that China and India are well endowed with coal, the most heavily polluting of the fossil fuels. Unless serious mitigation efforts are undertaken, the consequences for global climate change as these two demographic billionaires draw on their deposits for the rapidly growing economies will be serious.

As will be discussed later, to reduce the impending costs from global warming the world will need to shift to cleaner, more sustainable forms of energy. As Table 12.2(c) shows, oil, natural gas, and coal combined in 2010 to account for 87 percent of primary energy consumed in the world. For the OECD nations, the share of these fossil fuels was 83 percent. For the non-OECD nations, the share was 91 percent in 2010. Moreover, the developing nations relied relatively more on coal. Hydroelectricity and nuclear power each account for 5–7 percent of the total global commercial energy consumption, with renewables like solar, geothermal, and wind still under 2 percent. The disastrous meltdown at the Fukushima nuclear plant in Japan in March 2011 due to the earthquake and tsunami, however, has cooled interest in expanding this clean source of energy.

Table 12.2 Selected statistics on world energy

(a) Proven reserves in the world

Resource	End of 1990	End of 2000	End of 2010	R/P 2010 (years)
Oil (billion barrels)	1,003.2	1,104.9	1,383.2	46.2
Natural gas (trillion cu. meters)	125.7	154.3	186.6	58.6
Coal (million tons)	...	...	860,938	118

Note: Proven reserves are generally taken to be those quantities that geological and engineering information indicates with reasonable certainty can be recovered in the future from known reservoirs under existing economic and operating conditions.

The reserves to production ratio (*R/P*) indicates the length of time the reserves remaining at the end of any year would last if the rate of production prevailing in that year were to continue.

(b) Share of total reserves of the top five nations, 2010

Oil	Natural gas	Coal
Saudi Arabia (19.1%)	Russian Federation (23.9%)	United States (27.6%)
Venezuela (15.3%)	Iran (15.8%)	Russian Federation (18.2%)
Iran (9.9%)	Qatar (13.5%)	China (13.3%)
Iraq (8.3%)	Turkmenistan (4.3%)	Australia (8.9%)
Kuwait (7.3%)	Saudi Arabia (4.3%)	India (7.0%)
Top 5 total (59.9%)	Top 5 total (61.8%)	Top 5 total (75.0%)

(c) World primary energy consumption by fuel, 2010 (millions of tons of oil equivalent)

	Oil	Natural gas	Coal	Nuclear energy	Hydro-electricity	Renewables	Total
World	4,028.1	2,858.1	3,555.8	626.2	775.6	158.6	12,002.4
	(33.6%)	(23.8%)	(29.6%)	(5.2%)	(6.5%)	(1.3%)	(100%)
OECD	2,113.8	1,397.6	1,103.6	520.9	309.5	123.0	5,568.3
	(38.0%)	(25.1%)	(19.8%)	(9.4%)	(5.6%)	(2.2%)	(100%)
Non-OECD	1,914.3	1,460.5	2,452.2	105.3	466.1	35.6	6,434.1
	(29.8%)	(22.7%)	(38.1%)	(1.6%)	(7.2%)	(0.6%)	(100%)

Notes: Primary energy comprises commercially traded fuels, including modern renewables used to generate electricity. Renewables include wind, geothermal, solar, biomass, and waste.

OECD nations are: Australia, Austria, Belgium, Canada, Chile, Czech Republic, Denmark, Estonia, Finland, France, Germany, Greece, Hungary, Iceland, Republic of Ireland, Israel, Italy, Japan, Luxembourg, Mexico, Netherlands, New Zealand, Norway, Poland, Portugal, Slovakia, Slovenia, South Korea, Spain, Sweden, Switzerland, Turkey, United Kingdom, and the United States.

Source: BP Statistical Review of World Energy (June 2011), http://www.bp.com/statisticalreview.

Forestry

According to the Food and Agricultural Organization of the United Nations (FAO 2010), in 2010 the world's total forest area covered 4 billion hectares, approximately 31 percent of the total land area. Five nations, the Russian Federation, Brazil, Canada, the United States, and China, account for 53 percent of the total forest area.[4]

---

[4] The definition of "forest" used by the FAO (2010: 209) is "Land spanning more than 0.5 hectares with trees higher than 5 meters and a canopy of more than 10 percent, or trees able to reach these thresholds *in situ*. It does not include land that is predominantly under agricultural or urban land use."

Forestry is a major economic activity in many countries. With respect to logging, the primary commercial activity in forests, there are similarities with mining. Logging tends to be capital-intensive, given the heavy equipment needed to harvest and transport the timber. For those nations well endowed with forests, the export of timber can be a major source of foreign exchange.

Forests provide much more than lumber. Indeed, a second distinguishing feature would be the externalities associated with forests. Forests are an integral part of the environment, including the regional hydrologic cycles. The FAO (2010: 110) notes the protective functions provided by forests: for soils from wind and water erosion, for coasts from tidal erosion, and for mountains from avalanches:

Forests conserve water by increasing filtration, reducing runoff velocity and surface erosion, and decreasing sedimentation (which is particularly relevant behind dams and in irrigation systems). Forests play a role in filtering water pollutants, regulating water yield and flow, moderating floods, enhancing precipitation (e.g., "cloud forests," which capture moisture from clouds) and mitigating salinity.

Forests recycle carbon dioxide, helping to cleanse the earth's atmosphere. As reported by the Food and Agricultural Organization (2010: 11),

> Forests contain more carbon than the entire atmosphere. The world's forests store more than 650 billion tons of carbon, 44 percent in the biomass, 11 percent in dead wood and litter, and 45 percent in soil. While sustainable management, planting and rehabilitation of forests can conserve or increase forest carbon stocks, deforestation, degradation, and poor forest management reduce them.

Temperate forests are widely used for recreation such as hiking and camping. Astill (2010: 4, 7) lists other benefits naturally provided by forests including: housing for more than half the world's species of animals, birds, and insects; the basis for many modern medicines (e.g., aspirin derived from willow bark, and the breast cancer drug, Taxol, derived from Pacific yew bark); and livelihoods for some 400 million of the world's poorest people.

A note of alarm was sounded several years ago by the UNDP (2007: 158): "Rainforests are currently shrinking at about 5 percent a year . . . on one estimate, deforestation, peat land degradation, and forest fires have made Indonesia the third largest source of GHG emissions in the world."

Exports of natural resource-intensive products

Nations with substantial stocks of natural resources, especially mineral and fuel deposits and forest reserves, will likely enjoy a degree of international market power. That is, these nations will be price-setters, since the demand curves for their exports of the natural resources will be downward-sloping. There can be considerable volatility in export revenues, reflecting the international business cycle and economic conditions in foreign markets.

Minerals, fuels, and timber are basically inputs into further stages of production; for example, bauxite used for aluminum, coal for electricity, and timber processed into boards for construction. When the international economy is healthy, with expanding industrial outputs and construction activity, the derived demands for natural resources will increase. Revenues from mining and forestry will rise as market-clearing prices and quantities rise. In contrast, in periods of recession,

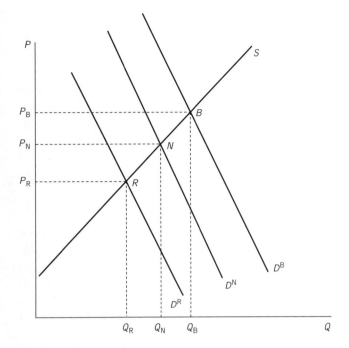

Figure 12.1 *Export revenue instability in natural resources*

The export revenues from natural resources can be highly variable, rising sharply in years of strong foreign demand, D^B and declining sharply in years of international recession, D^R.

industrial output and construction activity will decline. The derived demands for minerals, fuels, and lumber will fall, pulling down market prices and quantities sold.

In Figure 12.1 we illustrate the potential for the pro-cyclical boom and bust conditions in export revenues for a nation with natural gas reserves. With demand shifts, market prices and quantities move in the same direction. Over an international business cycle annual export revenues from natural gas for this nation could go from $TR_N = P_N \cdot Q_N$ in an average or normal year to $TR_B = P_B \cdot Q_B$ in a boom year or period of economic expansion to $TR_R = P_R \cdot Q_R$ in a recession year ($P_B > P_N > P_R$ and $Q_B > Q_N > Q_R$). If import expenditures are stable, the volatility in export revenues results in instability in the trade balance that can lead to other difficulties, including exchange rate variability or dependence on foreign credit during recessions. If, on the other hand, imports vary directly with exports, then the associated fluctuations in imports can be disruptive to the domestic economy. In periods when foreign demand is depressed and the inflow of foreign exchange from exports declines, the output of the domestic industries that depend on imported inputs may have to be cut back, increasing unemployment and reducing incomes in the nation. So too, shortages of foreign exchange may curtail domestic production and development projects that depend on imported inputs.

Conversely, in boom periods when export revenues are rising sharply, the nation may overextend itself—with inflation, budget deficits, and a run-up of external debt becoming problematic. We will illustrate this phenomenon, known as the Dutch disease, below. In short, nations with a high percentage of export revenues based on natural resources may be especially vulnerable to changing international economic conditions. Consequently, economic planning in the nation becomes more difficult.

In the long run the trend in real prices for many natural resources (i.e., the purchasing power of a physical unit of natural resources) has been downward. On the supply side, advances in technology and transportation have led to the discovery, recovery, and availability of greater quantities of natural resources. On the demand side, during the periods when natural resource prices have risen sharply, there are renewed efforts to conserve and to develop synthetic substitutes (or commodities that serve the same function but can be produced with fewer or cheaper resources). Plastic shutters replace wood shutters on houses and polyvinyl chloride piping replaces copper piping.

Tradeoffs in the short and long run

To illustrate the potential tradeoff between the short-run and long-run revenues, consider a nation with extensive reserves of natural gas. Refer to Figure 12.2, where the supply (S) and demand (D) curves for the natural gas exported by a nation are depicted. The aggregation of the demand curves of the foreign consumers of the nation's natural gas is illustrated by the D curve. Suppose that the initial market price is P_0, and that the nation is operating in the inelastic region (lower half) of the foreign demand curve at E_0. By levying a tax on the exports of natural gas the nation can increase the total export revenues while reducing the quantity exported.

A specific tax of t dollars per unit shifts the supply curve up in a parallel manner by t from S to S'. The quantity of natural gas exported during the period declines from Q_0 to Q_1, while the unit price foreign consumers pay rises from P_0 to P_1 (although not by the full amount of the tax). Total export revenues increase from $\text{TR}_0 = P_0 \cdot Q_0$ to $\text{TR}_1 = P_1 \cdot Q_1$. The price received by domestic producers falls from P_0 to P'_1 and their total revenues decline to $\text{TR'}_1 = P'_1 \cdot Q_1$ from TR_0. The government collects tax revenues of $(P_1 - P'_1) \cdot Q = t \cdot Q_1$, with foreign consumers' share of the tax revenues equal to $(P_1 - P_0) \cdot Q_1$. The share of the tax revenues borne by the nation's suppliers is equal to $(P_0 - P'_1) \cdot Q_1$. As long as the foreign demand is price-inelastic, raising the tax on exports will increase total export revenues in the current period.[5]

In the long run, however, relatively higher prices for natural gas exports will encourage conservation and substitution. For example, natural gas may be replaced by solar energy.[6]

Returning to Figure 12.2, in the long run conservation and substitution may reduce the foreign demand for natural gas to D'' (from D). Not only might the demand fall, but over time, with the greater possibilities for substitution, the demand curve would become more price-elastic.

---

[5] The OPEC cartel achieved much the same effect in the 1970s with quotas on oil production. With a price-inelastic demand for oil in the short run, oil prices and revenues sharply increased.

[6] In the case of petroleum, individuals not only turned down thermostats and carpooled more often, but also insulated their homes and switched to more fuel-efficient automobiles. Alternative sources of energy were used, including solar and natural gas. Finally, the sharply higher prices for gasoline and home heating oil during the 1970s and early 1980s prompted more exploration and recovery of petroleum reserves. Petroleum supplies on the market increased, not only as non-OPEC nations produced more, but also as the OPEC members exceeded their quotas. By the end of the 1980s, world prices for petroleum had declined back to the levels of the mid-1970s, and in real terms, were significantly less. Throughout the 1990s, world oil prices remained low (outside of the sudden spike during the 1991 Gulf War crisis), before rising again in the 2000s.

Currently China has a monopoly on rare earth minerals that are essential inputs into the manufacture of numerous green products, including compact fluorescent light bulbs, electric cars, and wind turbines. In fact, China mines over 90 percent of the world's light rare earths. Although not allowed by the World Trade Organization, unless imposed for environmental reasons and also applied domestically, China has levied export taxes on some of its rare earth minerals. Given the price-inelastic demand for rare earth minerals, China has benefited from its monopoly. Another reason for restricting exports of these rare earth minerals has been to induce high-technology foreign companies to move their production to China (Bradsher 2010). Bradsher also notes how China dominates in research and development of rare earth mineral technologies.

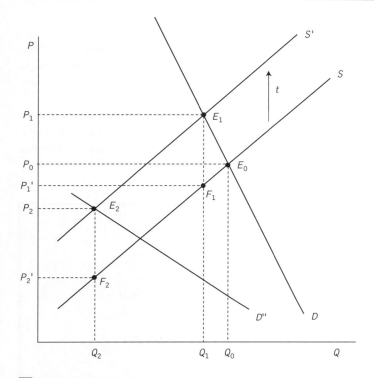

Figure 12.2 *Consequences of an export tax*

A nation well-endowed with natural resources may be able to increase its export revenues with an export tax when the foreign demand for its exports is price inelastic. The export tax reduces the supply curve, and in the short run the equilibrium shifts from E_0 to E_1. In the long run, foreign demand for the nation's natural resources may decline, with conservation and substitution, from D to D''. The export revenues from natural resources would then fall sharply.

Assuming an unchanged supply curve and specific tax, the quantity of natural gas exports would decline to Q_2 and the price paid by foreign consumers would decrease to P_2. (Note that the supply curve may well fall as nonrenewable resources are depleted and greater costs are incurred in accessing the remaining reserves.) Total export revenues are greatly reduced to $TR_2 = P_2 \cdot Q_2$. The price received by domestic producers is lowered to P_2'. Tax revenues are reduced to $(P_2 - P_2') \cdot Q_2$.

Thus, nations with market power in natural resources may face a tradeoff. The more aggressive they are in raising prices and generating export revenues in the short run, the more incentive provided to foreign consumers to conserve and develop substitutes. In the long run, export revenues may be greatly reduced.

In the case of natural gas, improvements in the technology of mining—in particular, **hydraulic fracturing** (fracking), where large volumes of water and chemicals are forcefully pumped underground to break up shale formations and access deposits—has significantly increased supplies in the US, driving down domestic prices for this fossil fuel.[7] The increased supplies have diminished the natural gas exports of other countries.

---

[7]There are environmental concerns, however, with this method of extracting natural gas, including the demands on water supplies and chemical contamination of underground sources of water; see http://www.epa.gov/hydraulicfracture.

DUTCH DISEASE

Another problem associated with an overreliance on export revenues and taxes on natural resources is known as the **Dutch disease**.[8] This phenomenon refers to the overextension of domestic economies that rely on revenues from a primary commodity, usually a fossil fuel, where an export boom is followed by economic recession and increased indebtedness.

Before we illustrate this phenomenon, we need to understand the distinction between nominal and real exchange rates. Nominal exchange rates are the stated foreign exchange values of currencies. Real exchanges rates are adjusted for the relative prices of the traded commodities in the two nations and determine international competitiveness. See Box 12.1.

BOX 12.1: REAL AND NOMINAL EXCHANGE RATES

In order to purchase goods or services from another nation, it is usually necessary to purchase the currency of that nation in the foreign exchange market. The **nominal exchange rate** is the price of one currency expressed in units of a foreign currency. Nominal exchange rates can be determined in the market, as in a flexible exchange rate system, or officially set by governments, as with a fixed exchange rate system.

Ceteris paribus, changes in the nominal exchange rate will affect the relative prices of domestic versus foreign commodities. For example, suppose that the nominal exchange rate between the Mexican peso (p) and the US dollar is 20p = $1.00 (the peso price of the dollar) or, equivalently, $0.05 = 1p (the dollar price of the peso). A nominal **depreciation** of the peso is indicated by an increase in the peso price of the dollar, say from 20 pesos to 25 pesos to the dollar (or $0.04 = 1p). (Note that this depreciation of the peso is equivalent to an appreciation of the dollar, indicated by a decrease in the dollar price of the peso.) This depreciation of the peso means that it costs 25 percent more pesos to purchase one dollar (or a dollar's worth of US goods and services). Consequently, we would expect to find fewer imports for Mexico from the US. The depreciation of the peso, however, lowers the dollar price of any peso-denominated Mexican good or service, and should boost exports from Mexico to the US.

Conversely, a nominal **appreciation** of the peso (a decrease in the peso price of the dollar, say from 20p = $1.00 to 16p = $1.00) should make Mexican goods and services less competitive internationally. The dollar price of a Mexican good selling for 20p increases from $1.00 to $1.25 with this appreciation of the peso (and depreciation of the dollar from $0.05 = 1p to $0.0625 = 1p). As the peso appreciates, the Mexican balance of trade should deteriorate as Mexican exports decline and imports rise.

The **real exchange rate** is the nominal exchange rate adjusted for the relative price levels of internationally traded goods and services in the two countries. Let *er* be the nominal exchange rate (e.g., the peso price of the dollar), *rer* the real exchange rate (also expressed

---

[8]This phenomenon was first applied to the Netherlands, when rapid increases in export revenues with the development of natural gas reserves during the 1960s and 1970s led to unbalanced growth, reducing the competitiveness of other sectors of the Dutch economy. For a brief description of the Dutch case, as well as case studies for Indonesia, Mexico, and Nigeria, see Gillis et al. (1987: 535–539).

as pesos per dollar), P_M the price index for traded goods and services in Mexico, and P_{US} the price index for traded goods and services in the United States. The price indices, P_M and P_{US}, represent the average price levels for goods and services in Mexico and the United States, respectively, that are internationally traded. The real exchange rate is equal to $rer = er \cdot (P_{US}/P_M)$.

The real exchange rate can change either due to a change in the nominal exchange rate, or a change in the relative price levels for traded goods and services (P_{US}/P_M). In particular, a real depreciation of the peso could reflect a rise in the peso price of the dollar ($er\uparrow$), a rise in the US price index ($P_{US}\uparrow$), or a fall in the price index in Mexico ($P_M\downarrow$). A real depreciation of the peso makes Mexican goods and services more attractive internationally.

Generally, nations with comparatively high rates of inflation experience nominally depreciating currencies. Whether a nation's real exchange rate depreciates, increasing its international price competitiveness, however, depends on the nation's relative rate of inflation versus the rate of nominal depreciation of the domestic currency. For example, if the Mexican peso depreciates from $20p = \$1$ to $25p = \$1$, while the Mexican price index rises from $P_M = 100$ to $P'_M = 125$, then with an unchanged US price index of $P_{US} = 100$, the real exchange rate is unchanged: $rer = 20 \cdot (100/100) = 20 = 25 \cdot (100/125)$.

The cycle of the Dutch disease

Consider a nation with substantial reserves of petroleum that is the beneficiary of sharply rising world prices for oil, such as triggered by the OPEC oil embargo in late 1973. Suppose further that this nation is not a member of OPEC and so is not bound by any agreement to restrict output in order to boost prices.[9]

The surge in petroleum export revenues initially results in a surplus in the nation's balance of trade. Flush with foreign exchange and tax revenues from petroleum exports, the government embarks on an ambitious program of spending and development projects. The rise in spending even outpaces the gain in revenues, and to cover the rising budget deficits the government turns to borrowing—both domestic and foreign. The central bank finances much of the domestic borrowing by printing money (monetizing the debt). While reducing the direct crowding-out effect on private investment spending from higher real interest rates, the expansion of the money supply induces inflation. Meanwhile, the robust export growth has triggered an acceleration of imports. In anticipation of the export boom continuing, the nation readily incurs foreign debt.

Because of the strong export earnings from petroleum, depreciation in the nominal exchange rate of the nation is modified. The high inflation, however, appreciates the real exchange rate. Sectors of the economy not involved in the petroleum trade, such agriculture and light manufacturing, suffer a loss in international competitiveness and may find their output and employment declining. These sectors may also find their access to credit and foreign exchange restricted as the

---

[9] The primary reason for the OPEC oil embargo in October 1973 was political. To punish the US for supporting Israel in the Yom Kippur War, the OPEC nations, dominated by the Arab states of the Middle East and North Africa, placed an embargo on oil exports to the US. The contrived shortage of oil led to panic in the world market, nearly quadrupling the price of a barrel of oil. The OPEC nations recognized their collective market power and have attempted since, albeit with decreasing success, to keep the world price of oil up by restricting their outputs.

rapidly growing sectors linked to petroleum receive preferential treatment. Those sectors benefiting from the rapid growth in the economy (e.g., transportation and construction) will encounter,
at some point, sharply higher marginal costs of production as bottlenecks and capacity constraints
arise. More inflation is generated as the economy moves along the highly inelastic region of the
aggregate supply curve. And, if price expectations of labor and other factor suppliers increase, the
aggregate supply curve shifts left, adding cost-push inflation.

Eventually the export boom ends and oil prices subside. If the export boom had been triggered
by rapid growth in the world economy, then foreign demand may return to more normal levels. Or
increased conservation by oil importing countries and the expansion of alternative energy sources
(coal, natural gas, solar) temper the demand for petroleum, while the discovery and recovery of
new international petroleum reserves increase the market supply. In any case, with the significant
decrease in export revenues, the nation is left with mushrooming budget deficits (due to aggressive
government spending set in motion overwhelming the tax revenues, now greatly reduced), high
inflation, increased foreign debt, and a currency that has appreciated in real terms (undermining
the nation's competitiveness). In short, with the Dutch disease, the nation goes from heady rates
of economic growth to stagnation.

Evidence from Mexico

Mexico offers a classic example of this boom to bust cycle. In 1973, at the time of the OPEC
oil embargo, fuels accounted for only 1 percent of Mexico's merchandise exports. The escalating
world price for petroleum provided Mexico and other nations with an incentive to increase the
exploration for, and recovery of, petroleum. Mexico discovered large oil deposits, and by the
latter half of the 1970s had emerged as a significant exporter of oil. Not a member of OPEC, and
so free to increase production, Mexico benefited from the second surge in world oil prices in late
1979, set off by the Iranian Revolution and the fall of the shah of Iran.

In 1981 more than two-thirds of Mexico's merchandise exports were fuel. While export revenues rose rapidly, imports grew faster. The merchandise trade deficit increased from $1.5 billion
in 1973 to $4.2 billion in 1981. Mexico's external debt exploded from under $10 billion to nearly
$80 billion. The government budget deficit increased from 3.8 percent of gross national income
in 1973 to 6.6 percent in 1981—largely due to the rapid expansion in public spending on capital projects. (In fact, until 1982 the government current budget balance, i.e., excluding capital
expenditures, was in surplus.) The government deficits were financed by printing money and
borrowing from foreign banks. Consequently, the impressive rates of economic growth Mexico
enjoyed were accompanied by accelerating inflation and rising debt.

In Mexico, while real national output increased by over 60 percent from 1973 to 1981,
the money supply (defined as currency in circulation plus checkable deposits) rose by over
650 percent. Not surprisingly, inflation soared, as measured by the percentage change in the price
deflator for gross domestic product. The GDP price deflator for Mexico increased 150 percent
more than the GDP price deflator for the US. The Mexican peso depreciated nominally from 12.5
pesos to the dollar in 1973 to 24.5 pesos to the dollar in 1981. In real terms, however, the peso
appreciated from 12.5 to 9.5 pesos to the dollar.[10]

---

[10]To calculate the real exchange rate here we use the ratio of the price deflators for GDP, which include the prices of all
final goods and services produced in the economies. If the data had been available, indices measuring the prices of only traded
goods and services would have been used. The data presented for Mexico in this case study come from the World Bank (1990:
392–395).

Then, with the oil-price declines in the 1980s, the Mexican economy hit the shoals. In August 1982, Mexico, nearly out of international reserves, announced that it could not meet the scheduled payments on its foreign debt. Additional loans, a moratorium of payments on the principal owed to commercial banks, and debt rescheduling were requested. Mexico also approached the International Monetary Fund for assistance. Recall, as discussed earlier in Chapter 5, Mexico's announcement focused attention on the larger international debt crisis that unfolded in the 1980s.

In response to its external debt problem, Mexico was forced to adopt tighter economic policies—including measures to reduce inflation, improve the trade balance, and attract foreign investment. Over the 1980s Mexico did manage to reform its economy, albeit with considerable hardships for large segments of its population. For the period 1980–90, the average annual growth rate in real GDP for Mexico was only 1.0 percent, down from the 6.5 percent average for the 1965–80 period. While the average rate of population growth in Mexico also declined—to 2.0 percent for 1980–90, down from 3.1 percent for 1965–80—Mexico experienced negative economic growth over the decade of the 1980s (World Bank 1992: Tables 1 and 26). In the early 1990s Mexico joined the US and Canada in the North American Free Trade Agreement (NAFTA), and in the 1990s, Mexico resumed modest economic growth.

Avoiding the Dutch disease

Lessons derived from the Dutch disease might be summarized as follows. First, if a nation experiences boom conditions for one or more of its exports, it should exercise self-discipline. In particular, an overly aggressive expansion of government spending on capital projects that exceed the absorptive capacity of the domestic economy should be avoided. Too rapid a push in investment, public or private, will encounter resource constraints and result in sharply escalating costs of production.

Second, a more balanced strategy may be called for, including more diversified exports. Clearly the temptation for a nation with exceptional growth in the exports of a sector is to "make hay while the sun shines." Too rapid an expansion in one sector, especially one like petroleum that is capital-intensive and has limited linkages to the other production sectors of the economy, may cause severe distortions by drawing resources away from these other sectors. Furthermore, when the export boom ends, these relatively neglected sectors may be weakened and internationally less competitive.

Third, the real exchange rate needs to be monitored. A depreciation in the nominal exchange rate need not translate into a depreciation of the real exchange rate. Often less developed countries set the nominal exchange rate and then fail to adjust frequently enough to compensate for their comparatively high rates of inflation. The result is a chronic overvaluation of the domestic currency and a loss in international price competitiveness. Fiscal and monetary discipline (i.e., avoiding large budget deficits and excessive expansion in the money supply) are needed to keep inflation down and maintain a competitive real exchange rate.

Finally, relying on nonrenewable resources is not a viable strategy for sustainable development. If fortunate to be well endowed with minerals or fossil fuels, a nation must invest the rents derived from those resources into human and physical capital formation.

In sum, avoiding the Dutch disease, where initially conditions for growth seem especially favorable, requires self-restraint and foresight. We now turn to the "natural resource curse," a more chronic and devastating affliction characterizing some developing nations endowed with natural resources.

367

THE NATURAL RESOURCE CURSE

Economists have observed that some developing nations, well endowed with minerals or fossil fuels, experience below average economic growth and development, a so-called **natural resource curse**. In contrast to the economic success stories of East Asia, where nations were not generally well endowed with nonrenewable resources and thus were compelled to develop their human resources, which provided a more stable foundation for sustainable development, these "cursed" nations have effectively squandered their gifts of nature.

There are a number of reasons given, most involving ineffective and corrupt leadership. In these nations often the elites and military authorities that rise to the top of government use the considerable natural resource revenues to enrich themselves and their patrons. Their concern is more with staying in power and suppressing opposition than with providing effective leadership and investing the rents from these resources for the development of the nation. Moreover, these rich sources of revenue engender rivalry among competing factions and continual strife, which can break out into civil war.

These natural resource rents are large enough not only for the enrichment of the controlling factions, but also for funding enough government activities so that effective tax systems for more sustainable public revenue generation need not be developed. Large armies can be financed to bolster the positions of the government leaders and the poor may be "bought off" with modest social welfare programs. Other institutions, whether legislative bodies for governance, a judicial system for upholding the rule of law and the administration of justice, or capital markets for the efficient allocation of financial resources, remain underdeveloped. Not surprisingly, income inequality tends to be great in natural resource cursed countries and a viable middle class and engaged civil society may not emerge.

In his extensive review of the literature on the natural resource curse, van der Ploeg (2011: 386) concisely captures the problems:

> Resource dependence elicits corruption and rent seeking via protection, exclusive licenses to exploit and export resources by the political elite, oligarchs and their cronies to capture wealth and political power . . . and crowds out social capital, erodes the legal system and elicits armed conflicts and civil wars.

As noted, natural resource-intensive sectors are capital-intensive and often rely on foreign technologies. Indeed, much foreign direct investment has been and is attracted to developing nations endowed with minerals and fossil fuels. Investments in human capital, especially education, are slighted. So, too, development of a more diversified, industrial base is forgone, when it is all too easy to rely on the natural resource intensive sectors. Nations under the natural resource curse are, not surprisingly, more prone to the Dutch disease.

A country widely cited as afflicted by the natural resource curse is Nigeria. The most populous nation in Africa, Nigeria is endowed with substantial oil deposits. As van der Ploeg (2011: 367–368) observes:

> Oil revenues per capita in Nigeria increased from US$33 in 1965 to US$325 in 2000, but income per capita has stagnated around US$1,100 in PPP terms since its independence in 1960 putting Nigeria among the fifteen poorest countries in the world. Between 1970 and 2000, the part of the population that has to survive on less than US$1 per day shot up from 26 to almost 70 percent.

Nigeria's history as an independent nation has been marked by political instability (with a series of corrupt and inept military dictators who siphoned off oil revenues for personal enrichment and ill-conceived public projects); a state-controlled economy burdened by monopolies, rent-seeking, bloated civil service, and little private enterprise; and regional factionalism (between Muslims predominately in the North and Christians in the South).[11] Despite an abundance of fertile farm-land, Nigeria has not developed its agricultural sector. Nigeria did elect a reform-minded, honest leader, Olusegun Obasanjo, in 1999, who served two full terms, and Nigeria has managed significant economic growth in the first decade of the twenty-first century (aided by higher oil prices). Nevertheless, poverty remains prevalent. In 2011, Nigeria's Human Development Index (0.459) ranked 156th out of 187 nations, and was even below the average for sub-Saharan Africa (0.463).

Collier (2007) devotes a chapter to the natural resource trap, one of the vicious cycles a poor country may fall into that stalls, or effectively prevents, economic development. According to Collier (2007: 39), "The societies of the bottom billion are disproportionately in this category of resource-rich poverty: about 29 percent of the people in the bottom billion live in countries in which resource wealth dominates the economy."[12]

Recall the regression analysis in Chapter 8, where for a sample of 68 low- and middle-income economies for the 2000–09 period, the average annual growth rate in real per capita GDP was found to be significantly inversely related to the share of resource rents for minerals and fossil fuels in national incomes—controlling for the net national saving rate, average annual growth rates in gross domestic investment and exports, and the initial per capita national income, ratio of the population 15–64 to the total population, and female youth literacy rate.[13]

As additional aggregate evidence of the "curse" of natural resource-intensive growth, we might contrast the average annual economic growth rates for 2000–10 for the Middle East and North Africa (2.9 percent) and sub-Saharan Africa (2.5 percent), and their respective shares of natural resource rents in GDP for 2010 of 18.7 percent and 16.7 percent, with the average economic growth rate for East Asia and the Pacific (8.6 percent) and South Asia (5.9 percent), and shares of natural resource rents in GDP in 2010 of 7.9 percent and 6.2 percent (World Bank 2012: Tables 2.1, 3.16, and 4.1).

Nations that are fortunate enough to be endowed with natural resources need not succumb to the curse. As noted earlier, Botswana is an example of a well-managed sub-Saharan African

---

[11] See Guest (2000) for an overview of Nigeria's sad history. Guest opened his survey with a quote from Chinua Achebe, a Nigerian novelist, who wrote in 1983:

> The trouble with Nigeria is simply and squarely a failure of leadership. There is nothing basically wrong with the Nigerian character. There is nothing wrong with the Nigerian land or climate or water or air or anything else. The Nigerian problem is the unwillingness or inability of its leaders to rise to the responsibility, to the challenge of personal example which are the hallmarks of true leadership.

[12] The other poverty traps Collier identifies are the conflict trap (political instability and civil strife), the "landlocked with bad neighbors" trap (referred to in the regression analysis earlier in Chapter 8), and "bad governance in a small country" trap (a combination of poor leadership in a nation too small to realize scale economies in industry or to generate a core of entrepreneurs). These traps are not mutually exclusive, and unfortunately poor nations may be stuck in more than one.

[13] In addition to the comprehensive review of van der Ploeg (2011), two useful studies on the natural resource curse are the influential early paper by Sachs and Warner (1995) and the more recent analysis of Dietz et al. (2007). Sachs and Warner find that developing nations with a high share of primary exports in GDP experienced significantly lower economic growth rates over the 1971–89 period, controlling for initial per capita incomes, the openness of the economies, gross domestic investment ratios, and an index for bureaucratic efficiency. Dietz et al. relate natural resource abundance with increased corruption and reduced adjusted net saving rates with panel data for over a hundred nations over 18 years.

nation that has used its abundant mineral resources, namely diamonds, to invest in its people and institutions. As van der Ploeg (2011: 368) points out, Norway, the nation with the highest HDI in 2011, is the third largest exporter of petroleum in the world and one of the least corrupt nations. Norway has established a sovereign wealth fund where income from its oil rents is used for public investment. The World Bank's comprehensive development framework, which was outlined earlier in Chapter 8, emphasizes effective governance and sound institutions, and like the market-friendly strategy of development, investment in human capital. Realizing effective governance and developing sound institutions, however, has proven difficult for many nations— especially those well endowed with natural resources.

RESOURCE SCARCITY

As discussed in earlier chapters, limits to economic growth reflect natural resource constraints. At one end of production, the supplies of nonrenewable resources as inputs into production are finite—even if all the available reserves of minerals and fossil fuels on Earth are not known and recoverable new deposits seem to found on a regular basis. The supplies of renewable resources, including arable land, fisheries, forests, fresh water, and clean air, can be extended indefinitely, provided these resources are not used beyond their regeneration capacities—although in any given period of time, the amounts of these resources available for use in production are set. At the other end, the ability of the environment to absorb the wastes generated is limited, at least without degradation of the environment. We will first discuss the evidence that natural resources as raw material inputs into production are limited. Then we will address the environmental thresholds.

Nonrenewable resources

If natural resources are limited, especially the nonrenewable resources of minerals and fossil fuels, then over time with economic growth due to increases in populations and per capita consumptions, the real prices of the resources should rise. After all, relative scarcities should be reflected in higher market prices. Over the last part of the twentieth century, however, real prices of nonrenewable resources generally fell.

Basically, four contributing factors may account for this counterintuitive trend in real prices for nonrenewable resources. One, as discussed in the first chapter, is that effective natural resources are the product of their physical quantities and indices of their qualities or inherent productivities. Advances in technology allow greater access to and more productive use of natural resources, increasing their effective supplies for given physical stocks on the planet.

We noted earlier in this chapter the new mining technology of hydraulic fracturing to access natural gas deposits in the US. Tapping the large reserves of oil sands in Canada is still too costly, but with further advances in the drilling and processing technologies, these sources of petroleum may well come into production (see Walsh 2012).[14] Ironically, global warming with the melting of Arctic sea ice is opening up new areas for offshore drilling.

---

[14] Walsh notes:

> Oil has never exactly been clean, but the new sources coming online tend to be more polluting and more dangerous than conventional crude. Producing oil from the sands in northern Alberta can be destructive to the local environment, requiring massive open-pit mines that strip forests and take years to recover from. The tailings from those mines are toxic. While some of the newer production methods eschew the open-pit mines and instead process the sands underground or in situ, which is much cleaner, they still require additional energy to turn oil sands into usable crude. As a result, a barrel of oil-sand crude usually has a 10% to 15% larger carbon footprint than conventional crude over its lifetime, from the

Second, to the extent relative prices do increase, consumers substitute less expensive alternatives. Induced technological change may even diminish the demands for the more expensive products, as lighter fiberglass replaces steel in automobile bodies (which also improves fuel efficiency) and composites replace granite countertops in kitchens.

Third, as will be illustrated later, market prices do not capture externalities. Usually present in the production or consumption of nonrenewable resources are negative externalities; as a result, market prices understate the true social prices.

Finally, while on a finite planet nonrenewable resources are absolutely limited, their market prices reflect relative scarcities; but in the past two centuries the exponential use of these natural resources by humankind has not suggested relative scarcities. These resources have been drawn on without regard to absolute limits and with insufficient concern for the environmental consequences.

Referring to Table 12.3 and selected commodity prices for energy, metals and minerals, we do see a downward trend in real prices over the last quarter of the twentieth century. Over the first decade of the twenty-first century, however, this trend has been reversed—with a notable exception for natural gas. On the demand side, consumption in the rapidly growing economies of China and India has pushed up prices. And, there is evidence of tighter supplies, in part reflected in the increased costs of accessing natural resources. The sharp declines in these resource prices in 2009 reflected the global recession, but the upward trend resumed with the world economic recovery.

Management of natural resources

Clearly, effective management of natural resources is critical for sustainable development. For nonrenewable resources, conservation and the substitution of synthetic for natural materials can reduce usage. Renewable resources should not be used beyond their regeneration capacities. Without such management, fishing stocks can easily be depleted and water tables can be quickly drawn down. Harvesting of forests without sufficient replanting may result in deforestation that, in turn, contributes to soil erosion and even desertification.

Twenty years ago, the World Bank (1992: 9–10), in observing the secular decline in nonrenewable resource prices, noted the evidence of rising scarcity in renewable resources:

> Prices of minerals have shown a fairly consistent downward trend over the past hundred years. They fell sharply in the 1980s, leading to gluts that threatened to impoverish countries dependent on commodity exports.
>
> With some natural resources, by contrast, demand often exceeds supply. This is true of the demand for water, not only in the arid areas of the Middle East but also in northern China, east Java, and parts of India. Aquifers are being depleted, sometimes irreversibly, and the extraction from rivers is often so great that their ecological functions are impaired and further expansion of irrigation is becoming severely limited.
>
> The reason some resources—water, forests, and clean air—are under siege while others— metals, minerals, and energy—are not is that the scarcity of the latter is reflected in market

---

well to the wheels of a car. Given the massive size of the oil-sand reserve—nearly 200 billion recoverable barrels—that's potentially a lot of carbon.

Table 12.3 Selected nonrenewable resource prices (2005 prices)

	1970	1980	1990	2000	2005	2006	2007	2008	2009	2010	2011
Energy	11	87	45	60	100	115	120	156	105	128	153
Coal: Australian ($/mt)	29	53	41	29	48	48	61	109	66	88	98
Natural gas: US ($/mmbtu)	1	2	2	5	9	7	6	8	4	4	3
Petroleum: ($/bbl)	4	48	24	32	53	63	66	83	56	70	85
Metals and minerals	112	89	75	67	100	151	171	154	110	159	167
Aluminum ($/mt)	2,050	1,910	1,695	1,734	1,898	2,516	2,430	2,198	1,523	1,924	1,953
Copper ($/mt)	5,219	2,863	2,752	2,030	3,679	6,580	6,557	5,943	4,711	6,672	7,181
Lead (cents/kg)	112	119	84	51	98	126	238	179	157	190	195
Nickel ($/mt)	10,492	8,553	9,167	9,669	14,744	23,742	34,293	18,035	13,406	19,313	18,637
Zinc (cents/kg)	109	100	157	126	138	321	299	160	151	191	178

Notes: Where possible the prices received by exporters are used; if export prices are unavailable, the prices paid by importers are used. The constant price series is deflated using a composite index of prices for manufactured exports from the fifteen major developed and emerging economies (converted to US $).

Abbreviations: mt = metric ton; dmtu = dry metric ton unit; mmbtu = millions of British thermal units; and bbl = barrel.

From: World Bank, *World Development Indicators 2012* (Table 6.5)

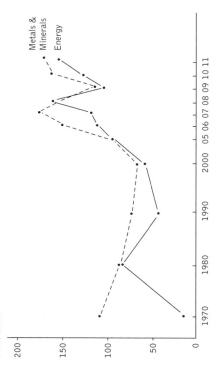

prices and so the forces of substitution, technical progress, and structural change are strong. The first group is characterized by open access, meaning that there are no incentives to use them sparingly. . . . This explains why the environmental debate has rightly shifted away from concern about *physical limits* to growth toward concern about incentives for *human behavior* and policies that can overcome *market and policy failures*.

For evidence on renewable natural resources, see Table 12.4. For the world, we find a decrease in the proportion of arable land in total land area from 10.9 percent in 1990 to 10.7 percent in 2009, despite significant increases in the low- and lower middle-income economies. For the upper middle- and high-income economies, a smaller share of total land area is under cultivation. Furthermore, world population growth has resulted in a decline of nearly 14 percent in arable land per capita, from 23.7 hectares (per hundred population) in 1990 to 20.4 hectares in 2009. As we will discuss in the next chapter on the global food supply, increased land pressures will have to be offset by greater productivity in agriculture. Regional variations are striking: from arable land accounting for over 40 percent of the total land area in South Asia (and over half in India) to less than 10 percent in sub-Saharan Africa, the Middle East and North Africa, and Latin America and the Caribbean. East Asia and the Pacific remains the most land-scarce region (indicated by arable land per capita), with South Asia, the Middle East and North Africa not far behind.

Table 12.4 *Selected statistics on renewable resources*

	ECONOMIES BY INCOME CLASSIFICATION							
	WORLD	Low	Lower middle	India	Upper middle	China	High	US
Proportion of land area:								
Arable land: 1990	10.9%	7.7%	14.8%	54.8%	9.2%	13.3%	11.7%	20.3%
2009	10.7%	9.6%	16.4%	53.1%	8.7%	11.8%	10.8%	17.8%
Forest: 1990	32.0%	31.2%	30.7%	21.5%	35.2%	16.8%	27.9%	32.4%
2010	31.1%	27.6%	27.9%	23.0%	34.6%	22.2%	28.8%	33.2%
Arable land in hectares								
per hundred people: 1990	23.7	23.8	18.7	18.6	18.9	10.9	42.5	74.4
2009	20.4	18.5	15.1	13.1	20.6	8.3	33.2	53.1
Average annual rate of deforestation:								
1990–2000	0.18%	0.63%	0.59%	−0.22%	0.10%	−1.20%	−0.14%	−0.13%
2000–2010	0.11%	0.61%	0.30%	−0.46%	0.01%	−1.57%	−0.04%	−0.13%
% of population in urban agglomerations of more than								
1 million: 1990	17%	8%	12%	10%	16%	9%	. . .	42%
2010	20%	11%	14%	12%	22%	18%	. . .	45%
Internal renewable freshwater resources per capita in cu. meters: 2009	6,258	5,381	3,277	1,197	8,718	2,113	8,305	9,186
Water productivity: GDP/water use in 2000 $ per cu. meter: 2009	10	2	1	1	6	5	31	24

Table 12.4 continued

	ECONOMIES BY REGION						
	Sub-Saharan Africa	Middle East & N. Africa	Europe & Central Asia	South Asia	East Asia & Pacific	Latin America & Caribbean	High-income economies
Proportion of land area:							
Arable land: 1990	6.6%	5.9%	11.6%	42.7%	12.1%	6.6%	11.7%
2009	8.5%	5.9%	10.5%	41.4%	11.5%	7.4%	10.8%
Forest: 1990	31.1%	2.4%	38.4%	16.6%	29.0%	51.6%	27.9%
2010	28.0%	2.4%	38.6%	17.1%	29.6%	47.0%	28.8%
Arable land in hectares per hundred people: 1990	32.1	22.5	68.5	17.8	12.0	30.3	42.5
2009	24.2	15.6	59.2	12.3	9.4	25.9	33.2
Average annual rate of deforestation:							
1990–2000	0.55%	−0.10%	−0.02%	−0.01%	0.08%	0.47%	−0.14%
2000–2010	0.48%	−0.15%	−0.04%	−0.29%	−0.44%	0.45%	−0.04%
% of population in urban agglomerations of more than 1 million: 1990	11%	20%	16%	10%	...	32%	...
2010	14%	20%	18%	13%	...	35%	...
Internal renewable freshwater resources per capita in cu. meters: 2009	4,634	695	12,887	1,236	4,506	23,323	8,305
Water productivity: GDP/water use in 2000$ per cu. meter: 2009	4	2	3	1	4	10	31

Notes: Land area is a country's total area, excluding area under inland water bodies and national claims to the continental shelf and to exclusive economic zones. In most cases, definitions of inland water bodies include major rivers and lakes.

Arable land is land defined by the Food and Agricultural Organization as under temporary crops (double-cropped areas are counted once), temporary meadows for mowing or pasture, land area under market or kitchen gardens, and land temporarily fallow. Land abandoned as a result of shifting cultivation is excluded.

Forest area is land under natural or planted stands of trees, whether productive or not.

Average annual deforestation is the permanent conversion of natural forest area to other uses, including agriculture, ranching, settlements, and infrastructure. Deforested areas do not include areas logged but intended for regeneration or areas degraded by fuelwood gathering, acid precipitation, or forest fires.

Renewable internal freshwater resource flows are internal renewable resources (internal river flows and groundwater from rainfall) in the country.

Water productivity is calculated as GDP in constant prices divided by annual total water withdrawals. Annual freshwater withdrawals are total water withdrawals, not counting evaporation losses from storage basins. Withdrawals also include water from desalination plants in countries where they are a significant source. Withdrawals can exceed 100% of total renewable resources where extraction from nonrenewable aquifers or desalination plants is considerable or where water reuse is significant. Withdrawals from agriculture and industry are total water withdrawals for irrigation and livestock production and for direct industrial use (including for cooling thermoelectric plants). Withdrawals for domestic uses include drinking water, municipal use or supply, and use for public services, commercial establishments, and homes.

Source: World Bank (2012: Tables 3.1, 3.4, 3.5, and 3.13).

The proportion of land area in the world covered by forest has declined over the past two decades, most notably in the low-income and lower middle-income economies where population pressures on the environment, especially forests, are likely to be greater. The average annual rate of deforestation in the world, however, declined from 0.18 percent over the 1990s to 0.11 percent for the first decade of the twenty-first century. This average too masks significant differences across countries that are better captured by geographic regions than income levels. Encouragingly, China and India have reversed their deforestation, and in the high-income economies we also find refor-estation. The loss of rainforests in Latin America (nearly 0.5 percent annual rate of deforestation between 1990 and 2010) and temperate forests in sub-Saharan Africa (slightly over 0.5 percent between 1990 and 2010), however, is troubling and undermines the sustainable development there as well as contributing to global warming.

As noted earlier, the world's population is for the first time in history more than 50 percent urban. Moreover, the growth of large cities is increasing, not just from natural increase but with rural to urban migration and urban sprawl and the physical expansion of urban areas. Economic development is accompanied by the need to feed a growing urban population, and only with increased productivity in agriculture can labor be released to industry. The rise in the percentage of the population in urban areas of 1 million or more may have advantages in terms of economies of scale in basic infrastructure and efficiencies in labor markets; but there are also attendant prob-lems with stress, congestion, crime, air pollution, and waste disposal. Recall Target 7.D of the Millennium Development Goals: to achieve by 2020 a significant improvement in the lives of at least 100 million slum dwellers. In the developing world, Latin America and the Caribbean is the most urban region, with over a third of the population living in urban agglomerations of a million or more. Sub-Saharan Africa and South Asia have the lowest urban concentrations, with less than 15 percent of their populations living in metropolitan areas of 1 million plus.

Finally, we see great diversity in freshwater resources per capita, which is more geographically determined than income-driven. For example, in 2009 renewable internal freshwater resources measured in cubic meters per capita ranged from 695 in the Middle East and North Africa and 1,236 in South Asia to 12,887 in Europe and Central Asia and 23,323 in Latin America and the Caribbean. Average per capita levels of water resources, however, may obscure significant variation across countries within a region. For example, compare the 2009 internal freshwater resources (in cubic meters per capita) of the four neighboring Central American nations of El Salvador (2,881), Honduras (12,877), Costa Rica (24,484), and Nicaragua (33,221). Globally, Grimond (2010: 4) notes:

> Water is not evenly distributed—just nine countries account for 60% of all available freshwa-ter supplies—and among them, only Brazil, Canada, Colombia, Congo, Indonesia and Russia have an abundance. America is relatively well off, but China and India, with over a third of the world's population between them, have less than 10% of its water.

Moreover, a high level of per capita water resources need not mean that the water is always available at the appropriate times. For example, for some countries, the monsoon rains in several months may account for nearly all of the rainfall received during the year. More volatile weather will accompany global warming, in particular greater variation and intensity of precipitation.

There are serious and growing concerns with the availability of freshwater in many parts of the world. Grimond (2010: 3) reports that the proportion of people living in countries chronically short of water is projected to increase over fivefold: from 8 percent (500 million persons) at the turn of the twenty-first century to 45 percent (4 billion) by 2050. While industry places heavy demands on water supplies, demands that rise with economic growth, agriculture is the major user. For example, agriculture used 70 percent of the annual freshwater withdrawals in the world in 2009 (see World Bank 20102: Table 3.5).[15] Declines in internal freshwater resources per capita

---

[15] For low-income economies in 2009, 90 percent of annual freshwater withdrawals were for agriculture, 2 percent for industry, and 8 percent for domestic use. For high-income economies in 2009, the shares of annual freshwater withdrawals were 41 percent for agriculture, 42 percent for industry, and 17 percent for domestic use.

may indicate unsustainable development unless improved efficiencies in the utilization of the water are realized.

In terms of water productivity, we see in general that output per unit of water consumed increases with economic development. The high-income economies have GDP per unit of water used that is 15 times greater than the low-income economies, which largely reflects the much higher share of economic activity in agriculture in the less developed nations. In the next chapter, we will discuss agriculture and fishing and the evidence of tighter global supplies of food, reflecting in large part renewable resource pressures. We turn now to evidence of environmental stress.

ENVIRONMENTAL CONCERNS

As defined in Chapter 11, with sustainable development the needs of the present generations are met without compromising the ability of future generations to meet their needs. There is considerable evidence of environmental stress, not the least of which is global warming, which well could compromise future generations. Three examples are offered:

> The world's wetlands provide an astonishing range of ecological services. They harbour bio-diversity, provide agricultural, timber, and medicinal products, and sustain fish stocks. More than that, they buffer coastal and riverside areas from storms and floods, protecting human settlements from sea surges. During the 20th Century, the world lost half of its wetlands through drainage, conversion to agriculture and pollution. (UNDP 2007: 102).

> Nearly two-fifths of the United States' 25,000 sewer systems illegally discharged raw sewage or other nasty stuff into rivers or lakes in 2007–09 and over 40% of the country's waters are considered dangerously polluted. Contaminated water lays low almost 20 million Americans a year. (Grimond 2010: 6).

> The burning of fossil fuels and other industrial processes can lead to the formation of other acids and hence a further reduction in the pH of rainwater. . . . The main culprits are the emission of sulphur dioxide (SO_2), which is a precursor of sulphuric acid, and nitrogen oxides (NO_x), which are precursors of nitric acid. The resultant acid "rain" [can cause] damage to buildings; the widespread death of plants, including trees; the removal of nutrients such as magnesium, calcium and potassium from soils; the release of toxic metals such as aluminum from soils; a reduction, often to zero, in reproduction and survival of fish, frogs, aquatic insects and other species; and calcium deficiency in fish leading to deformed or dwarfed individuals. (Coley 2008: 118–119)

To remedy environmental deterioration, manifested in reduced quality of the air, land, or water supplies, requires additional resource commitments to mitigate the pollution and clean up the damage as well as a modification of current practices (such as greater conservation and reduced consumption). With the loss of biodiversity that comes with the extinction of species, remedies are too late.[16]

---

[16]See *We Can End Poverty: 2015 Millennium Development Goals: Goal 7: Ensure Environmental Sustainability Fact Sheet* (United Nations Department of Public Information DPI/2650G, September 2010, http://www.un.org/millenniumgoals/pdf/MDG_FS_7_EN.pdf):

Technological progress and economic growth do not warrant a cavalier attitude towards natural resources and the environment. Even in the most advanced economies, where the knowledge and means to preserve the environment are readily available, signs of land, water, and air degradation are all too frequent, as the above example of water pollution in the United States illustrates. In fact, some technological progress may introduce new threats to the environment; for instance, the disposal of hazardous wastes from the generation of nuclear power and the water pollution from hydraulic fracturing to access natural gas.

CLIMATE CHANGE

A major concern, alluded to above, is climate change. The scientific evidence attributing global warming to human activity is now overwhelming. GHG emissions, largely from fossil fuel consumption but also from agriculture, changes in land use, and deforestation, have accelerated with the economic and population growth over the past two centuries. As Coley (2008) notes, the Intergovernmental Panel on Climate Change has issued four reports over the past two decades (in 1989, 1995, 2001, and 2007), each with increasing evidence that climate change is occurring and that humans are primarily responsible.[17]

Two reports by the UNDP (2007, 2010) addressed this unprecedented challenge to sustainable development. As asserted by UNDP (2007: 1–3):

> Climate change is the defining human development issue of our generation [which] demands urgent action now to address a threat to two constituencies with a little or no political voice: the world's poor and future generations. . . .
>
> Global warming is evidence that we are overloading the carrying capacity of the Earth's atmosphere. Stocks of greenhouse gases that trap heat in the atmosphere are accumulating at an unprecedented rate. Current concentrations have reached 380 parts per million. . .of carbon dioxide equivalent. . .exceeding the natural range of the last 650,000 years.

Five primary transmission mechanisms through which climate change can impact human development are identified. First, agricultural production will be adversely affected in the developing regions of sub-Saharan Africa, South Asia, and Latin America from changes in precipitation and warmer temperatures. Second, with the melting of glaciers, renewable water supplies will diminish over time, compromising especially Central Asia, China, and parts of South Asia. Third, the rise in sea levels could displace coastal populations and warming seas will generate more intense tropical storms. Fourth, warmer oceans also damage coral reefs and threaten marine ecosystems; and warmer climates endanger land species, pushing more to extinction. And fifth, diseases such as malaria and dengue fever will expand, especially in the developing regions, overtaxing already inadequate public health systems.

Nearly 17,000 species of plants and animals are currently at risk of extinction, and the number of species threatened by extinction is growing by the day. Despite increased investment, the main causes of biodiversity loss—high rates of consumption, habitat loss, invasive species, pollution and climate change—are not being sufficiently addressed.

[17] See Coley (2008: 131–134) for a discussion of the scientific evidence of climate change, as well as the claims of skeptics. The Intergovernmental Panel on Climate Change was created in 1988 by the World Meteorological Organization and the United Nations Environment Programme to "summarize the state of scientific knowledge about climate change in a periodic series of major assessments." See also World Bank (2010: 81).

See Box 12.2 for a short primer on the science of global warming.[18] The World Bank (2010: 70, 10), reflecting the scientific consensus, observed:

> If the world is able to limit the human-caused temperature increase to about 2°C above the preindustrial level, it might be possible to limit significant loss from the Greenland and West Antarctic ice shelves and subsequent sea level rise; to limit the increase in floods, droughts, and forest fires in many regions; to limit the increase of death and illness from the spread of infections and diarrheal diseases and from extreme heat; to avoid extinction of more than a quarter of all known species; and to prevent significant declines in global food production.

> . . .stabilizing global warming around 2°C above preindustrial temperatures [would necessitate] by 2050 that emissions be 50 percent below 1990 levels and be zero or negative by 2100. . . . [This implies] 450 ppm of CO_2 equivalent. . . .and. . . This would require global emissions to begin declining by about 1.5 percent a year. . . . A ten year delay in mitigation would most likely make it impossible to keep warming from exceeding 2°C.

Fossil fuels have greatly contributed to the economic progress of the industrial age and still account for the vast majority of the energy consumed throughout the world. Below we discuss present energy use. In Chapter 14 we look at policy options for reducing GHG emissions. Then in Chapter 15 we address sustainable energy policy.

ENERGY AND EMISSIONS

If the world population is to begin stabilizing somewhere between 9 and 9.5 billion near the middle of this century, then, currently with nearly 7 billion, we are already over 70 percent there. As noted, a stable world population does not imply zero population growth for all the nations in the world. Currently the developed nations and many developing nations, including China, have below replacement-level fertility, although some population momentum remains to be expended. High rates of population growth still characterize many of the poorest nations, and population increases will likely continue in these countries for some time. It will be in these nations that energy consumption will be increasing the fastest in the future.

BOX 12.2: A SHORT PRIMER ON GLOBAL WARMING

Four phenomena in global warming are described below. The first two are from David Coley (2008). The last two, on the oceans and coral reefs, are from the World Bank (2010).

1. Coley describes the carbon cycle as follows:

    the burning of fossil and other organic fuels, such as wood, releases carbon dioxide into the atmosphere. The growth of plants represents the reversal of this reaction: plants absorb carbon dioxide from the atmosphere and, though photosynthesis, use

---

[18]The World Bank (2010: 70–84) provides a good overview with "Focus A: The science of climate change."

sunlight to break the carbon dioxide into carbon and oxygen atoms, which are recombined with nitrogen and other elements to form carbohydrates, sugars, and other complex organic molecules essential to the plant. When plants decay, or burn in forest fires, the carbon in these compounds reacts once more with atmospheric oxygen to form carbon dioxide, thereby forming a carbon cycle. (Coley 2008: 18)

2. The Earth is regulated by a natural greenhouse effect:

[Radiation from the sun received by the Earth] must be re-radiated back into space, or the planet's temperature would continuously escalate... the composition of the atmosphere, which through the natural greenhouse effect ensures that the planet is about 33 °C warmer than it otherwise would be, and that life as we know it can exist. (Coley 2008: 80)

There are several **greenhouse gases** that contribute to global warming. Water vapor is the most prevalent and important GHG. The unprecedented accumulation over the past century of other GHGs, primarily carbon dioxide (CO_2), however, has accentuated this natural greenhouse effect and contributed to the global warming. Other GHGs include: methane (CH_4), which is released from ruminant animals, rice paddies, landfill sites, waterlogged soils and marshes, and melting permafrost; nitrous oxide (N_2O), which is released through fertilizers, deforestation, and fuel combustion; chlorofluorocarbons (CFCs), which are released through refrigeration, aerosols, and solvents; and ozone (O_3), which is a GHG in the lower atmosphere, whose depletion in the form of the ozone hole in the upper atmosphere over Antarctica has been a concern for the filtering of harmful ultraviolet light. (Coley, 2008: 105–110)

3. The oceans also serve as a sink:

The oceans have absorbed about half the anthropogenic emissions released since 1800, and more than 80 percent of the heat of global warming. The result is a warming, acidifying ocean, changing at an unprecedented pace with impacts across the aquatic realm. (World Bank, 2010: 156–157)

4. Coral reefs may symbolize the proverbial canary in the mine, providing an early distress signal:

Coral reefs, both tropical and deep cold water, are global centers of biodiversity. They provide goods and services of roughly $375 billion a year to nearly 500 million people. About 30 million of the world's poorest people directly rely on coral reef ecosystems for food.
Coral reefs are already being pushed to their thermal limits by recent temperature increases. Higher sea surface temperatures stress corals and cause coral bleaching (the loss or death of symbiotic algae), frequently resulting in large-scale mortality. An ecological "tipping point" is likely to be crossed in many areas if ocean temperatures increase to more than 2°C above their preindustrial levels, especially as ocean acidification reduces carbonate concentrations, inhibiting reef accretion. (World Bank, 2010: 78)

Energy use

Beginning at the top of Table 12.5 with selected statistics on energy and emissions, as expected we see that energy use increases with income. The production and consumption of goods and services requires energy. On a per capita basis, the high-income economies consume more than ten times the energy compared to the low-income economies. By itself, with less than 5 percent of the world's population, the US uses 18 percent of the world's commercial energy. We might ask whether the rest of the world, especially the low- and middle-income economies, will ever be able to consume energy at the same rate as the US. The development of renewable energy resources and improved efficiencies in the utilization of energy will be important for sustainable development. So may be absolute reductions in energy use in the developed nations.

The dominance of fossil fuels in total energy consumption is evident and unsustainable. Here, too, we see the share of fossil fuels in total energy consumption generally increasing with income, before leveling off at over 80 percent for the upper middle- and high- income economies.[19] The low-income and, to a lesser extent, lower middle-income economies rely relatively more on biomass. Clean energy production, encompassing noncarbohydrate energy like hydropower, nuclear, solar, and geothermal energy, does increase with income, although at less than 12 percent of total energy for the high-income nations in 2009, there is still much room for growth. As will be discussed in Chapter 15, there are nevertheless concerns with each of these other forms of clean energy.

We see considerable diversity in the sources of electricity. China and India relied on coal for generating respectively nearly 80 and 70 percent of their electricity, compared to less than 7 percent in the low-income economies and approximately a third in the high-income economies. Reducing the dependencies of these two giants on their ample coal deposits will be important for curbing global warming. Hydropower is most important in the low-income economies, while the sources of electricity are more varied in the high-income economies and include significant shares for gas, nuclear power, as well as hydropower.

Carbon dioxide emissions

The total and per capita emissions for carbon dioxide, the major greenhouse gas, are given. Paralleling the consumption of energy, carbon dioxide emissions vary greatly across the nations of the world. As noted by the World Bank (2012: 173):

> In combustion different fossil fuels release different amounts of carbon dioxide for the same level of energy use: oil releases about 50 percent more carbon dioxide than natural gas, and coal releases about twice as much. Cement manufacturing releases about half a metric ton of carbon dioxide for each metric ton of cement produced.

To repeat, that the world is experiencing global warming is almost universally accepted among scientists. In addition to the higher average temperatures and likely rises in the sea level, which could be devastating for coastal areas and some of the poorest nations such as Bangladesh, more volatile and severe weather can be expected.

---

[19] Of the fossil fuels, coal may be the most polluting, not only in terms of the direct mining of the coal, but with emissions of CO_2 and particulates, which can damage the lungs, as well as sulfur dioxide and nitrogen dioxide, which contribute to acid rain. Natural gas, on the other hand, burns "cleaner" than coal and oil. See Coley (2008) for an extensive discussion of these fossil fuels as well as other energies.

Table 12.5 *Selected statistics on energy and emissions*

	WORLD	Low	Lower middle	India	Upper middle	China	High	US
	ECONOMIES BY INCOME CLASSIFICATION							
Population, millions								
2010	6,895	796	2,519	1,225	2,452	1,338	1,127	309
		(11.5%)	(36.5%)	(17.8%)	(35.6%)	(19.4%)	(16.3%)	(4.5%)
Energy use								
Per capita (kilograms of oil equivalent)								
1990	1,661	386	607	362	1,375	760	4,649	7,672
2009	1,788	365	665	560	1,848	1,695	4,856	7,051
% of total energy								
Fossil fuel								
1990	80.9	41.5	65.1	55.4	83.7	75.5	84.2	86.4
2009	80.7	29.9	68.0	73.0	86.3	87.4	81.9	84.1
Combustible renewables and waste								
1990	10.2	54.7	30.7	42.1	12.0	23.2	2.8	3.3
2009	10.0	65.9	26.9	24.5	8.3	9.0	4.2	3.9
Alternative and nuclear energy production:								
1990	8.7	3.9	4.4	2.5	4.0	1.3	12.8	10.3
2009	9.2	4.1	5.3	2.3	5.3	3.7	13.8	11.9
Sources of electricity								
2009								
Coal	40.4%	6.9%	39.6%	68.6%	50.2%	78.8%	34.3%	45.4%
Gas	21.4%	20.4%	22.0%	12.4%	18.5%	1.4%	23.2%	22.8%
Oil	4.8%	4.7%	12.1%	2.9%	3.9%	0.4%	4.1%	1.2%
Hydropower	16.1%	45.7%	16.9%	11.9%	21.6%	16.7%	11.6%	6.6%
Nuclear power	13.4%	0.0%	5.3%	1.9%	4.4%	1.9%	21.3%	19.9%
Renewable	3.0%	0.9%	2.4%	2.2%	1.2%	0.8%	4.5%	3.7%
Other	0.9%	21.4%	1.7%	0.0%	0.2%	0.0%	1.0%	0.4%
Carbon dioxide emissions								
(billion metric tons)								
1990	22.3	...	2.0	0.7	7.3	2.5	11.5	4.9
2008	32.1	0.2	3.7	1.7	12.9	7.0	13.3	5.5
		(0.6%)	(11.5%)	(5.3%)	(40.2%)	(21.8%)	(41.4%)	(17.1%)
Per capita (metric tons)								
1990	4.2	...	1.1	0.8	3.6	2.2	11.8	19.5
2008	4.8	0.3	1.5	1.5	5.3	5.3	11.9	18.0

Carbon dioxide emissions have increased with production. On a per capita basis in 2008, the high-income economies emitted nearly 40 times as much carbon dioxide as low-income economies—and for the US per capita CO_2 emissions exceeded the low-income economies by a factor of 60. For the world per capita emissions increased between 1990 and 2008 by over 14 percent, from 4.2 to 4.8 metric tons.

Globally, the **carbon intensity of energy**, measured as the amount of carbon dioxide emitted from using one unit of energy in the production of goods and services, was unchanged between 1990 and 2008—significantly increasing for China and India, but declining in the high-income

Table 12.5 continued

	ECONOMIES BY INCOME CLASSIFICATION							
	WORLD	Low	Lower middle	India	Upper middle	China	High	US
Carbon intensity of energy (kilograms per kilogram of oil equivalent energy use)								
1990	2.5	0.6	1.8	2.2	2.8	2.9	2.5	2.5
2008	2.5	1.0	2.4	2.8	2.9	3.3	2.4	2.4
Carbon intensity of income (emissions in kilograms per 2005 PPP$ of GDP)								
1990	0.6	...	0.6	0.7	0.9	2.0	0.5	0.6
2008	0.5	0.3	0.5	0.5	0.7	0.9	0.4	0.4

Notes: Energy use refers to the use of primary energy (i.e., petroleum (crude oil, natural gas liquids, and oil from nonconventional sources), natural gas, solid fuels (coal, lignite, and other derived fuels), and combustible renewables and waste) before transformation to other end-use fuels, which is equal to indigenous production plus imports and stock changes, minus exports and fuels supplied to ships and aircraft engaged in international transport.

Fossil fuels comprise coal, oil, petroleum, and natural gas products.

Combustible renewables and waste comprise solid biomass, liquid biomass, biogas, industrial waste, and municipal waste. Biomass, also referred to as traditional fuel, comprises animal and plant materials (wood, vegetal wastes, ethanol, animal material/wastes, and sulfite lyes). Waste is comprised of municipal wastes (produced by commercial and public service sectors that are collected by local authorities for disposal in a central location for the production of heat and/or power) and industrial waste.

Alternative and nuclear energy production is noncarbohydrate energy that does not produce carbon dioxide when generated. It includes hydropower and nuclear, geothermal, and solar power, among others.

Electricity production is measured at the terminals of all alternator sets in a station. In addition to hydropower, coal, gas, and nuclear power generation, it covers geothermal, solar, wind, and tide and wave energy, as well as that from combustible renewals and waste. Production includes the output of electric plants designed to produce electricity only, as well as that of combined heat and power plants.

Sources of electricity are the inputs used to generate electricity: coal, gas, oil, hydropower and nuclear power. Coal is all coal and brown coal, both primary (including hard coal and lignite or brown coal) and derived fuels (including patent fuel, coke oven coke, gas coke, coke oven gas, and blast furnace gas). Peat also is included in this category. Gas is natural gas but not natural gas liquids. Oil is crude oil and petroleum products. Hydropower is electricity produced by hydroelectric plants. Nuclear power is electricity produced by nuclear power plants. Renewable sources are geothermal, solar, photovoltaic, solar thermal, tide, wind, industrial waste, municipal waste, primary solid biofuels, biogases, biogasoline, biodiesels, other liquid biofuels, nonspecified primary biofuels and waste, and charcoal. "Other" is the residual category for sources of generated electricity not shown.

Carbon dioxide emissions are emissions from the burning of fossil fuels and the manufacture of cement and include carbon dioxide produced during consumption of solid, liquid and gas fuels and gas flaring. The emission estimates for regions and countries exclude fuels supplied to ships and aircraft in international transport because of the difficulty of apportioning the fuels among benefiting countries.

Carbon intensity of energy is the ratio of carbon dioxide emissions to energy production and measures the greenness of energy production (i.e., the amount of carbon dioxide emitted as a result of using one unit of energy in the process of production).

Carbon intensity of income is the ratio of carbon dioxide emissions in kilograms per 2005 PPP dollar of GDP and is an indicator of the greenness of an economy.

Source: World Bank (2012: Tables 2.1, 3.7, 3.8, and 3.9).

economies. Carbon dioxide emissions per kilogram of GDP are inversely related to how clean the production processes are.

The **carbon intensity of income**, measured by carbon emissions per dollar of output (in 2005 PPP dollars), generally declines with economic growth, reflecting advances in technology (e.g., more energy efficient machinery), pollution abatement, as well as the increased share of services and decreased shares of agriculture and manufacturing with economic development (structural change that reduces the carbon intensity of the economy). Nevertheless, the technical efficiency gains reducing the carbon intensity of income have been outpaced by the growth in production, resulting in greater carbon dioxide emissions for the world. From 1990 to 2008, annual global CO_2 emissions increased by over 40 percent, from 22.3 to 32.1 billion metric tons, a trend that must soon be reversed.[20]

As noted in Box 12.2, carbon dioxide (from the combustion of fossil fuels and manufacture of cement), while the most prevalent greenhouse gas, is not the only one. Emissions of methane (largely due to agriculture, landfills, wastewater treatment, and forest fires), nitrous oxide (also from fossil fuel combustion, fertilizers, rainforest fires, and animal wastes), hydrofluorocarbons (from refrigeration and semiconductor manufacturing), perfluorocarbons (a by-product of aluminum smelting and uranium enrichment), and sulfur dioxide (used to insulate high-voltage electric power equipment) are other GHGs.[21]

As we will discuss in the final chapter, increased efforts within nations as well as international cooperation will be required to address climate change. Total emissions and concentrations of GHGs such as carbon dioxide in the atmosphere will continue to increase for some time, regardless of efforts in abatement, reflecting the momentum of global warming—just as there is population momentum from past high fertility. How high the concentrations will reach before stabilizing and then hopefully declining, however, will hinge on these national efforts to reduce emissions. Sustainable development will likely depend on such reductions in greenhouse gas concentrations.

CONCLUSION

The United Nations Development Programme (2007: 111–112) identified three foundations for success: putting a price on carbon emissions; behavioral change, involving consumers and investors shifting demand to low-carbon energy sources; and international cooperation, with rich countries taking the lead. In the concluding chapter these three foundations will be addressed, as will the policies for achieving sustainable development on our planet. In Chapter 14, we discuss market failures and the role of governments in economic development. But we turn now in the next chapter to the global food supply.

Agriculture illustrates many of the key dimensions of sustainable development: the Malthusian concern with feeding the global population; the importance of technological progress, embodied in genetically modified crops; the impact of climate change, which agriculture both contributes to

[20] In 2010, global emissions of carbon dioxide rose by 5.9 percent, the largest absolute increase ever recorded. In part, the sharp rise reflected the recovery from the recession. In 2009, global emissions declined by 1.4 percent. For the US, the world's second largest emitter of GHGs, carbon emissions fell by 7 percent in 2009 before increasing by 4 percent in 2010. Emissions grew by 10 percent in China, the global leader, about the same pace as GDP growth in 2010. Overall the annual growth rate in carbon emissions averaged 3 percent over the first decade of the twenty-first century, about triple the growth rate in the 1990s. See Gillis (2011).

[21] From World Bank (2012). While far less abundant, these other greenhouse gases are very powerful. As noted by the World Bank (2012: 177), a kilogram of methane and a kilogram of nitrous oxide are respectively 21 times and 310 times as effective in trapping heat in the earth's atmosphere as a kilogram of carbon dioxide within 100 years.

and is affected by; human behavior, with reduced, if not zero, population growth and changes in the meat-intensive diets that higher incomes allow; and international collaboration, in particular the responsibilities of the developed countries in assisting the less developed economies to mitigate and adapt to climate change.

KEY TERMS

appreciation	carbon intensity of energy
carbon intensity of income	depreciation
Dutch disease	greenhouse gases
hydraulic fracturing	natural resource curse
nominal exchange rate	real exchange rate

QUESTIONS

1. Has there been any movement in the Doomsday Clock since January 2012? To check, access the website of the *Bulletin of the Atomic Scientists* (http://www.thebulletin.org).

2. Compare the compositions of sources of electricity (coal, natural gas, oil, hydropower, and nuclear power) for Brazil, China, Russia, France, and the United States. What might account for the differences? (See the table on sources of electricity in World Bank's *World Development Indicators*.)

3. The reserves to production ratios (R/P), presented for oil, natural gas, and coal for the world in Table 12.2, indicate the length of time the proved reserves remaining at the end of any year would last if the rate of production prevailing in that year were to continue.

    (a) What can be concluded if the R/P ratio for a fossil fuel increases over time?

    (b) In 2009 the R/P ratios for oil, natural gas, and coal were 45.7, 62.8, and 119 years, respectively. In 2010, the R/P ratios were 46.2, 58.6, and 118 years, respectively. (Statistics are from the *BP Statistical Review of World Energy*, June 2010 and June 2011.) What does this suggest about fossil fuel supplies?

4. If the carbon dioxide emissions per capita of India in 2008 (1.4 metric tons) were to increase to the level of the United States in 2008 (19.3 metric tons of carbon dioxide emissions per capita), what would be the percentage increase in world carbon emissions (approximately 31 million metric tons) in 2008? Assume India's population is 1.2 billion and the US population is 315 million.

REFERENCES

Astill, James. 2010. "Seeing the wood: A special report on the forests," *The Economist*, September 25.

Bradsher, Keith. 2010. "US Called Vulnerable to Rare Earth Shortages," *New York Times*, December 15.

Coley, David. 2008. *Energy and Climate Change: Creating a Sustainable Future*. Chichester: Wiley.

Collier, Paul. 2007. "The Natural Resource Trap," in *The Bottom Billion: Why the Poorest Countries Are Failing and What Can Be Done about It*. New York: Oxford University Press: 38–52.

Dietz, Simon, Eric Neumayer and Indra de Soysa. 2007. "Corruption, the resource curse and genuine saving," *Environment and Development Economics*, 12: 33–53.

Food and Agriculture Organization of the United Nations. 2010. *Global Forest Resources Assessment 2010: Main Report*. Rome: FAO. http://www.fao.org/docrep/013/i1757e/i1757e.pdf.

Gillis, Justin. 2011. "Carbon Emissions Show Biggest Jump Ever Recorded," *New York Times*, December 4.

Gillis, Malcolm, Dwight Perkins, Michael Roemer, and Donald Snodgrass. 1987. *Economics of Development*, 2nd edition. New York: W.W. Norton.

Grimond, John. 2010. "For want of a drink: A special report on water," *The Economist*, May 22.

Guest, Robert. 2000. "Here's Hoping: A Survey of Nigeria," *The Economist*, January 15.

Hess, Peter and Clark Ross. 1997. "Natural Resources and the Environment," in *Economic Development: Theories, Evidence, and Policies*. Fort Worth, TX: Dryden Press: 353–386.

Sachs, Jeffrey and Andrew Warner. 1995. *Natural Resource Abundance and Economic Growth*, Working Paper 5398. Cambridge, MA: National Bureau of Economic Research.

United Nations Development Programme. 2007. *Human Development Report 2007/2008: Fighting Climate Change*. New York: Palgrave Macmillan for the UNDP.

United Nations Development Programme. 2010. *Human Development Report 2010: The Real Wealth of Nations; Pathways to Human Development*. New York: Palgrave Macmillan for the UNDP.

Van der Ploeg, Frederick. 2011. "Natural Resources: Curse or Blessing?" *Journal of Economic Literature*, 49(2): 366–420.

Walsh, Bryan. 2012. "The Future of Oil," *Time*, April 9.

World Bank. 1990. *World Tables 1989–90*. Baltimore, MD: Johns Hopkins University Press.

World Bank. 1992. *World Development Report 1992: Development and the Environment*. New York: Oxford University Press.

World Bank. 2010. *World Development Report 2010: Development and Climate Change*, Washington, DC: World Bank.

World Bank. 2011. *World Development Indicators 2011*. Washington, DC: World Bank.

World Bank. 2012. *World Development Indicators 2012*. Washington, DC: World Bank.

Chapter 13

Global food supply

Two centuries ago in a famous essay, Thomas Malthus, an English political economist, predicted that the rate of population growth, if unchecked, would tend to outstrip the food supply, yielding misery and vice. For Malthus, the ultimate check to population growth was the food supply, due to limited land and diminishing returns to labor. Malthus did not anticipate the tremendous growth in agricultural productivity due to advances in technology that were to follow. Nor did Malthus foresee the declines in birth rates that accompanied economic development with the demographic transition—although the declines in fertility did not reflect moral restraint as much as birth control, also enhanced by technological advances in contraception.

According to Paul Roberts (2008), what staved off the Malthusian specter was globalism and the emergence of an international food system made possible by free trade, advances in transportation networks (railways and shipping) and new preservation technologies. Expanding cultivation in United States, Australia, and Argentina helped feed growing populations in the industrializing countries (see Roberts 2008: 17–20).[1]

Even with the explosive population growth of the twentieth century, as the developing regions of the world began their demographic transitions, the world food supply kept pace, in part due to the Green Revolution in agriculture. As Roberts (2008: 25) observes:

> Between 1950 and the late 1990s, world output of corn, wheat, and the cereal crops more than tripled, which exceeded the more than doubling of the world population from 2.5 to 6 billion, so that the volume of food available per person rose from fewer than 2,400 calories per day to more than 2,700 calories per day.[2]

---

[1] In particular, in the United States, Roberts points to the creation of the Department of Agriculture, with a system of publicly funded farm programs to boost output and protect farmers from harvest failures, and the construction of dams, irrigation canals, and railroads to transport produce to urban areas and export outlets. New plant varieties and animal breeds were developed at federal and state research centers and land-grant universities. In the 1920s and 1930s, scientists came out with hybrid strains of corn with higher yields. A new nitrogen-based fertilizer process (Haber–Bosch) was developed that enhanced soil fertility.

[2] To illustrate the required daily caloric food intake to maintain current weight: a male, 30 years of age, who is $5^{1/2}$ feet tall, weighs 140 pounds, and is extremely active (with hard daily exercise or a physically demanding job) would require 2,983 calories. A female, 30 years of age, who is $5^{1/2}$ feet tall, weighs 120 pounds, and is moderately active (with moderate exercise three to five days a week), would require 2,075 daily calories to maintain her weight. Estimates are from Healthy Calculators at http://www.healthycalculators.com/calories-intake-requirement.php.

However, the World Bank (2007: 8) cautions:

> Agriculture has been largely successful in meeting the world's effective demand for food. Yet more than 800 million people remain food insecure, and agriculture has left a huge environmental footprint. And the future is increasingly uncertain.
>
> Models predict that food prices in global markets may reverse their long-term downward trend, creating rising uncertainties about global food security. Climate change, environmental degradation, rising competition for land and water, high energy prices, and doubts about future adoption rates for new technologies all present huge challenges and risks that make predictions difficult.

In this chapter we address the economic and environmental challenges in feeding the world population, both in technically producing enough food for the greater numbers expected, but also in ensuring that all have access to adequate diets.

HUNGER AND MALNUTRITION

That the global food supply has increased faster than population does not mean that all have enjoyed adequate nutrition. Hunger and malnutrition, where existing, reflect not limits in production, but poverty and the inability to purchase the food produced. The Nobel Laureate Amartya Sen (1981: 434) famously wrote that "starvation is a matter of some people not *having* enough food to eat, and not a matter of there *being* not enough food to eat."

Indeed, recall the first of the Millennium Development Goals agreed to by the leaders of the nations of the world at the turn of this century: to eradicate extreme poverty and hunger. The explicit target is to halve between 1990 and 2015 the proportion of people who suffer from hunger. The world, however, is not on target to reach this goal. The United Nations Department of Economic and Social Affairs (2011: 11–13) acknowledged that progress had stalled, with the share of the populations in the developing world going hungry leveling off at 16 percent in 2005–07, despite significant reductions in the incidence of extreme poverty. For children under age 5, while the proportion underweight had declined from 30 percent in 1990 to 23 percent in 2009, this is likely insufficient progress to meet the MDG target by 2015.[3] South Asia remains by far the region with the greatest problem, with 43 percent of children undernourished in 2009.

Inadequate nutrition undermines health and productivity. Undernourished adults may be unable to earn a living wage. The development of undernourished children may be impaired, perpetuating a vicious cycle of poverty. The nutrient deficiencies and inadequate protein for brain growth that characterize early insufficient food consumption result in potential intelligence loss and increased susceptibility to illness and disease. Undernourished and in poor health, children have reduced capacity for learning and subsequent diminished performance in school. These children may be more frequently absent from school and usually drop out earlier, failing to achieve even basic literacy and numeracy. Consequently, their labor productivity and socioeconomic mobility are undermined, locking them into low-income livelihoods. In turn,

---

[3] According to the World Bank and International Monetary Fund (2012: 14), "Rates of malnutrition have dropped substantially since 1990, but over 100 million children under age 5 remain malnourished. Only 40 countries, out of 90 with accurate data to monitor trend, are on track to meet the MDG target."

when they become parents, their children may face similar deprivation, perpetuating the poverty cycle.

The World Bank and International Monetary Fund (2012: 6) state that in developing countries:

> Child malnutrition accounts for more than a third of the under-five mortality—and malnutrition during pregnancy, for more than a fifth of maternal mortality. Other hard-to-reverse impacts include faltering growth (stunting, low height for age) and low school attendance. A malnourished child has on average a seven-month delay in starting school, a 0.7 grade loss in schooling, and potentially a 10–17 percent reduction in lifetime earnings—damaging future human capital and causing national GDP losses estimated at 2–3 percent. So malnutrition is not just a result of poverty—it is also a cause. Malnourished young children are also more at risk for chronic diseases such as diabetes, obesity, hypertension, and cardiovascular disease in adulthood.

Examples of the human costs of malnutrition, vividly reported by Michael Wines (2006), include:

> Well over half of sub-Saharan African children under five lack iron, vital to developing nervous systems. . . They often have trouble concentrating and coordinating brain signals with movements, like holding a pencil, that are crucial to education.
>
> Another 3.5 million children lack sufficient iodine, which can lower a child's IQ by 10 or more points. More than a half million suffer vitamin A deficiency, which cripples young immune systems.
>
> In most foods, these vital nutrients exist in traces—vitamins A and B12, iron, iodine, folic acid. Denied them in the womb and in infancy, children suffer irreversible brain and nervous system damage, even if they appear well fed.

As we will discuss later in the chapter, there are many food-insecure nations, with large percentages of their populations undernourished. Policy priorities for improving food supplies in these and other developing nations will be outlined.

We begin the analysis of whether there will be enough food produced to allow for an adequate diet for all of the world's population in the future with the underlying demand and supply factors. On the demand side, the size of the world's population and the average consumption of food, reflecting income and the compositions of diets, are the key determinants. On the supply side, the resources devoted to agriculture and the technology affecting the productivity of those resources are the primary determinants. Whether all have adequate diets, however, depends not only on the production of food, but also on poverty and politics.

THE DEMAND FOR FOOD

Increases in the demand for food accompany population growth and gains in per capita income. While the world population is expected to stabilize at somewhere around 9 billion by the latter part of the century, the population growth until then will be in the less developed countries where the demand for food, especially a more varied and protein-intensive diet, will rise with per capita incomes. In short, the world demand for food will increase significantly in the next few decades.

The North American diet, with reliance on animal products and processed foods containing relatively high amounts of fats and sweeteners, places great demands on the food supply. Lester Brown (2009: 233–234) calculates:

> Using round numbers, at the US level of 800 kilograms of grain per person annually for food and feed, the 2-billion ton annual harvest of grain would support 2.5 billion people. At the Italian level of consumption of close to 400 kilograms, the current harvest would support 5 billion people. At the 200 kilograms of grain consumed by the average Indian, it would support a population of 10 billion.
>
> ...Among the United States, Italy, and India, life expectancy is highest in Italy, even though US medical expenditures per person are much higher. People who live very low or very high on the food chain do not live as long as those at an intermediate level. People consuming a Mediterranean type diet that includes meat, cheese, and seafood, but all in moderation, are healthier and live longer.[4]

Undernourishment is characteristic of extreme poverty, which, as discussed above, has serious consequences for health and human productivity. A malnourishment more likely found among higher incomes is obesity, largely due to the overconsumption of food.

Obesity

A growing concern in the US and other high-income nations is obesity, reflecting unhealthy food consumption and lack of exercise. Skeel (2008) reports that two-thirds of adults in the US are overweight and almost a third are obese. The costs in terms of impaired health and the attendant medical expenditures, reduced labor productivity, and even the additional fuel needed to transport overweight people are substantial.[5] Bhattacharya and Sood (2011: 140) observe that while the US has the highest incidence of obesity among the high-income countries, obesity rates have also risen

---

[4] Brown (2008: 234) also notes:

Of the roughly 800 kilograms of grain consumed per person each year in the United States, about 100 kilograms is eaten directly as bread, pasta, and breakfast cereals, while the bulk of the grain is consumed indirectly in the form of livestock and poultry products. By contrast, in India, where people consume just under 200 kilograms of grain per year, or roughly a pound per day, nearly all grain is eaten directly to satisfy basic food energy needs. Little is available for conversion into livestock products.

Brown (2008: 226) also contrasts efficiencies in grain conversion into protein:

With cattle in feedlots, it takes roughly 7 kilograms of grain to produce 1-kilogram gain in live weight. For pork, the figure is over 3 kilograms of grain per kilogram of weight gain, for poultry it is just over 2, and for herbivorous species of farmed fish (such as carp, tilapia, and catfish), it is less than 2.

[5] From Shirley Skeel's 2008 article, "What if no one were fat?" (http://www.health-forums.com/misc-fitness-weights/msn-money-what-if-no-one-were-fat-55539.html). Skeel cites estimated savings based on the counterfactual that no one in America were fat, instead of the average American being at least 20 pounds overweight. Medical costs of obesity-related problems such as diabetes, stroke, and heart disease would be reduced by $140 billion, or more than 6 percent of all health care costs. Productivity in the workplace would increase as people took fewer sick days and spent less time at work feeling unwell, adding $257 billion in output from workers and their caregivers. The savings alone on fuel for cars and airlines due to their lighter loads would top $5 billion a year.

in Canada, Australia, every European country, and South Korea. Moreover, obesity is linked to higher incidences of diabetes and heart disease.[6]

A contributing factor is the meat-intensive American diet. Roberts (2008: 209) cites the average American consuming around 9 ounces of meat a day, nearly four times the government recommended intake for protein. And, this diet is spreading to the rest of the world:

> Between 1960 and 2002, per capita meat consumption in developing countries more than doubled, from 22 pounds to 56 pounds, and is on track to hit 74 pounds by 2030. That's still a fraction of the 220 pounds that each consumer in industrialized countries is expected to be eating by 2030. (Roberts 2008: 211)

Unfortunately, the problem is appearing in some developing nations. As shown in Table 13.1, more than two dozen low- and middle-income countries have 10 percent or more of their children under 5 who are overweight. (For each nation listed, the percentage of children under age 5 who are underweight is also given.) In general, poor nations have a relatively high percentage of undernourished children. Problems with overweight usually are found with higher incomes. And we do see developing nations with higher per capita incomes having relatively high percentages of overweight children. Noticeable here are the former socialist states in Eastern Europe and Central Asia. A number of Middle Eastern and North African countries also are found on this list. Particularly alarming, though, might be poor nations like Benin, Guinea-Bissau, Indonesia, Nigeria and Syria, who are beset with high percentages (10 percent or greater) of underweight and overweight children.

In sum, continued growth in food supplies will be needed in the future for the expected growth in demand. Stabilizing the world population and widespread adoption of healthier, more efficient, less meat-intensive diets may be essential for the adequacy of the available supplies. Before turning to the factors driving the production of food, we will review the trends in food prices, or the terms in trade in agriculture.

Trends in food prices

Prices of basic agricultural commodities have tended to be volatile. The lack of good substitutes for staple crops such as rice, corn, and wheat means that their price elasticities of demand are low. The supply of these commodities is also price-inelastic, as the natural growing season (i.e., the time between planting and harvesting) is fairly well set and limits the supply responses to price changes in the short run. Moreover, agricultural supplies are subject to exogenous shocks, with variations in weather, crop disease, and pests. The combination of price-inelastic demands and supplies with exogenous shifts in supplies means that agricultural prices can fluctuate significantly from one season to the next.

---

[6]Bhattacharya and Sood (2011: 139) cite the incidence of obesity among Americans aged 20–74 years increasing from 13.4 percent in 1962 to 35.1 percent by 2006. Obesity is commonly measured by a body mass index (BMI). Calculated as weight in kilograms divided by height in meters squared, a BMI between 25 and 30 is "overweight" and a BMI above 30 is considered to be "obese." For example, an individual who is $5^{1/2}$ feet tall and weighs 142 pounds would have a BMI of 23. If this individual weighed 155 pounds, his BMI would be 25 (marginally overweight); if his weight were 186 pounds, his BMI would be 30 (the lower limit for obesity). Bhattacharya and Sood also provide evidence that obese workers in the United States earn less.

Table 13.1 *Nations with 10% or more children under 5 under- or overweight*

Country	Overweight		Underweight	
	Male	*Female*	*Male*	*Female*
Albania ($8,520)	23.3%	23.4%	6.6%	6.0%
Algeria ($8,100)	13.4%	12.4%	3.7%	3.7%
Argentina ($15,570)	10.2%	9.5%	2.4%	2.2%
Armenia ($5,660)	13.9%	9.1%	3.4%	5.2%
Azerbaijan ($9,270)	14.9%	12.7%	8.7%	8.0%
Belarus ($13,590)	11.3%	8.1%	1.5%	1.0%
Benin ($1,590)	11.6%	11.3%	22.7%	17.6%
Bosnia & Herzegovina ($8,910)	27.4%	23.9%	2.2%	1.0%
Egypt ($6,060)	19.8%	21.2%	8.1%	5.4%
Georgia ($4,990)	21.3%	18.3%	1.3%	1.0%
Guinea-Bissau ($1,180)	17.6%	16.5%	16.6%	17.8%
Indonesia ($4,200)	11.3%	11.2%	20.7%	18.6%
Iraq ($3,370)	15.6%	14.3%	7.7%	6.6%
Kazakhstan ($10,770)	15.1%	14.5%	5.4%	4.3%
Kuwait (. . .)	10.0%	8.0%	2.0%	1.5%
Kyrgyz Republic ($2,070)	12.7%	8.6%	2.9%	2.5%
Libya ($16,880)	23.2%	21.6%	6.3%	4.8%
Macedonia FYR ($10,920)	16.6%	15.8%	1.7%	1.9%
Malawi ($850)	10.3%	8.2%	15.2%	12.6%
Mongolia ($3,670)	15.6%	12.6%	5.3%	5.3%
Nigeria ($2,170)	10.3%	10.7%	28.6%	24.8%
Serbia ($11,090)	20.4%	18.2%	2.2%	1.3%
Sierra Leone ($830)	10.3%	9.9%	24.2%	18.5%
Swaziland ($5,430)	11.8%	10.9%	6.3%	5.9%
Syria ($5,120)	17.8%	18.1%	11.5%	8.7%
Uzbekistan ($3,110)	13.1%	12.5%	4.6%	4.3%

Notes: Figures in parentheses are 2010 per capita incomes in PPP dollars.

The data refer to the most recent year available in the period 2005–10. Many nations are missing data for the percentages of children under 5 years of age who are overweight or underweight, including a number of high-income economies.

Prevalence of overweight children is the percentage of children under age 5 whose weight for age is more than two standard deviations above the median for the international reference population of the corresponding age as established by the World Health Organization child growth standards.

Prevalence of underweight children is the percentage of children under age 5 whose weight for age is more than two standard deviations below the median for the international reference population.

Source: World Bank (2012: Tables 1.1 and 2.20).

Nevertheless, up until recently, the long-run trend in real prices of food has declined, indicating relative increases in supply over demand.[7] That food prices declined despite increases in

---

[7] The demand for food, especially basic foodstuffs, tends to be income-inelastic, meaning that the proportion of income allocated for expenditures on food declines with higher incomes. To illustrate, in the US average per capita real disposable income more than doubled between 1965 and 2005, rising from $13,460 to $31,343. Over the same period, real personal consumption expenditures for food and beverages increased by a little over 12 percent (from $1,937 to $2,171). The percentage of disposable income spent on food and beverages declined from 16.8 percent (in 1965) to 7.4 percent (in 2005). The income-inelastic demand for food will moderate the rise in the demand for food with income growth, contributing to the secular decline in the real prices of food.

the world population and average consumption is largely due to the amazing growth in agricultural productivity with advances in technology unimagined by Malthus. The gains in productivity are indicated in greater yields per hectare of land, in turn reflecting improvements in seeds, pest control, management practices, as well as increased use of fertilizer and irrigation.

Economic development is accompanied by the need to feed a growing urban population. Only with increased productivity in agriculture can labor be released to industry. For example, the US has less than 2 percent of its labor force in agriculture, compared to approximately 20 percent in Brazil, 50 percent in Bangladesh, and 75 percent in Tanzania.[8]

Table 13.2 shows real prices in food and selected agricultural commodities over the past few decades. Overall, the food price index declined by almost half between 1980 and 2000. Over the first decade of the twenty-first century, however, food prices in general have increased—in 2008 returning nearly to the level of 1980. While the food price index fell during the global recession in 2009, it rose again in the next two years. In 2011, the food price index was 71 percent higher than in 2005. As can be seen, not all agricultural commodities move in lock step. For example, the price of chicken rose in 2009 and rice prices declined in 2010. And over the four decades, from 1970 to 2010, beef prices fell by nearly 40 percent, yet fishmeal prices doubled and banana prices increased by a quarter.[9]

To assess whether food prices will continue to rise, we need to consider the determinants of food supply. As we will see, given the limited ability to expand land under cultivation, growth in the supply of food will depend on gains in agricultural yields. Achieving the technological progress necessary to deliver these advances in farm productivity may be challenging, given the resource constraints and climate change.

THE SUPPLY OF FOOD

Modern growth in agricultural supply has been driven by science, which has significantly increased yields per hectare and output per farm worker. Most of the technological advancements in agriculture (improved seeds, fertilizers, pesticides, and herbicides, more efficient machinery, irrigation systems and cultivation techniques, including satellite technology to forecast and adapt to changing weather conditions) have been created in the developed countries and primarily for mechanized, chemical input-intensive farming. The Green Revolution is an important exception.

The Green Revolution

The **Green Revolution** refers to the enhanced production of basic crops that began in the 1960s with the development of high-yielding varieties of wheat (at the International Maize and Wheat Improvement Center in Mexico) and rice (at the International Rice Research Institute in the Philippines). Combined with irrigation and more intensive applications of fertilizer, the yields of these new varieties of wheat and rice could be two to three times those of the traditional varieties. By the late 1970s, over half the wheat acreage and one third of rice fields in developing countries were planted with the new varieties—especially in Asia, and to some extent in Latin

---

[8]According to the World Bank (2011: Table 2.3), the shares of male and female employment in agriculture, hunting, forestry, and fishing for 2005–08 are respectively: Tanzania (71 and 78 percent), Bangladesh (42 and 68 percent), Brazil (23 and 15 percent) and United States (2 and 1 percent).

[9]The World Bank and IMF (2012: 1–3) report that the sharp rise in world food prices in 2007–08 may have kept or pushed 105 million people in poverty. The rise in food prices in 2010–11 may have added nearly 49 million to the ranks of the poor.

Table 13.2 *Selected agricultural prices (2005 prices)*

	1970	1980	1990	2000	2005	2006	2007	2008	2009	2010	2011
Food Price Index	**165**	**163**	**94**	**86**	**100**	**108**	**128**	**159**	**142**	**150**	**171**
Maize ($/mt)	215	164	113	99	99	119	151	191	151	165	237
Rice ($/mt)	466	539	280	227	286	298	301	555	508	433	442
Wheat ($/mt)	231	250	162	165	198	212	277	388	275	277	358
Soybeans ($/mt)	431	389	255	237	275	263	354	447	400	398	440
Bananas ($/mt)	612	495	559	475	603	663	622	721	775	769	787
Beef (cents/kg)	481	362	265	216	262	249	240	268	241	297	329
Chicken (cents/kg)	...	99	112	147	163	149	159	159	173	168	157
Fishmeal ($/mt)	726	662	426	462	731	1,142	1,084	968	1,125	1,494	1,251

Notes: Where possible the prices received by exporters are used; if export prices are unavailable, the prices paid by importers are used. The constant price series is deflated using a composite index of prices for manufactured exports from the fifteen major developed and emerging economies (converted to US $).

Abbreviations are: *mt* = metric ton; *kg* = kilogram.

Food includes fats and oils (coconut oil, groundnut oil, palm oil, soybeans, soybean oil, and soybean meal), grains (barley, maize, rice, sorghum, and wheat), and other items (bananas, beef, chicken meat, oranges, shrimp, and sugar).

From: World Bank, *World Development Indicators 2012* (Table 6.5)

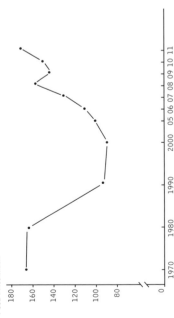

Food Price Index

America.[10] The World Bank (2007: 180) notes that cereal production in Asia doubled between 1970 and 1995, while the total land area cultivated with cereals increased by only 4 percent. The increased agricultural output and associated decline in food prices dramatically reduced poverty, particularly in Asia.

For example, by the mid-1990s, rice yields had risen in the Indian Punjab region (with its reliable water supply and history of agricultural innovation) to 6 tons per hectare, from 2 tons in the 1960s. Since the 1990s, India has become a major net exporter of rice. Yet, as noted earlier, undernutrition remains a major problem in India and South Asia. And, in many parts of Asia there are concerns with environmental damage stemming from an overuse of fertilizer, pesticides, and water (World Bank 2010: 150–151). There is evidence of slower growth in crop yields over the past decade. Planting two crops a year may be taxing the soil (see Barta 2007).[11]

Not all regions of the developing world, moreover, have benefited equally from the Green Revolution. For the most part, sub-Saharan Africa has not benefited much due its greater dependence on rain-fed agriculture (as opposed to irrigation), greater diversity of food crops, poor rural infrastructure, insufficient investment, weak agriculture extension services, and urban-biased policies, including suppressing prices paid to farmers.[12] The World Bank (2007: 180) observes:

> In areas not affected by the green revolution, there has been little if any agricultural intensification; instead, agriculture has grown through extensification—bringing more land under cultivation. This has led to environmental problems of a different kind—mainly the degradation and loss of forests, wetlands, soils, and pastures. Every year about 13 million hectares of tropical forest are degraded or disappear, mainly because of agriculture. Some 10–20 percent of drylands may suffer from land degradation (or desertification).

---

[10]For concise overview of agriculture in developing economies, see Rao (1989). Roberts (2008: 148–149) recounts the research of Norman Borlaug, working for the Rockefeller Foundation, who developed a high-yielding dwarf wheat that revolutionized farming in Mexico and southern Asia, and research at the International Rice Research Institute (another Rockefeller Foundation project) that developed a sturdy, nitrogen-tolerant rice variety that yielded up to six times as much rice as traditional plants and matured so quickly that two and sometimes three crops could be grown in a single year. Roberts (2008: 151) adds that, "because the new dwarf varieties were so short, they couldn't compete with weeds for sunlight and so were largely helpless without additional herbicides. And . . . high-yield plants needed massive amounts of nitrogen and other fertilizers." Parker (2011: 7) explains: "The Green Revolution had little to do with making plants bigger: rather, it produced higher yields by persuading more plants to grow in the same space and by getting them to put less effort into growing stalks and leaves and more into seedpods, the part people eat."

[11]In addition to soil exhaustion, Barta cites water shortages, lagging investment in agriculture, and climate change as contributing factors to the slowdown in the growth rate of crop yields. Hazell (2002) elaborates on the environmental damage:

> Excessive and inappropriate use of fertilizers and pesticides has polluted waterways, poisoned agricultural workers, and killed beneficial insects and other wildlife. Irrigation practices have led to salt build-up and eventual abandonment of some of the best farming lands. Groundwater levels are retreating in some areas where more water is being pumped for irrigation than can be replenished by the rains. And heavy dependence on a few major cereal varieties has led to loss of biodiversity on farms. . . . These problems are slowly being rectified without yield loss, and sometimes with yield increases, thanks to policy reforms and improved technologies and management practices, such as pest-resistant varieties, biological pest control, precision farming, and crop diversification.

[12]See World Bank (2007: 54–55). The dependence of Green Revolution technology on chemical fertilizer, as well as irrigation, encumbered African farmers, who had less access to market inputs, not only improved seeds, but fertilizers. Roberts (2008: 154) cites conservative estimates that more than a third of the yield increase came directly from using more fertilizer. . .in Africa yields fell unless farmers added steadily greater applications of nitrogen and other fertilizers.

Diversity in agricultural conditions

As illustrated throughout this text, there are significant differences across the regions of the developing world. This diversity also applies to agriculture. The World Bank (2007: Chapter 1) identifies three groups of developing nations. The first, agricultural-based economies, mostly in sub-Saharan Africa, are the least developed and the most food-insecure. In the second, transforming economies, mostly in Asia, the Middle East, and North Africa, the policy priorities are reducing rural–urban income disparities by addressing rural poverty. For the third group, urbanized economies, mostly in Eastern Europe and Latin America, the emphasis in policy is linking smallholders to modern food markets and bolstering productive employment.[13]

Some salient facts can be drawn from Table 13.3. With economic development, the share of agriculture in national output, as well as the share of the labor force in farming, declines. In 2010, a fourth of gross domestic product in the low-income economies was accounted for by agriculture (also encompassing forestry and fishing). In contrast, average shares were 8 percent for the upper middle-income economies and 1 percent for the high-income economies. This is reflected also in the faster growth in overall GDP than agriculture across all income levels and areas. Regionally, South Asia is still the most dependent on agriculture. Correspondingly, the least developed nations are the most rural—over 70 percent of their populations in 2010. The share of the population that is rural declines with economic development, despite higher rural than urban fertility rates, predominantly due to rural to urban migration. For the upper middle- and high-income economies, rural populations are declining in numbers, also due to the spread of urban areas. The developing regions of East Asia and the Pacific and Latin America and the Caribbean experienced rural depopulation over the first decade of the twenty-first century.

For the world, between 1990–92 and 2007–09, there was no change in the percentage of land area that is agricultural (including permanent pastures, arable land, and land under permanent crops). Land is most scarce in South Asia, where 55 percent of land area is agricultural, followed by East Asia and the Pacific with 49 percent and sub-Saharan Africa with 45 percent. In Latin America, in contrast, additional land could be brought under cultivation, but at the expense of deforestation. In sub-Saharan Africa, substantial land area is available, but will require heavy investment in infrastructure and agricultural extension services including disease control—both human and animal—in order to be productively used.[14,15]

Globally, land under cereal production declined by almost 3 percent between 1990–92 and 2008–10, although this aggregate masks significant differences: expansion in the low-income economies and contraction in the upper middle- and high-income economies. Sub-Saharan Africa increased its land under cereal production by a third between 1990–92 and 2008–10. Europe

---

[13] In agriculture-based economies, agriculture accounts for a quarter of more of national output (an average of 29 percent of GDP in 2005). Poverty is overwhelmingly rural, with small farmers producing for local consumption. In transforming economies, agriculture accounts for less than a seventh of national output (an average of 13 percent of GDP in 2005), and while still providing employment for over half of the labor force, opportunities for rural nonfarm employment are greater. Rural poverty remains high, and migration to urban areas is increasing. In the developing economies classified as urbanized countries, agriculture contributes less than a tenth of national output (an average 6 percent of GDP in 2005) and has become more integrated in the global market.

[14] Parker (2011: 8) notes that "Africa has some of the most exhausted soils in the world, with less than 1% of organic matter in them, half the level required for good fertility."

[15] In 2009, another 1.0 percent of land area was permanent cropland, defined by the World Bank as "land cultivated with crops that occupy the land for long periods and need not be replanted after each harvest, such as cocoa, coffee, and rubber. Land under flowering shrubs, fruit trees, nut trees, and vines is included, but land under trees grown for wood or timber is not."

395

Table 13.3 Selected statistics on agriculture

	ECONOMIES BY INCOME CLASSIFICATION							
	WORLD	Low	Lower middle	India	Upper middle	China	High	US
Share of agriculture in GDP:								
2010	3%	25%	17%	19%	8%	10%	1%	1%
Ave. annual growth rates 2000–10:								
Agriculture	2.5%	3.7%	3.3%	3.0%	3.6%	4.4%	0.7%	1.9%
GDP	2.7%	5.5%	6.3%	8.0%	6.5%	10.8%	1.8%	1.8%
Share of rural population:								
1990	57%	79%	68%	75%	56%	73%	27%	25%
2010	49%	72%	60%	70%	43%	55%	22%	18%
Agricultural land, (% of land area)								
1990–92	38%	35%	45%	61%	35%	57%	38%	46%
2007–09	38%	38%	47%	61%	34%	56%	37%	44%
Land under cereal production, (million hectares)								
1990–92	699.7	57.5	208.3	99.5	278.6	92.6	155.4	65.9
2008–10	681.9	90.7	209.3	92.6	239.0	90.1	142.9	57.5
Fertilizer consumption (kilograms per hectare of arable land)								
2007–09	122.1	25.9	118.9	167.8	159.4	488.4	104.3	109.3
Cereal yield (kilograms per hectare)								
1990	2,756	1,565	1,928	1,891	3,177	4,325	4,138	4,755
2010	3,568	2,075	2,718	2,537	3,831	5,521	5,319	6,988
Agricultural value added per worker (2000 $)								
1990	$781	$240	$472	$357	$487	$258	$14,129	$18,703
2010	$992	$288	$677	$489	$871	$545	$24,483	$51,120

Table 13.3 continued

ECONOMIES BY REGION

	Sub-Saharan Africa	Middle East & N. Africa	Europe & Central Asia	South Asia	East Asia & Pacific	Latin America & Caribbean	High-income economies
Share of agriculture in GDP:							
2010	13%	...	7%	19%	11%	6%	1%
Ave. annual growth rates 2000–10:							
Agriculture	3.2%	4.6%	2.7%	3.1%	4.1%	2.9%	0.7%
GDP	5.0%	4.7%	5.4%	7.4%	9.4%	3.8%	1.8%
Share of rural population:							
1990	72%	48%	37%	75%	71%	29%	27%
2010	63%	42%	36%	70%	54%	21%	22%
Agricultural land: (% of land area)							
1990–92	42%	24%	29%	55%	48%	34%	38%
2007–09	45%	23%	28%	55%	49%	36%	37%
Land under cereal production: (million hectares):							
1990–92	69.0	31.1	125.3	128.1	142.4	48.5	155.4
2008–10	92.0	27.7	92.8	125.9	150.6	50.0	142.9
Fertilizer consumption (kilograms per hectare of arable land):							
2007–09	10.5	79.5	38.8	176.0	...	92.2	104.3

Table 13.3 *continued*

	ECONOMIES BY REGION						
	Sub-Saharan Africa	Middle East & N. Africa	Europe & Central Asia	South Asia	East Asia & Pacific	Latin America & Caribbean	High-income economies
Cereal yield (kilograms per hectare):							
1990	1,033	1,471	2,596	1,926	3,796	2,089	4,138
2010	1,335	2,379	2,239	2,691	4,925	3,919	5,319
Agricultural value added per worker (2000 $):							
1990	$307	$1,796	$2,245	$373	$305	$2,221	$14,129
2010	$322	...	$3,204	$521	$585	$3,663	$24,483

Notes: Agriculture also includes forestry and fishing.

Agricultural land is permanent pastures, arable land, and land under permanent crops (including cocoa, coffee, rubber, and fruit trees, nut trees, flowering shrubs and vines).

Land under cereal production refers to harvested areas, although some countries report only sown or cultivated areas.

Fertilizer consumption measures the quantity of plant nutrients used per unit of arable land. Fertilizer products cover nitrogen, potash, and phosphate fertilizers, but do not include traditional nutrients such as animal and plant manure.

Cereal yield includes wheat, rice, maize, barley, oats, rye, millet, sorghum, buckwheat, and mixed grains.

Source: World Bank (2012: Tables 3.1, 3.2, 3.3, 4.1, and 4.2).

and Central Asia and the high-income economies decreased the land under cereal production by 26 percent and 8 percent, respectively.

In general, though, land is being used more intensively. The application of chemical fertilizer per hectare of arable land for 2007–09 varies from an average of 26 kilograms in low-income economies to 104 kg in high-income economies. This range, however, vastly understates the diversity across regions and individual countries. Reflecting generally drier conditions and less irrigation, sub-Saharan Africa averaged less than 11 kg of chemical fertilizer per hectare of arable land, compared with an average of 176 kg in South Asia, which, in turn, exceeded by nearly 70 percent the average in high-income economies. At 488 kg per hectare, China's fertilizer intensity is 2.5 times greater than South Asia's, and even so is less than in some other nations, including: Egypt (503), Chile (596), Malaysia (770), Costa Rica (827), New Zealand (1,232), Jordan (2,444), and Qatar (3,192); see World Bank (2012: Table 3.2). As noted earlier and will be discussed further below, there is evidence of diminishing returns, as well as negative externalities, from the use of chemical fertilizers in a number of nations.

In the last two decades, global cereal yields per hectare, a measure of land productivity, have increased by over a quarter. Here, too, substantial differentials can be found, although we should note due to changing weather, sharp shifts in crop yields can occur from one year to the next. Nevertheless, the greatest relative gains were found in the Middle East and North Africa (62 percent), Latin America and the Caribbean (44 percent), and the US (47 percent). In Europe and Central Asia, cereal yields actually fell by 14 percent between 1990 and 2010. In China, cereal yields per hectare in 2010 exceeded the average for the high-income economies, although were well below the US.

Agricultural labor productivity has increased across the board, measured by real value added per worker between 1990 and 2010. In sub-Saharan Africa, from a very low level of labor productivity in 1990, the gain was minimal (only 5 percent). This contrasts dramatically with the gains in the US (173 percent) and the high-income economies (73 percent). The enormous gaps in labor productivity (a ratio of 85 to 1) are evident between the farmers in the high-income economies and those in the low-income economies.

RESOURCE CONCERNS

A decade ago, the agricultural economist, Vernon Ruttan (2002), allowed that the world should be able to increase the production of food to accommodate the expected growth in the demand for food from the growth in population and incomes. There is room for many low-income and middle-income nations to improve agricultural productivity with the adoption of the improved technologies and practices and increased use of modern inputs including fertilizers, irrigation, and agricultural machinery. But he maintained this will require investments in agriculture in the less developed countries, including infrastructure (transportation networks, irrigation systems, storage facilities) and farmer education with agricultural extension services for the dissemination of technologies. Moreover, increased attention must be paid to sustainable development in agriculture—maintaining the capacity to grow food.

With a more cautionary stance, Lester Brown (2009: 5) points to environmental and resource constraints including:

> soil erosion, aquifer depletion, crop-shrinking heat waves, melting ice sheets and rising sea level, and the melting of mountain glaciers that feed major rivers and irrigation systems. In addition, three resource trends are affecting our food supply: the loss of cropland to non-farm uses, the diversion of irrigation water to cities, and the coming reduction in oil supplies.

The environmental concerns facing the world's farmers with deterioration in the resource base, co-evolution of pests and pathogens, and climate change, while interrelated, are addressed in turn below.

Soil conservation

With respect to soil loss and degradation, two issues affecting the food supply are frequently cited. First is the loss of arable land due to urban expansion. As noted, this is a particular concern in the densely populated Asian nations, where there is already evidence of diminishing returns to intensive agriculture. As shown in Table 12.4, in 2009 the world's population used 10.7 percent of the land surface to grow food, which was a decrease from 10.9 percent in 1990 (World Bank 2012: Table 3.1).

The World Bank (2010: 148–149) projects no net increase in the total land under cultivation over the next few generations—with moderate climate change, possible gains in land suitable for agriculture in the northern hemisphere will be largely offset by losses in the southern hemisphere. Consequently, increased crop production will have to rely on productivity gains. And if yields are arguably nearing their maximums in the developed economies, then output growth in agriculture will necessarily have to come from the developing nations as farmers adopt improved practices.

This makes all the more urgent the second concern, the degradation of arable land due to poor management, which has occurred in both developed and developing economies. Land degradation can reflect the overuse of land, for example, overgrazing of pastureland, excessive irrigation leading to waterlogging or salinization, depletion of nutrients with inadequate fallowing of land or too little rotation of crops, and soil erosion with insufficient attention to runoffs.

There are some fairly simple technologies, however, for maintaining the integrity of soils, including no-till farming, rotation of cover crops, planting of trees and the use of natural barriers near cultivated fields, and natural fertilization. For instance, with **zero tillage** or no-till cultivation, farmers do not plow up the fields after harvesting the crop, but use the crop residues as ground cover. Advantages of this technique include conserving soil and reducing greenhouse gas emissions. Zero tillage, though, may require additional herbicides to control the increased weeds, as well as investment in equipment to sink the seeds. Farmers in the US are increasingly adopting zero tillage.

The World Bank (2010: 154) estimated that 100 million hectares, or about 6.3 percent of global arable land, were farmed with minimum tillage in 2008, which was almost twice that in 2001. While mostly in the developed nations, there have been successful adoptions in the less developed economies.[16] For instance, the World Bank cites two states in India in 2007–08, where 1.26 million hectares of wheat were cultivated under minimum tillage. Not only were yields higher by some 5–7 percent, but also costs per hectare were reduced.

> Roberts (2008: 274–275) cites the advantages of simple crop rotation. In the US: using a four-year crop rotation, in which the usual corn-soybean regime is followed by nitrogen-fixing cover crops like alfalfa, and by encouraging populations of deer mice, crickets, and other seed predators that eat weed seeds. . .[farmers] can cut herbicide use by 85 percent and nitrogen inputs by 75 percent—without hurting yields. And because the soils are protected year-round by cover crops, this model dramatically reduces nitrogen leaching and volatilization [resulting in] an intensive legume rotation [that] can cut a farm operation's contribution to global warming by more than 60 percent.

Another green technology is found in southern Africa, where fast-growing "fertilizer" trees such as Gliricida, Sesbania, and Tephrosia have improved soil fertility, water infiltration, and holding capacity. Other benefits include the production of firewood and livestock fodder. In the Sahel, tree planting and simple, low-cost stone bunding (putting stones around the contours of slopes to keep rainwater and soil within the farming area) retain soil nutrients and reduce erosion, leading to higher and more stable yields and incomes (World Bank 2007: 164).[17] The World Bank (2010: 153) cites Zambia, where the "use of leguminous trees and herbaceous cover crops in improved

---

[16]For example, the World Bank (2010: 154) notes that 45 percent of the cropland in Brazil is under zero-tillage practice. Parker (2011: 9–10) discusses how the additional weeds accompanying no-till farming can be countered with plants that are genetically engineered to resist herbicides. Europe, however, has banned the use of this technology. And no-till agriculture was used on only 6 percent of farmland in developing countries in 2008.

[17]As noted by the World Bank (2007: 195), however, farmers will be reluctant to plant trees without secure property rights, accenting the importance of land reform where land holdings are concentrated. See also "New Study Finds 400,000 Farmers in Southern Africa Using 'Fertilizer Trees' to Improve Food Security," *Science Daily* (October 14, 2011) at http://www.sciencedaily.com/releases/2011/10/111014122317.htm. With these fertilizer trees, farmers were able to double the crop yields for maize (corn). Fertilizer trees improve soil fertility by disseminating nitrogen drawn from the air to the soil. The trees also improve water efficiency and reduce soil erosion.

fallow practices increased soil fertility, suppressed weeds, and controlled erosion, thereby almost trebling annual net farm incomes."

Mann (2008) describes measures taken by China to preserve its soils, including the "Green Wall" of China, an initiative begun in 1981, to be completed in 2050, where a 2,800 mile band of trees will retard the soil erosion from dust storms. Another proactive measure is the "three-three" system where Chinese farmers replant a third of their most erosion-prone land with grass and trees, a second third with orchards, and the remaining third intensively with food crops.

With respect to natural fertilization, Mann cites the *zai* technique used in sub-Saharan Africa, where farmers fill foot-deep holes in the fields with manure. Termites are attracted, not only digesting the organic matter, which enhances the nutrients available to plants, but also aerating the soils, which more effectively absorb the rains. Another technique is known as *terra preta*, where charcoal made by burning plants and refuse at low temperatures is spread over the land to improve soil fertility.

Water supply and irrigation

As noted, water scarcity is becoming an increasingly serious constraint in arid and semi-arid regions of the world. Large areas of China, South Asia, and the Middle East and North Africa are now maintaining irrigated food production through unsustainable extractions of water from rivers or the ground (World Bank, 2007: 64).[18] The advantage of irrigated over rain-fed agriculture is clear: irrigated farming is used on one-fifth of the world's farmland, but contributes two-fifths of the world's food output (Parker 2011: 9).[19] Yet, according to the World Bank (2010: 144), "there is little scope for increasing the total area under irrigation. Indeed, irrigated land is expected to increase by just 9 percent between 2000 and 2050."

Unfortunately, mismanagement is common with irrigated croplands, particularly in the failure to charge appropriate user fees. Those with access to the subsidized water, usually the better-off farmers, tend to over-irrigate, resulting in waterlogging (in humid regions) and salinity (in semi-arid and arid regions). Also we find problems with poorly designed and maintained drainage systems. Better management of water and the removal of policies that subsidize water usage will go a long way in addressing the problems of water scarcity. The most efficient water use in agriculture is **drip irrigation**, where pipes and hoses are spread through the fields to introduce water in measured amounts at the appropriate intervals to the base of the plants. Although requiring an initial investment in pipes and hoses as well as a source of water, drip irrigation can be adopted by small farmers.

The World Bank (2010: 144) notes that rain-fed agriculture provides livelihoods for the majority of the world's poor and accounts for more than half of the gross value of the world's crops. Whether rain-fed or irrigated, the productivity of the available water can be enhanced with more effective crop management, including mulching and zero tillage. Moreover, developing drought resistant crops and crops that can be grown in the winter months when less water is required will conserve water.

The demands on water supplies, in turn derived from the demands placed on agriculture by the growing world population and increased consumption of meat, are daunting. The World Bank

---

[18] According to the World Bank (2007: 182–183), an estimated 15–35 percent of total water withdrawals for irrigated agriculture are unsustainable, that is, beyond the regeneration capacities of the water sources. Moreover, the depletion of groundwater resources has required additional pumping of aquifers and resulted in damaging saline intrusion.

[19] Parker notes that farmers will likely need 45 percent more water by 2030, which will be difficult to provide given the expected increasing share of the world's population living in cities.

401

(2010: 148–149) reports that "by 2050 the production of beef, poultry, pork, and milk is expected to at least double from 2000 levels to respond to the demand from larger, wealthier, and more urban populations." And the water intensity of meat production is much greater: particularly beef (15,000 liters of water required per kilogram) versus pork (4,800 liters), chicken (3,900 liters), rice (3,300 liters), wheat (1,300 liters), milk (1,000 liters) and corn (900 liters).

Pesticides and fertilizers

As Ruttan (2002: 172) observes, pests have become an increasingly serious problem in spite of advances in technology—with the increased resistance of the pests and with the spillover effects from the chemicals used in pesticides on the environment and human health. Parker (2011: 10) adds: "Predators wage a constant war on plants, and if farmers do nothing the output of a new seed will decline by a percentage point or so every year. This is why new seeds are needed all the time." Climate change may accentuate the pest problems confronting farmers. Roberts (2008: 219–220) describes how developing nations, in switching from traditional crops to the primary grains such as wheat, corn, rice, and soybeans, often encounter a host of new pests which then require additional pesticide expenditures.[20]

Furthermore, there is evidence that the intensive use of chemical fertilizers is running into diminishing returns in crop yields, particularly in land-constrained Asia.[21] The environmental concerns associated with increased fertilizer use, whether runoffs contributing to water pollution or the emission of nitrous oxide contributing to global warming, are serious. For poor farmers, the increased input costs of chemical fertilizers with the rising prices of fossil fuels often make these inputs prohibitively expensive.

Climate change

As observed in Chapter 12, the phenomenon of global warming is almost universally accepted among climate scientists. The World Bank (2007: 200) illustrated the expected consequences of global warming for agriculture production:

> Under moderate to medium estimates of rising global temperatures (1–3°C) crop-climate models predict a small impact on global agricultural production because negative impacts in tropical and mostly developing countries are offset by gains in temperate and largely industrial countries. . . .

---

[20] Roberts (2008: 220) describes plant pathologists in Uganda in 1999 finding a fungus, known as stem rust, that was destroying the wheat crops. With spores spread easily by wind, the UG99 stem rust then migrated into Kenya, Ethiopia, and Yemen, and was moving north and east, threatening India, China, and even North America with a wheat crop failure.

[21] In particular, evidence of the diminishing returns from chemical fertilizers may be most striking in China. Parker (2011: 10) observes that Chinese grain production has been roughly stable since 1990, despite the increase of about 40 percent in the use of heavily subsidized fertilizer.

There are concerns also in the developed countries. The World Bank (2010: 149) reports:

> Highly productive agriculture, such as is practiced in much of the developed world, is usually based on farms that specialize in a particular crop or animal and on the intensive use of agrochemicals. This kind of farming can damage water quality and quantity. Fertilizer runoff has increased the number of low-oxygen "dead zones" in coastal oceans exponentially since the 1960s: they now cover about 245,000 square kilometers, mostly in coastal waters of the developed world. Intensive irrigation often causes salt to build up in soils, reducing fertility and limiting food production. Salinization currently affects between 20 million and 30 million of the world's 260 million hectares of irrigated land.

For temperature increases above 3°C, yield losses are expected to occur everywhere and be particularly severe in tropical regions. In parts of Africa, Asia, and Central America yields of wheat and maize could decline by around 20 to 40 percent as temperatures rise by 3 to 4°C. . . . Rice yields would also decline, though less than wheat and maize yields.

Later, the World Bank (2010: 133) concluded:

Climate change will make it harder to produce enough food for the world's growing population, and will alter the timing, availability, and quality of water resources. To avoid encroaching into already stressed ecosystems, societies will have to almost double the existing rate of agricultural productivity growth while minimizing the associated environmental damage.

At the same time, agriculture contributes to global warming, directly accounting for approximately one sixth of greenhouse gas emissions, including two of the most potent gases, nitrous oxide from fertilizers and methane released from digesting livestock. As noted by the World Bank (2010: 169), under the Clean Development Mechanism of the Kyoto Protocol (to be discussed in the next chapter), soil carbon sequestration projects in the developing world are unfortunately not eligible for carbon credits.

AN AGENDA FOR RESEARCH AND DEVELOPMENT

The need for increased investment in agriculture in low-income nations, especially land-abundant regions in Africa and South America, is clear. Yet, research and development of crops, seeds, and fertilizers suited for the environmental conditions in these poor countries, as well as assistance for investment in infrastructure and the deployment of improved agricultural technologies, have so far been overall insufficient.

The World Bank (2010: 154) reports that the share of official development assistance for agriculture decreased from 17 percent in 1980 to 4 percent in 2007, despite estimates that rates of return to investment in agricultural research and extension are extremely high (30–50 percent). Moreover, public expenditures on agricultural research and development by the developing nations, while increasing from $6 billion in 1981 to $10 billion in 2000 (2005 PPP dollars), are still modest. Private investments in agricultural research and development have been only 6 percent of this total. Recall that the Green Revolution technology began a half century ago with the development of higher-yielding seeds for wheat and rice at the international research institutes in Mexico and the Philippines. Renewed efforts are warranted to improve agricultural productivity in the low- and middle-income economies.

The Gene Revolution

Advances in technology with selective breeding and genetics with biotechnology (deliberate manipulation of plant DNA molecules to enhance certain characteristics) hold great promise. According to the World Bank (2007: 67), "The world is poised for another technological revolution in agriculture using the new tools of biotechnology to deliver significant yield gains."

In an opinion piece in the *Wall Street Journal* in 2007, Norman Borlaug, the American agronomist and winner of the 1970 Nobel Peace Prize, largely for his contribution to the

403

development of high-yielding wheat for developing nations, asserted that a **Gene Revolution** based on biotechnology could rival, if not surpass, the earlier Green Revolution. For example, herbicide-tolerant corn and soybeans would enhance the adoption of no-till agriculture. Borlaug (2007) argued for additional research on crops such as beans, peanuts, bananas, cassava and yams that are consumed by the poor and on measures to enhance their nutritional content with minerals and vitamins, such as iron, zinc, and vitamin A, deficiency in which can lead to blindness in children and increased susceptibility to infections.[22]

The World Bank (2010: 155) estimated that in 2007, out of the 114 million hectares planted with transgenic crop varieties (mostly insect-resistant or herbicide-tolerant), almost all (over 90 percent) was in just four countries (Argentina, Brazil, Canada, and the US). Moreover, the use of transgenic crops in developing nations has been largely confined to cotton (adopted especially in China and India) and crops used for animal feed (corn and soybeans), certain traits (insect resistance and herbicide tolerance), and countries with commercial farmers (such as Argentina and Brazil); see World Bank (2007: 177–178).[23]

As discussed, sub-Saharan Africa lags well behind other regions of the world in agricultural productivity, and has only marginally benefited from the Green Revolution, in part because of the generally more arid conditions and the overall lack of development. Thus, priority in research and the dissemination of appropriate technologies might be given to this part of the world. After more than 30 years of research, the International Maize and Wheat Improvement Center developed drought-tolerant maize varieties and hybrids that increased yields in eastern and southern Africa (World Bank 2007: 162).

Similarly, we find advances in livestock technology with cross-breeding of dairy cows and improved feeding practices that may be adopted by even small farmers. Nevertheless, while genetically modified crops and animals offer potential gains in productivity, the majority of developing-country farmers have not been able to take advantage, often due to the difficulties in delivering the new technologies to the farmers and their limited ability to afford market inputs. In addition, there is some risk-averseness on the part of the traditional farmers, given their modest educations and marginal incomes.

---

[22] As an earlier example, Monsanto announced in 2000 that it would give away certain patent rights to speed the use of genetically modified rice that could save millions of malnourished children in poor countries from dying or going blind. The so-called "golden rice" is enriched in beta carotene, a building block of vitamin A. See *Charlotte Observer* (August 4, 2000), page 19A. Later that month, it was also reported that:

> thousands of rice farmers in China have doubled the yields of their most valuable crop and nearly eliminated its most devastating disease—without using chemical treatments or spending a single extra penny.
>
> Under the direction of an international team of scientists. . .instead of planting the large stands of a single type of rice, as they have done, the farmers planted a mixture of two different rices. With this one change, growers were able to radically restrict the incidence of rice blast—the most important disease of this most important staple in the world. Within just two years, farmers were able to abandon the chemical fungicides previously used to fight the disease.

See "New strategy doubles rice farmers yields," *Charlotte Observer* (August 22, 2000), page 2A.

[23] The World Bank (2010: 151) also cautioned against dismissing traditional seeds varieties:

> older varieties of wheat or barley may grow faster and have an advantage over more modern varieties introduced in the late 20th century. Furthermore, the wild relatives of today's crops contain genetic material that may be useful to make commercial crops more adaptable to changing conditions.

The Svalbard Global Seed Vault, located in a mountain on an island between Norway and the North Pole, is a secure storage facility for duplicates of all the seed samples from the world's crops. It serves as a library for seeds—in effect, knowledge assets embodied in natural capital. See http://www.croptrust.org/main/content/svalbard-global-seed-vault?item=211.

Biofuels and food production

As shown earlier, in the last few years, the long-run downward trend in real agricultural prices has been reversed, with especially sharp increases in agricultural prices in 2008. In addition to the growth in the demand for food, especially from China and India, one of the contributing factors has been the increased diversion of crops from food and livestock feed to biofuels, intended to stem the sharply higher prices for gasoline. Parker (2011: 6) observed that ethanol accounted for less than 10 percent of the fuel for America's vehicles, but consumed almost 40 percent of the corn crop.

In the United States ethanol production, heavily subsidized by the government, is particularly unfortunate, since corn is not the most efficient crop to make biofuel. As noted by the World Bank (2007: 71), "The grain required to fill the tank of a sport utility vehicle with ethanol (240 kilograms of maize for 100 liters of ethanol) could feed one person for a year." In fact, most current biofuel programs are not economically viable so are possible only with substantial subsidization. An exception might be Brazil, widely recognized as the world's most efficient producer of biofuels, based on its low-cost production of sugar cane. The US, however, has restricted the imports of sugar-based ethanol from Brazil with high tariffs, protecting inefficient domestic ethanol production.[24]

This is not to say that biofuels will not have a role to play in renewable energy production. Continued research into more efficient, environmentally sustainable biofuels, with lower opportunity costs for food production, should be pursued. In particular, the World Bank (2010: 147) points to "second-generation biofuels under development, such as algae, *jatropha*, sweet sorghum, and willows, [that] could reduce competition with agricultural land for food crops by using less land or marginal land [although maybe resulting in] the loss of pasture land and grassland ecosystems."

THE NEED FOR POLICY REFORM

With the challenges facing world agriculture, there is need for policy reforms. In the industrial or developed nations, economic policies have been biased in favor of agriculture—notwithstanding the small shares of their labor forces engaged in farming—due to the influence of powerful agribusiness and strong agricultural lobbies. In the developing nations—despite the large shares of the labor forces engaged in farming—economic policies have tended to be biased against agriculture, a reflection of the lack of influence of the multitude of small farmers.

The developed countries

The industrial countries have often hindered the development of agriculture in the less developed nations through their farm policies. In addition to price supports and subsidies that directly bolster farm incomes, import barriers have been used to protect domestic farmers and, by extension, promote domestic agribusinesses.[25] The result often has been surplus agricultural production by

---

[24] Beginning in 2012 the federal tax credit for ethanol in the US expired, largely due to federal budget concerns. With the end of these subsidies, the nearly 40 percent share of the nation's corn crop going for ethanol production will certainly decline. In 2011 the tax credit cost the government nearly $6 billion (Pear 2012). Also, the US Congress eliminated the import tariff on ethanol, which should sharply increase Brazil's exports of sugar-cane-based ethanol (Mead 2012).

[25] Excerpts from a *Wall Street Journal* editorial ("The No Farmer Left Behind Act," November 14, 2007, p. A16) illustrate the problem:

the developed countries, which is then dumped on the world market, suppressing prices and incomes of farmers in developing countries.

Agriculture remains one of the most heavily protected sectors in world trade, to the detriment of agricultural development in the economically developing nations. As described by the World Bank (2007: 10–11), progress in trade liberalization has been slow: the average support to agricultural producers in OECD member nations declined only from 37 percent of the gross value of farm receipts in 1986–88 to 30 percent in 2003–05. The potential gains for the developing nations from the industrial nations in eliminating the agricultural trade barriers, however, were estimated to be five times the current levels of overseas development assistance to agriculture.[26]

The outlook for trade liberalization is uncertain at best. The latest round (i.e., the Doha Round) of multilateral trade negotiations foundered largely over the issue of agricultural protection by the US, the European Union, and Japan. In 2008, negotiations were effectively suspended. In fact, as the World Bank (2010: 160) reports, the sharp rise in agricultural prices in 2008, reflecting tight supply conditions, led some food-producing nations to restrict exports. For example, India banned exports of rice and pulses and Argentina increased export taxes on beef, maize, soybeans, and wheat.

Reducing scale

Roberts (2008) calls for a new system of agriculture in the US with more integrated farming through the promotion of mid-scale farms, between 50 and 500 acres in size, with greater attention to sustainable practices.[27] But he notes that small farms producing for local consumption, while appealing in terms of community identification and more organic methods, will not be able to meet the demand for food in the US, much less generate the surpluses for export. And, with respect to global warming, local production may not always be the best option. Roberts (2008: 286) gives the following example:

> because New Zealand farmers use far less fertilizer than their counterparts in the United Kingdom do and because New Zealand sheep feed almost entirely on grass whereas UK livestock are mainly grain-fed, consumers in the UK importing New Zealand mutton and dairy

---

About $4 out of every $5 in the Senate [farm] bill go straight into the pockets of the growers of five commercial crops: corn, cotton, rice, soybeans, and wheat.

. . .The powerful sugar, honey and dairy lobbies have also won expansions of their price supports. . .even though the WTO ruled last month that US cotton subsidies violate American trade agreements. The USDA says about two-thirds of this farm aid goes to the wealthiest 10% of farms.

. . .The biggest winners are corn producers, as corn prices have doubled in two years, thanks in part to new mandates for ethanol.

In 2012, however, largely due to federal budget concerns, the US Congress began sharply cutting back on subsidies to farmers.

[26]The World Bank (2010: 172) notes that the OECD member countries provide $258 billion every year in support to their farmers (23 percent of farm earnings). However, some reform is evident with the European Union's Common Agricultural Policy, making income support to farmers conditional on good environmental practices. The World Bank and IMF (2012: 8) remark: "Surprisingly, the aid directed toward agriculture, food, and nutrition—10 percent of total commitments in 2010—has not increased in response to the recent food price spikes or since the MDGs were agreed in 2000."

[27]Roberts (2008: 279) observes that in the US "just 163,000 mega-farms, representing a third of the agricultural land base, generate 60% of our food." Small farms are unlikely to be able to produce the volumes of food needed. The half million mid-size farms, however, could provide the foundation for a sustainable system of food production, one that might not only be more environmentally friendly, but also reduce the transport costs of getting the produce to the markets.

products actually cut energy use and climate impacts by 75% and 50%, respectively, over locally produced items.

Obstacles to reform include the large agribusinesses, from the corporate farms to the chemical companies, as well as consumers who might well resist paying higher prices for food produced more safely and incorporating all the involved externalities, such as water pollution and global warming. Moreover, sustainability in the world food supply will likely entail a modification of the Western diet, especially reduced consumption of meat.

Food safety

There is growing anxiety in the developed countries over the safety of the food supply. The increased reliance on chemicals in the mass production of food by the large agribusinesses that control markets has been controversial. Examples of unsafe products include the contamination of foods with salmonella (e.g., from tainted peanut butter in the US in 2010) and *E. coli* (e.g., from contaminated vegetables consumed in Germany in 2011), and the outbreak of new diseases (e.g., avian flu). Roberts (2008: 177) observes: "Despite dramatic advances in food production, preservation, and packaging, food-borne diseases continue to strike some seventy-six million Americans—one in four—each year...with 325,000 requiring hospitalization, and of these, anywhere from 5,000 to 9,000 die."

The promotion and use of genetically modified crops and livestock have met with some resistance. Reasons include a reluctance to increase reliance on powerful Western agribusinesses, fear of vulnerability to crop loss with greater genetic uniformity, and possible environmental and health risks. As the World Bank (2010: 155) clearly states, though: "After more than 10 years of experience, there has been no documented case of negative human health impacts from GM food crops, yet popular acceptance is still limited."

Nevertheless, continued vigilance is in order. For example, the increased use of antibiotics and other practices (e.g., cramped, filthy conditions for livestock and poultry) to maximize meat production not only may be unhealthy to humans but also is considered by many to be inhumane. So, too, the increased reliance of food companies on chemicals for sweetening, enriching the appearance, and preserving the shelf life of processed foods may yet prove unhealthy.

The less developed countries

The policy bias in the less developed nations against agriculture has been most severe in sub-Saharan Africa, a region plagued by political instability, corruption, disease, and poverty. Examples of policies that have discriminated against agricultural development include state marketing boards which suppressed the prices paid to farmers, overvalued currencies which undermined international competitiveness, and insufficient investment in agriculture, whether for rural infrastructure, research and development, or the dissemination of technology.

The potential for agricultural development with more enlightened policies can be dramatic. Consider China, where the World Bank (2007: 46) cites agricultural reforms, including user rights for rural households to farm the land, increased government procurement prices, and the adoption of higher-yielding varieties of rice as contributing to the decline in the incidence of rural poverty from 76 percent in 1980 to 12 percent in 2001.

One of the major contributions of the Green Revolution has been improving the incomes of small farmers, since this technology could be used on small farms when high-yielding seeds are complemented by irrigation and chemical fertilizers. The World Bank (2007: 46) also points to India, where rural poverty was reduced from 64 percent in 1967 to 34 percent in 1986, aided by land reform and rural credit. Yet, while dramatically increasing its food production to the point of exporting, many in India remain undernourished. As Table 10.4 showed earlier, over 40 percent of children under 5 in India are severely underweight or stunted.

In fact, the Food and Agriculture Organization of the United Nations estimated that 925 million people in the developing nations were undernourished in 2010 (FAO 2010). Twenty-two nations were identified as in a "protracted crisis," where the incidence of hunger is persistently high, 40 percent or more of the populations. Seventeen of these nations were in sub-Saharan Africa.[28] In these countries the chronic malnutrition more reflects turmoil and destitution than an inability to produce enough food.

In 2008, after sharp increases in food prices, Joachim von Braun, the head of the International Food Policy Research Institute (IFPRI), warned that "World agriculture has entered a new, unsustainable, and politically risky period."[29] Food riots in countries all along the equator (e.g., Haiti, Cameroon, and Egypt) were all too real evidence. Sharp increases in food prices especially hurt the poor, whose meager incomes already are stretched to provide for basic needs. In a provocative article, however, Banerjee and Duflo (2011) argue that even extremely poor households may have discretionary income, that is, more than enough to afford a minimal, albeit bland, diet.[30] Citing spending by poor households on alcohol, tobacco, festivals, ceremonies, and even televisions, Banerjee and Duflo suggest that subsidizing basic food stuffs to ensure essential nutritional needs may allow the poor to shift to a more varied, palatable diet. The World Bank and IMF (2012: 7–8), however, observe:

> The cereal import bill of low-income food-deficit countries was $31.8 billion in 2010–11 (29 percent more than in 2009–10), despite higher production in 2010 and the lower volume of cereal imports required. North Africa and the Pacific Islands suffered the largest negative impact, paying higher prices and importing more cereals to meet domestic demand. Although the estimated cereal import bill of the food-deficit countries is still below the record set during the 2008 food crisis, the increase in cereal costs, combined with price increases for other food and fertilizer imported by these countries, is cause for concern.

Rural poverty

The need to invest in agricultural development reflects not only the importance of boosting the supply of food, but also efforts to eradicate poverty. The World Bank (2007: 1) observes that:

> Three of every four poor people in developing countries live in rural areas—2.1 billion living on less than $2 a day and 880 million living on less than $1 a day—and most depend on agriculture for their livelihoods.

---

[28] The 22 nations (with per capita GNIs in 2010 in PPP dollars in parentheses, where available) identified in 2010 as being in a protracted crisis were: Afghanistan ($1,060), Angola ($5,410), Burundi ($400), Central African Republic ($790), Chad ($1,220), Congo ($3,220), Côte d'Ivoire ($1,810), Democratic People's Republic of Korea (–), Democratic Republic of the Congo ($320), Eritrea ($540), Ethiopia ($1,040), Guinea ($1,020), Haiti ($1,180), Iraq ($3,370), Kenya ($1,680), Liberia ($340), Sierra Leone ($830), Somalia (–), Sudan ($2,030), Tajikistan ($2,140), Uganda ($1,250), and Zimbabwe (–).

[29] From "The new face of hunger," *The Economist* (April 19, 2008), pp. 32–34.

[30] Banerjee and Duflo (2011) also argue that as arduous work declines with economic development, so would the calories required for a sufficient diet.

As defined by the FAO (2010: 8), food security exists "when all people, at all times, have physical, social, and economic access to sufficient, safe, and nutritious food that meets their dietary needs and food preferences for an active and healthy life." The key to food security is alleviating poverty. And essential for alleviating poverty is economic development and investing in people. As the parable states: give someone a fish and you feed them for a day; teach them how to fish and they can feed themselves.

Food-insecure countries should be a priority for international assistance, not just the humanitarian relief during crises of natural disasters, civil wars, and famine, but more regular aid to increase their capacities for producing food. Weak governance and unsustainable livelihood systems are common features afflicting nations identified by the FAO as in "protracted crises". Small farmers in developing nations, however, can be economically viable when they have secure land title and an incentive to invest in their farms, access to bank credit, market inputs (improved seeds, fertilizers, technical assistance), and receive fair prices for their produce. Often the rural infrastructure is sorely lacking, with insufficient storage facilities and means for transporting the produce to markets. Much of the food produced is lost to pests or is wasted due to inadequate storage or spoils on the way to the market.[31] One encouraging development has been the use of cell phones to allow farmers to check on prices in markets so that they know when to sell.

As illustrated with the Green Revolution, when given such support small farmers respond. Enhancing the domestic capacity for food production not only will increase the incomes of the farmers in developing economies, but also could significantly improve the nutrition of the poor. Greater access to the markets of the developed countries will allow these nations to realize their comparative advantages in agriculture.

Promoting smallholder agriculture is only part of rural development. Investing in schools, health clinics, public utilities that supply electric power and safe water, and microfinance institutions for saving and credit are all important. Accompanying the advances in agriculture will be growth of commerce and industry in nearby towns, providing livelihoods outside of farming. Described earlier in this chapter was an agenda for research and development of crops and techniques especially suited to the conditions in the developing nations, including hardier, drought-resistant, fortified plants, natural fertilizers, and renewable energy.

Better forecasting of weather with dissemination of meteorological information, especially with increased variability in climates, will be important for planting, growing, and harvesting. Satellite systems can collect and relay such information to farmers across the world.

We conclude this chapter on the global food supply with a brief discussion of fishing. In fact, the rise of aquaculture may be increasingly important for feeding the world population.

---

[31] Parker (2011: 10) documents the waste:

Both in rich countries and poor, a staggering 30–50% of all food produced rots away uneaten. . . .

In poor countries, most food is wasted on or near the farms. Rats, mice and locusts eat the crops in the fields or in storage. Milk and vegetables spoil in transit. . . .

Rich countries waste about the same amount of food as poor ones, up to half of what is produced, but in quite different ways. Studies in America and Britain find that a quarter of food from shops goes straight into the rubbish bin or is thrown away by shops and restaurants. Top of the list come salads, about half of which are chucked way. A third of all bread, a quarter of fruit and a fifth of vegetables—all are thrown out uneaten.

FISHING

As in farming, small-scale fishing operations can be economically viable, especially in developing economies. The necessary capital investment (mainly boats and nets) may be fairly modest for fishing in rivers, lakes, or near the sea coast. Deep-sea fishing, where the fish are caught, processed, and frozen on board factory ships, is a more capital-intensive venture. As with plantation agriculture and the growing of cash crops, large-scale fishing is often geared to export markets.

Fishing stocks can be sustained when properly managed, that is, when not fished beyond the potential for regeneration or damaged by pollution. But here is where an important difference with agriculture exists. In agriculture, access to the land is usually well defined, whether or not farmers actually working the land also own it. In contrast, property rights in fishing are less clearly established—especially in international waters. In some traditional fishing communities, the fishing grounds may be communally "owned"—with access determined by mutual agreement. Such common property resources, however, can break down with population growth (more fishermen competing for a livelihood) or technological change (yielding increased catches per fisherman). Unless carefully managed, common property can deteriorate into open access, with potential depletion of the fishing stocks. Unfortunately, this has already happened. As reported by the World Bank (2010: 157):

> Even without climate change, between 25 and 30 percent of marine fish stocks are over-exploited, depleted, or recovering from depletion—and are thus yielding less than their maximum sustainable yields. About 50 percent of stocks are fully exploited and producing catches at or close to their maximum sustainable yields, with no room for further expansion.

Further evidence that increased use of a resource results in diminishing productivity is provided by Grimond (2009: 12).

> in over-exploited waters the fish tend to be smaller and younger. Among those caught in the Pacific, the average length of an English sole fell from about 34 cm in the 1960s to 30 cm in 2002, a Pacific barracuda from nearly 80 cm in the 1950s to 65 cm in 1970, a bocaccio from over 50 cm in the 1970s to nearer 45 cm in the 1990s.

Consequently, there have been calls for increased regulation, including tradable fishing permits, to limit the catching of fish in the oceans within sustainable levels.[32]

Grimond (2009: 15–17) points to Iceland as a model for sustainable fishing within its 200-mile exclusive economic zone. Individual transferable quotas are allocated to fishing boats with shares based on the average catch over the previous three-year period. Any by-catch (collateral fish caught) has to be landed and counted as part of the individual quotas.[33] Some fishing grounds are closed during spawning season and nursery areas for fish are off-limits. Enforcement is strict, with fines, license suspensions, and even imprisonment for offenders.

---

[32] Sachs (2007) also calls for reduced subsidies for ocean fishing and outlawing bottom trawling, whereby the ocean dragged with large nets that sweep up large amounts of unintended fish in the by-catch.

[33] As Diamond (205: 480) explains, by-catch (including unwanted fish species, juveniles of the desired species, seals, dolphins, sharks, and sea turtles) accounts for one-fourth to two-thirds of the total catch, and is usually thrown overboard. He enjoins that by-catch can be reduced with improved fishing gear and diligence, citing a 50-fold reduction in dolphin mortality in the eastern Pacific tuna fishery.

A Blue Revolution

While yields from ocean fishing may be declining, the growth of **aquaculture**, or fish farm-ing, has been rapid—an average 7 percent annual rate in recent decades. Will there be a **Blue Revolution** in fish farming, one comparable to the earlier Green Revolution in agriculture? In fact, Sachs (2007) reports that aquaculture production increased 25-fold over the last six decades: from 2 million metric tons in 1950 to nearly 50 million metric tons in 2007. China alone accounts for two-thirds of total aquaculture harvested by volume and half by value. According to the World Bank (2010: 157), fish and shellfish supply about 8 percent of the world animal protein consumed, with aquaculture contributing 46 percent of the world's fish food supply in 2006. Yet, here too there are concerns.

With aquaculture, fish are raised in contained areas off coasts, so the issue of property rights is clearer. The concentration of fish, however, has consequences for the environment.

> Unfortunately, fish farming is still in its infancy and in some places may do more harm than good. In Indonesia, Thailand, Vietnam and other parts of Asia, huge swathes of coastline have been denuded of trees to make way for ponds and pens. Many fish farms create pollution too. Even if the water in which the fish are reared starts out fresh, the build-up of feces and uneaten food soon makes it foul. The mix is made even nastier by the pesticides and antibiotics needed to keep the crop alive. And to cap it all, aquaculture produces CO_2 and gobbles up energy.
>
> (Grimond 2009: 11)

The World Bank (2010: 158) adds: "Coastal aquaculture has been responsible for 20 to 50 percent of the loss of mangroves worldwide. . . . Aquaculture can also result in the discharge of wastes into marine ecosystems that in some areas contributes to eutrophication."

Farmed fish require feed, usually wild fish. The World Bank (2010: 158) illustrates: "the pro-duction of one kilogram of salmon, marine finfish, or shrimp in aquaculture systems is highly resource-intensive, requiring between 2.5–5 kilograms of wild fish as feed for one kilogram of food produced." Consequently, the growth in aquaculture might better be fueled by plant-based feeds for the raised fish, rather than fish meal.

Not surprisingly, climate change will compound the challenges.

> Rising seas, more severe storms, and saltwater intrusion in the main river deltas of the tropics will damage aquaculture, which is based on species with limited saline tolerance, such as catfish in the Mekong Delta. Higher water temperatures in temperate zones may exceed the optimal temperature range of cultivated organisms. And as temperatures rise, diseases affecting aquaculture are expected to increase both in incidence and impact.
>
> (World Bank 2010: 157–158)

In short, climate change will call for better management, including more sustainable feed for the farmed fish, better circulation of the water, and absorption of the wastes.

CONCLUSION

With renewed investments in agriculture, continued research and development and dissemination of knowledge, conservation of the environment with attention to soil loss, deforestation, and climate change, improved efficiencies in water use and organic fertilizers, and implementation of renewable energies on the supply side, combined with reduced population growth and adoption of healthier diets on the demand side, the world should be able to fend off the Malthusian specter of inadequate food supplies and achieve sustainable development in agriculture. This will not be easy.

It will take international cooperation and renewed efforts to be able to meet the first Millennium Development Goal: eradicating extreme poverty and hunger. Unfortunately, as assessed by the United Nations Development Group (2010: 6), the target of reducing by half the proportion of people who suffer from hunger is "among the worst performing of all MDG targets. . . . Reducing hunger and undernutrition will be critical to the success of the other MDGs, particularly those relating to poverty, education, gender, child mortality, maternal mortality and health."

In sum, the world has the means and the knowledge to eliminate hunger. Whether there is the will remains to be seen. In the next chapter we turn to the role of government in the economy, in particular, when government action is required to address market failures.

KEY TERMS

aquaculture	Blue Revolution
drip irrigation	Gene Revolution
Green Revolution	zero tillage

QUESTIONS

1. In the low-income nation of Guinea-Bissau, data indicate 17 percent of children under 5 are overweight and 17 percent are underweight. Discuss why child malnutrition is a concern. What policies should be implemented in Guinea-Bissau to improve child nutrition?

2. Do you think there is a relationship between the high income, time constraints, fast food, and obesity in the United States? As with cigarettes, should there be an additional excise tax on fast food and soft drinks? Discuss.

3. The World Bank (2007) classified Ghana, as an agriculture-based country, Thailand as a transforming country, and Mexico as an urbanized country. Using the latest *World Development Indicators*, collect data on the three economies for the share of GDP from agriculture (including forestry and fishing), the share of the population that is rural, the cereal yield (kilograms per hectare), and agricultural value added per worker.

4. What can the developed economies—in particular, the United States and the high-income nations in Europe—do to improve the global food supply?

5. Will the Gene Revolution ensure that the global food supply will keep pace with population? Discuss.

6. Is the Blue Revolution the answer to the depletion of the oceans fish stocks? Discuss.

REFERENCES

Banerjee, Abhijit and Esther Duflo. 2011. "More Than 1 Billion People Are Hungry in the World: But What If the Experts Are Wrong?" *Foreign Policy*, May/June.

Barta, Patrick. 2007. "Feeding Billions, a Grain at a Time," *Wall Street Journal*, July 28. http://online.wsj.com/article/SB118556810848880619.html.

Bhattacharya, Jay and Neeraj Sood. 2011. "Who Pays for Obesity?" *Journal of Economic Perspectives* 25(1): 139–158.

Borlaug, Norman. 2007. "Continuing the Green Revolution," *Wall Street Journal*, September 18: A15.

Brown, Lester. 2009. "Feeding Eight Billion People Well," in *Plan B 4.0: Mobilizing to Save Civilization*. New York: W. W. Norton: 216–238.

Diamond, Jared. 2005. *Collapse: How Societies Choose to Fail or Succeed*. New York: Viking.

Food and Agricultural Organization. 2010. *The State of Food Insecurity in the World: Addressing food insecurity in protracted crises*. Rome: FAO.

Grimond, John. 2009. "Troubled Waters: A Special Report on the Sea," *The Economist*, January 3.

Hazell, Peter. 2002. *Green Revolution: Curse or Blessing?* Washington, DC: International Food Policy Research Institute.

Mann, Charles. 2008. "Our Good Earth," *National Geographic*, September: 88–107.

Mead, Derek. 2012. With Tariff Gone, US and Brazil Can Trade Ethanol without Restrictions. *Greentech Media*, January 11. http://www.greentechmedia.com/articles/read/With-Tariff-Gone-U.S.-and-Brazil-Can-Freely-Trade-Ethanol/.

Parker, John. 2011. "The 9 Billion-people Question: A Special Report on Feeding the World," *The Economist*, February 26.

Pear, Robert. 2012. "After Three Decades, Tax Credit for Ethanol Expires," *New York Times*, January 1. http://www.nytimes.com/2012/01/02/business/energy-environment/after-three-decades-federal-tax-credit-for-ethanol-expires.html.

Rao, S. K. 1989. "Agriculture and Economic Development," in John Eatwell, Murray Milgate, and Peter Newman (eds), *The New Palgrave Economic Development*. New York: W. W. Norton: 43–51.

Roberts, Paul. 2008. *The End of Food*. Boston: Houghton Mifflin.

Ruttan, Vernon. 2002. "Productivity Growth in World Agriculture: Sources and Constraints," *Journal of Economic Perspectives* 16(4): 161–184.

Sachs, Jeffrey. 2007. "The Promise of the Blue Revolution (Extended Version)," *Scientific American*, June 17. http://www.scientificamerican.com/article.cfm?id=the-promise-of-the-blue-revolution-extended.

Sen, Amartya. 1981. "Ingredients of Famine Analysis: Availability and Entitlements," *Quarterly Journal of Economics*, 96(3): 433–464.

United Nations Department of Economic and Social Affairs. 2011. *The Millennium Development Goals Report 2011*. New York: United Nations.

United Nations Development Group. 2010. *Thematic Paper on MDG 1: Eradicate Extreme Poverty and Hunger*. New York: United Nations. http://www.undg.org/docs/11421/MDG1_1954-UNDG-MDG1-LR.pdf.

Wines, Michael. 2006. "Malnutrition Is Cheating Its Survivors, and Africa's Future," *New York Times*, December 28.

World Bank. 2007. *World Development Report 2008: Agriculture for Development*. Washington, DC: World Bank.

World Bank. 2010. "Managing Land and Water to Feed Nine Billion People and Protect Natural Systems," in *World Development Report 2010: Development and Climate Change*, Washington, DC: World Bank: 133–187.

World Bank. 2012. *World Development Indicators 2012*. Washington, DC: World Bank.

World Bank and International Monetary Fund. 2012. *Food Prices, Nutrition, and the Millennium Development Goals*, Global Monitoring Report 2012. Washington, DC: World Bank.

Chapter 14

Markets and the role of governments

In general, economists promote free markets, citing the market mechanism, where prices adjust to equilibrate demand and supply, as the most efficient method for allocating resources. Perfect competition is the embodiment of the market mechanism, just as democracy is the embodiment of a free and egalitarian political system. In perfect competition many buyers and many sellers of a homogeneous good compete, with no one party exerting any market power. Consumers vote with their dollars, seeking to maximize their satisfaction derived from their expenditures on goods and services. Firms compete for these dollar votes by producing the goods and services demanded. To maximize profits, a firm must produce the goods and services as efficiently as possible by minimizing its costs.

MARKET EQUILIBRIUM

To begin, a **market** is any arrangement by which buyers and sellers exchange a well-defined product. In a competitive market, many buyers and sellers interact to determine the market equilibrium price and quantity transacted over any given period. The **equilibrium price** is that price that equates the quantity demanded with the quantity supplied. In other words, the equilibrium price "clears" the market with zero excess quantity demanded.

Any departure from this market-clearing price would be corrected naturally by market forces. Too low a price results in an excess quantity demanded (shortage) that would induce a price increase. Conversely, too high a price gives an excess quantity supplied (surplus), resulting in a price decrease. In each case the price level would adjust to clear the market in that period.

Given the factors underlying the market demand (e.g., number of demanders, average incomes, tastes and preferences, and prices of related goods) and the factors underlying the market supply (e.g., input costs, technology, number of suppliers, and government regulations), this equilibrium would persist. A change in any one of these factors would shift the demand or supply curves and upset any initial balance in the system. The market would tend to adjust, however, and a new equilibrium would be achieved. For example, advances in the technology of production would increase the market supply (shifting the supply curve right or down), creating a surplus at the initial market equilibrium price. The price would fall, increasing the quantity demanded until a new and lower equilibrium price and higher quantity transacted were attained.

PERFECT COMPETITION

In perfect competition there are many demanders and many suppliers of a homogeneous good or service. An example of perfect competition would be the market for fresh shrimp in a coastal city: the shrimp caught are indistinguishable across the suppliers. As such, perfectly competitive firms are **price-takers**, accepting the market price (e.g., dollars per pound of fresh shrimp) as given.[1] Every market participant is a price-taker, accepting the market equilibrium price as given for all transactions. Moreover, **freedom of entry and exit** characterizes perfectly competitive markets. No potential demanders or suppliers are hindered from participating in the market, nor are there any restrictions on leaving the market. It may seem ironic, but perfectly competitive firms do not actually compete against each other. Examples that approach perfect competition are the market for unskilled labor and the markets for farm produce.

Adjustment with economic profits

With freedom of entry to the market, long-run equilibrium is defined by **zero economic profits**, that is, all firms are earning revenues sufficient to cover their costs of production, including a normal return on the invested capital. **Positive economic profits** would attract new firms. Existing firms enjoying positive economic profits may invest in additional physical capital—if not already operating at the minimum of their long-run average cost curves. The resulting increase in the market supply, the aggregation of the individual firm supply curves (the short-run marginal cost (MC) curves above the average variable cost (AVC) curves), would drive down the market price until zero economic profits prevailed.[2]

Negative economic profits, where firms' revenues fall short of their costs, including a normal return on the invested capital, may result in firms exiting the market, if their revenues do not even cover their variable costs, or downsizing, where firms do not replace the depreciated capital. With negative economic profits, the market supply curve shifts left. Consequently, the market price is driven up until zero economic profits are attained. As discussed in the previous example, in long-run equilibrium under perfect competition, the market price will just equal the average total cost of production for the firm.

Figure 14.1 illustrates the long-run equilibrium for a perfectly competitive firm i. The market price, P_0, is exogenous to the firm. The profit-maximizing output, Q_{i0}, is where the market price,

---

[1] The decision rule for a firm in selecting the profit-maximizing output is to set marginal revenue equal to marginal cost. To derive this condition, we begin with the firm's short-run profit function, $\Pi(Q) = R(Q) - STC(Q) = P(Q) \cdot Q - STC(Q)$, where the revenues of the firm, $R(Q)$ are the product of the firm's unit price, $P(Q)$, for its output and its output Q, and the short-run total costs of the firm, $STC(Q)$ are the sum of its total variable costs, $TVC(Q)$, and total fixed costs, TFC. To maximize profits, Π, the firm sets the first derivative of the profit function with respect to output equal to zero, $d\Pi(Q)/dQ = dR(Q)/dQ - dSTC(Q)/dQ = [dP(Q)/dQ] \cdot Q + P(Q) \cdot (dQ/dQ) - dSTC(Q)/dQ = 0$. The first two terms, $[dP(Q)/dQ] \cdot Q + P(Q) \cdot (dQ/dQ)$, represent the firm's **marginal revenue**, MR(Q). The firm's **marginal cost**, MC(Q) is given by $dSTC(Q)/dQ$. Thus the general condition for profit maximization is MR(Q) − MC(Q) = 0 or MR(Q) = MC(Q). That is, the firm sets output where the marginal revenue (the gain in revenue from the last unit produced) equals the marginal cost of production of the last unit.

A perfectly competitive firm takes the market price, P_0, as given, so $dP(Q)/dQ = 0$. Therefore the first-order condition for profit maximization is $P(Q) - MC(Q) = P_0 - MC(Q) = 0$, or the firm sets its output where the marginal cost of production equals the market price of the output, which equals the marginal revenue of the output for a firm that is a price-taker.

There is a second-order condition for profit maximization. Differentiating the first order condition again with respect to output gives $d[d\Pi(Q)/dQ]/dQ = d[dR(Q)/dQ]/dQ - d[dSTC(Q)/dQ]/dQ = dMR(Q)/dQ - dMC(Q)/dQ$. For a maximum we need $d[d\Pi(Q)/dQ]/dQ$ to be negative, which means $dMR(Q)/dQ < dMC(Q)/dQ$, that is, at the profit-maximizing output, the slope of the marginal revenue curve must be less than the slope of the marginal cost curve.

For a perfectly competitive firm the slope of the marginal revenue curve is zero, since the firm's marginal revenue curve is also its demand curve, which is perfectly elastic at the market price, P_0. Thus, only the positively sloped portion of the perfectly competitive firm's marginal cost curve is relevant.

[2] The short-run supply curve for a perfectly competitive firm is that portion of its marginal cost curve that rises above the minimum of its average variable cost curve. If the market price ever fell below the firm's average variable cost, the firm would cease production in the short run, minimizing its losses to its total fixed costs.

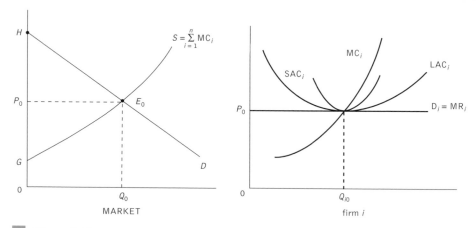

Figure 14.1 *Long-run equilibrium for a perfectly competitive firm*

Perfectly competitive firm i is a price taker. The market price, P_0, gives the firm's perfectly elastic demand and marginal revenue curve, $D_i = MR_i$. In long run equilibrium, the firm will be producing at the minimum of its long run average cost curve and the minimum of the associated short run average cost curve, earning zero economic profits.

also the firm's marginal revenue, MR_i, equals the marginal cost (MC_i). Due to freedom of entry and exit, in long-run equilibrium, the firm would be earning zero economic profits, that is, normal returns on the capital invested. The firm's short-run average cost (SAC) and long-run average cost (LAC) equal the market price. See the output Q_{i0} in Figure 14.1, where $SAC = LAC = P_0$. Furthermore, in a long-run equilibrium, a perfectly competitive firm would produce with the optimal amount of capital and labor (at the minimum of its long-run average cost curve) and its profit-maximizing output will coincide with its capacity output (the minimum of its selected short-run average total cost curve).[3] Since the perfectly competitive firm is a price-taker, then, in the long run, maximizing its profits is consistent with minimizing its average cost.

Allocative efficiency

An additional desirable feature of perfect competition is **allocative efficiency**. Refer back to Figure 14.1. At the equilibrium market quantity transacted, Q_0, made up of the outputs of the many firms in the market, the market price, P_0, equals the marginal cost of production (MC) of that last unit. The value consumers place on the good or service purchased is the price they

---

[3] The **long-run average cost curve**, LAC_i, gives the lowest unit cost of producing each rate of output in the long run, that is, when all the factors of production are variable. A **short-run average cost curve** gives the average cost of production for each rate of output in the short run when there is a fixed factor, usually physical capital. For any rate of output, the average cost of production in the short run will be greater than or equal to, at best, the average cost of production in the long run. At each point on the firm's long-run average cost curve, LAC_i, there is a tangential short-run average total cost curve, SAC_i, representing the optimal capital for producing that rate of output. Investing in additional capital would shift the firm to a new short-run average cost curve to the right along the long-run average cost curve.

The long-run average cost curve is generally drawn as U-shaped. Initially the long-run average cost declines as the firm increases output since there are economies of scale from the division of labor and more efficient capital-intensive production. The LAC curve will level off where there are constant costs of production. Higher levels of output may encounter diseconomies of scale, with rising long-run average cost due to management and communication problems and perhaps reduced worker productivity. Diseconomies of scale, however, are not to be confused with the short-run phenomenon of diminishing returns to labor, where the short-run marginal cost of production rises as more labor is employed for a given quantity of physical capital. Diminishing returns to labor account for the rising portions of the short-run marginal cost and average total cost curves.

are willing to pay, read off the market demand curve. The opportunity cost of producing a good is indicated by the marginal cost of production. Thus, at least in a private sense, the correct amount of the good is produced and consumed. Moreover, with the allocatively efficient condition, $P = MC$, the sum of consumer surplus and producer surplus is maximized.

Consumer surplus is the difference between the value consumers place on a given quantity of a good purchased, indicated by the area under the demand curve up to that quantity purchased, and the total expenditures required to purchase that quantity. In Figure 14.1, consumer surplus is measured by the area HP_0E_0. Intuitively, consumer surplus is the gain in welfare by being able to consume a good for a lower price than the individual would be willing to pay.

Producer surplus is the difference between the revenues suppliers receive for the sale of a good and the revenues they would be willing to accept to supply the good. In Figure 14.1, see the area P_0E_0G. Note that on the last unit sold, Q_0, the market equilibrium quantity transacted, there is no additional consumer or producer surplus.

MONOPOLY

If perfect competition represents one end of the theoretical spectrum of market structures, monopoly is at the other end. A **monopoly** exists when there is a single supplier or seller in a market. Thus, the market demand for the good or service is the actual demand facing the monopolist. Unlike a perfectly competitive firm, a monopolist can earn positive economic profits in the long run—provided that other firms can be prevented from entering the market.

Some barriers to entry are legal. A firm may have a patent, giving it exclusive rights to a specific product or process for a period of time. Pharmaceutical companies obtain patents on promising new drugs. Copyrights on original works also give monopoly power (e.g., Disney World and Mickey Mouse). The government may grant monopoly power, as in the case of the US Postal Service and first class mail or the single gasoline station and restaurant at service areas along interstate highways.

Alternatively, a firm may own a scarce resource, such as prime real estate around a picturesque lake used as a vacation resort or a snowy mountain used for a ski lodge. The national parks in the United States are examples of publicly owned monopolies.

Significant economies of scale may render competition in a market unfeasible—as has historically been the case with public utilities such as water, power, and natural gas. Usually these **natural monopolies** have been regulated by government-appointed commissions.[4]

A monopoly may arise simply because a market initially is too small to support more than one firm (e.g., a movie theater serving an isolated town). As the market demand grows, the monopolist may be able to discourage competition with aggressive price-cutting against any firm that attempts to enter. Such predatory behavior is illegal in the US; however, the threat of significant price discounting by a monopolist may be enough to deter the entry of potential competitors.

Monopoly profits

Unlike a perfectly competitive firm, which is a price-taker, facing a perfectly elastic demand curve for its output at the market-clearing price, a monopolist is a **price-setter**, facing a

---

[4] In the case of a natural monopoly, the regulatory commission will allow a fair or normal rate of return on the invested capital. The regulated output would be where the market demand curve intersects the monopolist's long-run average cost curve. The unit price, P, would then be equal to the long-run average cost of production, which includes a normal return on the invested capital.

417

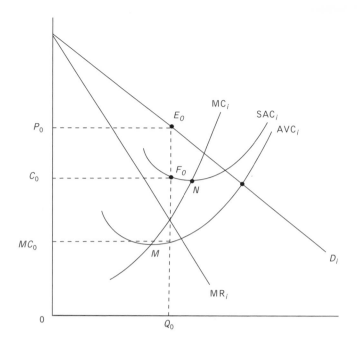

Figure 14.2 *Profit-maximizing output of a monopolist*

A monopolist is a price setter. To maximize profits, the monopolist would find the level of output where its marginal revenue equals its marginal cost, $MR_i = MC_i$. For this output, Q_0, the firm could charge a unit price of P_0. Here, the monopolist is earning positive economic profits equal $(P_0 - C_0) \cdot Q_0$, indicated by the area $P_0 E_0 F_0 C_0$.

downward-sloping market demand curve. In order to sell more output, the monopolist must lower the price, not just on the additional units sold, but on all units sold during the period. Thus, for a monopolist, its marginal revenue curve lies below its average revenue or demand curve.[5]

To determine the monopolist's economic profits, we need the short-run average cost curves—in particular, the short-run average total cost (SAC) curve. If at the profit-maximizing output, where marginal revenue equals marginal cost, $MR_i = MC_i$, the monopolist's price exceeds its average total cost, then positive economic profits are earned. See Figure 14.2. Here at the profit-maximizing output of Q_0, the monopolist is earning positive economic profits of $\Pi_0 = (P_0 - C_0) \cdot Q_0$ (given by the area $P_0 E_0 F_0 C_0$). As noted, positive economic profits may persist if there are sufficient barriers to entry to new firms. If firms do enter the market, the monopolist's demand curve would shift left. In fact, we would no longer have a monopoly.

---

[5] Suppose the demand curve facing the monopolist is given by $Q^d = a - bP$, or alternatively, $P^d = a/b - (1/b) \cdot Q$, where P^d is the demand price associated with any quantity sold. The total revenues of the monopolist are $R = P \cdot Q = [a/b - (1/b) \cdot Q] \cdot Q = (a/b)Q - (1/b)Q^2$. The **average revenue**, AR, is total revenue per unit of output, AR = TR/Q = $a/b - (1/b)Q = P$. In other words, average revenue and price are the same, so plotting the firm's demand curve, the relationship between the quantity demanded of output and the price of the output, is the same as plotting the average revenue curve. Marginal revenue, MR, the change in total revenue associated with a change in output, is MR = dTR/dQ = $a/b - (2/b) \cdot Q$. So, in the case of a downward-sloping, linear demand curve, the marginal revenue curve has the same vertical intercept, here a/b, but twice the slope, here $2/b = 2 \cdot (1/b)$, as the demand or average revenue curve.

A monopolist is not guaranteed to earn positive economic profits. The profitability of any monopolist depends on the demand for its product (and the substitutes for the monopolist's product) and the strength of the barriers to entry. Patents run out and demands shift with changes in tastes and preferences, population, and income. Also, cost conditions may change. For example, an increase in input costs, *ceteris paribus*, would reduce profits.

We note that the monopolist is allocatively inefficient in that the price of its output, P_0, exceeds the marginal cost of production, MC_0. Moreover, unlike the perfectly competitive firm in long-run equilibrium, the monopolist need not produce at its capacity output, where the short-run average total cost is minimized, which is illustrated in Figure 14.2 by the point N.

The allocative inefficiency of a monopoly

Whatever the underlying reason, a monopolist, by definition, exercises market power, which in the short run may be at the expense of consumer welfare. To illustrate, consider the following hypothetical scenario. Suppose a market is initially characterized by perfect competition. Refer to Figure 14.3, where the market demand and market supply curves intersect to yield a market-clearing price of P_c and quantity transacted of Q_c. Recall that in perfect competition the market supply, S, is the summation of all the individual firms' supply curves, or the rising portion of their marginal cost curves above their average variable cost curve. Here the market supply under perfect competition is

$$S_C = \sum_{i=1}^{n} MC_i$$

where n is the number of firms.

As discussed, perfect competition is characterized by allocative efficiency. On the last unit transacted in any period, here the Q_c unit, the price consumers are willing to pay, the market-clearing price, P_c, equals the marginal cost of production, $MC(Q_c)$. Moreover, in perfect competition, the sum of consumer surplus (given by the area HP_cE_c) and producer surplus (given by the area GP_cE_c) is maximized; since up to last unit sold there is still consumer surplus and producer surplus to be realized.

Now suppose that a wealthy private investor purchases all of the n firms or perhaps the government nationalizes all of the firms—in either case, turning a perfectly competitive market into a monopoly. Since there is no change in the cost curves of the individual firms, only a change in ownership, the market supply curve can be regarded as the marginal cost curve of the monopolist. See MC_m in Figure 14.3. In effect, we have a multi-plant monopolist. To maximize profits, the monopolist sets its marginal cost equal to marginal revenue: $MC_m = MR_m$. The profit-maximizing output is Q_m, less than the market quantity transacted under perfect competition. With the lower output, though, the monopolist can set a higher price, P_m.

With the monopolization of the market, consumer surplus is reduced to the area HP_mE_m. On net, producer surplus increases to the area P_mE_mFG. Part of the loss in consumer surplus is gained by the monopolist as producer surplus (the area $P_mE_mJP_c$). The area E_mJE_c is the known as the deadweight loss in consumer surplus, and the area JE_cF is the deadweight loss in producer surplus. A monopoly is allocatively inefficient. On the last unit sold, the Q_m unit, the price, P_m, exceeds the marginal cost of production, $MC(Q_m)$, illustrated by the gap E_mF. That is, the value consumers place on the last unit purchased is greater than the opportunity cost of producing that unit. Compared to perfect competition, then, a monopoly produces too little at too high a

419

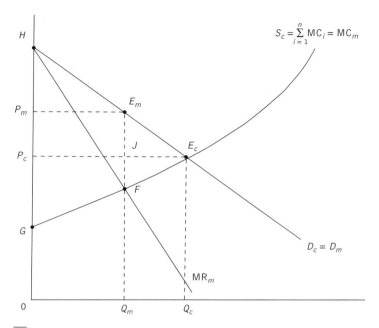

Figure 14.3 *Allocative efficiency: perfect competition and monopoly*

In contrast to a perfectly competitive market, a monopolist is allocatively inefficient. Compared to the perfectly competitive equilibrium at E_c, a profit-maximizing monopolist would produce less, $Q_m < Q_c$, and charge a higher price, $P_m > P_c$. Thus, the monopolist captures some of the consumer surplus. The deadweight losses in consumer surplus and producer surplus with the monopoly are equal to the area $E_m E_c F$.

price. A measure of the allocative inefficiency of the monopolist is the sum of the **deadweight losses**—in Figure 14.3, the area $E_m E_c F$.

Because they are able to earn positive economic profits in the long run, monopolies may be more innovative, affording research and development into better products and processes. Indeed, the patent system grants the inventor a monopoly for some 20 years to encourage such innovation. Moreover, in some cases where economies of scale are large relative to market demand, like with public utilities, natural monopolies arise. Rather than operating freely, however, the natural monopolist is usually regulated and allowed to earn only a normal return on the invested capital.

Despite the many attractive features of perfect competition (e.g., self-regulation and allocative efficiency), there are market failures. As a result there are pressures on governments to intervene in markets to ensure more socially acceptable results. Below we discuss the arguments for government intervention to regulate business and protect the public interest.[6]

---

[6] Perfect competition and monopoly are the theoretical extremes of market structure. The two other basic market structures are monopolistic competition and oligopoly. With **monopolistic competition** there are many firms producing slightly differentiated products. An example might be seafood restaurants in New Orleans. Like perfect competition there is freedom of entry and exit, so the long-run equilibrium is characterized by zero economic profits. Each monopolistic competitor, however, is a price-setter, like a monopolist, facing a downward-sloping, but highly elastic, demand curve for its product. **Oligopoly** is an market dominated by a few rival firms. Examples include the automobile industry, pharmaceutical companies, and personal computer manufacturers. The oligopolistic firms are well aware of their interdependence, and would be tempted to collude to restrict trade and bolster profits, but collusion is illegal in the US and other market economies. Like monopolies, however,

MARKET FAILURES

A **market failure** is a condition that arises when the unrestrained operation of a market yields socially undesirable results. Market failures include public and merit goods, regulation of business and consumer behavior for the social good, poverty and inequities in the distribution of income, and macroeconomic instability. There is considerable debate, however, on whether these all qualify as market failures warranting government involvement and, if so, the most appropriate form of government intervention.

Public goods

A pure **public good** is a good or service for which the consumption by any one individual does not reduce the consumption of others (i.e., nonrival consumption), and for which it is difficult to exclude anyone from consuming the commodity in question (i.e., nonexcludable consumption). The latter characteristic means that it would be difficult to charge users directly for the consumption of the commodity. Consequently, private firms would not find it profitable to produce a public good, and likely the population would not find it desirable for the commodity to be privately provided. Examples are national defense, lighthouses, public roads, the rule of law, and police protection. Restricting access to these public goods is not possible and asking for voluntary contributions to fund the provision of these goods is not effective because of the free-rider problem. As a result, these public goods are funded indirectly through tax revenues.

Merit goods

Merit goods are goods or services that society deems individuals should have, regardless of the ability to pay. That is, the consumption of merit goods is in the best interest of society and often generates positive externalities, to be discussed below. Merit goods are usually provided by the government and funded by tax revenues. Sometimes there may be user charges to defray part of the costs. Examples are public education, public health, and even public housing. An educated populace is in the best interests of a democratic society and a productive economy. Thus, for example, every child is entitled to schooling through high school in the US. The second Millennium Development Goal is to achieve universal primary education. Likewise, a healthy population is good for society, not only for improving the qualities and extending the quantities of lives, but also for labor productivity. Millennium Development Goals 4, 5, and 6 (reducing child mortality, improving maternal health, and combating HIV/AIDS, malaria, and other diseases) could be considered merit goods.

Government regulation

Rarely do we find markets characterized by perfect competition among equals. More likely, especially on the supply side, there is some market power (e.g., monopolies and oligopolies that can restrain trade and capture some of the consumer surplus). There may be monopsonies, or demanders with market power who can dictate prices paid (e.g., large employers in restricted markets suppressing the wages paid to labor).

---

barriers to entry may exist, for example, large economies of scale in production and heavy advertising expenditures and brand loyalty, that allow oligopolists to earn positive economic profits overtime. Internationally, oligopolistic cartels may form, like the Organization of Petroleum Exporting Countries, that can limit trade and influence prices.

SUSTAINABLE DEVELOPMENT

While not all monopolies are necessarily bad for the consumer—as noted, sometimes competition is not practical or even efficient, such as the case of natural monopolies—competition is generally believed to be socially desirable, as well as efficient. In the US and other industrialized economies, antitrust legislation is used to promote competition and break up attempts to control markets and restrict trade.

Moreover, in the pursuit of profits firms may not act in the public interest, for example, producing unsafe, if less expensive, medicines and goods, exploiting labor in the workplace, and improperly disposing of their wastes, which results in pollution of the environment. Thus, governments set standards to regulate businesses. In the US, the Food and Drug Administration, the Consumer Product Safety Commission, the Occupational Health and Safety Administration, and the Environmental Protection Agency are among the regulatory bodies that ensure the public interest.

EXTERNALITIES

A classic market failure arises with **externalities**, or third-party effects. Externalities exist when there is a divergence between the private and public (or social) net benefits of an action. **Negative externalities** occur when a private action, such as the production or consumption of a good or service, imposes costs on society. With negative externalities, third parties not directly involved in the primary activity experience a decline in their welfare. Pollution is the most commonly cited example of a negative externality. **Positive externalities**, on the other hand, result when society or third parties indirectly benefit from the actions of others. For example, individuals undergoing the expense and inconvenience of flu shots provide benefits to the general public since they are less likely to catch and pass along the flu. Basic research which adds to general knowledge with useful applications and cannot be appropriated entirely by the researchers themselves is another example of a positive externality.

Negative externalities

Free markets, driven by the individual pursuit of self-interest (i.e., utility maximization for consumers and profit maximization for producers) do not always capture all the consequences of the private economic activities in question. There may be externalities or spillover effects (positive or negative) on other parties not directly involved. With respect to the environment, negative externalities or adverse consequences seem to be more prevalent.

Consider a logging company's clear-cutting of a hillside forest that, with the heavy spring rains, leads to erosion of the nearby farmland; a chemical company's dumping of wastes in a river that threatens the fish and waterfowl; industrial air pollution that contributes to acid rain that damages forests and leads to respiratory problems that impair human health; the expansion of slash-and-burn agriculture into the tropical rainforests that adds to the greenhouse effect and global warming; the aggressive use of large nets for tuna fishing that also ensnare dolphins, seriously depleting the stocks of this gentle and intelligent creature; the radioactive wastes generated by nuclear energy that are temporarily stored while awaiting better solutions to be found by future generations. In each case there are costs of production not borne by the producers and consumers. The understating of the social costs of production results in market prices that are too low and quantities produced and consumed that are too high.

Refer to Figure 14.4, where the market demand and supply curves for a commodity whose production or consumption creates negative externalities are illustrated. The market supply curve

422

S reflects the private costs of producing the commodity. The supply curve S' incorporates the additional social costs, here associated with the degradation of the environment and impaired health. (Note that in some cases the social costs from the negative externalities are also borne by future generations who may inherit environmental blight, less biodiversity, or stockpiles of hazardous wastes.)

The free market would clear at P_0 and Q_0, with consumer surplus of HE_0P_0. Producer surplus is P_0E_0G. The social costs of the negative externality are equal to the area $GG'F_0E_0$. The total costs of providing the market output of Q_0 are given by the area $0G'F_0Q_0$, or the area under the comprehensive supply curve, S', inclusive of social costs, up to the output Q_0. The area $E_1F_0E_0$ indicates the welfare loss due to the uncovered social costs of producing the market output of Q_0. That is, between the socially optimal output of Q_1 and the market output of Q_0, the comprehensive marginal cost of production (read off the S' curve) exceeds the value consumers place on the additional output (indicated by the demand price). If the additional social costs from the production of this good were included, then the "social market-clearing" price would rise to P_1 and the quantity transacted would fall to Q_1, given by the intersection of S', the comprehensive supply curve, and D, the market demand curve.

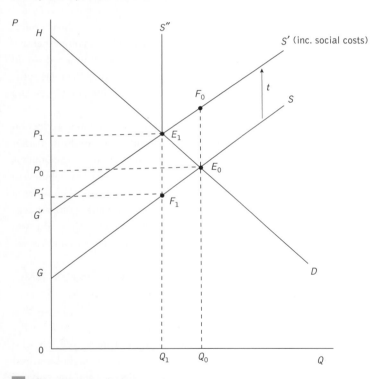

Figure 14.4 *Negative externality*

With a negative externality, too much of a good is produced at too low a price. Incorporating the social costs of the negative externality would shift the supply curve back from S to S', raising the price, from P_0 to P_1, and reducing the quantity transacted, from Q_0 to Q_1. To address this negative externality, the government could impose a tax of t on the suppliers, or limit production to Q_1 with quotas, or mandate that suppliers abide by government regulations that address the externality.

In sum, where there are negative externalities associated with the production or consumption of a commodity, too much of the commodity ($Q_0 > Q_1$) at too low a price ($P_0 < P_1$) tends to be produced in a free market. Resources are not being optimally allocated as had been implied by the market mechanism under perfect competition. There is a case then for government intervention in the market. There are several policy options for the government to attain the socially optimal outcome, here a unit price of P_1 and quantity transacted of Q_1, which account for all the costs of production, private and public.

Policy options for negative externalities

Consider the negative externality from chemical companies improperly disposing of the wastes resulting from their production of fertilizers. Nearby rivers and lakes are contaminated and as a result become unhealthy for the fish and hazardous for swimming. While the least expensive disposal of the chemical wastes through dumping into the public waterways is privately profitable for the chemical companies, there are social costs incurred in terms of public health and environmental degradation. Returning to Figure 14.4, the market demand and supply curves for the fertilizers are given as D and S, with the market-clearing price and quantity transacted as P_0 and Q_0. The market supply curve reflects only the private marginal costs of production of the chemical companies. If the additional social costs due to water pollution were included, the comprehensive supply curve would be S'. The price would then increase to P_1 and the quantity transacted would decline to Q_1, would which be the socially optimal outcome. In effect, the failure of the market for the fertilizers produced to account for these social costs results in too much production ($Q_0 > Q_1$) and consumption of these fertilizers, at too low a price ($P_0 < P_1$).

One option is an **output quota** set at Q_1. That is, the government could issue production licenses to the chemical companies allowing a total of Q_1 units of output. The resulting market supply curve would then be given by $GF_1 S''$, which becomes perfectly inelastic when the quota is reached at Q_1. The market price would rise to P_1. If the production licenses were distributed to the chemical companies according to some criterion, such as existing market shares, then the area given by $P_1 E_1 F_1 P_1'$, known as the **quota rent**, would be captured by the chemical companies as increased producer surplus. If, on the other hand, the government auctioned off the Q_1 production licenses, then the quota rent could be captured by the government, similar to tax revenues, since the market value of a production license would rise to $P_1 - P_1'$.

Infrequently are production licenses auctioned off, however, and when the licenses are distributed at the discretion of the government, corruption often will result. For instance, to secure a license to produce one unit of output, with a marginal cost of production of P_1', but with a market price of P_1, unethical chemical companies would be willing to pay a bribe up to $P_1 - P_1'$. In the extreme, the quota rents may be captured entirely by corrupt government officials who take the bribes in dispensing the production licenses. In practice, the quota rents might be shared by the chemical companies paying the bribes, if less than $P_1 - P_1'$ per license, and the corrupt government officials. On the other hand, if the government uses as a criterion for distribution the current market shares of the chemical companies, then the larger companies who might have been more responsible for the water pollution are favored. In any case, consumers of the fertilizer will pay a higher price.

A second option is for the government to impose an **excise tax** on the chemical companies, which would in effect shift the market supply curve up by the amount of the tax, here t, to S'. Now the negative externalities from the production of fertilizers are internalized or captured by the market. The market price inclusive of the tax would rise to P_1 and the quantity transacted would fall to Q_1. The government automatically collects tax revenues equal to $P_1 E_1 F_1 P_1'$. Taxing the production of fertilizers, moreover, is more flexible than imposing a production quota, since as the market demand for fertilizer increases and *ceteris paribus* the optimal quantity of fertilizer produced rises, the market adjusts. In contrast, under a production quota set at Q_1, increases in market demand would only drive up the market value of a production license. A concern, nevertheless, with increased fertilizer production to meet increases in market demand is that the resulting pollution from improperly disposing of the chemical wastes in public waterways may exceed environmental thresholds and irreparably damage the health of these waterways. Thus, even with a tax, future adjustments may be needed in the tax rate to reflect the social costs of the negative externality.

A third option to address a negative externality is through direct government regulation of production. Known as the **command and control** approach, the government sets and enforces environmental standards. In this example of the chemical companies improperly disposing of the wastes from their production of fertilizers, the government could mandate that all companies install proper pollution abatement equipment and adopt environmentally sound practices for the disposal of their wastes. For example, in the US, the Environmental Protection Agency began in 2011 a three-year phase-in of new restrictions on the emissions of mercury and other toxic metals from coal-fired power plants. Abiding by these government regulations will raise the costs of production, optimally shifting the market supply curve in Figure 14.4 up from S to S', in effect achieving the socially optimal price and output of P_1 and Q_1.

Pollution abatement

Clearly an important consideration is the optimal amount of pollution to be allowed, consistent with environmental thresholds and societal preferences. Given the total amount of pollution that would otherwise be generated (e.g., by chemical companies in their production of fertilizers), once the optimal, or at least acceptable, amount of pollution is determined, the optimal amount of pollution abatement can be derived.

In Figure 14.5 we illustrate the marginal costs (private and public) of pollution abatement, MC_A, which are likely to rise with the amount of pollution abated since the least-cost and most productive methods of abatement would be utilized first. Indeed, as we approach 100 percent abatement of pollution, if even attainable, the marginal cost is likely to accelerate. In contrast, the marginal benefit of pollution abatement, MB_A, is likely to decline as more pollution is abated, since the gains in public health and welfare initially are likely to be greater as the heaviest pollution is curtailed. Proceeding from clean water or air to pristine water or air is likely to add to social welfare, but at a diminishing rate.

A simple example might be helpful to illustrate. Consider college roommates who decide to clean up their dorm room after several weeks of neglect. With a little effort, they can make a big difference. For example, in 30 minutes they might throw away the pizza boxes, pick up the gym clothes from the floor, clean off their desks, and at least rearrange their clutter. Soon the health and esthetic benefits of a cleaner room are evident. Further efforts, however, become increasingly costly (e.g., vacuuming and dusting, even scrubbing the floor and washing the walls), while the benefits from additional cleaning will be declining and less noticeable. So the optimal amount of time spent cleaning the dorm room (abating the pollution), might be 50 minutes. Moreover, the

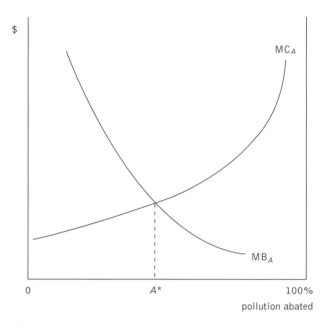

Figure 14.5 *Optimal pollution abatement*

The optimal pollution abatement is found where the marginal benefit equals the marginal cost of abatement. Here A* indicates the optimal abatement.

roommates, after their course in economic principles, realize the opportunity costs of the time spent cleaning their room (e.g., playing frisbee, studying, or visiting with friends).

In general, the optimal amount of pollution abatement is found where the marginal cost equals the marginal benefit, indicated in Figure 14.5 by the intersection of the MC_A and MB_A curves at A^*. While this seems straightforward enough, in practice determining the marginal costs and benefits of pollution abatement can be difficult. For example, what value should be placed on the preservation of a fish species threatened by water pollution or the esthetic pleasure associated with clean waterways or clear vistas?

Marketable pollution permits

Command and control tends to be the most expensive option for the government, generating no tax revenues or quota rents, but requiring outlays for enforcement. Moreover, the degree of enforcement of the government regulations can vary across political administrations. There is a variant of the command and control approach, though, that is gaining acceptance. With **marketable pollution permits**, the government decides on how much total pollution should be allowed, according to the marginal cost-marginal benefit criterion discussed earlier, and then issues pollution permits to firms consistent with this total. That is, as opposed to production licenses which are used for an output quota, pollution permits are used for a pollution quota. These pollution permits can be traded in the market. See Box 14.1 for a simple example of marketable pollution permits.

As with production licenses, the government must first come up with the optimal number of pollution permits to issue and then decide how to distribute them (e.g., based on historical shares of pollution emitted by the firms). The most efficient way and one that would generate revenues for the government would be to auction off the pollution permits. The underlying motivation with pollution permits is to allow the market to determine the most efficient way to abate the pollution. Also incentives are provided for firms to invest in pollution abatement measures to reduce their need to acquire pollution permits.

BOX 14.1: MARKETABLE POLLUTION PERMITS: A SIMPLE EXAMPLE

Suppose, for simplicity, that only two firms, A and B, are in the market, manufacturing a good where emissions of CO_2 are generated during the production process. Firm A, with the older plant, emits one unit of pollution per unit of output (Q_A) generated. Firm B has a newer plant and has invested in pollution abatement. Consequently, for each unit of output (Q_B) produced, there is only one half of a unit of pollution emitted. With no environmental standards, firm A might have the cost advantage, since it has not incurred the expense of investing in pollution abatement capital (e.g., scrubbers on smokestacks) like firm B.

Both firms are price-setters and face marginal revenue curves of MR_A and MR_B. Suppose further that the marginal cost curve of firm B is higher than that for firm A ($MC_B > MC_A$). Let the initial profit-maximizing outputs (where $MR = MC$) of the two firms be $Q_A = 30$ and $Q_B = 20$ and the pollution emitted by the two firms $e_A = 30$ units and $e_B = 10$ units.

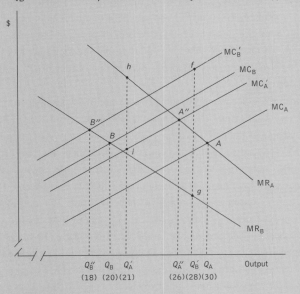

Figure B14.1 *Illustration of marketable pollution permits*

Initially the profit-maximizing outputs for firms A and B are $Q_A = 30$ and $Q_B = 20$. With the marketable pollution permits, however, the new profit-maximizing outputs are $Q_A'' = 26$ and $Q_B'' = 18$. To realize this firm A would have to purchase five pollution permits from firm B. Total output declines from 50 units to 44 units, which reduces the total pollution emitted from 40 units to 35 units, as intended.

Assume the government determines that the optimal pollution is 35 units ($e^* = 35$), a 12.5 percent reduction from the 40 units currently emitted. The government sells the two firms marketable pollution permits (pp) based on the current shares of market output. The total market output of the product is 50 units: $Q_A + Q_B = 50$. Each pollution permit gives the firm the right to emit one unit of pollution and costs x dollars. Then firm A would receive 60 percent of the pollution permits or $pp_A = 0.6 \cdot 35 = 21$ (paying $21x$), and firm B would receive 40 percent of the pollution permits or $pp_B = 0.4 \cdot 35 = 14$ (paying $14x$).

With the added cost of the pollution permits, the MC curves of the two firms would shift up by the cost per unit of output of a pollution permit—more for firm A (by x) than for firm B (by $0.5x$), however, since firm B can produce two units of output with each pollution permit, while firm A can produce only one unit of output for each pollution permit. See Figure B14.1, where the new MC curves are illustrated and still $MC'_A < MC'_B$ (although it could also be that $MC'_A \geq MC'_B$). Note that firm A only has enough pollution permits to produce 21 units of output ($Q'_A = 21$), while firm B has enough pollution permits to produce 28 units of output ($Q'_B = 28$). Neither of these are profit-maximizing outputs, however, where $MR = MC$. For firm A at Q'_A, $MR_A > MC'_A$ (illustrated by the distance between points h and i in Figure B14.1), so greater production would be profitable. For firm B at Q'_B, $MC'_B > MR_B$ (illustrated by the distance between points f and g), so less production would be profitable.

If the new profit-maximizing outputs are $Q''_A = 26$ and $Q''_B = 18$, then firm B could sell five pollution permits to firm A, for x each, say (although the market price need not equal the initial price set by the government). Thus, firm B receives $5x$ and with the remaining nine pollution permits, can produce the desired 18 units of output at Q''_B. (See point B'' where $MR_B = MC'_B$.) Firm A spends $5x$ for the five pollution permits and now has the needed 26 pollution permits required to produce its profit-maximizing output of $Q''_A = 26$. (See point A'' where $MR_A = MC'_A$.)

In this example, firm A, with the older plant, spends $26x$ on pollution permits; firm B, with the newer, cleaner plant, spends $9x$ on pollution permits; the government earns $35x$ in revenues from the initial issuance of the permits.

In sum, the government has reduced the amount of pollution emitted by the two firms from $e = 40$ to $e^* = 35$ units. The increased costs of production (due to the cost of the pollution permits which reflect the social costs of the pollution emitted) have resulted in higher prices for the firm outputs. Consequently, both firms have reduced their outputs— however, more so for firm A (by 13.3 percent, from $Q_A = 30$ to $Q''_A = 26$) than for firm B, with its investment in pollution abatement capital (by 10 percent from $Q_B = 20$ to $Q''_B = 18$). Firm A might have an incentive to invest in pollution abatement capital. Moreover, each year the government would issue new pollution permits and could reduce the total number of permits issued over time consistent with lower emissions targets.

Moral suasion

The fourth option to reduce the output and raise the price of this product with negative externalities is **moral suasion**. On the supply side the government could appeal to the public interests of the firms, exhorting them to adopt better methods of disposing of their wastes and reducing their pollution emissions. The problem with this approach is **dysfunctional selection**, in the sense that those producers that voluntarily comply incur additional costs which can put them at a competitive disadvantage in the market compared to the firms that do not comply. One way the government or other groups can induce firms to adopt environmentally more sound or safer methods of production is to publicize those firms that do comply. Labels certifying compliance would allow conscientious consumers to favor those more socially responsible producers.

Diamond (2005: 473–474) describes the certification process for sustainable forestry and sustainable fishing. The Forest Stewardship Council (FSC), an international nonprofit organization formed in 1993, set forth criteria for forestry products derived with sustainable and environmentally sound practices. These criteria include maintaining forest stocks with reforestation accompanying logging, conserving "old-growth" trees and preserving the natural variety, not resorting to monoculture tree plantations; respecting the valuable ecosystem services provided by forests, including havens of biodiversity, nutrient recycling, absorption of carbon dioxide, and prevention of soil erosion; as well as recognizing and honoring the livelihoods of indigenous people who depend on the forests. Forest products generated under such sustainable management and receiving FSC certification would be more expensive, but would appeal to environmentally conscientious consumers.

Similarly, the Marine Stewardship Council (MSC) was formed in 1997 to promote sustainable fishing. As Diamond (2005: 481) explains, the MSC criteria were developed jointly by fishermen, seafood processors, scientists, and environmentalists:

> The principal criteria are that the fishery should maintain its fish stock's health (including the stock's sex and age distribution and genetic diversity) for the indefinite future, should yield a sustainable harvest, should maintain ecosystem integrity, should minimize impacts on marine habitats and on non-targeted species (the by-catch), should have rules and procedures for managing stocks and minimizing impacts, and should comply with prevailing laws.

Whether there will be enough demand for the goods produced under sustainable management practices to warrant the additional costs incurred remains to be seen. In the case of the fisheries in the world's oceans, where property rights are not clearly defined, Hardin's (1968) tragedy of the commons may apply.[7] With open access to resources (e.g., common pastures for grazing livestock), individuals have an incentive to increase their harvest (add to their herds), since the gains from doing so (feeding their livestock) accrue entirely to the individuals, while the costs of environmental degradation (reduced productivity of the pastureland) are distributed across all the herders. Consequently, common resources, whether they are the oceans, public lands, or the atmosphere, tend to be exploited and diminished. And, in contrast to Adam Smith's "invisible hand," where individual pursuit of self-interest is in the public good, in the case of common resources with open access, an "invisible grab" may be more apt, where such competition is destructive. Hardin (1968) argues for "mutual coercion, mutually agreed upon" in order to address this tragedy of the commons. Examples include an international treaty that limits pollution or restricts fish harvests with sanctions for violators, an international tax on producers,

---

[7] In his classic essay, Garrett Hardin focused on what he saw as the world population problem. During the 1960s the annual world population growth rate had risen to 2 percent, implying a doubling of the world population every 35 years. The freedom to procreate, according to Hardin, without parents incurring all the costs of providing for their offspring, would result in overpopulation, just as open access to common pastureland would tend to result in overgrazing and the degradation of the land.

or marketable output licenses that are auctioned off. Without a supranational authority to monitor and enforce such measures, national compliance is more or less voluntary, which may be insufficient.

Elinor Ostrom, however, in her 2009 Economics Nobel Prize Lecture, is more optimistic with respect to self-regulation of common pool resources such as fisheries, forests, water systems or Hardin's pasture with open access to herders. She argues (2010: 641) that "Simply allowing communication, or 'cheap talk,' enables participants to reduce overharvesting and increase joint payoffs, contrary to game-theoretical predictions." She sets forth conditions that affect the level of cooperation, including when: communication is feasible for all the participants; the reputations of the participants are known; there are high marginal benefits per participant that increase the incentive to cooperate; capabilities exist for entry and exit of agreements; a longer planning horizon is taken; and agreed-upon sanctioning capabilities are recognized (2010: 661–662). For Ostrom, mutual trust is essential in building the social capital that promotes sustainable use of common resources.

Whether Ostrom's optimism (mutual trust) or Hardin's pessimism (mutual coercion) will carry the day remains to be seen. With respect to the global commons, like the world's oceans and atmosphere, where all nations have a stake, the challenge is considerably greater than a shared pasture for local herders.

Externalities can result also from the consumption of the goods. Consider automobile emissions. Mandated measures to reduce the harmful emissions include the switch from leaded to unleaded gasoline, excise taxes on gasoline, higher fuel efficiency standards for the automobile manufacturers, and the subsidization of mass transit. Some cities, such as London, have even imposed fees for driving within the city.

Or consider smoking, with the ill-effects of passive smoking, not to mention the higher health care costs incurred—but not entirely borne—by smokers. Measures to reduce smoking include excise taxes on the sale of cigarettes, laws on minors purchasing cigarettes, warning labels about the adverse health consequences, and moral suasion with advertising campaigns and public education to reduce the demand for cigarettes.

As Allcott and Greenstone (2012) discuss, in the US the government requires that information on energy efficiency be reported by producers, from average miles per gallon prominent on the stickers of automobiles to annual cost of electricity for running refrigerators. Consumers may not be aware of the cost savings that can be realized from more energy efficient products, savings that within a few years more than compensate for the higher initial purchase prices that reflect the improved products. Allcott and Greenstone argue, however, that taxes or marketable pollution permits are more efficient ways to address the externalities from energy production and consumption than the various command and control measures, such as direct pollution controls and mandated efficiency standards. Knittel (2012: 115) concurs, pointing out, that fuel economy standards are a second best policy that can induce the development of more fuel efficient automobiles, but that gasoline taxes would be more direct and effective.[8] As evidence, Knittel lists the excise taxes on motor fuel for the high-income OECD countries in 2010. Only the US (at $0.49 dollars per gallon) and Canada (at $0.96 per gallon) were under a dollar. Most OECD countries had gasoline taxes of well over $2 a gallon, ranging up to $4.19 in New Zealand.

---

[8] In the US, between 2007 and 2025 annual mileage improvement is mandated for cars. The Corporate Average Fuel Economy (CAFE) standards require average fuel economy for industry fleet-wide cars and trucks combined to reach 49.6 miles per gallon by the model year 2025. As Knittel (2012: 95–100) discusses, fuel economy standards can be undermined by loopholes and exemptions. For example, sports utility vehicles were classified as light trucks, which had lower miles per gallon requirements. And, large pick-up trucks were exempt from CAFE standards.

In sum, negative externalities evidenced in water and air pollution, unsustainable deforestation, often illegal, that results in habitat loss, soil erosion, and contributes to global warming, and the overfishing that depletes vulnerable stocks beyond their regeneration capacities need to be addressed.

Positive externalities

Not all externalities are negative, imposing social costs or decreasing public welfare. Positive externalities arise when the production or consumption of a good or service provides benefits to or improves the welfare of third parties or the general public. Consider basic scientific research into diseases and merit goods such as education.

For example, refer to Figure 14.6, where the supply and demand for college education is illustrated. The quantity, Q, might be measured as years of college education and the price, P, would be the annual tuition. If college education provides social benefits, in terms of a more informed, engaged, and productive population, then left to the private market there may be too little of this higher education produced, as with Q_0, where the market supply equals the demand for college education in a country. If the positive externalities of college education are included, then the comprehensive demand for this education would be reflected in the demand curve, D', which includes the public benefits. In other words, at Q_0, the market quantity of college education provided, the private value of a year of college education, P_0, is less than the social value, P_0', which includes the private and public benefits. The unrealized welfare gains of additional college education are indicated by the area $F_0 E_0 F_1$ in Figure 14.6. In effect, there is too little college education. In this example, the socially optimal quantity of college education would be Q_1, where D' and S intersect.

Options for reaching this socially optimal amount of college education would be for the government to subsidize higher education with public universities where students pay tuitions that are lower than the costs of the education. Also the government subsidizes private universities and colleges, sometimes directly through grants to the institutions, and often through scholarships and loans to students to make the education more affordable. The government subsidization of higher education shifts the supply curve, S, to the right to S'' ideally meeting the comprehensive demand for education, D' at the optimal rate of Q_1. (In Figure 14.6 the market supply curve would shift down, reducing the supply price by the amount of the subsidy, here s per unit.)

Alternatively, the government could enhance the private supply of this good with public production, in effect, shifting the supply curve down to S''. This is common with education, especially primary and secondary public schools funded by tax revenues. Public universities add to the supply of college education, although here, while still subsidized, much of the cost of public university education is covered through tuition and fees.

As with the other examples given, determining the optimal rates of production is difficult. Nevertheless, externalities are a classic market failure. When there are externalities present in a market, government intervention through taxes or subsidies, quotas, regulation, and moral suasion is warranted to increase social welfare.

POVERTY

A third general market failure may be poverty and undesirable income inequality. There are two issues here. The first is absolute poverty, where individuals fall below a minimum standard of

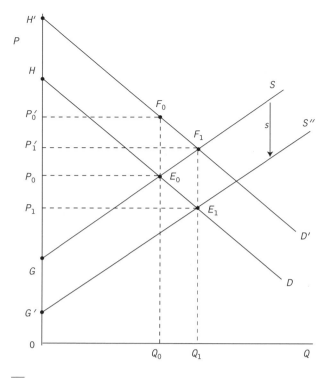

Figure 14.6 *Positive externality*

With a positive externality, too little of a good is produced at too high a price. Incorporating the benefits to society of the positive externality would shift the demand curve up to D' from D. The optimal quantity transacted would be Q_1. The government could subsidize suppliers, shifting the market supply down by s, or add to the private supply with public production.

living. The second is a high degree of income inequality, which may cause class conflict and the erosion of social capital.

Under the market mechanism, factor incomes earned reflect productivities. Indeed, in perfect competition each factor would be paid a real return equal to its marginal product. In the case of labor, wages and salaries received would equal the labor productivities, in turn a function of inherent abilities, education, and experience. Labor productivities also reflect the accompanying complementary factors, in particular technology and the physical and natural capital per unit of labor. In addition, those individuals with wealth (e.g., property and financial assets) receive incomes. Profits are the returns to owners of physical capital (e.g., stockholders in a corporation). Rent is the return to property owners, and interest is the return to savers.

The resulting distribution of incomes generated by free markets, however, does not guarantee that all will have adequate incomes. While those individuals with more capital, whether it is physical, human, or natural capital, will tend to earn more income, those with little capital will likely earn much less, perhaps even too little to escape poverty. Moreover, some in society are not able to earn income—children too young and seniors too old to work, as well as the disabled and infirm.

In 2008 approximately one-fifth of the world's population lived on less than $1.25 a day (in PPP dollars). The extreme poverty rate was over one-third in South Asia and nearly one-half in sub-Saharan Africa. Are there basic human needs (e.g., shelter, food, water, clothing, and health care) that should be met for all in society, regardless of the ability to earn income?

Even in the wealthiest economy in the world we find poverty, although not the extreme kinds found in the less developed world. In 2009, during the severe economic recession, 43.6 million people, 14.3 percent of the population, in the US, fell below the poverty line, a sharp increase from 39.8 million or 13.2 percent of the population in 2008. In that one year the US poverty rate for children under 18 years of age rose from 19.0 percent to 20.7 percent.[9]

Low-income households often cannot afford health insurance. In the US the number of people without health insurance increased from 46.3 million in 2008 to 50.7 million in 2009. Much of this increase reflected the loss of employer-provided health insurance with the rise in unemployment (DeNavas-Walt et al. 2010: 22). Individuals without health insurance may go without regular physical examinations and delay getting medical attention when ill, aggravating the health problems before resorting to highly cost-ineffective emergency room care. Concern with the lack of health insurance for so many Americans as well as the escalating costs of medical care motivated the Obama administration's health care reform, the Affordable Care Act of 2010.

In addition to absolute poverty, there is relative poverty, reflected in concentrated income distributions. Income inequality in the US has increased over the past quarter century. For example, in 1980, the poorest fifth of households received 4.2 percent of aggregate income, while the richest fifth received 44.1 percent. In 2009, the respective shares of the bottom and top quintiles of households were 3.4 percent and 50.3 percent.[10] Increased income inequality can create tension between the underclass and the privileged in society. A vibrant and growing middle class may be essential to building social capital in a nation.

Especially in developing nations, market failures that limit access to education, credit, and property will reduce economic growth when capable individuals cannot acquire these productive assets. The World Bank (2005: 2) points to inequality traps that persist across generations. For example:

> Disadvantaged children from families at the bottom of the wealth distribution do not have the same opportunities as children from wealthier families to receive quality education. So these disadvantaged children can expect to earn less as adults. Because the poor have less voice in the political process, they—like their parents—will be less able to influence spending decisions to improve public schools for their children. And the cycle of underachievement continues.

A particularly distressing example of stereotyping that reinforces inequality is given by the World Bank (2005: 8). In an experiment in India, in a general competition with simple exercises, such as solving mazes, low-caste and high-caste children performed equally well. When the castes were publicly announced before the competition, however, the low-caste children performed at a significantly lower level than the high-caste children. Such failure of individuals to realize their

---

[9] These statistics are from the US Census Bureau, *Highlights: Current Population Survey, 2010* Annual Social and Economic Supplement. In computing poverty status, the income used includes earnings, unemployment compensation, social security, retirement and pension income, and public assistance before taxes. Noncash benefits such as food stamps and housing subsidies are not included. In fact, an individual working 40 hours week at the federal minimum wage of $7.25 an hour would have earned slightly over $15,000 a year, which fell well below the official poverty line of $22,050 for a family of four in the US. As noted in Chapter 10, the US poverty rate rose further in 2010 to 15.1 percent of the total population (and 22.0 percent of the population under 18).

[10] These statistics on the share of aggregate income received by households are from the US Census Bureau (www.census.gov/hhes/www/income/income.html); see Table H-2.

potential is a loss not only for those individuals, but also for society. Opportunities to develop, to achieve and to excel should be open to all, beginning from the earliest ages.

MACROECONOMIC STABILITY

A fourth basic market failure might be macroeconomic instability. Unemployment or high inflation can have significant social costs and adversely affect the general welfare.[11] Whether the government through discretionary fiscal and monetary policies can help stabilize the economy and promote noninflationary economic growth is controversial. Macroeconomists are divided on the efficacy of demand-management policies.

The recent implosion of the financial markets in the US and severe recession, which spread to the rest of the industrial world, resulted in massive government intervention in the economy, from fiscal stimulus to increases in the money supply to greater regulation of financial firms' behavior to prevent systematic economic collapse.

Joseph Stiglitz (2010: 275–276), reflecting on the financial crisis which defined the Great Recession, asserted:

> The crisis exposed not only flaws in the prevailing economic model but also flaws in our society. . .We have gone far down an alternative path—creating a society in which materialism dominates moral commitment, in which the rapid growth that we have achieved is not sustainable environmentally or socially, in which we do not act together as a community to address our common needs, partly because rugged individualism and market fundamentalism have eroded any sense of community and have led to rampant exploitation of unwary and unprotected individuals and to an increasing social divide.

In the aftermath of the financial crisis, as part of the financial reform in the US, the Consumer Financial Protection Bureau was created, to promote transparency and fairness in consumer lending. This new agency will regulate credit cards, mortgages, and other financial products so that consumers are more clearly informed about the terms and conditions of the loans they are assuming.[12]

---

[11] In Chapter 6 we noted the aggregate economic costs associated with unemployment, including the loss of national output and incomes, the atrophying of labor skills, and deterioration in health. In an excellent review of the literature, Frey and Stutzer (2002: 419–422) summarize the research on the toll of unemployment and inflation on human happiness. For the unemployed, particularly as the duration of being out of work increases, the psychic costs (stress, depression, reduced self-esteem) and social costs (stigma of unemployment) add to the income loss. Inflation also adds detracts from reported happiness, particularly for those on relatively fixed nominal incomes, but is more diffuse. Frey and Stutzer cite a study of a dozen European countries for the period 1975–91 that attempted to quantify the aggregate tradeoff between unemployment and inflation on happiness and found that a one percentage point increase in the unemployment rate would be compensated for by a 1.7 percent decrease in the inflation rate. The policy implications would be to err on the side of full employment rather than price stability.

[12] The Consumer Financial Protection Bureau was established by the Dodd–Frank Wall Street Reform and Consumer Protection Act of 2010. According to the bureau's website at http://www.consumerfinance.gov/the-bureau (accessed May 11, 2012):

> The consumer bureau is working to give consumers the information they need to understand the terms of their agreements with financial companies. We are working to make regulations and guidance as clear and streamlined as possible so providers of consumer financial products and services can follow the rules on their own.

Among the charges of the new bureau are: supervision and enforcement of federal consumer financial protection laws, restricting unfair, deceptive, or abusive acts or practices; promoting financial education; and monitoring financial markets for new risks to consumers.

ECONOMIC GROWTH AND DEVELOPMENT

After World War II, many scholars advocated a greater role for government in directing economies, especially in those developing nations gaining their independence. The Soviet Union had emerged from the devastation of the war to rapid industrialization, quickly becoming a military superpower. While the Soviet-style command economy was considered to an extreme form of government control, not to mention the attendant political repression, there were advantages cited for governments, operating from the commanding heights, to manage economic growth and development. Resources could be marshaled for strategic industries. Public spending and credit could be so directed. Developing economies were considered to be too young for the free-for-all of capitalism, it was argued, and the guiding hand of the central authorities was needed for the welfare of the nation.

By the 1980s, however, the inefficiencies of state-controlled economies were increasingly apparent. Economic growth had stalled in these states. The rise to power of conservative leaders in the Western democracies, in particular, Ronald Reagan in the United States and Margaret Thatcher in the United Kingdom, reemphasized the importance of private enterprise and the "magic of the marketplace." With the dissolution of the Soviet Union in the 1990s and the transformation of former socialist systems, the triumph of capitalism, as well as democracy, seemed complete.

Yet, as discussed in Chapter 5, the difficulties experienced by Russia, the Commonwealth of Independent States, and the Western European economies in the 1990s as they adopted more market-oriented systems cooled somewhat the enthusiasm for capitalism. Then the financial crises that triggered the Great Recession in the US and the subsequent stresses in the European economies as they struggled with mandated austerity programs to address sovereign debt problems added to concerns with the soundness and sustainability of capitalism. The extraordinary economic growth of China, largely managed by the Communist Party, as well as the earlier successes of Asian economies under government direction, among them South Korea, Singapore, and Taiwan, provided further evidence for more active roles for the government.

At the same time, the forces of globalization are making nations more economically interdependent. National economic autonomies have been reduced by the increased mobility of capital, whether financial flows, where billions of dollars can be moved virtually instantaneously, or physical capital with multinational corporations and direct foreign investment. David Rothkopf (2012) observed:

> A key part of fixing capitalism will be reconciling the large and growing imbalances between the public and private sectors. National governments have, over the past few decades, seen the most basic pillars of their power erode. Globalization has undermined their efforts to manage their borders. The ability to control their own currency has been lost for all but a handful of major powers. . . .Meanwhile, corporations play nation states against one another as they venue-shop for more attractive tax or regulatory regimes. This regulatory arbitrage undermines nations' ability to enforce their own laws.

Woolridge (2012: 17) argues that "The rise of state capitalism constitutes one of the biggest changes in the world economy in recent years." In state capitalism, the government invests directly in strategic industries and sectors of the economy, eschewing state ownership and direct management for significant influence as a major shareholder of publicly traded stocks of the companies.

435

The government also enhances the growth of selected industries with preferential access to credit, research and development, assistance in trade and foreign investment, and public investment in supporting infrastructure. The favored companies, in turn, are increasingly engaged in the global market. While the leading example of state capitalism is China, in other emerging economies such as Russia and Brazil the government is also heavily involved. So, too, for many of the Middle Eastern oil-producing nations, the government has taken the lead in industrial policy, with directed investments and development projects. In fact, natural resources are typically the primary sectors for state control. Wooldridge (2012: 4) observes that the 13 largest oil companies and the biggest natural gas company in the world are all state-backed. He adds that state companies account for a large percentage of the total value of shares in the stock markets of China (80 percent), Russia (62 percent), and Brazil (38 percent).

On the downside, perhaps not surprisingly, state capitalism can be plagued by "cronyism and corruption," with party officials privy to inside information enriching their own nests. The bureaucracies associated with government stifle innovation and entrepreneurship. And those industries and companies not favored by the state capitalists will necessarily be at a disadvantage.

Another dominant characteristic of state capitalism is the sovereign wealth fund. Usually built from accumulated current account surpluses, these funds can be used for social welfare (as with Norway's Government Pension Fund) as well as investment in private companies (as with Abu Dhabi's investment in the high-technology sector as it seeks to diversify away from petroleum). Wooldridge (2012: 8) reports that the world's sovereign wealth control nearly $5 trillion in assets.

In fact, in the post-war era, governments of all nations, even market economies, increased their roles. Micklethwait (2011: 4) presents data on government spending as a share of national output for 13 industrial economies over the last half century.[13] From 1960 to 1980, on average, government spending in these nations increased from 28.4 percent to 43.8 percent of gross domestic product. Over the next 25 years, the average government share stabilized around 44 percent, before rising to 47.7 percent in 2009 with the recession. The greater incidence in government spending largely reflects entitlement programs. Micklethwait (2011: 5, 20) notes:

> Globalization. . .has increased many people's reliance on the state: greater job insecurity among the middle classes has increased the calls for bigger safety nets, and the greater inequality that comes with bigger markets has made voters keener on redistribution.
> . . .Unless Western governments start to reform entitlements, the state will swell again in line with their ageing populations. . . But governments also need to start redirecting social programs at the truly needy.

In sum, there is considerable controversy among economists, as well as politicians, as to the proper role of the government in the economy. John Kenneth Galbraith, in his classic work, *The Affluent Society*, first published in 1958, argued that there was excessive private consumption in affluent societies like the US. Driven by materialism and fueled by advertising, personal consumption expenditures were at the expense of more socially worthwhile public goods. He maintained (1998: 193, 223):

> Failure to keep public services in minimal relation to private production and use of goods is a cause of social disorder or impairs economic performance.

---

[13] The 13 nations are: Austria, Belgium, Britain, Canada, France, Germany, Italy, Japan, Netherlands, Spain, Sweden, Switzerland, and the United States.

...there are large ready-made needs for schools, hospitals, slum clearance and urban redevelopment, sanitation, parks, playgrounds, police and other pressing public services.

And, concerning poverty, Galbraith (1998: 239, 242) was equally provocative:

An affluent society that is also both compassionate and rational would, no doubt, secure to all who needed it the minimum income essential for decency and comfort.
...in the United States, the survival of poverty is remarkable. We ignore it because we share with all societies at all times the capacity for not seeing what we do not wish to see.

While public goods and externalities are widely recognized as market failures requiring government intervention, there is ongoing debate on the government's role in regulating business, addressing poverty, using macroeconomic policy to promote full employment, and directing the economy. Moreover, in each case, if government involvement is called for, the questions of what forms of intervention and which levels of government should intervene arise. Government can intervene though laws (e.g., environmental regulations and standards for product safety), through the market mechanism with taxes and transfers (as in the case of poverty assistance), through the direct provision of public goods (national defense, police protection and the judicial system) and merit goods (public education), and through state control of select industries and sectors (oil and natural gas).

In general, the primary advantage of intervention by state and local government is greater familiarity and perhaps less bureaucracy in dealing with the market failure (e.g., a system of community colleges for remedial education and job training). There can be greater variation in approaches, however, with state and local government intervention (e.g., differences in state income tax rates, environmental regulation, and poverty programs). Some public goods, notably national defense, can be provided only by the federal government. As noted earlier, market failures that transcend national boundaries pose greater challenges to address. Indeed, global warming may be the biggest market failure ever. We end this chapter with a examples of international cooperation that address the global commons.

INTERNATIONAL COOPERATION

The global commons encompass those natural resources, such as the oceans, atmosphere, and biodiversity, shared by all humans. Consequently, there is the danger of Hardin's tragedy of the commons, where open access seriously depletes and degrades these natural assets.

Oceans

The world's oceans are perhaps the most obvious of the global commons. As Grimond (2009: 3) observes, "Over half of the world's people live within 100 kilometers (62 miles) of the coast." The United Nations Convention on the Law of the Sea evolved over the second half of the twentieth century in an attempt to govern the resources of the oceans.[14] Recognizing that the resources of the oceans belong to all peoples—not just those current citizens of the developed nations able to

[14] See the United Nations Law of the Sea Treaty Information Center (http://www.unlawoftheseastreaty.org). For a history of the UN Convention on the Law of the Sea, see: http://www.un.org/Depts/los/convention_agreements/convention_historical_perspective.htm.

437

harvest these resources or even to those nations with coasts—and that open access could result in depletion and degradation of these common resources, especially the stocks of fish, the Law of the Sea Treaty, adopted in 1982, sought to establish guidelines for using the oceans for transport and research, for harvesting resources, and for protecting the marine environment.[15] Provisions are in place for the sharing of technology. Exclusive economic zones, however, give coastal nations jurisdiction over the management of the waters extending 200 miles offshore, which includes the vast majority of the fisheries as well as likely the recoverable mineral resources.[16] Yet, the World Bank (2010: 159) points out that, "despite the multibillion dollar-a-year international trade in fisheries, developing countries receive relatively little in fees from foreign fishing fleets operating in their waters." And overcapacity in foreign fishing fleets is contributing to the depletion of fishing stocks across the oceans.

Given the lack of a supranational authority to enforce any laws and the extensive exclusive economic zones and that less developed nations are often unable to exercise effective control of the waters off their coasts, it is not surprising that the oceans have increasingly been overfished and polluted.[17] The extraction of most minerals in the deep seas has so far been limited by the technology for accessing these resources in a cost-effective manner, but it may be only a matter of time before this mining is scaled up significantly. Collier (2010: 168–170) proposes that the United Nations assume control over the deep oceans by auctioning off rights for fishing, with the quotas set within sustainable limits. Likewise, rights for the exploration of minerals could be auctioned off, with an international tax imposed on any subsequent harvesting of minerals.

The Law of the Seas applies to the Arctic Ocean.[18] There is a concern, however, with an eventual scramble for the natural resources between the five nations (the US, Canada, Denmark, Norway and Russia) bordering the Arctic. Because the US has not ratified this treaty, its claim to exclusive rights to oil and natural gas exploration in the 200 miles of extended continental shelf in this Arctic region is less clearly established.[19]

Antarctica is also part of the global commons. The Antarctic Treaty, abided to by nearly 50 nations, attempts not only to ensure that the region be used for peaceful purposes, but also to promote scientific research and the conservation of the natural environment for all of

---

[15] It was not until 1994, however, that enough states ratified the convention for it to come into force. The US still has not ratified the treaty.

[16] As Grimond (2009: 5) discusses, the UN Convention on the Law of the Sea allows nations jurisdiction over greater areas off their coasts if they can demonstrate that the continental shelf extends beyond their 200-mile exclusive economic zones.

[17] That the oceans have been a receptacle for waste is vividly illustrated by Grimond (2009: 8) who reports that:

> between 1958 and 1992, the Arctic Ocean was used by the Soviet Union, or its Russian successor, as the resting-place for 18 unwanted nuclear reactors, several still containing their nuclear fuel. All over the world, oil spills regularly contaminate coasts.

> ...in the central Pacific...scientists believe as much as 100m tons of plastic jetsam are suspended in two separate gyres of garbage over an area twice the size of the United States.

[18] Grimond (2009: 7) notes that the Arctic Ocean has lost over 40 percent of its year-round ice since 1985, with a loss of 14 percent in 2004–05 alone, evidence that the melting from global warming is accelerating.

[19] Astill (2012: 12–13) reports:

> According to a 2008 study by the US Geological Survey, the Arctic may hold 90 billion barrels of oil and 1,669 trillion cubic feet of natural gas, respectively 13% and 30% of the world's estimated undiscovered reserves. Over 84% of this is thought to be offshore, with the continental shelves of the United States, Canada and Greenland likeliest to hold oil and Russia's and Norway's the best prospects for gas.

humankind.[20] Unfortunately, there is increasing evidence of environmental deterioration in this formerly pristine region of the world.

The atmosphere

Needless to say, clean air to breathe is essential for life. One of the major challenges of the last half-century has been protection the atmosphere, shared by all nations, owned by none. Air pollution does not respect national boundaries. Before the industrial era, emissions of pollutants into the atmosphere were little noticed. Increasingly, however, output and population growth have generated emissions of pollutants that exceed the natural capacity of the atmosphere for absorption without environmental deterioration. With advances in science that allowed for the measurement of air quality, the need for government intervention was recognized. Remedial action by any one nation, however, would be insufficient.

One of the earliest, and still most successful, examples of international cooperation to address this global concern was the agreement to protect the Earth's ozone layer, which filters out dangerous ultraviolet radiation that increases the incidence of skin cancer and can be harmful to eyes. The 1987 Montreal Protocol phases out the production of chlorofluorocarbons released through aerosol sprays and refrigeration. The initial treaty has been extended several times to aggressively reduce these ozone-depleting emissions. Virtually every nation in the world has signed up and the ozone hole above Antarctica has been reduced.[21]

Other efforts to addressing atmospheric emissions, however, have been less successful. The Kyoto Protocol was an international agreement to curb the emission of greenhouse gases through binding targets for developed economies to reduce their emissions, primarily of carbon dioxide, by roughly 5 percent from 1990 levels by 2012. Developing countries were not expected to reduce absolutely their emissions—in recognition both of their greater need for economic growth and industrialization and that the burden should be on the already developed economies that had been most responsible for the greenhouse gas accumulation in the atmosphere. Developing nations, however, were encouraged to adopt mitigation policies to limit their emissions. The Clean Development Mechanism of the Kyoto Protocol allowed for the developed nations to get credit for greenhouse gas reductions through financing projects in the developing nations that would reduce emissions below what otherwise would have occurred. There were provisions for emissions trading, as with the pollution permits. There were no provisions, however, for preserving forests that naturally absorbed carbon dioxide and generate positive externalities.

Perhaps not surprisingly, the Kyoto Protocol has not lived up to expectations.[22] In large part, the two major polluters in the world, the US and China, never adopted the treaty. The US, reluctant to agree to international treaties that might limit its economic growth or infringe on its sovereignty, objected to the exclusion of the developing nations from emissions reductions. China,

---

[20]For information on the Antarctic Treaty, see the National Science Foundation Office of Polar Programs at http://www.nsf.gov/od/opp/antarct/anttrty.jsp.

[21]For a brief overview, see "Recent International Developments in Saving the Ozone Layer" and "Amendments to the Montreal Protocol" on the US Environmental Protection Agency website at http://www.epa.gov/ozone/intpol.

[22]Carbon dioxide emissions in the world increased by 36 percent between 1990 and 2008. This aggregate figure, however, masks dramatic differences. The percentage changes in CO_2 emissions from 1990 to 2008 were +15 percent for the high-income economies (+12 percent for the US versus −3 percent for the euro area). For the developing regions of the world, the diversity in the total change in CO_2 emissions from 1990 to 2008 ranged from −20 percent in Europe and Central Asia to +48 percent for sub-Saharan Africa, +61 percent for Latin America and the Caribbean, +113 percent for the Middle East and North Africa, +154 percent for South Asia (+152 percent for India), and +185 percent for East Asia and the Pacific (+186 percent for China). These statistics are from the World Bank (2012: Table 3.10).

as a developing nation, was not obligated to accept reduced emission targets and placed greater emphasis on continuing its rapid economic growth. Even those nations accepting the Kyoto Protocol had only limited success in attaining the targeted emissions reductions. Russia, on the other hand, the nation whose adoption provided the critical mass to bring the treaty into force, was able to meet the emissions cutbacks not so much from due diligence, as from its declining economy over the 1990s.

In an assessment of the Kyoto Protocol, the United Nations Development Programme (2007: 54) concluded that the targets for emissions reductions were too modest, and even then were not binding, as evidenced in most countries falling short of their commitments. Moreover, any successful climate change agreement needs to be comprehensive, including all the major greenhouse-gas-emitting nations.

In place since 2005 has been the European Union Emissions Trading System (ETS), which is based on the "cap and trade" principle for pollution permits.[23] Covering 30 nations (the members of the European Union plus Iceland, Liechtenstein, and Norway), under the EU ETS companies (power stations and industrial plants) receive greenhouse gas emissions allowances. To be binding, the total allowances should be below the levels of emissions that otherwise would prevail under business as usual. The allowances or emissions permits are marketable. Companies with emissions exceeding their allowances face heavy fines. Under this scheme, the projected greenhouse gas emissions in 2020 will be 21 percent below the levels of 2005. While in principle an important effort to reduce greenhouse gas emissions, in practice the system has been criticized for the initially too high and overly generous allotment of allowances to the participating countries (see United Nations Development Programme 2007: 129–132). In retrospect, the initial cap was inadvertently actually above the then total emissions level, which not only greatly reduced the subsequent trading of allowances needed for efficiencies in emissions reduction, but also undermined the main objective of reducing emissions. Moreover, 95 percent of the allowances were given away to the countries, not auctioned off to generate state revenues for climate change mitigation. The allowances were distributed on the basis of historic emissions, not the most efficient criterion or even the fairest. Some companies, especially in the power sector, received windfall profits. Nevertheless, it is unreasonable to expect that any initiative, like the EU ETS, will be perfectly conceived and implemented. The lessons learned can inform future policy.

In December 2009, the nations of the world met in Copenhagen in an attempt to renew and strengthen the efforts to address global warming. Here too, consensus on a clear, binding strategy for curbing greenhouse gas emissions proved difficult to forge. Nevertheless, under the Copenhagen Accord, the goal of holding the increase in global temperatures to under 2°C was adopted and commitments for reducing emissions were made, both by developed and developing nations. Moreover, the developed countries pledged $100 billion in annual assistance to the developing nations by 2020 for their mitigation efforts; but as with past promises of aid, the actual delivery may be much less. The Accord also recognized the importance of forests with the establishment of an enhanced Reduced Emissions from Deforestation and Forest Degradation (REDD) scheme as part of a more comprehensive Clean Development Mechanism. Nations such as Brazil and Indonesia could receive payments for maintaining their rainforests.[24] Since the Accord, however, there is scant evidence of effective international mitigation.

[23] See European Commission Climate Action, "Emissions Trading System (EU ETS)," http://ec.europa.eu/clima/policies/ets.

[24] For a description of the Copenhagen Accord, as well as commitments by specific nations to emissions reduction, see Natural Resources Defense Council, "From Copenhagen Accord to Climate Action: Tracking National Commitments to Curb Global

Biodiversity

Biodiversity refers to all the variety of life on the planet: humans, animals, birds, insects, plants, and microorganisms. The importance of preserving these life forms, manifested in millions of species, is widely recognized—not only for the inherent value of the diversity for the myriad natural processes of life and for respecting the integrity of natural habitats, but also for the derived scientific knowledge, including new medicines and food sources.

In recognition of the need to preserve biodiversity, most clearly evidenced by the accelerated threat and realization of extinction of species, the Convention on Biological Diversity was created at the United Nations Conference on Environment and Development in Rio de Janeiro in 1992.[25] Consistent with the principles of sustainable development, nations are enjoined to preserve biodiversity through the protection of natural habitats for threatened species and through the preservation of indigenous cultures and their traditional knowledge. In particular, commercial trade which endangers wildlife, such as the slaughtering of elephants for the ivory in their tusks, the hunting of mountain gorillas for meat, and the capture of exotic animals for pets, is outlawed. Enforcing these prohibitions, however, has been difficult.

Natural resource management

As discussed in Chapter 12, without honest and able leadership, nations well endowed with natural resources, especially nonrenewable fossil fuels and minerals, can succumb to a "natural resource curse." All too often, poor nations have squandered the opportunities to use these gifts of nature to promote development. The rents from these natural resources have not been effectively invested in physical and human capital. Rather they have been expropriated by corrupt government leaders for their personal enrichment or captured by foreign companies. Competition for control over these resources has spawned conflict. Even when government are well intentioned, resource revenues can be mismanaged, particularly during export booms, as evidenced by the outbreaks of Dutch disease. Moreover, it has been all too easy for governments to live off the revenues from these resources, so that effective administrative, legislative, judicial, and financial institutions essential for economic development do not evolve.

The Natural Resource Charter is a global initiative, launched in 2009 at the annual meeting of the African Development Bank in Dakar, Senegal, by Paul Collier and other development scholars, to help nations use their natural resources effectively to promote sustainable development. Twelve precepts underlie the charter, including ensuring accountability and transparency in the management of the natural resources by governments and companies, sound investment of the resource revenues for the benefit of the greater society, and respect for the environment in extraction of the natural resources. In essence, the charter sets forth best practices for natural resource management: "The Charter is a living document that will continue to be refined in consultation with civil society organizations, policy makers, experts and other stakeholders involved in meeting the challenges associated with harnessing natural resource wealth."[26]

Warming," http://www.nrdc.org/international/copenhagenaccords. For example, the US committed to target reductions of greenhouse gas emissions below 2005 levels of 17 percent by 2020, 42 percent by 2030, and 83 percent by 2050.

[25] See Secretariat of the Convention on Biological Diversity, *Sustaining Life on Earth: How the Convention on Biological Diversity Promotes Nature and Human Well-Being*, http://www.cbd.int.

[26] See Natural Resource Charter at http://www.naturalresourcecharter.org. See also "AfDB Pledges Support for Natural Resource Charter," http://www.afdb.org/en/news-and-events/article/afdb-pledges-support-for-natural-resource-charter-4630.

A related endeavor is the Extractive Industries Transparency Initiative (EITI), which was launched by Tony Blair at the World Summit for Sustainable Development in Johannesburg, South Africa, in 2002.[27] A coalition of governments, companies, civil society groups, investors and international organizations, the EITI supports transparency and accountability through the publication and auditing of company payments and government revenues derived from oil, gas, and mining. By 2009, 30 countries had joined this coalition.

Finally, we should note the Kimberley Process, also a joint government, industry, and civil society initiative established in 2003 to reduce, if not eliminate, trade in "conflict" diamonds. The Kimberley Process Certification Scheme seeks to ensure that the rough or unprocessed diamonds entering into world trade are not illegal, in particular are not the conflict or so-called "blood" diamonds that have funded rebel movements in several sub-Saharan African nations. By the end of 2009, 75 countries, representing virtually all of the global production of rough diamonds, had joined the Kimberley Process. Through a process of verification, involving a warranty system by the World Diamond Council, trade in illicit diamonds has greatly been reduced to less than 1 percent, down from as much as 15 percent of the total rough diamonds in the 1990s. This success has deprived criminal and insurgency movements of what had been a key source of revenues, adding instead to the state revenues. For example, in Sierra Leone, legal exports of diamonds increased 100-fold since the end of the civil war in 2002.[28]

CONCLUSION

While free markets are an efficient system for the allocation of resources that underlie the production, distribution, and consumption of most goods and services, there are serious market failures. Public goods, merit goods, the regulation of business to protect social welfare, externalities, poverty, and macroeconomic instability call for government intervention. As we will discuss in the concluding chapter, achieving sustainable development in the world will require not only continued technological progress and efficiencies in resources allocation, driven in part by market incentives, but likely even greater government intervention in the economy, with unprecedented international cooperation, and ultimately fundamental reorientation in human priorities and practices.

KEY TERMS

allocative efficiency	average revenue
biodiversity	command and control
consumer surplus	deadweight loss
dysfunctional selection	equilibrium price
excise tax	externalities
freedom of entry and exit	long-run average cost curve
marginal cost	marginal revenue
market	market failure

[27]For a description of the Extractive Industries Transparency Initiative see http://eiti.org, from which this discussion is drawn. See also Collier (2010: 231–232).

[28]See "Kimberly Process: From Conflict Diamonds to Prosperity Diamonds," http://www. kimberleyprocess.com.

marketable pollution permits   merit good
monopolistic competition   monopoly
moral suasion   natural monopoly
negative economic profits   negative externalities
oligopoly   output quota
positive economic profits   positive externalities
price-setter   price-taker
producer surplus   public good
quota rent   short-run average cost curve
zero economic profits

QUESTIONS

1. Compare the insights from Adam Smith (the invisible hand) and Garret Hardin (the tragedy of the commons) for achieving sustainable development. Which perspective do you think is the more relevant? Why?

2. Suppose the market demand and supply curves in a competitive market are given by:

$$Q^d = 60 - 5P \quad \text{and} \quad Q^s = -10 + 2P$$

   (a) Find the market equilibrium price and quantity transacted. Calculate the consumer surplus and producer surplus.

   (b) Suppose that the production of this good generated negative externalities, so that the comprehensive supply curve, including social costs, is given by $Q^{s\prime} = -13.5 + 2P$. Find the socially optimal quantity produced and price.

   (c) Determine the excise tax on suppliers required to yield the socially optimal output. Calculate the tax revenues.

   (d) Suppose the market demand increases to $Q^{d\prime\prime} = 63.5 - 5P$. Find the new market equilibrium price and quantity transacted. Determine the new socially optimal quantity transacted.

3. Suppose the market demand and supply curves in a competitive market are given by:

$$Q^d = 40 - 4P \quad \text{and} \quad Q^s = -5 + 5P$$

   (a) Find the market equilibrium price and quantity transacted. Calculate the consumer surplus and producer surplus.

   (b) Suppose that the consumption of this good generated positive externalities, so that the comprehensive demand curve, including social benefits, is given by $Q^{d\prime} = 49 - 4P$. Find the socially optimal quantity produced.

   (c) Determine the subsidy to suppliers required to yield the socially optimal output.

4. What is the appropriate role for the government in an economy? That is, which of the market failures warrant government involvement? Who should determine this? Discuss.

5. With respect to global warming, do you think Hardin's mutual coercion or Ostrom's mutual trust will most likely address the problem? Discuss.

SUSTAINABLE DEVELOPMENT

REFERENCES

Allcott, Hunt and Michael Greenstone. 2012. "Is There an Energy Efficiency Gap?" *Journal of Economic Perspectives* 26(1): 3–28.

Astill, James. 2012. "The Melting North: Special Report: The Arctic," *The Economist*, June 16.

Collier, Paul. 2010. *The Plundered Planet: Why We Must—and How We Can—Manage Nature for Global Prosperity*. Oxford: Oxford University Press.

DeNavas-Walt, Carmen, Bernadette Proctor, and Jessica Smith. 2010. *Income, Poverty, and Health Insurance Coverage in the United States: 2009*, US Census Bureau, Current Population Reports, P60-238. Washington, DC: US Government Printing Office.

Diamond, Jared. 2005. "Big Business and the Environment: Different Conditions, Different Outcomes," in *Collapse: How Societies Choose to Fail or Succeed*. New York: Viking: 441–485.

Frey, Bruno and Alois Stutzer. 2002. "What Can Economists Learn from Happiness Research?" *Journal of Economic Literature*, 60(2): 402–435.

Galbraith, John Kenneth. 1998. *The Affluent Society*, 40th anniversary edition. Boston: Houghton Mifflin.

Grimond, John. 2009. "Troubled Waters: A Special Report on the Sea," *The Economist*, January 3.

Hardin, Garrett. 1968. "The Tragedy of the Commons," *Science*, 162: 1243–1248.

Knittel, Christopher. 2012. "Reducing Petroleum Consumption from Transportation." *Journal of Economic Perspectives* 26(1): 93–118.

Micklethwait, John. 2011. "Taming Leviathan: A Special Report on the Future of the State," *The Economist*, March 19.

Ostrom, Elinor. 2010. "Beyond Markets and States: Polycentric Governance of Complex Economic Systems," *American Economic Review*, 100(3): 641–672.

Rothkopf, David. 2012. "Command and Control: Fixing Capitalism Means Taking Power Back from Business," *Time*, January 30.

Stiglitz, Joseph. 2010. *FreeFall: America, Free Markets, and the Sinking of the World Economy*. New York: W.W. Norton.

United Nations Development Programme. 2007. *Human Development Report 2007/2008: Fighting Climate Change: Human Solidarity in a Divided World*. New York: Palgrave Macmillan for the UNDP.

Wooldridge, Adrian. 2012. "The Visible Hand: Special Report State Capitalism," *The Economist*, January 21.

World Bank. 2005. *World Development Report 2006: Equity and Development*. New York: Oxford University Press.

World Bank. 2010. *World Development Report 2010: Development and Climate Change*. Washington, DC: World Bank.

World Bank. 2012. *World Development Indicators 2012*. Washington, DC: World Bank.

444

Chapter 15

Policies and practices for sustainable development

How to achieve sustainable development, in all its ramifications, may well be the overriding issue facing humankind. We tend to focus on meeting our immediate needs, with perhaps too little concern for the long run and almost no concern for the welfare of generations yet to be born. This all too human myopia is perhaps understandable, but it is no longer sustainable.

If there are limits to the Earth's capacity to provide essential natural resources and environmental services, such as clean air and water, then there are limits to population growth and economic growth. Addressing climate change will drive the agenda for sustainable development. According to the United Nations Development Programme (2007: 2): "Climate change demands urgent action now to address a threat to two constituencies with a little or no political voice: the world's poor and future generations." In fact, the evidence of global warming, largely due to human activity, is mounting. The first decade of the twenty-first century was the warmest yet. And, with a global average temperature of 14.63°C, the year 2010 tied 2005 as the hottest in 131 years of record keeping (Giese 2011).[1]

In this concluding chapter, policies and practices for achieving sustainable development will be set forth. Underlying informed policy will be accurate measures of environmental change, including revisions to national income accounting. Markets will continue to play a role in the allocation of resources, but, as discussed in Chapter 14, the market failures of public goods, merit goods, externalities, poverty, and macroeconomic instability will still warrant government action. To deal effectively with the global challenges, such as climate change and environmental degradation, unprecedented international cooperation will be required. Continued technological progress will be important, but not enough. New human behavior is required, including a movement away from

---

[1] Giese (2011) added:

The earth's temperature is not only rising, it is rising at an increasing rate. From 1880 through 1970, the global average temperature increased roughly 0.03 degrees Celsius each decade. Since 1970, the pace has increased dramatically, to 0.13 degrees Celsius per decade. Two thirds of the increase of nearly 0.8 degrees Celsius (1.4 degrees Fahrenheit) in the global temperature since the 1880s has occurred in the last 40 years. And 9 of the 10 warmest years happened in the last decade.

...The Arctic has warmed by as much as 3–4 degrees Celsius (5–7 degrees Fahrenheit) since the 1950s. It is heating up at twice the rate of the earth on average, making it the fastest-warming region on the planet. Disproportionately large warming in the Arctic is partially due to the albedo effect. As sea ice melts, darker ocean water is exposed; the additional energy absorbed by the darker surface then melts more ice, setting in motion a self-reinforcing feedback.

consumerism, especially in the affluent nations. Conservation and shifts from fossil fuels to greater reliance on renewable and cleaner energy also will define sustainable development.

TWO GUIDING PRINCIPLES

It would be convenient to hope for, and continue to rely on, science and technology to solve the problems of natural resource scarcities, environmental thresholds, and human poverty. Hardin (1968: 1243) discounted, however, such dependence on technical solutions that "require a change only in the techniques of the natural sciences, demanding little or nothing in the way of change in human values or ideas of morality." Perhaps, then, two principles might guide the policies and practices for sustainable development. The first involves the adoption of a more cautious approach. The second promotes a more just society.

The precautionary principle

The **precautionary principle** basically reflects a "better safe than sorry" or a "minimizing future regrets" approach to policy (Rao 2000: 100–102). More concretely, the lack of complete information or irrefutable scientific evidence of the possible devastating consequences of human behavior does not warrant a cavalier attitude or postponing remedial action. Rather, preventative measures should be adopted as a precaution. For example, where there are threats of serious or irreversible damage, such as with climate change driven by population and economic growth, then adopting appropriate mitigating behaviors, including a moderation of consumption, is advised, just in case future technologies will not permit business as usual. Delays in action may not only limit future options, but will certainly increase the future costs of addressing the problem.

A personal example of the precautionary principle might be a parent's purchase of term life insurance. While the probability of dying before the end of the term, say age 65, may be slight, nevertheless, if early death does occur, then providing for one's dependents is important.

Setting global limits on greenhouse gas emissions or aggregate production of goods and services is hard enough. The more difficult issue then becomes the distribution of the costs and benefits associated with abiding by these limits. For example, as we discussed, zero population growth seems inevitable in the long run. The world's population size will eventually stabilize, likely in the neighborhood of 9 billion. The developed nations and many of the less developed nations have already attained replacement-level fertility. In fact, for the developed nations, fertility rates have been well below replacement level for some time and will soon result in population declines unless the rates rebound to at least replacement levels. In a steady-state global economy, should all nations be required to maintain replacement-level fertility? Zero population growth in a nation could also be achieved with net migration rates offsetting crude rates of natural increase. Will the developed countries with declining natural populations permit increased immigration to stabilize their population sizes? Of course, this begs the question of the optimum population sizes of the sending and receiving nations, quantities themselves contingent on technology and desired per capita resource consumption.

With an upper limit on the carrying capacity of the Earth and barring unforeseen advances in technology, the sustainable level of per capita consumption may be somewhere between the rates presently found in the high-income and low-income countries. Should there be convergence in future per capita incomes between the rich and poor nations? What degree of income and consumption inequalities across and within countries is tolerable? Should there be limits on per capita income and consumption to ensure the average sustainable levels are attained? Income could be redistributed through taxes and transfers to keep per capita incomes within the bounds consistent with sustainable consumption. Would such redistributions of income discourage the entrepreneurship, innovation, and technological progress that would allow for growth in output and per capita consumption?

The veil of ignorance

Virtually every policy change will make some in society better off, while making others worse off in terms of individual welfares. Nevertheless, policy change should be undertaken whenever there is an improvement in the overall social welfare. Determining this is difficult and inevitably controversial. There is a well-known bias among elected officials in favor of policies that provide benefits (especially to their constituents) in the short run, while delaying costs. Mitigating climate change, however, is likely to incur significant costs in the short run, with much greater benefits only in the long run.

One's perspective on the appropriate role for the government and the adopted policies for addressing these issues will likely depend on their position in the society. The political philosopher, John Rawls, recognized this vested interest. In contemplating what would constitute a 'just society,' Rawls (1971: 60–65 and 136–142) proposed a **veil of ignorance**. That is, when you conceive of being a member of a just society, you would not know your position in that society (i.e., your socioeconomic status, gender, race, religion, age, or inherent abilities). You might be the chief executive of a Fortune 500 company in the United States, or a beggar living on the streets of Delhi. You might attend a prestigious university in England or be a young girl sold into slavery in Sudan. You might be an acclaimed artist in Japan or an aged peasant farmer scratching a living off a small plot of land in Bolivia. You would not even know whether you were a member of the present or a future generation. Adopting this veil of ignorance, what kind of society would you prefer—particularly in terms of opportunities and redistributive institutions?

In a just society, Rawls favored the assurance of basic human rights and equality of opportunity. Moreover, Rawls suggested that no redistribution of resources within a just state would occur unless benefiting the least well off. In particular, in his principle of redress, Rawls (1971: 100) held that, "to provide genuine equality of opportunity, society must give more attention to those with fewer native assets and to those born into less favorable social positions." The United Nations Development Programme (2010: 104) echoed this sentiment: "Equity and poverty reduction must be at the forefront of policy design, not add-ons."

Can we extend this notion of a just society to the global society and to future generations who would inherit such a world? Perhaps whenever any policy is contemplated, the veil of ignorance should be adopted. Policy-makers would craft the policy as if they could be anyone in the affected population. Such policy may well be more just.

ACCOUNTING FOR SUSTAINABLE DEVELOPMENT

In Chapter 11 indicators of sustainable development were discussed, in particular, the adjusted net saving rate, the Human Development Index, and a new index of youth investment. These three comprehensive measures captured different dimensions of sustainable development: the rate of capital formation, average well-being, and investment in youth, respectively. We related how economic growth with increases in per capita income need not indicate sustainable development, but that there were many other statistics that would capture specific aspects of sustainable development, including the rate of deforestation, the loss of biodiversity, depletion of fishing stocks, greenhouse gas emissions, and access to safe water and adequate sanitation.

The limitations of national income accounting, in particular, the measures of aggregate output and income for indicating the average standard of living, have long been recognized.[2] Accurate indicators of well-being are needed not only for monitoring progress, but also for policy-making, identifying not only areas of priority investments but also initiatives that are successful and should be continued as well as those that fall short and should be discontinued.

Stiglitz et al. (2009) recognize the many dimensions of well-being that extend beyond material consumption to encompass education, health, voluntary leisure, economic and physical security, social activity, political participation, and the natural environment. How to quantify these dimensions in a few comprehensive measures remains a challenge. Also incorporating the distribution of benefits and costs, often obscured by averages, is important. For example, median income and median hours of voluntary leisure may be presented, along with statistics for the quintiles of population, to capture inequities in well-being.

National income accounting focuses on the measurement of economic output, essentially quantified by the costs of production of goods and services that enter the market. Included in GDP are defensive expenditures, such as for national defense, crime prevention and incarceration, commuting to work, and restoring the environment after oil spills, that are necessary but don't really enhance well-being. Netting out such expenditures would make per capita GDP more reflective of the average standard of living. As discussed earlier, net national product (and net national savings) deducts from gross output (gross national savings) the depreciation of physical capital, but not the depletion of natural capital or the change in the state of the environment. Along with the national income accounts, Stiglitz et al. argue for the collection and publication of an accompanying set of physical indicators on the environment, which could identify potential tipping points, for example, soil erosion, quantity and quality of freshwater supplies, days in the year with hazardous air pollution. Some of the most critical indicators would be global, such as greenhouse gas accumulations, state of coral reefs, depletion of fishing stocks.

In sum, monitoring the natural environment will be crucial for sustainable development. Consideration of the other dimensions beyond income is essential for accurately measuring the quality of life and enhancing the human condition.

THE ROLE OF MARKETS

As discussed in the previous chapter, externalities in the production or consumption of a commodity constitute market failures. In the case of a negative externality, government intervention in the form of a tax or regulation of the activity in question is justified. With positive externalities, where there are socially beneficial consequences from the private activities, government subsidization may be justified. For example, two decades ago, the World Bank (1992: 15) observed that "Investments in providing clean water and sanitation have some of the highest economic, social, and environmental returns anywhere." The policy implications are clear. In fact, this is Target 7.C. of the Millennium Development Goals. Yet, in 2010, still 12 percent (over 800 million) of the world population did not have access to an improved water source and 38 percent (2.6 billion) did not have access to improved sanitation facilities.

---

[2] Stiglitz et al. (2009) provide an excellent review of the limitations of present national income accounting centered on gross domestic product and gross national income for capturing the quality of life and sustainable development.

A first priority in natural resource policy would be "to get prices right." To incorporate the negative externalities from carbon emissions, taxes based on the carbon content of the goods and services produced could be assessed. A carbon tax not only could result in a more efficient allocation of resources, while providing incentives to reduce carbon dioxide emissions, but also would generate government revenues for funding projects to improve access to safe water and adequate sanitation, as well as adaptation to climate change. Similarly, current subsidies or tax breaks to fossil fuel producers should cease.[3]

As discussed in Chapter 8, an integral part of the market-friendly strategy of development is more open economies and freer trade. As natural resources become more limited with economic growth and population growth, greater efficiencies in the allocation of those resources must be realized. In the United States, subsidies for the domestic production of corn-based ethanol and the tariff on the more efficient sugar-cane-based ethanol produced in Brazil were dropped in 2012, a welcome development not only for the global food supply, but also for renewable energy.

Property rights

To encourage the conservation of scarce resources and the proper maintenance of renewable resources, property rights may need to be more carefully established. Traditionally common property rights enforced by convention or social sanctions may have been sufficient in small villages or agrarian communities as long as resources were relatively abundant. With economic growth and population increase, resource pressures can develop, that may stimulate technological progress and the recovery of new resources, but may also require clear property rights.

With the assignment of private property rights, individuals have the incentive to invest in and improve the resources under their ownership—the fertility of the land, stocks of fish, stands of trees. In the case of common resources considered as property of the state, access fees could be auctioned off—to mine the minerals, harvest the forests, and fish the oceans within the nation's territorial boundaries. Refundable deposits could be required to ensure environmentally responsible behavior—proper disposal of wastes, replanting of forests, restoration of the landscape after strip mining, or limiting fish catches to levels consistent with the regeneration potential of the fish stocks.

An earlier example of local management of common resources comes from Mexico, where, in 1993, the government ceded control over a 2,800 square mile forest reserve in the southeastern region of the country to a nonprofit organization, Pronatura Peninsula of Yucatan. Previously degraded by logging, the reserve was to be used by the indigenous population, with a protected area in the center to remain natural. As described at the time by Neumann (1993):

> Federal, state, local and Pronatura workers have trained residents to manage and protect timber and other resources they still remove illegally to make ends meet. Where logging is permitted—outside the reserve's virgin nucleus—residents practice reforesting methods. From their own nurseries, they plant mahogany and other native precious woods to harvest, as a family trust fund, in 25 to 50 years. They learn intensive organic agriculture methods that boost to 10 years from three the land's cultivability while bolstering staple corn and bean

[3] The International Energy Agency (IEA) is an autonomous agency established in 1974 to promote energy security and advise on energy policy. With 28 members, all OECD nations except for Turkey, the IEA (2010: 13) reports that worldwide fossil fuel consumption subsidies amounted to $312 billion in 2009, the vast majority of which were in non-OECD nations.

449

yields. They also plant commercial fruit and vegetables and develop apiaries employing the local high-yield Africanized bees.

...This sustainable development process is beginning to provide residents a dignified, stable livelihood.[4]

With resources, like the atmosphere, where property rights are not clearly defined, environmental standards need to be set and enforced. One way to incorporate the market into the process of environmental regulation is to auction off permits, as illustrated in Chapter 14. In addition to the carbon taxes, marketable permits could be auctioned off for other greenhouse gases and pollutants. An international agency could auction off access to scarce resources, like the fish in the oceans beyond the exclusive economic zones of countries, with overall quotas set within the regeneration capacities. For nonrenewable resources, such as the minerals lying beneath the oceans, permits could be also auctioned off, with the revenues used for research and development into renewable substitutes.

SUSTAINABLE ENERGIES

Considerable potential remains to be realized from renewable and environmentally sound sources of energy, such as solar, wind, and tidal. Currently, the reliance on fossil fuels largely reflects their relatively low market costs, which, as noted, do not incorporate the associated negative externalities of greenhouse gas emissions and environmental degradation. Scaling up renewable energies, while requiring considerable investments in the production and delivery infrastructure, will reduce unit costs. There is no silver bullet, however, for energy security. Each of the renewable energies comes with attendant challenges.[5]

Coley (2008: 78) defines **sustainable energy technologies** as those that contribute little to manmade climate change, are capable of providing power for many generations, and place no burden on future generations. Sustainable energies include solar, wind, tidal, small-scale hydropower, biomass, geothermal, fast nuclear reactors, and nuclear fission. In addition to fossil fuels, Coley classifies large-scale hydropower and thermal nuclear reactors as unsustainable energies. Briefly, we review some of the challenges of expanding sustainable energies.

With respect to global warming, nuclear power might seem an ideal substitute for fossil fuels in the generation of electricity, since no greenhouse gases are emitted. Worldwide there are over 440 nuclear reactors in 31 countries (Coley, 2008: 227). A handful of countries derive over half of their electricity from nuclear power.[6] As Barrett (2009: 60) observes, while uranium is an exhaustible resource, current estimates show remaining reserves could fuel 1,000 new reactors over the next 50 years. Yet, there are a number of concerns with nuclear power. The construction of the nuclear plants is costly, if not prohibitively expensive. The problem of storage of the radioactive wastes is ongoing. Furthermore, while slight, the potential for disaster exists—witness the Chernobyl nuclear power plant meltdown in Ukraine in 1986 and the more recent Fukushima nuclear power plant destruction in March 2011 from the earthquake and tsunami off the coast of

[4] For recent activity, see the Pronatura web site, www.pronatura-ppy.org.mx.
[5] See Coley (2008) for a comprehensive, but fairly nontechnical, treatment of the science of energy. Barrett (2009) provides a good discussion of renewable energy options.
[6] For example, in 2009, the percentage of electricity generated by nuclear power was 76 percent in France, 74 percent in Lithuania, 54 percent in the Slovak Republic, and 53 percent in Belgium. In numerous other nations nuclear power generates a significant share of electricity. See World Bank (2012: Table 3.8).

Japan. There is also the risk of nuclear weapons proliferation from the diversion of reprocessed extracted plutonium from the spent fuel. And, if this were not enough, leakage of radioactive tritium has been discovered in the aging US nuclear plants.[7]

Morton (2012: 5) notes that in 2010 nuclear plants provided 13 percent of the world's energy, compared to 18 percent in 1996. As a result of the meltdown at the Fukushima plant, Japan, which had generated 30 percent of its electricity from nuclear plants in 2010, shut down all but two of its 54 reactors. Some many not reopen. Germany, which produced 5 percent of the world's nuclear electricity in 2011, is phasing out nuclear power altogether. The dilemma, however, is captured by Morton (2012: 17):

> To have a reasonable chance of keeping the rise in temperature to less than 2°C, industrial countries need to reduce emissions by 80% by 2050. . . The IEA's 2011 World Energy Outlook calculates that, between now and 2035, an emission path that keeps the 2°C limit plausible would cost $1.5 trillion more if OECD countries were to stop building nuclear plants and other countries halved their nuclear ambition, largely because much more would have to be spent on renewables.

Developing countries may well proceed with nuclear power. For example, Morton (2012: 14) describes how China intends to add more nuclear capacity in the next decade than currently exists in France, yet this will only increase the share of nuclear generated electricity in China from 2 percent to 5 percent. Nevertheless, while there have been advances in the construction and safety of nuclear power plants, concerns persist.

Fusion, where atoms are fused or combined—as opposed to fission, where atoms are split—is the holy grail of nuclear power generation. As Coley (2008: 533) describes:

> In theory, the successful and economic application of nuclear fusion to generate heat, raise steam and thereby generate electricity could solve all the problems associated with our reliance on fossil fuels. This is because the basic fuel, hydrogen, could be provided in almost limitless quantities from seawater and nuclear fusion could provide four times as much energy per unit of fuel as nuclear fission.

Despite extensive research, the technology has yet to be developed, so the quest continues.

With hydropower, electricity is generated by dams and falling water. Coley regards large-scale hydropower as unsustainable due to the environmental degradation incurred in the flooding of valleys when the massive dams are constructed and thereafter by the tendency for the reservoirs to silt up, resulting in the release of methane with the decomposition of the vegetation. Small-scale hydropower, as well as tidal power, would require lower initial capital outlays and would be more manageable with lower maintenance costs and less environmental degradation. Where the rivers and tides are available, small-scale hydropower may be a sustainable energy option (see Coley 2008: Chapters 13 and 24).

---

[7]See Donn (2011), who reported that from at least 48 of the 65 commercial nuclear power sites in the US, radioactive tritium has leaked from corroded, buried piping, often into groundwater. Reflecting the aging facilities, the number and severity of the leaks has been escalating. On the 65 sites there are 104 nuclear reactors, almost all of which were built before 1990. Of the 104 reactors, 66 have been approved for 20-year extensions beyond their original 40-year leases, and 16 more extensions are pending. Davis (2012) describes how what appeared to be a revival of interest in nuclear power plant in the United States several years ago was undermined by the economic recession, the declines in natural gas prices, and the failure of Congress to advance legislation reducing carbon emissions. Morton (2012) discusses the high costs and increasingly lengthy times associated with the construction of nuclear power plants. In addition, there has been growing resistance from concerned communities in the intended sites.

Wave power could be harnessed by coastal nations, although here the challenge is maintaining the power infrastructure likely to be situated well off shore. Geothermal energy derived from heat below the Earth's surface is another renewable energy option for some nations.[8]

A renewable energy extensively utilized, especially in developing nations, is **biomass**, including wood, ethanol, vegetal wastes, and animal wastes. As shown earlier in Table 12.5, 10 percent of the total energy used in the world in 2009 came from combustible renewables and waste, including solid and liquid biomass, biogas, industrial and municipal waste. Two-thirds of the energy use of the low-income economies is derived from these sources. Concerns, however, with the burning of wood include deforestation and the release of greenhouse gases. And, the combustion of industrial and municipal wastes can result in the release of hazardous heavy metals.

Wind power holds substantial promise. It is clean and has one of the smallest environmental footprints. Barrett (2009: 56) points out that wind energy is already economic on a small scale. Massive investments in infrastructure, including installing wind turbines where wind is abundant (e.g., off coasts and in mountains) and providing for the transmission of the energy to population centers, will be required before wind energy makes a major contribution. The intermittent nature of winds and the challenge of storing the wind energy generated for future use may be limiting factors.[9] Overall, the objections seem relatively minor (e.g., noise from the turbines and infringing on the seascape or landscape). The hazard that the wind turbines pose to birds has been generally exaggerated.

There is also great hope for solar energy. For all practical purposes inexhaustible, solar energy is increasingly being used to heat water and homes and to generate electricity. Barrett (2009: 58) states:

> Solar energy tends to be abundant in places where wind energy is scarce (high pressure areas have fewer clouds but less wind). Photovoltaic systems, which convert solar energy to direct current electricity, are already in use, but they operate at low efficiency and are only economic in sun-rich off-grid areas.

As with wind power, massive investments in the infrastructure, including fields of solar collectors, storage and transmission facilities, are needed before solar energy becomes a significant source for electricity. The potential is there, however, to expand this clean source of energy. With economies of scale realized in the production of solar panels and transmission equipment, solar power will increasingly become affordable for individual homes and businesses. Without the ability to store solar power, back-up systems might still be necessary for times when the sun is not shining, for example, a stretch of overcast days.[10]

These are not the only future energy options. With advances in technology, we might be able to not only increase the productivity of nonrenewable sources, but also reduce the harmful emissions. This may be crucial in the near future. The International Energy Agency (IEA) predicts that fossil fuels will account for over half of the increase in total primary energy demand in the next quarter

---

[8] See Coley (2008: Chapters 23 and 26) for discussions of wave power and geothermal energy. Geothermal energy is mainly derived from radioactive decay of isotopes, deep within the Earth (e.g., geysers with ejections of boiling water or hot dry rocks, drawing on heat below the earth's surface).

[9] See Coley (2008: Chapter 22) for a discussion of wind power. As Coley (2008: 441) notes, "the core technology is simple and has been used by humankind for several thousand years. The earliest machines were used to raise water for irrigation, grind corn and to propel boats."

[10] See Coley (2008, Chapter 20) for a discussion of solar power. Coley (2008: 397) begins the chapter with the startling fact that "Every 10 minutes the surface of the earth receives enough energy from the sun to provide the primary energy needs of humankind for a whole year."

century. In its New Policies Scenario, which reflects the public commitments made by nations to reduce greenhouse gas emissions and phase out fossil fuel subsidies, the IEA projects world primary energy demand is to grow by 36 percent between 2008 and 2035, with China alone expected to account for over a third of this increase.[11]

The transition to cleaner, renewable energies will be aided by taxes on carbon emissions and marketable pollution permit systems. This transition should be led by the developed nations, particularly the United States generating one-sixth of the world's carbon dioxide emissions. But, as Borenstein (2012: 67) remarks, the political will for these more effective market-based policies of taxes and tradable permits has been lacking in the US. Without aggressive leadership, though, nations may rely on subsidies and mandates for renewable energy, which, while welcome, may be all together insufficient to mitigate climate change.[12]

AN AGENDA FOR TECHNOLOGY

Continued, if not accelerated, research and development of new technologies that conserve on scarce resources and preserve the environment are clearly needed. And simple technologies, already known, can be effectively utilized and further developed.

For example, given the likely reliance for the next few decades, at least, on the abundant, but highly polluting coal, carbon capture technologies could significantly reduce greenhouse gas emissions from coal-fired plants. As Barrett (2009: 61–63) explains, CO_2 released from coal combustion might be stored in geological formations such as oil and gas reservoirs, deep saline aquifers, and unminable coal beds. The technology, however, is still being developed. Simpler ways to reduce CO_2 emissions include the no-till agriculture discussed in Chapter 13 and reforestation, with the planting of new trees for absorbing the carbon in the atmosphere.

More advanced technologies for addressing global warming involve geoengineering and include reducing the amount of solar radiation striking the Earth by seeding clouds over the oceans with seawater spray from special ships and projecting sunlight-deflecting sulfate particles into the stratosphere—mimicking a volcanic eruption with the cooling effect.[13] A simple way to increase the reflectivity of the Earth's surface, reducing the absorption of heat from the sun, is painting the roofs of buildings white.

---

[11] See International Energy Agency (2010). Note that, under the New Policies Scenario, the goal of limiting the rise in mean global temperatures to $2°C$ would not likely be met. The IEA, however, also presents a 450 Scenario, with less growth in energy demand and relatively greater reliance on renewable energies that might limit the concentration of greenhouse gases in the atmosphere to 450 parts per million of CO_2 equivalent and so would more likely would hold the rise in global temperature to $2°C$.

[12] In addition to taxing fossil fuel emissions, stopping the subsidization of fossil fuels would be helpful. Borenstein (2012: 77) cites estimates of total subsidies of \$72 billion for fossil fuel production in the US in the period 2002–08. He also notes that 29 states and the District of Columbia mandate a minimum share of electricity be generated from renewables.

[13] See Barrett (2009: 71–73) for a discussion of geoengineering to address climate change. Barrett (2009: 72) cautions that these new technologies are unproven and that the attendant risks need to be considered:

> geoengineering would not address the related environmental problem of "ocean acidification"; stratospheric aerosols could destroy ozone; the cooling effect of geoengineering may not preserve the existing spatial distribution of climate; and a geoengineering experiment may have other effects, as yet unimagined. On the other hand, since particles will last at most a few years in the stratosphere (and sea spray only a few days), the geoengineering experiment could be turned off relatively quickly should its effects prove harmful overall.

New buildings throughout the world should incorporate environmentally sustainable technologies. The simplest relies on passive solar design, orienting the building and using the windows, walls, and floors to take advantage of the sun's energy for heat in the winter. Better insulation will conserve on energy loss. Leadership in Energy and Environmental Design (LEED) promotes green construction. In particular, LEED certification verifies that:

> a building or community was designed and built using strategies aimed at achieving high performance in five key areas of human and environmental health: sustainable site development, water savings, energy efficiency, materials selection and indoor environmental quality.[14]

Less developed economies

With their projected growth in population and the increases in per capita income and consumption required to alleviate poverty, the less developed countries will become the major force driving the sharply higher global demands for resources and commercial energy over the next few decades. As Wolfram et al. (2012: 119) note, in 2007 energy consumptions in OECD and non-OECD countries were roughly equal, but between 2007 and 2035 energy consumption in the latter is projected to increase by 84 percent, compared to only 14 percent in the OECD economies.[15]

The developing countries nevertheless might effectively leapfrog the fossil-fuel-intensive infrastructure that the advanced economies relied on for their economic growth—just as they might bypass the heavy investments in mainline telephone networks, moving instead to mobile cell phone systems. For example, for electricity, instead of investing in coal-fired power plants, developing nations can develop renewable and cleaner forms of energy, including wind and solar.

Advances in modern technology, such as genetically modified crops that are both hardier (e.g., drought-resistant) and more nutritious (e.g., fortified with key vitamins), have an increasingly important role to play. And there is a continuing agenda to develop intermediate technologies that may significantly improve the quality of life and environmental conditions for the poor in the less developed countries.

At present some of the technologies most appropriate to the conditions prevalent in much of the developing world are available, but not widely disseminated. Many poor, especially in rural areas, cook indoors over firewood. Simple solar cookers exist that can economically and environmentally be used in sunny climates. Such solar cookers, operating like natural crock pots, would not only reduce the deforestation caused by the burning of wood, but also save the time spent collecting the wood and eliminate in the indoor pollution from cooking over an open fire. In climates with less reliable sun, there are other inexpensive options. For example, in Nepal the Foundation for Sustainable Technologies, an indigenous nongovernmental organization, is promoting low-cost, intermediate technologies that are environmentally sustainable. One project introduced to a remote, poor village, small ovens fueled by briquettes made from local waste materials and

---

[14] From US Green Building Council, "What LEED Delivers," http://www.usgbc.org.

[15] Wolfram et al. (2012: 127) also observe that more than a fifth of the world's population live without electricity in their homes. With increases in income, the poor can afford appliances, with refrigerators usually one of the first purchases, after televisions. Energy growth follows a logistic pattern, beginning with minimal consumption for low incomes and rising at an accelerated rate, so that those on middle incomes are able to purchase consumer durables, before leveling off at higher incomes. In private transportation the transition may be from bicycles, to motor scooters, to economy cars, to SUVs. We also might expect the demand for air conditioning to rise with incomes in the developing economies.

organic debris. The use of these ovens not only is healthier for cooking, but also has initiated a local cottage industry in briquette-making.[16]

Other inexpensive technologies that can make a difference in the lives of the poor in rural areas include simple pit latrines that provide an effective way to upgrade sanitation. Contour-based agriculture may help prevent soil erosion. As noted in Chapter 13, drip systems can improve the productivity of water used for irrigation. In each of these cases, there is a continuing agenda to reduce costs and improve efficiency. The World Bank (2010b: 17) describes a sustainable soil-enrichment practice used by the indigenous population in the Amazon rainforest:

> Burning wet crop residues or manure (biomass) at low temperatures in the almost complete absence of oxygen produces biochar, a charcoal type solid with a very high carbon content. Biochar is highly stable in soil, locking in the carbon that would otherwise be released by simply burning the biomass or allowing it to decompose.

New practices

Conversion to lighter, more fuel-efficient hybrid automobiles, fluorescent light bulbs, and more energy-efficient, durable appliances will be important. Hawken et al. (1999: 16–19) discuss a future service flow economy where appliances and durable goods are not purchased, but leased, by consumers. Manufacturers would be responsible for not only servicing these goods, but would have to take back the goods at the end of their life cycles. If the goods were not satisfactorily performing, the users could return them to the manufacturers. Such a service flow economy would likely not only improve the quality of the goods produced with regular technological upgrades, but would encourage the effective recycling of the goods once returned to the original manufacturers. Other advantages include increased employment—as the natural resources used to produce the goods are recycled and the goods themselves are regularly serviced—and less volatility in the economy—as regular lease payments for the services rendered by these goods replace the periodic purchases of the durable goods. (As noted in Chapter 6, consumer durable and capital goods expenditures disproportionately contribute to fluctuations in the business cycle.)

Clean energy investments can be included in macroeconomic policy. For example, in addition to the American Recovery and Reinvestment Act of 2009, the fiscal stimulus plan of the Obama administration to deal with the severe recession, a "cash for clunkers" program, officially the Car Allowance Rebate System, was implemented for a brief period to give rebates of up to $4,500 to consumers who replaced their older vehicles with more fuel-efficient models.[17]

GLOBALIZATION

Globalization refers to the greater integration of nations, primarily economically through international trade in goods and services, foreign investment and labor migration, diffusion of technology, and the increased organization of production by multinational corporations on a

---

[16]See information on the Foundation for Sustainable Technologies, see http://www.fost-nepal.org. For a description of this briquette oven project, see "Dumrikharka Village Renewable Energy Program" in Papa's House News & Updates (April 24, 2009) at www.nepalorphanshome.org/news.asp.

[17]For an overview of the energy investments contained in the 2009 Recovery Act, see Council of Economic Advisers (2011: Chapter 6). More than $90 billion in federal expenditures were designated to improve energy efficiency, including investments in renewable wind and solar energy, high-speed rail, the development of smart grid technologies for electricity distribution, weatherization assistance for low-income households, and energy-efficient appliance rebates.

world-wide basis. One example is the share of exports in the world output, which rose from 20 percent in 1990, to 25 percent in 2000, and then to 28 percent in 2008, the year before the global recession. As such, national economic policies are more sensitive to the international economy, and autonomies of policy-makers over their national economies are consequently reduced.[18]

The advances in communications and transportation that have fueled the increased economic integration have also promoted greater awareness of events across the world. With the BBC and CNN one can witness natural disasters, violence, famine, political uprisings, and the latest consumer trends in any nation in real time. Providing for national securities has become more difficult, with international terrorism and the growth in illicit trade in drugs and weapons, as well as human trafficking.

As suggested, achieving sustainable development for the world, in particular, addressing climate change and extreme poverty, will require unprecedented international cooperation. The eighth Millennium Development Goal is to develop such a global partnership (refer back to Box 11.2 for the six targets associated with this goal). Table 15.1 provides selected economic statistics that reflect the extent of globalization. For 2010, the year following the severe recession in the developed nations, which also reduced the economic growth rates of the developing nations, we see that the share of exports of goods and services in the world GDP recovered to 28 percent (from 24 percent in 2009). Export shares, on average, are lowest for the low-income economies at 20 percent, which nevertheless is half again the 13 percent share for the US. At 32 percent, the low-income economies, however, have the highest import shares in GDP. Regional differences in export shares are significant, ranging from 20 percent and 22 percent for the still relatively closed South Asia and Latin America and the Caribbean to 37 percent for East Asia.

Table 15.1 Selected international statistics

2010	WORLD	Low	Lower middle	India	China	Upper middle	High	US
Share of exports in GDP	28%	20%	28%	22%	30%	29%	28%	13%
Share of imports in GDP	28%	32%	31%	25%	26%	27%	28%	16%
Foreign direct investment net inflows as share of GDP	2.3%	3.4%	2.1%	1.4%	3.1%	2.8%	2.1%	1.6%
Net ODA share of GNI	0.2%	9.6%	0.9%	0.2%	0.0%	0.1%	0.0%	...
Per capita ODA receipts	$19	$46	$16	$2	$1	$5	$0	...
Total external debt as share of GNI	...	28.5%	24.7%	16.9%	9.3%	19.7%	...	...
Military expenditures as share of GDP	2.6%	1.4%	2.1%	2.4%	2.0%	2.0%	2.9%	4.8%
Cell phone subscriptions per hundred people	78	33	72	61	64	84	111	90
Internet users per hundred people	30.2	5.6	13.5	7.5	34.4	34.1	73.4	74.2

ECONOMIES BY INCOME CLASSIFICATION

[18] For a vigorous promotion of the net benefits of globalization, see Bhagwati (2007). Statistics on export shares in world output are from Tables 4.8 and 4.9 of World Bank (2002, 2010a, 2011a, 2012).

■ **Table 15.1** continued

2010	ECONOMIES BY REGION						
	sub-Saharan Africa	Middle East & N. Africa	Europe & Central Asia	South Asia	East Asia & Pacific	Latin America & Caribbean	High Income Economies
Share of exports in GDP	30%	...	31%	20%	37%	22%	28%
Share of imports in GDP	32%	...	31%	25%	33%	22%	28%
Foreign direct investment Net inflows as share of GDP	2.3%	2.7%	2.8%	1.3%	3.1%	2.4%	2.1%
Net ODA share of GNI	4.3%	0.9%	0.2%	0.7%	0.1%	0.2%	0.0%
Per capita ODA receipts	$54	$41	$20	$9	$5	$16	$0
Total external debt as share of GNI	20.0%	14.1%	43.0%	19.2%	13.5%	21.7%	...
Military expenditures as share of GDP	1.6%	3.3%	3.0%	2.4%	1.9%	1.4%	2.9%
Cell phone subscriptions per hundred people	45	86	124	59	73	98	111
Internet users per hundred people	11.3	20.9	39.3	8.1	29.8	34.0	73.4

Notes: Share of exports (imports) in GDP is the ratio of exports (imports) of goods and services to gross domestic product.

Foreign direct investment includes equity capital, reinvestment of earnings, and other short-term and long-term capital flows between parent firms and foreign affiliates.

Net official development assistance is the flow (net of repayment of principal) of grants and the concessional loans from donor nations and multilateral organizations that promote development and welfare as the main objective.

Military expenditures include all current and capital expenditures on the armed forces, including peacekeeping forces, defense ministries, and other government agencies engaged in national defense projects.

Total external debt is the debt owed to nonresidents and comprises public, publicly guaranteed, and private nonguaranteed long-term debt, short-term debt, and use of IMF credit. This is expressed as a share of gross national income

From: World Bank (2012: Tables 4.8, 5.7, 5.11, 5.12, 6.9, 6.10, and 6.12).

For 2010 the share of net inflows of foreign direct investment in GDP for the world was 2.3 percent, and ranged from 1.3 percent for South Asia to 3.1 percent for East Asia and the Pacific. The net official assistance receipts as a share of gross national incomes averaged only 0.2 percent ($19 per capita) for the world, although for sub-Saharan Africa the share was 4.3 percent (and $54 per capita), far exceeding the assistance received in South Asia, the other region of mass poverty (at 0.7 percent and $9 per capita). External debt as a share of gross national income was highest for the low-income economies (28.5 percent), despite the debt relief extended to the poorest countries under the Heavily Indebted Poor Country Initiative.[19] The average external

---

[19] The Heavily Indebted Poor Countries Initiative (HIPC) was launched in 1996 to reduce the external debt for the least developed nations, conditional on their poverty reduction strategies that increased public investments and social spending (see http://go.worldbank.org/DO0DK39FO2).

debt ratio for the largely upper middle-income economies of Europe and Central Asia (43.0 percent) was twice that for the Latin America and the Caribbean in 2010, the developing region with the second highest average.

In 2010 the world spent 2.6 percent of its collective GDP on national defense. In general, the share of military expenditures in GDP (the so-called **military burden**) increases with income, rising from 1.4 percent for the low-income economies to 2.9 percent for the high-income economies—and 4.8 percent for the US. Again, regional differences are significant, with the military burden ranging from 1.4 percent for Latin America and the Caribbean to 3.3 percent for the Middle East and North Africa. The potential exists for reallocating these military expenditures toward mitigating climate change, a common security threat. For example, the World Bank (2010b: 198) estimated the mitigation costs of achieving the 450 ppm CO_2 equivalent accumulation that could limit global warming to an increase of $2°C$ to be 0.3–0.9 percent of global GDP in 2030.[20]

Finally, with regard to Target 8.F under MDG 8, increasing communications and access to information, two of the indicators are cellular subscriptions and Internet users per hundred people. As noted earlier, developing nations can move to the latest technologies, such as cell phones rather than fixed or mainline telephones, avoiding investment in the less efficient infrastructure. The incidence of cell phone subscriptions rises with income, although the gaps between the low-income and high-income economies are much smaller than for the fixed-line phones. For example, in 2010 the incidence of cell phone subscription for the economies of Europe and Central Asia (124 subscriptions per hundred people) exceeds the average for the high-income economies (111 subscriptions per hundred people). Access to the Internet also rises with income. In the low-income economies there are fewer than six users per hundred people compared with over 70 in the high-income economies. The rapidly decreasing costs of computers, however, should accelerate the rise in Internet use, especially for the developing economies. Gains in the diffusion of knowledge should be correspondingly significant.

POLICY IMPLICATIONS

The keys for achieving sustainable development are addressing climate change and reducing poverty, along with stabilizing the world's population and curbing, if not ceasing, economic growth in the high-income nations. Efforts on many fronts will be required, including continued technological progress, shifts to renewable and clean energy, trade liberalization, enhanced aid for developing countries, and reorientation of priorities in the developed nations. Perhaps the most pressing global priority is mitigating climate change.

---

[20] As reported by the World Bank (2010b: 202), this estimate assumes the most efficient mitigation efforts and has different implications for different nations:

> The 450 ppm CO_2e scenario assumes an additional annual investment of $110 billion to $175 billion for the United States (0.8–1 percent of GDP) and $90 to $130 billion for the European Union (0.6–0.9 percent of GDP) in 2030 [and] an additional annual investment for China of $30 billion to $260 billion (0.5–2.6 percent of GDP) by 2030.

For India, the additional annual investment would be $40 billion to $75 billion (1.2–2.2 percent of GDP) in 2030. The wide range for these estimates reflects the uncertainty about not only future economic growth, but also the growth in greenhouse gas emissions and the technological progress in mitigation.

Addressing climate change

Holding the rise in the average world temperature to $2°C$ above the preindustrial level would likely limit the more devastating effects of global warming, including catastrophic increases in the sea level from excessive melting of the ice sheets, significantly more volatile weather and incidences of drought, and accelerated biodiversity loss. As the World Bank (2010b: 79, 87) observes, however, the average temperature for the world has already increased by $1°C$ since preindustrial times, so even stabilizing atmospheric concentrations of greenhouse gases at 450 ppm CO_2 equivalent yields only a 40–50 percent chance of holding the rise to another $1°C$.[21]

A fundamental issue to be addressed at the outset is one of fairness. Most of the greenhouse gas accumulations currently in the atmosphere are the result of the economic and population growth of the developed countries, yet the majority of the adverse consequences from global warming will be borne by the developing nations. Presently the high-income economies with one-sixth of the world's population generate over 55 percent of the global income (in PPP dollars) and over 40 percent of the carbon dioxide emissions. Per capita energy use in the high-income economies averages more than four times that in the low- and middle-income economies. The US alone, with less than 5 percent of the world's population, generates 19 percent of the global income and 17 percent of CO_2 emissions (see World Bank 2012: Tables 1.1, 3.7, and 3.9).[22]

Moreover, without continuous degradation of the environment, the world cannot sustain the current population of 7 billion at the widely disparate levels of consumption, much less an expected future population of 9 billion at the average level of consumption presently found in the developed countries. Attaining sustainable development then implies a paring back of the consumption in the developed countries, while allowing continued economic growth in the less developed countries consistent with an eventual stabilization of greenhouse gas concentration in the atmosphere at 450 ppm CO_2 equivalent.

Even if there is a consensus on the goal of limiting CO_2 concentrations in the atmosphere to 450 ppm, how to achieve this target equitably and efficiently is contentious. One scheme, known as **contraction and convergence**, involves setting a global target for CO_2 concentrations and determining the per capita emissions consistent with attaining this goal (Coley 2008).[23] The underlying premise is that every person on the planet should have the right to emit same amount of carbon—a premise compatible with Rawls's veil of ignorance. Many low-income nations would be allowed to increase their carbon emissions as their economies grow. High-income economies and many other developing economies would have to reduce their carbon emissions. Countries would be issued marketable carbon permits consistent with the scheduled global reductions in

---

[21] To put this increase in the average global temperature of $2°C$ in perspective, the World Bank (2010b: 4) notes:

 Global atmospheric concentrations of CO_2, the most important greenhouse gas, ranged between 200 and 300 parts per million (ppm) for 800,000 years, but shot up to about 387 ppm over the past 150 years...mainly because of the burning of fossil fuels and, to a lesser extent, agriculture and changing land use....

 The more than $5°C$ warming that unmitigated climate change could cause this century amounts to the difference between today's climate and the last ice age, when glaciers reached central Europe and the northern United States.

[22] The income and population statistics are for 2010. The per capita energy use (in kilograms of oil equivalent) and CO_2 emissions are for 2009 and 2008, respectively.

[23] Coley (2008: Chapter 18) discusses the policy implications of such a scheme to limit greenhouse gas emissions and global warming. In particular, he provides a table with the required changes in carbon emissions for countries from 2005 to 2040 needed to limit CO_2 concentrations in the atmosphere to 450 ppm. Consistent with contraction and convergence, annual percentage increases in carbon emissions are allowed for developing nations, for example, Bangladesh (+3.9), Ethiopia (+4.3), and Honduras (+2.4). For the developed nations, and many other developing nations, annual percentage decreases in carbon emissions are required, for example, United States (−5.4), Germany (−4.4), China (−0.5), and South Africa (−4.4).

459

CO_2 emissions and the goal of converging to common per capita carbon emissions. Reducing annual carbon emissions, however, can be compatible with economic growth if accompanied by advances in energy efficiency and effective mitigation.

Since the annual number of global carbon credits would be reduced over time, the market value of the credits would increase. Clean energy and technologies to reduce carbon emissions would be stimulated. Developing countries well below the common convergence target, of say 0.4 tons of carbon emissions per capita (which is less than 10 percent of the world average for 2008 of 4.8 tons per capita), would be allowed to grow and could sell their surplus carbon credits to the developed countries, presently consuming well above the common carbon emissions target.

While this global cap and trade scheme for carbon emissions is straightforward in theory, there are clearly a number of challenges, not the least of which will be getting the developed nations to comply. With no supranational authority to enforce international treaties, compliance across nations is voluntary. As evidenced by the earlier Kyoto Protocol (never accepted by the US), which only set voluntary targets for individual countries to reduce CO_2 emissions, and the disappointing resolution of the Copenhagen Climate Conference in December of 2009, national sovereignty continues to trump international cooperation. Even if all nations were to accept the idea of contraction and convergence with marketable carbon emission permits, distributing the permits, monitoring compliance, and enforcing sanctions would require new international authority, perhaps an International Environmental Fund, modeled after the International Monetary Fund. Underlying such unprecedented international cooperation would have to be fundamental changes in the perspectives and priorities of the human race.

Another way to reduce carbon emissions would be a carbon tax. Collier (2010: 185) suggests a common tax, of say $40 per ton, on carbon. Nations seeking a competitive advantage in trade by not taxing carbon could be faced with countervailing tariffs, consistent with the carbon content of their exports. Short of a common global tax, other initiatives could be taken. For example, the European Union plans to regulate the carbon emissions of all planes using European airports using a cap and trade scheme for marketable carbon emissions permits. Airlines exceeding their emissions quotas would have to purchase additional permits.[24]

A provision in the Kyoto Protocol, the Clean Development Mechanism (CDM), allows investors in developed nations to purchase emissions reductions credits through funding projects in developing nations that reduce greenhouse gas emissions. The marketable certified emission reductions credits could be used by the developed countries towards meeting their Kyoto pledges to reduce their greenhouse gas emissions.[25]

While a useful initiative, the World Bank (2010b: 233) concluded that CDM has "so far brought little transformational change in countries' overall development strategies." Moreover, the World Bank (2010b: 269) notes that the CDM did not include agricultural soil carbon sequestration projects in the developing world, adding: "Carbon markets that cover greenhouse gases from

---

[24] See "Airlines and Carbon," Editorial, *New York Times* (August 2, 2011). The goal is to reduce carbon emissions by 3 percent relative to 2004–06. The estimated rise in ticket prices for European flights is 2.2–4.6 percent. Already there is strong resistance from outside Europe to this proposal–as there will be to any carbon tax. The editorial, which supports the European plan, notes the objections of the Obama administration, which prefers a global solution. Also reported in the article is the US Transportation Department's claim that American airlines reduced carbon dioxide emissions by 15 percent in the period 2000–09, while increasing the passenger and cargo loads by 15 percent.

[25] See http://cdm.unfccc.int for a description of the Clean Development Mechanism as well as the CDM projects around the world.

agricultural and other land-management practices could be one of the most important mechanisms to drive sustainable development in a world affected by climate change."

In 2005, nearly one-fourth of emissions in developing countries came from land-use change and forestry (see World Bank 2010b: 273).[26] In particular, an initiative discussed in the Copenhagen Climate Conference is Reduced Emissions from Deforestation and Forest Degradation (REDD), where developing nations are paid for preserving their forests, which provide numerous environmental services, including absorbing carbon dioxide emissions, and could provide income for indigenous people.[27] (Recall the earlier example of Pronatura in Mexico.)

Hopefully not only will REDD be implemented, but also the CDM will be extended, with provisions for agricultural soil carbon sequestration projects. As the United Nations Development Programme (2007: 2) stated: "The world lacks neither the financial resources nor the technological capabilities to act. If we fail to prevent climate change it will be because we were unable to foster the political will to cooperate." The same might be said for alleviating poverty.

Addressing poverty

Recall the first MDG: to eradicate extreme poverty and hunger. Here, too, a global partnership will be required to make significant progress. Consistent with MDG 8 and Target 8. A (developing further an open, rule-based, predictable, nondiscriminatory trading and financial system), would be completing the Doha Round of trade liberalization. Special attention should be given to the least developed nations, often relying on primary commodity exports, but needing to develop their manufacturing capacities. The protectionism in agriculture through tariffs and subsidies to domestic producers afforded by the developed nations should be significantly reduced and phased out over the next few years. Escalating import tariffs that hinder the processing and adding of value to primary products of the developing nations should be eliminated. Preferential treatment should be accorded to labor-intensive manufactured exports from the least developed nations. As nations move towards freer trade in goods and services, labor will be displaced in import-competitive sectors of economies. Thus, more liberal trade adjustment assistance will be needed to compensate and retrain those workers who lose their jobs from greater imports.

Some progress, however, has already been made. The United Nations (2011: 60–61) summarized the recent trends in trade, including the increased access of developing nations to developed country markets over the first decade of the twenty-first century. A reflection of international cooperation was that during the global downturn in 2009, despite declines in the volume of trade, nations did not increase protection. In fact, in 2009, developed country tariffs on agricultural products from developing countries continued to decline, albeit slowly, to around 8 percent (for

---

[26]The World Bank (2010b: 172) describes a pilot project for agricultural carbon finance in Kenya, listing sequestration activities that include reduced tillage, cover crops, residue management, mulching, composting, green manure, reduced biomass burning, and agroforestry. (Recall the earlier discussion of biochar.)

[27]For a description of the REDD program of the United Nations, see http://www.un-redd.org. For an example that dramatically illustrates the tradeoff between energy exploration and environmental preservation, see Walsh (2012), which describes the Ecuadorian government's proposal for indefinitely closing the Yasuni National Park to oil drilling in return for an international payment of $3.6 billion over a 13-year period. The park, covering some 4,000 hectares of Amazonian rainforest, is one of the richest areas of biodiversity in the world, with "nearly one-third of the Amazon basin's amphibian and reptile species, despite covering less than 0.15% of its total area." Yet, oil deposits of nearly 900 million barrels have been discovered there. As Walsh notes, the Yasuni plan would be one of the first to recognize the responsibility of the international community to help poor nations preserve nature. The plan would not only protect biodiversity, but also "prevent the emission of more than 800 million tons of carbon dioxide, an amount equal to Germany's annual greenhouse gas footprint." Proceeds from the plan would go into a capital fund, to be administered by the United Nations Development Programme, for the development of renewable energy in Ecuador and the welfare of the indigenous people in the Yasuni region.

461

the least developed nations, average agricultural tariff rates declined to under 2 percent). Developed country tariff rates on clothing and textiles from developing economies, however, were stable at approximately 8 percent and 5 percent, respectively. For the least developed countries the average tariff rates on textiles and clothing (often the first major manufactured exports of developing economies) remained some 2 percent lower, in the neighborhoods of 6 percent and 3 percent, respectively. Nevertheless, agricultural producers in the developed nations remain heavily subsidized, as discussed in Chapter 13.

To attract foreign direct investment, particularly in manufacturing and modern services, developing nations need political and economic stability, sound institutions, literate labor forces, and a core of infrastructure—for the most part lacking in the least developed nations. Economic liberalization is important for foreign investors, although developing economies may want to retain some capital controls on foreign portfolio investment to avoid the surges in capital that can occur with shifts in the international climate. (Recall the East Asian currency crisis in 1998, discussed in Chapter 5.)

To promote increased mobility of labor, nations could liberalize immigration; although, as noted in Chapter 10, there is strong resistance in many of the developed nations. On net, developing economies have exported skilled labor to the developed nations, the so-called brain drain addressed in Chapter 7. This loss in the developing nations' investments in education and training may be somewhat, even entirely, offset by the remittances the emigrants send home (a significant source of income and foreign exchange for some developing nations), the eventual return of the emigrants to their countries of origin (bringing back additional expertise and capital), and the stimulus to potential emigrants to get educated (to increase their prospects for migration, although many eventually cannot or will not leave).

With respect to Target 8.D (to deal comprehensively with the debt problems of developing countries), the debt relief extended under HIPC to the least developed nations was mentioned above. For the low- and middle-income economies collectively, total debt service fell from 18.0 percent of exports and income receipts on the balance of payments in 1995 to 11.3 percent in 2009. All regions of the developing world made progress, except for Europe and Central Asia, where the debt service ratio more than doubled from 10.9 percent to 26.9 percent between 1995 and 2009 (see World Bank 2011a: Table 6.11). Actually, in the aftermath of the severe recession of 2008–09, the greater concerns with national and external debt shifted to the developed nations, especially the US and several high-income members of the OECD, including Greece, Ireland, Italy, Portugal, and Spain.

The less developed nations, especially the least developed, will require foreign assistance to address their poverty and insufficient public investment in infrastructure and human capital, as well as for mitigation of climate change. Official development assistance (ODA), however, is highly controversial.[28],[29] On the left, critics argue that aid is mismanaged—whether wasted, poorly allocated or expropriated by corrupt officials—and is given, especially bilateral aid, more to promote the strategic and economic interests of the donor nations than to advance development and alleviate poverty in the recipient nations. On the right, critics see foreign aid as interfering with the market mechanism and creating dependencies. Moreover, many conservatives see official aid as an involuntary transfer of resources from taxpayers in the donor countries to less productive recipients

---

[28] In 2009, overall, world output declined by 1.9 percent; for the high-income economies, real GDP fell by 3.3 percent, while for the low- and middle-income economies, real output still increased, but at a slower rate of 2.7 percent (see World Bank 2011a: Table 1.1).

[29] For two contrasting views on the effectiveness of official development assistance, see Sachs (2005) and Easterly (2006).

in developing nations, impairing the economic growth in both. In truth, it is difficult to measure the effectiveness of aid, since some of the benefits may be intangible or significantly delayed, and often the recipients are the least developed, politically and economically, with weak institutions and histories of turmoil. Indeed, it is especially inhumane when emergency food aid is expropriated by warring factions in the afflicted nations, as evidenced in Somalia. There are numerous reforms to make aid more effective, however, including eliminating tied aid (whereby the recipients have to use the contributed funds to purchase goods and services from the donor nation), better coordination among the donors (reducing the burden of the recipient nations dealing with so many different monitoring and compliance systems), and more regular, reliable aid.

The United Nations (2011) cites the increased donor commitments made at the Gleneagles Group of Eight Summit and UN World Summit in 2005, with special attention to sub-Saharan Africa. For several decades the recommended target for developed nations has been 0.7 percent of national income allocated for official development assistance. In 2009, for example, net disbursements of ODA were $128 billion, up sharply from $50 billion in 2000. Still, ODA averaged only 0.31 percent of the national incomes of the developed countries in 2009, an increase from 0.22 percent in 2000.[30] Just a few of the developed nations attained the 0.7 percent goal. In 2009, the Western countries with shares of net ODA in gross national incomes exceeding 0.7 percent were: Sweden (1.12), Norway (1.06), Luxembourg (1.04), Denmark (0.88), and the Netherlands (0.82). These same countries continued to excel with development assistance in 2010.

For the low-income nation recipients of aid, the share of net ODA in gross national incomes increased from 7.0 percent in 2000 to 9.2 percent in 2009 (and from $18 to $47 in per capita net receipts). For the middle-income economies, between 2000 and 2009, the aid dependency ratio fell from 0.5 percent to 0.3 percent of gross national income, while per capita ODA receipts nearly doubled from $6 to $11.

Concerning Target 8.F (in cooperation with the private sector, to make available the benefits of new technologies, especially information and communications), the existing gaps in cellular phone subscriptions and Internet users between the high and low income economies were illustrated in Table 15.1. Nevertheless, information and communications technologies are rapidly expanding to the developing nations. The United Nations (2010: 72) observes, however:

> A challenge in bringing more people online in developing countries is the limited availability of broadband networks. Many of the most effective development applications of [information and communications technology], such as telemedicine, e-commerce, e-banking and e-government, are only available through a high-speed Internet connection.[31]

Generating revenues for development assistance, investments in technology, and climate change mitigation (e.g., the REDD) could be enhanced by an international tax. We noted earlier a common global tax on carbon emissions. Another proposal is a so-called Tobin tax, a levy on foreign exchange transactions, the vast majority of which are not for financing trade in goods

---

[30] The UN (2011: 58) observes that net aid disbursements amounted to nearly $129 billion in 2010 (or 0.32 percent of the combined incomes of the developed countries). The statistics on aid for 2000 and 2009 are from World Bank (2011a: Tables 6.14 and 6.16).

[31] The United Nations (2011: 63) observes that, by the end of 2010, fixed broadband penetration in the developing regions averaged only 4.4 percent, and was heavily concentrated in a few countries, compared to an average of 24.6 percent in the developed countries.

and services, but for foreign asset purchases and currency speculation.[32] Such a tax, even at a very low rate, would not only generate significant revenues that could be used for achieving the MDGs and climate mitigation, but also have the added benefit of reducing the unsettling volatility in the foreign exchange market due to currency speculation. For example, the average daily volume of foreign currency exchanges in April 2010 was in the neighborhood of $4 trillion. Applying a tax rate of 0.005 percent (or 5 cents on a $1,000 transaction) would yield perhaps $50 billion a year in tax revenues, or roughly 49 percent of the total net official development assistance received in 2010.[33] The foreign exchange tax revenues could be distributed by the World Bank and the United Nations for funding development and climate change mitigation projects around the world.

Fragile states and failed states

Consistent with MDG Target 8.B (to address the special needs of the least developed countries), particular attention should be given to the **fragile states**. The World Bank (2011b: 1) says that "One-and-one half billion live in areas affected by fragility, conflict, or large-scale organized criminal violence, and no low-income fragile or conflict-affected country has yet to achieve a single United Nations Millennium Development Goal."[34]

In the extreme, fragile states can become **failed states**, where the governments cannot provide for basic public services and the physical security of their citizens due to gross incompetence, corruption, insurgencies, invasion, or pervasive criminal activity.[35] In fragile and failed states, conflict, violence, and chaos compound the challenge of attaining sustainable development. Sound

---

[32] Such a tax on foreign exchange transactions was first suggested 40 years ago by James Tobin, a Nobel laureate in Economics. For a useful overview of Tobin taxes, see http://www.ceedweb.org/iirp/factsheet.htm. A resolution was introduced in the US Congress in 2001 for such a tax, the US Congress Concurrent Resolution on Taxing Cross-border Currency Transactions to Deter Excessive Speculation (see http://www.ceedweb/iirp/ushouseres.htm.)

[33] The estimate for the daily volume of foreign currency trading for all transactions (spot, forward, swaps, and options) for April 2010 comes from the Bank for International Settlements, *Triennial Central Bank Survey: Report on global foreign exchange market activity in 2010* (see http://www.bis.org/publ/rpfxf10t.pdf.). To get the estimate for the annual tax revenues, $0.2 billion per day (or $6 billion per month and $72 billion per year) was multiplied by 0.7 (an estimate derived from comparing the summed average daily volumes to the monthly volumes for foreign exchange transactions in the North American market for April 2011). See the Foreign Exchange Committee's FX Volume Survey (http://www.newyorkfed.org/FXC/volumesurvey/). This annual estimate of tax revenues from foreign exchange transactions is clearly rough, and in fact, assumes the volume of transactions is constant, when, in fact, the volume may slightly decline due to the tax, even at this minimal rate. Philippe Douste-Blazy, the French Foreign minister from 2005 to 2007, in an editorial, "A Tiny Tax Could Do a World of Good," *New York Times* (September 24, 2009), suggested a tax rate of 0.0005 percent on foreign exchange transactions involving the world's most traded currencies (the dollar, euro, pound, and yen) that would generate more than $33 billion a year for development.

[34] The World Bank (2011: xvi) defines fragility and fragile situations as "periods when states or institutions lack the capacity, accountability, or legitimacy to mediate relations between citizen groups or between citizens and the state, making them vulnerable to violence."

[35] For the 2011 rankings of countries, see "The Failed State Index 2011," *Foreign Policy* (August 18, 2011) at http://www.foreignpolicy.com/failedstates. The top ten nations in the Failed States Index for 2011 are, in descending order: Somalia, Chad, Sudan, Democratic Republic of Congo, Haiti, Zimbabwe, Afghanistan, Central African Republic, Iraq, and Côte d'Ivoire. See also The Fund for Peace, "The Failed State Index: Frequently Asked Questions" (http://www.fundforpeace.org/global/?q=fsi-faq). There are 12 indicators of state vulnerability: social (mounting demographic pressures; massive movement of refugees or internally displaced persons; legacy of vengeance-seeking group grievance or group paranoia; chronic and sustained human flight); economic (uneven economic development along group lines; sharp and/or severe economic decline) and political (criminalization and/or delegitimization of the state; progressive deterioration of public services; suspension or arbitrary application of the rule of law and widespread human rights abuse; security apparatus operates as a "state within a state"; rise of factionalized elites; and intervention of other states or external political actors). For each indicator, a rating from 0 to 10 is given, with 10 being the least stable. Somalia, at the top of the list of failed states in 2011, had a score of 113.4 (out of a maximum of 120). As noted in *Foreign Policy*, this was the fourth year in a row that Somalia has occupied the "top" spot.

The rankings are little changed in 2012, save for Yemen breaking into the top ten. Somalia retained its designation as the most failed state, its score increasing to 114.9 (see http://www.foreignpolicy.com/failed_states_index_2012_interactive).

institutions of governance and administration, as well as functioning markets, need to be developed or reestablished. The World Bank (2011b) argues that the emphasis in the short run should be on ensuring security, administering justice, and creating employment, especially for youth. Institution building takes longer, as does the formation of human and social capital, but is essential for sustainable development.

International support can be crucial is resurrecting fragile or failed states. In the case of widespread state violence (Syria, Libya, and Sudan being fairly recent examples), the United Nations, NATO, or regional peacekeeping forces may have to intervene to protect civilians. Such outside intervention, while an incursion on national sovereignty, can be justified by human rights. Indeed, the loss of innocent life from war and terrorism is a negative externality in the extreme. Other less aggressive, and hopefully proactive, international support for weak states would include more reliable and effective aid, especially for bolstering institutional capacities, regional cooperation in fighting terrorism and money laundering, human trafficking, and illicit trade in drugs and natural resources.

In short, with globalization and the world becoming increasingly smaller, instability and violence in any nation have repercussions for other nations. Like climate change, crime, terrorism and disease do not respect national boundaries. And, in line with Rawls's concern with the least fortunate in society, the international community should pay better attention to the least viable nations, as individuals born in those states deserve the same economic opportunities and human rights.

While continued technological progress, more enlightened national policies, and international cooperation on addressing poverty, mitigating climate change, and promoting development are essential, perhaps the key for achieving sustainable development for the world will be fundamental change in human behavior and social institutions.

REVOLUTION IN ATTITUDES

Achieving sustainable development will likely require fundamental changes in prevailing attitudes and priorities, especially in the wealthier nations. The World Bank (2010b: 44) puts the problem bluntly:

> By 2050 a large share of the population in today's developing countries will have a middle-class lifestyle. But the planet cannot sustain 9 billion people with the carbon footprint of today's average middle-class citizen. Annual emissions would nearly triple.
>
> . . .It is ethically and politically unacceptable to deny the world's poor the opportunity to ascend the income ladder simply because the rich reached the top first.

A paring back in consumption, even in the affluent societies, will not be easy, when the quality of life is measured by the quantity of income, consumption, and possessions, that is, if **materialism** is ingrained. Moreover, **relativism**, where individual welfare is assessed not on an absolute standard of achievement and comfort, but on comparisons with social reference groups (i.e., peers or idealized goals), may not only undermine individual satisfaction, but is unsustainable. For example, if you not satisfied unless you receive the highest salary, own the biggest house, etc. then you will not likely have a very satisfying life. Simply put, life is not like the NCAA basketball tournament, where only one team can be crowned the national champion. Indeed, all the teams in the tournament enjoyed successful seasons—as did many more who did not even qualify for the tournament.

On the other hand, one can argue that any attempts to restrict individuals in their pursuit of happiness by limiting the freedom to procreate or to earn income would be immoral and contrary to basic human freedom. Such limitations are counterproductive in the sense that any dampening of the desire to excel, acquire, and achieve may stifle the very creativity, ambition, and drive needed for the technological progress and advances in knowledge to fuel the economic growth that improves the standard of living, reduces absolute poverty and reverses environmental degradation.

Schumacher's Buddhist economics

The late British economist E. F. Schumacher was highly critical of Western economics, which he equated with capitalism, a system he believed to be neither humane nor sustainable. In his *Small is Beautiful: Economics As If People Mattered*, a book written before the energy crises of the 1970s, Schumacher castigates Western economics as justifying a lifestyle that is selfish and narrow—the single-minded pursuit of materialism, a quest that is without limits and is, therefore, inconsistent with a finite physical environment.[36] For Schumacher (1973: 33):

> The cultivation and expansion of needs is the antithesis of wisdom. It is also the antithesis of freedom and peace. Every increase of needs tends to increase one's dependence on outside forces over which one cannot have control, and therefore increases existential fear.

Western individuals do not see themselves as part of nature, but as a force to dominate and control nature. Therefore, Schumacher argues, Western-style development, with its emphasis on the quantitative goal of maximizing per capita output and income, is not an appropriate model for developing countries.

Schumacher proposes an alternative, which he calls **Buddhist economics**, his generic term for a type of development that is compatible with underlying cultures and spiritual values, and where "people matter"; the environment is respected; and natural resources are conserved. The principles of Buddhist economics are simplicity and nonviolence. The orientation is small-scale. The goal is qualitative growth whereby individuals seek the maximum well-being with the minimum of consumption. Dependence on natural capital, especially nonrenewable resources, should be minimized and the beauty and sustainability of land and renewable resources should be preserved.

Moreover, work is not just a means to an end—the generation of income for consumption. Work, an integral part of life, should be creative and satisfying. Schumacher (1973: 54–55) decries the unbridled pursuit of economic growth that fosters modern technologies based on an extreme division of labor. While assembly line production may yield the greatest output (permitting the greatest per capita consumption), the human workers are reduced to small cogs in an impersonal process. The fragmented, isolated work stations on the assembly line require continuous repetition of specific tasks. The problem is that for Western man, work has been reduced to a "means to an end"—the end being the generation of income for consumption.[37] In Buddhist economics, work

---

[36] This discussion is drawn from Hess and Ross (1997: 135–138).

[37] Layard et al. (2012: 66–69) discuss the value of work to human happiness. Citing a survey of workers in OECD countries, the authors report that, in order, security, interesting work, and autonomy are valued more than high income as very important job characteristics.

has a threefold function: to provide an opportunity for using and developing one's faculties; to enable one to overcome ego-centeredness by joining with others in a common task; and to bring forth the goods and services for a becoming existence.

Ultimately Schumacher (1973: 58–59) calls for a more humane development with spiritual growth.

> Simplicity and nonviolence are obviously closely related. The optimal pattern of consumption, producing a high degree of human satisfaction by means of a relatively low rate of consumption, allows people to live without great pressure and strain and to fulfill the primary injunction of Buddhist teaching: "Cease to do evil; try to do good." As physical resources are everywhere limited, people satisfying their needs by means of a modest use of resources are obviously less likely to be at each other's throats than people depending upon a high rate of use.

In Figure 15.1 a model of Buddhist economics is presented. For each individual there would not be the distinction found in the West between economic man and spiritual man. Rather each individual would seek "right livelihood," a dignified, satisfying existence consistent with man's place in nature. For the individual, education and spiritual growth produce enlightenment, which, combined with an optimal pattern of consumption and fulfilling work, yield and are influenced by right livelihood. Right livelihood is culture-specific. Schumacher's approach to development is clearly from the bottom up. Enlightened individuals build enlightened communities which form enlightened nations.

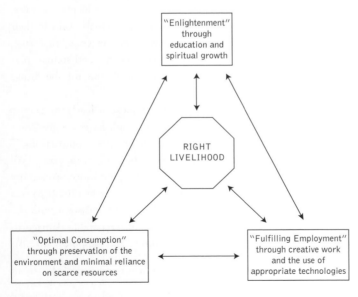

Figure 15.1 *Right livelihood for the individual*

For an individual, right livelihood is made up of optimal consumption, fulfilling employment, and enlightenment. All three dimensions interact and are in turn influenced by the pursuit of right livelihood to produce a satisfying existence.

Money and happiness

Does money buy happiness? Research on happiness suggests that, beyond a certain level, increases in per capita income are not correlated with increased life satisfaction. According to Frey and Stutzer (2002: 428):

> The empirical research on happiness has clearly established that at a given point in time, and within a particular country, persons with higher income are happier. Over time, however, happiness in western countries and Japan does not systematically increase, despite considerable growth in real per capita income. This can be attributed to the rise in aspiration levels going with increases in income.

Although studies also show that, on average, persons living in rich countries are happier than those living in poor countries, factors other than income, such as more stable democracies, better health, more economic freedom and ensured human rights may be responsible (see Frey and Stutzer 2002; see also Easterlin 2001; Kahneman and Kruger 2006; Di Tella and MacCulloch 2006). In fact, differences in income appear to account for comparatively little of the differences in reported happiness across persons.[38]

Based on their analysis of more than 450,000 responses to a daily survey of a thousand Americans, Kahneman and Deaton (2010) argue that emotional well-being or the perceived quality of everyday experience (e.g., joy, anger, affection, stress) rises with income, but only up to an annual income of approximately $75,000. Life evaluation, however, a longer-run assessment of personal well-being and satisfaction, seems to keep rising with incomes.

For one, there appear to be diminishing returns to income in yielding happiness. Indeed, if aspirations rise over time and with income, then higher incomes may not yield greater satisfaction as much as a sense of continually coming up short. Moreover, individuals evaluate their level of subjective well-being with regard to current personal circumstances (e.g., marriage, employment, health) and make comparisons to other persons (relative income and status), past experience (often remembered more fondly than warranted), and expectations for the future (perhaps inflated).

Research on happiness in America indicates that "older people are happiest." Clearly this state is conditional on good health, but the underlying reason may be that older people have accepted their lives, lowered their expectations for consumption, and are less motivated by peer comparisons.[39]

The research on happiness is extensive and increasingly considered to be relevant for policy. We noted earlier the high toll of unemployment, not only on national income, but more profoundly on human welfare. In his introduction to the *World Happiness Report*, Jeffrey Sachs (2012: 8) sets forth four sustainable development goals: ending extreme poverty by 2030 (consistent with the Millennium Development Goals); environmental sustainability (to avoid irreparable damage to the Earth's natural environment); social inclusion (meaning opportunity and happiness for all);

---

[38] Layard et al. (2012: 60) discuss what is known as the **Easterlin paradox**, that is, within any society, higher-income individuals tend to be happier, but that over time, reported happiness does not rise with income. With respect to the former, Layard et al. (2012: 63–64), using aggregate Gallup poll data for 139 countries, find the positive and highly significant coefficient for per capita income on reported "life satisfaction" in a simple regression to be more than halved when controlling for other influences. In particular, health (measured by healthy life expectancy), social support (i.e., having friends or relatives who can be depended on), and freedom (to choose one's life course) are all statistically significant determinants of average happiness in nations, while perceived corruption is a significant detractor.

[39] Mellowing is often associated with age. A dictionary definition of mellowing describes "having the gentleness, wisdom, or dignity often characteristic of maturity." See *The American Heritage Dictionary*, second college edition.

and good governance ("the ability of society to act collectively through truly participatory political institutions"). Moreover, in the concluding chapter to the report, Helliwell et al. (2012: 94) argue that government should "systematically survey the subjective well-being of the population."[40]

Below we modify a basic model of consumer behavior to incorporate relative consumption and leisure. This model can account for happiness not increasing with income and may be more compatible with sustainable development than the standard utility-maximizing model.

A MODEL OF CONSUMER BEHAVIOR

A basic model of household utility maximization subject to a budget constraint is extended to allow for relative income and what the economist Thorstein Veblen called **conspicuous consumption**. Writing over a century ago, Veblen argued that, with discretionary income, man's attention increasingly is given to emulation or conspicuous consumption. That is, individual utilities depend on the recognition and implicit approval of others (see Veblen 1934).[41] Utilities are interdependent. As incomes rise, so do aspirations and identification with higher social reference groups with greater demands for conspicuous consumption, so overall utility may not increase with incomes.

Utility maximization

A basic utility-maximizing model underlying consumer theory begins with an individual (or household) utility function, $U = U(I, L)$, where I is income earned, which allows for the ability to consume goods and services, and L leisure hours or activities not related to the production of goods and services. Consistent with standard theory, we assume positive, but diminishing, marginal utilities: $MU_I = \partial U/\partial I > 0$, $\partial MU_I/\partial I < 0$, and $MU_L = \partial U/\partial L > 0$, $\partial MU_L/\partial L < 0$.

To the individual utility function above we add an arguments for relative income and leisure, I/I^* and L/L^*, where I^* and L^* are the median income and hours of leisure of the social reference group the individual identifies with or aspires to. Individual utility is made up of inherent or absolute utility gained from consumption of goods and services made possible with the income earned and also the social or relative utility through what Veblen called "pecuniary merit." As Veblen (1934: 31) adds:

> an individual should possess as large a portion of goods as others with whom he is accustomed to class himself; and it is extremely gratifying to possess something more than others. But as fast as a person makes new acquisitions, and becomes accustomed to the resulting

---

[40] In the *World Happiness Report*, Ura et al. (2012) present a case study on Bhutan's Gross National Happiness Index. Bhutan, a small monarchy landlocked between India and China, is known for its emphasis on a more holistic measure of national welfare. Bhutan's 2010 Gross National Happiness (GNH) Index is based on a total of 33 indicators over nine domains: living standards (including per capita income); education (including knowledge and values); health (including mental health and disabilities); ecological diversity and resilience (including responsibility for maintaining a clean environment); good governance (including fundamental rights and political participation); time use (including balance between work and sleep); cultural diversity and resilience (including artisan skills and tradition); community vitality (including volunteerism); and psychological well-being (including life satisfaction and spirituality). Ura et al. (2012: 109) note the 2010 GNH index value was 0.737 and indicated overall that 41 percent of Bhutan's population could be considered "happy," with the remaining 59 percent enjoying "sufficiency" in 57 percent of the domains, on average.

[41] Veblen (1934: 154) hypothesized that "the human proclivity to emulation has seized upon the consumption of goods as a means to an invidious comparison, and has thereby invested consumable goods with a secondary utility as evidence of relative ability to pay."

new standard of wealth, the new standard forthwith ceases to afford appreciably greater satisfaction than the earlier standard did.

Empirical justification for including this relative income term, I/I^*, is given by Di Tella and MacCulloch (2006: 35), who conclude:

> the overall evidence is consistent with the hypothesis that an individual's happiness or utility is not just a function of income at a point in time, as in the standard model most often used by economists, but that happiness adapts to changes in income over time, and that at a point in time, happiness also comes from relative levels of income.

The same might be said for leisure.[42] On the importance of leisure for human well-being, Soper (2008: 1) remarks:

> The affluent lifestyle is increasingly now seen as both *compromised* by its negative by-products (the stress, pollution, congestion, noise, ill health, loss of community and personal forms of contact it entails) and as *pre-emptive* of other enjoyments. . .there is an overall sense that too much in the way of joy and relaxation is being sacrificed to the competitive spiral of the "work and spend" economy.

The utility function becomes $U = U(I, L, I/I^*, L/L^*)$, where positive but diminishing marginal utilities still characterize income and leisure. Utility is maximized subject to an income or budget constraint, given by the equation $I = (1 - t) \cdot (w/p) \cdot (H - L)$, where t is the tax rate on income, w/p the real wage rate per hour, and H the number of discretionary hours per month (outside of human maintenance, e.g., sleeping, eating, child care) to be allocated between work and leisure.

The tax rate and real wage are exogenous to the individual. The number of discretionary hours and the social reference group standards for income (I^*) and leisure (L^*) are predetermined by the individual. Using constrained optimization, we set up the Lagrangian function,

$$G(I, L, \lambda) = U(I, L, I/I^*, L/L^*) + \lambda \cdot [(1 - t) \cdot (w/p) \cdot (H - L) - I]$$

and derive the first-order conditions,

$$\partial G/\partial I = U_I + (1/I^*) \cdot U_I - \lambda = 0$$
$$\partial G/\partial L = U_L + (1/L^*) \cdot U_L - \lambda \cdot (1 - t) \cdot (w/p) = 0$$
$$\partial G/\partial \lambda = (1 - t) \cdot (w/p) \cdot (H - L) = 0 \text{ (i.e., the income constraint is met)}$$

From the first two marginal conditions, utility maximization would yield the combination where

$$\text{MU}_I = U_I \cdot (1 + 1/I^*) = \lambda = U_L \cdot (1 + 1/L^*)/(1 - t) \cdot (w/p) = \text{MU}_L/(1 - t) \cdot (w/p)$$

that is, the marginal utility of income equals the marginal utility of leisure per after-tax dollar earned. Alternatively, at the utility-maximizing combination of income and leisure, (I_0, L_0),

---

[42] Veblen (1934: 40) also developed the notion of "conspicuous leisure," stating that "the characteristic feature of leisure class life is a conspicuous exemption from all useful employment." For Veblen (1934: 43), conspicuous leisure connoted a nonproductive consumption of time to demonstrate "a pecuniary ability to afford a life of idleness." In our model, we use leisure to indicate the time not devoted to earning income, but to recreating and enjoying life. Clearly leisure often involves the consumption of goods and services made possible by the income earned.

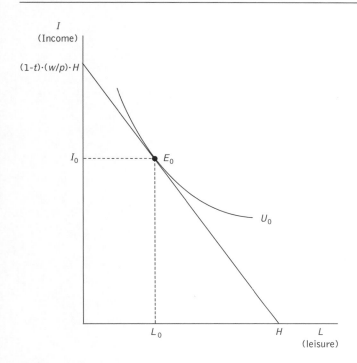

Figure 15.2 *Utility maximization*

At E_0, the utility-maximizing combination of income (I_0) and leisure (L_0), the slope of the income constraint, given by $-(1 - t) \cdot (w/p)$, is equal to the slope of the highest tangential indifference curve, U_0, given by the marginal rate of substitution, $MRS = MU_L/MU_I$.

illustrated in Figure 15.2 by point E_0 at the tangency of the income constraint, given by $I_0 = (1 - t) \cdot (w/p) \cdot (H - L_0)$, and the highest indifference curve attainable, U_0, we find $|(1 - t) \cdot (w/p)| = |MU_L/MU_I|$. That is, the slope of the income constraint (equal to the negative of the after-tax real wage) and the slope of the indifference curve (given by the marginal rate of substitution, $MRS = MU_L/MU_I$, the ratio of the marginal utilities of leisure and income) are equal. Note the marginal utilities of income and leisure each consist of an absolute component, U_I and U_L, and a relative component, U_I/I^* and U_L/L^*, respectively. *Ceteris paribus*, the higher the individual's social reference group standards, I^* and L^*, the lower will be the utility realized from given income and leisure hours.

Consistent with Easterlin (2001), increases in income and leisure over time may not be associated with greater utility if consumer aspirations rise accordingly. Graphically, increases in the social reference group standards would shift out the indifference curves.

A key then to happiness may be a change in income and leisure standards, from "keeping up with—or ahead of—the Joneses," to a sense of sufficiency and moderation, with a greater appreciation for those goods consumed and leisure taken. For example, traveling in a poor country on a hot day, one might especially value a drink of cool, clean water or a comfortable shirt—items taken for granted when living in affluent societies. And, anywhere a beautiful sunset or stunning mountain view can be appreciated. Indeed, Stiglitz et al. (2009: 41) point out that "individuals with greater capacities for enjoyment or greater abilities for achievement in valuable domains of life may be better off even if they command fewer economic resources." So, too, Jackson (2005)

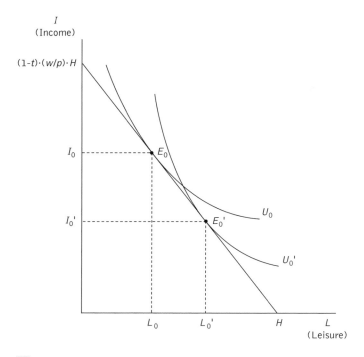

Figure 15.3 *New utility maximization with increased leisure*

An increase in the preference for leisure rotates the indifference mapping in a clockwise direc-
tion. Here the highest indifference curve that can be reached for the given income constraint is
now U_0'. The new utility-maximizing combination is at point E_0', with more leisure, L_0' and
less income, I_0'.

suggests that individuals might live better by consuming less, yielding a "double-dividend" for life
satisfaction and the impact on the environment.[43]

Utility and sustainable development

Important for sustainable development would be reducing the ecological footprint, indicated
here by a shift in preferences from income to leisure. Such a shift in tastes can be illustrated
by a clockwise rotation of the indifference curves, indicating a greater willingness to trade off
income (and the ability to purchase goods and services) for leisure (see Figure 15.3). For a given
income constraint, the utility-maximizing combination shifts from combinations E_0 to E_0', with
less income earned, but more leisure hours consumed.

We should be quick to note that not all leisure is equally rewarding and enriching. In particular, involuntary leisure due to unemployment can be demoralizing, due not only to the loss in
income earned, but also to the damage to self-esteem. Moreover, some forms of leisure activity
are more environmentally sustainable and healthy than others, (e.g., cross-country skiing versus
snowmobiling, sailing versus jet skiing, hiking versus driving all-terrain vehicles). Consistent with
more sustainable forms of leisure would be greater reverence for the environment.

---

[43] See Jackson (2005) for a review of the various perspectives—economic, philosophical, social, psychological—on human
behavior and consumption.

Brown and Leon (1999) discuss 11 personal actions that American consumers could take to make a difference for the environment (see Box 15.1). Americans are selected due to their relative profligacy. As Brown and Leon (1999: 5) point out:

> Even when we compare ourselves with people in other wealthy industrial countries, we generally emerge as the champion consumers. An average American uses twice as much fossil fuel (coal, oil, and natural gas) as the average resident of Great Britain and 2.5 times as much as the average Japanese. We consume over 3.25 pounds of boneless meat (mostly beef and chicken) each week, 1.5 times as much as the average Briton or Italian and more than 2.5 times as much as the average Japanese. . . The typical American discards nearly a ton of trash per person per year, two to three times as much as the typical Western European throws away.

These actions will not be easy. They will require a reorientation of priorities and sometimes, but not always, increased initial expenditures. Nevertheless, the changed behaviors may not only be more sustainable for the environment, but yield greater satisfaction with life.

Finally, reference group influences on consumption might promote the public good. The World Bank (2010b: 329) describes a psychological experiment on energy consumption in California, where the energy bills provided feedback on relative energy consumption. On all bills sent to the households in the study, the average household energy consumption was indicated. One group of low-energy households received positive feedback (a smiley face) on their energy bills, indicating approval. This group maintained their lower-than-average energy consumption. A second group of low-energy households did not receive positive feedback and actually increased their consumption to the average reported. The high-energy consuming households were given negative feedback (a sad face) on their energy bills, and as a result, tended to reduce their subsequent energy consumption. The World Bank adds that this approach has since been adopted by utilities in ten major metropolitan areas in the US, including Chicago and Seattle.

BOX 15.1: CONSUMER ACTIONS TO REDUCE ENVIRONMENTAL IMPACTS

Brown and Leon (1999: 86) state that "personal use of cars and light trucks is the single most damaging consumer behavior." Therefore, concerning transportation and the reliance of Americans on their automobiles, consumers should:

- Choose a place to live that reduces the need to drive. Consider living closer to the place of work or with convenient access to public transit.
- Think twice before purchasing another car. More careful planning as well as less driving may eliminate the need for a second or third car for each household.
- Choose a fuel-efficient, low polluting car. Increasingly fuel-efficient options are available, include hybrid cars.

- Set concrete goals for reducing your travel. Keep a log and try to reduce total miles driven in a typical month by 5 percent or more.
- Whenever practical, walk, bicycle, or take public transportation. Increasingly bike paths make this a healthier option. . . personally and for the environment, especially if the commute to work or school is shorter.

Concerning diet, modifications may not only reduce the environmental impact, but improve personal health. Thus, consumers are enjoined to:

- Eat less meat. Meat production is the most environmentally harmful food production.
- Buy certified organic produce. While more costly, largely due to the lower yields than chemical-intensive farming, organic farming has a significantly reduced impact on the environment.

Recognizing the trend over the last few decades for American houses to get bigger, while the average household size has gotten smaller, recommended actions center on affordable, energy efficient residences:

- Choose your home carefully. Avoiding larger houses than really needed will reduce the construction demands on the environment as well as the subsequent maintenance and operating costs.
- Reduce the environmental costs of heating and hot water. Consider upgrading to more energy-efficient systems (e.g., solar water heating or natural gas over home heating oil). Invest in home insulation.
- Install efficient lighting and appliances. Replacing old appliances with energy efficient ones often pays for itself within a few years. Likewise, compact fluorescent lighting, while initially more expensive, yields monetary and environmental savings in the long run.
- Choose an electric supplier offering renewable energy. Options that may be available include wind, solar, and hydropower. While currently more expensive, the environmental benefits are significant compared to fossil fuels, especially coal.

A sustainable economy

Tim Jackson (2009: 103) argues that "A macro-economy predicated on continual expansion of debt-driven materialistic consumption is unsustainable ecologically, problematic socially, and unstable economically." A blueprint for a sustainable economy is offered by the Sustainable Development Commission (see Jackson 2009: 102–107). The 12 components are:

- developing macroeconomic capability acknowledging natural resource constraints and environmental thresholds;
- investing in jobs and infrastructure, especially in renewable energy, public transit, and ecosystem maintenance;

■ increasing financial and fiscal prudence through financial reform with greater regulation of asset markets and fiscal discipline including higher taxes;

■ improving macroeconomic accounting to incorporate the state of the environment and the depletion of natural capital;

■ sharing work and improving the work–life balance with greater leisure along with more secure employment through shorter but more flexible work days;

■ tackling systematic inequality through progressive taxation, investments in education, and measures to combat discrimination;

■ developing measures of prosperity that better reflect human well-being and the common good;

■ strengthening human and social capital through increasing economic opportunities, promoting civil society, and investing in public and merit goods, such as museums, libraries, parks, and green spaces;

■ reversing the culture of consumerism involving stronger sanctions on advertising, enhanced support for public sector broadcasting, and promotion of more durable and sustainable products;

■ imposing clearly defined resource and emission caps as in ensuring sustainable yields from renewable resources and implementing a contraction and convergence model for greenhouse gas emissions;

■ reforming fiscal policy for sustainability with shifts to green taxes (e.g., carbon tax, nonrenewable depletion tax) from labor taxes (e.g., social insurance taxes);

■ promoting technology transfer and ecosystem protection by establishing a global technology fund to invest in renewable energy, energy efficiency, and climate mitigation.

Perhaps the most fundamental of the changes required to realize sustainable development for the world, even more so than the international cooperation in trade, aid, national defense spending, and climate change mitigation, will be the change in consumer attitudes in the affluent nations. Clearly, fairness dictates that if human resource consumption is to be reduced, then those with the greatest ecological footprints should take the lead. In fact, the poor in developing nations should be allowed to increase their consumptions from their present low levels. In the utility-maximizing model presented above, increasing the tax rates on higher incomes would lower consumption. More directly, carbon taxes would reduce consumption, especially of those goods and services with high carbon content. The tax revenues could be used for research and development of new sustainable technologies, climate mitigation, and poverty alleviation.

The decreased real incomes from the taxes need not reduce individual welfare if there is a corresponding shift in preferences from the consumption of goods to leisure, especially the more enriching forms of leisure, whether reading the classics, learning a new language, or enjoying good fellowship and conversation with friends and neighbors. Again, none of this will likely be readily accepted. To even suggest that more productive and satisfying forms of leisure are preferable to high consumption of goods and services may seem paternalistic, if not downright patronizing. But to repeat the insight of John Stuart Mill, a century and half ago:

> It is scarcely necessary to remark that a stationary condition of capital and population implies no stationary state of human improvement. There would be as much scope as ever for all kinds of mental culture, and moral and social progress; as much room for improving the

Art of Living, and much more likelihood of its being improved when minds ceased to be engrossed by the art of getting on.

CONCLUSION

As with the revolution in human attitudes, an overhaul of national policies that have been driven by the pursuit of economic growth will be challenging—to say the least. Herman Daly called for a steady-state economy, one with severe restrictions on reproduction, income, and natural resource use. Is such a steady-state economy inevitable, to be forced on the human race by natural resource constraints and climate change? Or will we voluntarily change our behavior so that we take greater care of the environment and show greater concern for the welfare of others, not only those less fortunate among us, but also future generations to come, not basing our satisfaction on improving our relative positions, but on improving the human condition?

KEY TERMS

biomass	Buddhist economics
conspicuous consumption	contraction and convergence
Easterlin paradox	failed states
fragile states	globalization
materialism	military burden
precautionary principle	relativism
sustainable energy technologies	veil of ignorance

QUESTIONS

1. The noted philosopher and inventor, Buckminster Fuller, was quoted in 1967 saying:

   Humanity's mastery of vast, inanimate, inexhaustible energy resources and the accumulated doing more with less of sea, air and space technology have proven Malthus wrong. Comprehensive physical and economic success for humanity may now be accomplished in one-fourth of a century.

   Compare Fuller's optimism with Herman Daly's (1977) call for a steady-state economy as discussed in Chapter 5. Which view do you think is more likely to hold in the future? Why?

2. Discuss whether there is a conflict between economic growth and sustainable development. How would you define sustainable development for the world? Is sustainable development possible with extreme poverty afflicting many throughout the world?

3. Are Rawls's veil of ignorance and the precautionary principles useful guides for achieving sustainable development? Discuss.

4. What is your assessment of the next half-century for the world population, average standard of living, and the condition of planet Earth? Discuss.

5. Why should we be concerned with the welfare of future generations?

6. Write down three things, conditions, or experiences that presently give you the most happiness or satisfaction. Which of these are dependent on income?

7. As you evaluate your life, say at age 80, what three things, conditions, or experiences do you think will have defined a "good life"?

REFERENCES

Barrett, Scott. 2009. "The Coming Global Climate-Technology Revolution," *Journal of Economic Perspectives*, 23(2): 53–76.

Bhagwati, Jagdish. 2007. *In Defense of Globalization*. New York: Oxford University Press.

Borenstein, Severin. 2012. "The Private and Public Economics of Renewable Electricity Generation," *Journal of Economic Perspectives* 26(1): 67–92.

Brown, Michael and Warren Leon. 1999. *The Consumer's Guide to Effective Environmental Choices: Practical Advice from the Union of Concerned Scientists*. New York: Three Rivers Press.

Coley, David. 2008. *Energy and Climate Change: Creating a Sustainable Future*. Chichester: Wiley.

Collier, Paul. 2010. *The Plundered Planet: Why We Must—and How We Can—Manage Nature for Global Prosperity*. Oxford: Oxford University Press.

Council of Economic Advisers. 2011. *Economic Report of the President 2011*. Washington, DC: United States Government.

Daly, Herman. 1977. *Steady-State Economics: The Economics of Biophysical Equilibrium and Moral Growth*. San Francisco: W. H. Freeman.

Davis, Lucas. 2012. "Prospects for Nuclear Power," *Journal of Economic Perspectives* 26(1): 49–66.

Di Tella, Rafael, and Robert MacCulloch. 2006. "Some Uses of Happiness Data in Economics," *Journal of Economic Perspectives*, 20(1): 25–46.

Donn, Jeff. 2011. "Radioactive Tritium Leaked from Most U.S. Nuclear Sites," *Charlotte Observer*, June 21: 1A, 5A.

Easterlin, Richard. 2001. "Income and Happiness: Towards a Unified Theory," *Economic Journal*, 111: 465–484.

Easterly, William. 2006. *The White Man's Burden: Why the West's Efforts to Aid the Rest Have Done So Much Ill and So Little Good*. New York: Penguin Books.

Frey, Bruno, and Alois Stutzer. 2002. "What Can Economists Learn from Happiness Research?" *Journal of Economic Literature* 60(2): 402–435.

Giese, Alexandra. 2011. "2010 Hits Top of Temperature Chart," Earth Policy Institute Release, January 18. http://www.earth-policy.org/indicators/C51/temperature_2011.

Hardin, Garrett. 1968. "The Tragedy of the Commons," *Science*, 162: 1243–1248.

Hawken, Paul, Amory Lovins, and L. Hunter Lovins. 1999. *Natural Capitalism: Creating the Next Industrial Revolution*. Boston: Little, Brown.

Helliwell, John, Richard Layard and Jeffrey Sachs. 2012. "Some Policy Implications," in John Helliwell, Richard Layard, and Jeffrey Sachs (eds), *World Happiness Report*. New York: Earth Institute, Columbia University. http://www.earth.columbia.edu/sitefiles/file/Sachs%20Writing/2012/World%20Happiness%20Report.pdf.

Hess, Peter and Clark Ross. 1997. *Economic Development: Theories, Evidence, and Policies*. Fort Worth, TX: Dryden Press.

International Energy Agency. *World Energy Outlook 2010: Executive Summary*. http://www.worldenergyoutlook.org.

Jackson, Tim. 2005. "Live Better by Consuming Less? Is There a 'Double Dividend' in Sustainable Consumption?" *Journal of Industrial Ecology*, 9(1–2): 19–36.

477

Jackson, Tim. 2009. *Prosperity without Growth? The Transition to a Sustainable Economy*. Sustainable Development Commission, March.

Kahneman, Daniel and Angus Deaton. 2010. "High Income Improves Evaluation of Life But Not Emotional Well-Being," *Proceedings of the National Academy of Sciences of the USA*, 107(38): 16489–16493.

Kahneman Daniel and Alan Kruger. 2006. "Developments in the Measurement of Subjective Well-Being," *Journal of Economic Perspectives*, 20(1): 3–24.

Richard Layard, Andrew Clark, and Claudia Senik. 2012. "The Causes of Happiness and Misery," in John Helliwell, Richard Layard, and Jeffrey Sachs (eds), *World Happiness Report*. New York: Earth Institute, Columbia University. http://www.earth.columbia.edu/sitefiles/file/Sachs%20Writing/2012/World%20Happiness%20Report.pdf.

Morton, Oliver. 2012. "The Dream that Failed: A Special Report on Nuclear Energy," *The Economist*, March 10.

Neumann, Holly. 1993. "Mexico Adopts a Bottoms-Up Environmental Policy, *Wall Street Journal*, June 25: A11.

Rao, P. K. 2000. *Sustainable Development: Economics and Policy*. Malden, MA: Blackwell.

Rawls, John. 1971. *A Theory of Justice*. Cambridge, MA: Harvard University Press.

Sachs, Jeffrey. 2005. *The End of Poverty: Economic Possibilities for Our Time*. New York: Penguin.

Sachs, Jeffrey. 2012. "Introduction," in John Helliwell, Richard Layard, and Jeffrey Sachs (eds), *World Happiness Report*. New York: Earth Institute, Columbia University. http://www.earth.columbia.edu/sitefiles/file/Sachs%20Writing/2012/World%20Happiness%20Report.pdf.

Schumacher, E. F. 1973. *Small Is Beautiful: Economics As If People Mattered*. New York: Harper & Row.

Soper, Kate. 2008. *Exploring the Relationship between Growth and Wellbeing*, Thinkpiece for the Sustainable Development Commission Seminar: Living Well—Within Limits. London: Sustainable Development Commission.

Stiglitz, Joseph, Amartya Sen, and Jean-Paul Fitoussi. 2009. *Report by the Commission on the Measurement of Economic Performance and Social Progress*. http://www.stiglitz-sen-fitoussi.fr.

United Nations Development Programme. 2007. *Human Development Report 2007/2008: Fighting Climate Change*. New York: Palgrave Macmillan for the UNDP.

United Nations Development Programme. 2010. *Human Development Report 2010: The Real Wealth of Nations*. New York: Palgrave Macmillan for the UNDP.

United Nations. 2010. *The Millennium Development Goals Report 2010*. New York: United Nations.

United Nations. 2011. *The Millennium Development Goals Report 2011*. New York: United Nations. http://www.un.org/millenniumgoals/11_MDG%Report_EN.pdf.

Ura, Karma, Sabina Alkire and Tshoki Zangm. 2012. "Gross National Happiness and the GNH Index," in John Helliwell, Richard Layard, and Jeffrey Sachs (eds), *World Happiness Report*. New York: Earth Institute, Columbia University. http://www.earth.columbia.edu/sitefiles/file/Sachs%20Writing/2012/ World%20Happiness%20Report.pdf.

Veblen, Thorstein. 1934. *The Theory of the Leisure Class: An Economic Study of Institutions*. New York: Modern Library.

Walsh, Bryan. 2012. "Rain Forest for Ransom," *Time*, February 6.

Wolfram, Catherine, Orie Shelef, and Paul Gertler. 2012. "How Will Energy Demand Develop in the Developing World?" *Journal of Economic Perspectives* 26(1): 119–137.

World Bank. 1992. *World Development Report: Development and the Environment*. New York: Oxford University Press.

World Bank. 2002. *World Development Indicators 2002*. Washington, DC: World Bank.

World Bank. 2010a. *World Development Indicators 2010*. Washington, DC: World Bank.

World Bank. 2010b. *World Development Report 2010: Development and Climate Change*, Washington, DC: World Bank.

World Bank. 2011a. *World Development Indicators 2011*. Washington, DC: World Bank.

World Bank. 2011b. *World Development Report 2011: Conflict, Security, and Development*. Washington, DC: World Bank.

World Bank. 2012. *World Development Indicators 2012*. Washington, DC: World Bank.

Glossary

(Note: the relevant chapter numbers are given in parentheses after each definition.)

Absolute advantage: A lower resource cost of production. (3)

adaptive expectations: the formation of price expectations based on previous prices. (6)

adjusted net saving rate: net savings adjusted for public education expenditures, depletion of natural resources, and pollution damage, expressed as a share of gross national income. (11)

adolescent fertility rate: the ratio of births to women aged 15–19 years to the mid-year population of women aged 15–19 years. (9)

adjusted coefficient of determination (**adjusted R^2**): the coefficient of determination adjusted for the number of observations in the sample and the number of coefficients to be estimated. (8)

age of degenerative and man-made diseases: the third of four stages of the epidemiological transition, where declining fertility rates are nearing the lower mortality rates. (10)

age of delayed degenerative diseases: the last of the four stages of the epidemiological transition, characteristic of modern societies, where most mortality occurs at the older ages. (10)

age of epidemics and famine: the first of four stages of the epidemiological transition, characteristic of early populations with high mortality. (10)

age of receding epidemics: the second of four stages of the epidemiological transition, where death rates have significantly declined. (10)

aged-to-child ratio: the ratio of the population 65 years and older to the population aged 16 years and younger. (9)

age-specific birth rate: the ratio of births to women of age x to the mid-year population of women of age x. (9)

age-specific death rate: the ratio of deaths to the population of age x to the mid-year population of age x. (9)

agglomeration: the benefits of concentration of economic activity in urban areas with economies of scale, specialization, interdependent industries, and large pools of labor. (7)

allocative efficiency: the condition that price (the value placed on the last unit purchased) equals the marginal cost of production. (14)

alternative hypothesis: the alternative to the null hypothesis, which holds if the null hypothesis can be rejected. (8)

application: the fourth stage of empirical analysis, where hypotheses that are confirmed by the evidence can be used for policy or forecasting. (8)

appreciation: a rise in the value of an asset; an increase in the foreign exchange value of a currency. (12)

aquaculture: fish farming or the cultivation of fish in enclosed areas. (13)

autarky: self-sufficiency; a nation under autarky does not engage in international trade. (3)

autonomous expenditures: aggregate expenditures that are independent of real income or the aggregate price level. (6)

average revenue: total revenue per unit of output; equivalent to the unit price. (14)

baby boom generation: the cohorts of Americans born between 1946 and 1964. (10)

barter terms of trade: the physical exchange ratio between two commodities, for example, three units of cloth for one unit of wine. (3)

behavioral equation: an equation that expresses the hypothesized relationship between variables. (5)

biodiversity: the variety of life forms. (14)

biomass: organic matter (wood, crops, wastes) that could be used as energy. (15)

Blue Revolution: the rapidly growing phenomenon of aquaculture. (13)

brain drain: the emigration of skilled labor from developing to developed economies. (7)

Buddhist economics: E.F. Schumacher's philosophy of development that is human-centered, small-scale, and respectful of the natural environment. (15)

burden of dependency: the ratio of the sum of the population under age 15 and over age 64 to the population between the ages of 15 and 64. (9)

business cycle: the periodic fluctuations in economic activity with expansions and contractions of real national output. (6)

capital-abundant: a nation with a relatively high ratio of physical capital to labor. (7)

capital account: the account in the international balance of payments that records international investment flows; now known as the financial account. (4)

capital deepening: an increase in the physical capital–labor ratio. (4)

capital flight: the rapid exit of financial capital from a national economy. (5)

capital widening: an increase in the physical capital stock proportionally equal to the increase in labor to maintain the physical capital–labor ratio. (4)

carbon intensity of energy: carbon emissions per unit of energy. (12)

carbon intensity of income: carbon emissions per dollar of output. (12)

carrying capacity: the maximum population an area can accommodate for the given technology, resources, and resource utilization rate without a deterioration in the environment. (2)

central rate: the ratio of events in a population per thousand mid-point population. (9)

children ever born: the average number of children ever born to a woman after the completion of her childbearing years. (9)

coefficient of determination (R^2): the proportion of the variation in the dependent variable that is explained by variation in the independent variables. (8)

cohort: a group of individuals that can be identified by a common demographic experience during a specified period of time. (9)

cohort component method: projection of a population by age groups using age-specific birth, death, and net migration rates. (9)

command and control: a method of government regulation that mandates certain standards of behavior. (14)

common market: a customs union among countries also with free movement of factors. (6)

comparative advantage: a lower opportunity cost of production. (3)

complementary factor: a factor that is used jointly in production with another factor. (7)

comprehensive development framework: The World Bank's holistic approach to economic development involving institution building, human capital formation, investment in physical and social capital, and urban management. (8)

conditional convergence: a convergence in per capita incomes across countries conditional upon international factor mobility. (7)

conspicuous consumption: Veblen's theory that individuals gain satisfaction by demonstrating their ability to purchase expensive goods and services. (15)

constant costs of production: the average cost of production does not vary with the rate of output produced. (3)

constant returns to scale: a proportional increase in inputs results in an equal proportionate increase in output. (1)

constrictive: a population pyramid shape where the base in narrower than the middle, indicating below replacement-level fertility and negative population momentum. (9)

consumer surplus: the gain in consumer welfare from purchasing a commodity for a lower market price than the consumer is willing to pay. (14)

consumption possibilities boundary: the combination of goods a nation can consume based on its production possibilities boundary and the international terms of trade. (3)

contraceptive prevalence rate: the percentage of a population (usually married women aged 15–59) using contraception. (2)

contraction and convergence: a method for reducing the gaps between nations in per capita carbon emissions (or any other output) where a common standard is set and nations above this would reduce their emissions, while nations below the standard would be allowed to increase their emissions until convergence is attained. (15)

convergence theory: the theory that poor countries will grow faster than rich countries so that per capita incomes will converge. (7)

correlation coefficient: a standardized measure of the linear relationship between two variables, which can range from -1 (a perfect negative linear relationship) to $+1$ (a perfect positive linear relationship). (8)

cost-push inflation: a rise in the aggregate price level due to a greater decline in aggregate supply than aggregate demand. (6)

covariance: a measure of the linear relationship between two variables with positive (negative) values indicating above average values of one variable are associated with above (below) average values of the second variable. (8)

crude birth rate: the number of births in a population of a given area over a year divided by the mid-year population. (2)

crude death rate: the number of deaths in a population of a given area over a year divided by the mid-year population. (2)

crude rate of natural increase: the difference between the crude birth rate and the crude death rate. (2)

current account: the account in the international balance of payments that includes the balance of trade in goods and services, net income flows, and net transfers. (4)

customs union: a free trade area among countries with common external trade barriers. (6)

cyclical unemployment: the unemployment due to insufficient aggregate demand. (6)

deadweight loss: a loss in consumer or producer surplus due to allocative inefficiency. (14)

decreasing returns to scale: a proportional increase in inputs resulting in a less than equal proportionate increase in output. (1)

degrees of freedom: the number of linearly independent observations used in calculating a sample statistic. (8)

demand-pull inflation: a rise in the aggregate price level due to a greater increase in aggregate demand than aggregate supply. (6)

demographic dividend: the boost to economic growth from an increase in the share of the labor force in the total population that accompanies the fertility transition. (1)

demographic transition: the movement of a population from a traditional equilibrium of high birth and death rates to a modern equilibrium with low birth and death rates. (2)

depreciation: a fall in the value of an asset; a decrease in the foreign exchange value of a currency. (12)

diminishing returns to labor: declines in the marginal product of labor in the short run with a given physical capital stock. (3)

discouraged workers: unemployed workers who drop out of the labor force discouraged by the poor job prospects. (6)

diseconomies of scale: a rise in the long-run average cost of production as the volume of production increases. (1)

division of labor: the breaking down of production into different stages to allow for greater efficiency. (1)

drip irrigation: an efficient method of irrigation whereby concentrated amounts of water are periodically directed through pipes and hoses to the base of the plants. (13)

dummy variable: an explanatory variable in regression analysis that represents a condition or attribute and is equal to 1 when the observation has that condition or attribute, but is equal to 0 otherwise. (8)

Dutch disease: a distorted type of development that arises with an export boom where a nation overextends its spending, resulting in inflation, increased government deficits and foreign debt, and real appreciation in the domestic currency. (12)

dysfunctional selection: adverse consequences from the behavior of socially irresponsible individuals. (14)

Easterlin paradox: the finding that within any society, higher-income individuals tend to be happier, but that over time reported happiness does not rise with income. (15)

ecological footprint: the demand placed on the natural environment by humans; can be measured by the total land area necessary to support current human production and consumption. (5)

economic contraction: a decline in real national output; the stage of the business cycle between a peak and a trough. (6)

economic development: the structural change, alleviation of poverty, and general improvement in welfare that accompany economic growth. (11)

economic efficiency: the use of the least-cost method of production. (4)

economic expansion: a rise in real national output; the stage of the business cycle between a trough and a peak. (6)

economic growth: a rise in real income per capita. (1)

economic model: a theoretical framework for explaining economic phenomena. (5)

economic profits: the difference between total revenues and the total costs of production, including the opportunity costs of the capital invested. (3)

economic rent: the difference between the price received by the owner of a factor of production and the minimum price they would be willing to accept. (3)

economies of scale: a decrease in long-run average cost of production as the volume of production rises. (1)

effective factor of production: the product of an index of the quality or inherent productivity of a factor and the physical quantity of the factor of production. (1)

Ehrlich identity: the equation ($I = PAT$) stating the total environmental impact (I) is equal to the product of population (P), per capita consumption or affluence (A), and environmental requirements per unit of output or technology (T). (11)

elasticity of substitution: the degree to which two factors can be substituted in production; given by the percentage change in the optimal ratio of the two factors divided by the percentage change in the ratio of their unit prices. (11)

elderly burden of dependency: the ratio of the population aged 65 and older to the population aged 15–64. (9)

endogenous growth theory: economic models that account for continuous growth in per capita incomes, whether through increasing returns to investment, embodied technological progress, or positive externalities for human capital formation. (7)

endogenous variable: a variable that is dependent on other variables and whose behavior is to be explained within the model. (5)

entrepreneurs: individuals who seek out profitable opportunities by starting, organizing, and operating business ventures. (7)

entropy: the energy that is no longer available for conversion into work. (5)

epidemiological transition: the changing patterns of mortality and morbidity with economic development. (10)

epidemiology: the study of health in populations, including the incidence of illness, disease, and epidemics. (10)

equilibrium condition: an equation defining the solution to a model; a condition where all the forces in a system are in balance. (5)

equilibrium price: the price that equates the quantity demanded with the quantity supplied. (14)

error term: a variable in regression analysis to account for specification error, including omitted explanatory influences, errors in the measurement of the dependent variable, and human variability. Also called 'disturbance term'. (8)

estimation: the second stage in empirical analysis where econometrics and data are used to quantify the relationship between a dependent variable and an independent variable or variables. (8)

exact ages: the age intervals in a life table that extend from age x up to, but not including, age $x + n$, where n is the length of the age interval. (9)

excise tax: a sales tax applied on each unit of a commodity sold. (14)

exogenous variable: a variable whose value is considered to be given or determined outside the scope of the model. (5)

expansive: a population pyramid shape where the base is wider than the middle, indicating above replacement-level fertility and positive population momentum. (9)

externalities: third-party effects, where the actions of primary parties involved in an activity have social consequences or impacts on the welfare of others. (14)

failed states: nations where the government can no longer uphold the rule of law, provide basic services, or protect the population. (15)

F-test: a test of the overall significance of a regression equation; the null hypothesis is that none of the estimated regression coefficients are statistically significant. (8)

fecundity: the biological capacity to bear children. (9)

fertility: the realization of fecundity with the bearing of children. (9)

fertility transition: movement of a population from high fertility rates to low fertility rates. (10)

First World: a term used for the developed nations, mainly the industrial democracies. (5)

fixed-coefficients production function: a production function with a fixed relationship between output and required inputs; no factor substitution is possible. (11)

flow: a variable defined over a duration of time. (2)

forecasting: the use of an estimated model to predict future values of the dependent variable. (8)

fragile states: nations where ineffective governance makes them vulnerable to turmoil and violence. (15)

freedom of entry and exit: a condition where there are no barriers to firms entering or exiting the market, characteristic of perfect competition. (14)

free trade area: an agreement among nations where there are no barriers to international trade between them. (6)

frictional unemployment: the unemployment due to the lag between the time individuals begin searching for employment and securing a job; reflects new entrants and reentrants to the labor force, as well as job leavers. (6)

full-employment real national output: the level of real national output that would be produced if the economy were operating at full employment, or with average rates of frictional and structural unemployment, no cyclical unemployment, and normal utilization of the capital stock. (4, 6)

fundamental equation of the Solow model: the equation for the change in the physical capital–labor ratio; equal to the difference between the net saving per unit of labor forthcoming and the net investment required to maintain the capital–labor ratio given the natural growth rate in labor. (7)

Gene Revolution: the advances in biotechnology and genetics that improve the yields of crops and livestock. (13)

general fertility rate: the ratio of births in a population over a year to the female population aged 15–49 at mid-year. (9)

Generation X: Americans born between 1965 and 1977, also known as the baby bust generation. (10)

Generation Y: Americans born between 1978 and 1995, as known as the baby boomlet and the Millennials. (10)

gestation: the carrying of a conception to term and successful birth. (9)

Gini coefficient: a measure of the income inequality in a population; varies between 0 (where the distribution of income is perfectly equal) and 1 (where all the income is received by one individual). (1)

globalization: the increased interdependence and economic integration of nations. (15)

gold standard: a fixed exchange rate system where each currency has an official gold price. (4)

Green Revolution: the higher-yielding seeds in rice, wheat, and corn that, combined with chemical fertilizer and irrigation, significantly enhanced the outputs of these staple crops in developing economies. (13)

gross domestic product: the total market value of all final goods and services produced in an economy over a year. (1)

gross national income : the total market value of all final goods and services produced by residents of a nation over a year. (1)

gross reproduction rate: the average number of daughters born to a woman if she were to live through the childbearing years and give birth at each age according to the current age-specific fertility rates. (9)

growth rate in total factor productivity: the growth rate in output due to neutral technical change and qualitiative improvements in the factors of production. (7)

headcount index: the absolute number of poor people in a nation or region. (1)

healthy life expectancy: expected average number of years lived in good health. (11)

heteroscedasticity: the variance of the error terms is not constant across observations in the sample. (8)

homoscedasticity: a constant variance of the error terms in a sample. (8)

homogeneous of degree n: the property whereby multiplying the arguments of a function by a scalar c multiplies the dependent variable by c^n. (11)

Human Development Index: an index created by the United Nations Development Programme to measure the general welfare of a population based on life expectancy at birth, education, and per capita income. (11)

hydraulic fracturing: extraction of natural gas by the forceful injection of water and chemicals into oil shale deposits. (12)

identity: an equation expressing a definition or accepted fact. (5)

IMF medicine: the set of policies promoted by the International Monetary Fund for countries with balance of payments difficulties.

incidence of poverty: the percentage of a population that is poor. (1)

income constraint: the combination of goods that can be purchased for a given income and unit prices of the goods. (10)

increasing returns to scale: a proportional increase in inputs results in a greater than proportionate increase in output. (1)

index of youth investment: an indicator of sustainable development that measures the investment in children, comprised as a geometric average of a quality-adjusted child survival rate and a quality-adjusted net secondary school enrollment rate. (11)

indifference curve: the combinations of goods that yield the same satisfaction. (10)

indifference mapping: a family of indifference curves, drawn for given tastes and preferences of the individual. (10)

infant mortality rate: deaths to infants under age 1 per thousand live births in a year. (9)

intensive production function: a production function where output per unit of labor depends on the capital–labor ratio. (7)

interest rate effect: the inverse relationship between the quantity demanded of real national output and the aggregate price level due to the effect of higher interest rates from an increase in the price level reducing interest-sensitive expenditures. (6)

international competitiveness effect: the inverse relationship between the quantity demanded of real national output and the aggregate price level due to the effect of an increase in the aggregate price level reducing net exports. (6)

international terms of trade: the international exchange ratio for two goods. (3)

invisible hand: Adam Smith's theory that individuals pursuing their self-interest in the market promotes the public good. (3)

involuntary migration: migration that is forced or coerced. (10)

isocost line: the combinations of inputs or factors that cost the same given their unit prices. (4)

isoquant: the technically efficient combinations of factors for producing a selected level of output. (4)

labor-abundant: a nation with a relatively low capital–labor ratio. (7)

labor theory of value: the classical theory that the costs of production of a good can be reduced to the labor hours required to produce the good. (3)

law of demand: the inverse relationship between the quantity demanded of a commodity and its unit price. (5)

law of supply: the direct relationship between the quantity supplied of a commodity and its unit price. (5)

life expectancy at birth: the average number of years a newborn would live if subject to the current age-specific death rates in that year. (9)

life span: the upper age limit for human life; the age beyond which less than 0.1 percent of the population lives. (9)

life table: a statistical device that summarizes the mortality experience of a population. (9)

line of best fit: an estimated regression equation based on a sample of observations of a dependent and explanatory variables. (8)

logistic curve: a curve that illustrates initially increasing growth and then diminishing growth in a variable, such as population. (2)

long-run average cost curve: the relationship between output and the minimum average cost of production in the long run. (14)

marginal cost: the change in total cost associated with a unit change in output. (14)

marginal factor cost of labor: the change in the total cost of labor associated with a unit change in labor. (6)

marginal product of labor: the change in output associated with a unit change in labor. (6)

marginal rate of factor substitution: the rate at which a firm can trade off or substitute two factors while maintaining the same rate of output. (4)

marginal rate of substitution: the rate at which an individual is willing to trade off or substitute two commodities for a given level of satisfaction. (10)

marginal revenue: the change in total revenue associated with a unit change in output sold. (14)

marginal revenue product of labor: the change in total revenue associated with a unit change in the labor used to produce a commodity. (6)

market: an arrangement by which demanders and suppliers exchange a well-defined commodity. (14)

marketable pollution permits: transferable licenses, initially distributed by the government, that allow for specified levels of emissions of pollutants. (14)

market failure: an outcome of an unrestricted market that is socially undesirable. (14)

market-friendly strategy: A World Bank strategy of development with four major components: competitive domestic markets, human capital formation, macroeconomic stability, and international integration. (8)

materialism: the association of individual welfare with consumption of goods and services. (15)

mean: the arithmetic average. (8)

mean duration of unemployment: the average number of consecutive weeks of unemployment for those who are unemployed. (6)

merit good: a good or service that society deems everyone should have access to regardless of their ability to pay. (14)

military burden: the share of military expenditures in national income. (15)

Millennium Development Goals: eight goals with specific targets set by leaders of the world in 2000 to improve the conditions of the poor. (11)

modern stage of demographic transition: the third stage of the demographic transition where birth rates and death rates have decreased to low levels and population growth is minimal. (2)

monetary union: an arrangement across countries with a common central bank, monetary policy, and currency. (6)

monopolistic competition: the market structure characterized by many firms producing slightly differentiated products. (14)

monopoly: the market structure characterized by one firm as the sole supplier of a product. (14)

moral suasion: attempt to convince individuals to act responsibly or in the public interest. (14)

most favored nation: a principle underlying trade liberalization where reductions in trade barriers between any two nations should be extended to other nations. (5)

multiple regression analysis: an estimation technique used to quantify the relationships between a dependent variable and explanatory variables based on a sample of observations. (8)

natural fertility: the fertility in a society where there is no individual discretion exercised over the number or spacing of births. (9)

natural monopoly: a good or service with economies of scale so significant relative to market demand that competition is not feasible. (14)

natural rate of output: the rate of real national output produced when the economy is at the natural rate of unemployment. (6)

natural rate of unemployment: the unemployment rate where the expected price level held by labor supply equals the actual aggregate price level; consistent with general equilibrium in the aggregate labor market. (6)

natural resource curse: the failure of a nation well endowed with natural resources to develop its economy and institutions. (12)

net flow of intergenerational wealth: Caldwell's theory that fertility levels reflect the net flow of wealth between parents and children. (10)

negative economic profits: an excess of total costs, including the opportunity cost of the invested capital, over total revenues. (14)

negative externalities: actions of primary parties involved in an activity that have adverse social consequences or impose costs on third parties. (14)

neoclassical growth model (Solow growth model): a model to explain growth in labor productivity based on an aggregate production function with factor substitution, net savings, and labor force growth.

net in-migration rate: the difference between immigrants to an area and the emigrants from the area over a year per thousand population in the area at mid-year. (2)

net reproduction rate: the average number of daughters born to a woman and surviving to the age of the mother, given the current age-specific fertility rates and survival rates. (9)

neutral technical change: an advance in knowledge that allows for an increase in output for a given set of inputs; also known as neutral technological progress. (1, 4)

nominal exchange rate: the price of one currency in units of a second currency. (12)

nonautocorrelation: the assumption that the error terms are independent. (8)

nonrenewable natural resources: natural resources with finite or exhaustible supplies, including fossil fuels and minerals. (1)

normal distribution: a symmetric probability distribution shaped like a bell curve. (8)

null hypothesis: the primary hypothesis, which usually is expected to be rejected with the evidence. (8)

official settlements account: the account in the international balance of payments that records transactions in official assets between governments and monetary authorities. (4)

oligopoly: the market structure characterized by the dominance of a few rival firms aware of their interdependence. (14)

one-tail test: A test of significance where, if the null hypothesis is that the true value of the parameter is zero, the alternative hypothesis is that it is greater than zero (or less than zero, but not both). (8)

ordinary least squares: the statistical technique where the criterion for estimating the coefficients of a regression equation is to minimize the sum of the squares of the residuals (prediction errors) of the observations of the sample. (8)

output-expansion path: the least-cost or economically efficient combinations of factors for producing various levels of output given the unit prices of the factors. (11)

output quota: an upper limit or ceiling on the production or import of a good over a given period. (14)

par value: the official exchange value of a currency. (4)

peak: the upper turning point of a business cycle, when real output ceases to increase and begins to decline. (6)

perfect competition: the market structure characterized by many firms producing a homogeneous good or service. (6)

perfect complements: goods or factors of production that must be used jointly and in fixed proportions. (11)

perfect information: the assumption that all economic actors know the price level. (6)

perfect multicollinearity: the condition where one explanatory variable can be written as a linear combination of one, several, or all of the other explanatory variables. (8)

perfect substitutes: goods or factors of production that are completely interchangeable. (11)

permanent income: the expected future income based on human capital, wealth, and employment. (10)

physical capital: the human-made aids to production; the buildings, equipment, and machinery used to produce goods and services. (1)

population forecast: the extrapolation of a population forward based on expected fertility, mortality, and net migration rates. (9)

population momentum: the inherent tendency for a population to change in size after the onset of replacement-level fertility. (9)

population projection: the extrapolation of a population forward based on assumed fertility, mortality, and net-migration rates. (9)

population pyramid: a bar graph of a population, where each bar represents the population of a certain age and sex. (9)

population regression line: a behavioral equation that expresses the theoretical relationships between a dependent variable and explanatory variables. (8)

positive checks to population growth: in Malthus's theory, the decreases in population growth from increased mortality due to violence, disease, famine, and natural disasters. (3)

positive economic profits: an excess of total revenues over total costs, including the opportunity cost of the invested capital. (14)

positive economics: economic analysis based on what is or will be; statements of testable propositions, not opinions or statements of what should be. (8)

positive externalities: actions of primary parties involved in an activity that have social benefits for third parties or improve the welfare of others. (8)

potential national output: See *full-employment real national output*.

poverty gap: a measure of the depth of poverty, indicating the average percentage shortfall of income below the poverty line for the population. (1)

precautionary principle: the approach that urges preventative measures in case there are uncertain, but potentially serious, consequences from current behavior. (15)

prediction error: the difference between the actual or observed value of a dependent variable and the value predicted from the estimated regression equation. (8)

preventative checks to population growth: in Malthus's theory, the decreases in population growth from reduced fertility due to birth control and moral restraint. (3)

price-setter: a firm that sets the unit price from the downwardly sloping demand curve for its output. (14)

price-taker: a perfectly competitive firm that accepts the market prices for its output or its inputs. (14)

probability: the chance that an event or outcome will occur. (9)

producer surplus: the gain in revenue equal to the difference between the price the supplier of a commodity receives and the minimum price the supplier would accept. (14)

production possibilities boundary: the combination of goods a nation can produce efficiently using all of its available resources. (3)

public good: a good or service that is nonrival and nonexcludable in consumption. (14)

purchasing power parity adjustment: conversion of national incomes or expenditures into internationally comparable dollars to account for differences in the cost of living. (1)

quota rent: the revenues available under an output quota; equal to the difference between the total expenditures on the restricted good and the total revenues of the suppliers. (14)

radix: the initial cohort of births in a life table, usually assumed to be 100,000 in number. (9)

random variable: a variable whose values are determined by probability or chance. (8)

rational behavior: behavior that is consistent with a given objective. (8)

rational expectations: the hypothesis that economic agents use all the available information to anticipate the price level. (6)

real exchange rate: the nominal exchange rate adjusted for the domestic and foreign price levels of internationally traded goods and services. (7, 12)

recession: a significant downturn in economic activity, evidenced by declining real national output over an extended period of time. (6)

reciprocity: a principle underlying trade liberalization where if one nation reduces its trade barriers to a second nation, then the second nation should reduce its trade barriers to the first nation. (5)

recycling of petrodollars: the lending of dollars earned by oil-exporting nations and placed in Western banks to developing nations to finance their oil imports. (5)

relative economic status: Easterlin's concept of an individual's comparison of their income prospects with their consumption aspirations. (10)

relativism: the evaluation of one's achievements in comparison with a relevant social reference group or aspired-to standard. (15)

renewable natural resources: natural resources that can be regenerated and with proper management will be available for use in future periods. (1)

replacement-level fertility: a total fertility rate just sufficient to maintain the size of successive generations and consistent with a crude rate of natural increase of zero in the long run. (9)

residual: the prediction error or the difference between the actual or observed value of a dependent variable and the value predicted from the estimated regression equation. (8)

sample regression line: the estimated line of best fit for a dependent variable and explanatory variable(s) based on a sample of observations. (8)

Say's law: the theory that supply creates its own demand so that the aggregate supply curve is vertical at full-employment national output. (3)

scatter diagram: a plot of the ordered pairs from a sample of observed values of a dependent variable and independent variable. (8)

Second World: a term used to identify the former socialist economies of the Soviet Union and the Eastern European countries under communism. (5)

short-run average cost curve: the relationship between output and the average cost of production in the short run. (14)

simple regression analysis: an estimation technique used to quantify the relationship between a dependent variable and an explanatory variable based on a sample of observations. (8)

simulation model: a model that extrapolates the values of dependent variables based on given equations and values of exogenous variables. (5)

social capital: the shared values, mutual trust, and social networks that give cohesion to a society and foster cooperation. (1)

social reference group: the relevant peer group of influence that sets the standard for individuals. (10)

specialization of labor: labor focused on a specific task or trained in a specific occupation. (1)

specialization in trade: a firm focused on producing a specific product; a country increasing production of those commodities for trade where it has a comparative advantage. (3)

specification: the first stage in empirical analysis where a model is set forth with assumed behavioral relationships between the variables of interest. (8)

stable population: a closed population where the age-specific birth and death rates have been constant for some time so that the age–sex structure of the population is unchanged. (9)

stagflation: the concurrence of inflation and falling real national output. (6)

standard deviation: the square root of the variance. (8)

standard error: the standard deviation of an estimated regression coefficient. (8)

stationary: a population pyramid shape that is fairly uniform until narrowing at the older ages, indicating replacement-level fertility and zero population momentum. (9)

stationary population: a stable population with a crude rate of natural increase of zero. (9)

steady-state equilibrium: the condition for equilibrium in a growth model. (7)

stochastic: random or determined by chance. (8)

stock: a variable defined at a point in time. (2)

strong sustainability: the condition where the total stocks of each capital (human, physical, natural, and social) are maintained over time. (11)

stunting: child malnutrition indicated by significantly below normal height for age. (10)

structural unemployment: unemployment due to a mismatching between the location or skills of the unemployed and the location or skills required for the jobs that are open. (6)

survival rate: the probability of living from one age to another. (9)

sustainable development: a development that meets the needs of present generations without compromising the ability of future generations to meet their own needs. (11)

sustainable energy technologies: clean energies that are renewable. (15)

t-**ratio**: a ratio of the difference between an estimated coefficient and its assumed true value to the standard error of the estimated coefficient under the null hypothesis that the true value of the coefficient is zero. (8)

t-**test** : the assessment of whether the *t*-ratio is statistically significant. (8)

technical efficiency: the condition in which no more of any factor is used than necessary to produce a given level of output. (4)

Third World: a term used to identify the less developed countries. (5)

total fertility rate: the average number of children a woman would have if she lived through the childbearing years and were subject to the current age-specific fertility rates. (2, 9)

traditional stage of demographic transition: the first stage of the demographic transition where birth rates and death rates are high and population growth is minimal. (2)

transitional stage of demographic transition: the second stage of the demographic transition where death rates have fallen before birth rates and population growth is significant. (2)

transfer earnings: the earnings necessary to have the factor supplied; the area under the factor supply curve up to the quantity transacted. (3)

trough: the lower turning point of a business cycle, when real output stops declining and begins to increase. (6)

two-tail test: A test of significance where, if the null hypothesis is that the true value of the parameter is zero, the alternative hypothesis is that it is nonzero. (8)

Type I error: the rejection of a true null hypothesis. (8)

Type II error: the failure to reject a false null hypothesis. (8)

unconditional convergence: two countries with identical production functions, saving rates and natural growth rates of labor, in the abscence of technological change, will converge to the same steady-state equilibrium. (7)

under-five mortality rate: the probability that a child born in a given year, if subject to the current age-specific mortality rates, will die before age 5, expressed as a rate per thousand live births. (9)

variance: a measure of the distribution of the values of a variable around its mean. (8)

veil of ignorance: Rawls's proposition that when one conceives of a just society, one should not know one's position in the society. (15)

verification: the third stage in empirical analysis where the estimated model is assessed for its statistical significance and robustness. (8)

voluntary migration: discretionary migration influenced by the perceived net benefits of moving. (10)

wasting: child malnutrition indicated by significantly below normal weight for height. (10)

weak sustainability: the condition where the total stock of capital (human, physical, natural, and social) is maintained over time, although the composition can change. (11)

wealth effect: the inverse relationship between the quantity demanded of real national output and the aggregate price level due to the effect of an increase in the price level reducing real wealth and the ability to consume goods and services. (6)

youth burden of dependency: the ratio of the population aged 15 or younger to the population aged 15–64. (9)

zero economic profits: total revenues are equal to the total costs of production, including the opportunity costs of the capital invested. (14)

zero tillage: the farming practice of not plowing up the fields after harvesting, but leaving the crop residue in place and planting seeds in the soil beneath the residue in the next season. (13)

Index

Note: page numbers in *italic* type refer to figures; those in **bold** refer to tables.

501

Declaration 7; and sustainable development 318; Universal Declaration of Human Rights 316, 334

United Nations Development Group 412

United Nations Development Programme (UNDP) 447; and climate change 379, 383, 440, 445, 461; Human Development Index 324–8, **327**, 330–2, **331**, **332**, 485

upper-middle income economies: adjusted net saving rate 322; and agriculture 395, **396**; average annual real GDP growth rates, 1970–2010, statistics 118, 122; cell phone subscriptions **456**; economic growth statistics 25, 26; emissions **377–8**; energy use 377; exports **456**; external debt **456**; fertility 242, **243**, 244, 291; foreign direct investment **456**; fossil fuel use 377, 382; health conditions 274; imports **456**; Internet users **456**; military spending **456**; mortality statistics **231**; natural resources **356**; negative output growth 29, **31**; official development assistance **456**; population growth statistics **50**; renewable natural resources 373, **373**; sustainable development 330, *see also* lower-middle income economies; middle-income economies

uranium 450

urban populations **291**; and agglomeration 182

urbanization 373, **374**, 375; and economies of scale 17; and European population growth 41; urbanized economies 395

Uruguay 223, **332**

US: 1970s/1980s economic situation 114; 1973–2001 economic situation 121–2; adjusted net saving rate 321, **322**; aged-to-child ratio 255–6, **256**; aggregate labor force participation 129, 131, **131**; aging population 295–7, **295**; and agriculture **396**, 398, 399, 406; and the Arctic Ocean 438; biofuels 405, 449; carbon dioxide emissions 25, 453; cell phone subscriptions **456**; consumer behavior 472–5; crude birth rate **292**, **298**; crude death rate 228, **292**, **298**; deflation 143; demographic transition 47; dependency rates 248, **251**; diet 389; economic growth 24, **25**, 77, **128**, 129–32, *130*, **131**, **184**; education 326; emissions **377–8**; energy use 25, **377**, 381–2; exports **456**; fertility 242, **243**, 244, 248, *250*, 291, **292**, **298**; forests 359; fossil fuels **359**; GNI statistics 25, 326; gold standard 101; in the gold standard era 79, 80; and the Great Depression 82–4, 87–8; greenhouse gas (GHG) emissions 459; happiness 468; health conditions 274; health insurance 433; Human Development Index 326, 327, **327**; imports **456**; and income inequality 185–6; inflation 129–30, **131**; Internet users **456**; and the Kyoto Protocol 439; labor force 25; labour productivity 129, 131–2, **131**; life expectancy **25**, 29, 238, 269, **298**; life tables 233, **234–5**, 236–8; migration **292**, 294, **298**; military spending **456**, 458; mortality 229, **230**, **231**, 269, **270**, 273; natural resources **356**;

North American diet 389; per capita income growth 4; population momentum **251**, 253; population pyramid 248, *250*, 251; population size **25**, **50**, 84–5, 88, 96, 227, **292**, **295**, **298**; post World War II era 99, 100, 101, 290–3, **292**; post-World War I era 81, 82; poverty 433; real GDP per capita 129, 131–2, **131**; recessions 115, 117, 122, 133n6, 143, 149–50, 151–3, 156, 434, 435; sustainable development 330–1, **332**; twentieth-century economic growth 5; unemployment 129–30, **131**, 133, 134; water resources **373**, 376

US dollar: and the Bretton Woods system 100; gold standard 101

utility: and sustainable development 472–4, *473*; utility maximization 469–72, *471*

Utopian School 65–6

Uzbekistan **31**, **356**, 391

van der Ploeg, Frederick 368–9, 370

variance 192, 491

Veblen, Thorstein 74n17, 469, 469–70, 481

veil of ignorance 447, 492

Venezuela 115, 223, **359**

verification 191, 492

Vietnam, regional classification 223

Volcker, Paul 114

voluntary migration 303, 304, 492

von Braun, Joachim 408

wage–rental ratio 91, *91*

wages 72, *72*; and aggregate supply 138, *139*

Walras, Leon 78

Washington Consensus 12

wasting, definition 492

water resources: access to improved sources **274**, **275**, 276, 277; and agriculture 401–2; and climate change 379; and forests 360; freshwater **373**, **374**, 375–6; productivity **373**, **374**, 376

wave power 452

weak sustainability 341, 342, 492

wealth effect 141, 492

Wealth of Nations, the see Smith, Adam

Weeks, John 38

Western Europe 435; economic growth, 1973–2001 period 121–2; fertility rates 242; in the gold standard era 79, 80; per capita income growth 4; population growth 39–42, 84; post World War II era 99, 101; vital rates **298**, *see also* Eastern Europe; Europe; Europe and Central Asia region

wetlands 376

wheat 392, **393**, 394, 403

Whelpton, Pascal 227

wind power 452

wine production example 60–4, *63*

Wines, Michael 388

Wolfram, Catherine 454

women: and development 218–19; and education 211–16, **213**, 223, 285, **291**, 341; life